Routledge Handbook of Asian Borderlands

In Asia, where authoritarian-developmental states have proliferated, statehood and social control are heavily contested in borderland spaces. As a result, in the post-Cold War world, borders have not only redefined Asian incomes and mobilities, they have also rekindled neighbouring relations and raised questions about citizenship and security.

The contributors to the *Routledge Handbook of Asian Borderlands* highlight some of these processes taking place at the fringe of the state. Offering an array of comparative perspectives of Asian borders and borderlands in the global context, this handbook is divided into thematic sections, including:

- Livelihoods, commodities, and mobilities
- Physical land use and agrarian transformations
- Borders and boundaries of the state and the notion of statelessness
- Re-conceptualizing trade and the economy in the borderlands
- The existence and influence of humanitarians, religions, and NGOs
- The militarization of borderlands

Causing us to rethink and fundamentally question some of the categories of state, nation, and the economy, this is an important resource for students and scholars of Asian Studies, Border Studies, Social and Cultural Studies, and Anthropology.

Alexander Horstmann is Associate Professor in Southeast Asian Studies at Tallinn University, Estonia.

Martin Saxer is an anthropologist based at LMU Munich, Germany.

Alessandro Rippa is a postdoctoral fellow at LMU Munich, Germany.

Section editors:

Christine Bonnin
Karin Dean
Swargajyoti Gohain
Caroline Grillot
Alexander Horstmann
Jean-François Rousseau

Routledge Handbook of Asian Borderlands

Edited by Alexander Horstmann, Martin Saxer, and Alessandro Rippa

LONDON AND NEW YORK

First published 2018
by Routledge
2 Park Square, Milton Park, Abingdon, Oxon OX14 4RN

and by Routledge
711 Third Avenue, New York, NY 10017

Routledge is an imprint of the Taylor & Francis Group, an informa business

© 2018 selection and editorial matter, Alexander Horstmann, Martin Saxer, and Alessandro Rippa; individual chapters, the contributors

The right of Alexander Horstmann, Martin Saxer, and Alessandro Rippa to be identified as the authors of the editorial material, and of the authors for their individual chapters, has been asserted in accordance with sections 77 and 78 of the Copyright, Designs and Patents Act 1988.

All rights reserved. No part of this book may be reprinted or reproduced or utilised in any form or by any electronic, mechanical, or other means, now known or hereafter invented, including photocopying and recording, or in any information storage or retrieval system, without permission in writing from the publishers.

Trademark notice: Product or corporate names may be trademarks or registered trademarks, and are used only for identification and explanation without intent to infringe.

British Library Cataloguing-in-Publication Data
A catalogue record for this book is available from the British Library

Library of Congress Cataloging-in-Publication Data
Names: Horstmann, Alexander, editor. | Saxer, Martin, 1971- editor. | Rippa, Alessandro, editor.
Title: Routledge handbook of Asian borderlands / edited by Alexander Horstmann, Martin Saxer and Alessandro Rippa.
Description: New York : Routledge, 2018. | Includes bibliographical references and index.
Identifiers: LCCN 2017037265| ISBN 9781138917507 (hardback) | ISBN 9781315688978 (ebook)
Subjects: LCSH: Borderlands—Economic aspects—Asia. | Asia—Commerce. | Asia—Emigration and immigration—Economic aspects. | Asia—Ethnic relations. | Social change—Asia.
Classification: LCC HC412 .R688 2018 | DDC 330.95—dc23
LC record available at https://lccn.loc.gov/2017037265

ISBN: 978-1-138-91750-7 (hbk)
ISBN: 978-1-315-68897-8 (ebk)

Typeset in Bembo
by Sunrise Setting Ltd, Brixham, UK

Contents

List of illustrations	*x*
Notes on contributors	*xii*
Acknowledgements	*xxi*
Asian borderlands in a global perspective *Martin Saxer, Alessandro Rippa, and Alexander Horstmann*	1

PART 1
Conceptual framing — 15

1. Violence in Asian borderlands — 17
   Reece Jones

2. Asia's gendered borderlands — 30
   Malini Sur

3. Intimate militarism: domesticating the border in rural Central Asia — 42
   Madeleine Reeves

4. Borders and bordering in Asia — 56
   Karin Dean

5. Zomia and beyond — 73
   Jean Michaud

PART 2
Livelihoods, commodities, mobilities — 89

Introduction — 91
Christine Bonnin

Contents

  6 Political livelihoods in the northeast borderlands of Cambodia: legacy of the past, territorial incorporation, and confrontation   94
Frédéric Bourdier

  7 Cross-border commodities: processual histories, commodity chains, and the yak tail trade   106
Tina Harris

  8 Old routes, new roads: proximity across the China–Pakistan border   114
Alessandro Rippa

  9 Making place within a geopolitical frontier: Mae Aw (Ban Rak Thai)   127
Carl Grundy-Warr, Jessica Teo, and Wei Jun Chin

10 Making connectivity work: exploring cross-border livelihoods between Kazakhstan and China   140
Henryk Alff

11 Ritual and issues of ethnic integration in the borderlands of the State of Rakhine/Arakan (Myanmar)   151
Alexandra de Mersan

PART 3
Physical land use and agrarian transformations   163

Introduction   165
Jean-François Rousseau

12 Genesis of state space: frontier commodification in Malaysian Borneo   168
Noboru Ishikawa

13 Frontier constellations: agrarian expansion and sovereignty on the Indonesian–Malaysian border   180
Michael Eilenberg

14 Beyond 'natural' pressures: Chinese agriculture in the Russian Far East   190
Jiayi Zhou

15 A failed market experiment and ignored livelihoods: jatropha expansion in the Sino–Vietnamese borderlands   202
Jean-François Rousseau

PART 4
Borders and boundaries of the state, governance, and the production of statelessness   213

    Introduction   215
    Karin Dean

16 Multiple borders and bordering processes in Kachin State   218
    Karin Dean and Mart Viirand

17 Turning your back to the border: federalism, territory, and claims for autonomy in the Nepal–India borderland   230
    Rune Bennike

18 A proliferation of border interfaces: ordering insecurity for migrants in the Thai–Burmese borderlands   242
    Adam Saltsman

19 The decision to move: post-exchange experiences in the former Bangladesh–India border enclaves   255
    Md. Azmeary Ferdoush and Reece Jones

20 The backdoors of resistance: identities in the Malay Peninsula's maritime borderlands   266
    Maxime Boutry

21 Ethnic reconstruction and Austronesian strategies at the borders: the Moken social space in Burma   277
    Jacques Ivanoff

PART 5
It's all about relations: re-conceptualizing trade and the economy in the borderlands   289

    Introduction   291
    Caroline Grillot

22 Accumulating trust: Uyghur traders in the Sino–Kyrgyz border trade after 1991   294
    Rune Steenberg

Contents

23 The "leech plot": discourses on alleged deception strategies among traders in the Sino–Vietnamese borderlands 304
Caroline Grillot

24 Nobody stops and stays anymore: motor roads, uneven mobilities, and conceptualizing borderland modernity in highland Nepal 315
Galen Murton

25 Cultivating consumer markets: ethnic minority traders and the refashioning of cultural commodities in the Sino–Vietnamese border uplands 325
Christine Bonnin

26 Invisible trade: sovereign decisions on the Sino–Russian border 334
Natalia Ryzhova

PART 6
Humanitarians, religion, and NGOs   345

Introduction 347
Alexander Horstmann

27 Humanitarian assistance and Protestant proselytizing in the borderlands of Myanmar: the Free Burma Rangers 349
Alexander Horstmann

28 The moral economy of the Myawaddy–Mae Sot border 361
Su-Ann Oh

29 Biosocial body of ethno-religious boundaries in a Tibetan marriage 376
Dan Smyer Yü

30 Development institutions and religious networks in the Pamirian borderlands 385
Till Mostowlansky

PART 7
Militarization of borderlands   397

Introduction 399
Swargajyoti Gohain

31 Border, checkpoint, bodies *Pradeep Jeganathan*	403
32 Musical crossings over the militarised borderland: a case study of the Ogasawara Islands *Masaya Shishikura*	411
33 Evaded states: security and control in the Sino–North Korean border region *Adam Cathcart*	422
34 Border and road regimes in Central Asia: ordering disorder at an Uzbek–Kazakh checkpoint *Rano Turaeva*	434
35 Bordered spaces: spatial strategies in a "disputed border" *Swargajyoti Gohain*	445
Index	*454*

Illustrations

Figures

9.1	Mr Jia Ta in KMT uniform with rifle taken from his tearoom display of KMT memorabilia	132
9.2	Mr Jia Ta's border restaurant in Baan Rak Thai	133
9.3	Li shares with us a photo of him dressed in his KMT uniform which he still keeps as a remembrance of his soldiering days	136
9.4	Entry point into the Shan border village near Ban Rak Thai	136
9.5	Based on interviews with one female migrant who is now a resident of Ban Rak Thai	137
14.1	Changes in sown area in RFE provinces between 1990 and 2014, in absolute hectare and percentage terms	194
14.2	Changes in sown area in Northeast China between 1990 and 2013, in absolute hectare and percentage terms	195
15.1	Abandoned jatropha plantation in Gaotong Cun	206
17.1	Gate at Panchhtar district headquarters	237
23.1	Móng Cái, Chinese traders carrying their load at the border gate with Vietnam	310

Maps

5.1	Van Schendel's original Zomia (2002) and its extension North and West (2007), which I call here Zomia+	74
5.2	The 'Hindu Kush-Himalayan' region (International Centre for Integrated Mountain Development (ICIMOD), Kathmandu, Nepal)	76
5.3	Over van Schendel's Zomia and Zomia+, are shown the Southeast Asian Massif (with a broad indication in darker shades of where the concentration of population is), and Scott's Zomia	77
5.4	The Southeast Asian Massif	79
6.1	Location of Ratanakiri province (Cambodia) in the Southeast Asian Massif	95
8.1	The Karakoram Highway (KKH) between Xinjiang and Pakistan	116
9.1	Map revealing places where we carried out research in the borderland. The focus of this chapter is on Ban Rak Thai near the northern borderland of Mae Hong Son, Thailand with Shan State in Myanmar	128
12.1	Malay maritime world	169
12.2	Sarawak and West Kalimantan (Dutch West Borneo)	170
12.3	Borneo border checkpoints	176

Illustrations

14.1	Map of the relevant areas in Northeast China and the Russian Far East	191
15.1	Approximate location of Gaotong Cun	204
16.1	Election cancellation in Kachin State 2010–2015	219
18.1	Map of Thai–Burmese borderlands highlighting mainland Southeast Asia Massif	244
20.1	Burmese migrations to the Malay Peninsula	272
21.1	Distribution of Moken groups in the Mergui Archipelago	278
21.2	The pivot system in action (Nyawi subgroup)	283
24.1	Nepal–China transborder road networks	316
27.1	Contested areas in Southeast Myanmar	350
27.2	Internally displaced people and refugees in Southeast Myanmar	351
30.1	Map of the Pamirian borderlands	386

Tables

| 1.1 | Border walls in Asia: more border walls in a borderless world | 23 |
| 4.1 | A survey of the geographic locations of the borders discussed during 1988–2008 | 58 |

Contributors

Henryk Alff is a postdoctoral researcher at the Leibniz Centre for Tropical Marine Research (ZMT) in Bremen, Germany, currently developing a project on China's Maritime Silk Road initiative. After completing his doctorate at the University of Potsdam, Germany, he held a postdoctoral research position in the competence network Crossroads Asia at the Centre for Development Studies (ZELF) of Freie Universität Berlin (2011–2016). His work on the transformation of bazaar trade across the former Sino–Soviet borderlands, drawing attention in particular to actor-based strategies of adaptation to changing border regimes and transformed ideas of development, has been widely published in journals such as *Central Asian Survey*, *International Development Planning Review* and *Eurasian Geography and Economics*. Henryk's research interests include development and transformation as well as border studies, translocality, and spatial theory.

Rune Bennike is a postdoctoral fellow at Copenhagen University's Department of Food and Resource Economics. His research deals with the spatiality of government and commodification of place in the Himalayan borderland between Nepal, China, and India. It explores the production and contemporary transformation of marginality through combined investigations into governmental history, national territorialism, local autonomy movements, land relations, post-disaster economies, tourism, and commodification of land and landscapes. Recent publications include 'Frontier Commodification: Governing Land, Labour and Leisure in Darjeeling, India' in *South Asia: Journal of South Asian Studies*, vol. 40 (2), 2017.

Christine Bonnin is an assistant professor in the School of Geography at the University College Dublin. She is the co-author of *Frontier Livelihoods: Hmong in the Sino Vietnamese Borderlands* (2015), and has conducted research on marketplaces, ethnic minority livelihoods, and issues relating to food security, food anxiety, and Hmong women's health in the China–Vietnam border region.

Frédéric Bourdier is a senior tenure anthropologist at the University of Paris Sorbonne (France) and at the Research Institute for Development (IRD: institute de recherche pour le développement). From 1989 to 2017, he lived for six years in South India (research on medical anthropology and social epidemiology of HIV/AIDS), five years in North Brazil (health and migration in Amazon frontiers with French Guyana and Surinam) and more than twelve years in Cambodia (anthropology of development among ethnic minorities, relation society – nature interactions, ethno-genetic investigations with non-Khmer populations, borderlands studies in the Northeast, malaria politics and policies in a context of resistance to the first line drugs, scaling up of antiretroviral treatment, ethno-history of oral civilizations, social movements related to land security). In most of his professional activities, he has been intensely involved in interdisciplinary research and some of his writings about this. He has been recently involved in the anthropology of political ecology in Southeast Asia, along with a particular effort to associate a conventional academic research with long term engagement and collaborative studies with some people that he uses to frequent.

Maxime Boutry obtained a PhD in Social Anthropology and Ethnology at the School for Higher Studies in Social Sciences (EHESS, Paris) in 2007, dealing with construction of a social space for the Burmese fishermen of the Myeik Archipelago (Myanmar). His research seeks to explore forms of continuity in the sociocultural changes affecting Burmese society through the study of 'frontiers' (borderlands, transition spaces). He is a research associate with IRD (French Institute for Research and Development, UMR PaLoc). His publications include *From Padi States to Commercial States: Reflections on Identity and the Social Construction of Space in the Borderlands of Cambodia, Vietnam, Thailand and Myanmar*, (Bourdier, F., Boutry, M., Ferrari, O., and Ivanoff, J., eds, 2015) and 'How far from national identity? Dealing with the concealed diversity of Myanmar', in Robinne, F. and Egreteau, R. (eds), *Metamorphosis: Studies in Social and Political Change in Myanmar*, NUS Press, pp. 103–126 (2015).

Adam Cathcart is a lecturer in Chinese history at the University of Leeds and the chief editor of the online journal *Sino–NK*. He has done extensive fieldwork in the Chinese–North Korean border region, and published peer-reviewed articles about the region in the *Journal of Cold War Studies, Korean Studies,* among others, and received fellowships and funding from the Academy of Korean Studies and the Beyond the Korean War Project at the University of Cambridge. With strong interest in the contemporary Sino–North Korean relationship, Dr Cathcart regularly publishes op-eds and source readings on this subject, and has presented related papers to the UK Foreign Office, Chatham House, International Institute of Strategic Studies, and the Korean Economic Institute.

Wei Jun Chin completed her masters in the Department of Geography, National University of Singapore in 2014. Her research concerns issues of 'homeland' in relation to Karenni refugees and people living within the northern borderlands of Thailand. She served as a teaching and research assistant on several human geography field investigations in both Thailand and Cambodia. Wei Jun is currently working with the Public Service in Singapore, safeguarding greenery and contributing to master planning for the nation. She returns to Thailand yearly for missions work.

Alexandra de Mersan, anthropologist, is associate professor at the Institut National des Langues et Civilisations Orientales (INALCO, Paris). She is an associate member of the Centre Asie du Sud-Est (CASE-CNRS, Paris). She has a PhD in social anthropology from the Ecole des Hautes Etudes en Sciences Sociales (EHESS, Paris). Since her doctoral dissertation, entitled: '*Ritual Space and the Making of a Locality. Contribution to the Ethnography of the Arakanese Population of Contemporary Burma*' (in French), she has been working on issues of territory and religion in Buddhist societies, mostly among Arakanese (or Rakhine). Her research in Burma (Myanmar) has also covered such subjects as ritual, migration, socio-religious dynamics, ethnicity, and nation building. Since 2012, her publications have been mainly dedicated to an improved understanding, from her anthropological research perspective, of the conflict between Buddhists and Muslims that has arisen in Arakan State.

Contributors

Karin Dean is a political geographer who has worked at the border regions of Southeast Asia since 2000. Her research focuses on boundaries, borderlands, power, and governance, and she employs ethnography to explore how contested spaces around these notions are navigated and negotiated by various actors. She has lived and worked in China, Thailand, Vietnam, and Singapore, and has experience in conflict resolution prior to her position as an associate professor at the School of Humanities, Tallinn University, since 2007. She holds a doctorate in Geography from the National University of Singapore and an MSc in Geography from the University of Idaho (USA).

Michael Eilenberg is Associate Professor of Anthropology at Aarhus University. His research focuses on issues of state formation, sovereignty, citizenship, and agrarian expansion in frontier regions of Southeast Asia with a special focus on the Indonesian–Malaysian borderlands. His studies are based on extended fieldwork and archival studies in British and Dutch archives. His monograph entitled '*At the Edges of States*' first published by KITLV Press (2012) and later reprinted by Brill Academic Publishers (2014) deals with the dynamics of state formation and resource struggle in the Indonesian borderlands. His recent articles have appeared in *Development & Change*, *Journal of Peasant Studies*, *Asia Pacific Viewpoint*, *Journal of Borderland Studies*, *Modern Asian Studies*, and *Identities: Global Studies in Culture and Power*.

Md. Azmeary Ferdoush is a Lecturer in Sociology at the University of Dhaka, Bangladesh and a PhD candidate in Geography at the University of Hawaii at Manoa. He is the co-editor of *Borders and Mobility in South Asia and Beyond*. His research interests include borders and enclaves, South Asia, citizenship, state, territory, and social theory.

Swargajyoti Gohain is Assistant Professor of Sociology and Anthropology at Ashoka University, Haryana, India. Before this, she taught for a couple of years at Indian Institute of Technology Kanpur. She received her PhD degree in anthropology from Emory University in 2013 and held a postdoctoral position at the International Institute of Asian Studies, Leiden, The Netherlands. Swargajyoti has conducted fieldwork in Arunachal Pradesh and Assam in Northeast India. Her main research interests are borders, cultural politics, roads, development, and mobility. Her doctoral research concerning contemporary cultural politics among the Monpas of Arunachal Pradesh, a Tibetan Buddhist minority in the Indo-Tibetan borderlands, has resulted in a number of publications, and her book, titled *Himalaya Bound*, has been accepted for publication by the University of Washington Press (estimated year of publication 2018). Her current project is to study the effect of highway construction among the people living along the road in the backdrop of huge investments on cross-border connectivity in Northeast India.

Caroline Grillot is a social anthropologist (Paris X-Nanterre University) and a sinologist (Institut National des Langues et Civilisations Orientales, INALCO). She spent 12 years in China, researching mainly on social margins. She has obtained a joint PhD in social anthropology at Macquarie University (Australia) and the Free University of Amsterdam (The Netherlands) under the supervisions of Professor Lisa Wynn and Professor Pál Nyíri (2013). Her research topic concerned cross-border marriages between Vietnamese women and Chinese men in borderlands, a topic on which she had previously published a book (*Volées, Envolées, Convolées...* 2010). She achieved a research fellowship at the Max Planck Institute for Social Anthropology (Germany) where she conducted research on traders' relationships in the Sino–Vietnamese borderlands. She then updated her earlier findings on cross-border marriages with Elena Barabantseva at the University of Manchester in order to publish her manuscript. She is now starting a new project on Chinese migrant beekeepers at the Ecole Française d'Extrême Orient.

Carl Grundy-Warr teaches political geography, geopolitics, global political ecologies, and field-based modules in the Department of Geography, National University of Singapore. He has written numerous articles on the political geography of cross-border forced migration, displacement, and refugees in mainland Southeast Asia. His current research focuses on the Mekong Basin, particularly geopolitics relating to ecological flows, hydro-power, and seasonal flooding. He is coordinating a project about water-based communities in the Tonle Sap and Lower Mekong Basin, under the Lee Kuan Yew School of Public Policy's Institute of Water Policy. He coordinates annual field schools in mainland Southeast Asia, including areas along the borderlands of Thailand, Myanmar, Cambodia, and Laos.

Tina Harris is an Assistant Professor in the Department of Anthropology at the University of Amsterdam and a member of the Amsterdam Institute for Social Science Research (AISSR) Moving Matters research cluster. Her research interests include airports, borderlands, commodities, labour, and mobilities. Her book, *Geographical Diversions: Tibetan Trade, Global Transactions* (2013) was a finalist for the International Convention of Asia Scholars (ICAS) Social Sciences Book Prize, and her articles have been published in journals such as *Political Geography, Material Religion, Antipode,* and *Environment and Planning D: Society and Space*.

Alexander Horstmann is Associate Professor in Southeast Asian Studies at the School of Humanities, Tallinn University, Estonia. He has held visiting positions at Tokyo University of Foreign Studies, Mahidol University and EHESS in Paris. His research interests include conflict, refugee studies, border studies, and religion. He is co-editor of the Berghahn journal *Advances in Research: Conflict and Society*. He published *Building Noah's Ark for Migrants, Refugees, and Religious Communities* (with Jin-Heon Jung, 2015), *Faith in the Future: Understanding the Revitalization of Religion and Cultural Traditions in Asia* (2012) and *Centering the Margins: Agency and Narrative in Southeast Asian Borderlands* (with Reed Wadley, 2006).

Noboru Ishikawa (PhD in Anthropology, Graduate Center, City University of New York) is Professor of Anthropology and Area Studies at the Center for Southeast Asian Studies, Kyoto University. His research focuses on the construction of national space, transnationalism, highland–lowland relations, plantation society, and the commodification of nature, based on more than two decades of fieldwork in Sarawak, Malaysian Borneo. His publications include *Dislocating Nation-States: Globalization in Asia and Africa* (2005), *Between Frontiers: Nation and Identity in a Southeast Asian Borderland* (2010), *Transborder Governance of Forests, Rivers and Seas* (2010), *Flows and Movements in Southeast Asia: New Approaches to Transnationalism* (2011), and *Anthropogenic Tropical Forests: Human-Nature Interfaces on the Plantation Frontier* (2018).

Jacques Ivanoff, has a PhD in ethnology (Ecole des Hautes Etudes, Paris) and is a researcher at the French National Research Council (Musée de l'Homme). He worked for many years among the Moken/Moklen sea gypsies in Thailand and Myanmar focusing on the roots of ethnicity through the strategies and ideology developed by the nomads. He works on multiple scales and studied the ethnic dynamics of the people living in the borderlands who use imaginary, political, and geographic limits as cultural tools to adapt in a globalized world.

He focuses on inter-ethnic relations and on social and economic consequences of national and international integration policies that expose the ideological construction of multi-ethnic states. He is responsible for the International Group of Research between Thailand, Mynamar, and France in order to build a museum, and has facilated research in the Myeik Archipelago (genetic, nomadism, preservation).

Pradeep Jeganathan is Professor of Sociology, in the School of Humanities and Social Science, Shiv Nader University, Delhi NCR, India. Previously he was a Senior Research Fellow at the International Center for Ethnic Studies (ICES), Colombo, Sri Lanka, where he was also a member of the board of management. At ICES, Jeganathan directed and participated in a number of multi-sited research projects, funded by Norwegian Agency for Development Cooperation (NORAD), Ford and International Development Research Centre, Canada (IDRC), and directed ICES's research partnership with the Senegal based The Council for the Development of Social Science Research in Africa (CODESRIA), on Afro-Asian nationalism. He has also served as McKnight Land Grant professor at the University of Minnesota, and taught at the New School for Social Research, New York. He is the author of *Living with Death* (2006), *At the Water's Edge* (2004) and co-editor of *Unmaking the Nation* (1995/2009/2017) and *Subaltern Studies X1* (2002), and number of articles on violence, grief, subaltern nationalism, and cyber subjectivity. He was educated at MIT and Harvard, and received his doctorate in Social Anthropology, with distinction, from the University of Chicago, in 1997.

Reece Jones is a Professor of Geography at the University of Hawai'i at Mānoa. He is the author of two books, *Border Walls: Security and the War on Terror in the United States, India and Israel* (2012) and *Violent Borders: Refugees and the Right to Move* (2016). He also edited *Placing the Border in Everyday Life* with Corey Johnson (2014, Routledge Border Regions Series), *Borders and Mobility in South Asia and Beyond* with Md. Azmeary Ferdoush (2018), and *Open Borders: In Defense of the Right to Move* (2018).

Jean Michaud is a social anthropologist and professor at Université Laval in Canada. Since 1987, he has conducted anthropological research in highland India, Thailand, Laos, Vietnam, and Yunnan on social change and responses to modernity among highland societies. He is the author of *'Incidental' Ethnographers. French Catholic Missions on the Tonkin-Yunnan Frontier, 1880–1930* (2007) and co-author of *Frontier Livelihoods: Hmong in the Sino–Vietnamese Borderlands* (2015) and *The Historical Dictionary of the Peoples of the Southeast Asian Massif – Second Edition* (2016). He co-edited *Moving Mountains: Ethnicity and Livelihoods in Highland China, Vietnam and Laos* (2011) and *Trans-Himalayan Borderlands: Frontiers, Modernities, Livelihoods* (2017). His research articles include 'Zomia and Beyond' (*Journal of Global History*, 2010), 'Hmong Infrapolitics: A View from Vietnam' (*Ethnic and Racial Studies*, 2012), and 'What's (written) history for? On James C. Scott's *Zomia*—especially Chapter 6½' (*Anthropology Today*, 2017).

Till Mostowlansky is a postdoctoral fellow at the Hong Kong Institute for the Humanities and Social Sciences, The University of Hong Kong, and a research associate at the Universities of Bern and Sussex. His main research interests include the study of infrastructure, modernity, development, charity, and Islam in contemporary Central Asia and at its historical crossroads between Russian, British, and Chinese spheres of influence. His research has been published in journals such as *Central Asian Survey*, *Modern Asian Studies*, and *Method and Theory in the*

Study of Religion, and he is the author of the monograph *Azan on the Moon: Entangling Modernity along Tajikistan's Pamir Highway* (2017).

Galen Murton is Assistant Professor of Geographic Science in the Department of Integrated Science and Technology at James Madison University in Harrisonburg, Virginia (USA). He completed his PhD in the Department of Geography at the University of Colorado Boulder with a dissertation on the development of borderland road networks between northern Nepal and Tibet. Broadly interested in the geopolitical and social impacts of infrastructure development throughout high Asia, his research project Road Diplomacy: China in South Asia is supported by a Marie S. Curie Action Individual Fellowship at Ludwig-Maximilians-Universität in Munich, Germany. His research has been published in journals such as the *Annals of the American Association of Geographers*, *Eurasian Geopolitics and Economics*, *South Asia: The Journal of South Asian Studies*, and *HIMALAYA: The Journal of the Association for Nepal and Himalayan Studies*.

Su-Ann Oh is a visiting fellow at the Institute of Southeast Asian Studies (ISEAS – Yusof Ishak Institute) in Singapore, with a doctorate from the University of Oxford. Her research interests include refugees, migration, education, and borders, with a geographical emphasis on Myanmar and its border with Thailand. She is currently writing a book on refugee education in camps on the Thai–Burmese border and is the editor of *Myanmar's Mountain and Maritime Borderscapes: Local Practices, Boundary-Making and Figured Worlds* (2016). She has written several articles, book chapters, and reports on education on the Thai–Burmese border. Su-Ann also serves as a board member at the Room to Grow Foundation, an organization that helps care for unparented children on the Thai–Burmese border.

Madeleine Reeves is Senior Lecturer in Social Anthropology at the University of Manchester and Editor of *Central Asian Survey*. She has published widely on questions of borders, state formation, everyday politics and migration in Central Asia, drawing on long-term ethnographic fieldwork in the Ferghana valley and Moscow. Her 2014 monograph, *Border Work: Spatial Lives of the State in Rural Central Asia* won the 2015 Rothschild Prize from the Assocation for the Study of Nationalities, and the 2016 Alec Nove Prize from the British Association of Slavic and East European Studies. She is currently directing a research project with Gulnara Aitpeava on dynamics of everyday conviviality in southern Kyrgyzstan.

Alessandro Rippa completed his doctorate in Social Anthropology at the University of Aberdeen with a thesis on the Karakoram Highway and China–Pakistan cross-border interactions. He is currently a postdoctoral fellow at Ludwig-Maximilians-Universität in Munich (LMU), part of the European Research Council (ERC)-funded project Remoteness and Connectivity: Highland Asia in the World, where he researches infrastructural development, cross-border trade and memory along the China–Myanmar and China–Laos borderlands.

Jean-François Rousseau is a development geographer. He is an assistant professor at the School of International Development and Global Studies at the University of Ottawa, Canada. He received his PhD from McGill University in 2014 and completed a postdoctoral fellowship at Simon Fraser University. His ongoing research is set in southwest China and investigates the interlinkages between infrastructure development and ethnic minority livelihoods, mostly focusing on agrarian and renewable energy projects. Some of his work was published by NUS Press, in *L'Espace géographique* and in the *Singapore Journal of Tropical Geography*.

Contributors

Natalia Ryzhova received the doctor's degree in economics from the Russian Academy of Science (RAS). She was also trained as anthropologist at Cambridge University. Now she works for Far Eastern Federal University as well as the Economic Research Institute of FEB RAS (Vladivostok). Her current project focuses on closeness and openness of the Russian border areas. She previously carried out research on informal economic practices in Sino–Russian border areas and has published books, articles, and book chapters in both English and Russian. Her recent publication is 'The Emergence of Cross-Border Electronic Commerce: Creativity and Declining Trust' in *Sino–Russian Trans-Border Economies. Risk, Benefit, and Trust*, edited by Caroline Humphrey (forthcoming).

Adam Saltsman received his doctorate in sociology from Boston College and is Assistant Professor in the Department of Urban Studies at Worcester State University in Massachusetts, USA. His research and teaching interests include migration, dispossession, political economy, and borderland social orders in Southeast Asia, especially along the Thai–Burmese border. He has also done advocacy on refugee rights in Thailand and in the Middle East. His current project focuses on transnational linkages between Burmese migrants moving through Southeast Asian borderlands and refugees relocating to de-industrialized towns of northeast USA. His research has been published in *Journal of Refugee Studies, Journal of Human Rights Practice*, and *Refuge*.

Martin Saxer is based at the Department of Social and Cultural Anthropology, Ludwig-Maximilians-Universität in Munich (LMU). He is the principal investigator of the European Research Council (ERC)-funded project Remoteness & Connectivity: Highland Asia in the World. Martin was a Clarendon scholar at Oxford and received his doctorate in 2010. He was a postdoctoral student at the Asia Research Institute in Singapore and a Marie Curie Research Fellow at LMU Munich. He has conducted extensive fieldwork in Siberia, Tibet and Nepal since 2003, directed two feature length documentary films, and runs the visual ethnography blog theotherimage.com.

Masaya Shishikura is an ethnomusicologist, and a lecturer of international studies at Tokyo University of Social Welfare. He is currently conducting research entitled 'Music, travel and translation towards trans-border humanity'. Through several stories of travelling songs, this research explores the chains of humanity that transcend the boundaries of the nation, ethnicity, and religion. For this research, Shishikura has been awarded a visiting fellowship from the International Institute for Asian Studies, Leiden (2014), and the Jawaharlal Nehru Institute of Advanced Study, New Delhi (2015), where he also gave several lectures. Shishikura received an MA from the University of Hawai'i at Mānoa (2007) and a PhD from the Australian National University (2014).

Dan Smyer Yü is Professor and Founding Director of the Center for Trans-Himalayan Studies at Yunnan Minzu University. Prior to his current faculty appointment, he was a research group leader at Max Planck Institute for the Study of Religious and Ethnic Diversity, a core member of the Transregional Research Network (CETREN) at University of Göttingen, and a New Millennium Scholar at Minzu University of China, Beijing. He is the author of *The Spread of Tibetan Buddhism in China: Charisma, Money, Enlightenment* (Routledge 2011) and *Mindscaping the Landscape of Tibet: Place, Memorability, Eco-aesthetics* (2015), and the co-editor of *Trans-Himalayan Borderlands: Livelihoods, Territorialities, Modernities* (2017). He has also published numerous book chapters and peer-reviewed journal articles. His current research interests are environmental humanities, transboundary state effects, hydraulic politics, climate change and heritage preservation, Buddhism and peacebuilding, and comparative studies of Eurasian secularisms. He is also a documentary filmmaker.

Rune Steenberg is a research scholar at Columbia University, New York. He received his PhD from Freie Universität Berlin in 2014. Rune's research focuses on kinship, social networks, and economic anthropology in Central Asia and China, especially Xinjiang. He currently works on local ethnographies published in Uyghur language in Xinjiang, PRC.

Malini Sur is a senior research fellow at the Institute for Culture and Society and teaches anthropology at Western Sydney University. Her research addresses three lines of inquiry – agrarian borders, urban space, and environment. The first examines fences, transnational flows, and citizenship. A second line of inquiry explores the relationship that mobility has to urban space, and specifically, with regard to bicycling and construction sites across Asian cities. Finally, she examines the afterlives of natural disasters, air pollution, and climate change. As an anthropologist, she researches these themes historically and with keen attention to visual representation. She has conducted fieldwork in Bangladesh and India, and with South Asian asylum seekers in Belgium. Malini's publications have appeared in academic journals such as *Comparative Studies in Society and History*, *HAU*, *Mobilities*, and *The Economic and Political Weekly*. She has co-edited a collection of essays entitled *Transnational Flows and Permissive Polities: Ethnographies of Human Mobility in Asia* (Amsterdam University Press, 2012). Photographs from Malini's fieldwork on South Asia's borders have been exhibited in Amsterdam, Berlin, Bonn, Chiang Mai, Gottingen, Heidelberg, Kathmandu, and Munich. Her first documentary film *Life Cycle*, about the politics of cycling in the city of Kolkata, has been screened internationally.

Jessica Teo undertook fieldwork for a project entitled From Roots to Routes where she focused on the politics of language and identity within the borderscape of Mae Hong Son. She graduated with honours in geography from the Department of Geography, National University of Singapore in 2014. Jessica participated in field investigations in Cambodia and Thailand. She served as a teaching assistant for field studies in Thailand where she was also able to undertake further research on the cultural and political landscape of the northern Thai–Myanmar borderland. Since then, Jessica has moved on to working in the Public Service in Singapore and the Meetings, Incentives, Conferences, and Events (MICE) industry.

Rano Turaeva is an associate researcher at Max Planck Institute for Social Anthropology in Halle Saale in Germany. She is currently working on the project 'The role of Mosques in integration of migrants in Russia' and has been writing on the topics of migration, enterpreneurship, informal economies, gender, border studies, identity, and inter-ethnic relations, among many other topics which she has published in such journals as *Central Asian Survey*, *Inner Asia*, *Communist and Post-Communist Studies*, and *Anthropology of Middle East*. Her book based on her PhD thesis was published by Routledge in 2016 under the title *Migration and Identity: The Uzbek Experience*.

Mart Viirand is a social anthropologist who has worked in the border regions of Southeast and Central Asia since 2010. His primary research uses ethnography and media analysis to study civil society organizations as development actors in Northern Myanmar. Against the backdrop of gradual economic and political change in this region, his work traces the tensions between Burmese statecraft, religious organization, and popular activism amongst the ethnic

Kachin. He has been a research fellow at Tallinn University and currently teaches as a visiting lecturer for the Oslo-Akershus University College and Kulturstudier.

Jiayi Zhou is a researcher at the Stockholm International Peace Research Institute (SIPRI), with a focus on geopolitics and sustainable development. She has an area studies background in the post-Soviet space, and has conducted fieldwork and research in the Caucasus, Central Asia, and Afghanistan. Her recent publications include 'Towards Pathways for Peacebuilding and Development to Reduce Violent Extremism' (*Journal of Peacebuilding and Development*, 2017), 'Chinese Agrarian Capitalism in the Russian Far East' (*Third World Thematics: A TWQ Journal*, 2017), and *The Silk Road Economic Belt: Considering Security Implications and EU–China Cooperation Prospects* (SIPRI, 2017).

Acknowledgements

When Routledge approached Alexander Horstmann with the idea of editing a *Handbook of Asian Borderlands*, a reference work on the topic for the following years, he accepted with enthusiasm. Quickly realizing the complexity of the task, Alexander approached Martin Saxer and Alessandro Rippa. The three of us worked together on this ambitious project for the following two years, skyping across continents from Tallinn to Munich, Kathmandu and the Tajik Pamirs. This handbook is the result of these shared efforts.

A special thank goes to Marlen Elders. Without her help in handling communications among us, the publisher, the part editors, and the contributors, this handbook would have been a much more daunting task. She proved invaluable in organizing the workflow, making us stick to our deadlines, and managing all sorts of issues that arose along the way. We were fortunate to have such a dedicated, smart, and hardworking editorial assistant.

This handbook would have not been possible without the help of the part editors, Christine Bonnin, Karin Dean, Swargajyoti Gohain, Caroline Grillot and Jean-François Rousseau. Alexander also doubled as the editor of Part 6 on humanitarianism, religion, and non-governmental organizations (NGOs). Their editorial work as well as their own contributions is what ties this volume together.

We owe considerable thanks to the scholars who have contributed essays to this volume. It is their work that makes this handbook a valuable resource for scholars and students interested in the world of Asian borderlands. Hailing from different fields and generations, they present new research on the social, political, cultural, and material realities at different borderlands across the region.

At Routledge, we are grateful to Asian Studies editors Georgina Bishop, Leanne Hinves, and Stephanie Rogers for their interest in our project and help throughout.

Martin and Alessandro as, respectively, principle investigator and postdoctoral fellow of the research project 'Remoteness & Connectivity: Highland Asia in the World', would also like to express their gratitude to the European Research Council for its generous support (Starting Grant 637764, Highland Connections).

In bringing together 35 different case studies and in-depth reflections, we hope that the handbook will set new standards for the scholarship on borderlands in Asia. We also hope that the chapters will stimulate even more work on Asian borderlands in the future, in the interest of both established scholars and students who might be first approaching this fascinating area of research.

Alexander Horstmann (Tallinn)
Alessandro Rippa (LMU Munich)
Martin Saxer (LMU Munich)
The editorial team,
Munich and Tallin

Asian borderlands in a global perspective

Martin Saxer, Alessandro Rippa, and Alexander Horstmann

Borderlands in post-Cold War Asia

At the end of the Cold War, globalization appeared on the world stage as a chimera of sorts, a three-headed fantastic beast with a lion's front, a goat's body, and a serpent as its tail. While the lion roared the promise of the final victory of capitalism and Western-style liberal democracy into the world (Fukuyama 1989; Ohmae 1990) – conjuring up a new era of unimpeded flows of goods, capital, and people – critics were quick to point to the creature's ordinary body and its dangerous serpent tail. Ever since, observers have argued that the promise of globalization was uneven at best, place became no less important, and borders were clearly not disappearing (Brenner 1997, 1999; Cox 1997; Dirlik 1997, 2011; Cunningham and Heyman 2004; Heyman et al. 2004; Gainsborough 2007; Cunningham 2009; Mezzardra and Neilson 2013; Jones 2016).

Looking back onto the past three decades, the evidence to this end is overwhelming. Rather than fading away, borders, and borderlands, have taken centre stage around the globe: today, in 2017, a little more than a quarter of a century after the fall of the Berlin Wall, plans for a new wall at the US–Mexico border are capturing worldwide public attention; European attempts at finding solutions to the ongoing refugee crises have given national borders new meaning; and the UK's decision to leave the European Union resonates with many similar nationalist and protectionist agendas elsewhere. Borders and borderlands matter more than ever.

The imaginary of unimpeded global flows for the benefit of humankind may have been little more than a delusion or a moment of hubris; however, there is no doubt that the lion's roar at the end of the Cold War heralded not only large geopolitics shifts; it also shaped opportunities, fears, and ambitions in the borderlands around the globe. While Western renderings of post-Cold War history tend to emphasize events like the independence of the Baltic states, the fall of the Berlin Wall, German reunification, and the subsequent disintegration of the Soviet Union, the end of the Cold War was an equally crucial juncture in Asia. 1989 was the year in which the Chinese leadership opted to crack down on the Tiananmen Square protests and thereby set the course for China's subsequent developments; it was the year when the insurgency in Kashmir flared up and led to increasing militarization; and rebel armies in northern Burma forged cease-fire deals with Myanmar's military junta, which brought about two decades of lucrative frontier capitalism (Woods 2011). The end of the 1980s were also the time when formerly sealed borders between China and the Soviet Union re-opened and the era of shuttle trade in Siberia and Central Asia began (Karrar 2013; Alff 2015; Billé 2017: 37; Ryzhova, Chapter 26, this volume).

Many of the cases analysed in this book are in one or the other way outcomes of post-Cold War dynamics, in which borders remained in place (and new ones were drawn) while becoming selectively and unevenly more permeable, thereby reversing a trend that began after World War II. When, after the end of colonial empires, the nation state became the norm throughout Asia, an era of border conflicts triggered a phase of closure. The Korean War, the Sino–Soviet split, partition in the Indian subcontinent, and the brief Sino–Indian and Sino–Vietnamese wars led in most cases to a reinforcement of borders. In the 1990s, the role and purpose of these borders began to change. While their role of protecting national sovereignty remained, they were no longer responsible for separating the ideological realms of socialism and the 'free' capitalist world. Superimposed onto the task of safeguarding national sovereignty, borders now also needed to facilitate exchange in the name of growth.

Following the lion head's neoliberal roar, foreign direct investment, availability of labour, and access to natural resources and consumer markets came to be seen as conditions *sine qua non* for economic development. Near-universal World Trade Organization (WTO) membership and a frenzy of free trade agreements around the world – from the North American Free Trade Agreement (NAFTA) in 1988/90, the Maastricht Treaty (1992) and the Association of Southeast Asian Nations (ASEAN) Free Trade Area (1992) to the Russian led Customs Union (2010) and Eurasian Economic Union (2014) – coincided with a shift of the gravitational centre of industrial production from the Euro-American West to Asia, the emergence of new Asian middle classes (Asian Development Bank 2010), and a stunning accumulation of capital in the new centres of global manufacturing.

Free trade agreements, promissory neoliberal rhetoric, and the boom of world manufacturing in Asia reverberated around the globe. These global developments met with fervent anti-globalization movements, new nationalist agendas and (at least since the 2007/2008 financial crises) widespread disillusionment with the model of the liberal Western democracy and the welfare state – in the West as well as in Asia. In particular, the dialectic between safeguarding national sovereignty and expectations of prosperity linked to free trade is the context in which borders and borderlands have reached ever deeper into the politics and discourses right at the heart of nation states.

This dialectic is a global rather than particularly Asian issue; however, compared to other borderlands around the world, the study of Asian borderlands faced an additional challenge: many of the borders this book is concerned with are not just engulfed in the legacies of colonialism, the Cold War, and its end; they also mark the very margins of South, Southeast, East, and Central Asian Studies – the traditional area studies disciplines in Asia. As Willem van Schendel (2002) famously argued, these area studies disciplines, with their journals, conferences, and academic career paths, created elaborate interdisciplinary 'geographies of knowing' at the heartlands of the respective disciplines. However, this approach to area studies also led to 'geographies of ignorance' along their fringes, to uncharted territories that tend to end up at the very margins of the maps, both printed and imagined, which area studies disciplines are used to work with. To tackle these geographies of ignorance, van Schendel suggests giving attention to unfamiliar spatial forms, such as lattices, archipelagos, hollow rings, and patchworks.

This agenda ties in with the larger project to think beyond geographical containers. The aim is thereby not to leave the nation state out of the picture in favour of a vague transnational or global rhetoric; the aim is rather to question well-established geographical containers as exclusive frames of reference, to overcome what John Agnew dubs 'the territorial trap' (1994),

Andreas Wimmer and Nina Glick Schiller (2002) call a 'methodological nationalism' at the core of social science disciplines, and to 'rescue history from the nation', as Prasenjit Duara (1995) puts it. What is at stake is thus far more than the uncharted terrains at the edge of nation states and area studies disciplines; what is at stake is a radical rethinking of nation states, areas, and globalization from the edge.

From refuge to roads

The terrain on which van Schendel's reflections on geographies of ignorance grew were the highlands of South, Southeast and East Asia – an unnamed area that he calls 'Zomia', derived from the term *zomi* denoting a highlander in several Tibeto-Burman languages (Schendel 2002: 653). The publication of his seminal paper in 2002 triggered a productive, and at times heated, debate on borderlands in Asia. James Scott's book *The Art of Not Being Governed. An Anarchist History of Upland Southeast Asia* (2009) famously used the idea of Zomia for a sprawling argument about highlanders and their relations to valley states and agricultural empires. His argument, in a nutshell, is that the hills and mountains of the Southeast Asian Massif (Michaud 2000, 2016) served as sanctuary for a variety of people seeking refuge from oppressive states and empires with their corvée obligations, diseases, and limited possibilities for upward mobility. Scott sees many of the shared sociocultural forms found in this area – from swidden agriculture and egalitarian political systems to linguistic diversity and fluid ethnic boundaries – as means to keep the state at arm's length. Scott's thesis of self-chosen refuge and a history of anarchism was met with much criticism from scholars working in the area, pointing out numerous flaws and imprecisions in his rendering of historical highland life and politics.

While Scott's take on Zomia, and the boldness of his thesis, arguably captured the debate to some extent, it also opened a perspective on Asian borderlands that has provided a point of reference and friction for a number of conceptually innovative works.[1] Scott understands Zomia not as a realm of primordial cultural forms and ageless traditions, but as a historical effect of state-making in the valleys and thereby as directly tied to larger geopolitical transformations. This raises the question whether similar dynamics were responsible for the making of remote peripheries elsewhere, and whether Zomia is a label that can be applied to other frontiers in Asia and elsewhere. Several chapters in this handbook grapple directly with this question (Jean Michaud, Chapter 5; Maxime Boutry, Chapter 20; Jacques Ivanoff, Chapter 21), and many more engage with the Zomia debate in their arguments.

Scott's thesis explicitly concerns pre-World War II history; he argues that after 1945, with the end of colonial rule and the formation of nation states throughout the region, new 'distance demolishing' technologies (roads, telecommunication) brought about the end of Zomia (Scott 2009: xii; cf. Harvey 1989). Indeed, the past couple of decades have seen a frenzy of transportation infrastructure projects in the borderlands of Asia. Thousands of kilometres of roads and railways were built or upgraded in the borderlands – some of them meant to tie peripheries more closely into states of which they are part, others with the dedicated purpose to foster border trade. Together with new roads came checkpoints, dry ports and customs facilities, all of them accompanied by rhetoric of progress, order, and security. In addition, thousands of kilometres of feeder roads were constructed, penetrating ever deeper into the last remaining jungles and highlands of Asia to access resources and turning sleepy rural villages into investment opportunities for agribusinesses and mining. Moreover, plans for even bigger infrastructural projects are on the horizon, many of them in relation to China's Belt and Road Initiative and other Silk Road phantasies (Callahan 2016; Johnson 2016; Sidaway and Woon 2017). Infrastructure – some promised, some built – has captured the minds and dreams of a vast portion of borderland residents in Asia. The pace at which infrastructure developments are currently reshaping livelihoods, opportunities, and ambitions is staggering.

However, as several anthropologists of infrastructure have noted, roads, corridors, and special economic zones seldom live up to the promise of mobility and prosperity on which they are built or planned (Nyíri and Breidenbach 2008; Campbell 2010; Dalakoglou and Harvey 2012; Lama 2013; Harvey and Knox 2015). At times, they even end up becoming obstacles rather than conduits for development and connectivity (Walker 1999; Pedersen and Bunkenborg 2012; Demenge 2013). In other words, roads and corridors do not always 'demolish distance' – they rather create nodes of legibility and state presence, but in the process they also increase the remoteness and illegibility of border areas outside their immediate scope. This means that while infrastructure and new technologies of surveillance overall bolster state efforts to regulate movement – and thereby turn borderlands into prime targets of biopolitical interventions – implementation often remains patchy. The fact that different arms of state authority often have contradictory agendas further complicates the state quest for legibility and control. As a result, one branch of state authority may easily become complicit in purposeful obfuscation, while another branch of the state may combat it. Accordingly, despite new roads, mobile phone connections along them, and new technologies of surveillance, states seem no less anxious about their presence and control in borderlands, and Zomia-like niches in which governance is weak or absent are not a thing of the past. In a certain sense, we presently witness even a return of old and familiar discourses about ungoverned frontiers (Andersson and Saxer 2016) – be it dangerous no-go areas in Mali, Syria, and Afghanistan (Andersson 2016) or special zones and casino towns in the borderlands between China, Laos, and Myanmar (Rippa and Saxer 2016).

A departure from Scott's narrow interpretation of Zomia as historical refuge in favour of a general reflection on state authority, identity, development, and infrastructure leads us back to van Schendel's original project of shedding light on what continues to be 'geographies of ignorance' in the larger debates on global issues of our times.

Mobility, military, and morality

The study of borderlands carries a paradox in its name. *Borderland* suggests a fixed territorial entity, an area at the edge of nation states that has a border as its main characteristic. The bread and butter of borderland studies, however, are its typically mobile actors, their connections across the border as well as to urban centres on both sides, and the movement of goods and capital in and out. Borderland scholarship has developed in parallel to the broader debates on mobility, migration, and transnationalism. This includes questions of immobility, moorings, and suspension that implicitly play a crucial role in these debates (Hannerz 1997; Gupta 2015; see also Harris, Chapter 7, this volume). While the scope of mobility studies goes far beyond the question of borders, and many of the conceptual innovations in this field are ethnographically rooted in urban settings (Urry 2000; Sassen 2002; Sheller and Urry 2006), borderlands are places where questions of mobility, migration, and transnationalism necessarily come to the forefront (cf. Cunningham and Heyman 2004).

Many contemporary studies of borderlands revolve around the act of border crossing, the obstacles, asymmetries, and materialities involved and the tactical manoeuvring necessary in day-to-day interaction (Sur 2013). Mobility, and the problems associated with it, shape life in borderlands – quite in contrast to the rural, static, sedentary imaginaries in which peripheries at the edge of nation states are often cast. Mobility is seldom a new phenomenon; it typically precedes borders, as David Ludden (2003: 1062) once remarked – it has a historical depth that the contemporary rhetoric of globalisation tends to ignore.

Given the dual task of borders in the post-Cold War era to safeguard sovereignty while fostering (orderly) exchange, the challenge for state authority is to separate 'good' from 'bad' mobility – terrorists from tourists, expats from illegal migrants, global trade from smuggling, foreign direct investment from capital seeking tax havens, etc. (cf. Jones, Chapter 1, this volume). This double task led to border situations in which state authority can be omnipresent while strangely absent at the same time. Much akin to Latour's argument (1993) that the work of separation so typical for the modern project always requires the work of translation, we see that state attempts at regulating and making legible cross-border interaction tend to go along with processes of exchange outside the channels set up for this purpose. The fenced and regulated border crossing and the trail through the jungle, the smuggler and the customs official, stand in an interdependent – and often intimate – relationship with each other. In this sense, bordering, or neighbouring, is not a trait but a generative process of antagonistic intimacy that ties the locality of a borderland situation into an ever-changing web of regional or global connections (Zhang and Saxer 2017).

In other words, taking a loan from Madeleine Reeves (2014), what many of the contributors to this volume are concerned with is 'border work' – the doing and undoing of contested borders by a wide range of players, including government institutions, border police, businesses, long-term residents, and newcomers, such as refugees, and humanitarian non-governmental organizations (NGOs). In this context, borders, and border work are not limited to international boundary lines; they are rather prolific and reach deep into state territory. Consider, for example, the immigration control of ethnic minority people in downtown Yangon or detention centres in Bangkok. Just like international borders, such boundaries are seldom sealed. On the contrary, they are typically purposefully semi-open. The gate of a refugee camp, for example, can be used to control the movement of international humanitarian organizations, while others bribe the guards and receive a special document to pass without being checked. In this sense, as Mezzardra and Neilson explain (2013), a border is a flexible, ultimately filtering membrane that can be wide open for the movement of capital and certain people, while being strictly closed for others.

This, in turn, raises questions of morality, identity, and legality. In the introduction to their seminal volume *Illicit Flows and Criminal Things. States, Borders, and the Other Side of Globalization*, Willem van Schendel and Itty Abraham (2005) disentangle these questions by separating legality from licitness, the former relating to law and the latter to morality. In brief, their argument is that exchange across a border is not always licit and legal, or illicit and illegal; often such exchanges can be technically illegal but locally conceived of as ethically licit, or the other way round: technically legal but ethically unjustified.

This distinction, which found entry into a great number of books and papers (see Kalir and Sur 2012 for a discussion), has been very productive in rethinking the notions of the 'shadow economy' or the 'informal sector'. In the context of Asian borderlands, the distinction between formal and informal seldom makes analytical sense, as the two are typically thoroughly entwined and embedded in ethical questions. Smuggling or trafficking typically takes place with the knowledge (and often the direct involvement) of military commanders or local officials, while documented legality is a resource that is often only accessible by elites with friends in high places. Informality and uncertainty, Rano Turaeva argues (Chapter 34, this volume), then become the very instruments of state power rather than being its obstacle.

Not only are borderland spaces, practices, discourses, and institutions 'contingent and mutually constitutive', as Adam Saltsman argues (Chapter 18, this volume), and thereby contribute to the manifold outcomes we observe; border regimes quickly become – for good or for bad – integral parts of the social and political fabric of borderlands. In some contexts, the presence of military and armed border guards becomes so routinized and the threat of force to settle communal disputes so perfectly normal, that, following Madeleine Reeves, it makes sense to see it as a form of 'intimate militarisation' (Chapter 3, this volume).

Thus, while there is little doubt that checkpoints and customs authorities are part of a state's security apparatus and thereby forcefully inserted into everyday life in the borderlands (Turaeva, Chapter 34, this volume), they themselves are continuously being 'digested' and made part of borderland situations in ways that state authorities hardly ever foresee. In this process, and despite the everyday disruption militarized border regimes may bring about, borders are sometimes reified by the very residents living close to them, and thereby serve as the moral basis for politics of identity and a variety of claims upon the state. The chapters by Rune Bennike (Chapter 17), Caroline Grillot (Chapter 23), Swargajyoti Gohain (Chapter 35), and Azmeary Ferdoush and Reece Jones (Chapter 19) in this volume are concerned with border situations that, while being contested, are at the same time taken for granted when used to make claims about identity, belonging, the neighbours across the border, or the duties of the state.

A patchwork of borderland situations

A handbook on Asian borderlands raises the question whether there is anything particularly Asian about the borderlands discussed. We would not support such a claim; the Asian borderlands analysed in this book are not fundamentally different from other borderlands around the world. However, over the past decade, Asian borderlands have been the setting from which a great number of novel and promising ideas about borders and borderlands emerged, highlighting important theoretical issues and furthering our conceptual understandings of the dynamics at stake. Most of the debates and concepts outlined above are rooted in deep and long-standing engagements with borderlands in Asia. Most of them have been intensively discussed and refined in the exponentially growing biannual conferences of the Asian Borderlands Research Network (ABRN). Furthermore, new journals like *TRaNS* and new book series like Asian Borderlands (Amsterdam University Press) are a testimony to the fertile terrain of these discussions (see Karin Dean, Chapter 4, this volume). The insights gained from Asian borderlands are of global relevance; they are important pieces in the puzzle to rethink globalization from the edge.

The hallmark of the chapters compiled in this handbook is not one particular theme or take on borderlands but rather the large gamut of borderland situations encountered in Asia today. While some border areas formerly engaged in intensive exchange were divided by new borderlines (Reeves, Chapter 3; Turaeva, Chapter, 34, this volume), others re-emerged as avenues for exchange (Alff, Chapter 10; Steenberg, Chapter 22, this volume). Some sensitive border regions formerly off-limits were turned into special economic zones and trading hubs (Rippa, Chapter 8, this volume), or became the target of large investments in agribusinesses that converted the forests between Yunnan and Indonesia into rubber, palm oil, or banana plantations (Eilenberg, Chapter 13, this volume; Rousseau, Chapter 15, this volume). Other border regions became frontier economies feeding the increasing consumer demands of new Asian middle classes for precious timber, medicinal plants, and exotic wildlife (Tsing 2005; Yeh 2012; Saxer 2013). Some border areas witnessed increasing militarization and securitization (Jones, Chapter 1, this volume), while in other areas remoteness became an asset in itself, facilitating exchange at the blurry edge of the state's field of vision or serving as hideouts for militias and drug lords. While in some borderlands people moved out in search of better lives, other borderlands attracted new populations seeking refuge, fortune, or target groups (Horstmann, Chapter 27, this volume).

How to make sense of this sheer variety of borderland situations? Typology is one answer. In his seminal book *Border People: Life and Society in the U.S.-Mexico Borderlands*, Óscar Martínez (1994) suggested a classification of borderlands into four types – alienated, coexistent, interdependent, and integrated – according to the relations between nation states and the respective restrictions on cross-border interaction. Critical of the reification of borders that come with this model, but ultimately in a similar vein, Michiel Baud and Willem van Schendel described the typical life cycle of borderlands: from infant to adolescent, adult, declining, and defunct (Baud and van Schendel 1997: 224–225). While useful as conceptual toolkit, however, these attempts at classification do not fully capture the patchwork of border situations we encounter in Asia today. In the chapters of this book, we find busy unofficial border crossings that continue to be used right next to fancy new checkpoints, state-sponsored special zones that foster practices the state aims to suppress, and customs officials or military personnel who themselves become major players in the very border economies they are meant to keep in check. In other words, borderlands can be both alienated and interdependent within a few miles: infant, adult, and declining at once.

More promising than a typology of characteristics or stages in a life cycle is an analysis of the underlying processes. We agree with Appadurai (2000) and others (Schendel 2002; Giersch 2010; Mielke and Hornidge 2014; Kreutzmann 2016) that a shift in spatialisation of social theory away from spatial containers like the nation state or the areas of area studies has to go hand in hand with an analytical move from a description of shared cultural, religious, social, and political 'traits' to a geography of processes – processes that necessarily reach far beyond the borderlands at stake while being right at the heart of their formation.

Outline of the book

This focus on processes lends this handbook its structure. The first part contains five longer chapters that prepare the ground for the themes of the subsequent parts. Reece Jones theorizes the shift towards hardened borders in Asia in the era of globalization, when restricting the movement of some people – the poor, the migrants, and other perceived threats to the security of often newly formed nation states – became the main purpose of borders. Building on this discussion, the chapter shows how violence derives from such hardening, and how it reduces the potentialities of those on the move. Moving from similar stories of displacement and violence along Asia's present-day national borders, Malini Sur explores the intersections between gender, nationalisms, and borders. Advancing that a gendered lens offers critical insights into the production of borderlands as contentious and sexualized territories, she invites scholars of borders and border societies to rethink women's roles in armed struggles and resettlement projects. Sur illuminates the manner in which women's political and economic participation in nation building and border projects have redefined gendered relations; and shows how women mobilize, circumvent, and challenge dominant gender hierarchies through their participation in trans-border trade and wage labour. The everyday dynamics of border securitization are, on the other hand, the focus of Madeleine Reeves's chapter. Reeves focuses on the contentious delimitation and regulation of borders in the Ferghana Valley, where Uzbekistan, Tajikistan, and Kyrgyzstan meet. Here, the disputed presence of borders and border claims, intertwined with the routinization of national geographies and of military presence, assume an 'intimate' quality – a matter of daily occurrence, negotiation, and concern. The remaining two chapters, by Karin Dean and Jean Michaud, respectively, while also dealing directly with the disputed nature of many Asian borders, take on directly the issue of scholarship on borderlands in Asia. Karin Dean, in particular, suggests that Asian borderlands have not yet become paradigmatic, despite the 'boom' in academic studies concerned with them, because they have been 'out of synchronization' with border studies in the West. She argues, however, that Asian borderlands can, and should, provide significant insights into this body of literature – something that is at the very core of this handbook's mission. One such insight is certainly the concern of Jean Michaud's chapter on Zomia, in which he weighs into the debate surrounding van Schendel and Scott's works on upland Southeast Asia.

Part 2 is concerned with livelihoods, commodities, and mobilities, bringing together places as distant as Kazakhstan and Myanmar. Frédéric Bourdier examines the Cambodia–Vietnam border as a site of contentious access to natural resources. Showing the ways in which both states have constructed these borderlands, and how these processes impact current local and geopolitical understandings of the regions, he describes how grassroots mobilization challenges larger development processes over access and control of natural resources. Competition, here as elsewhere, operates on both a concrete and a discursive level, with governments' attempts to 'modernise' local groups often going hand in hand with development projects highly disruptive of local livelihoods. Tina Harris, in her chapter, focuses on commodities in the study of borderlands. Focusing on one specific commodity – Himalayan yak tails – she argues, moving from a growing literature in the social sciences, that working through commodities can enlighten trans-border processes of great significance. Alessandro Rippa's chapter similarly draws on a *longue-durée* perspective to discuss cross-border trade relations between Xinjiang and Pakistan. He develops the notion of proximity in order to refer to the geographical, cultural, and historical closeness that affords specific economic opportunities to local traders, which is typical of many regions across Asian borderlands today. Historical legacies are at the core of the chapter by Carl Grundy-Warr, Jessica Teo, and Wei Jun Chin, in which the village of Ban Rak Thai in northern Thailand becomes a nexus of geopolitical and cultural forces spanning decades across the borders of China, Myanmar, and Thailand itself. The authors show that current cultural identities are shaped by intercultural and interethnic interactions, and generate a particular sense of belonging to a single national territory. Ethnic and national loyalties are also at the centre of Henryk Alff's discussion of the Kazakh Dungan community. Given its historical connection to China, Alff traces the successful engagement of the community in cross-border trade following the Sino–Soviet rapprochement in the late 1980s and the many opportunities arising in the subsequent two decades. The Dungans, Alff shows, have been able to take advantage of their socio-spatial liminality by situating themselves as influential brokers and facilitators of change between China and Central Asia. Alexandra de Mersan's chapter, on the other hand, addresses an issue of great current concern with the case of ethnic integration in Myanmar's Rakhine/Arakan state. Through an original analysis of spirit cults and rituals, the chapter shows the inclusive role of such rituals in a society increasingly segmented along ethnic lines.

Part 3 looks at cases of agrarian transformation and changes in the use of forests in the borderlands of Asia. Noboru Ishikawa explores the making of state boundaries in relation to the commodification of forest products in Sarawak, Malaysia. He argues that in the case of Borneo, the genesis of borderlands are less an issue of extending state power into the frontier; rather, they are better understood as an effort in re-imagining the region as *terrae nullius* with the purpose of accessing its resources in the process of transnational commodification. On the other side of the border between Indonesia and Malaysia a similar story takes place. Michael Eilenberg shows how in Kalimantan, a master plan introduced by the Indonesian government aims at integrating unproductive borderlands and local populations into the national economy by allocating land to private oil palm concessions in combination with a military intervention to make this possible. Along similar lines, Jean-François Rousseau shows how in Yunnan terrain traditionally used in an extensive way by local farmers was classified as wasteland and thus ready for an experiment in commercial jathropa biodiesel production. The heavily subsidized experiment in Chinese development failed, but the species introduced in the course of this agrarian transformation does not allow for a return to prior forms of usage. Another different type of agrarian transformation is taking place in the Russian Far East. Jiayi Zhou's chapter discusses the evolution of Chinese farming on Russian territory from small Chinese tenant farmers producing vegetables in greenhouses to capital intensive agribusinesses renting thousands of hectares of land for mechanized grain and pulse production. The shared underlying story in all four cases presented in this part is the re-imagining of a frontier as unproductive wasteland to kickstart a certain kind of development based on capital-intensive agribusiness and resource extraction.

Part 4 – Borders and Boundaries of the State, Governance, and the Production of Citizenship and Statelessness – takes on issues of identity politics, belonging, and citizenship. It revolves around questions of how boundary making can be both a curse and a resource for minorities at the margin to make claims on the state. Karin Dean and Mart Viirand show how national borders, the main subjects of this handbook, are but one kind of boundary shaping movements and livelihoods. Through the case of Kachin State, in northern Myanmar, they discuss multiple borders as ordering devices enacted by both state and non-state actors. International borders, they conclude, can also emerge – or perform their role – well inside state territory, while the actual border line remains porous and poorly enacted. Rune Bennike looks at how territorial autonomy is discursively constructed in a borderland region of eastern Nepal. By distinguishing between a indigeneity-oriented *politics of culture* and a state-emulating *culture of politics*, he argues that political mobilization represents a 'balancing act' across the different scales that these two dimensions relate to. In Adam Saltsman's chapter borders are not only multiple – they proliferate. Discussing the numerous characterizations of the Thai–Myanmar borderlands, he argues that the experience of borders often challenges simplistic notions of free trade and/or national security. Borders, on the other hand, manifest themselves as heterogeneous assemblages through which different populations experience territory, sovereignty, and governance in varying ways. Azmeary Ferdoush and Reece Jones's chapter deals with a different kind of border mobility: enclaves at the India–Bangladesh border that, after decades, saw their precarious administrative status settled. Local groups were thus faced with the decision of whether to move to their country of citizenship (a new country) or get settled within the country they had grown to call their own. In this exchange the enclaves, formerly little more than abandoned spaces, became a symbol of nationalism in the region, the objective of development programmes, and a bargaining chip between two states. The issue of mapping and administering territories at the edge of the nation state is also at the centre of Maxime Boutry's chapter. Discussing the case of sea gypsies in the Malay Peninsula against the backdrop of James Scott's Zomia, the chapter shows how littorals can be seen as increasingly important places of resistance against the state. Sea nomads of the Malay Peninsula are also the focus of Jacques Ivanoff's chapter, in which the case of the Moken is dealt with in detail. Ivanoff employs the notion of the 'pivot system' to show how certain cultural and social traits can be 're-activated' at particular times despite migration and the necessary adaptation to new political systems. Once again, James Scott's work on Zomia serves as a point of departure in thinking through such processes.

Part 5 – It's all About Relations – follows the revival and current crises of small-scale trade and brokerage. Natalia Ryzhova retraces the history of shuttle trade between Russia and China across the Amur River since the end of the 1980s and discusses questions of legality, visibility, and sovereignty in these economic niches. Facing increasing pressure from a series of state regulations, the old shuttle trade became less and less lucrative. However, online shopping in China combined with payment and delivery services have emerged as a new opportunity for a new kind of brokers. Rune Steenberg tells a similar story about Uyghur shuttle traders doing business between Xinjiang and Kyrgyzstan. Perfectly positioned to make use of this economic niche when it appeared in the early 1990s, small Uyghur traders have since faced harsh competition by Kyrgyz and Han-Chinese traders with better access to capital and state officials.

However, the relations Uyghur traders forged in the Kyrgyzstan trade are now used to venture into other fields of business. Galen Murton's contribution looks into the construction of a road to Mustang in northern Nepal and the effect of infrastructure development on social relations formerly at the heart of trans-Himalayan trade. Strained relations are also the topic of Caroline Grillot's contribution on the Sino–Vietnamese border. Following the story of an alleged plot by Chinese traders against the Vietnamese, Grillot discusses ethnopolitics and moralities in the context of boom and bust in a frontier economy. The chapters in this part discuss brokerage based on intensive relation-making from different angles, and raise the question what happens to these relations when the very niches in which they grew come under pressure. Christine Bonnin's chapter looks at the tactical adaptation strategies of Hmong ethnic minorities in the Sino–Vietnamese borderlands. Over the last decade, the industrial production of textiles in China made to emulate Hmong traditional designs has flourished, and the chapter focuses on the import of such new, ethnic minority-oriented 'cultural commodities' into the remote border uplands of Vietnam. Through a case study of the trade in factory-made textiles, Bonnin demonstrates how consumer markets 'on the margins' are being actively crafted through the actions of Hmong small-scale traders, and how the emergence of new technologies of production for these cultural commodities has worked to enliven, strengthen, and diversify the use and trade of Hmong textiles.

Part 6 explores the arrival of faith-based NGOs and their partnerships with international humanitarian organizations on the stage of Asian borderlands. It offers a number of analytical takes on the ways their work combines global notions of humanitarianism and development with religion. Till Mostowlansky discusses the 'political theology of development' that the Aga Khan Development Network (AKDN) introduced in the Pamirian borderlands after the collapse of the Soviet Union, focusing on how different actors participate in the redrawing of borders and states. Su-Ann Oh analyses humanitarian NGOs in the framework of a new kind of moral economy in the Thai–Myanmar borderlands and the role that emotion and affect play in soliciting the support of donors. Situated in the same borderlands, Alexander Horstmann addresses the ideological and practical power of the Free Burma Rangers, an American evangelical organization working clandestinely in Burma, vis-à-vis the generalized morality of humanitarian organizations like Médecins Sans Frontières. His contribution discusses the biopolitical intervention of the Free Burma Rangers in the dangerous borderlands of Myanmar as an act of political community-making in the global arena. Finally, the chapter by Dan Smyer Yü looks at the role of religion, morality, and community from the perspective of a Tibetan woman eloping with a Muslim man in northwestern China, and the issue of embodiment in relation to ethnoreligious boundaries. The chapter illustrates the extension and multiplication of boundary making on the personal level of cultural intimacy.

The final part – Militarization of borderlands – follows up on a theme initiated by Madeleine Reeves in Part 1 and touched upon by many of the chapters throughout this handbook: state authority enforced by military power and exercised at checkpoints and borders. The chapters by Pradeep Jeganathan and Rano Turaeva describe the logic of everyday violence and authority at checkpoints. Swargajyoti Gohain discusses militarization in the context of a disputed border, in her case two districts in Arunachal Pradesh claimed by China. Adam Cathcart discuss fear, security, and control at the Sino–North Korean border, the issue of North Korean trans-border violence, and Chinese–North Korean cooperation. Masaya Shishikura, finally, takes us to the residents of the Ogasawara Islands who aim at transcending these militarized border islands with musical crossings.

The six themes that the various chapters address, are, of course, far from comprehensive. What they do, we hope, is help to foster comparisons between borderland situations across Asia not by enumerating their characteristics, or their similarities and differences, but by focusing on a number of underlying processes that are at work throughout Asian borderlands and, probably, across borderlands worldwide.

Note

1 See, for example, the special issue in the *Journal of Global History* edited by Jean Michaud (2010).

References

Agnew, John. 1994. 'The Territorial Trap: The Geographical Assumptions of International Relations Theory.' *Review of International Political Economy* 1 (1): 53–80.
Alff, Henryk. 2015. 'Profiteers or Moral Entrepreneurs?: Bazaars, Traders and Development Discourses in Almaty, Kazakhstan.' *International Development Planning Review* 37 (3): 249–67.
Andersson, Ruben. 2016. 'Here Be Dragons: Mapping an Ethnography of Global Danger.' *Current Anthropology* 57 (6). www.journals.uchicago.edu/doi/10.1086/689211 (accessed 19 May 2017).
Andersson, Ruben, and Martin Saxer. 2016. 'Remoteness Redux? Anthropological Takes on the Return of #remoteness.' *Allegra Lab*. http://allegralaboratory.net/introduction-to-the-week-remoteness-redux/ (accessed 19 May 2017).
Appadurai, Arjun. 2000. *Globalization and Area Studies: The Future of a False Opposition*. Amsterdam: CASA – Centre for Asian Studies Amsterdam.
Asian Development Bank. 2010. 'The Rise of Asia's Middle Class.' In *Key Indicators for Asia and the Pacific 2010*. Manila: Asian Development Bank.
Baud, Michiel, and Willem van Schendel. 1997. 'Toward a Comparative History of Borderlands.' *Journal of World History* 8 (2): 211–42.
Billé, Franck. 2017. 'Bright Lights across the River. Competing Modernities at China's Edge.' In *The Art of Neighbouring. Making Relations Across China's Borders*, edited by Martin Saxer and Juan Zhang, 33–56. Amsterdam: Amsterdam University Press.
Brenner, Neil. 1997. 'Global, Fragmented, Hierarchical: Henri Lefebvre's Geographies of Globalization.' *Public Culture* 10 (1): 135–67.
Brenner, Neil. 1999. 'Beyond State-Centrism? Space, Territoriality, and Geographical Scale in Globalization Studies.' *Theory and Society* 28 (1): 39–78.
Callahan, William A. 2016. 'China's "Asia Dream": The Belt Road Initiative and the New Regional Order.' *Asian Journal of Contemporary Politics* 1(3): 1–18.
Campbell, Ben. 2010. 'Rhetorical Routes for Development: A Road Project in Nepal.' *Contemporary South Asia* 18 (3): 267–79.
Cox, Kevin R. 1997. *Spaces of Globalisation: Reasserting the Power of the Local*. New York: The Guilford Press.
Cunningham, Hilary. 2009. 'Mobilities and Enclosures after Seattle: Politicizing Borders in a "Borderless" World.' *Dialectical Anthropology* 33 (2): 143–56.
Cunningham, Hilary, and Josiah Heyman. 2004. 'Introduction: Mobilities and Enclosures at Borders.' *Identities* 11 (3): 289–302.
Dalakoglou, Dimitris, and Penny Harvey. 2012. 'Roads and Anthropology: Ethnographic Perspectives on Space, Time and (Im)mobility.' *Mobilities* 7 (4): 459–65.
Demenge, Jonathan P. 2013. 'The Road to Lingshed: Manufactured Isolation and Experienced Mobility in Ladakh.' *Himalaya, the Journal of the Association for Nepal and Himalayan Studies* 32 (1): Article 14.
Dirlik, Arif. 1997. *The Postcolonial Aura. Third World Criticism in the Age of Global Capitalism*. Boulder, CO: Westview Press.
Dirlik, Arif. 2011. 'Globalization, Indigenism, Social Movements, and the Politics of Place.' *Localities* 1: 47–90.
Duara, Prasenjit. 1995. *Rescuing History from the Nation: Questioning Narratives of Modern China*. Chicago: The University of Chicago Press.
Fukuyama, Francis. 1989. 'The End of History?' *The National Interest* 1989 (Summer): 1–18.
Gainsborough, Martin. 2007. 'Globalisation and the State Revisited: A View from Provincial Vietnam.' *Journal of Contemporary Asia* 37 (1): 1–18.
Giersch, Charles Patterson. 2010. 'Across Zomia with Merchants, Monks, and Musk: Process Geographies, Trade Networks, and the Inner-East-Southeast Asian Borderlands.' *Journal of Global History* 5 (2): 215–39.

Gupta, Akhil. 2015. 'Suspension.' *Cultural Anthropology.* https://culanth.org/fieldsights/722-suspension (accessed 19 May 2017).

Hannerz, Ulf. 1997. 'Flows, Boundaries and Hybrids: Keywords in Transnational Anthropology.' *Mana* 3 (1): 7–39.

Harvey, David. 1989. *The Condition of Postmodernity: An Enquiry into the Origins of Cultural Change.* Cambridge, MA: Blackwell.

Harvey, Penny, and Hannah Knox. 2015. *On Roads. An Anthropology of Infrastructure and Expertise.* Ithaca, NY & London: Cornell University Press.

Heyman, Josiah McC., Hilary Cunningham, Jonathan D Hill, and Thomas M Wilson. 2004. 'Special Issue: Movement on the Margins: Mobility and Enclosures at Borders.' *Identities* 11 (3): 287.

Johnson, Christopher K. 2016. *President Xi Jinping's 'Belt and Road' Initiative.* Center for Strategic & International Studies. www.uschina.org/sites/default/files/President%20Xi%20Jinping%27s%20Belt%20and%20Road%20Initiative.pdf (accessed 19 May 2017).

Jones, Reece. 2016. *Violent Borders: Refugees and the Right to Move.* New York: Verso.

Kalir, Barak, and Malini Sur. 2012. *Transnational Flows and Permissive Polities: Ethnographies of Human Mobilities in Asia.* Amsterdam: Amsterdam University Press.

Karrar, Hasan. 2013. 'Merchants, Markets, and the State.' *Critical Asian Studies* 45 (3): 459-80.

Kreutzmann, Hermann. 2016. *Mapping Transition in the Pamirs.* Cham: Springer.

Lama, Sonam. 2013. 'Road from Nowhere to Nowhere.' *Nepali Times.* http://nepalitimes.com/article/nation/Nation-road-from-nowhere-to-nowhere,549 (accessed 19 May 2017).

Latour, Bruno. 1993. *We Have Never Been Modern.* New York: Harvester Wheatsheaf.

Ludden, David. 2003. 'Presidential Address: Maps in the Mind and the Mobility of Asia.' *The Journal of Asian Studies* 62 (4): 1057–78.

Martínez, Óscar Jáquez. 1994. *Border People: Life and Society in the U.S.-Mexico Borderlands.* Tucson: University of Arizona Press.

Mezzardra, Sandro, and Brett Neilson. 2013. *Border as Method, or, the Multiplication of Labor.* Durham, NC & London: Duke University Press.

Michaud, Jean. 2000. *Turbulent Times and Enduring Peoples: Mountain Minorities in the South-East Asian Massif.* Richmond: Curzon Press.

Michaud, Jean. 2010. 'Editorial – Zomia and beyond.' *Journal of Global History* 5 (2): 187–214.

Michaud, Jean. 2016 'Seeing the Forest for the Trees: Scale, Magnitude, and Range in the Southeast Asian Massif.' In *Historical Dictionary of the Peoples of the South-East Asian Massif.* Second Edition, edited by Jean Michaud, Meenaxi B. Ruscheweyh, and Margaret B. Swain, 1–40. Lanham, Boulder, CO, New York, & London: Rowman & Littlefield.

Mielke, Katja, and Anna-Katharina Hornidge. 2014. 'Crossroads Studies: From Spatial Containers to Interactions in Differentiated Spatialities.' Crossroads Asia Working Paper Series, No. 15, www.ssoar.info/ssoar/bitstream/handle/document/39751/ssoar-2014-mielke_et_al-Crossroads_studies_from_spatial_containers.pdf?sequence=1 (accessed 26 September 2017).

Nyíri, Pál, and Joana Breidenbach. 2008. 'The Altai Road: Visions of Development across the Russian–Chinese Border.' *Development and Change* 39 (1): 123–45.

Ohmae, Kenichi. 1990. *The Borderless World: Power and Strategy in the Interlinked Economy.* New York: Harper Business.

Pedersen, Morten Axel, and Mikkel Bunkenborg. 2012. 'Roads that Separate: Sino-Mongolian Relations in the Inner Asian Desert.' *Mobilities* 7 (4): 555–69.

Reeves, Madeleine. 2014. *Border Work: Spatial Lives of the State in Rural Central Asia.* Ithaca, NY: Cornell University Press.

Rippa, Alessandro, and Martin Saxer. 2016. 'Mong La: Business as Usual in the China-Myanmar Borderlands.' *Cross-Currents: East Asian History and Culture Review* 19: 240–52. https://cross-currents.berkeley.edu/e-journal/issue-19/mong-la/essay (accessed 19 May 2017).

Sassen, Saskia. 2002. 'Locating Cities on Global Circuits.' In *Global Networks, Linked Cities*, edited by Saskia Sassen, 1–36. New York and London: Routledge.

Saxer, Martin. 2013. 'Between China and Nepal: Trans-Himalayan Trade and the Second Life of Development in Upper Humla.' *Cross-Currents: East Asian History and Culture Review* 8: 31–52.

Schendel, Willem van. 2002. 'Geographies of Knowing, Geographies of Ignorance: Jumping Scale in Southeast Asia.' *Environment and Planning D: Society and Space* 20 (6): 647–68.

Schendel, Willem van, and Itty Abraham. 2005. *Illicit Flows and Criminal Things. States, Borders, and the Other Side of Globalization.* Bloomington, IN: Indiana University Press.

Scott, James C. 2009. *The Art of Not Being Governed. An Anarchist History of Upland Southeast Asia.* New Haven, CT & London: Yale University Press.
Sheller, Mimi, and John Urry. 2006. 'The New Mobilities Paradigm.' *Environment and Planning A* 38 (2): 207–26.
Sidaway, James, and Chih Yuan Woon. 2017. 'Chinese Narratives on 'One Belt, One Road' (一带一路) in Geopolitical and Imperial Contexts.' *The Professional Geographer* 69 (4): 591-603.
Sur, Malini. 2013. 'Through Metal Fences: Material Mobility and the Politics of Transnationality at Borders.' *Mobilities* 8 (1): 70–89.
Tsing, Anna Lowenhaupt. 2005. *Friction: an Ethnography of Global Connection.* Princeton, NJ: Princeton University Press.
Urry, John. 2000. *Sociology beyond Societies. Mobilities for the Twenty-first Century.* London: Routledge.
Walker, Andrew. 1999. *The Legend of the Golden Boat. Regulation, Trade and Traders in the Borderlands of Laos, Thailand, China, and Burma.* Honolulu: University of Hawaii Press.
Wimmer, Andreas, and Nina Glick Schiller. 2002. 'Methodological Nationalism and Beyond: Nation-State Building, Migration and the Social Sciences.' *Global Networks* 2 (4): 301–34.
Woods, Kevin. 2011. 'Ceasefire Capitalism: Military-Private Partnership, Resource Concessions and Military-State Building in the Burma-China Borderlands.' *The Journal of Peasant Studies* 38 (4): 747–70.
Yeh, Emily T. 2012. 'Transnational Environmentalism and Entanglements of Sovereignty: The Tiger Campaign across the Himalayas.' *Political Geography* 31 (7): 408–18.
Zhang, Juan, and Martin Saxer. 2017. 'Neighbouring in the Borderworlds along China's Frontiers.' In *The Art of Neighbouring. Making Relations Across China's Borders*, edited by Martin Saxer and Juan Zhang, 11–29. Amsterdam: Amsterdam University Press.

Part I
Conceptual framing

1
Violence in Asian borderlands

Reece Jones

Introduction

In the years 2015 and 2016, media headlines were dominated by stories about refugees, borders, and violence. In 2015 alone, 1.2 million people applied for asylum in the European Union, up from 197,000 in 2006 (Eurostat 2016). The images of dead children washed up on beaches and millions of people struggling to move to new homes for safety competed with images of new barbed wire fences under construction at borders and stories about the rise of anti-migrant politicians in many countries around the world. In 2015 alone, Austria, Bulgaria, Estonia, Hungary, Kenya, Saudi Arabia, and Tunisia all announced or began the construction of walls and fences on their borders (see also Brian and Laczko 2014). Many European countries reinstated internal border checkpoints after a decade of free movement. Donald Trump was elected President of the United States by promising to build a massive wall on the US–Mexico border and to temporarily ban all Muslims from entering the USA.

What was often missing from many of these stories was the experience of borders in Asia. How do Asian borders compare to the hardening and militarization of borders in the USA and Europe? Has there been a similar transformation of borderlands across Asia? Of course, the situation varies at different borders and even the same borderlands can be dramatically different in different locations. The India–Bangladesh border, for example, is a site of extreme violence in some sections and over 1,000 people have been killed by the Indian Border Security Force (BSF) since the year 2000 (Odhikar n.d.). At the same time, on other parts of the border, the BSF allows cross-border market days where traders from both sides come together to sell their wares (Boyle and Rahman 2018). Other contributors to this volume lay out the multitude of different border spaces, but the focus of this chapter is how Asian borderlands are situated within the global trend toward hardened and violent borders.

A number of scholars have begun to analyze the hardening of borders in Asia and the resultant violence including a recent special section of the International Institute for Asian Studies (IIAS) newsletter edited by Swargajyoti Gohain (2015). Gohain argues that although borders are the edges of state territories, they are not peripheral to the practice and performance of authority. Instead, 'Our focus on militarized borders brings to light the many ways in which militarization aids the nation-state project in the national peripheries' (Gohain 2015: 22). The changes at the edge of the state have both discursive and material effects, simultaneously symbolizing the idea of state territory and control while materializing those claims on the ground. 'It has powerful spatial and ideological effects, changing the visual landscape, the language and social norms, and the local and global economy' by normalizing the idea of the border (Gohain 2015: 22).

Traditionally, scholars have maintained a distinction between different types of violence, using direct violence to refer to intentional actions that result in harm, and structural violence to refer to how systems, rules, and procedures produce violence through neglect, foreclosing safety, or forcing people into dangerous situations (Galtung 1969). At borders, an example of direct violence is when an Indian Border Guard shoots someone in the India–Bangladesh borderlands. Structural violence would be the regulations that sends migrants to more dangerous routes and locations, for example the citizenship laws in Myanmar that deny citizenship to Rohingya people and force them to cross the border into Bangladesh or, increasingly, to board a ship in the hopes of finding safety in other more distant Southeast Asian locations.

In recent years, scholars have begun to question these divisions and instead argue that maintaining a distinction hides the intentionality in much of the structural violence. James Tyner and Joshua Inwood (2014: 779) suggest that

> Instead of focusing on the uncritical distinction between structural and direct violence, as though each of these forms has its own a prior existence in and of itself, we need to unite these seemingly opposite abstract forms into their historical and geographical totalities.

They continue 'if we abstract violence as any action that affects the material conditions of another, thereby reducing one's potentiality, the distinction between "direct" and "structural" violence collapses' (Tyner and Inwood 2014: 779).

This chapter follows Tyner and Inwood by suggesting that the hardening of borders in various locations across Asia demonstrates the violent outcomes of border work that denies people the right to move adversely affects their material conditions, and reduces their potentiality. This violence is evident in both deaths at borders and also restricted life chances for many individuals who are contained by borders and cannot access opportunities in other locations both within Asia and beyond. The next section provides a theoretical background to border studies with a focus on how walls and other security infrastructure have been used to manage movement at the edges of the state. Three global trends at borders are identified: the externalization and internalization of border work away from the border line; the turn to walls as a symbolic and material device; and the militarization of border spaces as technologies, mentalities, and strategies from the military transform how border police work is done. The third section turns to Asian borderlands to analyze the extent of these trends at different borders throughout Asia. The conclusion argues that even while some borders in the region are still relatively open and lightly guarded, many of the global changes are evident at borders in Asia, which have been transformed during the era of globalization as new technologies alter how security is practiced.

Theoretical background

Over the past decade, the field of border studies has matured as scholarly attention to borders and movement restrictions has expanded rapidly (Amilhat Szary and Giraut 2015; Johnson et al. 2011; Mountz 2015; Parker and Vaughan-Williams 2009; Paasi 2011, 2012; Vallet 2014). The traditional view of borders as taken for granted containers of state space is largely obsolete and has been replaced by the view that borders are performative and socially constructed ideas that are reproduced through events, narratives, and performances of state sovereignty and authority. A key aspect of this literature is the expansion of security infrastructure at borders, which has transformed the landscape of the borderlands, the everyday lives of borderland residents, and the experiences of people and goods moving through border spaces. Three prominent trends in the field are research into the externalization of borders as much of the work of borders is done both within and beyond the edge of the state, often quite far from the actual borderland; the return of the wall as a significant tool for states to mark and enforce sovereignty claims at the border; and the militarization of the practice of border enforcement as new technologies and techniques derived from the military are deployed for policing borders.

Border externalization

A growing debate in border studies is over how to situate border lines within the broadening zone of where border work is done (Amilhat Szary and Giraut 2015; Johnson et al. 2011; Jones and Johnson 2014). Contemporary borders are the product of negotiations between state authorities over the territorial extent of the sovereignty and most borders begin first as lines on the map that are later located on the ground through surveys and then inscribed into the landscape with boundary markers, patrols, and more recently walls and fences (Harley and Woodward 1987). Consequently, border work is predicted on the existence of the line on a map and the corresponding line on the ground (Reeves 2014; Rumford 2008). However, it is increasingly clear that much of the work that goes into protecting the border happens far away from the actual line. A number of states have put in place policies that externalize the border by transferring much of the work of border enforcement to neighbouring states who patrol for migrants and smugglers to prevent them from even reaching the actual border (Collyer and King 2015). This externalization has been closely studied in the European Union and the United States. The European Union and individual member states signed agreements with neighbouring states such as Turkey and Morocco to cooperate on border enforcement. In practice, this means that these states round up migrants, detain them, destroy smuggling infrastructure, and even build border fences, like Morocco's new barbed wire fence around the Spanish enclave of Melilla (European Commission 2013).

A second way that border enforcement has become externalized is through patrols in ocean spaces, often beyond the 12 nautical mile territorial waters or even the 200 nautical mile exclusive economic zone of the state as defined by the United Nations Law of the Sea Convention. Frontex, the European Union-wide border agency, has implemented over a dozen operations in the Mediterranean Sea and Atlantic Ocean that push border enforcement away from the coastline into these liquid spaces of the sea (Heller and Pezzani 2014). In Asia and the Pacific, Australia is at the forefront of maritime border enforcement and island detention, as is described in depth below (Coddington and Mountz 2014).

The work of border enforcement has also been internalized in many states as borders are enforced in zones that can stretch from meters to hundreds of kilometers away from the border line. In the United States, for example, the border zone is defined as within 100 miles (161 km) from borders and coastlines. In this area, the Border Patrol has special authority to conduct searches and seizures without warrants if the agent has 'articulable facts' that justify a search. In the 1975 Brignoni-Ponce decision, the US Supreme Court established what qualifies as an articulable fact, which included being near the border, driving a station wagon, and having a Mexican-style haircut (Jones 2014). In the European Union the internalization of border enforcement has meant a reversal of the Schengen Agreement's open internal borders. For almost a decade there had been individual cases of EU states reinstating internal border controls in response to specific events. However, in 2015 many states, including Germany and France, began to check documents at the borders to screen for migrants and filter out people making asylum claims from countries other than Syria, a practice that targets migrants from Asia, particularly Afghanistan.

For Stuart Elden (2013a, 2013b) the changing geography of security means that the focus should be less on territory as a two dimensional plane and more as a three dimensional zone. Thinking of security in a volumetric rather than a territorial sense allows for a broader understanding of the scope of new infrastructure that includes walls and fences on the ground, but also drones in the air and ground penetrating radar that can detect tunnels under borders. The volumetric approach also emphasizes the zone of the borderlands that stretches away from the actual line in both directions, in some ways mirroring the concept of frontier in the past.

Finally, much of the sorting of people moving across borders, whether at checkpoints or at airport passport controls, is done through computer algorithms housed in facilities far from the border itself (Amoore 2013; Popescu 2012). This data driven migration policing means that the work of security is often taken out of the hands of people and placed in the sphere of artificial intelligence that looks for patterns of trusted travellers in order to identify people who could be perceived as a threat to the state.

With so much of the work of bordering being done away from the border itself and by computers, private security contractors, and other non-state actors, the significance of the border line is under question. However, it is critical not to lose sight of the fact that all of these other bordering practices are based on the existence of a line-on-the-ground border. Indeed, the border line is a symbolic space to project the actions of the state to secure its territory and people. The border line is where the performance of sovereignty is most evident and the border line is also where migrants come into contact with the material consequences of border enforcement, which often means violence, detention, and death. It is also at the border line where the most visible symbolic object of border exclusion is built: the wall.

Border walls

Walls are important objects for the study of borders and border violence. Although walls themselves do not stop movement or cause violence, they are material objects that symbolize the desire of a group of people to protect a piece of land or a particular resource (Brown 2010; Jones 2012; Till et al. 2013; Vallet 2014). They territorialize the claim of authority and control over a space and they reify the line on the map by materializing it as a visual marker on the landscape (Sack 1986). Although there has been a rapid expansion in the construction of walls globally in the past 30 years, walls are also one of the oldest technologies used to control access to resources and protect privileges that have accrued in a particular place.

For many people, the Great Wall of China represents the fact that countries have built border walls for thousands of years. US President Donald Trump has repeatedly used the Chinese wall as an example of how easy it would be to build a wall on the US–Mexico border. On 2 March 2016 he stated 'The Great Wall of China, built 2,000 years ago, is 13,000 miles, folks, and they didn't have Caterpillar tractors' (Beckwith 2016). As with many Trump claims, this version of the Great Wall turns out to be false. The most familiar sections of stone walls snaking through mountains are only about four hundred years old and a few hundred kilometres long. Earlier Chinese states did built multiple walls over a 1,500 year period to prevent nomadic raiders from taking their resources stored in sedentary settlements, but most of these discontinuous walls were thought of as failures and taken down within a few decades of their initial construction (Lovell 2009; Rojas 2010; Sterling 2009; Waldron 1989). Even the most famous sections that have been rebuilt as tourist sites today were overrun within a few decades of their construction.

Walls were more successful historically when used to control a much smaller area that could be more effectively guarded, in a way similar to the use of prison walls today. Most ancient cities in North Africa and the Middle East had a wall complex, the pueblos of Mesoamerica were essentially settlements built into the shape of a wall to provide protection in the event of an attack, and in the Middle Ages, political power in Europe was organized through city states that had walls around the central settlement that allowed resources to be protected in the event of a siege or invasion. Long walls that were hundreds or thousands of kilometres long were extremely rare. Furthermore, prior to the modern era, the idea of a fixed border as a line on a map did not exist (Elden 2013a; Winichakul 1994). Consequently, border walls are also a modern phenomenon and a very recent one. In the 19th century, city walls fell out of favour because they were an impediment to growing cities and most in Europe were torn down. New ones were not built on the emerging borders of sovereign states because walls are not particularly effective against modern weapons such as tanks, missiles, and airplanes. However, the past 30 years has been characterized by a return to the wall, but in a new longer form, as dozens of countries around the world fortified borders and built walls. While in 1945 there were less than five border walls anywhere in the world, in 2016 there are almost 70 (Jones 2012; Vallet 2014).

Border militarization

Another trend at borders globally, and in Asia specifically, is the militarization of border spaces (Gohain 2015). In the past, some borders were militarized zones as the lines on the ground represented the edges of the political space of the state and the point to defend against invasion. However, as the United Nations system of mutually recognized borders was formalized around the world during the 20th century, borders become less about military and defence and more about lines to mark different juridical, political, and economic systems (Murphy 1996, 2013). During this period, it was uncommon for states to securitize borders with a heavy military presence or border infrastructure like walls and fences, because they are expensive and not necessary to simply depict different political regimes. Instead, boundary markers were common ways to mark the edge of the state territory while most of the state infrastructure was deployed at crossing points to check documents and impose customs duties on goods passing into the state. There were a few lingering examples of the older purpose of borders as defensive lines, but the exceptional nature of the Demilitarized Zone in Korea and the Line of Control between India and Pakistan illustrate the fact that most other borders were not well marked and fairly open during the middle of the 20th century.

During the era of globalization, the purpose of borders has shifted again towards being the locations to stop the movement of unauthorized civilians, whether migrants or smugglers. The result has been a new era of border militarization as the violent hardware of state warmaking has been redeployed to border lines, but not to protect against an invasion or an existential threat to the state but rather to prevent unauthorized movements (Dunn 1996, 2001, 2009; Heyman and Campbell 2012; Jones and Johnson 2016; Slack et al. 2016). The militarization of borders has meant surveillance technologies such as drones and high tech sensors, as well as military weapons including tanks, armoured personnel carriers, and battle weapons are increasingly used to monitor for these civilian movements in borders. Furthermore, at many borders the changing practice of enforcement has meant that what was previously a policing job that focused on arrest has become a security job that uses violence to deter movement in the first place.

Peter Kraska (2007: 503) defines militarism as 'a set of beliefs, values, and assumptions that stress the use of force and threat of violence as the most appropriate and efficacious means to solve problems'. Kraska, whose work focuses on police, sees four dimensions where a military ideology and strategy can alter policing. The first dimension is material as new gear and technologies developed for the military are deployed in policing settings. The second is a cultural shift in which police forces that previously relied on minimal force techniques shift towards a language, style, and belief in a maximum force military approach. The third dimension Kraska identifies is an organizational shift as police adopt the military strategy of maintaining elite tactical squads for particular situations but which get used for increasingly quotidian purposes. The fourth dimension is operational in which the daily approach to the job that treats every interaction as a life or death struggle of the battlefield.

Countries around the world classify border patrols differently, but in most instances they are closer to police forces that look for violations of laws rather than militaries that engage in armed conflict. However, the militarization of border policing has meant that many borders around the world have become increasingly militarized zones where the border crossers are the same as they have been for decades—workers looking for higher wages, smugglers making a profit off of different regulations—but the response has becoming increasingly violent as the border guards rely on a security first mentality to prevent terrorist infiltrations into the state. The clear result of these changes at borders is a dramatic increase in violence as more people are killed directly by border agents or indirectly as people are funnelled to ever more dangerous routes cross borders. The International Organization for Migration reported that from 2005 to 2014 over 40,000 people died attempting to cross a border (Brian and Laczko 2014; Weber and Pickering 2011).

Violence and militarization in Asian borderlands

The historical arc of borders in Asia mirrors the global trend. In the 16th and 17th centuries in South and Southeast Asia, empires and states were organized through a tributary system that created affiliations between different cities and loose frontier zones between rival centres of power (Scott 1998, 2009). Borders were not historically fixed lines on the ground, but rather fluid zones where the authority of one state ended and another state, or more frequently a non-state, space began. Contemporary borders in Asia are primarily legacies of colonialism. The British colonized South Asia and left behind the current borders through the 1947 partition (Chatterji 1994; Chester 2008; Edney 1997; Zamindar 2007). Southeast Asia is marked by the boundaries of Dutch, English, French, and Portuguese colonial claims, which were transformed into international borders with the independence of the current sovereign states. Even the borders of Thailand, a country that was never colonized, are shaped by the boundaries of colonial encroachment around its edges (Winichakul 1994). For most of the 20th century, many of these newly created borders were relatively lightly guarded and open, but over the past 30 years a number of borders have been fortified in ways similar to the United States and European Union. The construction of walls, the externalization of border enforcement, and state violence directed towards migrants is evident at many borders throughout Asia.

Border walls

Approximately 40 percent the border walls in the world are located in Asia. While a few of the barriers are defensive military lines along disputed territories, such as on the Korean Peninsula and the Line of Control in Kashmir between areas occupied by India and Pakistan (Datta 2015), most of the walls in Asia have been built in the past 30 years in the era of globalization and often target migrants and smugglers rather than a military threat from the neighbouring country.

The justification for these walls varies depending on the local politics, but in government announcements most walls are proposed as a response to the perceived threat posed by terrorism, smuggling, or migration (Table 1.1). Almost all the walls are built unilaterally by one country with protests and resistance from the state on the other side. The one exception to this is the Thailand–Malaysia barrier, which was built jointly by the two states in order to work against

Table 1.1 Border walls in Asia: more border walls in a borderless world

Building country	Against	Year	Building country	Against	Year
North Korea	South Korea	1977	Saudi Arabia	Iraq	2006
India	Bangladesh	1989	Kazakhstan	Uzbekistan	2006
India	Pakistan	1990	China	North Korea	2006
Kuwait	Iraq	1991	Israel	Egypt	2010
Israel	Gaza	1993	Iran	Pakistan	2011
Uzbekistan	Kyrgyzstan	1999	Israel	Syria	2013
Iran	Afghanistan	2000	Thailand	Malaysia	2013
Israel	Lebanon	2001	India	Myanmar	Planned
Uzbekistan	Afghanistan	2001	India	Bhutan	Planned
Turkmenistan	Uzbekistan	2001	Israel	Jordan	Planned
Israel	West Bank	2002	Iran	Turkey	Planned
Saudi Arabia	Yemen	2003	Malaysia	Brunei	Planned
Brunei	Malaysia	2005	Malaysia	Indonesia	Planned
Saudi Arabia	United Arab Emirates	2005	Malaysia	Thailand	Planned
Saudi Arabia	Oman	2005	Pakistan	Afghanistan	Planned
United Arab Emirates	Oman	2005	Saudi Arabia	Qatar	Planned

Source: Author data; Élisabeth Vallet; The Economist (2016)

what they perceived to be shared threats of a cross-border insurgency and smugglers (Cosmas 2015). Interestingly, while there is a substantial literature on the construction of some of the walls such as India–Bangladesh (McDuie-Ra 2014), Israel (Dolphin 2006), and in Korea (Kim 2013), many of the others have not received substantial scrutiny in the media or in the academic literature.

Externalization of border work

In addition to the construction of walls and fences, there is also substantial evidence of the volumetric approach to border security proposed by Elden (2013b) and the externalization of security practices beyond the sovereign territory of the state in Asia (Andersson 2014; Casas-Cortes et al. 2015; Collyer and King 2015). A number of boundaries in Asia lie across ocean and sea spaces and many of these zones were militarized in the past decade as they have become closed straights where unauthorized ships are interdicted and prevented from reaching the coastline (Rosière and Jones 2012). There are three particularly prominent examples of these closed straights: in the Bay of Bengal, particularly targeting Rohingya refugees from Myanmar, the seas around Australia, and the straits of Taiwan. Each of these represents the externalization of border enforcement as states push the border out to prevent people on the move from even reaching edges of the state at the border line.

The Rohingya are a Muslim minority population of approximately 1.1 million people that lives in Rakhine State in the northwestern corner of Myanmar. Myanmar as a whole is a predominately Buddhist country and the government of Myanmar has long contended that the Rohingya are not natives of Myanmar, but instead are immigrants who crossed over from Bangladesh. Consequently, they are not given citizenship and are persecuted in Myanmar (Human Rights Watch 2013). A 2015 study produced by the Allard K. Lowenstein International Human Rights Clinic at Yale Law School found 'persuasive evidence that the crime of genocide had been committed against Rohingya Muslims' (Lindblom et al. 2015). Bangladesh denies the Rohingya originated in Bangladesh, and only provides basic services in refugee camps for over 200,000 people. Bangladesh lacks the resources to adequately deal with the refugees and wants them to return to Myanmar. 'The Rohingya are the citizens of Myanmar and they must go back', H.T. Imam, a Bangladesh official, explained in 2015 to a Reuters reporter, 'We feel for them, but we are unable to host them any longer' (Miglani 2015). In August and September 2017, over 600,000 more Rohingya fled to Bangladesh after a crackdown by the Myanmar government.

Without a safe home in Myanmar or Bangladesh, many Rohingya are setting out in boats in search of better opportunities in other countries in Southeast Asia. In the first four months of 2015, the United Nations High Commissioner for Refugees estimated that 25,000 Rohingya departed in boats from the Myanmar–Bangladesh border area (United Nations High Commissioner for Refugees 2015). Several boats were reportedly pushed away from the coasts of Indonesia, Malaysia, and Thailand before Indonesia and Malaysia, under growing international pressure, eventually took them. The Deputy Home Minister of Malaysia, Wan Junaidi, explained the position of the receiving countries, 'What do you expect us to do? We have been very nice to the people who broke into our border', he told The Associated Press. 'We have treated them humanely, but they cannot be flooding our shores like this. We have to send the right message that they are not welcome here' (Fuller and Cochrane 2015). In addition to hundreds of people who have died on the trip, Malaysia discovered several mass graves near its border with Thailand that were reported to be of Rohingya migrants who died or were killed by smugglers. Because the Rohingya are stateless and lack documents that prove their identity, some governments deny them the protection of the status as a refugee. The Australian Foreign Affairs Minster Julie Bishop said in 2015 most were Bangladeshi 'illegal laborers' not refugees (Stewart and Balogh 2015).

Another example of border externalization in Asia are the seas off the coast of Australia, a country that has extremely strict border policies which do not allow boats to reach its shores (Coddington and Mountz 2014). With easier crossings from the Indonesian island of Timor closed, many migrants are funnelled to the more dangerous journey across the open Indian Ocean towards Christmas Island, an Australia territory, 400 km (250 miles) away. As migrants began to arrive at Christmas Island in the early 1990s, the Australian government reclassified the island as outside Australian territory for immigration purposes, which means that today migrants who arrive cannot automatically apply for asylum in Australia.

Migrants who still attempt the trip are often detained at sea before they reach Australia. The government of Australia has agreements to house these migrants in detention facilities in other countries including East Timor and Nauru, which means they never actually set foot on Australian soil while their claims are adjudicated. The conditions in some of the Australian detention facilities are atrocious and the long delays in the claim process means that some migrants are stuck there for years at a time (Coddington and Mountz 2014). In April and May 2016 two people held at the facility set themselves on fire to protest the conditions. Hadon, a refugee from Somalia, set herself on fire days after Omid Masoumali, a 23 year old from Iran, died after self-immolation (Australian Border Deaths Database n.d.; Davidson and Doherty 2016).

Violence and death at the border

The hardening and militarization of borders across Asia has resulted in thousands of deaths both directly at the hands of border guards and as a consequence of easier routes across borders closing down and funnelling migrants to ever more dangerous locations. The International Organization for Migration counted 917 border-related deaths in Asia in 2015, which is far less than the 3,770 at the edges of Europe, but also double the number of deaths in the Americas (448) and triple the number in Africa (244) (International Organization for Migration n.d.).

One of the most violent borders in the world in terms of direct violence by border guards is the India–Bangladesh border (Cons 2012, 2016; Cons and Sanyal 2013; Shewly 2013; Sur 2013). From 2000 to 2015, over 1,000 Bangladeshi civilians were killed by the Indian Border Security Force along the border. India has the most extensive border fencing network of any country in the world in terms of total length and the largest border security force with over 200,000 members. India has walls and fences on 1,926 km (1,198 miles) of the 2,308 km (1,434 mile) border with Pakistan and on sections of its 1,624 km (1,009 miles) border with Myanmar. At the Bangladesh border, there are 3,500 km (2,175 miles) of fence along the 4,090 km (2,541 mile) border. The agents are tasked with being the front line against terrorism in India and have standing orders to shoot to kill if they perceive there is a terrorist infiltration threat (Kabir 2005). In 2015, India's Home Minister Rajnath Singh reiterated that the government planned to 'completely seal' the border. 'We want to take all possible steps to check illegal immigration. All loopholes have to be plugged' (bdnews24 2015).

The killing of Bangladeshi citizens in the borderlands became international news with the killing of 15-year-old Felani Khatun as she climbed the fence with her father in order to return to Bangladesh to look for a husband (Sur 2015). The images of her body hanging on the barbed wire fence elicited sympathy for the victims in the way that the routinized stories of another cattle smuggler shot and killed did not. Nevertheless, the agent who shot her was still acquitted by an Indian special court (*The Economist* 2011). The BSF is also regularly accused of kidnapping or abusing people in border areas, often if they refuse to pay a bribe. One case of abuse was videotaped on 9 December 2011 and caused outrage across India and Bangladesh. Mohammad Habibur Rahman, a 24-year-old Bangladeshi who traded in cattle across the border, had gone to the Charmouroshi camp of the BSF. When he did not have enough money to pay the requested bribe, he was beaten and humiliated by the border guards. The cell phone video shows the brutal attack from beginning to end as he was first stripped, his arms tied bound behind his back, and then repeatedly beaten as he pleads for mercy. The attack happened in broad daylight with dozens of BSF border guards and other civilians milling around, watching the gruesome event, and participating in the attack. He was eventually left unconscious at the border. After the video was broadcast on Indian television, eight border guards were suspended and in 2014 the Indian government gave Habibur Rahman a cheque for 50,000 rupees as compensation (*Daily Star* 2014).

There are many other examples of deadly borders in Asia. The International Organization for Migration reports that 615 migrants died at borders in Southeast Asia in 2015, predominately in the Bay of Bengal as Rohingya attempted to flee Myanmar. Myanmar's western border with Thailand is also a militarized and deadly space as landmines have been laid to control the movement of insurgent groups (Horstmann and Cole 2015). At the India–Pakistan border, fewer civilians are killed by border forces, in some part due to the fact that less of the border runs through dense farmland than the India–Bangladesh border. Nevertheless, there are skirmishes between security forces that result in occasional deaths and in November 2014 a bomb blast killed 60 people and injured 100 more at the Wagah border during the daily border closing ceremony. The South China Sea dispute is another example of a militarized and hardened frontier zone where the various states claim parts of the sea as exclusive economic zones and the islands as territories. China and Vietnam have recently built new islands and most of the states have increased their military presence in the disputed area.

Finally, a significant proportion of migrants who have lost their lives on the way to Europe are of Asian origin. The nationalities of migrants who die at sea are often difficult to ascertain, but the total number of asylum applications in Europe from different countries provides a good rough estimate of the total number of people on the move from various countries. In 2015, there were 1.2 million asylum applications to the EU of which approximately two thirds were from Asian countries (Eurostat 2016). Consequently, it is likely that roughly two thirds of the people who have lost their lives on the way to Europe, a total of almost 24,000 from 2005 to 2015, were from Asia.

Conclusion

The violence of borders is evident in many different locations in Asia as formerly open and lightly guarded borders are increasingly patrolled by militarized border security forces and marked by walls and other border infrastructure. The hardening of borders has both symbolic and material impacts on the border landscape, on borderland residents, and on migrants. The symbolic impact of hardened borders is the reification of the idea of sovereignty and territorial control. It brings into being the territorial edge of the state and it clarifies precisely where one state ends and another begins. The walls and security infrastructure have a material impact on the landscape by disrupting the habitats of plants and the migratory routes of animals. For example, the route of the Indian border fence around Bangladesh cuts through a traditional elephant migration route, forcing the animals into populated areas. In the decade after the construction, 226 people and 62 elephants were killed as more people and elephants came into contact with each other. In early 2016, India agreed to reopen a corridor to allow for elephant migrations (Siddique 2016). The hardened borders materially affect cross-border connections between borderland communities that are often used to regular interactions with the people on the other side but are increasingly cut off as security personnel dominate daily life. Finally, the hardening of borders has the real material impact on migrants as easier routes across borders are closed and migrants are forced to take ever more dangerous routes to move.

Over the next 20 years borders and migration related debates will continue to take a more central position in global politics as a series of factors coalesce in a way that will encourage and force more people to move in search of better opportunities for themselves and their families. These factors include global income divergence as the gap between the wealthiest and the poorest continues to grow, population growth that pushes more people out of rural areas to crowded cities in search of jobs, wars over resources, political power contained by artificial borders that are the remnants of colonialism, and the spectre of climate change induced migration, which could displace hundreds of millions of people as sea levels rise and new climate patterns alter agriculture (Baldwin 2012, 2014; Wright 2012).

Across Asia these challenges will encourage people to do what people have done for centuries: set out across the landscape to move to a new place and establish a new existence there. What distinguishes the current era from most of human history is that states have established increasingly firm control over their territory through internal surveillance and increasingly violent and militarized control over border lines. These newly hardened borders include walls and fences, more border guards, and new technologies from high tech sensors to drones that transform how these lines are monitored. As more people try to move, more will come face-to-face with the violent reality of border enforcement across Asia.

References

Amilhat Szary, A.-L. and Giraut, F. (2015) Borderities and the Politics of Contemporary Mobile Borders, London: Palgrave Macmillan.
Amoore, L. (2013) The Politics of Possibility: Risk and Security Beyond Probability, Durham, NC: Duke University Press.
Andersson, R. (2014) Illegality, Inc.: Clandestine Migration and the Business of Bordering Europe, Oakland, CA: University of California Press.
Australian Border Deaths Database. (n.d.) Available at: http://artsonline.monash.edu.au/thebordercrossing observatory/publications/australian-border-deaths-database/
Baldwin, A. (2012) 'Orientalizing Environmental Citizenship: Climate Change, Migration, and the Potentiality of Race', Citizenship Studies, 16, 625–640.
Baldwin, A. (2014) 'Pluralising Climate Change and Migration: An Argument in Favour of Open Futures', Geography Compass, 8, 516–528.
Bdnews24 (2015) 'Delhi Plans to Seal India-Bangladesh Border to Check Illegal Migration', 11 August, http://bdnews24.com
Beckwith, R. T. (2016) 'Read Donald Trump's Super Tuesday Victory Speech' Time Magazine, 2 March, available at: http://time.com/4245134/super-tuesday-donald-trump-victory-speech-transcript-full-text/
Boyle, T. and Rahman, Z. (2018) 'Border Layers: Formal and Informal Markets along the India-Bangladesh Border', in Jones, R. and Ferdoush, M. A., eds. Borders and Mobility in South Asia and Beyond, Amsterdam: Amsterdam University Press.
Brian, T. and Laczko, F. (2014) Fatal Journeys: Tracking Lives Lost during Migration, Geneva: International Organization of Migration.
Brown, W. (2010) Walled States, Waning Sovereignty, New York: Zone Books.
Casas-Cortes, M., Cobarrubias, S., and Pickles, J. (2015) 'Riding Routes and Itinerant Borders: Autonomy of Migration and Border Externalization', Antipode, 47, 894–914.
Chatterji, J. (1994) Bengal Divided, Cambridge: Cambridge University Press.
Chester, L. (2008) 'Boundary Commissions as Tools to Safeguard British Interests at the End of Empire', Journal of Historical Geography, 34, 494–515.
Coddington, K. and Mountz, A. (2014) 'Countering Isolation with Use of Technology: How Asylum-seeking Detainees on Islands in the Indian Ocean Use Social Media to Transcend Their Confinement', Journal of the Indian Ocean Region, 10, 97–112.
Collyer, M. and King, R. (2015) 'Producing Transnational Space: International Migration and the Extraterritorial Reach of State Power', Progress in Human Geography, 39, 185–204.
Cons, J. (2012) 'Histories of Belonging(s): Narrating Territory, Possession, and Dispossession at the India-Bangladesh Border', Modern Asian Studies, 46, 527–558.
Cons, J. (2016) Sensitive Space: Fragmented Territory at the India-Bangladesh Border, Seattle: University of Washington Press.
Cons, J. and Sanyal, R. (2013) 'Geographies at the Margin: Borders in South Asia, An introduction', Political Geography, 35, 5–13.
Cosmas, N. (2015) 'Stay Where You Are Until Our Backs Are Turned': Imagining the Border from Kuala Lumpur and Bangkok, MA Thesis, University of Hawaii.
Daily Star (2014) Available at: www.thedailystar.net/bsf-apologises-compensates-10968
Datta, A. (2015) 'Far Away, So Close', IIAS Newsletter, 71, 26–27.
Davidson, H. and Doherty, B. (2016) 'Second Refugee at Australian Detention Centre in Nauru sets Herself on Fire', The Guardian, 02 May, available at: www.theguardian.com/world/2016/may/02/second-refugee-sets-themselves-alight-on-nauru
Dolphin, R. (2006) The West Bank Wall: Unmaking Palestine, New York: Pluto Press.
Dunn, T. (1996) The Militarization of the U.S.-Mexico border, 1978–1992: Low-intensity Conflict Doctrine Comes Home, Austin, TX: CMAS Books.
Dunn, T. (2001) 'Border Militarization via Drug and Immigration Enforcement: Human Rights Implications', Social Justice, 28, 7–30.
Dunn, T. (2009) Blockading the Border and Human Rights: The El Paso Operation that Remade Immigration Enforcement, Austin: University of Texas Press.
Edney, M. (1997) Mapping an Empire: The Geographic Construction of British India 1765–1843, Chicago: Chicago University Press.
Elden, S. (2013a) The Birth of Territory, Chicago: The University of Chicago Press.

Elden, S. (2013b) 'Secure the Volume: Vertical Geopolitics and the Depth of Power', Political Geography, 34, 35–51.
European Commission. (2013) Migration and Mobility Partnership Signed between the EU and Morocco (Press Release). European Commission, Brussels, available at: http://europa.eu/rapid/press-release_IP-13-513_en.htm
Eurostat (2016) Available at: http://ec.europa.eu/eurostat/statistics-explained/index.php/File:First_time_asylum_applicants_in_the_EU-28_by_citizenship,_Q4_2014_%E2%80%93_Q4_2015.png
Fuller, T. and Cochrane, J. (2015) 'Rohingya Migrants from Myanmar, Shunned by Malaysia are Spotted Adrift in Andaman Sea', The New York Times, 14 May.
Galtung, J. (1969) 'Violence, Peace, and Peace Research', Journal of Peace Research, 6, 167–191.
Gohain, S. (2015) 'Militarized Borderlands in Asia', IIAS Newsletter, 71, 21–35.
Harley, J.B. and Woodward, D. (1987) The History of Cartography, vol 1, Chicago: The University of Chicago Press.
Heller, C. and Pezzani, L. (2014) 'Left-to-die-boat', in Weizman, E., ed. Forensis: The Architecture of Public Truth, London: Sternberg Press, 637–656.
Heyman, J. and Campbell, H. (2012) 'The Militarization of the United States-Mexico Border Region', Revista de Estudos Universitários, 38, 75–94.
Horstmann, A. and Cole, T. (2015) 'State Violence, State Building', IIAS Newsletter, 71, 24–25.
Human Rights Watch (2013) 'All You Can Do Is Pray:' Crimes Against Humanity and Ethnic Cleansing of Rohingya Muslims in Burma's Arakan State, New York: Human Rights Watch.
International Organization for Migration (IOM) (n.d.) 'The Missing Migrant Project', available at: https://missingmigrants.iom.int/
Johnson, C., Jones, R., Paasi, A., Amoore, L., Mountz, A., Salter, M., and Rumford, C. (2011) 'Interventions on Rethinking "the Border" in Border Studies', Political Geography, 30, 61–69.
Jones, R. (2012) Border Walls: Security and the War on Terror in the United States, India, and Israel, London: Zed Books.
Jones, R. (2014) 'Border Wars: Narratives and Images of the US-Mexico border on TV', ACME: An International E-Journal for Critical Geographies, 13 (3) 530–550.
Jones, R. and Johnson, C. (2014) Placing the Border in Everyday Life, London: Routledge.
Jones, R. and Johnson, C. (2016) 'Border Militarization and the Rearticulation of Sovereignty', Transactions of the Institute of British Geographers, 41, 187–200.
Kabir, E. (2005) Border Fencing: A Major Irritant in Indo-Bangla Relations, Dhaka: News Network.
Kim, D. (2013) 'Borders as Urbanism: Redrawing the Demilitarized Zone (DMZ) between Democratic People's Republic of Korea and Republic of Korea', Landscape Architecture Frontiers, 1, 150–157.
Kraska, P. (2007) 'Militarization and Policing—Its Relevance to 21st Century Police', Policing, 1, 501–513.
Lindblom, A., Marsh, E., Motala, T. and Munyan, K. (2015) 'Persecution of the Rohingya Muslims: Is Genocide Occuring in Myanmar's Rakhine State? A Legal Analysis', Allard K. Lowenstein International Human Rights Clinic, Yale Law School.
Lovell, J. (2009) The Great Wall: China Against the World, 1000 BC–AD 2000, New York: Grove Press.
McDuie-Ra, D. (2014) 'The India-Bangladesh Border Fence: Narratives and Political Possibilities', Journal of Borderlands Studies, 29, 81–94.
Miglani, S. (2015) 'Rohingya Huddled in Bangladesh Camps Fear Plan to Move Them On', Reuters, 02 June.
Mountz, A. (2015) 'Political Geography II: Islands and Archipelagos', Progress in Human Geography, 39, 636–646.
Murphy, A. (1996) 'The Sovereign State System as Political-Territorial Ideal: Historical and Contemporary Considerations', in Biersteker, T. and Weber, C., eds. State Sovereignty as Social Construct, Cambridge: Cambridge University Press, 81–120.
Murphy, A. (2013) 'Territory's Continuing Allure', Annals of the Association of American Geographers, 103, 1212–1226.
Odhikar (n.d.) Atrocities by Indian Border Security Force (BSF) against Bangladeshi Citizens, 1 January 2000–28 February 2017, Bangladesh–India Border Violence, available at: http://odhikar.org/wp-content/uploads/2016/04/Statistics_Border_2000-2017-Jan-Feb.pdf.
Paasi, A. (2011) 'A Border Theory? An Unattainable Dream or a Realistic Aim for Border Scholars?', in Wastl-Walter, D., ed. The Ashgate Research Companion to Border Studies, London: Ashgate, 11–31.
Paasi, A. (2012) 'Border Studies Reanimated: Going Beyond the Territorial-Relational Divide', Environment and Planning A, 44, 2303–2309.

Parker, N. and Vaughan-Williams, N. (2009) 'Line in the Sand? Towards an Agenda for Critical Border Studies', Geopolitics, 14, 582–587.
Popescu, G. (2012) Bordering and Ordering the Twenty-first Century: Understanding Borders, Lanham, MD: Rowman & Littlefield Publishers.
Reeves, M. (2014) Border Work: Spatial Lives of the State in Rural Central Asia, Ithaca, NY: Cornell University Press.
Rojas, C. (2010) The Great Wall: A Cultural History, Cambridge, MA: Harvard University Press.
Rosière, S. and Jones, R. (2012) 'Teichopolitics: Re-considering Globalisation through the Role of Walls and Fences', Geopolitics, 17, 217–234.
Rumford, C. (2008) 'Introduction: Citizens and Borderwork in Europe', Space and Polity, 12, 1–12.
Sack, R. (1986) Human Territoriality: Its Theory and Practice, Cambridge: Cambridge University Press.
Scott, J.C. (1998) Seeing Like a State: How Certain Schemes to Improve the Condition Have Failed, New Haven, CT: Yale University Press.
Scott, J.C. (2009) The Art of Not Being Governed: An Anarchist History of Upland Southeast Asia, New Haven, CT: Yale University Press.
Shewly, H. (2013) 'Abandoned Spaces and Bare Life in the Enclaves of the India-Bangladesh Border', Political Geography, 32, 23–31.
Siddique, A. (2016) 'Elephant Corridor through Indo-Bangla Border in Talks', Dhaka Tribune, 17 February, available at: www.dhakatribune.com/bangladesh/2016/feb/17/elephant-corridor-through-indo-bangla-border-talks
Slack, J., Martínez, D., Lee, A., and Whitford, S. (2016) 'The Geography of Border Militarization: Violence, Death, and Health in Mexico and the United States', Journal of Latin American Geography, 15, 7–32.
Sterling, B. (2009) Do Good Fences Make Good Neighbors? What History Teaches Us about Strategic Barriers and International Security, Washington, DC: Georgetown University Press.
Stewart, C. and Balogh, S. (2015) 'Boatpeople "Labourers" not Rohingya: Indonesia', The Australian, 23 May.
Sur, M. (2013) 'Bamboo Baskets and Barricades: Gendered Landscapes at the India-Bangladesh border', in Kalir, B. and Sur, M., eds. Transnational Flows and Permissive Polities: Ethnographies of Human Mobilities in Asia, Amsterdam: IIAS Publications, 127–150.
Sur, M. (2015) 'Spectacles of militarization' IIAS Newsletter, 71, 28–29.
The Economist (2011) 'Felani's Last Steps', 03 February, available at: www.economist.com/node/18073333
The Economist (2016) 'More Neighbours Make More Fences', 07 January, available at: www.economist.com/blogs/graphicdetail/2016/01/daily-chart-5
Till, K., Sundberg, J., Pullan, W., Psaltis, C., Makriyianni, C., Zincir Celal, R., Samani, M., and Dowler, L. (2013) 'Interventions in the Political Geographies of Walls', Political Geography, 33, 52–62.
Tyner, J. and Inwood, J. (2014) 'Violence as Fetish: Geography, Marxism and Dialectics', Progress in Human Geography, 38, 771–784.
United Nations High Commissioner for Refugees (2015) South-East Asia: Irregular Maritime Movements, January–March 2015, available at: www.unhcr.com
Vallet, E. (2014) Borders, Fences and Walls: State of Insecurity? Farnham: Ashgate.
Waldron, A. (1989) The Great Wall: From History to Myth, Cambridge: Cambridge University Press.
Weber, L. and Pickering, S. (2011) Globalization and Borders: Death at the Frontier, Lanham, MA: Palgrave Macmillan.
Winichakul, T. (1994) Siam Mapped: A History of the Geo-Body of a Nation, Honolulu: University of Hawai'i Press.
Wright, S. (2012) 'Policing Borders in a Time of Rapid Climate Change', in Scheffran, J., Brzoska, M., Brauch, H., Link, P., and Schilling, J. eds. Climate Change, Human Security and Violent Conflict: Challenges for Societal Stability, Berlin: Springer, 351–370.
Zamindar, V. (2007) The Long Partition and the Making of Modern South Asia: Refugees, Boundaries, Histories, New York: Columbia University Press.

2
Asia's gendered borderlands

Malini Sur

For refugees who are crossing Syria and Iraq's devastated war zones to seek safer shores in Europe, states and humanitarian agencies have struggled to guarantee basic protection from violence and exploitation. Refugee women experience sexual and financial abuse from smugglers, security staff, and other refugees during their journeys and upon their arrival in Europe (Amnesty International 2016). In 2016, while appoximately 1 million refugees requested asylum in Europe, 4.8 million Syrian refugees fled to Turkey, Lebanon, Jordan, Egypt, and Iraq. In addition, 6.6 million people are internally displaced within Syria (Syrian Refugees 2016). In late 2016, Myanmar's security forces raped Rohingya women and girls during security operations in the northern Rakhine state (Human Rights Watch 2017). Rohingyas, who the Burmese state has perscuted in large numbers in Myanmar, have desperately sought relocation in Bangladesh and India. While Bangladesh's border forces have pushed them back into Myanmar (Sherwood 2016), India has proposed to deport them as illegal migrants (Chauhan 2017).

Contemporary refugee movements remind us of Asia's 20th-century partitions that caused large-scale displacement and gendered violence. Their legacies are visible along Asia's present-day national borders, where wars, conflicts, legal disputes, and human rights abuses prevail. Even where state armies and militias battle over borders, the role of women in armed struggles for nationhood, aspirations for transborder trading and employment, and uncertain resettlements come together to shape gendered identities in uneven ways.

This chapter explores the intersections between gender, nationalism, and borders in Asia. If scholars specializing in borders have transcended disciplinary boundaries and nationalist intellectual traditions to offer comparative frameworks (Baud and Van Schendel 1997: 212; Jones 2009; Wilson and Donnan 2012: 20; Cons 2016), ones who investigate nationalism, partitions, and wars in relation to gendered violence and citizenship have also richly counter-narrated the nation (Yuval-Davis 1997; Menon and Bhasin 1993; Butalia 1999; Bagchi and Dasgupta 2006; Das 2007; Banerjee 2010). The productive convergences between these two bodies of scholarship invite the former to locate women's actions as pivotal to the production of space, and the latter to interrogate how borders reconfigure nations and everyday life.

The following pages situate women's contemporary mobility for labour and trade in the context of Asia's mid-20th century history of partitions, emphasizing women's suffering and political burdens. It foregrounds the multiple ways in which women have mobilized border resources and taken risks to circumvent national policies and state control of borders. The first section engages with the gendered outcomes of the partitions of Palestine and the Indian subcontinent (1947) and the Bangladesh independence war (1971) that created contentious boundaries between Palestine and Israel, India and Pakistan, and India and Bangladesh. These divisions have led to numerous wars and conflicts. Given their cumulative length – a total of 8,142 kilometres (approximately) – is substantially longer than the US land and water boundary with Mexico, which is 3,111.5 kilometres (Beaver 2006), gendered identities along Asia's partitioned borders merit in depth investigation. Highlighting women's subjectivities in refugee camps in Pakistan, Lebanon, and India since then, it is shown how women's political and economic participation in national and border projects have redefined gendered relations.

The second section analyzes how partitions and wars continue to restructure women's lives and activism in border zones. In addition to the Israel–Palestine and India–Bangladesh borders, it is shown how nation-building projects in Northeast India and Kashmir, Chittagong Hill Tracts, and the Rakhine state in Myanmar have disrupted women's lives. However, discussions on gender and violence have multiple currents. Drawing on illustrations from South Asian, Southeast Asian and China's borderlands, this section further illuminates how women have mobilized borders as resources and taken risks to circumvent and challenge dominant gender hierarchies through their participation in transborder trade and wage employment.

The final section analyzes women's international migration from the Philippines, Indonesia, and India for domestic employment in Singapore, Hong Kong, and the United Arab Emirates. It underlines the relationship between the rapid economic advancement of Asian nations that encourage privileged women citizens to undertake formal employment and the arrival of domestic workers from the region's relatively poorer nations. These processes have spatialized gender hierarchies across nations, and in public and domestic spheres (Yeoh and Huang 1998). State control and regulation of foreign domestic workers' labour, sexualities, and reproductive capacities show how 'gendered geographies of power' operate within and across multiple scales (Mahler and Pessar 2001: 441–442; Mahler and Pessar 2006). It is suggested that border studies should seriously consider women's labour mobility for domestic work, remittances, and risks to query questions of geographical scale and sexuality.

Gendered nationalism and displacement

In the 20th century, partitions created new nations and borders in Asia. The partition of Palestine and the Indian subcontinent led to large-scale displacement and suffering. In the 1940s, Britain suffered enormous losses during World War II, which prompted its leaders to end Britain's burdensome financial and military responsibilities, privilege global alliances, and quickly abdicate responsibility for violence (Chester 2008: 495, 513). Subsequently in Palestine and Israel, despite the participation of women in nationalist projects that raised political consciousness, their reproductive roles assumed salience (Yuval-Davis 1997; Sharoni 2001). The contrasting participation of women in the two phases of Palestinian resistance *(intifada)* against Israeli occupation makes this evident. In the first phase of the *intifada* (1987–1993), women participated in direct confrontations with the Israeli army in ways that blurred the boundaries between the home and the battlefield. However, in the second phase of resistance (2000–2005), gendered relations were more complex. Women experienced painful maternal contradictions. Israel accused Palestinian mothers of encouraging their sons to die as martyrs. Furthermore, the disabilities that Palestinian men faced as a consequence of the conflict, along with their dependence upon Israeli border checkpoints to make a living, increased women's maternal and economic burdens (Johnson and Kuttab 2001).

Although Israeli men and women have both participated in the armed forces, the contribution of Israeli women to nation building has been measured in terms of their reproductive roles as mothers. For decades, women conscripted for the Israel Defense Forces were marginalized in subservient military positions. Furthermore, as family members of male armed forces, women performed laborious domestic tasks that supported men's military participation. The demographic war between Israeli Jews and Palestinian Arabs, that intensified and reproduced gendered hierarchies, have made Jewish women's demographic contributions critical (Mayer 2012: 36–37).

In contrast to Palestine and Israel's historic 'womb war', the newly independent India 'recovered' abducted Hindu women who had resettled in Pakistan. The partition of the Indian subcontinent in 1947 resulted in 14 million people moving across the borders of the newly created countries of India and Pakistan. India's concerns surrounding 30,000 Hindu women who were abducted by opposing religious and political groups during the partition riots, surfaced soon after independence. India's attempts to recover these women disregarded their desires and interests, and undermined the maternal and marital attachments that they had established in Pakistan. Instead of acknowledging these women's altered roles in a resettled context as wives and mothers, and their new religious identities, India initiated an exchange of 'abducted' women. This urgency to recover Hindu women from Pakistan and hand over Muslim women to Pakistan overshadowed these women's voices (Menon and Bhasin 1993: WS 6). It exemplified India's partriachal communalism.

Veena Das has cogently argued that India's national anxiety surrounding women's sexuality and purity mobilized the iconic image of the raped woman to reinstate the Indian nation as a 'pure and masculine space'. She illuminates how large-scale efforts to 'recover' abducted women and restore them to their relatives as gestures of national honour – what she calls the 'orderly exchange of women' – not only reinforced the figure of the abducted woman with its associated imagery of social disorder as sexual disorder, but also helped build the new nation on the notion of social contracts between men (Das 2007: 19–24, 37). State and social workers recovered women against their wishes, compelling them to relinquish their children. Once forcibly resettled, the women preferred lives of anonymity and the relative autonomy of rehabilitation centres rather than return to their families (Menon and Bhasin 1993: WS6). Unlike Israeli and Palestinian nationalism that privileged women's reproductive and maternal roles in building and defending territories, India's actions infantilized women as citizen-daughters.

Similar issues on national honour and women's sexuality influenced Bangladesh's early nation building. In 1971, following a prolonged war with Pakistan, Bangladesh became an independent nation state. The Bangladeshi state valorized women who the Pakistani armed forces had raped, as war heroines *(birangonas)*. However, the 1971 war failed to make any revolutionary impact upon gender relations as official narratives refused to recognize women's roles in the war. The official title of war heroines did not entitle women the honour accorded to freedom fighters. Although they were able to gain economic independence, they could not socially liberate themselves from traditional gendered boundaries (Guha-Thakurta et al. 2010). Bangladesh's rehabilitation programmes enabled women to gain employment in social work and family planning. The state governed these women's lives outside the institution of marriage, and state policies compelled women to operate within cultural norms of femininity (Mookherjee 2015: 129–130, 157). Bangladesh's disciplining of women's bodies and sexuality, including their maternal sentiments, dispersed the pastoral care of social workers and doctors as sovereign mechanisms (Mookherjee 2015: 58). The efforts of compassionate social workers to integrate women also reflected patriarchal values. In addition, families were reluctant and refused to accept the women back (D'Costa 2011: 121–122, 125–126).

Nation-building projects have regulated, abused, and deprived women of their reproductive capacities and desires. The nation state's control over women's lives and bodies as citizens and border crossers recall Nira Yuval Davis' claims on gender relations in nationalist projects. She argues that, although women played crucial roles in biological, cultural, and political reproductions of the nation and other collectives, gender relations have defined constructions of citizenship, the cultural conceptions of collectives and their boundaries (Yuval Davis 1997: 630).

Anxieties surrounding women's sexuality and reproduction still dominate resettlements. In Palestinian refugee camps in Lebanon, in the 1990s, the historical forces that impinged upon questions of women's sexuality further restructured notions of the home. At specific junctures that prompted early refugee movements, poverty led to coercive marriages altering women's labour and fertility. In addition, women's participation in collective resistance generated dilemmas (Sayigh 1998). In the face of prolonged destitution and the feeble prospect of a return to Palestine, Palestinian women have demonstrated exemplary courage through education, revolutionary activities, and efforts to rebuild a sense of community (Holt 2007).

In the city of Calcutta (now Kolkata) in eastern India, the early 1950s witnessed a gradual shift in the transformation of the partition refugee from an iconic figure of human devastation to an emergent political actor. Here, Hindu Bengali refugees led a well-organized land-grabbing/squatting movement in the face of inadequate state rehabilitation. Women deliberately moved forward to protest against evictions, playing a central role in protecting their settlements against police attacks and evictions. In addition to rebuilding homes, they set up schools and libraries, and sought to rebuild communities (Chakrabarti 1990; Chatterjee 1992; Weber 1995: 205).

For Afghan women refugees, who fled Afghanistan's oppressive Mujahideen and Taliban governments and came to reside in camps in Pakistan (since the 1980s), insecurities continued even after their relocation. Refugee women came to live alongside those who represented groups that they were fleeing from in Afghanistan. To add to their burdens, the killings of Afghan men compelled women to undertake sex work to survive. Women also had to care for disabled children and spouses. When Afghan women refugees in Pakistan suffered trauma and depression, health services did not provide mental health services, limiting assistance only to problems related to their reproductive issues. While women refugees across social classes and educational backgrounds suffered, refugee men lived with imposed masculine notions that enabled them to perpetrate violence against other men and women (Khattak 2002, 2007).

Even today, developing regions accommodate 86 percent of the world's refugees (12.4 million persons), the highest number in more than two decades (International Organization for Migration 2015). Given the international media's focus on Europe, the scale of refugee movements within Asia is easily forgotten. Out of the estimated 19.5 million refugees globally, Turkey, Pakistan, Lebanon, and Iran host the highest numbers.

Until February 2014, more than a million Rohingya refugees have been living in precarious conditions in Bangladesh, Saudi Arabia, Malaysia, India, and Pakistan (Azad 2017). In January 2017, Bangladesh sanctioned a controversial plan to resettle Rohingya refugees on a remote island until they were repatriated (Habib 2017). Myanmar's security forces have renewed attacks on the stateless Rohingyas since 2015, using the garb of Islamic terror to rape women and most recently to kill infants and children (Bulman 2017). Violence, rape, and the burning down of Rohingya villages from July to September 2017 have pushed almost 500,000 refugees into Bangladesh. These actions have tacit support from the Burmese leader and Nobel Peace Prize winner Aung San Suu Kyi who leads the National League for Democracy (NLD). Her silence and lack of action endorses the violent nationalism that placates Burma's Buddhist ruling elites, the military as well as the clergy.

Out of the 1.7 million Syrian refugees who are registered in Jordan and Lebanon, the majority are women living in dangerous conditions. In 2014, seven in ten registered Syrian refugees living in Jordan and Lebanon were considered poor. They usually reside on the margins of urban and semi-urban areas (World Bank 2015). Protection eludes women even when they find their way into refugee camps. Syrian women refugees in Jordan's camps report feelings of insecurity, fear, and shame. Militant groups in this region have used women's bodies as human shields and rape as a weapon of war. Women are compelled to submit to early marriages as a survival option. In addition, they experience high levels of domestic violence, harrassment from local men, and sexual violence during food distributions and in shared toilets (Greenwood 2013). Given that the majority of Syrian refugees are women and 70 percent of refugees are living in poverty, the correlation between gendered displacement and the feminization of poverty is evident.

Humanitarian organizations in Asia operate in ways that reproduce dominant gendered divisions of labour in refugee camps. A comparison of the participation of refugee communities in Bangladesh and Thailand established that humanitarian interventions which solicit female participation reinforce women's gendered and familial roles, in contrast to men, whose participation is not desired as they are held to be corrupt and politicized. Humanitarian efforts encourage women refugees to be involved in community projects as governable and docile subjects. In the case of Burmese refugees in Thailand, when women functioned in ways that went contrary to the roles that humanitarian agencies had prescribed, they came to be labelled as unruly and problematic (Olivius 2014: 54–58).

Economies of violence

Nation building and militant nationalism render women's lives and border crossings precarious. At the India–Bangladesh border, human rights organizations have documented that Indian border forces have shot dead approximiately 1,000 undocumented travellers since 2000 (Human Rights Watch 2010). Among them was an adolescent girl, Felani Khatun. Like many others, Felani was a school dropout whose adolescence in India was to lead to an early marriage in Bangladesh. On a cold and foggy January morning in 2011, Felani was travelling with her father, Nurul Islam, who lived in the Indian state of Assam. Islam had paid money to border brokers for the journey. In early 2011, an Indian border constable shot Felani. Felani's body hung from India's new border fence with Bangladesh, a project under construction that substantially reconfigures the agrarian landscape (Sur 2013, 2014). The total number of killings at the India–Bangladesh border would be far higher if the area investigated included portions of the international boundary that cuts across Northeast India. Northeast India not only shares complex borders with Bangladesh, but India has also militarized this region to control demands for independent homelands (Baruah 1999).

Similarly, the scale and intensity of gendered violence would be greater if one were to include India's complicated internal borders with states in Northeast India and Kashmir. Here, excessive state militarization and exceptional violence are seen as prerequisites to contain armed struggles for independence, and terrorist and territorial threats from Bangladesh, Burma, China, and Pakistan. The Armed Forces Special Powers Act (1958), which is in operation in most of the states of Northeast India and Kashmir, sanctions armed impunity, suspends democratic functioning, and exposes residents to constant state surveillance (McDuie-Ra 2009: 255). Here, protracted battles between the Indian armed forces and ethno-nationalist militant groups have led to a 'frontier culture of violence'. These have affected women's intimate and familial lives (McDuie-Ra 2012:

330–333). For instance, in the India–Naga conflict (from the 1960s to the 1990s) Naga men were either killed by Indian security forces or they joined Naga nationalist groups. Militarization created women-headed households, increasing women's domestic burdens. In addition, political violence and gendered norms that privileged women's chastity, helped to sustain a culture of violence that specifically targeted women (Kikon 2016).

Although the partition of the Indian subcontinent (1947) still influences politics and ensures that violence and displacement structures everyday life in Kashmir and along its borders, scholars have rarely studied Kashmir (Zutschi 2015: 266, 270). Since the partition, India and Pakistan have fought over Kashmir. Kashmiri women live with the threat of rape from security forces and armed groups. Protracted armed conflicts that have targeted and killed men have increased women's economic and emotional burdens. In Kashmir, the presence of Indian armed forces, and local and non-local armed groups have redefined the interior of the rural Kashmiri homes and have made routine agricultural activities along the India–Pakistan border uncertain. Armed conflicts have compelled women to assume new roles to ensure survival (Dasgupta 2012: 86–88). Along the highly disputed, intensely nationalistic, and politically charged Line of Control (LOC) in Kashmir, women who encounter the line as border residents, border crossers, and wives of soldiers experience violence. Female residents along the LOC are evicted from their homes, families, and communities without support, and the state closely monitors their mobility (Hans 2000: 84). Furthermore, despite Kashmiri women belonging to families where men have mysteriously 'disappeared', and their claiming public spaces in ways that make mourning a political act (and collectively seeking justice), Kashmir's prolonged militarization has led to gender inequities (Zia 2016: 172).

Bangladesh's militarization of the Chittagong Hill Tracts has dispossessed the Chakmas, a Buddhist minority, as well as other minority residents of this region (Moshin 2004). Kalpana Chakma – an activist with the Hill Women's Federation in the Chittagong Hill Tracts – penned a diary before her disappearance in June 1986. Her words illuminate how Bangladesh's military and settler-related politics resulted in rapes and abductions. She wrote,

> Life means struggle and here are some important notes of a life full of struggle… On the one hand, the woman faces the steam roller of rape, torture, sexual harassment, humiliation and conditions of helplessness inflicted by the military and Bengalis; on the other hand she faces the curse of social and sexual discrimination and a restricted lifestyle.
> *(quoted in Guha Thakurta 2010: 74)*

Bangladesh is yet to bring Kalpana's military abductors to task for her disappearance.

At the Israel–Palestine border, militarized checkpoints control and prevent the movement of Palestinians into Israel (Bornstein 2008; Tawil-Souri 2011). The regulation of Palestinian lives and labour through checkpoints not only influences mainstream Israeli discourses of national security regarding the occupation, but also activism related to this issue. If the masculine body of the Palestinian terrorist reinforces Israel's national security concerns, for leftist activists, Palestinian women in labour who give birth at checkpoints symbolize injustice. Scholars have argued that the division between a masculine bomber exercising violent agency and a feminine victim justifies humanitarian discourses to support and sustain the occupation (Kotef and Amir 2007: 978, 980).

However, women's capacity to cross militarized borders makes them important actors. Along the Northeast India–Bangladesh border that India especially patrols to contain Islamic dissidence from Bangladesh and armed struggles, militarization has resulted in greater transborder mobility for indigenous women. India's militarization marks Muslim and indigenous men as potential terrorists and political dissidents, rendering them immobile. In contrast, indigenous women traders are able to navigate border fences and checkpoints without passports and identity documents (Sur 2014). While border militarization disciplines male bodies as suspects, it creates possibilities for women to trade and labour. Women's border crossings challenge the dominant understandings of militarized borders as spatially liminal and sexually predatory. The transborder mobility of women, even along heavily patrolled borders where the threat of rape and sexual oppression is always present, is gendered in ways that make border crossings relatively easier for women than conventionally imagined (Sur 2012, 2013).

Illustrations from Southeast Asian and China's borderlands similarly show the unevenness of gendered expectations and roles. The Thailand–Myanmar borderland that provides sanctuaries for female soldiers and economic opportunities for transborder traders and wage labourers is an interesting case. Here, women soldiers belonging to the Shan nationalist groups (who demanded independence against the Burmese state) operated for several years. The role of Shan women in nationalist projects involved an extension of the domestic sphere. Since the home extended to the army barrack, the participation of women in armed rebellions served to reproduce their feminized functions as nurses, food providers, and messengers. Furthermore, the reinforcement of this gendered division of labour in Shan nationalism ensured social order in both the private and the public sphere (Leungaramsri 2006: 82–83). Even during intense periods of conflict between the Burmese state and ethnonationalist groups (1960s to 1990s), Shan women crossed the Thailand–Myanmar border to trade. They provided rebel militias with goods in exchange for border passage and protection. In fact, Shan women mobilized village and ethnic ties to make a living and profit from a volatile border (Lertchavalitsakul 2015: 677, 704).

Burman migrants, Myanmar's largest ethnic group, who arrive at the Thailand–Myanmar border, escaping traditional systems of gendered oppression in their villages, negotiate its ambivalent borderland culture. The border provides women with resources and opportunities for wage labour and transborder trade. Women migrants take advantage of the weak state control at this remote location. Their new role as border entrepreneurs radically changed their prior status as farmers who the Burmese state exploited. Their economic participation reduced their household duties and led to a greater influence in their villages of origin (Kusakabe and Oo 2004).

Studies on border trading further show how women traders skilfully negotiate trade regulations and routes along Southeast Asian borders (Walker 1999: 160–161). Along this region's borders with China, female traders who speak multiple languages are important entrepreneurs. Since 1989, the opening of the China–Vietnam border has improved their prior status of economic marginality in a region that was greatly affected by the Sino–Vietnamese War and border animosities. Women capitalized upon the economic opportunities that the opening of the Sino–Vietnamese border created, and increased their role in border employment and trade. In their new roles, women have disrupted dominant notions of trading defined by male leadership in family-run establishments. Furthermore, they have also invested in their children's education and in themselves (Guangmao 2000).

Labours of domesticity

If we review another important border-crossing by women as foreign domestic workers, we see that gender hierarchies transcend national boundaries. These journeys and relocations show how spatial mobility is a densely interconnected phenomenon operating simultaneously in the realm of global economies and specific cultural landscapes (Silvey 2006: 68). Since the 1990s, these factors enabled women from the Philippines, Indonesia, and India to arrive in large numbers to Hong Kong, Singapore, and the United Arab Emirates to undertake domestic work. The rapid economic development that encouraged women citizens of economically advanced nations to enter the workforce paved the way for impoverished women to labour as foreign migrants. However, their presence and visibility in public spaces created moral panic. In the 1990s, Singapore's employment policies constrained foreign domestic workers' spatial access to the city. In addition, Singaporean women employers worked out a series of economic and cultural mechanisms to further limit their domestic workers' access to public space. Employers permitted migrant women to undertake additional employment and generated anxieties about sexual trafficking to circumscribe domestic workers' movements. However, foreign women workers successfully reclaimed and routinely colonized public spaces. For instance, Filipino women were a boisterous presence in shopping malls that specially catered to them; their actions were a means to reject their subordinated status within domestic spaces (Yeoh and Huang 1998). In recent years, Indonesian domestic workers have successfully established monetarily profitable relationships with their Singaporean employers for extra income and emotional relationships with their families and children. Complex monetary and affective relationships that women migrants establish show how border crossings are gendered and transnational (Yeoh et al. 2016).

Labour migration regimes in Singapore, Hong Kong, and the United Arab Emirates reinforce women domestic workers' subordinate and transient status by excluding them from citizenship, long-term residence, and reproductive roles. Nicole Constable shows how Hong Kong's state policies not only legally prohibit foreign domestic workers from travelling with family members, but also how employers limit women's freedom to establish romantic relationships. Notwithstanding restrictions, women do establish romantic relationships. If pregnant, and forced to leave, women do not shy away from filing torture claims against the state. They seek legal recourse to prolong their stay as mothers desiring to reside with their partners and children. This, even when pregnant workers are aware that the state will reject their claims, and will imprison them for illegal overstays (Constable 2015:103–107). Furthermore, domestic workers have redefined themselves as good mothers who are able to support their children. Even when they were compelled to return to their home countries, they re-established their economic and social contributions through remittances. While the potential to earn money offered a way to remedy gendered transgressions, it created a self-perpetuating 'global capitalist cycle of inequality' reinforcing differences between citizens and migrants (Constable 2014: 231–232). The actions of returning foreign domestic workers in Hong Kong convey why remittances must be measured through gendered relations, rather than only in monetary terms.

National policies in labour-exporting countries have either encouraged or prohibited women's migration for foreign domestic work. Some states have mobilized religion to shape migration policies. For instance, during the Indonesian New Order (1965–1998) and the post-Suharto phase, Indonesia proactively used Islamic religious reasons to encourage Muslim women to migrate to Saudi Arabia in order to work. Invoking affective religious ties to a unified Islamic pious space reinforced Indonesia's subordinate position in its relationship to Saudi Arabia and made women migrants vulnerable to state and domestic violence (Silvey 2007). In contrast, India tried to curtail women's labour migration for domestic work from the state of Kerala to the United Arab Emirates on religious grounds. Policies that prohibited women from crossing borders for domestic work associated the religious imagery of non-Muslim Indian women working under oppressive Muslim Arabs. State policies assumed that women's migration from 'safe' communities within national territories to foreign states posed risks to their lives and well-being. Policies restricting women's migration, expose them to greater risks and illegality during their journeys and in their work situations. (Pattadah and Moors 2012).

Conclusion

Considering the large numbers of female refugees who are crossing borders, as well as the 11.5 million domestic workers who are international migrants, we need to carefully review how nationalism, conflicts, religion, and patriarchy shape women's displacement and mobility. This chapter advanced that gendered conjunctures shape national geographies and claims to contested territories, and illuminated how women's contemporary border crossings persist despite restrictions. Even under distressing political and economic circumstances, women's revolutionary and political participation has blurred domestic/public areas in refugee camps. In other instances, such as within labour migration regimes, women have crossed many borders to encounter new ones in resettled contexts.

The hardening of borders in the 21st century has resulted in the increased construction of walls, fences, and checkpoints. Today, states increasingly restrict (often forcefully) refugee movements as well as labour migration, using Islamic terror, cultural nationalism, and local job losses as reasons. Globalization is on shaky ground, and one of the principal consequences is the difficulties faced by women refugees and migrants. Despite daunting odds and political persecution, women's resilience and adaptivity will continue to remind us of their capacity to use borders as resources, even as high walls divide nations and societies.

Acknowledgements

I am grateful to Shahnaz Rouse, Nausheen H. Anwar, Rakesh Kumar, and Alessandro Rippa for their suggestions.

References

Bagchi, J., and S. Dasgupta, eds. (2006). *The Trauma and the Triumph*. Kolkata: Stree.
Banerjee, P. (2010). *Borders, Histories, Existences: Gender and Beyond*. New Delhi: Sage Publications.
Baruah, S. (1999). *India Against Itself: Assam and the Politics of Nationality*. Philadelphia: University of Pennsylvania Press.
Baud, M. and W. Van Schendel (1997). "Towards a Comparative History of Borderlands." *Journal of World History* 8 (2): 211–242.
Bornstein, A. (2008). "Military Occupation as Carceral Society: Prisons, Checkpoints, and Walls in the Israeli-Palestinian Struggle." *Social Analysis* 52 (2): 106–130.
Butalia, U. (1999). *The Other Side of Silence: Voices from the Partition of India*. Karachi: Oxford University Press.
Chakrabarti, P. K. (1990). *The Marginal Men: The Refugees and the Left Political Syndrome in West Bengal*. Kalyani: Lumière Books.
Chatterjee, N. (1992). Midnight's Unwanted Children: East Bengali Refugees and the Politics of Rehabilitation. PhD Dissertation, Brown University.
Chester, L. (2008). "Boundary Commissions as Tools to Safeguard British Interests at the End of Empire." *Journal of Historical Geography* 34 (3): 494–515.
Cons, J. (2016). *Sensitive Space: Fragmented Territory at the India-Bangladesh Border*. Washington: University of Washington Press.
Constable, N. (2014). *Born Out of Place*. Berkeley: University of California Press.
Constable, N. (2015). "Temporary Shelter in the Shadows: Migrant Mothers and Torture Claims in Hong Kong." In *Migrant Encounters: Intimate Labor, the State, and Mobility across Asia*, edited by Sara L. Friedman and Pardis Mahdavi, 92–112. Philadelphia, PA: University of Pennsylvania Press.
Das, V. (2007). *Life and Words: Violence and Descent into the Ordinary*. Berkeley: California University Press.
D'Costa, B. (2011). *Nationbuilding, Gender and War Crimes in South Asia*. London: Routledge.
Dasgupta, S. (2012). "Borderlands and Borderlines: Re-negotiating Boundaries in Jammu and Kashmir." *Journal of Borderland Studies* 27 (1): 83–93.
Guangmao, X. (2000). "Women and Social Change along the Vietnam-Guangxi Border." In *Where China Meets Southeast Asia: Social and Cultural Change in Border Regions*, edited by Grant Evans, Christopher Hutton and Kua Khun Eng, 321–337. Singapore: ISEAS.

Guha Thakurta, M. (2010). "Resistance Politics in the Hills." In *Between Ashes and Hope*, edited by Naeem Mohaimmen. Dhaka: Dristipat Writers Collective.

Guha Thakurta, M., H. Hossain, and M. Sur (2010). *Freedom from Fear? Freedom from Want? Rethinking Security in Bangladesh*. New Delhi: Rupa.

Hans, A. (2000). "Women across Borders in Kashmir: The Continuum of Violence." *Canadian Woman Studies: Downsview* 19 (4): 77–87.

Holt, M. (2007). "The Wives and Mothers of Heroes: Evolving Identities of Palestinian Refugee Women in Lebanon." *The Journal of Development Studies* 43 (2): 245–264.

Johnson, P., and E. Kuttab (2001). "Where Have All the Women (and Men) Gone? Reflections on Gender and the Second Palestinian Intifada." *Feminist Review* 69: 21–43.

Jones, R. (2009). "Geopolitical Boundary Narratives, the Global War on Terror and Border Fencing in India." *Transactions of the Institute of British Geographers* 34 (3): 290–304.

Khattak, S. G. (2002). "Floating Upwards from History: Afghan Women's Experience of Displacement." *Development* 45 (1): 105–110.

Khattak, S. G. (2007). "Living on the Edges: Afghan Women and Refugee Camp Management in Pakistan." *Signs* 32 (3): 575–580.

Kotef, H., and M. Amir (2007). "(En)Gendering Checkpoints: Checkpoint Watch and the Repercussions of Intervention." In *War and Terror I: Raced-Gendered Logics and Effects in Conflict Zones*, edited by Mary Hawkesworth and Karen Alexander, *Signs* 32 (4): 973–996.

Kusakabe, K., and Z. M. Oo (2004). "Gender and Power at the Burmese Border." Centre for International Borders Research (CIBR), Electronic Working Papers Series, 2004: 1–28.

Lertchavalitsakul, B. (2015). "Shan Women Traders and Their Survival Strategies along the Thai-Myanmar Border." *Sojourn: Journal of Social Issues in Southeast Asia* 30 (3): 675–709.

Leungaramsri, P. (2006). "Women, Nation and the Ambivalence of Subversive Identification along the Thai-Burmese Border." *Sojourn: Journal of Social Issues in Southeast Asia* 21 (1): 68–89.

Mahler, S. J., and P. R. Pessar (2001). "Gendered Geographies of Power: Analyzing Gender Across Transnational Spaces." *Identities: Global Studies in Culture and Power* 7: 441–460.

Mahler, S. J., and P. R. Pessar (2006). "Gender Matters: Ethnographers Bring Gender from the Periphery Toward the Core of Migration Studies." *International Migration Review* 40 (1): 27–63.

Mayer, T. (2012). "The Struggle Over Boundary and Memory: Nation, Borders, and Gender in Jewish Israel." *Journal of International Women's Studies* 13 (4): 29–50.

McDuie-Ra, D. (2009). "Fifty-year Disturbance: The Armed Forces Special Powers Act and Exceptionalism in a South Asian Periphery." *Contemporary South Asia*, 17: 255–270.

McDuie-Ra, D. (2012). "Violence Against Women in the Militarized Indian Frontier: Beyond 'Indian Culture' in the Experiences of Ethnic Minority Women." *Violence Against Women* 18 (3): 322–345.

Menon, R., and K. Bhasin (1993). "Recovery, Rupture, Resistance: Indian State and Abduction of Women during Partition." *Economic and Political Weekly* 28 (17): WS2–WS11.

Mookherjee, N. (2015). *The Spectral Wound: Sexual Violence, Public Memories, and the Bangladesh War of 1971*. Durham, NC: Duke University Press.

Moshin, A. (2004). "Gendered Nation, Gendered Peace." *Indian Journal of Gender Studies* 11 (4): 43–64.

Olivius, E. (2014). "(Un) Governable Subjects: The Limits of Refugee Participation in the Promotion of Gender Equality in Humanitarian Aid." *Journal of Refugee Studies* 27 (1): 42–61.

Pattadah, B., and A. C. E. Moors (2012). "Moving between Kerala and Dubai: Women Domestic Workers, State Actors, and the Misrecognition of Problems." In *Transnational Flows and Permissive Polities: Ethnographies of Human Mobility in Asia*, edited by Barak Kalir and Malini Sur, 151–169. Amsterdam: Amsterdam University Press.

Sayigh, R. (1998). "Gender, Sexuality, and Class in National Narrations: Palestinian Camp Women Tell Their Lives." *Frontiers: A Journal of Women Studies* 19 (2): 166–185.

Sharoni, S. (2001). "Rethinking Women's Struggles in Israel/Palestine and the North of Ireland." In *Victims, Perpetrators or Actors: Gender, Armed Conflict and Political Violence*, edited by Carolina Moser and Fiora Park, 85–98. London: Zed.

Silvey, R. (2006). "Geographies of Gender and Migration: Spatializing Social Difference." *International Migration Review* 40 (1): 61–81.

Silvey, R. (2007). "Mobilizing Piety: Gendered Morality and Indonesian–Saudi Transnational Migration." *Mobilities* 2 (2): 219–229.

Sur, M. (2012). "Bamboo Baskets and Barricades: Gendered Landscapes at the India-Bangladesh Borderlands." In *Transnational Flows and Permissive Polities: Ethnographies of Human Mobility in Asia*, edited by Barak Kalir and Malini Sur, 127–150. Amsterdam: University of Amsterdam Press.

Sur, M. (2013). "Through Metal Fences: Material Mobility and the Politics of Transnationality at Borders." *Mobilities* 8 (1): 70–89.
Sur, M. (2014). "Divided Bodies: Crossing the India–Bangladesh Border." *Economic and Political Weekly* 46 (13): 31–35.
Tawil-Souri, H. (2011). "Qalandia Checkpoint as Space and Non-Place." *Space and Culture* 14 (1): 4–26.
Walker, A. (1999). *The Legend of the Golden Boat: Regulation, Trade and Traders in the Borderlands of Laos, Thailand, Burma and China*. Richmond: Curzon Press.
Weber, R. (1995) "Re(creating) the Home: Women's Role in the Development of Refugee Colonies in South Calcutta." *Indian Journal of Gender Studies* 2 (2): 195–210.
Wilson, T. M., and H. Donnan, eds. (2012). *A Companion to Border Studies*. Vancouver: Wiley-Blackwell.
Yeoh, B. S. A., and S. Huang (1998). "Negotiating Public Space: Strategies and Styles of Migrant Female Workers in Singapore." *Urban Studies* 35 (3): 583–602.
Yeoh, B. S. A., M. Platt, C. Y. Khoo, T. Lam, and G. Baey (2016). "Indonesian Domestic Workers and the (Un)-Making of Transnational Livelihoods and Provisional Futures." *Social and Cultural Geography*, 17 May: 1–20. Available at: www.tandfonline.com/doi/full/10.1080/14649365.2016.1185800. Accessed on 31 January 2017.
Yuval-Davis, N. (1997). *Gender and the Nation*. London: Sage.
Zia, A. (2016). "The Spectacle of a Good-Half Widow: Performing Agency in the Human Rights Movement in Kashmir." *Political & Legal Anthropology Review* 39 (2): 169–175.
Zutschi, C. (2015). "An Ongoing Partition: Histories, Borders, and the Politics of Vivisection in Jammu and Kashmir." *Contemporary South Asia* 23: 266–275.

Reports and newspaper articles

Amnesty International (2016). "Female Refugees Face Physical Assault, Exploitation and Sexual Harassment on Their Journey Through Europe." 18 January. Available at: www.amnesty.org/en/latest/news/2016/01/female-refugees-face-physical-assault-exploitation-and-sexual-harassment-on-their-journey-through-europe/. Accessed on 5 February 2017.
Azad, A. (2017). "Life in Limbo: The Rohingya Refugees Trapped Between Myanmar and Bangladesh." *The Wire*, 7 February. Available at: https://thewire.in/106344/life-limbo-rohingya-refugees-trapped-myanmar-bangladesh/. Accessed on 7 February 2017.
Beaver, J. C. (2006). "U.S. International Borders: Brief Facts." *CRS Report for Congress*. Available at: www.fas.org/sgp/crs/misc/RS21729.pdf. Accessed on 12 May 2011.
Bulman, M. (2017). "Burma: Rohingya Muslim Babies and Children "Being Slaughtered with Knives", UN Warns." *The Independent*, 3 February. Available at: www.independent.co.uk/news/world/asia/burma-rohingya-muslim-babies-children-slaughtered-knives-massacre-genocide-un-warns-a7561711.html. Accessed on 6 February 2017.
Chauhan, N. (2017). "NHRC to Oppose Govt's Deportation Plan for Rohingyas." *The Times of India*, 16 September. Available at: http://timesofindia.indiatimes.com/india/nhrc-to-oppose-govts-deportation-plan-for-rohingyas-likely-to-fight-for-refugees-in-sc/articleshow/60704936.cms. Accessed on 1 October 2017
Greenwood, P. (2013). "Rape and Domestic Violence Follow Syrian Women into Refugee Camps." *The Guardian*, 23 July. Available at: www.theguardian.com/world/2013/jul/25/rape-violence-syria-women-refugee-camp. Accessed on 6 February 2017.
Habib, H. (2017). "Rohingya Refugees to be Relocated on Remote Island." *The Hindu*, 7 February. Available at: www.thehindu.com/news/international/Rohingya-refugees-to-be-relocated-on-remote-island/article17205798.ece. Accessed on 7 February 2017.
Human Rights Watch (2010). "'Trigger Happy' Excessive Use of Force by Indian Troops." 9 December. Available at: www.hrw.org/report/2010/12/09/trigger-happy/excessive-use-force-indian-troops-bangladesh-border. Accessed on 13 April 2013.
Human Rights Watch (2017). "Burma: Security Forces Raped Rohingya Women." 6 February. Available at: www.hrw.org/news/2017/02/06/burma-security-forces-raped-rohingya-women-girls. Accessed on 6 February 2017.
International Organization for Migration (2015). World Migration Report 2015. Available at: www.iom.int/world-migration-report-2015. Accessed on 20 January 2017.

Kikon, D. (2016). "Sexual Violence and the Culture of Impunity in Nagaland." *Open Democracy*, 10 May. Available at: www.opendemocracy.net/5050/dolly-kikon/sexual-violence-and-culture-of-impunity-in-nagaland. Accessed on 5 February 2017.

Sherwood, H. (2016). "Rohingya Muslims Fleeing Myanmar 'Turned Away by Bangladesh'." *The Guardian*, 25 November. Available at: www.theguardian.com/world/2016/nov/25/rohingya-muslims-fleeing-myanmar-turned-away-by-bangladesh. Accessed on 5 February 2017.

Syrian Refugees (2016). "The Syrian Refugee Crisis and its Repercussions for the EU." Available at: http://syrianrefugees.eu/. Accessed on 5 February 2017.

World Bank (2015). "Syrian Refugees Living in Jordan and Lebanon: Young, Female, at Risk." The World Bank Press Release, 16 December. Available at: www.worldbank.org/en/news/press-release/2015/12/16/syrian-refugees-living-in-jordan-and-lebanon-caught-in-poverty-trap. Accessed on 7 February 2017.

3
Intimate militarism
Domesticating the border in rural Central Asia

Madeleine Reeves

The boundaries that separate the five post-Soviet states of Central Asia (Kazakhstan, Kyrgyzstan, Tajikistan, Turkmenistan, and Uzbekistan) remain relative outliers in the comparative study of Asian borderlands. These international borders are constitutionally and empirically new, marking the territorial limits of independent states only since 1991. Significant sections of these states' boundaries with one another remain subject to ongoing processes of delimitation and demarcation, including half of the Kyrgyzstan–Tajikistan border (451 kilometres) and up to 60 separate sections, totalling 371 kilometres, of the Kyrgyzstan–Uzbekistan border (Polat 2002; Alamanov 2005).

The texture of everyday life along and across these new international boundaries remains comparatively under-researched, given the significant practical, institutional, and security challenges to conducting sustained cross-border fieldwork.[1] We should also be wary of extrapolating from research in one region to a depiction of Central Asian borders as a whole: the border is always more than (and sometimes not even) a line on a map, and this has implications for the way that borders locally are worked and made to work (Reeves 2014). In some areas concrete border posts, deep trenches and lines of razor wire stretch into the horizon as far as the eye can see, cutting through the middle of villages, dividing settlements from their fields, neighbours from neighbours, even houses from their outhouses (see, e.g. Megoran 2002: 181; Troscenko 2016). In others, the border traces the line of a river or irrigation canal, and is monitored by soldiers and observation towers to warn off any potentially unauthorised crosser. Along many of its stretches, however, the 'border' is impossible to read from the landscape with the juridical boundary indexed only by the pockets of trade that cluster around it: a concentration of oil-tankers moving gasoline from Kyrgyzstan to Tajikistan; a series of *Kamaz*-trucks parked at the unmarked border selling coal to middlemen from nearby villages. In other stretches still, where the border coincides with zones of dense residential settlement, the presence of the border provides lucrative opportunities for homes to be turned into store-houses and back yards to serve as informal, untaxed crossing points, sometimes just a few metres away from the official border post: a so-called 'back door' (*chernyi khod*) that is a critical, if legally unrecognised, part of border infrastructure and of local economies (Orlova 2003).[2]

Rather than attempting to present an encyclopaedic survey of Central Asian borders, this chapter focuses ethnographically on the everyday dynamics of border securitisation at the southern edge of the Ferghana Valley, a densely populated intra-montane basin where three of the Central Asian states, Uzbekistan, Tajikistan, and Kyrgyzstan, meet. This is a region where the delimitation and regulation of these post-Soviet borders remain both politically contentious and sometimes violently disputed (International Crisis Group 2002; Megoran 2004; ACTED/OSCE 2005). It is also a region where ties of kinship, of trade, and of ritual visiting have been most dramatically ruptured by post-Soviet restrictions on cross-border mobility, as Uzbekistan maintains a visa regime with both of its Ferghana Valley neighbours. Land exchanges throughout the 20th century between what were constituent republics of a single Soviet state have resulted, upon independence, in juridical boundaries that transect settlements that had previously constituted a single moral community, bound by ties of 'giving and taking' daughters (*kyz berüü, kyz aluu*) in marriage and reciprocal attendance at funerals and family celebrations (*jamanchylyk* and *jakshylyk toilar*). It has also resulted in the appearance of some of the world's largest sovereign enclaves (or exclaves, depending upon the particular state perspective): administrative units of one state, in some cases with populations in the tens of thousands, enclosed within the territory of another (Thorez 2003).

The extent of juridical non-determination means that one encounters stretches of disputed borderland in this region where formal prohibitions upon construction and cultivation have been ignored due to shortages of irrigated land. This administrative impasse has resulted in discrepancies between the maps that are taken to be authoritative in the respective Ferghana Valley states, just as it has between the international boundaries that Google Maps claims to be authoritative and the de facto distribution of villages and infrastructure subordinate to the respective state authority. It has also rendered infrastructure contentious and politicised. At the foothills that fringe the Ferghana basin to the north and south one finds reservoirs, irrigation canals, and dams legally owned by one state, but maintained by the down-stream neighbour that benefits from their use. One can see flags painted by hand on tea houses, bridges, or petrol stations to signal that this otherwise unmarked spot is the border, and this local landmark is the sovereign territory of Kyrgyzstan, Uzbekistan, or Tajikistan; and one can find roads with sections allocated as 'green', meaning that passengers are exceptionally able to enter the neighbouring state without being subject to border controls. Such arrangements, characterised by varying degrees of formality and informality, can become objects of public commentary, popular mobilisation and—exceptionally—of violent confrontation at moments of heightened inter-state tension. It is little surprise, perhaps, that Central Asian examples feature widely in texts on 'anomalous borders' or 'political oddities' (Diener and Hagen 2010); or that Central Asian film-makers have explored the poignant ironies of relatives and co-ethnics who find that they need to apply for a visa to attend a wedding or visit a deceased relative who happens, now, to be the citizen of a neighbouring state (Alykulov 2006; Raev 2007).

Exceptional borders?

Given the violent intrusion that borders represent to ordinary life in Central Asia it may seem incongruous to explore borders as anything other than exceptional. Popular literature on the region often points precisely to this quality: borders in Central Asia are described as 'arbitrary', 'incongruous', 'contorted', or the object of cynical manipulation by early Soviet authorities bent on a policy of divide and rule (see, e.g. Lewington 2010; Shishkin 2013). As ethnographers of other new, or 'anomalous' borders have shown, however, even exceptional places become part of one's everyday (Cons 2013), just as bullet-pocked buildings can become part of the taken-for-granted backdrop of one's urban surroundings (Nucho 2016). This chapter, accordingly, focuses less on borders' geopolitical or material 'exceptionality' in Central Asia than on the way that such spaces become part of that which is unmarked or everyday; how they become banal. In part this is a story of borders' routinisation; the embodied practices and institutional forms through which certain routes through a landscape become marked as 'safe' and 'unsafe', 'normal', and 'transgressive', such that a border comes to be reproduced and take on social salience, even in the absence of regular border checks. But it is also more than that; for what is striking in large parts of the Ferghana Valley—a setting that is shot through with existential uncertainty over collective village futures in contexts of strained inter-ethnic relations and declining economic opportunities—is the way that borders, and more specifically, the military presence with which they are associated, come to be normalised and even desired as an index of social and geographical legibility to the state.

I argue in this chapter that taking seriously borderland residents' concern to be 'gridded' (Jansen 2014)—to be recognised as legible to the state; to count and be counted, rather than to evade the state—is critical for understanding the contemporary escalation of force that we see in the Ferghana Valley. For village residents and rural officials alike, I suggest, being identified as a 'border village' has become a way of being seen by the state and thus of accessing material and symbolic benefits in a context otherwise marked by consistent state withdrawal. As a school teacher commented to me in 2005, reflecting on the differential benefits accorded both by government agencies and various non-governmental organisations (NGOs) to the school where she taught: 'we had the good fortune, it turns out, to be considered a border village; you know, "strategically important"' (*'strategicheskoe vazhnoe' ekenbiz!*) Rather like the uniformed citizens who take it upon themselves to check on the identity of a visiting journalist and accuse her of 'not knowing the map' (Geine 2016), becoming 'strategically important', like becoming a 'border village'—a designation that carries both privileges and responsibilities for local men to participate in the monitoring of border movement—is becoming part of the logic and language of self-identification for borderland residents at a time when the provision of public goods is increasingly strained.

Intimate militarism

I develop the category of 'intimate militarism' to explore this dynamic, drawing upon fieldwork that I have conducted in a side valley of the Ferghana basin, along the Isfara River, over the course of a more than a decade. I draw in particular upon research that I have conducted in and around the village of Ak-Sai, a Kyrgyz-majority village (population 1,160) established in the 1970s on the border with Tajikistan's Vorukh exclave. Along the length of the Isfara River, the borders between Kyrgyzstan and Tajikistan have the quality of being at once apparently indistinct, with few conventional markers of membership in the form of flags, signs, and border posts *and*, at the same time, highly politicised and occasionally the site of violent confrontation. For all the lack of conventional border infrastructure, this is a setting where variant logics of national membership—manifest in differences of state ideology, school curricula, modes of tolerated dress, language policy, and even the time zone that is locally operative on two sides of the border—have come to structure everyday life along increasingly national lines. An important insight from this region is that borders do not need to materialise in the forms of walls and fences to be experienced as real. Indeed, it is the very capacity of the border to appear, suddenly and consequentially, in the form of a conscript soldier, a customs officer, or a member of the security services patrolling a mountain road, that gives 'border' here the sense of being nowhere and potentially everywhere at one and the same time.

To explore this quality in more depth, I turn to a kindred scholarly field. In his now classic monograph on 'banal nationalism', Michael Billig (1995) argues that nationalism should be located not so much in the domain of political ideology as in the mundane, embodied practices that lie beyond conscious reflection or deliberation. In this national order of things, according to Billig, the citizenry's reminders of political membership are 'so familiar, so continual, that it is not consciously registered as reminding'. The social correlate of this is not the flag that is being fervently waved by a nationalist politician, but the flag that hangs unnoticed on the public building (Billig 1995: 8–9).

Billig's 'deixis of homeland-making' can be identified in multiple domains of life in rural Central Asia, from the country-shaped icons that often decorate local taxis to the branding of local beer as *nashe pivo*, 'our beer', in the colours of the local flag (Marat 2009). Yet there are two qualifications to Billig's thesis that are generative for thinking about the routinisation of bordered geographies in the Ferghana Valley. First, Billig is primarily interested in the symbolic register of this national flagging: in the reading of weather forecasts, in the production of national newspapers, in the learning of selective national histories, or the invocation by newsreaders of a national 'we'. But banal nationalism is also a *material* and spatial practice, and the work of nation flagging may be particularly salient in states where the geographic coordinates of national territory are disputed or contentious (cf. Billé 2014). Furthermore, in many global settings, the nation that is being flagged and rendered banal is a *securitised* nation: a nation that is always already under threat, and which can only survive as a nation by being (collectively) on its guard (compare Ochs 2011). The 'ban' in banal derives etymologically from the compulsory (and thus *banal*, common-to-all) call to arms. To invoke Billig's formulation again, the 'banal' in 'banal nationalism' gestures not just to what is boring or unremarkable: *it is more specifically the unmarked routinisation of being-on-one's guard*: to the national citizen as watchman or vigilante.

This nuance is significant for reflecting on the particular modalities of nationalism that figure in Central Asian public culture. In Uzbekistan, for instance, the sense of the nation being under permanent threat (whether from substandard goods being imported across the border to vermin that need to be kept under control by a vigilant citizenry to armed incursions of Islamist militants) is a staple, not just of official political discourse, but also of pop culture, *estrada* music, and high-school pedagogy (Megoran 2008; Koch 2011; Klenke 2015). In Tajikistan, scholars have pointed out how President Rahmon uses the threat of 'radical Islam' as 'a vehicle to justify popular repression, to eliminate rivals, and to obtain material aid for the RT [Tajikistani] security apparatus, both internal and military' (Foster 2015: 152). In Kyrgyzstan, meanwhile, concerns about the illicit movement of people and goods across excessively 'porous' borders have resulted in a number of policies explicitly aimed at preventing out-migration and 'strengthen[ing] the military-patriotic preparation of the population' of territories accorded special border status, just as they have in a range of public statements about the threat of so-called 'creeping migration': the cultivation (and de facto appropriation) of territory that is legally disputed between neighbouring states (Reeves 2009; Proekt 2011).

These discourses, while deriving from elite concerns about political and territorial stability, also have considerable local traction. Along Kyrgyzstan's southern border with Uzbekistan at the perimeter of the Sokh enclave, for instance, I found that my own critique of borders' increasingly militarised presence—manifest in barbed wire military controls, and the repurposing of public buildings for military ends—did not necessarily resonate with my informants. For many of my Kyrgyz interlocutors, having a defended border was spoken of, both as a critical index of 'normal' statehood *and* as the only meaningful brake upon the increasing demands of Uzbekistan's border guards, who would often aggressively question Kyrgyzstani citizens as they sought to reach their homes, or pester them for 'tea money' (*choi pul*) for alleged driving offences. As the director of a border market (*bazarkom*) asked me rhetorically in 2005, pinning his hopes on the new president that had been propelled to power by a popular uprising in March that year,

'Doesn't England have a border? The new President has to define and give us the border!' (*chek arany taktap berish kerek!*) (Reeves 2011)

In the ethnography that follows, I proceed by exploring three modalities through which the new international borders in the Ferghana Valley have become 'intimately militarised'. First, they manifest in the habitual reproduction of border geography: the way, that is, that a new international border comes to shape patterns of movement and avoidance; where people choose (or are permitted) to travel and not to travel; to shop and not to shop; to visit and not to visit. Second, they manifest in the normalisation of military presence itself: in the everyday presence of conscript soldiers and their military barracks; in the presence of soldiers asking for lifts, purchasing goods, checking passports, or offering services (such as the provision of a barracks bathhouse for local use). And third, it appears in the domestication of state force: in the appeal to armed conscript soldiers and officers for the resolution of mundane, neighbourly disputes, and in the blurring of boundaries between 'state' and 'vigilante' control of borders. In the final section, I suggest how such an approach might offer a more nuanced account of how popular concerns for recognition and incorporation within state space intersect with, and become enmeshed within, elite-led agendas of securitisation.

Becoming bordered: changing habitual geographies

In the spring of 2004, when I first travelled to Ak-Sai, the journey from the provincial centre of Batken took over two and half hours in the yellow *Pazik* bus that had been servicing this route for the past 30 years. The journey was frequently interrupted by unscheduled stops: to coax the ageing engine into gear on a gravelly incline; to tie an extra large bundle to the roof of the bus; to fit a milk pail or carpet in among the passengers squatting and standing along the bus's middle. Travelling on this route was a sociable affair: children and packages might be passed to seated strangers to be cared for until we reached our destination; seats would be rearranged or given up to allow an elderly passenger the opportunity to rest her feet; other seats would be created from small wooden planks across the middle of the rows. This bus, designed to accommodate no more than 30 passengers, probably transported more than double that number on each of its daily routes from Batken to Ak-Sai and back again. Its route tacked westward from Batken until it reached the Tortgul Reservoir before following the line of the Isfara River itself, dipping in and out of Tajikistan and Kyrgyzstan in the process.

Along our route, river, road, and border continuously crossed and recrossed, such that our route took us back and forth, in and out of Kyrgyzstan and Tajikistan, no fewer than six times in the course of the journey. None of these crossing points was marked by a permanent border post or fence, and few, indeed, by any obvious indicators of being at an international border crossing, such as a road-side sign or flag. The move from one state to another had to be read in other ways: here prices were listed in Kyrgyz som, there in Tajik somoni; here the licence plates on passing cars took one form and there another; here the announcements advertising mobile phone contracts were in the Kyrgyz language, there in Tajik. My fellow passengers could identify 'Kyrgyz' and 'Tajik' villages in an instant: there were differences in the density of dwelling, the style of domestic construction, and the size of the local mosques. There were differences in habitual modes of male and female dress; even the preference for particular models of imported car.

But the social space of cross-border public transport was not marked in 'national' terms, and while the bus was operated from the bus station in Batken town, and ended its journey in the Kyrgyz village of Ak-Sai, its route knitted all of the border villages along its route, whether in Tajikistan or Kyrgyzstan, in a single social space. More importantly, perhaps, the 15 or so villages that lay along our route were ones on which everyone on the bus had certain kinds of claim.

Everyone knew that to buy livestock, one went to Samarkandek, a sprawling, parched, and rather desolate Kyrgyz village that came alive on market day. To buy petrol one went to the Kyrgyz side too; for coal, you went to the Tajik side, where canvas-covered trucks brought coal directly from sole functioning mine in the once flourishing border town of Shorab. In this space of intense social and linguistic mixing, the Russian rouble often served as the convertible currency of choice; just as Uzbek, understood to a greater or less degree by most Kyrgyz and Tajik adults, served as an informal lingua franca. During my earliest period of research here, what was striking in the Isfara valley was precisely how *little* international borders seemed to matter. There were other differences that made a difference (Green 2005): notably those of ethnicity, language, wealth, mode of life, or one's commitment or not to pietist forms of Islam. Sometimes these differences were objects of commentary of contention: there were whispered conversations about the big traders who hid narcotics in their apricot harvest and who had managed to build lavish two-storey houses. But these were not, by and large, seen as differences that mapped onto state boundaries; still less, as sources of threat.

Looked at from a distance of 13 years, what is striking in the villages along the Isfara River is less a sudden moment of border closure than a progressive shifting of habitual geographies, practices, and registers of identification, such that social life is increasingly conducted and framed within the administrative and geographical confines of the nation state. Some of these shifts are subtle and not driven by any explicit nationalist agenda. The ending of the state-run bus service between Batken and Ak-Sai and the replacement of this route by private mini-buses (*marshrutki*) has meant, for instance, that ordinary people spend much less of their week in this space of trilingual (Kyrgyz, Uzbek, and Tajik) mixture. These private *marshrutki* typically run from a single end village to the respective district centre (Batken in Kyrgyzstan, Isfara in Tajikistan), such that citizens of Kyrgyz and Tajik villages have fewer reasons to take the *mashrutka* of the 'other' state than in the recent past, when a single vehicle serviced all of the villages along its route. The orienting of domestic livelihoods towards labour migration in Russia has also had a transformation effect. On both sides of the border, young men now typically leave to work in Russia straight after school, registering to take exams 'by correspondence' (*zaochno*) if they wish to register—at least notionally—on a degree course. Yet the patterns of migration in Kyrgyz and Tajik villages in the valley are strikingly different: young men are channelled through different national systems of transport, work in different Russian cities, and rely on different networks of friends and relatives to help in securing work and accommodation. Middle-aged interlocutors on both sides of the border often reflected on this difference: in the late Soviet period, there was a lot of habitual interaction among Kyrgyz- and Tajik-speakers, both in school and leisure time: with few television sets in the valley until the 1980s, for instance, everyone would go and watch the Bollywood movies in a make-shift movie theatre in the Vorukh house of culture. Today, with the exception of sponsored events aimed at fostering 'inter-ethnic tolerance' (which meet with varying degrees of cynicism and commitment), there are few opportunities among young people for spontaneous social interaction across linguistic and national boundaries.

Other infrastructural interventions have been more explicitly concerned to shape local geographies of movement and identification. The road network throughout Kyrgyzstan dips in and out of the neighbouring states: as a mountainous republic within the Soviet Union it was largely bypassed by the highway network. Until the early 1990s, to travel from Batken to the republican capital of Frunze (today's Bishkek), one would travel the faster, easier 'lowland' route, via Tajikistan, Uzbekistan, and Kazakhstan. Kyrgyzstan had few highways of its own, and the single two-lane road across southern Kyrgyzstan was puckered with potholes, not fully tarmacked along its length, and was frequently unpassable in winter. Reaching any other town in southern Kyrgyzstan, meanwhile, involved crossing international borders—through Uzbekistan's Sokh exclave to reach the city of Osh to the East—and through Tajik Surh and Chorkuh to reach the western-most district of Leilek. This fact fed into characterisations of Batken in public culture as itself a kind of 'enclave' (even though, legally and administratively, it is not), just as it inflected local discourses in Ak-Sai about the village's 'strategic significance'. As I was often told by acquaintances and village officials, Ak-Sai's geographical location—squeezed in between two large settlements in Tajikistan, and acting as a buffer between their apparently relentless expansion—was the only thing that prevented Batken itself from being 'cut in half'. That was one reason why it was important for the village's border status to be 'seen' in Bishkek, and why a vocal strand of ethnonationalism had considerable traction here. As one village official put it, leaders had to encourage local patriotism to 'defend the border' against much larger, neighbouring villages, 'for there are just 1,000 of us, and how many in Vorukh? 25,000? 30,000? You can do the maths!'

It is in this context of territorial anxiety that we need to understand the importance attached, locally and in Bishkek, to the building of so-called 'independent roads' (*nezavisimye dorogi*): roads that would lie entirely within the borders of the Kyrgyzstani state. In Batken in 2008, as part of a larger national project of road 'rehabilitation' construction work began on a new bypass road that was explicitly intended to obviate the need for Kyrgyzstani border-residents in the Isfara valley to have to cross into the territory of Tajikistan to reach their district centre of Batken. In a speech to mark the opening of the bypass, which circumvented the large Tajik settlements of Surh and Chorkuh, the provincial governor celebrated the road's completion as a mark of national-territorial fulfilment. The smooth asphalt bypass, he argued, would, for the first time, give the people of Batken the 'taste of genuine freedom, the taste of independence' by providing a means of circumventing 'foreign enclaves' (*innostrannye anklavy*) (Anarkulov 2008). Kyrgyzstan's prime minister, meanwhile, announced that the new road would turn Kyrgyzstan from a country of dead ends into a country of transit (*iz tupikovoi strany v tranzitnuyu*) (Kabar 2008). Nor was it just political leaders who saw the expressly territorial and military significance of the road. In publicly available documents, the World Bank acknowledged that, in addition to the economic benefits of the new road (cutting down journey times and limiting time-consuming customs checks), the renovated section in the territorially contentious Isfara valley would 'serve to define the nearby border into the future and reduce the risk of encroachment' (World Bank 2009: 5), both through its material form and through the facilitation of border guards' foot patrols.

Celebrated in Kyrgyz public discourse as a 'road of peace' (*tynchtyk jolu*) (e.g. Nazaraliev 2014), it is clear that within a few years of its construction, the new road had served significantly to reshape local geographies of movement and confinement. In part this is because, from Kyrgyz border villages such as Ak-Sai, it made little sense to travel to the market in Chorkuh, Tajikistan, despite its geographical proximity, when the Kyrgyz market in Batken could now be reached much more comfortably and speedily along smooth asphalt. It is also, however, because the new road, running more-or-less along the line of the previously unmarked border, enabled the border itself to be policed much more visibly and systematically, both by border guards and by vigilante groups seeking to stop the felling of trees for firewood and the gathering of *mumio* (a marketable mountain gum, valued for its medicinal properties) on what was now more obviously 'Kyrgyz' land.

Domesticating the border guard

The Batken–Ak-Sai road provides a salutary lesson in the ways that well-intentioned initiatives of borderland infrastructural provision can generate a range of unexpected consequences, the most striking of which, a decade after the road's opening, is the way that local patterns of mobility are now habitually conducted in 'national' terms, to the extent that a 'Kyrgyz' car on a 'Tajik' road is remarked upon locally as anomalous, or that Kyrgyz girls are discouraged from taking the 'Tajik *marshrutka*' for fear of inappropriate glances or gestures from unrelated men. The road also reminds us that 'border infrastructure' can take many forms, and that it is not just wire, walls, or watchtowers through which a new international boundary can come to materialise. Roads, like rivers, can divide as well as connect.

An equally significant factor in the everyday securitisation of the Isfara valley, however, is the increasing presence of military and security personnel and associated infrastructures of surveillance. In Ak-Sai, for instance, the largest and best-equipped building in the village is the military barracks, situated prominently on the village's central street. The walls of the barracks are today painted with a stencil design showing a border guard looking out over a mountainous landscape. The accompanying lettering reminds passersby, in Russian and Kyrgyz, that they are 'At the Border' (*Na granitse/ Chegarada*) and that the border is necessarily a place where one should naturally be on one's guard.

Although the barracks are a space set apart within the village, with high walls, metal gates, and a metal watchtower, the awareness of border-as-threat is routinised through the very intimacy of its militarisation. The barracks here are *banal* in the dual sense described above. For one thing, the barracks are a source of livelihood to several in the village as one of the major consumers of local flour, rice, and potatoes. The area immediately in front of the entrance gate serves as an informal meeting ground and taxi pick-up stop, where petrol can also be purchased and where village news is exchanged. One family I knew regularly used the barracks bathhouse to wash their clothes because they and their neighbours lacked a bathhouse of their own. This sense of military 'closeness' worked the other way, too: driving east out of Batken, one might encounter conscript soldiers at the side of the road requesting a lift to their duty station or barracks. Officers were a regular presence in Batken, and often rented rooms from local families if they had been posted to the district from elsewhere. When, in 2014, special forces (*OMON*) were sent to Ak-Sai in the wake of an escalation of cross-border violence precipitated by the construction of a new stretch of contested road between Ak-Sai and its mountain pastures, these elite troops were temporarily housed in the hall of the village school. Cars bearing Kyrgyz number plates, moreover, would rarely stop for Kyrgyz military patrols. 'They are our lads' (*Özübüzdün baldarabyz!*) the driver would typically comment to the passengers—implying that there was no need to stop, as they would not be seen as a source of threat.

This military intimacy had a particular quality in border villages such as Ak-Sai. In many routine situations of intra- and inter-village dispute, the authority of informal village leaders, whether the elected head of the administrative district of the *ak-sakals* ('white beards') who in many villages constitute a semi-formal court of elders, has come to be overshadowed by a much younger 'face of the state' (Navaro-Yashin 2002): that of the local head of the border unit, a figure with direct and immediate connections 'upwards' to the state bureaucracy, backed up by threat of force. In Ak-Sai, 35-year-old Azamat (a pseudonym), the officer responsible for the local border unit, was a well-known figure in the village and frequently called upon in times of dispute. Many men in the village had his telephone number and would refer to him through the informal pronoun, *sen*.

The physical and social 'closeness' of this military presence is significant to its mode of operation. Azamat's authority works *both* because he is familiar—a young man with local knowledge and extensive local contacts, who is a regular at weddings and other celebrations—and because his words and actions have the capacity to speak to, and on behalf of, the state. On several occasions, I witnessed what was essentially a trivial dispute between young Kyrgyz and Tajik men (had someone pushed someone else deliberately? Had a car with Tajik number plates been travelling too recklessly through Ak-Sai?) first escalate through phone calls between young men warning each other that things had 'kicked off' (*topolong bashtaldy*), to be followed by calls to 'invite Azamat' (*Azamatty chakyryp koichu!*) to serve as a mediator whose words could be backed up by threat of force. A critical aspect of intimate militarisation, then, is not just the routinisation of military presence, but rather the *normalisation of appeal to threat of force to resolve habitual disputes*, such that the non-local head of the border unit comes to be spoken of and appealed to, locally, as the best meaningful guarantor of local peace and de facto arbiter at times of inter-communal dispute.

Escalating force?

Writing of the US/Mexico border in the 1990s, Josiah Heyman described what he calls the 'state escalation of force'—the process of 'adding increments of force to a failing or incomplete system of control' (Heyman 1999: 285). In the Isfara valley, we can see traces of a rather similar dynamic. In Tajik border villages throughout the valley (and now, increasingly, in online forums and videos), the intensification of border controls, facilitated by and materialised through the new road that bypasses Chorkuh and Surh, has exacerbated the sense of relative neglect by a political elite that is geographically and socially distant. It has also fed into a lingering feeling of territorial injustice; of having been repeatedly 'cheated' of land in a cycle that goes back to the middle of the 20th century (e.g. Ismoil 2013).

The official response to increased local tension, however, has less been to find transboundary solutions than to intensify state presence, whether in the form of border guards, police officers, or members of the security services. An example from my fieldwork can illustrate here. The period 2009–2011 was marked by an increase in local incidents of low-level cross-border crime in the Isfara valley, including theft, arson, and the retaliatory pelting of 'foreign' cars with stones by young boys observing traffic along the new roads. Many of these incidents had, it seems, been exacerbated by the new restrictions on cross-border mobility and the difficulties of accessing irrigation water resulting from the bypass road, particularly for young men from Chorkuh and Surh in Tajikistan whose own local mobility had been constrained by the new road. In the wake of political upheaval in Kyrgyzstan and ethnically marked violence in Kyrgyzstan's southern city of Osh, there was a palpable sense among my Tajik interlocutors in 2010 that their own concerns were being ignored, not least by a political elite in Dushanbe that cared little about the remote Isfara district. Reporting in February 2010 on an altercation along the bypass road between a Kyrgyzstani border guard and an elderly woman from Chorkuh village who was struggling to climb the steep incline that now separated her village from the road, a Tajik journalist described the journey from home to work for the communities now circumvented by the road as a 'real trial' (*nastoyashchee ispitanie*). It was also, she implied, a historical injustice:

> While citizens of Tajikistan have to overcome a difficult mountain path and constantly have to fend for their rights with the organs of law and order, citizens of Kyrgyzstan are able to move about freely in the streets of Chorkuh [in Tajikistan]. […] Citizens of both states hoped for their transport problems in the borderland to be solved. But so far, the new road has brought only difficulties (*s novoi trassoi voznikaiut tol'ko slozhnosti*).
>
> *(Komilova 2010)*

From the perspective of state officials, however, it was precisely the increase in incidents of hooliganism associated with the road that was cast as the source of threat: a threat that is to be contained with more force and more state presence. In a vivid illustration of Heyman's 'increments of force', the interim President of Kyrgyzstan, Roza Otunbaeva, announced in February 2011 that she would be sending an additional 500 troops to Batken district to guard the oblast's borders with Tajikistan and Uzbekistan. Speaking to activists gathered in the Batken regional administration building, Otunbaeva noted that her decision had been prompted by the increase in incidents of cross-border violence over the preceding year. While just one violent cross-border conflict had been recorded on the Kyrgyzstan–Kazakhstan border in 2010, 26 had been recorded on the Kyrgyzstan–Uzbekistan border, and 24 on the Kyrgyzstan–Tajikistan border. Had it not been for the 'decisive action of the relevant state organs', Otunbaeva argued, 'many of these incidents could have turned into armed conflicts. The most dangerous thing is that each of these disputes [*sporov*] has the potential to turn into an inter-ethnic and inter-national conflict' (Otunbaeva, quoted in Centrasia.ru 2011).

Otunbaeva's narrative framing, pitched as much for a national television audience as it was at the local Batken activists, situated the urgency of political intervention within a global risk of threat. 'The whole civilized world has declared that it is fighting against subversive and terrorist activity from international extremist terrorist organizations', Otunbaeva argued. 'And if we consider that, because of our geopolitical specificity our state is currently the centre of attention of a variety of external powers, then the importance of the border forces is difficult to over-estimate' (Otunbaeva, quoted in Centrasia.ru 2011). Otunbaeva's language effectively subsumed local actions of cross-border violence into a larger discourse of threat, ignoring both the specificity of these local dynamics in 2010 and obviating the question of whether border controls that are experienced as arbitrary, draconian, or coercive might themselves be a factor in provoking borderland incidents of violence. Her response begs the question of who is provoking whom, and whether, in the context of a region where livelihoods on both sides of the border are precariously dependent upon equitable access to water and pastures, more force might not, as Heyman suggests, lead to more retaliation. Certainly, the dynamic of transboundary relations in the half decade since Otunbaeva delivered her speech would give credence to such an interpretation.

There is something else about this incident, however, that may be equally important for our understanding of the region and of the progressive escalation of force that can be seen in the borderlands of the Ferghana Valley. For while the increased presence of border patrols was certainly a source of concern when it referred to the military of the neighbouring state, in Ak-Sai, Otunbaeva's words resonated with, and gave credence to, a rather different set of local concerns: to see and be seen by the president when she visited the provincial capital. 'It's good that she came to Batken', I was told by one of the selected *aktivisty* who had heard the president speak in the Batken administration building. 'It's good when she listens to us.' For the village social worker who made these comments, a state employee whose task was compiling lists of families with invalids or veterans that would entitle them to compensatory payments, the concern was less whether the 500 new border forces proposed by Otunbaeva were a good or bad thing, than with being legible to the state in a context where the basic material resources for making a life—the infrastructures of water provision; the institutions of medical care; the payments made to pensioners and to those requiring humanitarian aid (*gumanitarnaia pomosch'*)—were both chronically insufficient and unequally allocated. In such a context, reiterating one's status as a 'border village' that is the locus of 'threat' (still more, as Otunbaeva's words suggest, the locus of unspecified geopolitical danger) had become a crucial vehicle for establishing a direct connection to the capital city and its perceived sources of material and political protection.

Conclusion

The category of 'intimate militarism' that I have sought to develop in this chapter conveys a double dynamic in the Ferghana Valley. It refers, first, to the routinisation of national geographies and of military presence at new international borders. It also signals a shift in the way that habitual disputes over water allocation, pasture-use, and access to canals, springs, or goods that are treated as common property (such as mountain herbs, animal dung, or gravel for construction from the Isfara river) come to be framed as 'transboundary' issues that can only be resolved through the intervention of state officials, backed up by the threat of force.

This dynamic is consequential for our understanding of the (strained) work of social ordering in rural Kyrgyzstan. The kinds of everyday disputes that occur within and among villages along the Isfara River, including the allocation of irrigation water from a shared irrigation infrastructure (and associated maintenance of a decaying irrigation network), access to pastures and the 'de facto' privatisation of common grazing land, the polluting of down-stream water sources by up-stream users, the (deliberate or accidental) destruction of crops by grazing livestock, and inequitable access to a limited supply of piped drinking water, are by no means confined to this or any other border region. As scholars of Central Asia have long argued, communal disputes, between neighbours, relatives, landlords, and tenants, up-stream and down-stream water users, or different ethnolinguistic communities, are part of the fabric of everyday social life (Bichsel 2009). Such disputes may coexist with a popular discursive emphasis upon social 'harmony' (*yntymak*) and considerable informal coercion to prevent social relations from breaking down beyond repair (Beyer 2016). But contention, in a context of limited and unequal resource access, is itself unremarkable: and in the Isfara valley there are well-developed mechanisms for allocating and regulating a shared and unpredictable supply of irrigation water (Pak et al. 2013). This has, after all, always been a region where sedentary and pastoral livelihoods have depended upon a limited supply of both water and irrigated land.

The framing of such disputes here as 'national' issues means that over the course of the last decade, my interlocutors have often spoken of relations having 'broken down' (*buzuldu*) between the Kyrgyz-majority villages that depend on the Isfara River and the more populous Tajik-speaking communities of Vorukh, Chorkuh, and Surh with which they are geographically contiguous. These villages used to be connected through multiple ties of trade, ritual visiting, religious learning, kolkhoz labour, and military service (though not, except in rare cases, through kinship or marriage). More importantly, there were dense ties of connection between elders from the various communities, such that disputes between young people were quickly resolved through the intervention of respected figures of authority, or symbolic acts of 'everyday diplomacy' (Marsden et al. 2006) in order to prevent a neighbourly dispute from escalating (see, e.g. UNDP 2011: 70).

This has implications, I suggest, for a broader anthropological conversation about how and when the state—in this case, a state that is able to 'defend its borders' and protect its territorial integrity—becomes a register through which ideas of political membership, existential security, and concerns for the possibilities of a 'normal life' gain social salience (Obeid 2010; Reeves 2011; Jansen 2014). As Jonathan Spencer argued in a 2007 study of the postcolonial state in South Asia, much anthropological literature on the state, whether drawing inspiration from post-structuralist critique or studies of everyday bureaucratic evasion, has tended to treat 'the state', analytically as an 'an absolute externality' which can be conceived, only as 'a force to be resisted, with more or less heroism, by the plucky subjects of our field research'. Such an approach is unconvincing, Spencer argues, not just because it presumes that we know what the state, in any given situation, is and does. It is also unconvincing because it 'fails to account for the moral investment that many people make in the idea of being owners, or at least members, of a state of their own' (Spencer 2007: 102).

It is in this realm of moral investment, I suggest, that we need to understand the *intimacy* of militarism in rural Central Asia. While much of the growing scholarly and policy literature on Central Asia's borders has focused productively on the way that borders and their agents are resisted, bypassed, subverted, or undermined by those seeking to get people, goods, valuables, and ideas across them (e.g. Dolina mira 2004; Jackson 2005; Megoran et al. 2005), there has been less attention to the complex alignments between the routinisation of military presence, the formalisation of dispute resolution, and the dynamics of territorial desire. For marginalised border residents, I have suggested, belonging to a 'border village'—a village that is, moreover, explicitly and visibly protected by uniformed border agents—has become a vehicle for anticipating and enacting certain kinds of claim upon the state that demand recognition and response. This dynamic may yet prove consequential for the local practices through which everyday peace is enacted and sustained in contemporary Central Asian borderlands.

Notes

1. For instance, one of the few sustained initiatives of cross-border monitoring and violations of civilian rights conducted in the early 2000s by a network of Kyrgyzstani, Tajikistani, and Uzbekistani NGOs, *Dolina mira* ('Valley of Peace'), was abruptly halted following political upheaval in Kyrgyzstan and subsequent crack-downs on civil society organisations in Uzbekistan in 2005. See Dolina mira (2004).
2. In 2016, for example, Uzbekistan's security services announced the discovery of a 120 metre-long tunnel running 6 metres underground between houses in Burbalyk (Uzbekistan) and Kyrgyz-Kyshtak (Kyrgyzstan) that was being used for the smuggling of contraband. While the authorities in Tashkent warned that the tunnel had been used for the illicit transfer of 'arms, military equipment, explosives, anti-constitutional literature, narcotics and militants' (Sputnik 2016), this particular pair of villages is well-known in the border region as one of the main crossing points for potatoes, macaroni and other foodstuffs that find their way into local border markets (see Reeves 2014: 153).

References

ACTED/OSCE. 2005. 'Borders of Discord: An Appraisal of Sources of Tension in Villages on the Kyrgyz-Uzbek Border in the Ferghana Valley.' Unpublished Report.

Alamanov, Salamat. 2005. *Kratkaia istoriia i opyt resheniia pogranichnykh problem Kyrgyzstana*. Bishkek: Friedrich Ebert Stiftung.

Alykulov, Murat. 2006. *Chegara/Granitsa*. DVD Film. Bishkek: Oy-Art Productions.

Anarkulov, Nurbek. 2008. 'Kirgizskii Batken zakanchivaet stroitel'stvo avtodorog, obkhodyashchikh inostrannye anklavy'.' *Kabar*, July 15.

Beyer, Judith. 2016. *The Force of Custom: Law and the Ordering of Everyday Life in Kyrgyzstan*. Pittsburgh: University of Pittsburgh Press.

Bichsel, Christine. 2009. *Conflict Transformation in Central Asia: Irrigation Disputes in the Ferghana Valley*. Abingdon: Routledge.

Billé, Franck. 2014. 'Territorial Phantom Pains (and Other Cartographic Anxieties).' *Environment and Planning D: Society and Space* 32 (1): 163–178.

Billig, Michael. 1995. *Banal Nationalism*. London and Thousand Oaks, CA: Sage Publications.

Centrasia.ru. 2011. 'R. Otunbaeva:V peregovorakh po anklavam s Uzbekistanom mozhet idti rech' tol'ko o ravnotsennom obmene zemel.' February 8. Available at: www.centrasia.ru/newsA.php?st=1297167300.

Cons, Jason. 2013. 'Narrating Boundaries: Framing and Contesting Suffering, Community, and Belonging in Enclaves along the India-Bangladesh Border.' *Political Geography* 35: 37–46.

Diener, Alexander and Joshua Hagen. 2010. *Borderlines and Borderlands: Political Oddities at the Edge of the Nation-State*. Lanham, MD: Rowman & Littlefield.

Dolina mira. 2004. *Analiz situatsii po perekhodu granits v Ferganskoi Doline*. Osh: Dolina mira.

Foster, Douglas. 2015. 'Militarism in Tajikistan: Realities of Post-Soviet Nation Building.' PhD diss., University of Oregon.

Geine, Khloya. 2016. 'Spetzreportazh: Kak uzbekskie bronetransportery obnazhili prigranichnye problemy.' March 29. Available at: http://kloop.kg/blog/2016/03/29/spetsreportazh-kak-uzbekskie-bronetransportery-obnazhili-prigranichnye-problemy/.

Green, Sarah. 2005. *Notes from the Balkans: Locating Marginality and Ambiguity on the Greek-Albanian Border*. Princeton, NJ: Princeton University Press.

Heyman, Josiah. 1999. 'State Escalation of Force: A Vietnam/US-Mexico Border Analogy.' In Josiah Heyman and Alan Smart, eds., *States and Illegal Practices*. Oxford and New York: Berg, 285–314.

International Crisis Group. 2002. 'Central Asia: Border Disputes and Conflict Potential.' *Asia Report* 33. Osh and Brussels: International Crisis Group.

Ismoil, Tolib Usmon. 2013. 'Vorukh- ne Anklav!' Asia Plus, September 5. Available at: http://news.tj/en/node/170036.

Jackson, Nicole. 2005. 'The Trafficking of Narcotics, Arms and Humans in Post-Soviet Central Asia: (Mis) perceptions, Policies and Realities.' *Central Asian Survey* 24 (1): 39–52.

Jansen, Stef. 2014. 'Hope for/Against the State: Gridding in a Besieged Sarajevo Suburb.' *Ethnos* 79 (2): 238–260.

Kabar. 2008. I. Chudinov prinyal uchastie v torzhestvennom sobranii ko Dnyu rabotnikov avtomobil'nogo transporta', *Kabar*, October 10.

Klenke, Kerstin. 2015. 'On the Politics of Music: Estrada in Uzbekistan.' PhD diss., Hochschule für Musik, Theater und Medien, Hannover.

Koch, Nathalie. 2011. 'Security and Gendered National Identity in Uzbekistan.' *Gender, Place and Culture: A Journal of Feminist Geography* 18: 499–518.

Komilova, Khosiat. 2010. 'Zhizn' na prigranich'e.' Stan.tv, March 5. Available at: www.stan.tv/news/14897/.

Lewington, Richard. 2010. 'The Challenge of Managing Central Asia's New Borders.' *Asian Affairs* 41 (2): 221–236.

Marat, Erica. 2009. 'Nation Branding in Central Asia: A New Campaign to Present Ideas About the State and the Nation.' *Europe-Asia Studies* 61 (7): 1123–1136.

Marsden, Magnus, Diana Ibañez-Tirado and David Henig. 2006. 'Everyday Diplomacy: Introduction to Special Issue.' *The Cambridge Journal of Anthropology* 34 (2): 2–22.

Megoran, Nick. 2002. 'The Borders of Eternal Friendship? The Politics and Pain of Nationalism and Identity along the Uzbekistan-Kyrgyzstan Ferghana Valley Boundary, 1999–2000.' PhD diss., University of Cambridge.

Megoran, Nick. 2004. 'The Critical Geopolitics of the Uzbekistan–Kyrgyzstan Ferghana Valley Boundary Dispute, 1999–2000.' *Political Geography* 23 (6): 731–764.

Megoran, Nick. 2008. 'From Presidential Podiums to Pop Music: Everyday Discourses of Geopolitical Danger in Uzbekistan.' In Rachel Pain and Susan Smith, eds., *Fear: Critical Geopolitics and Everyday Life*. Aldershot: Ashgate Publishing, 25–36.

Megoran, Nick, Gaël Raballand and Jerome Bouyjou. 2005. 'Performance, Representation and the Economics of Border Control in Uzbekistan.' *Geopolitics* 10 (4): 712–740.

Navaro-Yashin, Yael. 2002. *Faces of the State: Secularism and Public Life in Turkey*. Princeton, NJ: Princeton University Press.

Nazaraliev, Meder. 2014, December 30. *Kök-Tash – Ak-Sai: Tynchtyk jolu*. KTRK: Bishkek, Kyrgyzstan.

Nucho, Joanne. 2016. *Everyday Sectarianism in Urban Lebanon: Infrastructures, Public Services, and Power*. Princeton, NJ and Oxford: Princeton University Press.

Obeid, Michelle. 2010. 'Searching for the Ideal "Face of the State" in a Lebanese Border Town.' *Journal of the Royal Anthropological Institute* 16 (2): 330–346.

Ochs, Joanne. 2011. *Security and Suspicion: An Ethnography of Everyday Life in Israel*. Philadelphia: University of Pennsylvania Press.

Orlova, Tat'iana. 2003. 'Detektiv, ili Lenin pmeshal?' *Moia Stolitsa – novosti*, August 18.

Pak, Mariya, Kai Wegerich and Jusipbek Kazbekov. 2013. 'Re-Examining Conflict and Cooperation in Central Asia: A Case Study from the Isfara River, Ferghana Valley.' *International Journal of Water Resources Development* 30 (2): 230–245.

Polat, Necati. 2002. *Boundary Issues in Central Asia*. Leiden: Transnational Publishers.

Proekt. 2011. *Proekt zakona Kyrgyzskoi Respubliki o pridanii osobogo statusa Otdel'nym prigranichnym territoriiam Kyrgyzskoi Respubliki i ikh razvitii* [Draft law of the Kyrgyz Republic on according special status to certain border territories of the Kyrgyz Republic and their development], debated in Parliament 8 April 2011.

Raev, Sultan. 2007. Last Will. Radio play, broadcast as part of *Seven Wonders of the Divided World*. BBC Radio 3, September 9.

Reeves, Madeleine. 2009. 'Materialising State Space: "Creeping Migration" and Territorial Integrity in Southern Kyrgyzstan.' *Europe-Asia Studies* 61 (7): 1277–1313.

Reeves, Madeleine. 2011. 'Fixing the Border: On the Affective Life of the State in Southern Kyrgyzstan.' *Environment and Planning D: Society and Space* 29 (5): 905–923. doi: 10.1068/d18610.

Reeves, Madeleine. 2014. *Border Work: Spatial Lives of the State in Rural Central Asia*. Ithaca, NY: Cornell University Press.
Shishkin, Philip. 2013. *Restless Valley: Revolution, Murder, and Intrigue in the Heart of Central Asia*. New Haven, CT and London: Yale University Press.
Spencer, Jonathan. 2007. *Anthropology, Politics and the State: Democracy and Violence in South Asia*. Cambridge: Cambridge University Press.
Sputnik. 2016. 'Uzbekistan i Kyrgyzstan unichtozhat tunnel' kontrabandistov na granitse.' Sputnik Uzbekistan, March 25. Available at: http://ru.sputniknews-uz.com/politics/20160325/2286816.html.
Thorez, Julien. 2003. 'Enclaves et enclavement dans le Ferghana post-Soviétique.' Cahiers d'études sur la Méditerranée orientale et le monde turco-iranien, Centre d'études et de recherches internationales 2003: 28–39.
Troscenko, Elina. 2016. 'With a Border Fence in the Backyard: Materialization of the Border in the Landscape and Social Lives of Border People.' In Tone Bringa and Hege Toje, eds., *Eurasian Borderlands: Spatializing Borders in the Aftermath of State Collapse*. New York: Palgrave Macmillan, 87–106.
UNDP. 2011. *Potential for Peace and Threats of Conflict: Development Analysis of Cross-Border Communities in Isfara District of the Republic of Tajikistan and Batken District of the Kyrgyz Republic*. Vorukh: Jamoat Resource Centre.
World Bank. 2009. *National Roads Rehabilitation Project: Osh Isfana Section. Updated Feasibility Study. Resettlement Action Plan*. Bishkek: World Bank.

4

Borders and bordering in Asia

Karin Dean

Introduction

Studies of Asian borderlands are sailing in the wind of growing interest in borders worldwide both empirically and theoretically. With obvious links between practices and theoretical conceptualizations, various events and developments on the ground have been shaping our understanding of borders and borderlands across the globe. The supply of theoretically challenging developments on the ground has led to booms in border studies, while their perceived absence caused temporary busts. All in all, border studies have hugely expanded since their 'geographically bounded beginnings in the nineteenth century' (Kolossov and Scott 2013: 2) culminating in what has become to be understood as the contemporary proliferation, transformation, and multiplication of borders (Mezzadra and Neilson 2013). After the 'long period of oblivion' during much of the second half of the 20th century (Amilhat Szary and Giraut 2015: 1), the following events and developments are consistently listed as the source for the reinvigorated interest in borders and borderlands in most overviews of border studies scholarship: the 1990s trumpeting of a (neo-liberal) borderless world where the convergence of communication and information technology and the unobstructed flows of capital would gradually lead to the disappearance of borders; the fall of the Iron Curtain that removed old boundaries and established new ones; the EU enlargement and the issues around its external borders and surrendering of state sovereignties to the EU; and the 9/11 attacks in the USA that led to the (re-)construction of borders on both sides of the Atlantic. The most recent EU efforts to expand its ability to control its southern borders and the so-called immigration crisis can be added to this list of what Newman (2015: 14) has called the 'changing historical and political contingencies'—significant developments that alongside the processes of globalization are impacting the meanings and functions of boundaries both in theory and practice.

What these 'historical and political contingencies' shaping our understanding of borders have in common is that all are located in the so-called West or Global North. Even the work on reterritorialization of large parts of the Middle East in the wake of Islamic State territorial claims across many current state boundaries (see Newman 2015: 14) and the emerging research on European/Turkish/Mediterranean/African borderscapes (Andersson 2014, 2016; Brambilla 2015) are not exceptions, in the sense that this work is relevant to the politics of the

USA and the EU. Similarly, the vast body of research on the US–Mexican boundary since the 1980s and the related institutional concentration in the area, inspiring much of earlier border work until new foci emerged, is connected to the US interest in controlling cross-border flows.

At the same time, Asia has witnessed many significant developments since the end of the Cold War, which could potentially contribute to a better theoretical understanding of borders more generally. The list would include, among others, the clarion call to turn 'battlefield to marketplace,' originally voiced by the Thai Prime Minister Chatichai Choonhavan in 1988 in relation to Indochina and its post-war opportunities; the consequent regional integration in transportation, communication, diplomacy, and business bolstered by powerful rhetoric of opening borders and new gateways; or the Association of Southeast Asian Nations (ASEAN) model of enlargement *not* impinging on the sovereignty of its individual states. Constituting insightful empirical material for understanding statehood around the world are the many separatist movements in Asia, and particularly the processes of peace-building in Indonesia, the Philippines, and Myanmar where issues of autonomy or devolution of power are central to ending armed conflicts, thus highlighting the importance of arrangements related to borders as '*central ordering devices* at the core of societies both in symbolic and material terms' (Popescu 2015: 49, *emphasis added*). The attempts to 'reterritorialize' the South China Sea add new and original dimensions to what borders can do both horizontally and vertically in terms of also 'securing the volume,' by adding a dimensionality such as depth to the scrutiny (Elden 2013). Finally, some of the world's most geopolitically charged borders are in Asia, including the territorial conflict in Kashmir between India and Pakistan, the border between the two Koreas, and China's claims in the East and South China Sea.

The array of active and operational spatio-political arrangements effectively performed across the world, on one hand, and the existing West-centred scholarship and its reliance on certain paradigmatic cases located in Europe and North America, on the other, urgently demand to widen the empirical-theoretical grasp in scholarship. In fact, many fields of social studies that have overlapping concerns with border studies strive for 'new geographies of theory' (Roy 2009). For example, the work of Risse (2013: 2) challenges the governance debates' bias towards modern nation states, pointing to the problematic issue of 'one of the key concepts of modern social sciences [being] not applicable to two-thirds of the international community.' Or, as Forsyth et al. (2013), writing on surfaces, conclude: 'there has been a close and powerful alignment of Western notions of objectivity, democracy, and agency with capitalist constructions of commodities, exchange, and property ownership, granting aesthetic power to a range of surfaces.' Or, as Bunnell et al. (2012) spell out in their introduction to an *Urban Studies* special issue on Asian cities: there continues to be a disjuncture between the locations where most cities in the world can be found and those from which knowledge about cities and urban processes is derived. We can say the same about borders: there continues to be a disjuncture between the volume of borders in the world and those from which our knowledge about borders and bordering is actually derived. Furthermore, certain (types of) borders (just as cities) taken as paradigmatic or as somehow leading edge have so far been concentrated in Western Europe and North America, as have powerful border related academic organizations, journals, and conferences. The now Finland-based Association for Borderlands Studies (ABS), established in 1976 in Arizona with the main objective of studying the USA–Mexico border, had a North American focus and management, and only recently started to expand its scope and membership. The ABS runs the *Journal of Borderlands Studies* and has annual meetings, and in 2014 held the first ABS World Conference. Others include the International Boundaries Research Unit (IBRU) at Durham University (established

Karin Dean

Table 4.1 A survey of the geographic locations of the borders discussed during 1988–2008 in the *Journal of Borderlands Studies*

Location	Number of appearances	Percent of appearances
Africa	6	2.1
Arctic	1	0.4
Asia	5	1.8
Borderlands – General	3	1.1
Canada	18	6.4
Caribbean	2	0.7
Europe	48	17.0
Mexico	6	2.1
Middle East	3	1.1
North America	4	1.4
South America	5	1.8
United States	7	2.5
U.S.–Canada	10	3.6
U.S.–Mexico	158	56.2
N/A	5	1.8
Total	281*	100.0

Source: Pisani et al. (2009: 14). © Association for Borderlands Studies, reprinted by permission of Taylor & Francis Ltd, on behalf of Association for Borderlands Studies.
*More than one geographic area possible.

in 1989); the informal Border Regions in Transition (BRIT) network and its conferences since 1994; the Nijmegen Centre for Border Research; and some large EU-funded projects (e.g. East-BordNet, EUBORDERSCAPES). A survey of the geographic locations of the borders discussed during 1988–2008 in the *Journal of Borderlands Studies* revealed that 72 percent were located in North America, 17 percent in Europe, 2.1 percent in Africa, and 1.8 percent in Asia (Table 4.1) (Pisani et al. 2009; see also Brunet-Jailly 2010). The authors of the articles were from North American institutions in 77 percent of the cases and from Europe in 19 percent of the cases. Brenner (2013: 10–11) who did a similar study for 2001–2011 noted that even with the special issues devoted to 'under-researched geographic areas,' there remains a hegemonic influence of theoretical constructs with focus on the global North. While the share of North American scholars was decreasing in these later years at the expense of Europeans, the cases from Asia still amounted to only 3 percent, while Africa figured in 10 percent of studies (Brenner 2013: 12).

Why have the political developments in Asia *not* become *the* historical contingencies that shape the wider understanding of borders? This chapter tries to explain why the developments or concepts originating from Asia have not been perceived as influential and paradigmatic. The main reason is the sheer absence of Asian scholars and borders in the scholarship, and the chapter tries to elucidate this dearth. It suggests that the spatio-political developments and the challenges these pose in Asia have been *out of synchronization* with those in the West or Global North supplying the bulk of empirical material for border studies mostly driven by the Anglo-American intellectual engagement. It argues that Asian borders—and the current boom in Asian border scholarship—can provide extremely important insight more widely, but for this, a *longue durée* take is imperative in order to grasp the fluctuation of scholarly and practitioner interest and the issues around conceptualization related to borders. This *longue durée* take needs to go back to at least the origins of the contemporary nation states—that in most of Asia means less than a hundred years—but possibly earlier strata could be uncovered. Finally, the chapter also delineates the pitfalls and possibilities for Asian border studies and for further merging these two scholarships that until now have very seldom touched.[1]

Borders: from bust to boom

Border has been a key word for geographers since the end of 19th century, when it was regarded as a measure and expression of power of the organic state (Paasi 2013). In earlier scholarship, these physical lines of separation between states in the international organization of space were described and classified into different categories, typologies, legal statuses, or functions (Brunet-Jailly 2005; Rumford 2006; Newman 2011: 34). In parallel, borders were observed and described as symbolic lines bounding people and groups into a variety of social and spatial compartments, designating various social, cultural, or political group affiliations. The interest since the 1990s intensified in reaction to the destruction of the many Cold War borders and the post-Cold War 'borderless' world thinking arising from the belief that the converging information, communication, and transportation technologies accompanied by accelerating commercial and financial flows would erase borders. In anthropology, the earlier view of cultures as autonomous and bounded in 'naturally disconnected' space (for the critique, see Gupta and Ferguson 1992: 8) was challenged by new scape-suffixed and 'trans'-words, and appellations such as 'flows,' 'permeability,' 'fluid,' 'porous,' 'conflation,' 'fragmentation,' 'hybridization,' 'creolization,' 'multiculturalism,' 'transversal solidarities,' and 'intercultural reflexivity' became the catch-terms (Bloul 1999). In political geography, the notion of 'territorial trap' by Agnew and Corbridge (1995) signified a succinct warning against an intellectual trap implicit to the notion of state territories as fixed units of sovereign space (Grundy-Warr 1998: 41). The view of states and their associated territories as containers of society was famously challenged by Taylor (1995), while 'the idea of a simple parallelism between social boundaries and state borders' (Agnew 2015: 44) has been decried in an extensive body of border studies scholarship (Paasi 1995, 1996; Baud and van Schendel 1997; Newman and Paasi 1998; Wilson and Hastings 1998; Grundy-Warr 1998; Anderson and O'Dowd 1999; Sidaway 2002). Most political geographers argued against the 'naïve, post-Cold War "borderless" world discourses' (Johnson and Jones 2011: 61) as the lived world saw many new borders and even walls constructed and various technology aided 'security measurements' selectively exploited against those who were not welcome. 'We woke up to our borderless world only to find that each and every one of us, individuals as well as groups or States with which we share affiliation, live in the world of borders which give order to our lives' (Newman 2006: 172). Sociologists and social theorists have also identified the changing meanings and roles of borders in the centre of societal transformations such as cosmopolitanization, or geopolitical events such as the 9/11 attacks as creating a new spatiality of politics (see Rumford 2006). In short, major transformations in the geopolitical landscape re-introduced political borders as 'highly salient objects of research' (Paasi 2011: 11) everywhere.

The general trends, messages, and ideology of bordering emanating from Anglo-American scholarship in the early 1990s—presenting borders as increasingly permeable for flows of people and goods, and the state surrendering some of its sovereignty to the so-called neo-liberal forces, or supra-regional blocks such as the EU—clearly diverged from the political developments in much of Asia of the time. Asian borders, particularly those traversing extensive wilderness and land mass, had hardly functioned as barriers for vast amounts of people, nor even delineated state sovereignties. With exceptions, borders in Asia were widely permeable and embroiled in lively cross-border social, economic, kith and kin ties. Instead of surrendering some of their sovereignties, many states in Asia in the 1990s struggled to establish full internal sovereignty and strengthen statehood, aided by the officially sanctioned forms of economic (and political) cooperation at both regional and sub-regional levels (see Grundy-Warr 1998: 73).

The complex and fluid local cross-border power domains in many cases, the violent conflicts and securitized state presence and control in others, or the mere transportational and bureaucratic logistics have also not favoured scholarly access to many Asian borders and border communities. This difficulty is epitomized in van Schendel's (2002b) example of borderland settlements of Gohaling, Zayü, Sakongdan, and Dong in the eastern Himalayas, about 50 km apart from each other but belonging to three states—thus making a study of local dynamics logistically challenging for a border scholar who first needs visas from Beijing, Yangon, and New Delhi. Furthermore, the scholar would not be able to travel between those villages, but enter each from the state it belongs to as there are no official border crossings. Many border scholars in Asia have elaborate stories (and, thus, unique methodological challenges) related to accessing their borders.

But the scholars who traversed borderlands in the mid-1990s, observed the following (for China, Vietnam, Laos, and Cambodia):

> [b]orders may become porous, but that does not make them borderless. They were only borderless in the past when Akha or Muslim caravaners, or other ethnic groups in the region wandered across it without paying attention to borders drawn up in far-off capitals. But those days are gone.
>
> *(Evans et al. 2000: 2–3)*

It has been the states' economic opening-up along the borders that started to close the frontier in large parts of Asia since late 1990s (Evans et al. 2000). Walker (1999) goes beyond the celebration or condemnation of the increasing state level interconnectedness, and explores regulatory practices in the four corner area of Thailand, Laos, China, and Myanmar. He highlights what he calls 'one of the most important paradoxes of contemporary borders: as trade and passage becomes more liberalized, the opportunities and incentives for regulation flourish' (Walker 1999: 16). By focusing on the experiences of borderland residents, he demonstrates how they not only struggle against central authorities, but often actively collaborate in regulatory activities if benefits and opportunities arise.

This gradual strengthening of statehood and regulation at the border—the 'closure' of the frontier—at many of Asia's borderlands, was, by contrast, concealed by powerful state rhetoric and practices of 'opening borders.' Much in the tailwind of the borderless world construction elsewhere but also, emerging from the particular geopolitical conditions in the region, the states across Asia—from India's Look East policy to China's relations with ASEAN—started to formally and rhetorically 'open' borders. The latter referred to establishing new official border gates for trade, tax, and 'facilitation' of regional interconnectedness. Powerful discourses of emerging cross-border connections and gateways for trade exploited 'a value judgement that the opening of borders is "good" and desirable' (Newman 2015: 16), thus attributing the state a benevolent role of spearheading the 'changes' towards what was constructed as a progressive development (such as liberalization of trade). Such constructs helped to conceal the fact that trade, and social and political connections, had always been the business at borders even when these were nominally 'closed' by states for ideological or other reasons. In short, as synopsized by a Chin trader at one such 'newly opened' border gates at Champai, between Chin state (Myanmar) and Mizoram (India): '[b]efore [the opening of the gate] we could do as we liked. Now we have to go through the gate. Before the trade was illegal, now it is legal' (Champai, 28 February 2004). Long before this Mizoram 'new gateway' 'opened,' most Mizos had been to the idyllic and tranquil heart-shaped lake just 22 km from the border in Myanmar's Chin State that is believed to be the place where the souls—of Chin and Mizo alike—pass to their eternal abode.

In short, the contexts of the spatio-political developments related to states' practices at their borderlands, diverged between the Anglo-American and the many South and Southeast Asian contexts. The efforts by the then scanty number of border scholars did not resonate with the interests of (mainstream) border scholarship located in the USA, Canada, and Europe. In the wider context of imagining and constructing states and nations, it did not even take Benedict Anderson and his *Imagined Communities* (2006), with an imposing travel history, to insert Southeast Asia into the paradigm of social sciences, although he was a Southeast Asianist by training and perhaps by preference, and devoted an entire chapter ('Census, Map, Museum') to Southeast Asia in the book's second edition. In the preface to the volume, Anderson admits that the Thai historian Thongchai's 'brilliant' doctoral thesis was his inspiration for adding the chapter. Regardless, the work of border scholars of the late 1990s and early 2000s at Asia's borders laid firm cornerstones for the current boom to come. From Thailand, Thongchai's treatise of the first encounters between Western and Siamese understandings of space, borders, and mapping, and how the Siamese court learned to exploit Western mapping that together with the military served to carve out a distinct geo-body for its own, became the indispensable text in Southeast Asian scholarship. It inspired, initiated, and launched numerous studies on 'local,' 'autonomous,' 'seditious,' 'borderless,' and 'unravelling' histories challenging the predominantly statist historiographies in the region (see, respectively, Sunait and Baker 2002; Reynolds 2006; Nhung Tuyet Tran and Reid 2006; Grabowsky 2011). From the complex borders of northeast Myanmar and western Cambodia, Grundy-Warr (1998) argued that the impression of stability, reflected in the brightly coloured blocks of sovereign territorial states, was false and presented powerful examples of hidden de facto political geographies. From the Akha villages in Southern China and Northern Thailand during 1996 and 1997, Sturgeon (2005) documented the transfiguring of small pre-modern principalities and chiefdoms into the major nations states and the tensions arising from the borders as both dividing and linking territories. Drawing attention to the importance of non-state spaces in the making of nation states, van Schendel (2002a: 126) describes the 197 enclaves located in the India–Bangladeshi borderlands (out of the 250 world's enclaves in total) as 'miniature societies attempting to survive in the interstices of the modern world state system.' Viewing these as privileged locations from which to study nations, he argues that enclaves cannot be considered as 'a mere footnote to state formation' (van Schendel 2002a: 139) because of their important position in the national imaginations (as in India and Bangladesh) and the challenges to the assumed territorial contiguity and generally straightforward (statist) historiographies. A *Political Geography* special issue by Sidaway et al. (2005) argued that Southeast Asian sovereignties and territorialities were not reducible to experiences in Europe (see also Dean 2005). In the first half of the 2000s, Horstmann and Wadley (2006) called upon anthropologists to take a comparative approach by focusing on agency and narrative in the borderlands of Southeast Asia.

More in dialogue with border studies elsewhere in the world has been Willem van Schendel, who together with Baud (Baud and van Schendel 1997) argued for studying borderlands as constituting a region, one unit of analysis, on both sides of a state border. His fieldwork at the India–Bangladeshi borderlands (van Schendel 2001, 2002a, 2002b) has contributed to the general understanding on enclaves, providing a non-statist perspective, and it has also led to his equally relevant criticism on how scales have been imagined, naturalized, and structured as regions. In his article in *Environment and Planning D* (van Schendel 2002b), he effectively demonstrates how the usual premises behind area construction such as geopolitics (of the Cold War), centrality of states, and academic support have led to the Asian regions we have—and not others such as the one that he invokes and labels as Zomia. This work initiated wide academic collaboration on interregional linkages, with the themes of borderlands and flows of goods, people, and ideas as the driving force, building up for the current boom. A definite push for focusing on the border regions, as criticized by van Schendel (2002b), was given by the establishment of the Asian Borderlands Research Network (ABRN) that held its first conference in Guwahati in 2008.[2]

However, it was James Scott's *The Art of Not Being Governed: An Anarchist History of Upland Southeast Asia* (2009) that chimed beyond regional studies and borders, and resulted in it being 'impossible to discuss the uplands of Southeast Asia in the same way again,' making 'some who had never discussed them before … discussing them for the first time' (Sadan 2017). In his bold 'anarchist' history, Scott borrows van Schendel's Zomia and argues that vast areas of the contiguous and spatially interconnected upland of South, Central, Southeast, and East Asia remained outside the control of the state until the early 20th century when modern technologies allowed the state to make inroads into its borderlands. While it is generally agreed to be a thought-provoking and necessary synthesis and intervention, its sweeping 'bird's-eye view' (Michaud 2010: 209) of a huge area makes it susceptible of various degrees of criticism (see Jonsson 2010; Lieberman 2010; Michaud 2010; Brass 2012; Sadan 2017). Broadly speaking, an overall sweeping gaze, weak documentation, a degree of selectiveness, idealization, and anti-state bias have been pointed out by the critics. The importance of Scott's argument for the study of borders lies in the fact that it demonstrates how studies of highland social groups within the restrictive frame of one given nation state 'curb, and sometimes erase, the dimensions that otherwise concern an entire trans-border society' (Michaud 2010: 209). Importantly, too, both praise and criticism have helped to deploy a huge variety of borders in Asia from their putatively peripheral locations to the centre of the study by a snowballing number of scholars since the end of 2000s.[3]

Asian borderlands have also intruded into flagship academic journals. In 2013, *Political Geography* ran a special issue on *Geographies at the Margins: Borders in South Asia* with the stated aim, as Cons and Sanyal (2013: 6) put it, to use the 'rich palate' of South Asia's borders and margins as material to theorize on borders' 'troubling linkages' to nation and state, thus rethink postcolonial history, geography, and politics. The 2014 special issue on Asian borderlands of the *Journal of Borderlands Studies* focuses on people's state-evading practices at borderlands through the themes of permeability, strategic use of borders, and local meanings of borders, aimed at encouraging comparative research on borderlands in order to develop 'truly global' borderlands studies (van Schendel and de Maaker 2014: 8). As van Schendel and de Maaker (2014: 4) say, Asian border(land)s promise exciting conceptual and methodological innovations, while, so far, this research has remained 'somewhat self-referential and rather isolated from borderland studies elsewhere in the world.' Thus the next step should be that of seeing the inclusion of insights from Asian borderlands as equally contributing and enriching the understandings of borders and the spatialities of power in redefining territory and contemporary statehood, whether in special issues, or as a part and parcel of research published *in every issue of flagship and other journals*, or in new, devotedly trans-regional journals (such as, for example, the *Trans-Regional and -National Studies of Southeast Asia*, or *TRaNS*, launched in 2013). This means penetrating what is constructed as universal concepts (Chakrabarty 2000), challenging the 'asymmetrical "ignorance" within international scholarship' (Robinson 2003: 275), and extending the geographical and analytical scope of theorizing (e.g. see McFarlane 2006). In short, this means engaging in studies of borders in reciprocal manner, so that North American and European borders are not the template against which all other borders are judged (see Edenson and Jayne 2012: 1 for an analogical statement on cities).

A *longue durée* take

States and borders in most parts of Asia, rather than emerging from a slow and gradual process of change, adaptation, and development, have been created through military conquest or indirect acquisition as a part of colonialism by outside powers. There are many important progressions and schemes buried from view at such borders, borderlands, and states that simply are not present or relevant in Anglo-American contexts, from where border studies overwhelmingly draws its empirical material. First, the establishment of most Asian borders can be traced down to very concrete reasons and even dates.[4] Colonial boundaries emerged when distant European powers agreed upon territories to avoid future disputes between different colonial authorities over space and societies where the 'concept of a frontier was uncommon, if not unknown' (Tarling 1998: 47). The colonial boundaries were inherited by the nation states that emerged, with their governments attempting to entrench a whole set of new meanings to these lines by devising some coercive or not so coercive ways to spatially socialize the communities within (see Paasi 1996 for the concept of spatial socialization). The young governments of the developing geo-bodies inherited the arbitrary and ill-defined lines created by alien interests and a conceptual approach derived from the social sciences and political practice strongly influenced by the experiences of Western modernity and statehood, universalized in the international system of states. This relates to the second reason why insights from Asian borders are important more widely: a far greater diversity of borders and related spatialities than studied so far need to be scrutinized for conceptualizing developments or arrangements that are constructed as global or universal, including the state and its corollaries.

Many Asian contemporary experiences with borders, particularly those related to its persisting non-state spaces and actors, have been viewed, both empirically and theoretically, as exceptions, challenges, misfits, dysfunctions, or incompletes demanding special attention, or (isolation in) special issues. What has given rise to this perspective is their *aberration from conceptualizations derived from a slow and gradual process of change, adaptation, and development* that have led to what Risse (2013: 1) calls 'an "ideal type" of modern statehood—with full internal and external sovereignty, a legitimate monopoly on the use of force, and checks and balances that constrain political rule and authority.'

The framing of various spatio-political developments in the non-Western world thus becomes that of limited statehood, ineffective state apparatuses, failed states, weak states, non-state actors, fiefdoms, state-like actors, warlords, states within states, and state evasions. All these are further qualified as 'dysfunctional' and normalized as a 'deplorable deficit of most Third World and transition countries that has to be overcome' (Risse 2013: 2). While the diversity of status quos in many states of the Global South point to aberrations from the idealized type of statehood, such enunciations are also hegemonic and constitutive of a limited approach to theory and the geographies of theory. Or, they take the generally dominating construction of borderlands as places that are unruly, subversive, uncontrollable, or disruptive of the order, particularly where the state has not made tangible inroads as is the case at many Asian borders. Qualifications such as shadow, illegal, or criminal are often associated with such borderlands, although none of these elements is absent from cities or from any society at large. Providing a nuanced study on illicitness, Abraham and van Schendel (2005) conceptually distinguish between what states consider legitimate ('legal') and what people involved in cross-border networks may consider legitimate ('licit'). They (Abraham and van Schendel 2005: 7) challenge the statist perspectives arguing that borders and the associated regulations were imposed on human mobilities from the position that enjoyed 'a monopoly of regulated predation and redistribution of proceeds (i.e., taxation and state expenditure) … based on the delegitimization of other forms of predation that are constructed as robbery, piracy, fraud, warlordism, or racketeering.' There is thus a view that borderlanders and their various cross-border activities, many constituting mobilities and capabilities of centuries-long social, economic, and political relations, *challenge* the international boundaries. Rich material meticulously excavated in countless ethnographic case studies at various Asian borderlands demonstrates *how the border*, imposed on local communities in the lifetime of many contemporary borderlanders, has instead interfered in or *challenged the lived spaces at borderlands* in every possible way by altering peoples' lives permanently by requiring adaptation and generating new dynamics.

All this becomes visible, however, only if taking a longer perspective: '(i)n our interpretations of the political map ... we should also look "backwards" so that we can peel away the historical layers that are masked by the snapshot spatial impression of our current political map' (Grundy-Warr 1998: 74).

This spatial snapshot still continues to be 'the assumption that the nation/state/society is the natural social and political form of the modern world,' designated as 'methodological nationalism' by Wimmer and Schiller (2002: 302), and that the territorial state is the predominantly acknowledged unit for organizing space. Much of our thought still remains territorially trapped, with statehood, the political, and the territorial tightly intertwined intellectually (Agnew 2015). This is while places from regions to cities are increasingly recognized as assemblages of relations, policies, governance, processes, and phenomena across time and space in ways that emphasize the depth of the context (Allen and Cochrane 2007; McFarlane 2011; Robinson 2013). This depth is seen as emerging from 'the crucial role of multiple and overlapping histories in producing habits of practice, ways of going on, and trajectories of policy and economy' (McFarlane 2011: 209). The call to take a *longue durée* critical historical perspective when trying to bridge borders worldwide is thus by no means an original one. Many scholars working on non-Western spaces have done so (Baud and van Schendel 1997; Dick and Rimmer 1998; Grundy-Warr 1998; Horstmann and Wadley 2006; Risse 2013; van Schendel and de Maaker 2014; Ren and Luger 2016). This chapter emphasizes a particular dimension to this call—by arguing that the *longue durée* perspective is necessary in order to recognize Asian borders' potential contribution to theoretical and practical understandings of the driving forces at work at and around borders.

Particularly as many of the 'unfitting' Asian experiences, such as 'limited statehoods,' alternative polities, 'non-traditional' arts of conducting relations, or the so-called *challenging* borderlands persist in the 21st century, the conceptualization of their trajectories of evolvement need to be included in order to see the logics of such outgrowth. A *longue durée* perspective enables the inclusion of such particularities. It is the ultimate time to insert such arrangements into mainstream research, value their achievements, and explore the issues around their discretion and legitimacy, recognizing their theoretical value. In short, the concepts we use are based on their *longue durée* evolvement in the Western thought and practice, while universalized and applied to a variety of contemporary (and historical) contexts across the world, resulting in cases that do not fit. Viewing border thought and practices in Asia also in *longue durée* perspective needs to become a part of the general conceptualization.

From borders to bordering, from pitfalls to possibilities

The sovereign state delimited by boundaries has undoubtedly remained the primary unit of identifying and organizing space in practice, regardless of its porosity, mobilities, or the various alternative spatial or virtual regimes. While border studies as a field relies on borders as its primary object of study, it is also important to reiterate that the study of borders and borderlands is intrinsically connected to the central workings of the state and its characteristics. The processes and institutions embedded in power, physically distant from the borders, have in fact never been absent from the (study of) borders which has always been heavily driven by centre–periphery or inside–outside tensions of political, economic and social character. Soguk (2007: 284) articulates this in a poignant way:

> If there is any constant to borders in time and place, particularly in the order of the national territorial state, it is the logic of the statist and territorial governmentality, which political borders are compelled to reflect and embody. Often overlooked in those studies of borders that take actual fences and walls as sites of a border's enunciation and actualization, this statist logic is nevertheless central to border practices as limit markers. It is this logic that lurks behind fences and walls. More important, it is the same logic that shows us how fences and walls are not the only borders that can be deployed as borders.

For Asia, particularly, as the framing tenets of border thinking did not evolve at the (to-be) borders or borderlands, but at the centres of power often thousands of kilometres away and in very different social settings, hierarchies and cultures, the governmental logic has been detrimental (even if not visible) at the borders. Its shaping power has gradually reached most boundaries even if the institutions stayed behind. The life advancement strategies, the perceptions of possibilities and perils by the borderlanders, cannot be understood without closely scrutinizing state authorities even where other organizations exercise de facto control, as for example, at many of Myanmar's borderlands. In many cases, the response taken by the borderlanders may speak more of the institutions or processes located elsewhere than about the local communities or border areas. For example, being trapped in the camps for the Internationally Displaced Persons (IDPs) near borders has less to do with the border site per se and more with the politics of discrimination, repression, or exclusion conducted from the centres of political power. Thus issues related to institutional governance and state power, even if these were contested or skirted (as is often the case) at the edges of the state, are always present in the practices at borders in some form.

The emphasis on the power and practices of bordering has led to thinking of borders as a process rather than as a pattern (Newman 2006). Consequently, in Anglo-American border scholarship, borders are seen as diversifying, multiplying, and popping up in many places—and, importantly, far away from their physical sites. The shifts in border enforcement resources and practices, and the mobility of enforcement officials in North America, Australia, and at Europe's borders have led to 'discovering' boundaries at new (and previously) unexpected sites. Such spaces can be away from the respective state itself (such as offshore detention and processing), but also inside states' sovereign territory (such as interior checkpoints or spaces where immigration and security officials operate). Borders have become to be viewed as biological through biometric passports (Amoore 2006) and other bio-political practices exploited when inspecting, screening and classifying mobile subjects (Mountz 2011: 64; Paasi 2013). There is also a recognition of a diversity of scales from global to local: borders can be non-geographical and -spatial, such as the vertical social and cultural categories within which society is ordered, where both welfare or economic belonging, for example, are as much issues of demarcation and power relations as are the physical borders (Newman 2015: 15). In this 'borders are everywhere' (Balibar 2002) vision, 'the traditional almost excusive concern with borders between States in the international system becomes but just one scale category of borders' (Newman 2015: 15). Brambilla (2015) sees this as a part of the (wider) processual (conceptual) turn in border studies, related to the dis- and re-locating of borders and the multiplication of their forms, functions, and practices. Such new understandings have also benefitted from inputs from multiple disciplines that have contributed not only with new insight, but also with entirely new forms of borders to study.

On the other hand, this has led several political geographers to ask where the border in border studies is (Johnson et al. 2011).

While in the Anglo-American scholarship, a growing body of literature is now exploring how borders have been reconstituted away from the physical border, what these new border sites are and how and why border enforcement takes place in these new sites, in Asia, most border-related interest clearly remains attached to the edges of the states. An exception in this sense is Piliavsky (2013: 41) who invites borderlands scholars to turn their attention to borders as key structuring mechanisms of the states, and thus away from borderlands per se to recognize the processes around national borders also 'deep inside the territories of states.' Her ethnography in India's Rajasthan State demonstrates how both territorial police jurisdictions and the divisions of rank among the police, order communities through processes usually attributed to national borders.

One of the main concerns of Asian border scholarship, however, involves the dynamics, livelihoods, and communities at its extensive physical borderlands; the passages, flows, and mobilities that transverse these; their regulations and reproductions. The attention of Asian border scholars has been deeply captivated by the borderland communities involved in, adapting to, and enduring the state- and nation-making processes in Asia (e.g. Wijeyewardene 1990; Rajah 2002, 2008; Duncan 2004; Sturgeon 2005; McCaskill et al. 2008; Fiskesjö 2010; Pinkaew 2013; Sadan 2013; Turner et al. 2015). Scholars have been intrigued by the communities' relations with the new states, but also with kith and kin across the borders 'who have been longstanding partners in realms as diverse as trade, agriculture, religious practice and marriage' (van Schendel and de Maaker 2014: 3). The lion's share of analyses have ethnicity, ethnic–state (i.e. minority–majority) relations and tensions, and marginalized livelihoods at the centre of the study, with Michaud (2010: 208–209) criticizing the studies that have taken a country-based approach justified by the logic that states generate minority policies. A relevant theme in this nexus is mobilities, both historical and contemporary, at uplands, coasts, and otherwise traversing long distances, recognized as having always easily criss-crossed the edges of the polities (e.g. Davis 2003; Tagliacozzo 2005; Chang 2009; Harris 2013). Borders as the zones of refugees (e.g. Lang 2002; Grundy-Warr 2002; Decha 2006; Horstmann 2014), or of globalized production and migrant labourers (e.g. Lindquist 2010; Kusakabe and Pearson 2010; Arnold and Pickles 2011), have led to presentations of borderlands as multiple, contested, blurred, hierarchical, multilayered, or tense sites. The multiple growth triangles and quadrangles in the region have also received scholarly attention, while the national level regionalization efforts in the disguise of economic complementarity and the 'borderless world' in the Indonesia–Malaysia–Singapore (IMS) borderlands have attracted criticism from scholars who work at borders (Sparke et al. 2004; Bunnell et al. 2006). What all studies related to Asia's borderlands also have in common is that the ethnographic nature of investigations has been generating an exponentially growing progression of case studies.

Case studies are important for investigating borders as by default single border cases provide in-depth access for wider audiences to many kinds of dynamics and interactions, while creating deep and situated contextual knowledge. Several border scholars have argued for the importance of ethnography, for example Megoran et al. (2005: 714) have called for the study of discursive representation of borders in national politics in tandem with 'the quotidian experiences of people negotiating and living alongside them' when studying Uzbekistan's tightening border regime since 1999. Ethnographies producing the crucial ken and intricately excavating material from hidden lived spaces have been a part and parcel of discovering the borders that have 'intruded' into various horizontal but also vertical spaces, unexpected locations, and our everyday lives. That border case studies spawn is inevitable with the proliferation of the border itself across space, areas of study, and methods. However, in mainstream border studies, this has led to some (little concealed) questioning as to where or how far border studies should go by complementing and commending case studies, with the prospect of 'diminishing marginal returns' as a result (Sidaway 2011: 974). In mainstream border studies, the shift of gaze from borders (the place, pattern) to bordering (the process) as one of the most important developments is related to the recognition that this broad interdisciplinary field is unable to theoretically capture the multiplicity and complexities of the borders—and this is surely true for Asia. It is for this reason that James Sidaway (2011: 974–975) argues for toppling border studies with the study of bordering: 'perhaps this moment and aspiration might be expressed polemically as: down with border studies per se – long live scrutiny of social bordering as a mirror to the ways of the world!' There has been a realization among many scholars that studying borders as a process, as an 'epistemic angle' (Mezzadra and Neilson 2013) informs us more usefully of the complexities and nuances of the social world. It is because the binary distinction between inclusion and exclusion, inside and outside, here and there, attributed to borders, is increasingly becoming less clear as bordering processes criss-crossing spaces are investigated. A trend seems to be emerging that distances from the classical paradigm of border studies relying on the comparison of unique case studies, assuming that the latter are inherently different, and instead regards bordering as a wider and non-local process (Mezzadra and Neilson 2012: 65). The latter opens more spaces for studies (or cases) of bordering in Asia for dialogue with border studies more widely.

Conclusion

Borders as the object of scholarly interest has a long history. This intellectual process has changed and adapted to the historical contingencies and geopolitical developments feeding into the thinking. Border thinking has mainly been advanced from North America and Europe where most empirical cases, border scholars, journals, conferences, and institutions have been located.

Most Asian borders have directly or indirectly evolved from a relatively short spatial-temporal experience where these were imposed on social and ecological landscapes over pre-existing cultures and political histories, definitely not following any logic of mapping territorial integrity or social cohesion. Thus, when the Anglo-American-led scholarship discovered the porosity of borders as something novel owing to particular post-Cold War developments in Europe, many of the Asian borders were still yet on track for more demarcation, militarization, and state presence, concealed behind the powerful state-led rhetoric of trade liberalization and interconnectedness. Therefore, the themes of interest in borders between the Anglo-American and Asian scholarly research have been out of synchronization, and the scanty research in Asia before the 2000s, while laying foundations for the regional border studies, was not able to penetrate 'mainstream' scholarship. The state-centric views and methodological nationalism hampering the understanding of many of the political and social dynamics in the non-Euro–American world has nevertheless been building slowly and stirring up vivid scholarly attention on the Asian borderlands in the last decade.

Insight from Asian borders is important for reworking statehood and border constellations into a more inclusive concept—such that would not denigrate any aberrations from an ideal type of statehood as temporary dysfunctions that need to be overcome. It is because many of the current conceptualizations in use—while these have been developed over long periods of time in Anglo-American scholarship and passed as universal theories—continue to be applied to places or issues are taken out from contemporary snapshots elsewhere. Thus, a *longue durée* conceptual perspective needs to be taken vis-à-vis borders in Asia in order to see the contemporary outcomes as logical, rational, or pragmatic consequences—for practical reasons, but also for enriching the wider thought of what borders are.

We can say that the two border scholarships have converged in the sense that there is currently a boom of interest in both. In Anglo-American border scholarship, there has been a shift of interest from the border as an object to the process of bordering, where the analysis of power relationships at the borders or borderland communities has moved to discussing the power of bordering and viewing this as the mechanism in the making of the world order. This has led to the recognition that while the functions of the borders (divisions, regulation, and control) have remained the same, their form and material expression have, aided by technologies, undergone substantial changes (Amilhat Szary and Giraut 2015). The influential 'political contingencies' such as the European refugee crisis, Brexit, and new US policies on migration, consolidate the role of borders in selectively controlling the flows of people and goods.

While the border has increasingly been conceptualized as mobile and potentially everywhere in Anglo-American border studies, in Asian scholarship it is more 'fixed' to borderlands. This is because the scrutiny of the driving forces, interactions, and relations in borderlands exposes the often deadly incompatibility of nations and states—the latter remaining an important aspect both in the politics and studies of Asian borders. Various transregional mobilities and the attendant flows of people, ideas, practices, and goods also have wide currency in Asia. Ethnographic case studies have been vividly demonstrating the continuous making and re-making of (territorial) borders, constituting the cornerstone of Asian border studies. Dialogue with wider scholarship will emerge with complementary theoretical insights into the processes of (b)ordering. Borders can play a strategic role in the fabrication of the world (Mezzadra and Neilson 2013: vii). The concurrent convergence of interests in borders in both scholarships can chip in to protracted interest in borders globally, enhancing the explanatory power for understanding our social worlds.

Acknowledgements

The research leading to this chapter was funded by the Estonian Research Agency grant IUT 3-2 'Culturescapes in transformation: Towards an integrated theory of meaning making.'

Notes

1. This chapter does not want to construct Asian borders as a distinct type or category. Rather, 'Asian borders' is shorthand for boundaries in Asia, of which the immense diversity in dynamics and trajectories of evolvement is simultaneously recognized. The scope and argument inevitably demand generalization.
2. Its planning committee included Stuart Blackburn (SOAS, London), Erik de Maaker (Leiden University), Willem van Schendel (University of Amsterdam), Mandy Sadan (University of Oxford), and Sanjib Baruah (Indian Institute of Technology, Guwahati and Bard College, New York).
3. A good indicator of the ongoing boom is the exponential growth in the numbers of applicants to the Asian Borderlands Research Network's conferences. For the first conference in 2008 in Guwahati, the number of applicants was 88. The call for the third conference in Singapore (in 2012) yielded 210 applicants and proposals for 24 panels, while the fifth conference in Kathmandu (in 2016) had 400 applicants and proposals for 62 panels. Only about 40 percent of the applicants were accepted for the last conference, due to the limitations in organizational capacity and the principles of acceptance (Communication, ABRN Academic Committee and Martina van den Haak, 15 February 2017).
4. It is beyond the scope of this chapter to discuss the polities and spatial thinking that dominated before the formal acceptance of the colonial/Western concept of borders and statehood, while as a part of political culture this is highly relevant. Thongchai's (1994) work discussing the different conceptualization of space and governance, when the British colonial authorities embarked on establishing clear lines between its territories and the Siamese kingdom, or the various conceptualizations of pre-modern state in Southeast Asia, provides interesting insight.

References

Abraham, I. and van Schendel, W. (2005). Introduction: The Making of Illicitness. In: van Schendel, W. and Abraham, I., eds., *Illicit Flows and Criminal Things: States, Borders, and the Other Side of Globalization*. Bloomington: Indiana University Press, pp. 1–38.

Agnew, J. (2015). Revisiting the Territorial Trap. *Nordia Geographical Publications* 44(4), pp. 43–48.

Agnew, J. and Corbridge, S. (1995). *Mastering Space: Hegemony, Territory and International Political Economy*. London and New York: Routledge.

Allen, J. and Cochrane A. (2007). Beyond the Territorial Fix: Regional Assemblages, Politics and Power. *Regional Studies* 41(9), pp. 1161–1175.

Amilhat Szary, A.-M. and Giraut, F. (2015). Borderities: The Politics of Contemporary Mobile Borders. In: Amilhat Szary, A.-M. and Giraut, F., eds., *Borderities and the Politics of Contemporary Mobile Borders*. Basingstoke and New York: Palgrave Macmillan.

Amoore, L. (2006). Biometric Borders: Governing Mobilities in the War on Terror. *Political Geography* 25(3), pp. 336–351.

Anderson, B. (2006). *Imagined Communities*. London and New York: Verso.

Anderson, J. and O'Dowd, L. (1999). Borders, Border Regions and Territoriality: Contradictory Meanings, Changing Significance. *Regional Studies* 33(7), pp. 593–604.

Andersson, R. (2014). Hunter and Prey: Patrolling Clandestine Migration in the Euro-African Borderlands. *Anthropological Quarterly* 87(1), pp. 118–149.

Andersson, R. (2016). Europe's Failed 'Fight' Against Irregular Migration: Ethnographic Notes on a Counterproductive Industry. *Journal of Ethnic and Migration Studies* 42(7), pp. 1055–1075.

Arnold, D. and Pickles, J. (2011). Global Work, Surplus Labor, and the Precarious Economies of the Border. *Antipode* 43(5), pp. 1598–1624.

Balibar, E. (2002). *Politics and the Other Scene*. London: Verso.

Baud, M. and van Schendel, W. (1997). Toward a Comparative History of Borderlands. *Journal of World History* 8(2), pp. 211–242.

Bloul, R.A.D. (1999). Beyond Ethnic Identity: Resisting Exclusionary Identification. *Social Identities* 5(1) pp. 7–30.

Brambilla, C. (2015). Exploring the Critical Potential of the Borderscapes Concept. *Geopolitics* 20, pp. 14–34.

Brass, T. (2012). Review Article: Scott's 'Zomia,' or a Populist Post-modern History of Nowhere. *Journal of Contemporary Asia* 42(1), pp. 123–133.

Brenner, C.T. (2013). The Role of Comparative Analysis in Borderlands Studies. EASTBordNet Relocating Borders Working Paper No. 117, available at www.eastbordnet.org/working_papers/open/.

Brunet-Jailly, E. (2005). Theorizing Borders: An Interdisciplinary Perspective. *Geopolitics* 10(4), pp. 633–649.

Brunet-Jailly, E. (2010). The State of Borders and Borderlands Studies 2009: A Historical View and a View from the Journal of Borderlands Studies. *Eurasia Border Review* 1(1), pp. 1–15.

Bunnell, T., Goh, P.S.D., Lai, C.-K. and Pow, C.P. (2012). Introduction: Global Urban Frontiers? Asian Cities in Theory, Practice and Imagination. *Urban Studies* 49(13), pp 2785–2793.

Bunnell, T., Sidaway, J.D. and Grundy-Warr, C. (2006). Introduction: Re-mapping the 'Growth Triangle': Singapore's Cross-border Hinterland. *Asia Pacific Viewpoint* 47(2), pp. 235–240.

Chakrabarty, D. (2000). *Provincialising Europe: Postcolonial Thought and Historical Difference*. Princeton, NJ: Princeton University Press.

Chang, W.-C. (2009). Venturing into 'Barbarous' Regions: Transborder Trade among Migrant Yunnanese. *The Journal of Asian Studies* 68(2), pp. 543–572.

Cons, J. and Sanyal, R. (2013). Geographies at the Margins: Borders in South Asia—An Introduction. *Political Geography* 35, pp. 5–13.

Davis, S. (2003). Premodern Flows in Postmodern China: Globalization and the Sipsongpanna Tais. *Modern China* 29(2), pp. 176–203.

Dean, K. (2005). Spaces and Territorialities on the Sino-Burmese Boundary: China, Myanmar and the Kachin. *Political Geography* 24(7), pp. 808–830.

Decha, T. (2006). Taking Flight in Condemned Grounds: Forcibly Displaced Karens and the Thai-Burmese In-Between Spaces. *Alternatives* 31(4), pp. 405–429.

Dick, H. and Rimmer, P. (1998). Beyond the Third World City: The New Urban Geography of SE Asia. *Urban Studies* 35(12), pp. 303–321.

Duncan, C.R. (ed.) (2004). *Civilizing the Margins: Southeast Asian Government Policies for the Development of Minorities*. Ithaca and London: Cornell University Press.

Edenson, T. and Jayne, M. (2012). *Urban Theory beyond the West*. London: Routledge.

Elden, S. (2013). Secure the Volume: Vertical Geopolitics and the Depth of Power. *Political Geography* 34, pp. 35–51.
Evans, G., Hutton, C. and Eng, K.K. (2000). Introduction. In: Evans, H. and Eng, K.K., eds., *Where China Meets Southeast Asia: Social & Cultural Change in the Border Regions*. Bangkok: White Lotus and Singapore: Institute of Southeast Asian Studies, pp. 1–6.
Fiskesjö, M. (2010). Mining, History, and the Anti-state Wa: The Politics of Autonomy between Burma and China. *Journal of Global History* 5(2), pp. 241–264.
Forsyth, I., Hayden, L., Merriman, P. and Robinson, J. (2013). Guest Editorial: What Are Surfaces? *Environment and Planning A* 45, pp. 1013–1020.
Grabowsky, V. (ed.) (2011). *Southeast Asian Historiography: Unravelling the Myths*. Bangkok: River Books.
Grundy-Warr, C. (1998). Turning the Political Map Inside Out: A View of Mainland Southeast Asia. In: Savage, V.R., Kong, L. and Neville, W., eds., *The Naga Awakens: Growth and Change in Southeast Asia*. Singapore: Times Academic Press, pp. 29–86.
Grundy-Warr, C. (2002). Geographies of Displacement: The Karenni and the Shan across the Myanmar-Thailand Border. *Singapore Journal of Tropical Geography* 23(1), pp. 93–122.
Gupta, A. and Ferguson, J. (1992). Beyond 'Culture': Space, Identity, and the Politics of Difference. *Cultural Anthropology* 7(1), pp. 6–23.
Harris, T. (2013). Trading Places: New Economic Geographies Across Himalayan Borderlands. *Political Geography* 35, pp. 60–68.
Horstmann, A. (2014). Stretching the Border: Confinement, Mobility and the Refugee Public among Karen Refugees in Thailand and Burma. *Journal of Borderland Studies* 29(1), pp. 47–61.
Horstmann, A. and Wadley, R.L. (2006). *Centering the Margin: Agency and Narrative in Southeast Asian Borderlands*. New York and Oxford: Berghahn Books.
Johnson, C. and Jones, R. (2011). Rethinking 'the Border' in Border Studies. In: Johnson, C., Jones, R., Paasi, A., Amoore, L., Mountz, A., Salter, M. and Rumford, C. eds., *Interventions on Rethinking 'the Border' in Border Studies. Political Geography* 30, pp. 61–69.
Johnson, C., Jones, R., Paasi, A., Amoore, L., Mountz, A., Salter, M. and Rumford, C. (2011). Interventions on Rethinking 'the Border' in Border Studies. *Political Geography* 30, pp. 61–69.
Jonsson, H. (2010). Above and Beyond: Zomia and the Ethnographic Challenge of/for Regional History. *History and Anthropology* 21(2), pp. 191–212.
Kolossov, V. and Scott, J. (2013). Selected Conceptual Issues in Border Studies. *Belgeo* 1, pp. 2–15.
Kusakabe, K. and Pearson, R. (2010). Transborder Migration, Social Reproduction and Economic Development: A Case Study of Burmese Women Workers in Thailand. *International Migration* 48(6), pp. 13–43.
Lang, H. (2002). *Fear and Sanctuary: Burmese Refugees in Thailand*. Ithaca and New York: Cornell University Press.
Lieberman, V. (2010). Review Article: A Zone of Refuge in Southeast Asia? Reconceptualizing Interior Spaces. *Journal of Global History* 5(2), pp. 333–346.
Lindquist, J. (2010). *Singapore's Borderlands: Tourism, Migration and the Anxieties of Mobility*. Singapore: NUS Press.
McCaskill, D., Leepreecha, P. and He, S. (eds.) (2008). *Living in a Globalized World: Ethnic Minorities in the Greater Mekong Region*. Bangkok: Mekong Press.
McFarlane, C. (2006). Crossing Borders: Development, Learning and the North–South Divide. *Third World Quarterly* 27(8), pp. 1413–1437.
McFarlane, C. (2011). Assemblage and Critical Urbanism. *City* 15(2), pp. 204–224.
Megoran, N., Raballand, G. and Bouyjou, J. (2005). Performance, Representation and the Economics of Border Control in Uzbekistan. *Geopolitics* 10, pp. 712–740.
Mezzadra, S. and Neilson, B. (2012), Between Inclusion and Exclusion: On the Topology of Global Space and Borders. *Theory, Culture & Society* 29(4/5), pp. 58–75.
Mezzadra, S. and Neilson, B. (2013). *Border as Method, or, the Multiplication of Labor*. Durham, NC: Duke University Press.
Michaud, J. (2010). Editorial – Zomia and Beyond. *Journal of Global History* 5, pp. 187–214.
Mountz, A. (2011). Border Politics: Spatial Provision and Geographical Precision. In: Johnson, C., Jones, R., Paasi, A., Amoore, L., Mountz, A., Salter, M. and Rumford, C., eds., *Interventions on Rethinking 'the Border' in Border Studies, Political Geography* 30, pp. 61–69.
Newman, D. (2006). Borders and Bordering: Towards an Interdisciplinary Dialogue. *European Journal of Social Theory* 9(2), pp. 171–186.

Newman, D. (2011). Contemporary Research Agendas in Border Studies: An Overview. In: Wastl-Walter, D. ed., *The Ashgate Research Companion to Border Studies*. Burlington, VT: Ashgate, pp. 33–47.

Newman, D. (2015). Revisiting Good Fences and Neighbors in a Postmodern World After Twenty Years: Theoretical Reflections on the State of Contemporary Order Studies. *Nordia Geographical Publications* 44(4), pp. 13–19.

Newman, D. and Paasi, A. (1998). Fences and Neighbors in the Postmodern World: Boundary Narratives in Political Geography. *Progress in Human Geography* 22(2), pp. 186–207.

Nhung Tuyet Tran and Reid, A. (eds.) (2006). *Viêt Nam Borderless Histories*. Madison: University of Wisconsin Press.

Paasi, A. (1995). Constructing Territories, Boundaries and Regional Identities. In: Forsberg, T., ed., *Contested Territory: Border Disputes at the Edge of the Former Soviet Empire*, Aldershot: Edward Elgar Publishing Ltd, pp. 42–61.

Paasi, A. (1996). *Territories, Boundaries and Consciousness: The Changing Geographies of the Finnish-Russian Border*. Chichester: John Wiley.

Paasi, A. (2011). A Border Theory: An Unattainable Dream or a Realistic Aim for Border Scholars? In: Wastl-Walter, D., ed., *The Ashgate Research Companion to Border Studies*, Burlington, VT: Ashgate.

Paasi, A. (2013). Borders and Border-Crossings. In: Johnson, N.C., Schein, R.S. and Winders, J., eds., *The Wiley Blackwell Companion to Cultural Geography*. London: Wiley-Blackwell, pp. 478–493.

Piliavsky, A. (2013). Borders Without Borderlands. On the Social Reproduction of State Demarcation in Rajasthan. In: Gellner, D., ed., *Borderland Lives in Northern South Asia*, London: Duke University Press, pp. 24–46.

Pinkaew, L. (2013). Contested Citizenship: Cards, Colors and the Culture of Identification. In: Marston, J.A., ed., *Ethnicity, Borders, and the Grassroots Interface with the State: Studies on Southeast Asia in Honor of Charles F. Keyes*. Chiang Mai: Silkworm Books, pp. 143–164.

Pisani, M.J., Reyes, J.C. and García, B.G. Jr. (2009). Looking Back Twenty-three Years: An Analysis of Contributors and Contributions to the Journal of Borderlands Studies, 1986 (volume 1, number 1) to 2008 (volume 23, number 2). *Journal of Borderlands Studies* 24(1), pp. 1–17.

Popescu, G. (2015). Topological Imagination, Digital Determinism and the Mobile Border Paradigm. *Nordia Geographical Publications* 44(4), pp. 49–55.

Rajah, A. (2002). A 'Nation of Intent' in Burma: Karen Ethno-nationalism, Nationalism and Narrations of Nation. *The Pacific Review* 15(4), pp. 517–537.

Rajah, A. (2008). Remaining Karen: A study of Cultural Reproduction and Maintenance of Identity. ANU e-press, available at: http://epress.anu.edu.au/karen_citation.html (1986 PhD reprinted in tribute).

Ren, J. and Luger, J. (2016). Comparative Urbanism and the 'Asian City': Implications for Research and Theory. *International Journal of Urban and Regional Research* 39, pp. 145–156.

Reynolds, C.J. (2006). *Seditious Histories: Contesting Thai and Southeast Asian Pasts*. Seattle and London: University of Washington Press; Singapore: Singapore University Press.

Risse, T. (2013). Governance in Areas of Limited Statehood. In: Risse, T., ed., *Governance Without a State? Policies and Politics in Areas of Limited Statehood*. New York: Columbia University Press, pp. 1–35.

Robinson, J. (2003). Postcolonialising Geography: Tactics and Pitfalls. *Singapore Journal of Tropical Geography* 24(3), pp. 273–289.

Robinson, J. (2013). 'Arriving at' Urban Policies/the Urban: Traces of Elsewhere in Making City Futures. In: Södeström, O., Randeria, S., Ruedin, D., D'Amato, G. and Panese, F., eds, *Critical Mobilities*. Lausanne: EPFL Press.

Roy, A. (2009) The 21st-century Metropolis: New Geographies of Theory. *Regional Studies* 43, pp. 819–830.

Rumford, C. (2006). Theorizing Borders. *European Journal of Social Theory* 9(2), pp. 155–169.

Sadan, M. (2013). *Being and Becoming Kachin: Histories Beyond the State in the Borderworlds of Burma*. Oxford and London: Oxford University Press and the British Academy.

Sadan, M. (2017). Review of *The Art of Not Being Governed: An Anarchist History of Upland Southeast Asia*, (review no. 903), available at: www.history.ac.uk/reviews/review/903.

Scott, J. C. (2009). *The Art of Not Being Governed: An Anarchist History of Upland Southeast Asia*. New Haven and London: Yale University Press.

Sidaway, J.D. (2002). Signifying Boundaries: Detours Around the Portuguese-Spanish (Algarve/Alentejo-Andalucía) Borderlands. *Geopolitics* 7(1), pp. 139–164.

Sidaway, J.D. (2011). The Return and Eclipse of Border Studies? Charting Agendas. Book Review Essay. *Geopolitics* 16, pp. 969–976.

Sidaway, J.D., Grundy-Warr, C. and Park, B.-G. (2005). Editorial. Asian Sovereigntyscapes. *Political Geography* 24(7), pp. 779–783.

Soguk, N. (2007). Border's Capture: Insurrectional Politics, Border-crossing Humans, and the New Political. In: Rajaram, P.K. and Grundy-Warr, C., eds., *Borderscapes: Hidden Geographies and Politics at Territory's Edges*. Minneapolis and London: University of Minnesota Press, pp. 283–308.

Sparke, M., Sidaway, J.D., Bunnell, T. and Grundy-Warr, C. (2004). Triangulating the Borderless World: Geographies of Power in the Indonesia–Malaysia–Singapore Growth Triangle. *Transactions of the Institute of British Geographers* 29, pp. 485–498.

Sturgeon, J.C. (2005). *Border Landscapes: The Politics of Akha Land Use in China and Thailand*, Seattle: University of Washington Press and Chiang Mai: Silkworm Books.

Sunait, C. and Baker, C. (eds) (2002). *Recalling Local Pasts: Autonomous History in Southeast Asia*, Chiang Mai: Silkworm Books.

Tagliacozzo, E. (2005). *Secret Trades, Porous Borders: Smuggling and States Along a Southeast Asian Frontier, 1865–1915*. New Haven: Yale University Press.

Tarling, N. (1998). *Nations and States in Southeast Asia*. Cambridge: Cambridge University Press.

Taylor, P.J. (1995). Beyond Containers: Internationality, Interstatedness, Interterritoriality. *Progress in Human Geography*, 19 (1), pp. 1–15.

Thongchai, W. (1994). *Siam Mapped: A History of the Geo-Body of a Nation*. Chiang Mai: Silkworm Books.

Turner, S., Bonnin, C. and Michaud, J. (2015). *Frontier Livelihoods. Hmong in the Sino-Vietnamese Borderlands*, Seattle: University of Washington Press.

van Schendel, W. (2001). Working Through Partition: Making a Living in the Bengal Borderlands. *International Review of Social History* 46, pp. 393–421.

van Schendel, W. (2002a). Stateless in South Asia: The Making of the India-Bangladesh Enclaves. *The Journal of Asian Studies* 61(1), pp. 115–147.

van Schendel, W. (2002b). Geographies of Knowing, Geographies of Ignorance: Jumping Scale in Southeast Asia. *Environment and Planning D: Society and Space* 20, pp. 647–668.

van Schendel, W. and de Maaker, E. (2014). Asian Borderlands: Introducing their Permeability, Strategic Uses and Meanings. Introduction to the Special issue. *Journal of Borderlands Studies* 29(1), pp. 3–9.

Walker, A. (1999). *The Legend of the Golden Boat: Regulation, Trade and Traders in the Borderlands of Laos, Thailand, China and Burma*. Honolulu: University of Hawai'i Press.

Wijeyewardene, G. (ed.) (1990). *Ethnic Groups Across National Boundaries in Mainland Southeast Asia*. Singapore: Institute of Southeast Asian Studies.

Wilson, T.M. and Hastings, D. (1998). *Border Identities: Nation and State at International Frontiers*. Cambridge and New York: Cambridge University Press.

Wimmer, A. and Schiller, N.G. (2002). Methodological Nationalism and Beyond: Nation-State Building, Migration and the Social Sciences. *Global Networks* 2(4), pp 301–334.

5
Zomia and beyond[1]

Jean Michaud

Introduction

What is 'Zomia'? A brief explanation helps locate the object of this chapter. This exotic sounding name was coined in 2002 by Dutch social scientist Willem van Schendel. Van Schendel presented a macroscopic and thought-provoking analysis, in which he probed and challenged the fixed boundaries of classical 'Area Studies'. He proposed to consider the highlands of Asia, from the Tibetan Plateau, and all the way to the lower end of the Peninsular Southeast Asian highlands, as a political and historical entity significantly distinct from the usual area divisions of Asia: Central (Inner), South, East, and Southeast. 'Zomia' constituted, he argued, a neglected – an invisible – transnational area, which overlapped segments of all four sub-regions without truly belonging to any of them. It is an area marked by a sparse population, historical isolation, political domination by powerful surrounding states, marginality of all kinds, and huge linguistic and religious diversity. Then, in 2007, following discussions with scholars of the Western Himalayas reacting to his 2002 proposition, Van Schendel tentatively opted to further extend Zomia westward and northward, including southern Qinghai and Xinjiang within China, as well as a fair portion of Central Asia, encompassing highlands of Pakistan, Afghanistan, Tajikistan, and Kyrgyzstan.[2] In this way, van Schendel logically extended his gaze into the high grounds west of the Himalayas, much as he had into the east. A visual representation of this process can be seen in Map 5.1.

Testing Zomia from the perspective of the Southeast Asian Massif

This chapter concerns an unusual cross-border locale at the heart of the Asian continent, covering an area comparable to Europe. Following its inception in 2002, Willem van Schendel's idea of Zomia, its magnitude, and its countercurrent quality to an academic world profoundly determined by political borders and institutionally enshrined Area Studies, proved challenging enough to keep social scientists at bay for a while, triggering relatively little reaction. However, it did get noticed by scholars of the area, to whom it spoke directly, showing consistency with what they had been observing on the ground. The most prominent case of this interest is the latest book by political scientist James C. Scott, which focuses on the eastern part of van Schendel's Zomia (Scott 2009). Further west, scholars of the Himalayas saw relevance in this

Jean Michaud

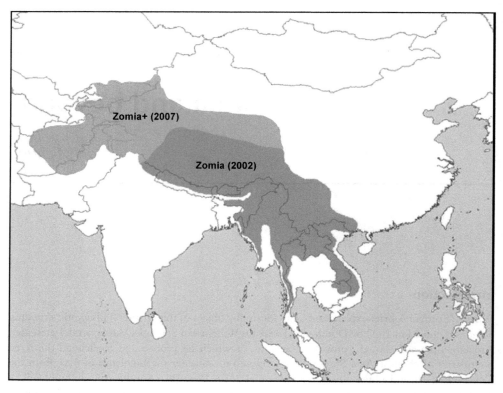

Map 5.1 Van Schendel's original Zomia (2002) and its extension North and West (2007), which I call here Zomia+[3]
Map by Michaud 2010: 188

large-scale corroboration. Some agreed that the populations of this high region shared a heritage that could not simply be explained by the political and cultural influence of Tibet, a rare example of a highland Asian imperial power. Others working east of the Tibetan plateau have also shown a liminal interest for a transnational approach to this area and its populations (Lim 1984; Wijeyewardene 1990; Evans et al. 2000). John McKinnon and I realized the importance of the transnational nature of minority populations in what we called the Southeast Asian Massif, and proposed to disembed social science research on peripheral societies there from intellectually binding national settings (McKinnon and Michaud 2000).

Although not empty of human settlements, the relief and climate of mountains set them apart from the surrounding more densely inhabited lands, while still allowing for trade routes to develop. What makes Zomia a space of interest to global historians and social scientists alike lies not just in its transnationality, and its trans-regionality in terms of the accepted Asian sub-areas, but also in terms of a space linking neighbouring polities together in a unique way. It can be argued that its interest as a large-scale space lies in part in the global trade that contributed to link the Asian highlands together, as well as with the outside world. For centuries, trade in this region has been conducted on all scales: from one valley to the next, from one fiefdom to others around it, and at the macro scale through long-haul trade in shapes such as those popularized by intercontinental notions such as the Silk Road. Though never really central to the trade linking the Far East to South Asia, the Middle East, and Europe, these highlands have been an integral part of trading patterns, due to caravan trails crossing them, and the provision of prized and rare items (Hill 1998; Clarence-Smith 2004). Such items have included hardwoods, animals and animal parts, cotton and hemp, medicinal plants, precious metals such as silver, and gemstones. Two examples, maize and opium, will suffice to make this point (Michaud 2006: 149–150, 183–186).

Maize (*Zea mays* L.) was unknown to Asia before its introduction from America by the Iberians in the 16th century. It quickly became a popular crop in China's southwestern mountainous periphery. It required neither rich soils nor irrigation, it could be planted on slopes, and it was perfectly suited to the temperate climate of the highlands. As a crop, maize proved extremely attractive to highlanders. Easy to grow, to harvest, and to stock, it does not deplete the thin highland soil of too much of its nutrients. Its root system helps to consolidate slopes, and it can profitably be grown on the same plot concurrently with beans, peas, or opium poppies. Grounded to fine flour with portable milling stones, which practically every household historically owned a pair of, maize often became an essential element of pigs' diets, and was occasionally consumed by humans. Last but not least, maize became a favourite raw material to produce homemade distilled alcohol, consumed in large quantities in the highlands and subject to a thriving trade.

This particular grain has thus been instrumental in helping local highland populations to root themselves successfully in a demanding environment. Concurrently, maize has also helped the Han Chinese masses in the lowlands to deal with demographic pressure by facilitating their movement into the less fertile hills and plateaus, and settling where previously only mountain groups had been dwelling. Together with excessive state infringement and relentless taxation, this invasion constituted an important cause of conflict between the Han administration and highland minorities, the latter trying to preserve their integrity vis-à-vis the imperial central government, as well as regional rulers and warlords.

Opium (*Papaver somniferum*) provides an even more telling example of global integration. Due to the marketing of large quantities in China by Europeans and Indians, a high level of consumption emerged in the 19th century (McCoy et al. 1989; Chouvy 2009). This trend was significantly stimulated and skillfully maintained by the British East India Company. Early on, China's leaders became worried by the huge outflow of silver that the importation of thousands of tons of opium implied. By the Treaty of Nanking (Nanjing) in 1842, China was forced to allow Westerners to trade almost freely with the huge Chinese market. The only option left to the Chinese to compete with the intruders was to promote and support national production of opium. The populations dwelling in areas suitable for this production, that is, the limestone mountains and plateaus of the southwest, were then encouraged to grow the poppy and produce raw opium to be sold to the government. The state in turn processed the raw substance and sold it on the interior market (Bello 2005).

Many of these same producers in the southwest highlands were also courted by the British and the French, who were able to reach 'Chinese Zomia' through Burma and Indochina. Processed opium was thus also shipped from Saigon or Calcutta to European trading posts on the Chinese coast, and elsewhere around the world where Chinese migrants had settled (Descours-Gatin 1992; Le Failler 2001). Highland minorities in Zomia were thus becoming actors in a fierce international competition. The violent revolts and rebellions that shook southern China during the second half of the 19th century, such as the Panthay and Miao Rebellions, and the subsequent waves of migration into the highlands of the Peninsula, can be linked, at least in part, to the strong urge to control the production and sale of opium.

Then, into the second half of the 20th century, being in control of opium production and trade remained crucial for various belligerent groups, for whom it provided a means of financing their armed struggles. Even American forces during the Second Indochina War (1954–1975) were instrumental in the transportation, storage, distribution, and consumption of opium and its

Jean Michaud

derivatives, heroin and morphine. But when wars in the region subsided, national governments saw more harm than good in this peculiar trade, and started putting an official end to it. They were financially assisted by countries that now had to contain a drug addiction problem brought home by returning troops. All countries sharing the eastern part of Zomia were eventually to sign the 1988 UN Drug Convention. Massive opium production and its train of consequences have now moved to another major war zone sitting this time on the Western edge of greater Zomia, Afghanistan, and the highlands of Central Asia. The global interconnectedness of this region continues.

Naming and defining Zomia

What is commendable about Willem van Schendel's idea is his call to academics to pay more attention to areas and societies dwelling on the periphery of bona fide states and civilizations, which are otherwise neglected as merely peripheral, exotic, or backward. In doing so, van Schendel acknowledged the inspiration from predecessors, embodied in Map 5.2 here, which shows a telling representation of the highlands under the name of the 'Hindu Kush-Himalayan region'. This representation was proposed in the 1980s by a development group based in Nepal, the International Centre for Integrated Mountain Development, whose aim in circulating this map was more informative than academic. It did not yield a great deal of scholarly discussion at the time, but it interests us here as an evident ancestor to greater Zomia (van Schendel 2002: 655).[4]

Van Schendel has been astute. Zomia, like Shangri-la or Xanadu, is a catchy name and makes for a wonderfully enticing sound bite. It may well stick with media and academic publishers, who have a penchant for the scent of mystery it carries. I also suspect that we are closer every day to the creation and popularization, in generalist academic circles as well as in the informed public, of a 'new and exciting' Asian population, the Zomians with 'Zomian studies' to follow. But we should keep in mind that Zomia remains an awkward choice of name in relation to

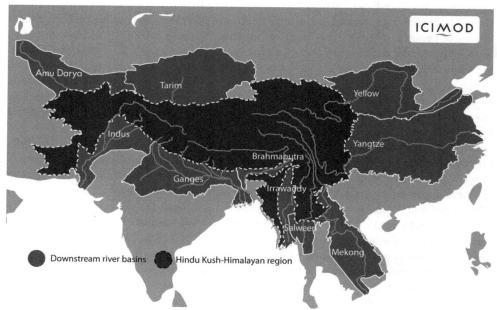

Map 5.2 The 'Hindu Kush-Himalayan' region (International Centre for Integrated Mountain Development (ICIMOD), Kathmandu, Nepal)

Zomia and beyond

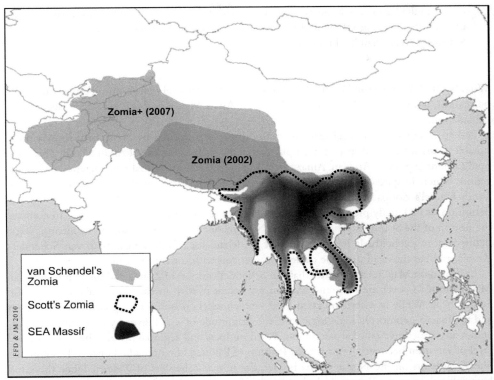

Map 5.3 Over van Schendel's Zomia and Zomia+, are shown the Southeast Asian Massif (with a broad indication in darker shades of where the concentration of population is), and Scott's Zomia

Map by Jean Michaud 2017

an enormous and vastly diverse reality. To use a North American analogy, this is the equivalent of naming the Rockies, the English language name for a giant mountain range spreading from Central America to Alaska, from a vernacular ethnonym employed by, say, the Athabaskan of eastern Yukon. As an alternative, the notion of Haute Asie, High Asia, widely used in French Himalayan studies circles, may have offered a more promising option. But, I suppose there is no purpose in insisting that van Schendel's neologism should be perfect, and Zomia may well be here to stay. The question that really matters is whether the reality behind the name can bear significance for social and historical research on highland societies in Asia.

To date, the most prominent use of Zomia comes in James C. Scott's 2009 book, *The Art of Not Being Governed: An Anarchist History of Upland Southeast Asia*. Scott explicitly refers to van Schendel's work and makes Zomia the locale for his analysis. However, one can immediately see from Map 5.3 that the area Scott calls Zomia differs significantly from van Schendel's proposition.

As a justification for this discrepancy, Scott simply states in his preface, without further detail:

> Zomia is a new name for virtually all the lands at altitudes above roughly three hundred meters all the way from the Central Highlands of Vietnam to northeastern India and traversing five Southeast Asian nations (Vietnam, Cambodia, Laos, Thailand, and Burma) and four provinces of China (Yunnan, Guizhou, Guangxi, and parts of Sichuan). It is an expanse

of 2.5 million square kilometers containing about one hundred million minority peoples of truly bewildering ethnic and linguistic variety. Geographically, it is also known as the Southeast Asian mainland massif.

(Scott 2009: ix)

What Scott chooses to call Zomia does not match van Schendel's proposition, but as this quote points out, it fits what others call the Southeast Asian Massif, and this similarity deserves an explanation.

Perhaps a non-geographical term such as Zomia, as suggested by Scott, may seem a more suitable name for a social space than a physical name such as Southeast Asian Massif. This same predicament applies to Andean, Amazonian, Mediterranean, or Himalayan societies and civilizations which, in spite of this concern, have widely and profitably used such names for decades. Van Schendel's Zomia remained somewhat imprecise in its geographical, cultural, or linguistic definition, as he chiefly proposed broad political criteria and no precise boundaries. In contrast, the notion of the Southeast Asian Massif has been made more operational, and its intrinsic logic defined more explicitly. It has been subject to debate for a little longer than van Schendel's Zomia, and has thus had the time to be characterized with some precision.

As shown on Map 5.3, the locales that van Schendel's notion of Zomia and the Southeast Asian Massif mean to cover are different, with an important overlap in eastern Zomia, which is also Scott's locale. While to a certain extent I see van Schendel's reason for his greater Zomia project and the macro-geomorphologic logic to it, the magnitude of social diversity it encompasses precludes any conclusive cultural assessment. Based on local and regional history, there is a colossal level of variation between the pastoralist Pashtun of Pakistan, the nomadic Gujar of Kashmir, the Sherpa peasants on the Nepal–China border, the nomadic herders of Western Tibet, the Chin horticulturalists on the Burma–India border, the 'feudal' Yi and Bai in central Yunnan, the heavily sinicized Zhuang in the western half of Guangxi, the Hui (Chinese Muslim) merchants present amongst many of these societies, and the kinship-based Austronesian groups divided between southern Laos and Vietnam. This to name but a slim sample of the range of ethnicities that greater Zomia is meant to encompass. Based on cultural factors such as language families, religious systems, forms of social organization, migration patterns, sources of outside influence and so on, as a social anthropologist I question how operational such an idea can be in terms of providing a coherent unit for social research. I also accept, however, that van Schendel uses a macroscopic, historical, and political science viewpoint. He is thus not bound to be as concerned as social anthropologists or human geographers with the details of cultural distinction on the ground.

A few years ago, while researching the first edition of the *Historical Dictionary of the Peoples of the Southeast Asian Massif* (Michaud 2006), I had to devise a workable definition of what I encompassed within the label 'Southeast Asian Massif' (Map 5.4). This name is derived from Lim Joo Jock's seminal *Territorial Power Domains, Southeast Asia, and China: The Geo-strategy of an Overarching Massif* (Lim 1984). At the time, despite having used the term in articles and in my edited *Turbulent Times and Enduring Peoples: Mountain Minorities in the South-East Asian Massif* (Michaud 1997a, 1997b, 2000), neither myself nor other scholars had felt the need or obligation to actually define the region. To do so for the dictionary (Michaud 2006), I decided to involve regional historical processes, political crystallization, linguistic diffusion, ethnic groupings, migrations, and geographical features.

Starting with the palpable physical dimension, it was neither realistic nor helpful to bound the area in terms of precise altitude, latitude and longitude, with definite outside limits and internal subdivisions. This was due to the extremely complex geomorphology of this large space, and to constant population movements.[5] Broadly speaking, however, at their maximum extension,

Zomia and beyond

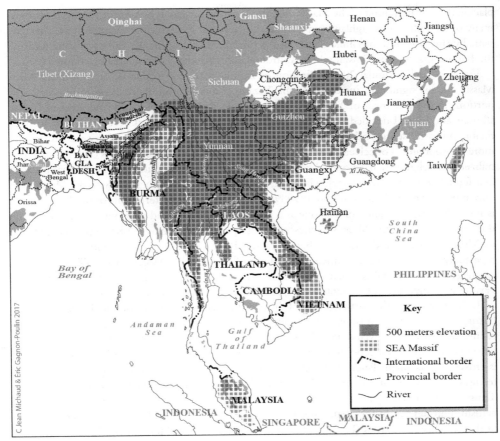

Map 5.4 The Southeast Asian Massif
Map by Jean Michaud 2017

these highland groups are scattered over a domain mostly situated above an elevation of about 300 to 500 metres, within an area approximately the size of Western Europe. Stretching from the temperate Chang Jiang (Yangtze River), which roughly demarcates the northern boundary, it moves south to encompass the high ranges extending east and south from the Himalayas and the Tibetan Plateau, and the monsoon high country drained by the basins of the Brahmaputra, Irrawaddy, Salween, Chao Phraya, Mekong, Song Hong (Red River), and Zhu Jiang (Pearl River). In China, it includes extreme eastern Tibet, southern and western Sichuan, western Hunan, a small portion of western Guangdong, all of Guizhou and Yunnan, north and west Guangxi, and the highlands of Hainan Island. Spilling over the Southeast Asian peninsula, it covers most of the border areas of Burma with adjacent Tibeto-Burman speaking segments of Northeast India and southeastern Bangladesh, the north and west of Thailand, all of Laos above the Mekong valley, borderlands in northern and central Vietnam along the Annam Cordillera, and the northeastern fringes of Cambodia.

Beyond the northern limit of the Massif, I do not include the Chongqing basin, because it has been colonized by the Han for over one millennium, and the massive influx of population into this fertile 'rice bowl' of China has spilled into parts of central and western Sichuan above 500 metres. The same observation applies to highlands further north in Gansu and Shaanxi provinces,

79

placing the northern limit of the Massif roughly along the Yangtze River. At the southern extreme, many of the indigenous highland populations of peninsular Malaysia, the Orang Asli, are Austroasiatic by language, and thus linked to groups in the Massif such as the Wa, the Khmu, the Katu, or the Bahnar. Likewise on Taiwan where Austronesian highlanders can arguably be counted in too.[6]

Van Schendel's original 2002 definition of Zomia was close to that of the Southeast Asian Massif, bar his significant inclusion of the Xizang (Tibet) Autonomous Region plus adjacent portions in the provinces of Xinjiang, Qinghai, and Sichuan, as well as upland areas in Nepal, Bhutan, and India. I decided not to include that area within the Massif because, despite its irrefutable minority status within China, Tibet and the Tibetan cultural periphery are historically more appropriately conceived of as a distinct entity. The Tibetan world has its own logic: a centralized and religiously harmonized core with a long, distinctive political existence that places it in a 'feudal' and imperial category, which the societies historically associated with the Massif have only rarely developed into (Goldstein 1989). In this sense, the western limit of the Massif, then, is as much a historical and political one as it is linguistic, cultural, and religious. Again, this should not be seen as clear-cut. Many societies on Tibet's periphery, such as the Khampa, Naxi, Drung or Mosuo in Yunnan, the Lopa in Nepal, or the Bhutia in Sikkim, have switched allegiances repeatedly over the centuries, moving in and out of Lhasa's orbit. Moreover, the Tibeto-Burman language family and Tibetan Buddhism have spilled over the eastern edge of the plateau. The perimeter is anything but straightforward, pertaining instead to a blending of cultural heritages.

To further qualify the particularities of the Massif, a series of core factors can be incorporated: history of course, but also languages, religion, customary social structures, economies, and political relationships with lowland states. What distinguishes highland societies may exceed what they have in common: a vast ecosystem, a state of marginality, and forms of subordination. The Massif is crossed by six major language families, none of which form a decisive majority. In religious terms, several groups are Animist, others are Buddhist, some are Christian, a good number share Taoist and Confucian values, the Hui are Muslim, while most societies sport a complex syncretism. Throughout history, feuds and frequent hostilities between local groups were evidence of the plurality of cultures (Lombard-Salmon 1972; Jenks 1994; Herman 2007). The region has never been united politically, not as an empire, nor as a space shared among a few feuding kingdoms, not even as a zone with harmonized political systems. Forms of distinct customary political organizations, chiefly lineage based versus 'feudal',[7] have long existed. At the national level today, political regimes in countries sharing the region (democracies, three socialist regimes, one constitutional monarchy, and one military dictatorship) simply magnify this ancient political diversity.

Along with other transnational highlands around the Himalayas and, indeed, around the world, the Southeast Asian Massif – let alone van Schendel's Zomia – is marginal and fragmented in historical, economic, as well as cultural terms. It may thus be seen as lacking the necessary significance in the larger scheme of things to be proposed as a promising area subdivision of Asian studies. However, my point here is not to become a flag bearer for such a new area studies subdivision, but to stress that we have to rethink country-based research, addressing transborder and marginal societies.

Careful inquiries on the ground throughout the Massif show that these peoples actually share a sense of being different from the majorities, a sense of geographical remoteness, and a state of marginality that is connected to political and economic distance from regional seats of power. In cultural terms, these highland societies are like a cultural mosaic with contrasting colours, rather than an integrated picture in harmonized shades – what Terry Rambo has dubbed 'a psychedelic nightmare' (Rambo 1997: 8). Yet, when observed from the necessary distance, which is precisely what van Schendel and Scott do and must be given credit for, that mosaic can become a distinctive and significant picture, even if an imprecise one at times.

States, borders, and agency in Zomia

Despite Scott's thesis that until about a century ago Zomia constituted a non-state space, an array of small states have in fact mushroomed there, such as the Tai-speaking *muang* of Sip Song Phan Na in Yunnan, Sip Song Chau Tai in Vietnam, Lan Xang in Laos, the Shan states in Burma (Rispaud 1937; Condominas 1976), or the well-established 'feudal' regimes of Dian and Nan Chao, and those of the Yi, the Dong, and the Bai in Yunnan and Guizhou. In fact, the Massif was not characterized by the lack of states. Instead, it was home to a plethora of small, weak, loosely connected states, at various stages of formalization. They subjugated egalitarian groups in their orbit, but never united, and were never totally integrated into surrounding polities. Risky but operational caravan trade routes contributed to keeping these political entities economically connected, while remaining physically separated.

Before European influence took root in Southeast Asia, a mandala model of state administration was dominant. The outskirts of the fiefdoms and empires' cores were conceived as buffer zones, inhabited by less- or non-civilized people, with whom tributary relations generally sufficed to ensure the core's political security and stability (Winichakul 1994; Wolters 1999; Bruneau 2002). In contrast, the current, widely accepted division of the large cultural continental sub-areas into South, East, Central (Inner), and Southeast Asia, is based chiefly on the European and Chinese notions of the nation state and linear borders.

Later, this crystallized into the dominant subdivisions of Asian studies within such academic entities as the American Association for Asian Studies, where panels and papers have to be located in one given sub-area. The rare non-specific panels straddling two or more sub-regions have been bundled together in a recently established 'border-crossing' section, reflecting a belated though welcome interest in trans-regional analysis. Coherent with such a vision, and in a way as a consequence of it, most political scientists more or less consciously infer that because minority policies are country based, minority issues ought to be studied in country specific contexts. Christopher Duncan's edited volume, *Civilizing the Margins: Southeast Asian Government Policies for the Development of Minorities* (Duncan 2004) – albeit important in its own right – provides an example of this position, with each country being allocated one chapter with a roughly equal share of pages. No room is allowed for transborder analyses.

However, the category of 'minority' and its corollaries, remoteness and marginality, only makes sense from a lowland perspective. It works when referring to one or several national cores that produce authoritative knowledge about such peripheries, from the occasional depictions in ancient Annals to recent studies of the exotic other – or antique self – within.[8] Studying highland social groups within the restrictive frame of one given nation state moves them from coherent cultural entities to binaries of majority–minority, modern–ancient, and civilized–barbarian. Pre-set labels are applied uncritically, such as 'national minorities' and 'minority nationalities'. Scores of country-based studies produced throughout the Massif and Zomia for over a century, in an array of disciplines, provide telling examples of how national factors curb, and sometimes erase, dimensions that otherwise concern an entire transborder society. The same applies elsewhere: one can think of the Kurds, the Gypsies, the Inuit, the Nuer, the !Kung, the Dayak, and many others. Borders, by their very political nature, artificially break up the historical social and cultural fabric of transborder subjects and reduce the validity of country-based findings to what applies to a splinter group, with the larger entity disappearing beyond the nation's borders.[9]

Without denying in any way the importance of the national context and its implications, social anthropologists argue that ethnic groups divided by international borders should also be studied in their cultural integrity in a transnational way, and not solely as part of one nation state. Scholarly consideration of Zomia and the Massif as a transnational social space helps to do just that

(Michaud 2000; Michaud and Forsyth 2011). On a larger scale, transborder studies contribute to raising the international level of awareness about a more than significant portion of the world population that otherwise has consistently ended up, throughout history, being misrepresented and, thus, disempowered.

In this regard, James C. Scott's book contributes a great deal to reappraising that history, and to assigning agency to highland dwellers. Using a bird's-eye view familiar to political scientists, Scott draws a chart of human settlements and political relationship over (his definition of) Zomia. His thesis is:

> Zomia is the largest remaining region of the world whose peoples have not yet been fully incorporated into nation-states. Its days are numbered. Not so very long ago, however, such self-governing peoples were the great majority of humankind. Today, they are seen from the valley kingdoms as 'our living ancestors,' 'what we were like before we discovered wet-rice cultivation, Buddhism, and civilization.' On the contrary, I argue that hill peoples are best understood as runaway, fugitive, maroon communities who have, over the course of two millennia, been fleeing the oppressions of state-making projects in the valleys — slavery, conscription, taxes, corvée labor, epidemics, and warfare. Most of the areas in which they reside may be aptly called shatter zones or zones of refuge.
>
> (Scott 2009: ix)

While this bold thesis had not yet been proposed in such a thorough, forceful, and documented way, ideas compatible with Scott's point have been debated before. More often than not, it has been anthropologists who started the debates, thanks to investigations on the ground with actors displaying such avoidance strategies. Working among various groups in the northern Amazon basin in the 1960s, French anthropologist Pierre Clastres published in 1974 a short polemical essay entitled 'La société contre l'État' ('Society against the State') (Clastres 1974). His argument was that the absence of a complex stratified social organization amongst many so-called primitive societies in the pre-Columbian Americas did not mean they had not 'yet' discovered social stratification. Instead, Clastres surmised that these societies had developed through time a capacity to refuse its promises and keep it at bay. To him, so-called primitive societies were built to avoid the emergence of the state among them. At the time, Clastres' thesis triggered ferocious debates. Most forcefully, he was accused of romanticizing the Noble Savage in his splendid resistance against the evils of modernity, a critique that some feel compelled to extend to Scott.

Scott acknowledges his debt to Pierre Clastres 'whose daring interpretation of state-evading and state-preventing native peoples in post-Conquest South America [...] has come, in the wake of subsequent evidence, to seem clairvoyant' (Scott 2009: xiii). Scott also notes Owen Lattimore's study (1962) of southwest China's small societies running up the mountains to evade Han assimilation, Robert Hefner's work (1985) on the highlands of Java, where the Hindu Tenggeri sheltered themselves from the powerful Muslim states controlling the island, and Keesing's conclusions (1976) about the Ifugao of the Northern Cordillera area of Luzon in the Philippines. He also makes great use of Edmund Leach's influential analysis (1954) of highland Burma, where Kachin egalitarian social organization could oscillate, according to circumstances and strategic objectives, between their kinship-based form of local power and the more centralized political organization of their feudal neighbours, the Shan (Sadan and Robinne 2007). To this already convincing list, one could add Patterson Giersch's detailed study (2006) of how Qing China gradually took political control over Sip Song Phan Na (today Xishuangbanna) in Yunnan. Or again, there are Bernard Sellato (1994) and Jérôme Rousseau's (1990) rich studies of highland Borneo, an area very comparable to Zomia, in which both observed that Punan nomads kept their distance from Dayak farmers, precisely to avoid being subjected to them. Similarly, Alain Testart (1985) states that the mobility of enclaved hunting-gathering societies all over the world reflects their desire to distance themselves from the domination of peasants surrounding them.

A fertile element of Scott's analysis pertains to what he calls the 'friction of terrain' (Scott 2009: Chapter 2). For Scott, this notion is part of the explanation of why small societies in Zomia elected remote highlands as refuge. A difficult and poorly accessible terrain provided a degree of safety, and landscape could also be socially engineered to amplify friction. Conversely, for the enterprising state wishing to reach and control such populations, the friction of terrain can be reduced by an array of 'distance-demolishing technologies':

> Bridges, all-weather roads, forest-felling, accurate maps, and the telegraph. The advanced techniques of defoliation, helicopters, airplanes, and modern satellite photography further diminish that friction. Friction is thus not simply 'there' in some mechanical way; it is constantly being sculpted for one purpose or another.
>
> *(Scott 2009: 166)*

Logically, Scott observes that for those wishing to maximize the friction of terrain as a strategy to counteract the state's controlling actions,

> a host of countervailing strategies are available: destroying bridges, ambushing or booby-trapping passes and defiles, felling trees along roads, cutting telephone and telegraph wires, and so forth. A great part of the literature on guerrilla warfare (that part that is not about techniques for gaining intelligence) is about efforts to manage the landscape to one's advantage.
>
> *(Scott 2009: 166)*

Thus, the inhabitants of Zomia are not just passive subjects, they can also perform as agents. As Nicholas Tapp stated in his review of *The Art of Not Being Governed*,

> Scott is concerned to lend agency to those who have been thought to be without it, to see conscious political choices and strategising in the historical practice of swidden agriculture, segmentary kinship structures, and oral traditions.[…] This is a strikingly different picture from the generally accepted [one] of these people as reluctant, hapless victims of state agency, losers in history, robbed of productive lands, or fossilised relics of some pre-historic past.
>
> *(Tapp 2010: 12)*

What James Scott is trying to tell us about these 'barbarians by design' (Scott 2009: 8) is that they receive outside prescriptions, try to indigenize them as best they can with regards to their particular circumstances, and craft tailored responses in creative, culture specific ways that may not be easily decipherable by outside observers.

Conclusion: Zomia and beyond

I call this chapter 'Zomia and beyond' for several reasons. I chose to use the name Zomia because, in spite of its lack of precision and contested definitions, the very term appears capable of generating debate. It has the invaluable quality of attracting international attention for an amalgam of distinct societies and little researched histories which richly deserve to be better known. I used 'beyond' because it highlights the fact that many authors have now tested the Zomia proposal against reality, through grounded research in locations and during time periods each has expertise on. Such authors come from a range of disciplines, contributing to weighing up the relevance of the Zomia scheme beyond any specific intellectual coterie. Most share a degree of reservation towards the Zomia idea, conceived and expressed in ways that were probably not foreseen by its creator(s). The result pushes the intellectual boundaries of scholarship on this notion, as well as on the peoples that it is meant to encompass.

One question has yet to be addressed: Who exactly needs a notion such as Zomia? I surmise that it is probably not the nation states sharing these highlands. If a variety of vernacular terms in national languages in each of the countries sharing Zomia do exist to designate the highlands within national borders, to the best of my knowledge none of these countries has produced a functional term to talk about the uplands beyond their own borders. We can also suppose that notions such as Zomia, the Southeast Asian Massif, the Himalayan Massif, or High Asia, have never been needed by the subjects themselves. Up in the mountains, vernacular languages have hundreds of terms labelling the local habitat, sometimes referring explicitly to a specific element of topography. But I suspect such an overarching notion as Zomia has never been proposed locally by any of the societies dwelling there customarily. Most specialists of one or another of these highland groups can confirm that that scale of things simply does not make sense, either practical or symbolic, for highlanders.

Characteristically, social anthropologists, but also linguists and indeed 'incidental' ethnographers (Michaud 2007: 67), will have specialized on one particular highland group, not several, and often within the limits of one country. Hundreds of dissertations and monographs on the Lisu, the Naga, the Zhuang, the Yao, the Mnong, the Dai, the Hani, the Dong, the Buyi, and many, many more prove this trend. I also suspect that most of these locally rooted scholars would be of the opinion that the general notion of Zomia is defined on an overly macroscopic scale, rather than constituting an operational object in their disciplines.

While neither the highlanders themselves, nor their national rulers, nor academic specialists are likely to require a notion like Zomia, it will appeal to international organizations and academics who want to articulate their thoughts on 'High Asia' and its peoples at a macroscopic level, for institutional, intellectual, research, or teaching purposes. Other transnational labels have recently appeared in this way such as Circumpolar Studies, for indigenous societies around the Arctic Circle.[10] Amazonian Studies, referring to a similar venture on the forested transnational margins of central South America, are also established. These underline a need for a macroscopic vision of large portions of humanity spreading over vast territories, but also of a desire to transcend political borders and disciplinary boundaries, in order to assess the current and future state of local societies differently.

In Asia in the long term, the relevance for history and for the social sciences in general of the notion of Zomia and similar terms is open to speculation. Despite its current appeal, it could prove to be short lived. An increasing density of road and rail networks crossing these uplands, a near complete coverage by technologies of communication (television, mobile phone, internet), massive internal migrations, and the gradual opening up of borders to trade and tourism may soon erase the 'friction of terrain'. This would fuse these populations into wider Asia. Conversely, multitudes of highland people have left the rural settings where their ancestors tilled the land, and now reside in lowlands and urban areas in and all around Zomia. The range this movement covers is impressive. Karen and Lahu farmers have become peri-urban unskilled labours in Bangkok. Tay, Thai, and Nung men and women represent their constituencies in the People's

Assembly in Hanoi. Naga operate tourist businesses in cities in northern India. Educated Naxi, Bai, and Yi work as civil servants in Kunming or Chengdu. Yao, Dong, and Buyi academics teach in Guiyang. Zhuang computer programmers promote their skills in Nanning and Hong Kong. Miao men are busy in the taxi industry in Shanghai. Ethnic pop stars occasionally top the charts in various parts of Zomia.

Each of the countries sharing Zomia has promoted, or is still promoting, a relocation policy for lowland dwellers to pursue their economic dreams in the highlands, where demographic pressure on the land is below national averages. This ranges from the New Economic Zones scheme in Vietnam in the 1960s, to the Go West scheme in southwest China in recent years. A typical highland town has thus evolved over the last hundred years or so, from being a mainly indigenous entity to becoming the seat of vast cultural hybridization. Indigenous highland societies in Zomia may sooner or later be integrated or overtaken by populations with outside origins, making this distinct social space less relevant.

However, contemporary connections may just as well refashion Zomia once again, rather than efface it. Tourists demand difference, not sameness. The majority of upland populations still live and work in the countryside and are much less directly touched by migration from the lowlands, be it of people, technologies, or ideas. As a consequence, highland zones are still largely ethnically distinct from the lowlands, and diverse ethnicities will persist in the region for many years to come. Whether flight, refuge, and resistance to assimilation will still be high on the agenda remains to be seen. Faced with this modernization dilemma, James Scott thought it prudent to specify, in *The Art of Not Being Governed*, that his reading of the situation could only be considered valid until roughly the first half of the twentieth century. Yet, his own earlier works on 'infrapolitics' and everyday resistance strongly suggest that this modernization process might also proceed less seamlessly than its proponents forecast (Scott 1985, 1990; see also Kerkvliet 2009).

Notes

1   This chapter is a version, shortened and lightly edited, to fit the needs of this collection, of the original article 'Editorial. Zomia and Beyond' (Michaud 2010).
2   Personal communication, February 2008. To my knowledge van Schendel has not published this expansion to his original 2002 Zomia.
3   I drew this map based in part on van Schendel's schematic map in his 'Geographies of Knowing, Geographies of Ignorance,' p. 653.
4   The ICIMOD describes itself as 'a regional knowledge development and learning centre serving the eight regional member countries of the Hindu Kush-Himalayas – Afghanistan, Bangladesh, Bhutan, China, India, Myanmar, Nepal, and Pakistan'. (Accessed online at: www.icimod.org/.)
5   See for instance, on Borneo, Bernard Sellato, *Nomads of the Borneo Rainforest: The Economics, Politics, and Ideology of Settling Down* (1994). In the Indonesian context Tania Murray Li, 'Marginality, Power, and Production: Analyzing Upland Transformations (1999).
6   See the extended definition of the Southeast Asian Massif in the second edition of the *Historical Dictionary of the Peoples of the Southeast Asian Massif* (Michaud 2016).
7   See the Introduction in Michaud (2006).
8   For instance Ma Touan Lin, *Ethnographie des peuples étrangers à la Chine. XIIIe siècle, traduit du chinois et commenté par le Marquis d'Hervey de Saint-Denys* (1883). Zhang Tan, "'Zhai men" qian di shi men kan: Jidu jiao wen hua yu Chuan Dian Qian bian Miao zu she hui' [The Stone Threshold in Front of the "Narrow Door": Christian Culture and Miao People's Society of the Border Regions of Sichuan, Yunnan and Guizhou Provinces] (1992).
9   Thailand, in this regard, is exemplary, with hundreds of monographs having been produced from the 1960s to the 1990s on 'the Hmong', 'the Karen', or 'the Akha' while the number of representatives of each group there amounts in each case to a few per cent of the whole group. See for instance Gordon

Young, *The Hill Tribes of Northern Thailand* (1962), Inga Lill Hansson, *A Folktale of Akha in Northern Thailand* (1984), Paul E. Durrenberger, 'Misfortune and Therapy among the Lisu of Northern Thailand' (1979), Robert G. Cooper, 'Sexual Inequality among the Hmong' (1983).
10 See the map by the Makivik Cartographic Services, 2000, Canada, at: www.makivik.org/. The University of the Arctic now offers an undergraduate degree in Circumpolar Studies.

References

Bello, David. A., 2005, Opium and the Limits of Empire. Drug Prohibition in the Chinese Interior, 1729–1850. Cambridge, MA: Harvard U. Asia Center.
Bruneau, Michel, 2002, 'Évolution des étagements ethnopolitiques dans les montagnes sino-indochinoises', Hérodote, 10, 4: 89–117.
Chouvy, Pierre-Arnaud, 2009, Opium. Uncovering the Politics of the Poppy. London: I.B. Tauris Publishers.
Clarence-Smith, William G., 2004, 'Horse Breeding in Mainland Southeast Asia and its Borderlands': 189–210, in P. Boomgaard and D. Henley (eds.), Smallholders and Stockbreeders. History of Foodcrop and Livestock Farming in Southeast Asia. Leiden, Netherlands: KITLV Press.
Clastres, Pierre, 1974, 'La société contre l'état'. Paris: Editions de Minuits. [Society Against the State: Essays in Political Anthropology, trans. Robert Hurley, New York: Zone, 1987.]
Condominas, Georges, 1976, 'Essai sur l'évolution des systèmes politiques thaïs', Ethnos: Journal of Anthropology, 41, 1–4: 7–67.
Cooper, Robert G., 1983, 'Sexual Inequality among the Hmong': 173–187, in John McKinnon and Wanat Bhruksasri (eds.), Highlanders of Thailand. Kuala Lumpur and New York: Oxford University Press.
Descours-Gatin, Chantal, 1992, Quand l'opium finançait la colonisation en Indochine. Paris: L'Harmattan.
Duncan, Christopher R. (ed.), 2004, Civilizing the Margins: Southeast Asian Government Policies for the Development of Minorities. Ithaca, NY: Cornell University Press.
Durrenberger, Paul E., 1979, 'Misfortune and Therapy among the Lisu of Northern Thailand', Anthropological Quarterly, 52, 4: 204–210.
Evans, Grant, C. Hutton, and K.-E. Kuah (eds.), 2000, Where China Meets South-East Asia: Social and Cultural Change in the Border Regions. Singapore and Canberra (Australia): Institute of Southeast Asian Studies – Allen & Unwin.
Giersch, Patterson, 2006, Asian Borderlands: The Transformation of Qing China's Yunnan Frontier. Cambridge, MA: Harvard University Press.
Goldstein, Melvyn C., 1989, A History of Modern Tibet, 1913–1951: The Demise of the Lamaist State. Berkeley: University of California Press.
Hansson, Inga Lill, 1984, A Folktale of Akha in Northern Thailand. Copenhagen: University of Copenhagen.
Hefner, Robert W., 1985, Hindu Javanese: Tengger Tradition and Islam. Princeton, NJ: Princeton University Press.
Herman, John E., 2007, Amid the Clouds and Mist: China's Colonization of Guizhou, 1200–1700. Cambridge, MA: Harvard University Press.
Hill, Ann Maxwell, 1998, Merchants and Migrants, Ethnicity and Trade among the Yunnanese Chinese in Southeast Asia. New Haven, CT: Yale University Press.
Jenks, Robert D., 1994, Insurgency and Social Disorder in Guizhou. The Miao Rebellion, 1854–1873. Honolulu: University of Hawaii Press.
Keesing, Felix M., 1976, The Ethnohistory of Northern Luzon. Stanford: Stanford University Press.
Kerkvliet, Benedict J. Tria, 2009, 'Everyday Politics in Peasant Societies (and Ours)'. Journal of Peasant Studies 36, 1: 227–243.
Lattimore, Owen, 1962, 'The Frontier in History', in Studies in Frontier History: Collected Papers, 1928–58. London: Oxford University Press.
Le Failler, Philippe, 2001, Monopole et prohibition de l'opium en Indochine. Le pilori des Chimères. Paris: L'Harmattan.
Leach, Edmund, 1954, The Political Systems of Highland Burma: A Study of Kachin Social Structure. Cambridge, MA: Harvard University Press.

Li, Tania Murray, 1999, 'Marginality, Power, and Production: Analyzing Upland Transformations': 1–44, in Tania Murray Li (ed.), Transforming the Indonesian Uplands. Amsterdam: Harwood.
Lim, Joo Jock, 1984, Territorial Power Domains, Southeast Asia, and China: The Geo-Strategy of an Overarching Massif. Singapore: Institute of Southeast Asian Studies.
Lin, Ma Touan, 1883, Ethnographie des peuples étrangers à la Chine. XIIIe siècle, traduit du chinois et commenté par le Marquis d'Hervey de Saint-Denys. Paris: Ernest Leroux.
Lombard-Salmon, Claudine, 1972, Un exemple d'acculturation chinoise: la province du Guizhou au XVIIIe siècle. Paris: Publication de l'École Française d'Extrême-Orient, vol. LXXXIV.
McCoy, Alfred W., C. B. Read and L. P. Adams III, 1989, The Politics of Heroin in Southeast Asia. Singapore: Harper Torchbooks.
Mckinnon, John and Jean Michaud, 2000, 'Presentation. Montagnard Domain in the South-East Asian Massif': 1–25, in J. Michaud (ed.), Turbulent Times and Enduring Peoples. The Mountain Minorities of the South-East Asian Massif. London: Curzon Press.
Michaud, Jean, 1997a, 'Economic Transformation in a Hmong Village of Thailand', Human Organization, 56, 2: 222–232.
———, 1997b, 'From South-West China into Upper Indochina: An Overview of Hmong (Miao) Migrations', Asia-Pacific Viewpoint, 38, 2: 119–130.
———, 2000, Turbulent Times and Enduring Peoples: The Mountain Minorities of the South-East Asian Massif. London: Curzon Press.
———, 2006, Historical Dictionary of the Peoples of the Southeast Asian Massif. Lanham, MD: Scarecrow Press. [Reprinted in 2009 as A to Z of the Peoples of the Southeast Asian Massif.]
———, 2007, 'Incidental Ethnographers': French Catholic Missions on the Tonkin-Yunnan Frontier, 1880–1930. Leiden and Boston: Brill, Studies in Christian Mission 33.
———, 2010, 'Editorial. Zomia and Beyond'. Journal of Global History 5, 2: 187–214.
———, 2016, 'Introduction. Seeing the Forest for the Trees: Scale, Magnitude, and Range in the Southeast Asian Massif': 1–40 in Jean Michaud, Meenaxi B. Ruscheweyh and Margaret B. Swain, Historical Dictionary of the Peoples of the Southeast Asian Massif. Second Edition. Lanham, MD, Boulder, CO, New York, London: Rowman & Littlefield.
Michaud, Jean and Tim Forsyth (eds.), 2011, Moving Mountains: Highland Livelihoods and Ethnicity in China, Vietnam and Laos. Vancouver: University of British Columbia Press.
Rambo, A. T., 1997, 'Development Trends In Vietnam's Northern Mountain Region': 5–52, in D. Donovan, A. T. Rambo, J. Fox and Le Trong Cuc (eds.), Development Trends In Vietnam's Northern Mountainous Region. Hanoi: National Political Publishing House.
Rispaud, J., 1937, 'Les noms à éléments numéraux des principautés taï', Journal of the Siam Society 29, 2: 77–122.
Rousseau, Jérôme, 1990, Central Borneo. Ethnic Identity and Social Life in a Stratified Society. Oxford: Oxford University Press.
Sadan, Mandy and François Robinne (eds.), 2007, Social Dynamics in the Highlands of South East Asia: Reconsidering 'Political Systems of Highland Burma' by E. R. Leach. Leiden: Brill.
Scott, James C., 1985, Weapons of the Weak. Everyday Forms of Peasant Resistance. New Haven: Yale University Press.
———, 1990, Domination and the Arts of Resistance: Hidden Transcripts. New Haven: Yale University Press.
———, 2009, The Art of Not Being Governed: An Anarchist History of Upland Southeast Asia. New Haven: Yale University Press.
Sellato, Bernard, 1994, Nomads of the Borneo Rainforest: The Economics, Politics, and Ideology of Settling Down. Honolulu: University of Hawaii Press.
Tan, Zhang, 1992, 'Zhai men' qian di shi men kan: Jidu jiao wen hua yu Chuan Dian Qian bian Miao zu she hui [The Stone Threshold in Front of the "Narrow Door": Christian Culture and Miao People's Society of the Border Regions of Sichuan, Yunnan and Guizhou Provinces]. Kunming, China: Yunnan jiao yu chu ban she [Yunnan Education Press].
Tapp, Nicholas, 2010, 'Review of James C. Scott's "The Art of Not Being Governed"', ASEASUK News 47 (Spring).
Testart, Alain, 1985, Le communisme primitif, Vol. 1: Economie et idéologie. Paris: Editions de la Maison des Sciences de l'Homme.

van Schendel, Willem, 2002, 'Geographies of Knowing, Geographies of Ignorance: Southeast Asia from the Fringes'. Environment and Planning D: Society and Space 20, 6: 647–668.
Wijeyewardene, Gehan, 1990, Ethnic Groups Across National Boundaries in Mainland Southeast Asia. Singapore: Institute of Southeast Asian Studies.
Winichakul, Thongchai, 1994, Siam Mapped: A History of the Geo-Body of a Nation. Honolulu: University of Hawaii Press.
Wolters, O. W., 1999, History, Culture and Region in Southeast Asian Perspectives. Revised Edition. Ithaca, NY: Cornell Southeast Asia Programme, and Singapore: Institute for Southeast Asian Studies.
Young, Gordon, 1962, The Hill Tribes of Northern Thailand. Bangkok: The Siam Society.´

Part 2
Livelihoods, commodities, mobilities

Introduction

Christine Bonnin

Dramatic transformations are currently underway throughout Asia's borderlands, as states attempt to assert a dominant spatial imagination on these frontiers, transforming them from supposedly disconnected, marginal, and remote places into efficient economic corridors and booming cross-border trading zones. Investments in large-scale infrastructural projects geared at overcoming the frictions of distance and terrain abound (Scott 2009). With state support, domestic and international private investors race to cash in on the ever more accessible frontier resource bounty by enclosing these spaces and moving them swiftly towards new forms of market-based production, with often deleterious effects on local livelihoods. Within such challenging and rapidly changing environments, how do individuals, households, and communities residing across Asia's borderlands work to support their own efforts to build resilient and meaningful livelihoods? In what ways do cross-border mobilities and flows contribute to sustaining these livelihood endeavours? In this part, we shift the lens towards the lived spaces of Asia's borderlands in order to explore how these places are being reshaped not only through the efforts of powerful state and market actors, but also through the everyday struggles, activities, and pursuits of borderland residents. Through careful ethnographic studies of different segments of these borderlands and their cross-border dynamics, the contributors to this part add to recent case studies that look at how frontier people strive to make a living (Sturgeon 2005; Forsyth and Michaud 2011; Harris 2013; Turner et al. 2015).

Livelihoods, understood as how people make a living through modifying their economic and natural resource base, have long been of interest to social scientists, and a number of different "livelihood frameworks" are now employed by scholars and development practitioners alike. All of these share a holistic, actor-focused conceptualization of how people work to create and sustain certain means of living within difficult contexts of vulnerability, marginality and/or poverty. By acknowledging the complexity of reality, this livelihoods focus has contributed to a clearer recognition of the multi-faceted nature of "what people do". Despite its appeal, however, a recurring criticism of the livelihoods approach has been the tendency to privilege material access and capital while often neglecting historical, geographical, social, cultural, and political dimensions (e.g. Turner et al. 2015). The contributors to this part tie economic considerations in with an examination of the ways that history, culture, locality, identity, and emotion are also intimately intertwined in borderland practices of making a living.

Christine Bonnin

De Mersan's chapter focuses on the borderlands of the State of Rakhine/Arakan, Myanmar. Historically a very diverse social landscape, evidence of social and economic linkages and interdependencies between groups has become today highly politically contentious and largely absent from official documents. Departing from the usual spaces of livelihoods analysis, De Mersan shows how local spirit beliefs reflect traces which evidence social and economic interconnectivities. Through her analysis of local borderland ritual practices relating to spirit and local territorial cults, De Mersan demonstrates how it becomes possible to detect an alternative discourse revealing an enduring inter-relationship between different social components for livelihoods and commodities exchanges.

In the multi-ethnic space of the highland Cambodian–Vietnamese borderlands, Bourdier introduces the concept of political livelihoods, which stands out starkly from a more "neutral" traditional livelihoods approach by situating questions of power, agency, and resistance at the centre of the analysis. Local highlanders perform resistance to contemporary land grabs and threats to resource access through politically strategic use of ethnic and collective identities, joining transnational social movements and adopting international laws as a powerful new form of "capital". Through the concept of political livelihoods, Bourdier draws attention to the expanding spaces of the legal system for livelihoods struggles and practices of "jumping scale" where highlanders successfully manage to get the powerful multilateral development funders on their side, although the tangible material outcomes of this have yet to be truly realized.

The instrumentality of identity "positioning" in the borderlands, in terms of its use as a livelihood resource, is also a theme addressed in Alff's chapter, which concentrates on the social processes entangled in the emerging cross-border livelihoods of ethnic Dungan traders between Central Asia and China. The focus here is on the productive role of socio-spatial liminality in gaining access to resources and opportunities. For Dungan traders, occupying this in-between space is the outcome of an imposed diasporic position by Kazakhstani and Chinese nation-building imperatives in tandem with a strategic self-representation as a group that is historically connected to the Silk Road. Successfully drawing upon this intangible resource, Dungans have emerged as influential brokers between China and Central Asia.

The contributors to this part highlight how borderlanders have access to particular livelihood resources as an outcome of a shared history of inhabiting these diverse frontier spaces, such as multilingualism, longstanding cross-border networks and mobilities, and an intimate local knowledge of borderland geographies. In Rippa's chapter on the Kashgari in the China–Pakistan frontier, borderlanders use friction and illegibility to their advantage as they instrumentalize border "assets" in the pursuit of economic activities such as cross-border trade. Rippa aptly proposes the notion of "proximity" in reference to these sorts of border-specific livelihood resources, here based on historical, geographical, and cultural "closeness".

Borderland narratives as disconnected places and the binary of backwards 'margins' and modern 'centres' endures within state discourse and policy, mainstream thinking, and applied development circles. By contrast, Harris' chapter shows us that by devoting specific attention to the historical and contemporary workings of cross-border and transnational exchanges, we come away with a rather different picture that highlights the dynamics of flows, interconnections, and active spaces – challenging the dominant model of stagnancy and disconnect. As with the Himalayan yak tail, many of the goods that are part of current-day cross-border and global trade flows hold historical significance within the livelihoods of borderland residents. Harris' focus on the "social life of things" and commodity chains illuminates processes of accommodation, re-working, and sometimes resistance as values and meaning are transformed as these products are commoditized and as new interest groups arrive on the scene.

Movement, of people, goods, money, and ideas, as rapidly sped-up and enhanced, has become an implicit meta-narrative of mainstream theorizing on globalization. Yet, in the borderlands, where the state is deeply preoccupied with overcoming friction, and as we find in Harris' chapter, it is more often the case that the mobilities for some things (and groups of people) are becoming more highly regulated, monitored and constrained/directed, even as their movements are intensifying. Grundy-Warr, Teo, and Chin approach border mobilities in a refreshing new light as they chart the transformation of Mae Aw in the Thai–Myanmar borderlands from a strategic crossing point for illicit goods during the Cold War and drug trading period into a "developmental space" of tea plantations, fruit trees, and cultural tourism. They approach their analysis of this complex geopolitical landscape through a humanistic understanding of place-making by former Kuomintang soldiers and other groups who have made these borderlands their home. In so doing, the authors demonstrate how people's sense of place and belonging in the past and present is continually being (re)shaped in this geo-body space through migration, mobilities, cultural coexistence, and proximity.

Livelihoods, commodities, and mobilities are key themes that weave throughout the contributions to this part. These are the core elements that need to be considered by anyone undertaking research on the dynamics of local borderland economies. The individual chapters that follow work to complement more macro-level panoramas of Asia's borderlands (e.g. van Schendel 2002; Michaud 2006; Scott 2009) by pairing these with rich accounts of how these border spaces are being made from below.

References

Forsyth, T. and J. Michaud. 2011. *Moving Mountains: Ethnicity and Livelihoods in Highland China, Vietnam and Laos*. Vancouver: University of British Columbia Press.

Harris, T. 2013. *Geographical Diversions: Tibetan Trade, Global Transactions*. (Geographies of justice and social transformation; No. 18). Athens: University of Georgia Press.

Michaud, J. 2006. *Historical Dictionary of the Peoples of the Southeast Asian Massif*. Lanham, MD: Scarecrow Press.

Scott, J.C. 2009. *The Art of Not Being Governed: An Anarchist History of Upland Southeast Asia*. New Haven, CT: Yale University Press.

Sturgeon, J.C. 2005. *Border Landscapes: The Politics of Akha Land Use in China and Thailan*. Seattle: University of Washington Press.

Turner, S., C. Bonnin, and J. Michaud. 2015. *Frontier Livelihoods. Hmong in the Sino-Vietnamese Borderlands*. Seattle: University of Washington Press.

van Schendel, W. 2002. Geographies of Knowing, Geographies of Ignorance: Jumping Scale in Southeast Asia. *Environment and Planning D: Society and Space*, 20: 647–668.

6
Political livelihoods in the northeast borderlands of Cambodia
Legacy of the past, territorial incorporation, and confrontation

Frédéric Bourdier

Southeast Asian borderlands, it has been argued, stimulate the creation of new identities and alternative management of natural resources (Scott 2009). However, the spatial proximity between Vietnam and Cambodia, characterized by episodic geopolitical tensions in the borderland region of the Southeast Asian Massif, has not yet been investigated in this regard. In order to fill this gap in the literature on the region we chose Ratanakiri province, with an area of 12,561 km^2, located 600 km from the Cambodian capital, as our case study.

Ratanakiri is the ancestral home of eight ethnic minorities, also called highlanders in the scholarly literature (the last census from 2008 lists a total population of 100,000 with 70 percent of it made up by highlanders), traditionally practicing swidden agriculture and relying on forest products for their livelihoods. Their social organization differs: some have a matrilineal clan system (Jarai, Tampuan, and Kachoh') while others (Brao, Kreung, Lun, Kaveth, and Bunong) have a cognatic descent system. All follow matrilocal residential rules. The Jarai (the second most numerous group after the Tampuan) live in the border heartland,[1] close to Vietnam, and they maintain relationships with their Vietnamese counterparts. Particular attention will be given to the social fabric of their management of the borderlands and their livelihood approaches, which nevertheless share common patterns with the other ethnic groups.

The anthropology of frontiers begins, in the historical context of the area, with an anthropology of political negotiation and contest, as will be discussed in the next section. Major changes occur after the mid-20th century. National borders become zones wherein negotiations of internal and international relations take place, mostly for access to and control over natural resources. Under these circumstances, borderlands are also those areas liable to be extended across borderlines.

This chapter proposes, as detailed below, an approach towards grasping 'political livelihoods' in these relatively unknown borderlands, an analysis which may also be of relevance to other borderland contexts.

Political livelihoods of Cambodia

Map 6.1 Location of Ratanakiri province (Cambodia) in the Southeast Asian Massif
Map by Frédéric Bourdier

Perspectives on borderlands and livelihoods

For centuries, the highlanders of Ratanakiri—today known as Ratanakiri province (Map 6.1) in north-east Cambodia—did not have institutionalized borders. Living in a hinterland caught between two empires, they could travel without restriction. They relied on natural resources for their habitat, food, health, agriculture, and other cultural practices. Recent top-down development interventions by the state in this remote territory created a new paradigm: villages were settled, families started to grow cash crops, and individuals began to supplement their incomes with trade and wage labour. Another characteristic of Ratanakiri's development since the early 1990s has been the rapid and uncontrolled exploitation of natural resources (NGO Forum 2015) with exacerbated competition for access and control over land by Khmer migrants and agro-industrial businesses. Distant Cambodian territories have become a resource frontier for national and external investors (mostly Vietnamese and Chinese), private companies, and a complex nexus of local/national/international legitimate and illegitimate loggers. The livelihoods of local borderland residents have been transformed.

What do we mean by livelihoods? Ordinarily, they are understood as the means by which people make a living. However, Amartya Sen, quoted by Michaud and Forsyth (2011: 13), proposes that 'livelihoods are a means of achieving capabilities, or the range of a person's life options, and are not only a means of achieving an economic income'. Consequently, a livelihood approach focuses on activities, on access to these, and on how changing economic, social, political, and environmental contexts might transform the underlying means by which people seek suitable livelihoods on a long-term basis. In Ratanakiri, long-established livelihoods are challenged by national development interventions, and a heartening response of the highlanders facing external pressures is to associate with transnational social movements. In that context, the concept of political livelihoods – rather than the elusive and neutral concept of sustainable livelihoods stressed by many authors – is more adequate for deploying an integrated framework encompassing the dynamics of changing livelihoods along with the way people assert their needs, make daring decisions, and forge worldwide alliances.

Such an orientation follows the concerns of a political economy under cultural ecology, which gives rise to the concept of political ecology (Peet and Watts 1996). The latter can be defined as the study of the manifold articulations of history and biology, and the cultural mediations through which such articulations are necessarily established, with the aim of examining the manifold practices through which the biophysical has been incorporated into history (Escobar 1999: 3). It is assumed that the notion of political livelihoods can receive a similar scientific consideration insofar as livelihoods cannot be simply understood as survival adaptations to the surrounding environment or as a homeostasis of the local culture of the people in their natural and social settings. A cultural ecology, deliberately minimizing parameters that rely on political and economical forces, has been criticized for its theoretical tendency to support superficial and unoriginal explanations (Peluso 1993). These consider overpopulation, ignorance, and irrationality of locals as the main causes of recent worldwide environmental degradations. This is an accusation that exaggerates highlanders' responsibility for the deprivation of their livelihood. To the contrary, a contemporary study of borderlands must take into account regional market integration, commercialization, and the dislocation of customary forms of resource management—a tendency that has been quite neglected in earlier conventional anthropological studies concentrating on isolated rural communities. Most recent works on borderland peoples, which have moved well beyond such a view of untouched and homogenous rural communities, explore the very issues mentioned, and do so by using too often the somewhat ill-defined and multipurpose concept of political capital (Casey 2008).

In line with this theoretical approach, Cambodian borderland political livelihoods relating to land can be defined as the combination of external/internal forces committed to transforming the ecological landscape into large agro-industrial territories. These forces challenge local dynamics that are willing to permit ancestral rights for access to and control over land, which is the core of people's livelihoods. Both (unequally) affect the others: a national movement strengthened by worldwide corporations violates most villages' territories, while local movements, supported by external actors, try to counteract this process by forging social networks and international alliances. Three components deserve particular attention for a better understanding of the political livelihoods: the contextual sources of the borderlands, the existing uneven co-management of natural resources, and the emerging social movements associated with livelihood impoverishment.

Based on this triad (borderland construction, contemporary development, and grassroots mobilization), this text is divided into three parts. The first insists on the historical dynamics — how both states have constructed their borderlands—which shape the present situation. The two following sections pay direct attention to the ways in which Cambodia–Vietnam borderlands deal with state policies. We switch from a linear, state-centred approach to a localized, multi-centred approach, in which competition for access and control over natural resources is balanced by grassroots mobilization challenging giant development processes. We focus on the Cambodian side. Taking the northeastern Ratanakiri borderland as a starting point for anthropological research facilitates a better understanding of the sociocultural, ecological, and political dynamics that are quickly changing in the area. The second part deals with the encounter between customary practices relating to the management of natural livelihoods and the attempts of the government to 'modernize' them, by capturing ecological resources for large-scale projects under the guise of development. We will see that some highlanders with political patronage, that is government and private connections, may take advantage of this, to the detriment of those who have been left out. The third part deals with highlander social movements driven by uncertainty about the fate of future generations, converging on land insecurity and natural resources depletion.

Disjointed borders

The ways in which the two nation states of Vietnam and Cambodia envision the borderlands have been transformed. On the Khmer side, the notion of frontier was not originally conceived in the same way as the Vietnamese Confucian notion of frontier. The perception that the kingdom had of its frontiers was of an ethnic Khmer dominant territory corresponding, as in Thailand, with a type of mandala model (Winichakul 1994: 82), which served as an extension of royal power. The Angkor agrarian state grouped together smaller units into principalities that were constituted more from the centre than from their own hypothetical geographical limits. Three concentric aureoles existed: at the centre, the capital of the king with his palace and the sanctuaries, surrounded by a territory under direct control. A second aureole of principalities was in the hands of some royal family members and aristocrats. A third external aureole was made up of tributary states and unsubdued territories (Bruneau 2001: 44). This third aureole, where northeastern highlanders were established, was far more fluctuant. Local inhabitants were not conscious of, and probably not interested in, a clear distinction between Cambodia and Vietnam: the centre was far away, and it was not *their* centre. They could secure a social distance: for instance the Jarai territory, at least in its moving fringe, encompassed a huge zone caught in the interstices of the two countries, but comprising their own established territory. They maintained a relative autonomy strengthened by the establishment of diplomatic relations, through exchanges of prestigious gifts, with the courts of Hue and Phnom Penh.[2]

At the beginning of the colonial area, no single map of Cambodia existed. The royal chronicles and epigraphy show that territorial limits were unclearly defined (Lafont 1989: 136–37). But these historical documents rely on states' attitudes and neglect the incessant links among the borderlanders attested by recurrent exchanges, similar social organizations, common kinship, and shared mythology. The borderland area was officially considered as a no man's land, a non-aligned space inhabited by independent, belligerent ethnic groups. It was a buffer zone with barely penetrable evergreen forests that none of the kingdoms ever tried to control.

More important and worrisome for the Cambodians had been the progressive attempt of the Siamese to gain control over the north, including its eastern part where Ratanakiri province is now located. The Thaïs were interested in collecting natural resources and recruiting human slaves via a system of vassalage with the Champassak Kingdom in Laos, which persisted up to the time of the French decision prohibiting slavery.

At the beginning of the Protectorate in 1863, the French had no idea of the approximate limits between the two kingdoms. They tried, unconvincingly, to push forward to the northeastern borderlands by establishing a limit with the aim of delineating a frontier, visibly distinguished, relying on natural obstacles and prominent physical characteristics. The French discovered the complexity of the situation between Cambodia and Vietnam: two hostile valley populations with a serious bone of historical contention, and a totally permeable border inhabited by similar groups, with the Bunong and the Stieng in present-day Mondulkiri and with the Jarai and the Kachoh' in present-day Ratanakiri.[3] The existing porous border became a matter of challenge for the colonizers who tried by themselves, lacking precolonial statecraft liable to exert a powerful influence over colonial administration, to develop their modern conception of state along with a closer definition of borders. But the establishment and the demarcation of the border was prepared without further control. They identified who was living there, what they were doing, and what needed to be modified. The French classified the ethnic groups and imposed, ineffectively, a corvée system with a ban on swidden agriculture. The production of a national frontier political line nevertheless split the territories of highlanders' societies who belonged thereafter either to Ratanakiri/Mondolkiri, or Pleiku/Gia Lai in Vietnam.

Simultaneously, the elusive border turned to be a matter of political unrest for the Vietnamese after 1954 when the independent Hanoi government decided to export communism into Laos and Cambodia through its northwestern border covering 350 km from the Dragon tail up to Kratie province. In a 'revolutionary situation', the state territory was about to be fragmented. Vietminh military troops and commissioners percolated the northeastern region and commenced political indoctrination of the highlanders. Before Cambodian Independence, some of these highlanders, mostly the Jarai, were trained as 'Khmer Issarak' (freedom fighters) against the French. Oral testimonies[4] attest to the presence of sanctuaries, political training centres, hospitals, munitions and food warehouses on the northern side of the Sésan River. Moreover, numerous Ho Chi Minh Trails coming from Vietnam to Cambodia via Laos had been active over a period of ten years (1962–1972), which made the region subject to intensive American bombings.

Ratanakiri had already become a rebellious borderland before the rise of the Khmer Rouge, with some local leaders, trained and influenced by Vietminh, refusing the authority of the Sihanouk state's intervention on their land, and later denunciating American bombings since 1962 as an imperialist attempt to subjugate the highland borderlanders. The future Khmer Rouge leaders, escaping the government repression, took refuge in the heartland of the borderlands in the mid-1960s, and collaborated with the Vietminh. After the overthrow of Sihanouk in early 1970, relations deteriorated between the two camps, and abruptly ended in 1972. The Khmer Rouge decided that the 'liberated province' would become an irrigated rice border. Such external and internal geopolitics greatly affected the livelihood conditions of borderlanders, facing terror and deprivation during the Khmer Rouge's repression up to 1979.

Borderlands and development: multi-centred confrontations

Political boundaries often create conflicts of interest between central authorities and people who live near borders (Grundy-Warr 1993: 42). While the functions of the first are inner-oriented and bound up with the concepts of nation state and territorial sovereignty, the activities and interests of local villagers in border regions are, in Ratanakiri, outer-oriented and directed across political boundaries. It means that despite attempts by central states to control their borderlands and to promote an imported national culture, local highlanders on both sides maintain ties: they visit each other's homes for religious festivities; kinship members join for funeral and wedding celebrations; adolescents intermarry; natural products and modern goods are exchanged. All these events have the latent function of maintaining ties and developing socioeconomic and political affiliations among borderlanders.

The central government resents border cultures, yet it promotes international trade and does not try to suppress cross-border ties, which otherwise could create diplomatic embarrassments. Meanwhile, the Master Economic Plan[5] promotes a national culture through imposed values aimed at showing the unity of the nation, implemented by such methods as Khmer language education, decentralized administration, and by encouraging Khmers to settle in the borderlands.

If the physical delimitation of a territory and the notion of borderlands had been evasive before being formulated in the 1960s by the state, borderlanders have adjusted and incorporated these fluctuating concepts with their own rationalities. Until recently, in the Cambodian borderlands highlanders have had a cultural perception of their 'social space' (Condominas 1983: 11–19) as consisting of a village territory with a residential unit, a forest that can be burnt for swidden agriculture, and a prohibited area devoid of human intervention (cemetery, sacred forests). The limits of the village territory may change according to demographic pressure and ecological characteristics.[6] Assimilating immutable complementary natural elements within a territory that is home to the gods and spirits is highly significant (Lafont 1989: 27), providing a symbolic sense of their ancestral origin. It also allows for a reliance on indestructible elements, easily identifiable by those who know the area, which is intimately connected with their daily life. Ontologically, movements of human beings and circulations of non-human beings coexist. The two living entities whose mutual and uncompetitive presence is encrusted in Nature (trees, hills, streams, etc.) and beyond Nature (human artefacts, posts, etc.) have to share on earth a social space where unavoidable encounters take place.

After Vietnamese troops' withdrawal in 1989, Cambodian political-economic interests prioritized the capture of natural resources through cross-border diplomacy and salient cooperation. But the gate is not open in the same way for everybody: a first segmentation process allows top-ranking Cambodian officials to develop lucrative deals in the borderlands, including smuggling wood with the blessing of the two governments. Local populations can do the same, on a smaller scale, but at their own risk. Owing to growing competition for access to natural resources, control of coveted territories, and accumulation of capital, a second social segmentation mixed with identity negotiation occurs. Villagers are less and less in a position to respect the ecological niches of the others and the pre-existing social spaces, because of large-scale land appropriations and internal scissions/conflicts. Such conflicts occur when some members use pretexts to assume abusive ownership over collective resources (forests, cultivated lands) by accomplishing advantageous economic transactions with outsiders. Indeed, it happens that well-connected highlanders, irrespective of their ethnic affiliation, and those enjoying administrative positions use state institutions for their own ends and develop patronage systems in imitation of what the Khmers have been doing so successfully.

The 'fertile border', with its rich, basaltic soils, makes the indigenous population particularly vulnerable to alternative forms of commercialization and to human colonization. The rapid expansion of Economic Land Concessions (ELCs), the diminishing access and control over natural resources owing to intensive forest loggings (NGO Forum 2015), and land dispossession constitute the major concerns for highlander societies. Thousands of evicted, dispossessed, and landless Khmers, Cham, and Vietnamese have moved to Ratanakiri in the last 20 years for agricultural purposes and for national/transnational business. Due to increasing land inaccessibility, recent newcomers become seasonal workers in family plantations or in real estate.

Countless stories attest to compulsory land purchases at the village level by wealthy well-connected absentee owners, even if some of these narratives, subjectively formulated by well-minded outsider and insider activists with a blind faith in the authenticity of the highlanders, forget to mention the deliberate decision of villagers to sell their land—such villagers knowing that well-intentioned non-governmental organizations (NGOs) would help them to recover the supposedly illegally sold land.

Agro-industrial expansion has a deleterious impact on socioecological landscapes (Bourdier 2015). The latest reliable figures from 2015 show that the 2001 Land Law (allowing national/international investors to be granted up to 10,000 hectares) authorized the creation of 26 ELCs plus 29 exploring mining licences in Ratanakiri. Most of this land, covering 300,000 hectares (the average size of each ELC is around 7,500 hectares), has been converted for monoculture plantation (rubber, cassava, coffee, soybean). Two thirds of them are located in the central plateau where most highlanders live. The mining areas, bigger than the ELCs, with a surface covering 20,000 up to 72,000 hectares (for a total exceeding 350,000 hectares), are located in two national parks in the north and in the south, and in the central forests previously inhabited by villagers.

The eastern borderland, the border heartland, is by far the most affected area. Four companies have been granted ELCs, which run end to end from a 31-km frontier along the Vietnamese border through the districts of O'Yadao, Andong Meas, and Thaveng. More than 40,000 hectares have been cleared for rubber: the first company received the first government agreement in 1996 (20,000 hectares), two in 2007 (5,080 and 5,120 hectares), and the fourth in 2012 (9,380 hectares). Initially granted separately to four Vietnamese agribusiness ventures, the concessions have since made their way into the hands of a single one, Corp 15, an arm of the Vietnamese People's Army stationed across the border in Gia Lai province. Authorities respond to people's concern by explaining that ELCs are needed to develop the country's remote areas with the ostensible benefits—jobs, roads, and schools—that they bring to the communities (more than 30 villages, with an average population of 500) on which they are imposed. The reality is different: since 2010, when the first rubber trees were planted, villagers discovered that, without prior negotiations, the four ELCs were encroaching on communal land, destroying spirit forests and burial grounds, and illegally exporting luxury-grade timber across the porous border.[7] Families came to know that a huge territory was in the hands of the companies claiming to have the right to expel the locals, the majority of whom have no 'official' ownership documents, only customary rights, to prove it was their land.

Borderland forests are decreasing at an alarming rate. The land transfers to investors are usually accompanied by illegal logging and prohibited forestland encroachment. Most concessions systematically cut all forested areas in their circumscriptions. These forestland encroachments stray beyond the allocated land and cut precious woods for export to China via Vietnam.[8] The Community Forestry, managed by the Forestry Administration Department, is supposed to reduce deforestation and support livelihoods through the local management of forests. So far, however, the provincial government has not approved the many proposals for a community forest site.

Due to a drastic reduction of the territory previously used by highlanders, swidden cultivation is decreasing—sometimes abandoned—and a good amount of non-timber forest products and game has become difficult to find. Upland rice rotational farming is difficult to maintain in deforested, shrinking territories, and rare are the families having sufficient rice for the whole year. Additionally, there is a reduction in the variety of grown rice, fruits, vegetables, and other products from the upland fields. Daily food items can be obtained from neighbours, but they are frequently bought from Khmer/Cham groceries. Most villagers engaged in cashew nut production, with an average of 2 hectares per household, and the wealthiest invest in family rubber plantations. Cash crops are also a way to secure land more permanently through private land titling, which is on the rise.

Another strategy to secure livelihoods consists in work diversification at the household level: while maintaining agriculture as *the* traditional rural activity, even if reduced in size, indigenous people are appointed to government jobs, or employed by NGOs (more than 100 highlanders are currently working with local/international agencies), while others become reluctant daily wagers for the agro-industrial companies. Business is usually in the hands of Khmers, Cham, and Chinese. Informal and lucrative trading, which allows cross-border linkages to flourish to the advantage of this migrant population, is also practiced by a smaller number of well-connected highlanders.

Ratanakiri is therefore in a gloomy situation, wherein the state, which is run by political, military, and bureaucratic elites, honours special interest groups rather than the borderlanders as a whole, while paradoxically directing a hostile rhetoric towards the same interest groups as a strategic act of deceptive courtesy towards the international media interpreting such official bogus discourses as a step forward to democracy and human rights.

All these activities have created socioeconomical fragmentations among highlander groups, who do not provide a homogenous picture anymore, if ever it has been the case. Similarly, the diffracted notion of community is challenged. But highlanders do not consent passively to the livelihoods menaces they suffer, and they are prompt in reacting to them. In the next section, we are going to see the reverse: how unequal development is leading to the rise of collective awareness and efforts to defend resource access and livelihoods.

Temporary quiet borderland, insecure livelihoods, and social movements

The notion of a 'quiet' borderland, compared to the 'unruly' and 'rebellious' designations applied to it, refers to a situation where the state, regional elite, and local populations are knit in a coherent power structure in which tensions are very low. So far, sporadic confrontations existed in Ratanakiri, but they were rarely displayed openly. But the times are changing, and local discontent is on the rise.

Conflict with the establishment derives from highlanders' consciousness of their own political vulnerability, and also because borderlanders have increasingly become aware of themselves as a collective entity in response to their consistent identification by national developers and leaders as a social problem. Most of the inhabitants now perceive outside interferences, especially those promoting agro-industrial development, as a threat to the pursuit of their own access and control over natural resources. Such feelings are justified, according to them, by outsiders and officials engaged in land grabbing and forest products dispossessions that they used to rely on. In such circumstances, in areas adjoining the eastern bank of the Sésan River, intensive contacts have been established among highlanders, with local highlanders' associations involved in land conflict resolutions and identity safeguards.

As a preamble, it remains important to acknowledge that the emergence of resistance is not consensual. Those who get material and symbolic benefits from the government expect to maintain their elitist and politico-administrative connections: adhesion, with a visible indication of sympathy for the social movements, can be a 'setback' to their diligent acquisition of wealth. For some others, one may wonder about the tactical use of ethnic identity, mostly when supported and valued as a prerequisite by external bodies (NGOs, regional agencies and worldwide entities such as the United Nations). Personal enquiries show that the quest for ethnic authenticity was not initially part of the agenda among sections of highlanders, until some leaders became aware that it had to be highlighted for receiving funds, being sponsored to travel for seminars, and for receiving recognition from the global proponents of autochthonous self-determination. Last, if the ascription of a group's identity has been the subject and outcome of a cross-boundary struggle for control, as with the Jarai in both countries, the social identity of a group can be contested within the group itself, on grounds related to cross-boundary interactions and restrictions, therefore minimizing unity for a growing expected transnational movement.

Others expect to be protected from further encroachment and to obtain decent livelihood prospects. Organization and professionalization have been the first steps, beginning in the early 2000s with the creation of local, indigenous NGOs. Most indigenous activists are young, educated, and they frequently marry each other. They share this capacity to contain and insulate their culture and worldview with routine interactions (with other villagers, scientists, and developers) when they make claims to government bodies (for challenging national policies), and when they advocate in front of people who support them (United Nations, international lobbyists, and so on). The great majority have become absorbed in hybrid forms, having simultaneously learnt the appropriate responses to give to their manifold interlocutors. Plasticity and assimilability are integral parts of their personalities. Their first objective is to make local people aware of their rights. And effectively, based on this knowledge, villagers do not hesitate, as before, to organize protests, demand information, issue letters of complaint (with the assistance of community-based organizations and local activists), and participate in stakeholder meetings. A concrete example given below is more explicit in helping to understand the dynamics of social mechanisms in this matter.

Andong Meas is one of the three Ratanakiri districts bordering Vietnam, with an estimated population of 8,000 in 2016. Predominantly inhabited by ethnic Jarai, Kachoh', and Tampuan, some of the 21 villages are also inhabited by Lao, Cham, Khmer, and Vietnamese peoples. As already mentioned, the district is severely affected by ELCs and private investors. When companies started growing rubber trees, after having fenced off a territory already used for rice cultivation in some parts, headmen, elders, and younger representatives of the 13 affected villages complained to the district and provincial officials, but to no avail. A litany of abuse complaints was thereafter transmitted to human rights associations, who publicized these cases in the media and at the national/regional level for social visibility. Once the villagers became confident of their rights, an inter-village committee was spontaneously created for establishing relations with indigenous and local/international associations operating in the province.

Altogether, national advocacy was not considered sufficient. In each affected village, two individuals volunteered to make the link between local inhabitants and outsiders supporting their cause. Five international and national NGOs—notably the local Highlander Association (HA), Cambodian Indigenous Youth Association (CIYA), and Equitable Cambodia (EC)—had long-established regional and international networks: travelling for training and seminars in the Philippines, Thailand, Switzerland, and the USA became routine for outspoken grassroots leaders, who acquired expertise in receiving funds from donors, including the United Nations who supported indigeneity empowerment. Having understood international laws, regulations, and procedures, local and non-local peoples joined together in order to conduct a field investigation, which concluded that the company had violated ELC standards (size) and practices. Highlanders were now ready to use their political rights, first by starting a dialogue with the company and by taking legal action if negotiations did not work.

Highlanders summoned the national delegate of the Compliance Advisor Ombudsman (CAO),[9] an independent body from the World Bank (WB), to come to the district to verify whether the incriminated company was respecting the International Finance Corporation (IFC) guidelines and safeguards.[10] The CAO recognized that ethical considerations highlighted by the WB were not met owing to economic, environmental, and social malpractices. Consequently, the IFC, as the financial arm of the WB, could in theory force its institution to withdraw loans requested by the company in Ratanakiri. This pronouncement prompted the investor/company to adopt a shift in attitudes towards the affected people. The widely publicized announcement of the IFC's possible action came as a surprise to the investor, who realized that the villagers could sue them, with the risk of returning their granted loan to the Dragon Bank. At the current time of writing, the company has accepted engaging in dialogue with the affected communities; it has removed security guards, allowed locals to enter the concession (for pasture and collecting products like honey), made a written promise not to extend its territory, and is expecting to reach an agreement with villagers for compensation.

Borderlanders are now aware of their capacity to be major agents of change in sociopolitical processes of significance to people beyond their locality and beyond their state. An old Kachoh' woman assumed, with pride, 'My kinship does not live in isolation, and most of the problems that we are trying to resolve, for legal access to justice and land reform, are publicized in distant places [...] we receive many visits from supporters!' Such perceived worldwide attention may as well influence the official position of the government, insofar as national sociopolitical engagements (expanding intensive cash crops and promoting small credit for encouraging people's investments in cash crops) depend also on local communities for their support and the successful achievement of their aims, as was shown elsewhere (Donnan and Wilson 1994: 2). But for the moment, such expected dialectic between 'bottom' and 'top' does not bring concrete results to the local populations. Investors' and government's reactions restrict their efforts to asking forgiveness of the affected communities by organizing religious ceremonies for the spirits residing in sacred forests that have been cut for growing rubber trees or cassavas. Real compensation, either with cash or with land redistribution, is still a project with no definitive decisions after more than two years of negotiation.

Borderlanders in Andong Meas have developed intensive contacts among themselves and also with other development actors expecting them be mobilized in order to protect their land and have better access and control over natural resources. Some highlanders, but not all, join together with the aim of becoming an organized group recruited on the basis of their shared characteristics (Ross 1975: 54). If the majority of highlanders who are concerned with livelihood deprivation are not all directly involved, they do have at least some representatives from their communities who speak, use smartphones, act, and network on their behalf. Assemblies of villagers act as a formal organization once they know that they are supported by regional and international agencies, expecting a clear response from private and public bodies threatening their land. Additionally, individuals who have frequent contacts with their supporters promote the development of a sense of collective identity (*cheunchiet yeung*: we the indigenous peoples) to their fellow villagers, who had, until then, remained isolated. Resistance, in that case, is affected by the perceived cultural disintegration that highlanders, mostly elders and local associations' working forces, are eager to prevent. Receiving a collective land title for regaining the 'social space' depicted above is one of the options.

Conclusion

Some border societies are increasingly strong and have become very vocal about their grievances vis-à-vis land grabs and illegal logging. They are well represented by highlanders in Ratanakiri, as well as in Preah Vihear and Mondulkiri provinces, which are located in other borderlands of the country. They are not confined within a passive 'everyday resistance of the poor' (Scott 1977), but in a long, active process of engagement and persuasion. Some of them enlarge their vision by not being contained within a single tradition that is their own. 'We need to know what happens outside, because we can learn from it', asserted an elder. 'Transculturalism' (Augé 2009: 50) is being instilled in these societies, and one of the most interesting mainstream ideas is that, for borderlanders, cultural diversity has an appropriate meaning when it percolates each individual.

Traditional livelihoods have been unable to maintain the same guarantees as before. Alternatives and innovations have been hampered by the presence of valley peoples, who have been more reactive in this changing economic environment. Despite a few successful responses, a sense of insecurity has given birth to social movements. These grassroots mobilizations have been accompanied by a complex series of actors making the link from the village to the highest international agencies and the powerful banks. If improvement of livelihoods remains a principal concern, the positive outcome, felt as such by local inhabitants, would be that each phalanstery is a worldwide scene. Borderlands have been infiltrated, and the notion of political livelihoods is not a mere academic concept, but a practical concern appropriated by the populations.

Notes

1. A classification of three components of borderlands (Baud and Van Schendel 1997: 221–23) encompasses the whole province of Ratanakiri. The 'border heartland' is abutted on the border and dominated by its existence. The 'intermediate borderland' is the area that feels the influence of the border but in varying intensities. The 'outer borderland' is affected by the border in specific circumstances, the Master Plan (discussed after) being one of them.
2. The diplomatic relations were not an indication of salient allegiance, but a treaty based on mutual recognition of the other's sovereignty. In Cambodia, it was expected that the Jarai would prevent any potential invasion from the Vietnamese side to the Khmer empire.
3. Both provinces were created in 1959.
4. Personal enquiries, 2015.
5. Ministerial agreement, ratified in 2004, between nine neighbouring provinces of Vietnam, Laos, and Cambodia for promoting agro-industrial regional development.
6. In 1994, most provincial inhabitants believed that natural resources were almost unlimited. The territories of some villages could be subject to fluctuation and expansion.
7. Satellite imagery shows dozens of improvised roads, tracks, and trails crossing the border.
8. The highest authorities have allowed all confiscated timber to be bought by a timber magnate, close to the prime minister, who has the exclusive right to take all the wood in the government depots which fuels illegal logging across the country.
9. See: www.cao-ombudsman.org.
10. See: www.ifc.org.

References

Augé, M. 2009. Pour une anthropologie du la mobilité, Paris: Payot.
Baud, M. and Van Schendel, W. 1997. 'Towards a Comparative History of Borderlands', Journal of World History 8(2): 211–42.
Bourdier, F. 2015. 'Socio-Ecological Transformations in a Tributary Region of the Mekong in Cambodia: Culture of Resistance or Resistance of Culture?', Asia Pacific Viewpoint 56(2): 282–96.
Bruneau, M. 2001. 'La notion de frontière et sa signification dans la Péninsule indochinoise', Mousson 3: 33–55.
Casey, M. 2008. Defining Political Capital: A Reconsideration of Bourdieu's Interconvertibility Theory, available at: https://about.illinoisstate.edu/critique/Documents/Spring%202008/Casey.pdf
Condominas, G. 1983. L'Exotique est quotidien, Paris: Plon.
Donnan, H. and Wilson, T.M. 1994. Border Approaches: Anthropological Perspectives on Frontiers, Lanham, MD: University Press of America.
Escobar, A. 1999. 'After Nature: Steps to an Anti-Essentialist Political Ecology', Current Anthropology 40(1): 1–30.
Grundy-Warr, C. 1993. 'Coexistent Borderlands and Intra-State Conflicts in Mainland Southeast Asia', Singapore Journal of Tropical Geography 14(1): 42–57.
Lafont, P.B. 1989. Les frontières du Vietnam. Histoire des frontières de la péninsule indochinoise, Paris: L'Harmattan.

Michaud, J. and Forsyth, T. (eds.). 2011. Moving Mountains: Ethnicity and Livelihoods in Highland China, Vietnam, and Laos, Vancouver: UBC Press.
NGO Forum. 2015. Logs and Patronage, Systematic Illegal Logging and the Destruction of State Forests and Protected Areas in Rattanakiri and Stung Treng Provinces, Phnom Penh.
Peet, R. and Watts, M. 1996. Liberation Ecologies: Environment, Development, Social Movements, London: Routledge.
Peluso, N.L. 1993. 'Coercing Conservation? The Politics of State Resource Control', Global Environmental Change June: 199–217.
Ross, J.K. 1975. 'Social Borders: Definitions of Diversity', Current Anthropology 16(1): 53–72.
Scott, J.C. 1977. The Moral Economy of the Peasant: Rebellion and Subsistence in Southeast Asia, New Haven, CT: Yale University Press.
Scott, J. C. 2009. The Art of Not Being Governed: An Anarchist History of Upland Southeast Asia, New Haven, CT: Yale University Press.
Winichakul, T. 1994. Siam Mapped: A History of the Geo-Body of a Nation, Chiang Mai: Silkworm.

7
Cross-border commodities
Processual histories, commodity chains, and the yak tail trade

Tina Harris

Introduction

A vendor sells a brocade coat lined with sheep wool along the Barkhor, the main pilgrimage route and marketplace in Lhasa, Tibet. The silky purple outer layer, with its pattern of Buddhist endless knots and brocade trim, is apparently made in a small factory in Varanasi, India, brought by trucks through India, Nepal, and up to Lhasa. The wool lining is likely from a sheep located in the Changtang in central Tibet. The silver-plated buttons are made in Kathmandu and delivered by women who cross the Chinese border once every few months for trading purposes. The vendor himself is Tibetan, born in the border town of Dram, who spent much of his life shuttling goods like cheap perfume from Nepal. What do we learn from commodity journeys like this, journeys that take place along multiple paths in and across the borderlands of Asia? Which objects become more (or less) important during which periods in history, and why? What kinds of items travel more easily over borders than others? Who controls the flow of commodities in borderland areas, and under what conditions might this control be overturned? This chapter focuses on a rich set of studies that investigate the intersections between mobility, commodities, and borders in Asia by asking similar kinds of questions. It argues that commodity-level research is ideally placed to draw out broad, dynamic themes that can expand the study of borders and borderland processes in Asia, themes such as state and territory formation, changing consumption meanings and values, and the direction of global capital.

In the social sciences and humanities, studies of commodities have been characterized by several different theoretical lines; however, this chapter will highlight two threads that are particularly useful in the study of Asian borderlands. First, 'processual histories' such as Fernand Braudel's three-volume *Civilisation and Capitalism* (1979) and Eric Wolf's *Europe and the People Without History* (1982) focus on the labour and people involved in the paths of objects and resources in order to provide a fuller picture of the large-scale, transnational flows of goods that are crucial to the making of states and territories over a *longue durée* history. The study of commodities—especially in Asian borderland regions where diverse groups struggle to maintain control over states and territories that solidify and loosen over the course of time—necessarily needs to be embedded in a wider context of global historical and geopolitical change.

Second, although there are numerous excellent studies of the transformation of material culture in Asia such as the marketization of 'ethnic' crafts in Thailand (Cohen 2000), the relationship of individual lives to wearing a sari (Banerjee and Miller 2003), and even the Intel anthropologist Genevieve Bell's study of changing mobile phone use (Bell 2006), the focus of this chapter is on the production and consequences of the mobility—and immobility, in many cases—of goods across borders. Thus, the chapter focuses on scholarship influenced by the notion of the 'commodity chain' (Gereffi and Korzeniewicz 1994), as well as the idea of creating a 'cultural biography' of an item (Appadurai 1986), where both approaches emphasize the movement of commodities and their transformation as they pass through the hands of diverse groups, especially in the so-called 'margins' of states. While tracing the production, exchange, and consumption of an object across borders is methodologically difficult (Where does one begin? Which branches of exchange do you follow?), it works well as a heuristic tool for addressing *processes*, both the time period and the spatial paths that an object traverses. Exploring the commodity in borderlands is less about what kind of object it is, but what meanings are given to it at specific moments in its 'life' as it travels (Appadurai 1986: 13).

This chapter is organized in three main parts. First, it outlines why some processual histories or 'process geographies' have been useful for informing more contemporary studies of commodities in Asian borderlands. Second, it looks at a small selection of the scholarship on specific commodities in Asian borderlands, emphasizing three main themes that emerge: how focusing on flows of commodities in regions that are often considered 'remote' can also highlight state regulatory mechanisms; how various groups come to have profoundly differential access and control over certain commodities; and how the very idea of 'Asian borderlands' itself might be challenged through studies of the cross-border movement of commodities. Finally, in order to draw out these themes in more detail, the chapter concludes with a brief consideration of one specific commodity: the Himalayan yak tail.

'Processual' histories and geographies

Many of the studies of the movement of commodities across borderlands have been informed by comparative, *longue durée* histories of production, distribution, and exchange across the globe. It is worth giving a nod to these studies of interrelated political, economic, and social processes for their overarching view of how commodities move across time and space from production to exchange to consumption. One prominent example is Fernand Braudel's extended documentation of capitalism and trade, emphasizing the production and circulation of goods as they travelled through the hands of merchants and middlemen from the 15th to the 18th centuries (Braudel 1979). Paying close attention to the 'material life' and livelihoods of people involved in the trade of goods such as calico from India to France reveals hierarchies and dependencies that are produced amongst merchants, distributors, and officials in everyday exchange, where the 'upper stories can't exist without the lower stories' (Braudel 1979: 22). Traces of this *longue durée* approach are clear in Eric Tagliacozzo's work on the illicit flow of narcotics and humans across maritime Southeast Asia, for instance (Tagliacozzo 2005).

The sharp critique of the mid-20th century disciplinary split in the social sciences separating social, political, and economic as autonomous spheres of study has also proven crucial for many scholars of commodities, who work with the understanding that these processes are inextricably intertwined. Immanuel Wallerstein's 'world systems' idea was one of these critical frameworks, where the world economy is seen as made up of two interdependent regions: core and periphery, both of which are geographically and culturally different, one focusing on labour-intensive production, and the other on capital-intensive production (Wallerstein 2000). However, from the perspective of studies in and across Asian borderlands, this approach has been highly criticized for being too dependent on the notion that a marginalized, powerless 'periphery' has less agency than the more powerful regions in the 'core' parts of the world (Wolf 1982; Walker 1999). Thus, critiquing the idea of border regions as 'traditional' and 'static' has been extremely important to scholars who work on commodities in these regions. In particular, drawing out the histories of commodities 'from below' demonstrate that borderland populations were dynamically—and often violently—drawn into commodity production (such as rubber, palm oil, and sugar) to supply people in power for territorial expansion and capitalist accumulation (Wolf 1982: 352–353).

Eric Wolf's description of the movement of rice across South and Southeast Asia is one case in point. When Britain colonized Burma in 1855, nearly all of the Burmese rice began to be exported to British colonies. Yet the crop was not meant for the British people living there (their consumption habits did not include much rice), but instead for sustaining the huge numbers of Indians labouring on British tea and rubber plantations in Ceylon and Malaya, the sugar plantations of the West Indies, and in India itself. Bringing these 'marginal' and mostly non-Western commodity stories to the forefront, according to Wolf, means that 'both the people who claim history as their own and the people to whom history has been denied emerge as participants in the same historical trajectory' (Wolf 1982: 23). By tracing the (often violent) acquisition of raw materials, the processing of goods, and their consumption across multiple territories, these 'process geographies' (or processual histories as they have been called) necessarily shift the focus away from national centres or state boundaries to the diverse humans involved in the creating of, the transport of, and the struggle over goods and resources (Appadurai 2000: 7; van Schendel 2002). What is especially significant for this chapter is that these processes more often than not occur within and across so-called 'remote' locations in the borderlands of states and territories. When the mundane commodity and its producers, handlers, and consumers take centre stage, this approach can simultaneously pay attention to local dynamics expressed at the human level as well as more macro-level changes in geopolitics, as the commodity bumps up against state-based restrictions such as border closures. And yet these stories are not simply tales of dichotomous top-down state regulations versus bottom-up resistance or resilience. One of the other common approaches is to look at these very stories themselves through the commodity biography approach.

Commodities in Asia and in Asian borderlands

The 'mystical character of the commodity', as Karl Marx has put it, often obscures the social relations and labour that generate its production and exchange (Marx 1857: 164). The commodity chain approach, then, is one way to examine the complex 'network of labour and production processes whose end result is a finished commodity' (Gereffi and Korzeniewicz 1994: 1). Critical versions of this approach have attempted to move beyond fixed production and consumption nodes in the commodity chain as well as to expose the deeper inequalities and unevenness produced by such chains (Hartwick 1998; Cook et al. 2004). Ted Bestor's work on the global sushi supply chain, for example, follows fishermen off the coasts of Maine and Spain, to auctions at the Tsukiji fish market in central Tokyo, to the discourse and effects of this chain on global tuna sustainability (Bestor 2001, 2004). Focusing on a specific commodity or set of commodities often requires a multi-sited methodological approach, which is particularly useful for scholars working across multiple Asian border regions (Marcus 1995). But commodities do not necessarily flow easily across such borders; they are stopped, they are taken away, they are restricted, and their direction of movement may very well be reversed. At other moments, they are waved through, concealed, disguised as other kinds of commodities, or welcomed. In-depth studies of commodities across borders can help illuminate the wider political, social, and economic contexts that lead up to these very moments. This section will therefore highlight selected narratives of specific commodities from several border regions in Asia, emphasizing three overarching themes that emerge from the literature: how looking closely at the paths of commodities demonstrate that borderlands are *not* peripheral and powerless; how the study of commodities reveal the ways that diverse groups have differential access and control over such goods; and how the very idea of 'Asian borderlands' itself might be challenged through studies of the cross-border movement of commodities.

Lying in the margins of states, borderlands are often represented as peripheral and beholden to the power of those who rule from the centres. On the contrary, borderland scholars have shown that people who move commodities across borders intersect daily with the state or state power, as well as contribute to the hardening of these very borders (Walker 1999: 7). For instance, Andrew Walker's work on cross-river boat operators in the economic quadrangle of Laos, Burma, China, and Thailand demonstrates that although the livelihoods of people in the 'margins' 'have mobility at the heart of their identity' they have 'no problems with participating in the maintenance of borders' (Walker 1999: 8). It is indeed common to depict borderlands as lawless frontiers, but when commodities move across border areas, this very movement often presents a contradiction: as trading becomes more liberalized, opportunities for regulation flourish (Walker 1999: 7). States perform a balancing act where they must 'pursue their neoliberal dream of a borderless economy and at the same time barricade their borders' (Abraham and van Schendel 2005: 23). Wen-chin Chang has written on similar processes in the jade trade from Burma to Thailand during the 20th-century period when Burma declared border trade illegal. She shows that instead of being a 'passive geographical margin' it is precisely because of restrictions on the flow of commodities that this borderland becomes a 'scene of intense interactions' and that pragmatic reasons for making profits overshadow the cultural meanings of jade (Baud and van Schendel 1997: 216; Chang 2014).

There is a second thematic argument that stems from much of the literature on the movement of specific commodities across Asian borderlands. Such studies reveal the tensions between various stakeholders vying for power in the borderlands and their profoundly differential access to control over territory and goods. For instance, Laura Schoenberger and Sarah Turner's research has shown that Lao cross-border traders sell small volumes of goods such as ribbons, skirts, cardamom, and sandals precisely because they gain a more concentrated minority market, putting them at an advantage vis-à-vis their Kinh competitors in the same region (Schoenberger and Turner 2008). On the other hand, Rune Steenberg shows that the trade in one kind of rubber sandal in two cross-border locations in Kyrgyzstan and Xinjiang is based on long-term community building efforts between people from the same town and along the nodes of the sandal supply chain (Steenberg 2014: 11–12). While they are technically each other's main competitors, they must share knowledge about infrastructure, prices, and often share living spaces as well. Finally, Malini Sur has explored how both rice cultivators and the military raided each others' harvests in order to survive in the India–East Pakistan borderlands before 1971, illustrating how the rice itself became central to the production of Indo-Bangladesh borders that are still contested today (Sur 2016). Research on specific commodity flows across Asian borderlands is therefore fruitful for showing not only how ethnic groups vie for recognition vis-à-vis states, but also vis-à-vis each other at crucial historical moments.

Finally, the last thematic point is that cultural biographies of commodities across Asian borders are not always about Asian borders. As mentioned above, tracing a commodity across distance is often methodologically difficult, and necessarily involves far-flung networks that may have distribution centres in Brazil and manufacturing hubs in Indonesia. Several works on the movement of commodities in Asia, particularly those that investigate more flexible or neoliberal accumulation strategies, explore those who are in nodes or hubs of chains that are scattered around the world. One example is Ted Bestor's work on the sushi chain (mentioned earlier), and another is Anna Tsing's collaborative research on the extraction of value in the high-value matsutake mushroom trade, from the wealthy mushroom buyers in Japan, to Lao, Hmong, and Cambodian mushroom harvesters in the Pacific Northwest of North America (Tsing 2015). In each of these cases, it is clear that the approach to following specific commodity histories involves expanding or questioning what the 'Asian borderland' actually is. As the Southeast Asian refugees use the jungle skills they learned while surviving in war-torn homelands to successfully pick profitable mushrooms while reminiscing about village life, who is to say that the idea of an Asian borderland cannot also be produced in the forests of Oregon?

The yak tail: a borderland story

A 2013 article in *Vanity Fair* magazine titled 'Creating *The Hobbit*'s Oscar-Nominated Yak Beards' discusses hair-and-makeup designer Peter King's need to procure up to 80 kilos of yak hair, ideal for making dwarves' thick, flowing beards in the fantasy film (Hanel 2013). When imagining commodities that are clearly linked to global demand and geopolitical change, the yak tail—unlike sugar, salt, or timber—is not usually on the top of this list. But in answering the question of how studies of cross-border commodities can help us to understand changing socio-economic dynamics in Asia and beyond, the journey of a yak tail can be a fruitful case study of how both its origin and use are linked to the production and negotiation of Asian borders. Using the 'commodity biography' framework mentioned in the sections above, the narrative below investigates these issues through three 'windows': the yak tail's changing uses and meanings, its role and representation in 20th century geopolitics, and how its movement is affected by border closings and re-openings.

The yak—a shaggy haired, fairly docile bovid—lives in high altitude areas along the Himalayas and the Central Asian plateau. It is commonly used in a number of ways: as a pack animal, for meat, for dung for fuel, and for milk (from the female yak, the *'bri*). In Edward Schafer's study of Tang dynasty trade and tributary items, the tails of yaks have been traded across Asia as Buddhist, Jain, and Hindu ritual implements, as fly whisks, and as decorations for hats of nobility since the 8th century (Schafer 1985: 74). The tails are sturdy, waterproof, and easy to curl, which also made them—particularly the white tails—ideal for costume wigs and beards in Chinese dance and opera performances. In the mid-20th century, the yak tail was one of the main items in the *Tibet Mirror* newspaper, which featured the commodity prices of various goods that were traded along the route linking Lhasa, Tibet with Kalimpong, and India. Wool, animal skins, musk, and yak tails all made their way down the Himalayas into India, and further down to the port of Calcutta for their eventual trade to Europe and North America. It is unclear exactly when yak tails began to be exported to the United States, but sometime during the late 1940s, reports of the desirability of expensive yak-tail beards used for Santa Claus costumes began to emerge, as Santa Clauses became more common in malls and shopping centres in North America during the post-World War II commoditization boom (Harris 2014).

While sales of Santa Claus costumes boomed in North America, political tensions with China continued to intensify. Soon after the Chinese People's Liberation Army (PLA) entered eastern Tibet in 1950, Tibet came under the control of the Chinese state. The US embargo on goods from China meant that wool and yak tails from Tibet (i.e. China) would be stopped from leaving India. Yak tails began piling up in warehouses in Tibet and India, prevented from crossing over the border and beyond to North America. In response, the already-sky high prices of this luxury commodity skyrocketed. Here, the humble yak tail begins to be implicated in geopolitical marketing manoeuvres: in order to continue the profitable trade with wig retailers and suppliers in the United States, Kalimpong-based traders and sellers began to say that the yak tails—and by extension the yak—were not from Tibet (read: China) at all, but were mixed with yak hair from other places in the surrounding Asian borderlands: Bhutan, India, and even Russia. It is at this point that the borders in this region come into sharper focus. Even though the Tibetan yak do not necessarily follow national boundaries and could very well have mixed with Bhutanese yak, the fact that the nationality of the yak tails must now be declared in order to generate potential profits across borders paradoxically dovetails with the hardening of nation state borders.

Our borderland yak tail story is not yet over. In 1962, the Sino–Indian War resulted in the closing of all borders between the two countries, and the commodities that once travelled along the Lhasa–Kalimpong route trickled to a halt. But in 2006, over 40 years later, the Nathu-la mountain pass along the old Lhasa–Kalimpong trade route was re-opened in order to increase trade between China and India, during a time when both countries were pushing rapid development agendas in their hinterlands. The opening of borders is often simultaneously a hardening of borders, bringing with it increased fences, walls, gates, security, and limitations of what can and cannot be brought across. With Nathu-la, the yak tail was one out of only 15 items that were allowed by the Indian government for fear of Chinese goods 'flooding' the weaker market on the other side. Not a hugely lucrative commodity by any means at this point, yak tails are instead displayed in the border markets as 'ethnic souvenirs' from Tibet for foreign and Chinese tourists. Other, more profitable items go across illicitly, such as white goods that are brought as 'gifts' for cross-border friends and family, blurring the commodity-versus-gift distinction so prominent in early social science work on material culture. This leads to a hierarchy of items that can cross borders: 'women's goods' such as kitchenware or 'shopping' are seen as less important, for instance, but at the same time can often travel more quickly across border crossings (Konstantinov 1996; Harris 2013; Sur 2014). What commodity biographies across Asia also do is to situate 'Asia' in a more complex arena of transnational networks and nodes. To what extent is a hobbit's beard part of an Asian borderland story or part of a more global story?

Conclusions

Recently, there have been numerous examples of the increased infrastructural connections between China and the rest of its Asian borders, such as reports of seven border openings between Arunachal Pradesh and Tibet, and new civilian airports in western Tibet, Sikkim, and southwestern Yunnan. Through the implementation of the Chinese-led 'One Belt One Road' maritime and overland infrastructure network throughout Asia, the nostalgic revival of the 'ancient Silk Road' or the Tea-Horse Road features strongly in the representation of how commodities will travel across Asia in the *future*. There is indeed a need for better infrastructure in many margins of states where local roads and routes are liable to be washed out due to landslides or poor maintenance, but for whom will these new infrastructural changes be meant for? Do border openings increase the power of some groups while creating closings for others? Do these new road connections mean that certain goods will saturate the market, and what consequences will this have? There is a tendency to treat the study of goods and objects as static 'material culture', isolated from contemporary geopolitics. But tracing the movement of specific commodities across Asian borderlands allows for multiple lenses onto where and when they can get across, why they may be halted or banned, and where they may very well go next. Far from the celebratory fanfare of globalization ushering in a unified 'borderless' world, borders are brought into even sharper focus from the perspective of the comparative-historical commodity biography in most of the studies mentioned here.

References

Abraham, I. and W. van Schendel, eds., (2005) Illicit flows and criminal things: states, borders, and the other side of globalization. Bloomington: Indiana University Press.
Appadurai, A., ed., (1986) The social life of things. Cambridge: Cambridge University Press.
Appadurai, A., (2000) "Grassroots globalization and the research imagination." Public Culture 12(1), pp. 1–19.
Banerjee, M. and D. Miller, (2003) The sari. Oxford: Berg Publishers.
Baud, M. and W. van Schendel, (1997) "Toward a comparative history of borderlands." Journal of World History 8(2), pp. 211–242.
Bell, G., (2006) "The age of the thumb: a cultural reading of mobile technologies from Asia." Knowledge, Technology, and Policy 19(2), pp. 41–57.
Bestor, T., (2001) "Supply-side sushi: commodity, market, and the global city." American Anthropologist 103(1), pp. 76–95.
Bestor, T., (2004) Tsukiji: the fish market at the center of the world. Berkeley, CA: University of California Press.
Braudel, F., 1992 (1979) Civilization and capitalism, 15th–18th centuries (3 vols.). translated by Siân Reynolds, Berkeley, CA: University of California Press.
Chang, W., (2014) Beyond borders: stories of Yunnanese Chinese migrants of Burma. Ithaca, NY: Cornell University Press.
Cohen, E., (2000) The commercialized crafts of Thailand: hill tribes and lowland villages. Honolulu: University of Hawaii Press.
Cook, I. et al., (2004) "Follow the thing: papaya." Antipode 36(4), pp. 642–664.
Gereffi, G. and M. Korzeniewicz, eds., (1994) Commodity chains and global capitalism. Westport, CT: Praeger.
Hanel, M., (2013) "Sketch to still: creating *The Hobbit's* Oscar-nominated yak beards, hand-painted blood vessels, and glowing elf-skin makeup." Vanity Fair Magazine, February. Available at: www.vanityfair.com/hollywood/2013/02/the-hobbit-oscar-yak-hair-beard. Accessed 10 June 2016.
Harris, T., (2013) Geographical diversions: Tibetan trade, global transactions. Athens: University of Georgia Press.
Harris, T., (2014) "Yak tails, Santa Claus, and transnational trade in the Himalayas." The Tibet Journal 39(1), pp. 145–155.
Hartwick, E., (1998) "Geographies of consumption: a commodity-chain approach." Environment and Planning D: Society and Space 16, pp. 423–437.
Konstantinov, Y., (1996) "Patterns of reinterpretation: trader-tourism in the Balkans (Bulgaria) as a picaresque metaphorical enactment of post-totalitarianism." American Ethnologist 23(4), pp. 762–782.
Marcus, G., (1995) "Ethnography in/of the world system: the emergence of multi-sited ethnography." Annual Review of Anthropology 24, pp. 95–117.
Marx, K., (1992 [1857]) Capital, vol I. London: Penguin.
Schafer, E. H., (1985) The golden peaches of Samarkand: a study of T'ang exotics. Berkeley, CA: University of California Press.
Schoenberger, L. and S. Turner, (2008) "Negotiating remote borderland access: small-scale trade on the Vietnam–China border." Development and Change 39(4), pp. 667–696.
Steenberg, R., (2014) "Network or community? Two tropes for analysing social relations among Uyghur traders in Kyrgyzstan." Crossroads Asia Working Paper Series, No. 18.
Sur, M., (2014) "Divided bodies: crossing the India-Bangladesh border." Economic and Political Weekly 49(13), pp. 31–35.
Sur, M., (2016) "Battles for the golden grain: paddy soldiers and the making of the Northeast India–East Pakistan border, 1930–1970." Comparative Studies in Society and History 58(3), pp. 804–832.

Tagliacozzo, E., (2005) Secret trades, porous borders: smuggling and states along a Southeast Asian frontier, 1865–1915. New Haven, CT: Yale University Press.

Tsing, A., (2015) The mushroom at the end of the world: on the possibility of life in capitalist ruins. Princeton, NJ: Princeton University Press.

van Schendel, W., (2002) "Geographies of knowing, geographies of ignorance: jumping scale in Southeast Asia." Environment and Planning D: Society and Space 20, pp. 647–668.

Walker, A., (1999) The legend of the golden boat: regulation, trade and traders in the borderlands of Laos, Thailand, China, and Burma. Honolulu: University of Hawaii Press.

Wallerstein, I., (2000) The essential Wallerstein. New York: New Press.

Wolf, E., (1982) Europe and the people without history. Berkeley, CA: University of California Press.

8

Old routes, new roads
Proximity across the China–Pakistan border

Alessandro Rippa

In today's China, new projects of transnational connectivity, generally brought together under the 'One Belt, One Road (*yidai yilu* 一带一路)' umbrella, often allude to old trading routes. In Xinjiang, Western China, where I conducted research between 2009 and 2013, almost every project involving roads, railways, or Special Economic Zones (SEZ) along the region's borders is branded in connection to the old Silk Road. For instance, at the 2013 Kashgar Central & South Asia Commodity Fair, an entire stand was dedicated to the new Kashgar Special Economic Zone (*Kashi tequ* 喀什特区). A poster highlighted Kashgar city's strategic position for cross-border trade, describing it with the slogan 'five ports (of entry) through eight countries, a road connecting Europe and Asia (*wu kouan tong ba guo, yilu lian ouya* 五口岸通八国，一路连欧亚)'. Kashgar, according to the same panel, was 'China's great entryway to Central Asia, South Asia, the Middle East and even Europe'. Another poster showed the vision for the city's new Finance and Trade district, complete with skyscrapers, high-rise apartment buildings, and a lake. All of this, in the various panels, brochures, and presentations, was framed explicitly within the context of Kashgar's traditional role as a major hub along the Silk Road, its thriving bazaars, and geographical proximity to Central and South Asia.

Most recently Xinhua, the official press agency of the People's Republic or China (PRC), reported that China has started construction work on a massive China–Pakistan logistics complex in the remote border town of Tashkurgan, about 300 km south of Kashgar along the Karakoram Highway, as part as the China–Pakistan Economic Corridor (CPEC). The project should include 'an Internet service administration center, a cross-border e-commerce enterprise incubator, and a modern warehousing and logistic center', but also an exhibition centre, hotels, and entertainment facilities.[1] The logistics centre, expected to cost 3 billion *renminbi* (US$464 million), highlights China's commitment to invest in its border regions, foster cross-border exchanges, and increase its economic presence among neighbouring countries.

Although the Kashgar SEZ and the CPEC have a history that precedes Xi Jinping's launch of the One Belt, One Road (OBOR) in late 2013, both projects have currently been included into this new initiative. Anyone who has recently been to China, or regularly follows its news from outside the country, knows how often such projects are mentioned and how pervasive the OBOR rhetoric has become.

This renewed interest in developing cross-border exchanges and further increasing trade with neighbouring countries, comes at a time when Beijing has achieved firm control over these very borderlands. It might be argued that the opening up of border posts and the construction of special trade zones and roads all along its frontiers is a direct consequence of China's successful attempt to secure its border regions: an opening, to put it in another way, that follows an (en)closure. However, if we look at this process from such a perspective, it becomes rather easy to forget that many of these border regions have had a long history of cross-border interactions and exchanges that precedes the establishment of the current borderlines. To be sure, in many cases these interactions survived and persisted following the closure of these borders in 1949 and throughout the Mao era. To analyse the One Belt, One Road initiative from a merely macroeconomic or geopolitical angle, in other words, carries the risk of overlooking long-lasting transnational dynamics that have characterised these border areas for centuries. In fact, the rhetoric of 'opening up' borders and cross-border trade so often employed today, not only seems to imply the false assumption of a pre-existing empty frontier space (Tsing 2005; Harris 2017), but also often produces precisely the opposite results for local traders and residents, thus curbing their previous mobility, rather than enhancing it.

Such local dynamics are rooted in what I call proximity: the geographical, cultural, and historical closeness which characterises – at least some – border regions on China's peripheries. In order to show this, in this chapter I describe the historical trajectories of cross-border trade in the Karakoram region, and analyse the cases of a few cross-border communities and activities drawn from my fieldwork in both Xinjiang and Pakistan.[2] Despite its specificity, I find the case of the Karakoram Highway rather representative of a more common pattern along China's borderlands. Building on this material, I eventually define proximity as a combination of local knowledge, social networks, and territorial rootedness that affords specific economic opportunities to the people who live in these regions. I then conclude by showing how contemporary fantasies of transnational connectivity seemingly eradicate proximity, by attempting to bring the centres of power closer together through frictionless corridors of trade and exchange.

Karakoram connections

Karimabad's Baltit Fort is one of the most impressive buildings of the Hunza valley, in the northern part of Gilgit-Baltistan, Pakistan, about 200 km south of the Chinese border (see Map 8.1). Overlooking the villages of Karimabad and Altit, and offering splendid views of the valley and of the Karakoram Highway (KKH), the Fort was inhabited by various rulers – *mir* or *tham* – of Hunza until 1945 (Hussain 2015). After decades of abandonment, the Fort was restored during the 1990s by the Aga Khan Trust for Culture, and represents today Karimabad's main tourist attraction. If the Fort is a symbol of Hunza's power, various objects exposed inside tell a story of frequent relations with the kingdom's northern neighbour, China. In its small and dark rooms visitors are shown a picture of Safdar Khan, the *tham* who escaped to Xinjiang following the British military intervention in 1891. In another room, a couple of old Chinese documents recount the long relations between Hunza and Kashgar, while a picture shows former Chinese premier Zhou Enlai shaking hands with the last *tham* of Hunza during a visit in 1960. One of the most impressive items is a big carpet hung in one room where the *tham* used to entertain his guests with music and dancing during the cold months, a wonderful and seemingly quite old piece from Xinjiang's southern oasis of Khotan, once famous for its beautiful and unique carpets. Testament to ancient trade routes, similar carpets can also be found in Ladakh, northwest India, where they are used in mosques during Ramadan. During a visit in 2013, not far from the Baltit

Alessandro Rippa

Map 8.1 The Karakoram Highway (KKH) between Xinjiang and Pakistan
Source: Cartographic base: Google Maps; design by the author

Fort, in an antiques shop in the small village of Altit, I found another reminder of China's proximity. As I browsed through jewellery, semiprecious stones, and seemingly ancient documents in various languages, I discovered a few banknotes featuring both Chinese and Uyghur scripts. They came from Xinjiang and were issued in Kashgar in the 20th year of the Republic of China (1931). Called Kapiao 喀 票 (Wang 2007), the history of those banknotes goes back to the early days of the Republic in Xinjiang, when the region was under its first warlord, Yang Zengxin, and on the brink of bankruptcy.[3] In the 19th century, Xinjiang's economy heavily relied on subsides from the Qing government. The withdrawal of those funds, combined with the collapse of trade with Russia following the First World War and the Russian Civil War, inevitably left the region in grave financial crisis (Forbes 1986; Yu 1987). Yang's solution for Xinjiang was an intuitive one: extensively issue its own currency in the form of paper notes called Xinpiao and Shengpiao. These currencies were not, however, backed by official reserves, and their value suffered an enormous decline from the moment they were issued. The Kapiao were slightly more successful and had a higher credit, as Kashgaria – less connected to both Russia and the heart of the Qing Empire – suffered less from the overthrow of the Manchu dynasty. The Kapiao, however, had one major problem in common with the other currencies available in Xinjiang: they had no value outside the province. Foreign merchants were thus forced to exchange the Kapiao with silver or other merchandise before leaving the region, a business which in the south of Xinjiang was partly in the hands of Indian traders and moneylenders (Warikoo 1996; Thampi 2010).

Both the Kapiao and the objects exposed in the Baltit Fort are testaments to old trade routes connecting the two sides of the Karakoram. For centuries, a complex network of routes connected Kashgar and Yarkand in today's Xinjiang to Srinagar, Leh, Rawalpindi, and Peshawar (Warikoo 1996; Rizvi 1996, 1999; Kreutzmann 1998). This form of trade dried up from the 1930s onwards due to various factors, such as disturbances in Xinjiang (Thampi 2010), the Second World War, the Chinese Civil War, and the Kashmir impasse that followed the partition of British India (Lamb 1991). The region did not, however, lose its strategic relevance even as it fell into economic oblivion, and local cross-border trade continued via Gilgit during the Second World War. Chiang Kai-shek even proposed to the British the construction of a supply route through the Karakoram, which he thought would help his efforts against the Japanese and the communists (Kreutzmann 2009). While the road was not built, the idea of an all-weather road connecting Western China to the subcontinent survived both nationalist China and British India, when following the partition of the subcontinent (1947) and the Chinese Revolution (1949) the northern areas of Pakistan and western Xinjiang changed from being important hubs of transit between South and Central Asia, to an under-connected cul-de-sac and strategic frontline (Stellrecht 1997, 1998).

This does not mean, however, that between the late 1940s and 1978 – when the KKH was officially inaugurated – contact between the two sides of the Karakoram simply ended. From a political perspective, the newly established PRC and the Islamic Republic of Pakistan began to discuss the construction of a road to Xinjiang in the early 1960s. Most importantly, during these decades several hundred families of Uyghur migrants from Xinjiang continuously crossed the high passes of the Karakoram into Pakistan, where many settled down and can still be found today (Rippa 2014). Even in the dramatic years of famine during the Great Leap Forward and the Cultural Revolution, when China remained closed and isolated, these migrants and their stories provided important information about one of the world's most secretive regimes. Moreover, as I will show in the next section, this group of Pakistani Uyghurs – generally known in Pakistan as 'Kashgari' – played a central role in the revival of cross-border trade that followed the opening of the Karakoram Highway in 1978. Their story, that I will outline in the next section, shows how a combination of local knowledge, social networks, and territorial rootedness – or what I call proximity – was fundamental for the establishment and maintenance of cross-border trade relations across the Karakoram.

Uyghur traders

The first time I met a Kashgari was neither in Pakistan nor in Xinjiang. Salman, in 2012, was a master's student in one of China's most prestigious universities, Tsinghua, in Beijing. He came from a successful family of Kashgari traders, and his education was sponsored by a Chinese government scholarship dedicated to overseas Chinese conducting part of their studies in China.[4] On a nice autumn day, as we sat down in his tidy dormitory room for some tea and home-cooked biriani, Salman told me the story of his family. Before the partition of the subcontinent, in 1947, Salman's grandmother, who was originally from Kashgar, went together with her family to Mecca for the Hajj. Back then, the whole journey could take up to two years, or even more, and the long and tiring route was generally shared with other pilgrims. When Salman's grandmother left, something like 60 or 70 families were travelling by foot together through the Karakoram into South Asia and then, by sea route, to the Arabian Peninsula. On the way back from the pilgrimage, as the group was passing through the mountainous region of today's Gilgit-Baltistan, Salman's grandmother's sister died of an unspecified illness, as was not uncommon back then. The whole family halted their journey in order to hold the funeral, but then decided to stay on where they had stopped. During this time, Salman's grandmother met her future husband, a Kyrgyz–Iranian trader who could speak Uyghur, and eventually decided to settle down with him in Gilgit. Then, as Salman put it to me, 'Pakistan was made in 1947 and … [China] in 1949, so in two years they made the borders.'[5] Salman's grandmother would have to wait for over 30 years, until after the end of the Cultural Revolution, to go back to her homeland – this time together with her own children – to see what remained of her family there.

Over the course of my fieldwork, I heard many other stories similar to Salman's. In general, the oldest Kashgari migrants I managed to interview moved to Pakistan just before the partition of the subcontinent (1947) and the foundation of the People's Republic of China (1949). Many simply left Xinjiang for the Hajj, but then could not get back because the border was sealed, while others decided to stay in Pakistan for their faith or out of fear of the communists. I was told, for instance, that in 1948–49 about 500 people moved to Pakistan from Yarkand, southwestern Xinjiang, apparently afraid of the People's Liberation Army advance into Xinjiang. Some of them were rich families of traders with an established network of contacts in the region, while others were farmers with little or no experience of the world outside their native villages. Many, for these very reasons, moved in the years following the establishment of the PRC, when the new government did not thoroughly control Xinjiang's border and crossing out of the country was still relatively easy. Frequently mentioned in the course of my interviews was an uprising which took place in the southern oasis of Khotan in 1954 (Dillon 2004: 54), after which many Uyghurs involved decided to leave Xinjiang fearing repercussions against them and their families (Rahman 2005).

Most Kashgaris, moreover, seem to have moved to Pakistan during the 11 years of Ayub Khan's presidency, between 1958 and 1969. He, the second president of Pakistan, facilitated their transfer to the newly established Islamic Republic due to the Kashgaris' family ties with the subcontinent. As Abdulaziz, a Kashgari trader from Gilgit, told me during one interview: 'There are four kinds of us [Kashgaris]: those who are originally Pathan [Pashtun], those who are originally from Baltistan and those who are originally from [Indian] Kashmir. And there are those, like us, who are 100 per cent Uyghurs.' In fact, most Kashgaris seem to have South Asian origins, as before the 1940s it was not rare for Kashmiri or Pashtun traders to marry Uyghur women and move to south Xinjiang (Warikoo 1996; Rizvi 1996, 1999; Thampi 2010). Although I have also heard stories of families who lied about their South Asian origins and still managed to enter Pakistan, in most cases it was the fact that those migrants carried a British passport that allowed them to move back to Pakistan during Ayub Khan's government.

Such is, for instance, the story of Sultan Khan. Sultan Khan's father was born in Baluchistan, today Pakistan's westernmost province, and was a trader who travelled through Afghanistan, British India, and Xinjiang. In 1949, as Mao's Red Army took control of the country, he found himself on the wrong side of the border, in south Xinjiang. Back then, the partition of the subcontinent into two hostile states, India and Pakistan, had already triggered a war, and the situation south of the Karakoram Range did not appear promising. He decided to stay, hoping that life under the communists would bring him fortune, and married a local woman in Yarkand. After a few years, however, when the Maoists had confiscated all his properties and the failure of the Great Leap Forward had brought famine upon the country, Sultan Khan's father decided that he had had enough. As a former British subject he still had a British passport, and could thus apply to the Pakistani authorities for expatriation. Years later, in 1967, he was eventually allowed to move to his native country with his wife and three children. Once in Gilgit, Sultan Khan learned from his father the art of trading. With the Chinese border still sealed, they established a successful business importing goods from Afghanistan and 'down country'. In 1985 Sultan Khan's father died in Gilgit, and one year later Sultan Khan took his mother to his native town, Yarkand, through the newly opened Karakoram Highway.

Like Sultan Khan, Salman's father also had to look elsewhere for business in the 1950s and 1960s, before the opening of the KKH. Together with his brother, and similar to many other Pakistanis, he spent several years working in Saudi Arabia. As soon as the KKH opened, however, they came back, and with the money they earned in Saudi Arabia started off an extremely lucrative business importing Chinese silk to Pakistan. Later on he would open a travel company, and since 1978 he has been to China countless times.

The stories of the many Kashgari families in Pakistan are too various to be analysed according to a single framework. Despite their differences, however, as soon as the Karakoram Highway opened virtually all of them went back to Xinjiang to visit what was left of their families, or to see the land of their fathers. What is more, thanks to their network of contacts, linguistic skills, and freedom of movement, they were the first to start trading in the early 1980s. In many cases, it was simply a form of small-scale trade that allowed them to pay off travel expenses to and from Xinjiang, not dissimilar to what Muslim pilgrims have been doing for centuries during their travels to Mecca. In other cases, such as Salman's father, this became a real profession and a source of significant wealth. For all Kashgari, however, Xinjiang was more than just an option among several others. The decision to invest in cross-border trade was only partly the result of a considered analysis; rather, it was also a way to return to their fathers' business and to re-establish an old trade route, one that many Kashgari had heard of since a young age. It was a choice driven by their emotional attachment to the land beyond the Karakoram, of which they could only dream of before 1978. Proximity, I argue, brings together those different trajectories of geographical closeness, economic opportunity, and historical rootedness. Sultan Khan's decision to move most of his business to Xinjiang was not, in other words, merely an economic choice. It was driven by business interests as much as by an emotional — perhaps even nostalgic — bond with his homeland and his father's tales of trans-Karakoram trade. Furthermore, his ability to succeed in such endeavour was partly due to his language skills and kinship relations that were still in place when he first visited Xinjiang. A similar argument could be made for Salman's father's silk business, and certainly for Salman himself. Proximity, in other words, works on different levels — economic, geographical, and emotional — to the extent that without taking even one of those into account, it would be impossible to understand the case of the Kashgari traders in Xinjiang.

Uncertainties

If the Kashgaris had a significant advantage, at least initially, they were not the only ones with intimate knowledge of what lay on the Chinese side of the border. As previously described with the case of the Baltit Fort and the Hunza valley, people from the northern part of Gilgit-Baltistan also shared a long history of cross-Karakoram relations. Such is, for instance, the case of Karim and his family.

Karim has a wife and a young daughter in Pakistan, yet his trading business keeps him away from his family for a large part of the year. He is from Gojal, in the upper Hunza valley, not far from Sost and the Chinese border at Khunjerab Pass. Karim is Isma'ili and his mother tongue,

Wakhi, is shared by the Tajik minority in Tashkurgan, Xinjiang, where he has a few relatives. It is in Tashkurgan that, 19 years ago, Karim's father started his business together with his brother. According to Karim they were the first Pakistanis who bought a property there: a two-storey house that they still use as a shop, warehouse, and domicile. Ten years ago, Karim's father opened another shop in Kashgar, near the Idgah mosque, which had moved only a few months before our first encounter into a new shopping centre for jade and other semi-precious stones not far from Kashgar's People Square, in a new part of town. Karim, who has a degree in software engineering, has been working with his father for only a couple of years, and when I met him for the first time in 2012 he was designing the company's website.

Karim's business is a family enterprise and the two shops in Tashkurgan and Kashgar are managed by a number of brothers and cousins from the same family, who take turns with their monthly trips to China. They all have a border pass, and often use those continuous trips across the border to take some goods with them, as everything carried in luggage is 'tax free'.[6] Bigger items, however, are sent yearly in a single container and divided between the Kashgar and Tashkurgan shops. In China they sell various handicrafts, mostly in marble and brass, but they also have an interesting selection of precious and semi-precious stones and carved wooden pieces. In the Tashkurgan shop they sell imported soaps, perfumes, and other beauty products, which seem particularly popular among the local female population. It is a 'one-way business', as most of the goods come either from Gilgit-Baltistan or Karachi. Some stones – such as the famous lapis lazuli from Badakhshan – are imported from Afghanistan and taken to Xinjiang through the Karakoram Highway.

The first time I met Karim he was working in the Kashgar shop. The following year he moved to the Tashkurgan shop, and as I visited him there he kept complaining about how boring the small border town was. Kashgar, on the other hand, was different, and he later spent part of the winter period studying Mandarin in Islamabad with the purpose of returning there on a more permanent basis. 'China is our future', he told me once, 'I think people in Hunza should study Chinese.' Not only this, he was trying to teach his wife and mother, back home, how to use chopsticks. As he put it once: 'for us it takes two days to go to Islamabad, the capital of Pakistan. But if I leave my home in the morning, I can be in Kashgar in the evening. What's more convenient?'

For Karim, as it became clear to me throughout our conversations during long afternoons in Tashkurgan, this 'convenience' was not only a matter of geographical proximity. He would often tell me about the history of the region, highlighting Hunza's former control of many of the areas within China's current borders. Similarly, he would stress time and again that Wakhis from the Hunza valley and the Tajiks of Tashkurgan were, in fact, the same people. Old connections have not been forgotten in those dry highlands. Doing business in China then, for Karim as well as for many traders from the northern parts of Gilgit-Baltistan, was not merely a choice. Neither, as I was often told, was it a strict necessity – in different periods the same traders would resort to different activities, in different sectors and areas. Rather, it seemed like the natural outcome of the particular position, history, and cultural orientation of the region they were originally from. It was, given China's rise, an opportunity – one rooted into the history of the area and the long-lasting connections between the two sides of the Karakoram.

Similarly, Saxer (2017) argues that contemporary trans-Himalayan trade must be understood against the background of old trade routes, seasonal entrepôt, and brokering practices. Focusing on two new roads in Western Nepal, Saxer convincingly argues that 'rather than leading to modernity (for good or for bad), the new roads are primary conceived of as ways back to what is remembered as prosperous trans-Himalayan exchange' (2017: 76). Although with significantly different economic asymmetries and border regimes, those 'new' trades remain, at least initially, in the hands of the same 'old' suspects: local dealers, brokers, and re-invented traders.

According to this kind of analysis, it did not come as a surprise that following the 2010 Attabad landslide that dammed the Hunza River, causing a 30-km-long lake that submerged the Karakoram Highway in the north of Gilgit-Baltistan, it was 'China traders' who were responsible for the introduction of the large wooden boats that began to transport goods and passengers across it, thus reconnecting the area north of the lake with the rest of Pakistan (Sökefeld 2012). As the construction of the new road around the lake by the China Road and Bridge Corporation was completed only in 2015, the boat service was still the only option available at the time of my fieldwork, in 2012-13. If the crossing itself did not usually take more than 90 minutes, the operations of loading and unloading made the trip extremely expensive and time consuming. The inevitable result was a sharp – and visible – reduction of trucks plying the KKH on the Pakistani side, with many non-local traders shifting their businesses elsewhere. Although with lower profits then, at the time of my fieldwork, most small-scale cross-border trade was yet again in the hands of traders from Gilgit-Baltistan.

Natural disasters, moreover, are only one of many uncertainties that traders have to learn to navigate across the China–Pakistan border. For instance, on 31 October 2014, the online news blog 'Sost Today' reported large protests by Pakistani traders in Sost, Pakistan's border town, over China's decision to ban the transport of trade goods on the daily public buses between Tashkurgan and Sost. Although no official explanation was offered by Chinese officials, the ban highlights the ongoing attempts at hardening the border regime and regulating informal exchanges. According to the article, protesters asked for the lifting of the ban, claiming that due to the small-scale nature of the exchanges most traders could not afford any type of container truck. Chinese immigration officials, on the other hand, pointed out that traders from Gilgit-Baltistan could transport goods destined only to their region, but not to other markets in Pakistan. Pakistani customs officials, eventually, said that 'two trucks will be assign[ed] in a week for the local traders and baggage carriers of GB [Gilgit-Baltistan] and a person can take 500kg [of] goods in each trip'.[7] The news was not taken up by any other outlet, but those traders I managed to speak to confirmed that similar incidents occurred regularly.

In general, it comes as little surprise that Chinese immigration would change its policy over this issue, and several of my contacts expected it to happen sooner or later. In fact, Chinese import taxes are subject to constant – and seemingly arbitrary – fluctuations, and local traders have grown accustomed to navigating such shifts in the regulatory framework. For this reason, in the case of the ban, nobody seemed overly worried. Despite their regular complaints, local traders are confident in their ability to navigate these unexpected changes, finding compromises or ways to exploit apparently adverse schemes. This confidence is not reckless, as at first I was temped to judge it, but rather grounded in their experience and knowledge of border practices along the Karakoram Highway. In what, in other words, I call proximity.

Proximity

As the first section of this chapter described, the people of Gilgit-Baltistan have a rich history of cross-border contacts with China, Kashmir, and Central Asia. The China–Pakistan Economic Corridor and the PRC's most recent involvement in the region do not, for borderland residents, represent an exception or a turning point. Rather, it is a sign of continuity, a reminder of the centrality – economic, political, and cultural – that for many people in Gilgit-Baltistan remains the main characteristic of their land. As Amjad, a Gilgiti whose mother was originally from Afghanistan, told me once: 'We [from Gilgit-Baltistan] want our borders open: the borders with China,

India, Tajikistan. If borders are open, then we can develop' (Interview, Gilgit May 2013). Amjad's opinion, shared by many in the region, is also not unusual in the borderlands of Highland Asia (Harris 2017), where geographical remoteness is often paired with long-lasting trading routes, and political marginality with ambitious commercial enterprises. Hence local dynamics, as the cases of the Kashgaris and of the traders from Gilgit-Baltistan show, always occur at the nexus of a number of trajectories – border policies and regulations, the opening of infrastructures, the friction of the terrain (Scott 2009), and so on – that traders necessarily need to learn how to navigate. Those factors, or uncertainties, are often illegible for external actors. Yet locals, as traders in Attabad and Sost demonstrated, not only have the ability to circumnavigate those obstacles, but also often seem to profit from them. This ability, I argue, is rooted in what I call proximity.

With this notion, my aim is not to introduce a new concept or analytical tool, but rather to highlight, to bring the focus to, the historical trajectories of cross-border relations, on continuities, rather than abrupt ruptures and political changes, and on the very terrain where these take place. When, for instance, traders such as Karim and Amjad talk about China there is both a sense of distancing – from an alien culture, language, and a political system – but also a feeling of intimacy, of shared memories and histories. China, here, is no stranger; but neither is it a brother: it is, rather, an old acquaintance, too close to not be affected by it, but also too far to be subjugated by it.

Most importantly, I find, it is because of this shared history and the geographical closeness that I call proximity, that locals are often able to find and exploit new opportunities triggered by external decisions, such as the construction of a road or the opening of the border. So for instance, the first group of people that took advantage of the opening of the KKH were the Kashgari families who had left Xinjiang only a few decades earlier. Many of those traders came from families of mixed background, rooted in trans-Karakoram trade. For them, the decision to invest in China–Pakistan trade in the early 1980s was triggered precisely by these experiences, and by the network of contacts and set of expertise that they possess. The case of the Kashgaris is not the only one where we can see the forces of proximity at work. As I have shown, in the aftermath of the Attabad landslide, it was 'China traders' who re-established the connection between Gojal – and therefore China – and the rest of Pakistan. In a moment of great economic difficulties, when many Punjabi and Pashtun traders went elsewhere, traders from Gilgit-Baltistan kept travelling to Tashkurgan and Kashgar, purchasing cheap Chinese manufactured goods or selling gemstones and Afghan dry fruit – and quite often both. To be sure, following the landslide traders from other parts of Pakistan did not, in many cases, interrupt their business relations with Xinjiang. However, they relied on traders from Gilgit-Baltistan for arranging and managing the transportation of the goods between Kashgar and Gilgit. The disaster, in other words, created a situation of uncertainness within which only a combination of local knowledge, social networks, and territorial rootedness made it possible for business relations to persist.

Proximity, then, is not defined simply by a passive geographical closeness, although it is rooted in a particular terrain that favours certain kinds of routes over others. Proximity also implies a degree of cultural familiarity, and an active effort to keep those connections alive. It is, in this sense, close to what Zhang and Saxer call 'neighbouring': a set of practices that 'entails both a geographical reality of living in proximity, and a flexible construction of social relations that can be stretched across time, space, and distance' (2017: 23). As with neighbouring, proximity is based on a certain kind of geographical closeness, but it is by no means defined only by it. Rather, it implicates a certain effort, a 'doing' that often, as in the case of the Kashgari community, overcomes distance, political barriers, and generations. Unlike neighbouring, however, the concept of proximity is less bound to specific geopolitical conditions, and more attentive to the terrain through which encounters occur. Practices of proximity, then, should be analysed according to a broader historical spectrum, stretching generations and ever-changing political configurations.

Proximity, I find, is especially relevant in a context in which borders are not actually sealed, yet crossing them is for one or another reason difficult. In such contexts, smooth highways and official border-crossing procedures often seem to benefit outside elites, while bad roads, legal uncertainty, or obstacles such as the Attabad Lake bring old networks and social relations again to the forefront. To put it simply: it needs some form of friction for the forces of proximity to play out. It is these forces, I argue, that often afford economic opportunities to specific groups. Large-scale projects, state investments, and bigger players from outside the region, generally come only later. The paradox, then, is that the bureaucratic and infrastructural obstacles that often characterise border areas, and about which local traders constantly complain, are ultimately responsible for their very own success. By making the border landscape illegible (Scott 1998) to outsiders, those obstacles – or what I have called friction – become an advantage for those who can make sense of it due to their experience and contacts. It is a fragile benefit, as I shall briefly explain in the last section of this chapter.

Eventually, the concept of proximity helps us to avoid the risk – which I find present in much of the literature on borders – of overly focusing on the institutional side of cross-border relations. The celebrated opening of border crossings, for instance, often seems to complicate things for local cross-border interactions, rather than simplifying them. Or, as in the case of the Karakoram Highway, while the strategic and economic implications of the China–Pakistan Economic Corridor are widely discussed, the issues of those who are most directly influenced by the project are rarely addressed. With this chapter, my attempt is rather to switch the attention from the somewhat overstated importance of regulatory and economical differentials characteristic of border areas, focusing instead on the century-long history of trans-Karakoram relations, and on how these can influence the current situation in the region and local people's visions for its future. This is, I find, where the concept of proximity can help the most.

Conclusion: the end of proximity?

Border practices along the Karakoram Highway remain largely illegible for external actors. The bulk of the trade is dominated by small-scale traders, often with decades of experience. Like Karim's, these are often family businesses, cultivated on skilful diplomacy on both sides of the border, and on the network of contacts and local knowledge that I have called proximity. In other words, proximity entails legibility for these involved, making cross-border practices not only possible, but also economically profitable.

In the case of the Karakoram Highway the particular geopolitical situation of the area might have amplified this contrast. On the one hand, as I have shown, the KKH did not only re-open an ancient trade route to China, but also channelised a sparse and often-changing network of routes into one single infrastructure. This is not to say, however, that the rationale behind the construction of the road was trade, or economic development. Rather, as with other similar projects in the remote highlands of Asia (Ispahani 1989; Kreutzmann 1991, 1998, 2013), the main rationale behind the construction of the KKH was clearly strategic – giving Pakistan access to previously inaccessible frontier regions and consolidating Sino–Pakistani control over territory that India claims as its own (Small 2015).

Although the Karakoram Highway today maintains this role as strategic – and indeed, symbolic – infrastructure, rhetoric on both sides of the border has in recent years focused on its potential economic role as a trade corridor. The CPEC and the OBOR initiative, in this regard, represent China's attempt to develop its border regions, enhance cross-border trade, and reaffirm its commitment to a strategic ally such as Pakistan. The – purposely provocative – argument with which I aim to conclude this chapter, is that Economic Corridor and One Belt, One Road fantasies might accomplish yet another goal: to do away with proximity. In other words, the quest for a frictionless corridor that brings the centres closer together undermines the relevance of proximity in remote border areas such as southern Xinjiang and Northern Pakistan. Proximity, as I have shown, takes advantage of a certain kind of friction and illegibility. Without it, larger companies with significant economic power can easily take over the bulk of trans-Karakoram trade, leaving little room for local forms of exchanges. The risk, then, to use Pedersen and Bunkenborg's (2012) expression, is that China's new strategy for infrastructure development in the borderlands will become a new, larger, 'technology of distantiation', curbing the quality and quantities of interactions between local actors.

To what extent the 'end of proximity' is part of China's plan remains open for discussion. What is certain is that proximity, entailing both intimate cross-border relations and a certain kind of illegibility for non-local actors, can be seen as threatening for central authorities, particularly in an area that generates all sorts of geopolitical and security anxieties. Therefore, the 'Silk Road' to which Chinese rhetoric often refers, as I mentioned in the opening paragraph of this chapter, is not the Silk Road of proximity. It is not, in other words, made of local contexts, intimate knowledge, and long-term relations. It rather represents an ontogenetic concept: something that produces an imaginary of frictionless global connections that does not exist, never existed, and probably will never exist – at least in this form.

Acknowledgements

Research for this chapter was conducted as part of my doctoral fieldwork and written with the generous support of the European Research Council (Starting Grant 637764, Highland Connections). I would like to thank my PhD supervisors Tanya Argounova-Low, Martin Mills, and Andrea Teti for their help throughout my doctoral studies, as well as Martin Saxer, Christine Bonnin, and Alexander Horstmann for their insightful comments on various versions of this chapter.

Notes

1 'China-Pakistan logistics complex breaks ground in Xinjiang', Xinhua, 1 April 2016. Available at: http://news.xinhuanet.com/english/2016-04/01/c_135243654.htm. [Accessed May 2016].
2 Research for this chapter was mostly carried out over a 12-month period between 2012 and 2013, in multiple locations along the Karakoram Highway in both China and Pakistan. Ethnographic methods such as participant observation and semi-structured interviews with various actors engaged in cross-border trade were employed throughout the research.
3 I am particularly grateful to Dr Shinmen Yasushi for his help in shedding light on the history of the Kapiao.
4 Such scholarships are quite common in China today. In 2012, at the time of my first meeting with Salman, over 20 Uyghurs from overseas communities in South Asia, Central Asia, and Turkey were studying in Beijing.
5 Interview, October 2012.
6 The 'Border Pass' is a document which allows residents of Gilgit-Baltistan to visit Xinjiang – only through the Khunjerab Pass – without having to apply for a visa. The Border Pass is valid for one year, it is not expensive (1500 Rupees, about US$14) or difficult to obtain, and it allows multiple visits for a maximum stay of one month each time. This kind of permit is not exceptional to the China–Pakistan area, but it can be found in other contexts along China's borders (Schoenberger and Turner 2008; Shneiderman 2013).

7 'Trade Snag: Traders and private transporters blocked KKH, traffic remain suspended for many hours at Sost', Sost Today, 31 October 2014. Available at: http://sosttoday.com/trade-snag-traders-and-private-transporters-blocked-kkh-trafic-remain-suspend-form-many-hours-at-sost/#.WdOZlK-2B2Rs. [Accessed October 2017].

References

Dillon, M. 2004. Xinjiang: China's Muslim Far Northwest. London and New York: Routledge.
Forbes, A. D. W. 1986. Warlords and Muslims in Chinese Central Asia: A Political History of Republican Sinkiang, 1911–1949. New York: Cambridge University Press.
Harris, T. 2017. The Mobile and the Material in the Himalayan Borderlands. In Saxer, M., and Zhang, J. (eds). The Art of Neighbouring: Making Relations Across China's Borders. Amsterdam: Amsterdam University Press, 145–163.
Hussain, S. 2015. Remoteness and Modernity: Transformation and Continuity in Northern Pakistan. New Haven, CT and London: Yale University Press.
Ispahani, M. Z. 1989. Roads and Rivals: The Politics of Access in the Borderlands of Asia. London: I.B. Tauris & Co.
Kreutzmann, H. 1991. The Karakoram Highway: The Impact of Road Construction on Mountain Societies. Modern Asian Studies 2(4): 711–736.
Kreutzmann, H. 1998. The Chitral Triangle: Rise and Decline of Trans-montane Central Asian Trade, 1895–1935. Asien Afrika Lateinamerika 26: 289–327.
Kreutzmann, H. 2009. The Karakoram Highway as a Prime Exchange Corridor between Pakistan and China. In Kreutzmann, H., Amin Beg, G., Lu, Z., and Richter, J. (eds). Proceedings of the Regional Workshop Integrated Tourism Concepts to Contribute to Sustainable Development in Mountain Regions Gilgit/Pakistan-Kashgar/P.R.China, October 8–14, 2008. Bonn: InWEnt.
Kreutzmann, H. 2013. The Significance of Geopolitical Issues for Internal Development and Intervention in Mountainous Areas of Crossroads Asia. Crossroads Asia Working Paper Series, No. 7.
Lamb, A. 1991. Kashmir. A Disputed Legacy 1846–1990. Hertingfordbury: Roxford Books (reprint: Karachi: Oxford University Press, 1992).
Pedersen, M., and M. Bunkenborg. 2012. Roads that Separate: Sino-Mongolian Relations in the Inner Asian Desert. Mobilities 7(4): 555–569.
Rahman, A. 2005. Sinicization Beyond the Great Wall: China's Xinjiang Uighur Autonomous Region. Leicester: Matador.
Rippa, A. 2014. From Uyghurs to Kashgaris (and Back?): Migration and Cross- border Interactions between Xinjiang and Pakistan. Crossroads Asia Working Paper Series, No. 23.
Rizvi, J. 1996. Ladakh: Crossroads of High Asia. Oxford: Oxford University Press.
Rizvi, J. 1999. Trans-Himalayan Caravans: Merchant Princes and Peasant Traders in Ladakh. Oxford: Oxford University Press.
Saxer, M. 2017. New Roads, Old Trades: Neighbouring China in North-Western Nepal. In Saxer, M., and Zhang, J. (eds). The Art of Neighbouring: Making Relations Across China's Borders. Amsterdam: Amsterdam University Press, 73–92.
Schoenberger, L., and S. Turner. 2008. Negotiating Remote Borderland Access: Small-Scale Trade on the Vietnam-China Border. Development and Change 39(4): 667–696.
Scott, J. 1998. Seeing Like a State: How Certain Schemes to Improve the Human Condition Have Failed. New Haven, CT: Yale University Press.
Scott, J. 2009. The Art of Not Being Governed: An Anarchist History of Upland Southeast Asia. New Haven, CT: Yale University Press.
Shneiderman, S. 2013. Himalayan Border Citizen: Sovereignity and Mobility in the Nepal-Tibet Autonomous Region (TAR) of China Border Zone. Political Geography 35: 25–36.
Small, A. 2015. The China-Pakistan Axis: Asia's New Geopolitics. London: Hurst & Company.
Sökefeld, M. 2012. The Attabad-Landslide and the Politics of Disaster in Gojal, Gilgit-Baltistan. In Luig, U. (ed.). Negotiating Disasters: Politics, Representation, Meanings. Frankfurt: Peter Lang, 175–204.
Stellrecht, I. 1997. Dynamics of Highland-Lowland Interaction in Northern Pakistan since the 19th Century. In Stellrecht, I., and Winiger, M. (eds). Perspectives on History and Change in the Karakoram, Hindukush, and Himalaya. Köln: Köppe, 3–22.

Stellrecht, I. 1998. Trade and Politics: The High Mountain Region of Pakistan in the 19th and 20th Century. In Stellrecht, I., and Bohle, H. (eds). Transformation of Social and Economic Relationships in Northern Pakistan. Köln: Köppe, 5–92.

Thampi, M. 2010. Indian Traders in Xinjiang in the Nineteenth and Twentieth Centuries. China Report 46(4): 371–385.

Tsing, A. 2005. Friction: An Ethnography of Global Connection. Princeton, NJ: Princeton University Press.

Wang, Y. 2007. Xinjiang Lishi Huobi [Historical Money of Xinjiang]. Beijing: Zhonghua Shuju.

Warikoo, K. 1996. Trade Relations between Central Asia and Kashmir Himalayas during the Dogra Period (1846–1947). Cahiers D'Asie centrale 1(2): 113–124.

Yu, S. 1987. The governorship of Yang Zengxin in Xinjiang, 1912–28. University of Hong-Kong: Unpublished MPhil Thesis.

Zhang, J., and M. Saxer. 2017. Neighbouring in the Borderworlds along China's Frontiers. In Saxer, M., and Zhang, J. (eds). The Art of Neighbouring: Making Relations Across China's Borders. Amsterdam: Amsterdam University Press, 11–29.

9
Making place within a geopolitical frontier
Mae Aw (Ban Rak Thai)

Carl Grundy-Warr, Jessica Teo, and Wei Jun Chin[1]

Introduction: a border piece within a larger geopolitical jigsaw

Our contribution focuses on a tiny sliver of the Thailand–Myanmar borderland, part of the northern border of Mae Hong Son Province with southwestern Shan State. We focus on a border village called Ban Rak Thai (บ้านรักไทย), literally 'Thai-Loving Village', located in Mae Hong Son, Thailand (Map 9.1). Formerly the village was named Mae Aw (แม่ออ in Thai or 密窝村, *m Thai* in Chinese) and its history and origins lie largely as a strategic borderland cross-point for its mostly Chinese Kuomingtang (KMT), Shan, Pa-O, and Wa residents. The village has a quasi-formal border crossing with a Shan, Pa-O, and Wa enclave on the Myanmar side of the border, in southern Shan State, called Kong Mung Mong. This border area is historically part of a geopolitical frontier known as 'the Golden Triangle' (covering parts of southwest China's Yunnan province; northeast Myanmar; northwest Laos; and northern Thailand). 'Golden' derives from the prime currency in the upland borderlands from poppy cultivation and a lively transnational opium and heroin trade, which helped to finance both ethno-nationalist and Cold War battles (Lintner 1991). Thus, the Mae Aw-Kong Mung Mong borderland is one piece in a very complex cross-border geopolitical jigsaw, particularly as it relates to the political territoriality of a remnant KMT army originally from Yunnan Province in China, and now spread across northeastern Myanmar and into northern Thailand (Chang 2014; Hung and Baird 2017), and territorial-ethnic politics relating to the Shan, Wa, and Pa-O in relation to the Myanmar geo-body.

What may ethnographic and political geographic research uncover from a microcosm of a bigger borderland and historical frontier? Our research is based upon periodic ethnographic research involving frequent stays in the village, enhanced by observations, interviews in Mandarin and in Thai, with the help of local translation when other languages are more dominant.[2] In this chapter we wish to focus on three dimensions. First, we draw upon personal imaginaries of the place as part of a hotly contested Cold War battlefield. Second, we wish to examine how geopolitical migrants and soldiers have developed a sense of place and belonging at the rough permeable edges of the Thai, 'Shan', and Myanmar geo-bodies. In the last two decades, commercial tea production, orchards, and cultural tourism have helped to transform the political

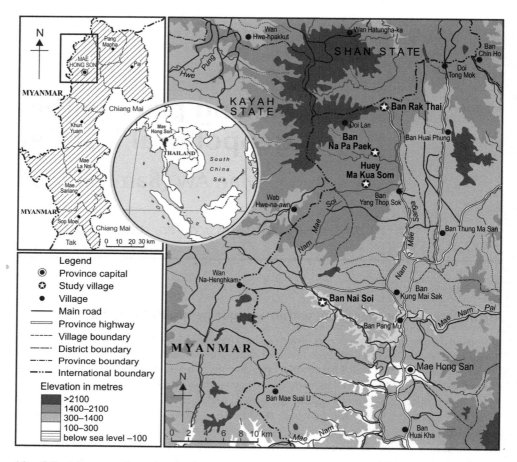

Map 9.1 Map revealing places where we carried out research in the borderland. The focus of this chapter is on Ban Rak Thai near the northern borderland of Mae Hong Son, Thailand with Shan State in Myanmar

economic space and attachments to this borderland. Finally, we wish to argue that for many borderland residents, their cultural identities are shaped as much by intercultural and interethnic interaction over time as by issues of 'national belonging' and a sense of being part of a single national territory. Borderlands attachments are part of a sense of self and community, as much, if not more than past or present nationalist sentiments.

Fixed territories, cross-border mobility, and ethnic identity

Pre-boundary frontiers, Keyes (1987: 20) observes, were 'constantly shifted in accord with the relative strengths' of local overlords in relations with larger polities, but the imposition of colonial 'territorial boundaries deprived local tribal chiefs of any role in determining relationships on the frontiers'. In so doing, the boundaries of territorial sovereignty bisected previously more fluid contact zones and made border crossings increasingly subject to central state interference, surveillance and control, albeit with rather patchy application across difficult terrain and complex human landscapes. Inter-territorial state relations between major polities became complicated by pockets of de facto geopolitical control by non-state entities and would be nations-of-intent. Even so, the powerful territorialised 'grid of the modern mind' (Winichakul 1994: 96) changed the political landscape for those indigenous polities and peoples of the frontier, whose voices were submerged by 'the major nations'. As Ludden (2003: 1064) critically observed:

> Modernity cast a harsh eye on mobile forms of social life in all of its mapped constituencies, from the micro-domain of the village to the macro-domain of the national state. Territorialism became a cultural passion. Being a native insider became the only firm basis for social status in each mapped territory. A mobile past became a cultural liability that faded from memory for people who sank roots in native places, where being alien became more perilous as societies attached themselves more firmly to modern maps.

Thus, static boundaries became instruments for cultural ordering, as well as a territorial rationale for bordering and re-ordering people in accordance with 'national graphics'. Thus there was a tendency for indigenous spaces to be buried 'inside national territory under symbols of orderly geography' (Ludden 2003: 1064). However, we view territories as geopolitically contingent, socially malleable, and permeable entities, which have never really entirely produced an orderly national geographic, especially in zones of intense inter- and intra-cultural mingling such as the highland borderland of northern Mae Hong Son and southern Shan State.

The case outlined in this chapter fits with border scholarship that has opened up research into multiple social identities, histories, and cultural lives that are in fact active agents in forging places and making border-landscapes over time (cf. Horstmann 2002; Gellner 2013; Turner et al. 2015). Borders may be sites for spatial socialisation practices in relation to national territory (Paasi 1996), but they are also sites of active place-making by non-state agents and actors. By focusing on the 'grassroots negotiation of modernity' rather than on state-centred national imaginaries, we may raise interesting questions about differing experiences, perceptions, and imaginations of national belonging, as well as issues of 'suspended' and 'flexible citizenship' (Marston 2014). It is imperative to consider how different people experience and negotiate border space. Such 'grassroots negotiation' relates to countless personal socio-spatial narratives and experiences, for 'borders look different depending on who you are, and crucially, where you come from' (Delaplace 2012: 12). Historically informed ethnographic political geography (Megoran 2006) may help to reveal how borderland social identities are 'shaped by continual negotiations across the nationalist divide' (van Schendel et al. 2000: 299) and also help to 'de-centre' perceived 'margins' (Horstmann and Wadley 2006). Furthermore, a focus on indigenous and personalised border histories means that borders cease to be purely 'national' geo-bodies, for there are often coalescing and overlapping histories of border space as opposed to a singular dominant national 'geo-body' narrative. As Winichakul (2003: 11) puts it: 'we should explore all the extremities where the domain of national history ends and another history begins'. Indeed, local indigenous polities, communities, and individuals may be very active agents in transforming border spaces (Turner et al. 2015) through their abilities to 'manoeuvre between border-as-margin and border-as-connecting line' (Sturgeon 2005: 25). The following account focuses on people who migrated to Ban Rak Thai, particularly former KMT soldiers and their families, but their experiences first need to be placed within the broader geopolitics of the 'Golden Triangle' during the Cold War and its aftermath.

A Cold War frontier and disorderly geopolitical space

During the early 1950s when Communist forces were driving the Chinese Nationalist government to Taiwan, some of the nationalist anti-Communist KMT forces viewed Burma (Myanmar) as a 'back door' for escape from Yunnan and as a base to launch cross-border attacks on the Red Army of China (Chang 2002). Shan historian, Sai Aung Tun (2009: 304) expressed this as an alien 'incursion' into 'Shanland', transforming it into 'a theatre of war' subject to the machinations of bigger powers, such as China, the USA, smaller powers and neighbouring states.

> No prohibition, no supervision, no restrictions, and no immigration laws existed to prevent the illegal immigrants brought along with the Kuomintang. Many Yunnan migrants who did not wish to live under the Communist regime slipped through many points along the border into the Shan States without any difficulty.
>
> *(Sai Aung Tun 2009: 312)*

As opium was the most lucrative commodity of the Golden Triangle, the KMT coerced local hill farmers to grow more poppy crops in order to fuel the transborder trade to purchase more arms and support troops. Distant support for the KMT from the Nationalist government of Taiwan plus 'clandestine CIA operations' meant that the KMT received arms, ammunition, and military equipment, often through Thailand's borders (Lintner and Black 2009: 52). This secret war served Cold War geopolitical imaginaries as the KMT forces were viewed as a thorn in the side of the Communist Party of Burma (CPB), in addition to competing for resources and territory with various Shan nationalist and ethno-military forces in northern Burma (Myanmar).

Over time, the KMT force began to merge into the cultural tapestry of the mountain frontier zone as they employed local ethnic militia, married local women, and brought family members from Yunnan into Shan territory (Chang 2014: 55). Initially, KMT forces were focused heavily along the Burma (Myanmar)–Shan border as well as along key trade routes well inside Shan territory. Cross-mountain tracks and trails were well known to Yunnanese traders who traversed the frontier well before, during, and after the imposition of modern political geography, and the KMT soldiers became just one, albeit a very politicised element, in a rich history of cross-frontier traffic and mobility linking distant trading places of southwest China, South Asia, and Southeast Asia.

Following international pressure from the United Nations in 1961, many KMT soldiers went to Taiwan, but the KMT did not totally desert the Golden Triangle. Two military elements, the Third Regiment (93rd Division) and Fifth Regiment (95th Division) remained as remnant KMT forces in northern Burma (Myanmar). Eventually, Thailand, concerned about possible CPB links with communists in Thailand, welcomed the KMT forces, led by Generals Li Wen-huan (李文煥) leader of the Third and Duan Xiwen (段希文) leader of the Fifth respectively, to assist in protecting its borders, facilitate caravan trade, and prevent linkages between Thai and Burmese Communist groups (Chang 2002; Transnational Institute 2009). The KMT divisions spread their troops in scattered locations along the northern borders of Chiang Rai, Chiang Mai, and Mae Hong Son.

At the height of the Cold War, the Thai State seemed to use the KMT as 'a buffer and unofficial border police' (Lintner and Black 2009: 56), as they were ideologically acceptable and viewed as potentially 'loyal members' of a 'territorial power domain' straddling national geo-bodies (Lim 1984: 90). According to one personal narrative by a Yunnanese trader there was significant collusion between the Thai Border Patrol Police, traders, and the KMT involved in cross-border traffic:

> Several KMT villages were entry bases for Yunnanese caravan traders from Burma. Many traders would go to Mae Aw, Piang Luang, Arunotai, Xincun/Ban Mai Nongbour, or Mae Salong and pretend to be village residents so they could apply for a permit from the BPP [Border Patrol Police] to go to Chiang Mai or Chiang Rai to purchase Thai merchandise.
>
> *(Chang 2014: 167)*

Geopolitical 'traffic line' to multicultural border home

As a crossing point along the Thai–Myanmar border, Mae Aw was viewed as a geostrategic location by Wa, Shan, Pa-O, and KMT soldiers among others, especially for trade across rough highland terrain from southwest Shan State. Effectively Mae Aw became a crossing point for market goods, contraband, drugs, and weapons. According to Mr Jia Ta, a former KMT soldier in his late 40s, Mae Aw was known as 'the traffic line' (交通线 *jiāotōng xiàn*) where high amounts of taxes and trade tariffs could be collected. Thus, this was one piece of territory which was coveted by Khun Sa (张奇夫 Zhāng Qífū– the Chinese name of Khun Sa), who was at once a self-proclaimed Shan national leader of the Mong Tai Army and self-styled warlord overseeing a thriving cross-border trade in heroin and gemstones (Lintner 1991). One former KMT soldier in his mid-50s, Mr Liu recounts:

> That fateful fight, 30 years ago, I remember it was the 17th of the second month of the lunar calendar at around six in the morning. The KMT soldiers had hid guns outside [Mae Aw] which the [Thai] military did not seize. Khun Sa had an army of more than a thousand soldiers, while we only had 500 to 600 people. The Thais were incapable of fighting this battle so we stepped up to defend our land. We used guns like A60, M16, and cannons to surround them. More than 100 people died in battle but (on that day) we defeated Khun Sa and he retreated on the 20th.[3]

For military veterans, the space of Ban Rak Thai (formerly Mae Aw) is imbued with geopolitical meaning. Jia Ta has been living in the village for 33 years. He experienced fighting as a boy soldier and lived in the mountains of Shan State during his youth (Figure 9.1). Now he is the owner of a tea plantation, a small farm, buffalo herd, and a restaurant. As the second oldest child of the family, he decided that he would take on the family responsibility of joining the KMT army in place of his brothers when he was a boy. Between the ages of 11 and 15, Jia Ta travelled through the Shan mountains on the back of a mule, and later became an expert muleteer. Thus, he played a small part in the centuries' long tradition of mule caravans from Yunnan to upper mainland Southeast Asia (Chang 2006, 2014). He was one of many young Chinese soldiers who ventured 'into barbarous regions' (Chang 2009). He learnt how to use guns and cannons living and fighting in the Shan hills, and sometimes fought alongside Shan fighters when factions split and fought one another. Several KMT soldiers adopted the homemade 'stick and poke' tattoos of Shan words. Jia Ta beamed proudly as he discussed how these tattoos served for identification purposes and were also a symbol of strength and good luck for the soldiers. Like many soldiers in the village, Jia Ta speaks Mandarin with a Yunnan accent, fluent Shan, which was essential for his survival, and practical Thai, essential for his new life as a farmer, restaurant owner, and local businessman.

Jia Ta's life story reflects very well the transformation of borderland space from the Cold War and drug trading days into the more peaceful developmental space, particularly since the end of

Figure 9.1 Mr Jia Ta in KMT uniform with rifle taken from his tearoom display of KMT memorabilia
Photo by the authors (with kind permission of Mr Jia Ta)

the Cold War. The village has since become a zone of tea plantations, initially supported with Taiwanese aid, training, and technology, fruit orchards, and cultural tourism focusing on Chinese identity. This transformation of borderland space, in Mae Aw (renamed Ban Rak Thai in the early 2000s), and more so in larger KMT settlements in Chiang Mai and Chiang Rai provinces, was partly encouraged by the Thai State and Royal Thai Army in order to turn unruly spaces, former battlefields, and poppy cultivation zones into a more regular and legible border landscape with a settled population, including many former KMT soldiers granted Thai identity and parcels of land (Hung and Baird 2017).

Before living in Mae Aw, many KMT soldiers agreed they were deemed 'placeless', living a life of impermanence, with little sense of having deep roots in any particular place. While the initial KMT muleteer contacts with Mae Aw were primarily as a way station for cross-border traffic, it eventually became a more permanent site for the soldiers as the Thai authorities and Royal Thai Army recognised these soldiers were useful in 'proxy' battles against potential security threats. Winichakul (1994: 169) states that 'communism … is simply Enemy Number One of Thainess and thus external to Thainess'. Thus, the KMT soldiers who protected Thai borders from perceived communist infiltration and other perceived security threats provided a geopolitical sense of closeness helping to 'internalise' the Chinese KMT soldiers into the national geo-body. As they try to recall the past, it is clear that many of the KMT veterans have invested deep emotional attachments into former army camps across the border and into the site which eventually became a new home away from home for them and their families: Mae Aw. Geopolitical memories infuse lasting cultural associations through past sacrifices and battles where friends and comrades fought and died, and due to their eventual adoption of this strategic

Making place within a geopolitical frontier

Figure 9.2 Mr Jia Ta's border restaurant in Baan Rak Thai
Photo by the authors (with kind permission of Mr Jia Ta)

cross-place as home. Recalling the above-mentioned battle with Khun Sa's forces, ex-KMT soldier Li commented: 'We were not afraid that *Zhang Qifu* had twice as many soldiers, for we were brave in battle.'[4] These stories exemplify a geopolitical 'sense of place' (Relph 1976; Shamai 1991), reflecting their knowledge of, belonging to, and defensiveness towards not just Mae Aw, but the strategic territory that straddles the international boundary. There used to be a KMT military camp based just outside Mae Aw, formally inside Burma (Myanmar), but in a piece of land that has long been a sort of no-state-land enclave, and is currently a base for the Shan State Army – South (SSA-S).

Mae Aw was a vital border crossing for Shan, Wa, and Pa-O migrants facing military confrontation inside southern Shan State. For instance, it was a cross-border getaway for Pa-O soldiers and their families when Khun Sa overran a Pa-O National Organisation base on the other side of the border (Christensen and Sann Kyaw 2006: 55). For five decades of Myanmar's/Burma's modern history there were numerous forcible relocations caused by warfare between the *Tatmadaw* (Burma Army) and 'insurgent' ethnic armies, as well as territorial and resource rivalries between warlords and factional in-fighting (Smith 1999). Nevertheless, the history of border space is also one of intercommunal cooperation and resettlement irrespective of official territorial arrangements, and Mae Aw was often a vital cross-border refuge for different groups – Wa, Pa-O, Shan, and KMT, among others.

Place-making began at Mae Aw shortly after the Thai authorities allowed them the space to resettle. Figure 9.2 illustrates a local KMT restaurant that commemorates the KMT history in Ban Rak Thai. This idea of place-making necessarily implicates what Penrose (2002: 279) terms as the 'latent emotional power of space' transforming a node of a 'traffic line' into a border 'home'.

Migdal (2004: 7) asserts that 'boundaries are constructed and maintained by people's mental maps' which incorporate 'the loyalties they hold, the emotions and passions that groupings evoke and their cognitive ideas about how territory is constructed'. However, spatial socialisation that comes from residence in a new place has resulted in the first-generation KMT villagers developing secondary national attachments to Thailand in spite of maintaining a strong notion of an original 'homeland' in Yunnan. As one long-time resident elaborated, 'The Thai government has offered us with a place to stay and land to settle in. We are grateful for the place provided. Now, we are considered as Thai citizens and we want to live a normal life',[5] albeit one that is simultaneously embedded within cross-border relations and shared histories of a geopolitical frontier. Sometimes, the ex-soldiers identify themselves as Thais, having once defended the 'border' and are now gratefully living in the country, as former soldier 'Li' said: '我们是老百姓，是泰国人' (wǒmén shì lǎobǎixìng, shì tàiguó rén; 'we are commoners, we are Thais').[6] Hall (1995: 183) suggests that 'cultures work like languages. They cannot be fixed, but shift and change historically.' From this perspective, cross-border migration and borderland residence has lessened attachments to Yunnan over time, while helping to produce hybrid borderland–national identity that recognises the security of residence within the Thai geo-body.

Growing attachments to the Thai geo-body does not mean they lessen their wish to bolster Chinese culture. Within each Chinese household in the village, Mandarin, spoken in the Yunnan dialect, is the dominant language. Interviews with several parents revealed the importance of mother tongue in communication with their children:

> '要保存语言和文化，要懂得讲自己的话，不然是野人' (yào bǎocún yǔyán hé wénhuà, yào dǒng de jiǎng zìjǐ de huà, bùrán shì yěrén; 'we have to preserve language and culture, [we] have to know how to speak in our own language, if not we would be uncouth').
>
> (Jia Ta, ex-KMT soldier[7])

> '自己的文字不可以忘记，要遗传下去的' (zìjǐ de wénzì bù kěyǐ wàngjì, yào yì chuán xia qù de; 'one cannot forget one's own language and literature, [we] have to pass them on').
>
> (Fang, second generation Thai Chinese, female tea shop owner[8])

The younger generation has a greater sense of familiarity with their Thai identity and this is a cause of cultural anxiety for parents who hold onto their Yunnan cultural roots. Jia Ta jokes that his daughters have forgotten how to write their own Chinese names because they find it difficult to learn Mandarin given their lengthy exposure to Thai language and culture in high school. Therefore, some parents send their children for Mandarin tuition classes in Qinghua Primary School. Mr Luo, a 46-year-old Mandarin language teacher in the school, claims that should his children speak to him in Thai or any other language at home, he would not respond to them. He recognises that their proficiency in Mandarin can only improve through habit. Chinese language channels on local TV enable parents to engage their children in programmes at home to encourage them to speak more Chinese. So while the 'Thai-Loving Village' (the name of Ban Rak Thai) is increasingly embedded in the national geo-body, there are quiet everyday acts to preserve ethnic culture and language. Even so, out-migration for education and jobs is strengthening the use of Thai among the younger generation.

It seems that among the younger generation of Ban Rak Thai there has been a notable shift in terms of the way in which personal identification with a Chinese identity is made. One of the KMT veteran's daughters, 'Juying' expressed that she was mostly ignorant of and unable to feel a connection with the KMT history, in spite of her father's passionate recollections of being a soldier in the borderlands. However, if given the opportunity, she would like to continue learning Mandarin as it links her to her Chinese heritage and is a useful skill for her future. Similarly, discussions with children from the local schools (Thai and Chinese), reveal that the use of mother tongue languages (especially Mandarin and Shan) in home spaces is common, despite a lack of in-depth knowledge of their family's cultural roots. This suggests that the mixed cultural composition of Ban Rak Thai means that most residents are still able to use different languages for practical purposes even though deeper historical cross-border linkages and geopolitical roots are weakening.

Another vitally relevant aspect of Ban Rak Thai's identity is that it continues to be a cross-border home for non-Chinese residents, including people who were previously geopolitical refugees. Most recent migrants came over to Thailand in search of economic opportunities or to stay with kith and kin who had already migrated. One of our respondents, a woman in her early 20s, Lao, is one of them. Identifying herself as of Shan ethnicity, she recounted her story with a shy smile:

> I was travelling from Burma to find a job. I tried searching for work in Burma and China but I could not find any. In Namong (Shan state), I lost my way, but luckily I met Ahxiang, who was visiting friends and relatives. She took me in and brought me to work on her tea plantations and farms here. She helped me to apply for the hill tribe ID card, which allows me to work and live in Thailand for 10 years. Not long after I started working in Thailand, I met my husband and he works in the city now. So I spend most of my time looking after my son and plucking tea leaves for a living.[9]

KMT soldiers were exposed and accustomed to the Shan culture and language, and some of these soldiers were not ethnically Chinese. Mr Ga, a Wa man in his 50s and former KMT-fighter, for example, likes to listen to the Shan radio every day, with his good friend, Mr Li, another Wa and former soldier in his 70s (Figure 9.3), who visits him frequently. They have conversations reminiscing about their past in a mixture of Shan, Yunnan Chinese, and Thai languages, which are used interchangeably and sometimes include bi- and tri-lingual sentences. Younger border residents also can converse across languages, sometimes mixing Chinese, Shan, and Thai. As there is no high school in the village, and almost all students leave for the provincial capital for higher grade study in Thai language, there is concern among the Chinese people in particular that Thai traits will eventually dominate over Chinese ones as younger people move away for educational advancement and eventually migrate for job opportunities in faraway cities.

Regular cross-border mobility also defines the borderland. Daily, there are movements of migrant workers who commute across the border on motorbikes via a muddy track to go for work in tea plantations, orchards, and hillside farms around Ban Rak Thai. The two sides of the border are effectively a complementary economic zone for one side needs labour and the other side has people in need of jobs. Indeed, given the difficult mountain terrain and poor roads on the Myanmar side of the border, the Shan, Pa-O, and Wa enclave of Kong Mung Mong seems closer economically to the Thai side than it is to the geo-body of Myanmar.

Since the Cold War era, the enclave has been a de facto base for several ethnic armies, including the Shan State Army – South (Figure 9.4). In fact, there have been many historical connections between the two sides of the border. KMT soldiers remember a camp they established there a couple of decades ago and they have many old friends, including some former foes, who now live in Kong Mung Mong. The Royal Thai Army used to collaborate with the KMT to

Figure 9.3 Li shares with us a photo of him dressed in his KMT uniform which he still keeps as a remembrance of his soldiering days

Photo by the authors

Figure 9.4 Entry point into the Shan border village near Ban Rak Thai

Photo by the authors

Making place within a geopolitical frontier

bring goods and contraband across the border, and there is a history of long-term communications between the Thai Army and Shan State Army. Kong Mung Mong is a semi-autonomous de facto enclave where several armies coexist with their families, each with their own 'national' insignia, emblems and symbols, although the longer term economic viability of this border place will depend as much on future relations with the rest of Myanmar as well as continued cross-border ties with the Thai side.

On both sides of the border, cross-cultural marriages are common. Thus, many children have learnt how to speak in different languages even before they start school. One of our respondents called Lao shared her family's multilingual background and how her four-year-old son 'Gao'[10] was already capable of speaking bits of various languages quite well. Even so, Lao admitted that learning standard Thai had been challenging since migrating across the border to work and reside in Ban Rak Thai. The mixed ethnic heritage of this family incorporates six languages, which is indicative of the intercultural connections that are common within this borderland, as well as the family history of migrating from place to place within the borderland. Cultural coexistence and proximity helps to shape place identity and a unique sense of togetherness within a foreign land dominated by a distinct national language (Thai) from one's mother tongue. Lao's family language tree (Figure 9.5) represents in microcosm the complexity of vernacular mobility, linguistic, and ethnic geography within and across border space. The geo-body at the Mae Hong Son margins is a highly differentiated and layered landscape due to various personal and group histories of movement and cross-border connections. Residents and migrants are 'capable of drawing on different maps of meaning, and of locating themselves in different imaginary

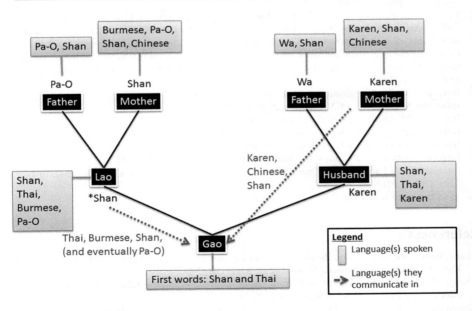

Figure 9.5 Based on interviews with one female migrant who is now a resident of Ban Rak Thai
Source: Authors

geographies at one and the same time' (Hall 1995: 207). Chinese, Wa, Pa-O, and Shan (among other) migrants have contributed their own imaginaries to the multi-layered meanings of borderland and place at Ban Rak Thai.

Mobility 'in' a borderland place

Ban Rak Thai is at once an intercultural and Chinese–Thai place, but the place's future continues to be defined by human mobility and migration, both within and across the international border. Many young people leave for high school or colleges in the provincial capital of Mae Hong Son or move to the city of Chiang Mai, and eventually they end up working within the larger Thai economy making only occasional visits home. In this sense, cross-border migration defines the past and will continue to shape the political economic landscape, but out-migration of persons of working age is likely to dilute the distinctiveness of this bit of not-so-Thai geo-body space. Everyday cross-border labour migration is another essential element of making this border space. Borderlands are shaped and reshaped by human interactions and movements over time, producing different ethnographic layers to notions of national geo-bodies on each side of the international boundary. Ban Rak Thai's residents and those living in the neighbouring Shan enclave have been active agents in creating a cultural landscape replete with layers of geopolitical iconography and personal histories that are indelibly tied to transgressing borders and forging new de facto homes within the borderland.

Notes

1 Carl Grundy-Warr teaches Geopolitics, Political Geography and Field Studies at the Department of Geography, National University of Singapore (NUS). Jessica Teo and Wei Jun Chin both undertook field research in Ban Rak Thai and helped to coordinate the NUS Field Studies module in northern Thailand in previous years.
2 In effect, the research for this chapter relates to different projects, by Carl Grundy-Warr during the early 2000s until today; by Wei Jun Chin in 2010–11; and by Jessica Teo in 2013–14; and enhanced by subsequent visits in 2015 and 2016. All the interviews were carried out in Chinese or Thai language, except for those in Shan and Wa where local translation support was available owing to the fact that most of the borderland inhabitants were able to speak at least two or more local languages in addition to Chinese or Thai.
3 Interview, Mr Liu Xueguang, Ban Rak Thai, 20 July 2013.
4 Interview, Mr Li, former KMT soldier, 25 June 2014.
5 Interview, Mr Lu Jinzhi, Ban Rak Thai, 22 July 2013.
6 Interview, Mr Li, former KMT soldier, 25 June 2014.
7 Interview, Mr Huang Jia Ta, Ban Rak Thai, 26 June 2014.
8 Interview with Fang, a Chinese tea shop owner, Ban Rak Thai, 17 July 2013.
9 Interview with Lao, a migrant from Shan State, Myanmar, working on a tea plantation in Ban Rak Thai, 19 July 2013.
10 'Gao' is a given nickname.

References

Chang, Wen-Chin (2002) 'Identification of leadership among the KMT Yunnanese Chinese in Northern Thailand', Journal of Southeast Asian Studies, 33, 1: 123–146.
Chang, Wen-Chin (2006) 'Home away from home: Migrant Yunnanese Chinese in northern Thailand', International Journal of Asian Studies, 3, 1: 49–76.
Chang, Wen-Chin (2009) 'Venturing into "barbarous" regions: Transborder trade among migrant Yunnanses between Thailand and Burma, 1960–1980s', The Journal of Asian Studies, 68, 2: 543–572.
Chang, Wen-Chin (2014) Beyond Borders. Stories of Yunnanese Chinese Migrants of Burma, Ithaca, NY: Cornell University Press.

Christensen, R. and Sann Kyaw (2006) The Pa-O. Rebels and Refugees, Chiang Mai: Silkworm Books.
Delaplace, G. (2012) 'A slightly complicated door: The ethnography and conceptualization of North Asian borders', in Frank Billé, Grégory Delaplace and Caroline Humphrey (editors) Frontier Encounters. Knowledge and Practice at the Russian, Chinese and Mongolian Border, Cambridge: Open Book Publishers, 1–19.
Gellner, D.N. (editor) (2013) Borderland Lives in Northern South Asia, Durham, NC and London: Duke University Press, 214–244.
Hall, S. (1995) 'New cultures for old', in D. Massey and P. Jess (editors) A Place in the World?, Oxford: Oxford University Press, 176–213.
Horstmann, A. (2002) Class. Culture and Space. The Constriction and Shaping of Communal Space in Southern Thailand, Tokyo: Springer-Verlag.
Horstmann, A., and Wadley, R.L. (editors) (2006) Centering the Margin. Agency and Narrative in Southeast Asian Borderlands, New York and Oxford: Berghanh Books.
Hung, P.-Y., and Baird, I.G. (2017) 'From soldiers to farmers: The political geography of the Chinese Kuomintang territorialisation in northern Thailand', Political Geography, 58: 1–13.
Keyes, C. (1987) 'Tribal peoples and the nation-state in mainland Southeast Asia', in Cultural Survival Inc (editor) Southeast Asian Tribal Groups and Minorities: Prospects for the Eighties and Beyond. Proceedings of a conference co-sponsored by Cultural Survival, Inc., and the Department of Anthropology, Harvard University, Cambridge, MA: Cultural Survival, Inc., 19–26.
Lim, Joo-Jock (1984) Territorial Power Domains, Southwest Asia, and China. The Geo-Strategy of an Overarching Massif, Singapore: Institute of Southeast Asian Studies and the Strategic and Defense Studies Centre, Australian National University.
Lintner, B. (1991) 'Cross-border drug trade of the Golden Triangle (Southeast Asia)', Territory Briefing series, Durham: International Boundaries Research Unit (IBRU).
Lintner, B., and Black, M. (2009) Merchants of Maadness. The Metamphetamine Explosion in the Golden Triangle, Chiang Mai: Silkworm Books.
Ludden, D. (2003) 'Presidential Address: Maps in the mind and the mobility of Asia', The Journal of Asian Studies, 62, 4: 1057–1078.
Marston, J.A. (editor) (2014) Ethnicity, Borders and the Grassroots Interface with the State. Studies on Southeast Asia in Honor of Charles F. Keyes, Chiang Mai, Thailand: Silkworm Books.
Megoran, N. (2006) 'For ethnography in political geography: Experiencing and re-imagining Ferghana Valley boundary closures', Political Geography, 25: 622–640.
Migdal, J. (2004) Boundaries and Belonging. States and Societies in the Struggle to Shape Identities and Local Practices, Cambridge: Cambridge University Press.
Paasi, A. (1996) Territories, Boundaries and Consciousness: The Changing Geographies of the Finnish-Russian Border, Chichester and New York: J. Wiley & Sons.
Penrose, J. (2002) 'Nations, states and homelands: Territory and territoriality in nationalist thought', Nations and Nationalisms, 8, 3: 277–297.
Relph, E. (1976) Place and Placelessness, London: Pion.
Sai Aung Tun, U. (2009) History of the Shan State: From its Origins to 1962, Seattle: University of Washington Press.
Shamai, S. (1991) 'Sense of place: An empirical measurement', Geoforum, 22, 3: 347–358.
Smith, M. (1999) Burma. Insurgency and the Politics of Ethnicity, London and New York: Zed Books.
Sturgeon, J.C. (2005) Border Landscapes. The Politics of Akha Land Use in China and Thailand, Chiang Mai: Silkworm Books.
Transnational Institute (2009) Neither War Nor Peace: The Future of the Cease-Fire Agreements in Burma, available at: www.tni.org/en/publication/burma-neither-war-nor-peace, accessed November 2009.
Turner, S., Bonnin, C., and Michaud, J. (2015) Frontier Livelihoods. Hmong in the Sino-Vietnamese Borderlands, Seattle: University of Washington Press.
van Schendel, W., Mey, W., and Dewan, A.K. (2000) The Chittagong Hill Tracts. Living in a Borderland, Bangkok: White Lotus.
Winichakul, Thongchai (1994) Siam Mapped: A History of the Geo-body of a Nation, Chiang Mai: Silkworm Books.
Winichakul, Thongchai (2003) 'Writing at the interstices: Southeast Asian historians and postnational histories in Southeast Asia', in Abu Talib Ahmad and Tan Liok Ee (editors) New Terrains in Southeast Asian History, Singapore: Singapore University Press, 3–29.

10
Making connectivity work
Exploring cross-border livelihoods between Kazakhstan and China

Henryk Alff

Introduction

Few other sections of Almaty's wholesale and retail bazaar agglomeration ('Barakholka' or flea market, as it was called locally), under mounting threat of state-imposed closure, were as busy as the one trading shoes in bulk one May morning in 2014. Recently relocated to a more peripheral position from its formerly central base at the Ayan and Olzha bazaars, after these were hit by a massive fire disaster the year before, the shoe wholesale entrepreneurs were already busy stocking their warehouse containers with autumn and winter boots, 'Made in China', for the upcoming sales season and negotiating deals with customers from all over Kazakhstan. Intriguingly, Dungans provided for a large part of the trade entrepreneurs in this branch of the bazaar, adding to its distinctive atmosphere. Along with Russian as the principal language of interethnic communication in Kazakhstan, Dungan and Chinese were constantly to be heard, be it in interpersonal conversations between traders or in rushed negotiations via mobile phone with their business partners in Urumqi, Beijing, or Guangzhou. Several months of prior research, between 2012 and 2014, suggested that few other trading groups at Almaty's Barakholka have been more proficient than the Dungans in doing large-scale wholesale business with Han Chinese as well as *hueitsu*[1] or *huizu* (as Dungans are generally referred to in the People's Republic of China (PRC)) partners in mainland China. In fact, many of my interlocutors at Almaty's bazaars and beyond, irrespective of their ethnic background and individual professional history, claimed that Dungan trade entrepreneurs were among the first in Kazakhstan to establish reliable, pragmatic, and long-standing business links to China before and shortly after the Soviet break-up.

The following contribution traces these translocal interconnections of the Dungans between Kazakhstan and China and the practices and sociospatial positioning they invoke. It explores ethnographically how and with what consequences Dungans in Kazakhstan have negotiated their social belonging (elsewhere conceptualized as 'translocal' (Alff forthcoming)), and affiliation with influential economic and political circles, both in Kazakhstan and in China, with the increasing permeability of the (former) Sino–Soviet border since the late 1980s. Through their activities, Dungan entrepreneurs gain from (and somewhat contribute to) fostering China's rapidly growing economic and political impact in Kazakhstan. The latter role of Dungans as 'gatekeepers' for Chinese companies especially does not go undisputed, even among many members of the group, as Chinese influence contributes to feelings of threat regarding their ethnic and social distinctiveness. It is argued here that many Dungans succeeded in gaining socioeconomically from changing border regimes between the PRC and Central Asia in the long run, thanks to their ability to position themselves flexibly vis-à-vis powerful economic and political circles. The present chapter thus gives an account of the opportunities, challenges, and renegotiation of social–cultural boundaries that come with the dynamics of border regimes. It also shows how the Dungans managed to situate themselves as influential brokers in the political arena, thereby making use of their sociospatial liminality between China and Central Asia. As will be discussed in greater detail below, this liminality evolves partly from the diasporic position that is imposed upon the Dungans by both the Kazakhstani and Chinese nation-building projects, but also from their self-representation as a group being produced by historical processes along the Silk Road.

Through its focus on the Dungan case, the current study sheds light on the social processes of emergent cross-border livelihoods between China and the Central Asian republics, which so far have been subject to rather limited research (Gladney 1996; Sadovskaya forthcoming) and addressed mostly Uyghur groups (see Roberts 2007; Dautcher 2009; Steenberg 2016). Furthermore, the chapter contributes more broadly to ethnographic scholarship on the interrelated negotiation of political borders and sociocultural boundaries (Donnan & Wilson 1999).

As part of a larger research project on the transformation of trade and exchange processes across the borderlands of Kazakhstan, Kyrgyzstan, and the PRC since 1991, the analysis is based on six months of multi-sited fieldwork in Almaty, Bishkek, and several Dungan-inhabited villages along the Kazakhstan–Kyrgyzstan border between April 2012 and May 2014. Semi-structured biographical interviews ($r=18$), more informal conversations and participant observation served as major means of research.

The following section provides brief historical and sociocultural background information on Kazakhstan's Dungans. The remainder of the contribution then deals in a more detailed way with their strategies and practices in establishing cross-border economic and political cooperation.

Sociocultural and historical background

Kazakhstan's Dungans, a group of Sinophone Muslims totalling about 56,000, predominantly live in a cluster of compact settlements in Zhambyl *oblast'* in the southeast of the country (Agenstvo po statistike 2012) and in a few suburban communities in Kazakhstan's largest city and commercial centre Almaty. They are also one of the largest minority groups in the Chuy and Issyk Köl *oblast'* of neighbouring Kyrgyzstan. Nonetheless, while Dungans in the Central Asian public (and in China, where they are subsumed under the ethnic category of *huizu*)[2] are widely considered to be a more or less coherent ethnic group, those originating from the Shaanxi and Gansu provinces of China speak distinct dialects of Mandarin[3] and often inhabit distinct settlements (Jimenez Tovar 2013). In Kyrgyzstan, those claiming their origins in Gansu province dominate among the 60,000 Dungans and form the intellectual elite.[4]

The Dungan communities in Zhambyl *oblast'* and in Almaty, where they form the dominant group in the former collective farm Zarya Vostoka ('Dawn of the East'), are almost exclusively descendants of refugees hailing from the Chinese province of Shaanxi. During the late 1870s they fled Qing China under the guidance of Muhammad Ayub Biyanhu, one of the military leaders of the Hui Revolts (Vansvanova 2000). Having escaped annihilation in the Qing Empire, Dungan refugee groups were settled by Tsarist authorities a few kilometres north of the garrison of Tokmak (Sushanlo 1967), now a regional centre across the border in Kyrgyzstan with a sizeable Shaanxi Dungan community (Jimenez Tovar 2016). Along the fertile valley of the Chu River, the Dungan refugees cultivated former pasture land and established irrigated farms, making use of their advanced agricultural skills and seeds they brought from China. On the basis of Dungan-dominated settlements in southwestern Kazakhstan, collective agricultural production units were formed in the early Soviet period. Some of them, like the collective farm 'Kommunisticheskiy' in Shortobe, were renowned for their high productivity in growing corn, potatoes, and garden vegetables throughout the Soviet period. Dungans were also involved in the distribution of agricultural products through formal and informal channels across Central Asia and Siberia as far north as Yakutsk and Norilsk.[5]

The dismantling of the Soviet Union and subsequent independence of the republics of Kazakhstan and Kyrgyzstan as sovereign states in 1991 brought about fundamental change to Kazakhstan's Dungan population. On the one hand, collective farming and the distribution of their products, the main source of employment and subsistence in the early 1990s, owing to the loss of state subsidies and the decreasing purchasing power of the population, showed transient signs of disintegration. On the other hand, Dungans were among the first rural dwellers in Kazakhstan to gain from the relaxation of travel and foreign trade regulations across the formerly closed Sino–Soviet border. Drawing on their ethnolinguistic (and religious) affiliation with *huizu* and Han-Chinese, Dungan community leaders from Shortobe, in the late 1980s and early 1990s, started to develop close interpersonal relations with partners across mainland China (Laruelle & Peyrouse 2012: 123) and even as far as Malaysia. Trans-Eurasian trade and transport, linking manufacturing centres in China's seaboard, Xinjiang, with post-Soviet states, offered an important source of income even for rural Dungan settlements. Furthermore, hundreds of Dungan students studied in universities in Xi'an, Lanzhou, and other cities of mainland China, partly receiving scholarships financed by the Chinese state.

The end of the Soviet Union, however, also brought about a religious revival and an exchange of ideas of Islam among the Dungan population of Kazakhstan. Dungans consider themselves pious Muslims and usually follow their religious obligations more strictly than Kazakhs. A great deal of attention is attributed among Dungans to the regular five-times daily prayer, travelling for 'hajj' at least once (but often even twice or to 'umroh')[6] in a lifetime, and renouncing the consumption of alcohol and tobacco.[7]

Islam plays an important role in the Dungans' self-identification and has certainly contributed to the solidarity and the expansion of *huizu*–Dungan business relations, as the strict pious Muslim self-definition among both Dungan and *huizu* has generated mutual trust and contributed to notions of honesty regarding each other.[8] The process of trust generation on the basis of Muslim piety is flanked by a general tightening of state control, particularly in China but also in Kazakhstan, over what could be perceived from a top-down perspective as expressions of religious extremism and the construction of suspicious religious networks. As this is obviously a highly sensitive topic, religious aspects of Dungan–*huizu* relations are not studied in greater detail in the present study. Consequently, religious affiliation will not be addressed more thoroughly in the following section on the Dungans' reconstruction of socioeconomic and cultural links.

(Re-)building ties to China

In the late Soviet era, Dungans were considered in Kazakhstani society as a compact ethnic group[9] of successful, efficient, and particularly hard-working agriculturalists (Hong 2005: 138). Collective farms in predominantly Dungan-populated rural settlements such as Dunganovka (on the outskirts of the city of Taraz) and the village cluster around Shortobe (in Korday *rayon* of Zhambyl *oblast'*) were in fact among those with the highest productivity in irrigated vegetable farming in the south of the Kazakh Soviet Socialist Republic. In-depth knowledge of and access to distribution networks, due to providing agricultural produce from collective farms to formal state structures and surplus production to informal farmers' markets in large cities in Soviet Central Asia and Siberia, were key to becoming one of the central groups in the private trade sector after the Soviet break-up.[10] When private wholesale and retail bazaars like the Dordoy Bazaar in Bishkek and the Barakholka agglomeration in Almaty replaced state-controlled provision schemes at the beginning of the 1990s, Dungan entrepreneurs, and first of all Husey Daurov, introduced below, actively facilitated this process in particular by strategically (re-)extending and building cultural and business ties to China.

In fact, before, in the 1970s, Dungans on Soviet Union territory had already lost any kinship links to China (Rimsky-Korsakoff Dyer 1978), owing to both a century of geographical separation and the strained political climate during the Sino–Soviet conflict. With the Sino–Soviet rapprochement since the mid-1980s, cross-border communication with and travel from the Soviet Union to China, however, became less restricted. Husey Daurov, a former history teacher in Shortobe's secondary school and then the secretary of Shortobe's collective farm 'Kommunisticheskiy', was the first to build up new ties with *hueitsu* and Han political and economic circles in China. Daurov thereby became the pioneer for the extensive interpersonal relations that link many of Kazakhstan's Dungans with China nowadays – as one of my interlocutors, a local businessman from Shortobe, stated:

> Husey Shimarovich [Daurov] has done a lot for the Dungans, in particular for those here in Shortobe. In fact, all of the people doing business with Chinese partners have received contacts and built their business through him. He is the moral authority of our people.[11]

In search of family links in China, Daurov, in the late 1980s, ventured to the village in Shaanxi province from where his ancestors claimed to hail. While he did indeed find distant kin, he also made contact with the local and regional *huizu* community, establishing initial ties for later fruitful cultural and socioeconomic cooperation. Based on Daurov's initial contacts, cultural and later economic exchange between Dungan communities in Shaanxi province and Central Asia, and especially in Kazakhstan, revived with increasing pace shortly before and after the Soviet break-up and with the subsequent increasing permeability of the (former) Sino–Soviet border. Daurov encouraged a more institutionalized form of exchange by founding and becoming the long-standing president of the Association of Kazakhstan's Dungans in the early 1990s, which became responsible for organizing the exchange of scholars specializing in Dungan/*huizu* culture and of Dungan students to Chinese universities (Laruelle & Peyrouse 2012). Since the 1990s, Daurov has also served as the central figure in mediating business ties between Dungan trade entrepreneurs in both Kazakhstan and Kyrgyzstan, and Han and *huizu* business circles across China. Many of the thriving Dungan-run wholesale trade and manufacturing businesses in Kazakhstan cooperating with Chinese partners nowadays originally came into being on Daurov's initiative and thanks to his increasingly extensive network of contacts in China. The following section draws attention to the dynamics these evolving socioeconomic and cultural relations had (and have) on the Dungans' socioeconomic activities between Kazakhstan and China.

Cross-border livelihoods

Medium- to large-scale agricultural production for the Kazakhstani and Russian markets on at least 13,000 hectares of long-term-leased land[12] still accounts for the better part of household income among many Dungan families in Kazakhstan. Since the 1990s, international trade, thanks to increasing cooperation with Chinese partners, however, has gained major importance even for the rural Dungan population. In up to 80 per cent of the Dungan households in Shortobe and Masanchi, one or more of its members are self-employed as trade entrepreneurs, importing consumer goods from China, or as shopkeepers (*realizatory* in Russian) on Almaty's Barakholka. One of my Dungan interlocutors at Bayzat Bazaar in Almaty noted that:

> [i]n some sections of Barakholka almost every shop is Dungan-owned, and all of them are selling imported household items from China. Even now, after Kazakhstan entered the Customs Union with Russia and Belarus, which led to rising customs duties, this is still a lucrative business. It's also still possible for Dungan youth to enter the China business market without providing founding capital, for example as shopkeepers for Dungan wholesalers.[13]

The first economic activities arising from connections between Dungan and *huizu*/Han entrepreneurs in the 1990s comprised the export of scrap metal and Soviet-era industrial installations from Kazakhstan and Kyrgyzstan to China. The highly profitable wholesale importation of Chinese-made consumer goods, such as textiles, shoes, and household items to the bazaars in Kazakhstan that started to flourish in the late 1990s, and the organization of transport schemes between coastal China, Kyrgyzstan, Kazakhstan, and Russia, facilitated the outflow of people from Dungan villages to Bishkek and Almaty. According to estimates made by Husey Daurov, at least 20 per cent of Dungan-run trade businesses in Kazakhstan nowadays turnover more than US$1 million each, some of them even tens of millions US$.[14] Smaller retail trade businesses mainly rely on supplies from a wholesale bazaar agglomeration in Urumqi known locally as *bingtuan*.[15] Those people running well-established wholesale trade businesses, however, travel directly to the manufacturing centres on China's eastern seaboard for supplies on a regular basis. Some of them, together in cooperation with their Han Chinese and *huizu* partners, have even founded manufacturing facilities for the production of textiles, furniture, and construction materials in neighbouring Kyrgyzstan, where workers, energy, and water are considerably cheaper than in Kazakhstan. Another professional niche filled by Dungans, particularly in Kyrgyzstan, is the one of shop assistants and interpreters for Han Chinese trade entrepreneurs (Zhaparov 2009).

A sense of solidarity and loyalty between Dungan and *huizu*, as well as Han Chinese business partners, based on ethnic, linguistic (and religious) affiliation, has contributed to a greater degree than with Kazakh, Kyrgyz, and Uyghur competitors in the evolving China trade business and resulted in the establishment of enduring, trustful, and often exclusive commercial and political alliances[16] (Laruelle & Peyrouse 2012). The trust inherent in Dungan–Chinese business relations will be illustrated in the example of Dungan businesses affected by the fire disasters that hit several bazaars at Almaty's Barakholka in September and again in November 2013 (Forbes 2014). During interviews at the newly opened shoe wholesale bazaar section, I met many traders, among them numerous Dungans, who had suffered loss of investment and goods worth several tens of thousands US$. While they complained bitterly about the fire, which most of them considered as having being caused by arson organized by influential circles within Kazakhstan's political elite, some, like the 52-year-old Dungan trader quoted below, did not lose hope regarding their future business opportunities:

> I started trading here in the mid-1990s, when Barakholka just got up on its feet. Since that time, I have gained and learnt a lot from doing business with the Chinese. Even last year, after I lost a large part of the goods I had ordered for the pre-New Year sales, due to the fire,

which brought me to the brink of bankruptcy, my suppliers in Guangzhou called me and asked if they could help me out.[17]

My interlocutor claimed that his Chinese business partners were well-informed about which sections of Barakholka had been affected by the fire and who suffered the heaviest material losses. Given his desperate situation, his long-standing business partners offered to send him substantial new supplies, in order to keep him in the business. He said:

> Like me, dozens of other neighbours and colleagues lost their only means of income. Bazaar trade here has been quite profitable for many years, and every one of us Dungans has at least one relative in the trading sector. Few of us saw this disaster coming, though. But apart from that, few of those that suffered from the criminal activities attempting to close our bazaars, were granted as much support as me.[18]

In fact, my interviewee did not claim his preferable treatment as being a direct outcome of being Dungan. He, like several other of my Dungan interlocutors, however, asserted that their ethnolinguistic and religious affiliation with both Han and *huizu* would at least contribute to more understanding and closeness in day-to-day business operations with his partners in China, often over many years. The following section seeks to take a closer look at the ongoing negotiation of social boundaries that comes with many Dungans' leading roles in cross-border trade, but also with their liminal position as a diasporic group in Kazakhstan and of China, socially constructed by exchange processes along the Silk Road.

Renegotiating social boundaries

In conversations at Almaty's Barakholka it became apparent that Dungan trade entrepreneurs in Kazakhstan gained significantly from China's increasing economic and political influence in Central Asia. Dungan business people generally appear to be much less hesitant and more pragmatic (than, for example, Uyghur) in cooperating with Han Chinese (Laruelle & Peyrouse 2012). In fact, some of my interlocutors emphasized that they relied mainly on *huizu* and Han partners for supply and transport services, leaving members of other ethnic groups effectively excluded from their wholesale trade schemes. The profitability of business operations arising from the close cooperation with Chinese partners in Kazakhstani society, where the increasing impact of the eastern neighbour is generally viewed anxiously, raises the risk of negative sentiments. However, Dungan wholesalers, for several reasons, are less frequently accused of being profiteers acting against 'national interests' than, for example, successful Kazakh trade entrepreneurs in the China business arena (Alff 2014).

The status of the Dungan community as a diaspora people within Kazakhstan, claiming ancestry from China, can be regarded as one of these reasons (Jimenez Tovar 2016). Jimenez Tovar (2016: 393) points out that the discursive 'diasporization' of the Kazakhstani society 'is a way of "othering" the non-Kazakh population while arguing for Kazakh indigeneity'. The diasporization of ethnic minorities in Kazakhstan legitimizes the revival and maintenance of historic social or cultural ties to their places of origin, as long as territorial integrity is not threatened (Jimenez Tovar 2016: 7). Along with the diasporization process, a form of civic nationalism, often described as 'Kazakhstanization', is imposed by the nation-building project to foster social cohesion in the ethnically diverse Kazakhstani society (Davenel 2012).

Following this ethnonational set-up, community leaders, like the principal of a school in the village, are eager to present the Dungans' multiple links to China as vital for themselves (and for China–Kazakhstan relations as a whole), while their belonging to Kazakhstani society is constantly reconfirmed:

> Dungans are a bridge, a connecting link between China and Kazakhstan. Our culture is Eastern, close to the Chinese one, but we are living in multi-ethnic Kazakhstan, where the policy of one nation – the united Kazakhstani nation – was, I think, rightly introduced [by president Nazarbaev]. [...] Now they are no longer speaking of peoples of Kazakhstan but of the Kazakhstani people, of which Dungans are a part.[19]

Further corroborating the legitimacy of the Dungans' important role in cross-border exchange with China, and at the same time confirming their belonging to Kazakhstani society, Husey Daurov, among others, has put much effort into positioning his group as the product of a historical Silk Road and as quintessential brokers and intermediaries on the newly evolving Silk Road:

> Dungans are in fact a product of the Silk Road. Centuries ago, Persian and Arab groups played an important role in trade on the historic Silk Road between Europa and Asia. It is how Islam came to China. And we came here through the Silk Road, too. Today the Chinese and Kazakhstani governments are investing huge funds in the new Silk Road, into the construction of overland roads and railroad lines. It is up to us Dungan, as a people constituted by the Silk Road, to utilize these historic opportunities as much as possible.[20]

The Dungans' role as brokers between Kazakhstan and China has taken a number of different forms. At the political level, their intermediary position becomes evident in the frequent participation of Dungan businessmen in Kazakhstani government delegations visiting China. During a conversation with Husey Daurov in May 2014, he told me that he and several other Dungan entrepreneurs would be accompanying an official visit of CEOs of Kazakhstani government companies, vice-ministers and the father of then Kazakhstan's prime minister, Karim Massimov, Kazhymkhan, to the International Silk Road EXPO in the city of Xi'an.[21] In fact, Daurov was also responsible for negotiating a partnership agreement between Shaanxi province, considered by many Dungans in Kazakhstan as their ancestral homeland (*istoricheskaya rodina* in Russian), and Zhambyl *oblast'* in southeastern Kazakhstan in 2007 (Laruelle & Peyrouse 2012). At the everyday level, many of the former Dungan exchange students, after their studies at the universities of Xi'an, Lanzhou, or Guangzhou, found employment in branches of Chinese companies in Kazakhstan, thereby valorizing their language skills and intercultural knowledge. The centrality Dungans gained in Kazakhstan–China trade and exchange processes has, among others, evoked calls for a more profound standard of Chinese language instruction in Dungan community high schools. Increasing sociocultural approximation and '"recovering" the Chinese connection' (Jimenez Tovar 2016: 398), however, do not go undisputed among Kazakhstan's Dungans. Thus, a Dungan elder I interviewed in Shortobe highlighted tendencies of 'sinicization':

> We are Dungans, here speaking the Dungan language. It is true that our ancestors came here from China more than 130 years ago. But our culture, our traditions were always distinct, as is our language. Chinese tourists, when visiting our villages here in Kazakhstan, keep telling us that our Dungan way of living has long-vanished in China. It may be useful for our youth to know better how to speak proper Chinese nowadays, but we should be more conscious about our own heritage.[22]

The negotiation of social–cultural boundaries through alignment and othering, along with intensified cross-border connectivity to China, therefore appears to lead in different directions and is subject to both pragmatism and flexibility in the Dungan's social practice. These seemingly divergent social processes can be associated with liminality understood as a state of in-between-ness in the identity work literature, or what Turner (1967) has called 'betwixt and between'. According to Beech (2011: 286), social liminality refers to a form of dynamic dialogue between projections of the self to the outside, the definition of identity through external discourses, and enacts changing markers, narratives, or symbols of identity and belonging. Horvath and her colleagues emphasize the unpredetermined attribute of liminality evolving from radical sociopolitical change stating that the concept 'captures in-between situations and conditions characterized by the dislocation of established structures, the reversal of hierarchies, and uncertainty about the continuity of tradition and future outcomes' (Horvath et al. 2015: 2). Liminality in this sense characterizes a highly fluid, processual positioning of individual agents or groups, which is shaped by their interstitial social situatedness and external ascriptions. While liminality can enforce processes of disorientation, social exclusion, or marginalization and therefore of the construction of boundaries, it can also contribute to increasing reflexivity and flexibility as illustrated by many Dungans' positionality as brokers, close to what Alessandro Rippa has called proximity in his description of the China–Pakistan trade (Chapter 8, this volume).

Conclusion

The case of Kazakhstan's Dungans provides a valuable insight into both the opportunities and challenges that cross-border groups are facing when state borders and sociocultural boundaries reconfigure in a rather unexpected way, a theme that is in the centre of border research in post-Soviet Central Asia and particularly in the Ferghana Valley (Megoran 2007, 2013; Reeves 2007; see also Reeves' Chapter 3, this volume). With the Sino–Soviet border becoming more permeable since the mid-1980s, it was on the initiative of a single community leader that connections between Dungans, who had left Qing China more than a century before, and *huizu* communities in China revived. While cultural exchange was the dominant factor in Dungan reconnections to their ancestral homeland in the beginning, business cooperation, particularly in the form of flourishing wholesale trade between China and Central Asia, became the determining moment from the mid-1990s onward. Ethnolinguistic affinity, pragmatism, and trust generated from engaging with Han and *huizu* business partners, put Dungan trade entrepreneurs in a favourable position vis-à-vis Kazakh, Kyrgyz, or Uyghur competitors. Dungans thus have become one of the most influential groups in highly profitable trade operations between east coast China and Kazakhstan.

As a contribution to the emerging border studies literature in Asia (van Schendel & de Maaker 2014), this chapter shows from an ethnographic perspective how changing state border situations and sociocultural boundaries in motion interrelate and impact upon each other in a complex way on the livelihoods of a cross-border group (see also Horstmann & Wadley 2006; Eilenberg & Wadley 2009; Turner et al. 2015 for examples from other stretches of Asia). At the same time, the study illustrates how groups such as the Dungan harness these border and boundary changes and therefore valorize their agency and relations in what Reeves (2014) has called upon as border work. Thus, the chapter has emphasized how Dungan cross-border livelihoods have evolved since the final years of the Soviet Union through the rebuilding of cross-border social ties, on the one hand, and the flexible negotiation of sociocultural boundaries on the other. The Dungans' diaspora status in Kazakhstan, it is argued, allows them to legitimize close interactions with *huizu* and Han business partners in China, without raising Sinophobe sentiments in the Kazakhstani public. At the same time, Dungan community leaders have made great efforts to position themselves as brokers or intermediaries in Kazakhstan–China cooperation in the political arena, thereby receiving a positive reception from leading political circles in Kazakhstan. However, despite the increasing sociocultural approximation of Kazakhstan's Dungans with China, an emphasis of distinctiveness and othering remains a prominent feature of many Dungans' identity. These seemingly divergent identity formations arrive from a state of in-between-ness or social liminality. As has been shown in this contribution, liminality refers to the dynamic, interlinked process of self-representation, ascription through external discourses, and the emergence of changing markers, narratives, and symbols. While social segregation and exclusion are often outcomes of liminality, in the case of Kazakhstan's Dungan community liminality has fostered a rather favourable sociospatial positionality between Central Asia and China. While geostrategic and geopolitical aspects of new Silk Road(s) and economic corridors dominate the scholarship on interactions across the former Sino–Soviet border, this contribution highlights the social processes of connectivity and the negotiation of borders and boundaries in the production of cross-border livelihoods that invite further scholarly inquiry (Alff 2016).

Acknowledgements

The research for this chapter was funded by the German Federal Ministry for Education and Research (BMBF) within the framework of the competence network 'Crossroads Asia' (2011–16). The author thanks both BMBF and Crossroads Asia for their support. He is also grateful to Christine Bonnin (University College Dublin) and to the editors of this handbook for their helpful comments on an earlier draft of this chapter.

Notes

1. *Hueitsu* is sometimes used among the Dungans alongside the ethnonym of *huizu* as a denomination for the respective *minzu* or national minority in the PRC.
2. See the extensive work by Dru Gladney (1991, 1996, 2004) for a thorough ethnographic study of the *huizu* in China.
3. In Dungan studies, as well as by the Dungans themselves, their language, however, is regarded not as a form of Chinese but as a language proper, see for example Rimsky-Korsakoff Dyer (1978).
4. The chair of Dungan Studies (*dunganovedenie* in Russian) at the Kyrgyz Academy of Sciences is the only scholarly institution in the former Soviet Union dedicated to the study of the Dungan language, history, and culture. It is also responsible for the editing of Dungan school textbooks, which are based on the Gansu dialect of Dungan.
5. Interview, Husey Daurov, Almaty, 9 October 2012.
6. Hundreds of Dungans from Kazakhstan leave for hajj every year on charter flights, appropriating a considerable part of the Kazakhstani government quota for these journeys.
7. In shops across the village cluster around Shortobe, alcoholic beverages and tobacco products are banned from sale on the decision of the local elders.
8. The aspect of Muslim solidarity between Dungan and Hui plays out, for example, in the organization of hajj tours. During an interview on 4 April 2012, a female head of a Bishkek-based Dungan travel agency explained how she arranged journeys predominantly for Hui from Xinjiang, making use of the comparatively relaxed religious policies in Kyrgyzstan and bypassing the limited annual state quota for hajj travel in China.
9. The inward-orientation of the Dungan community in conversations with trade entrepreneurs in Almaty was directly linked several times to their short-lived demands for political autonomy in the Korday district going back to the early post-Soviet period.
10. Dungan-run restaurants and canteens offering 'Oriental and Chinese cuisine' (*Vostochnaya i kitayskaya kukhni* in Russian), being fairly popular in all major cities of Kazakhstan, are also major recipients of agricultural produce from Dungan farms.

11 Interview, Shortobe, 19 May 2014.
12 Interview, Husey Daurov, Almaty, 8 October 2012.
13 Interview, Almaty, 16 May 2014.
14 Interview, Husey Daurov, Almaty, 9 October 2012.
15 *Bingtuan* refers to the Xinjiang Production and Construction Corps (XPCC), which used to be a paramilitary organization of farms and production units that played an important role in settling and cultivating, or colonizing, large swathes of land, but in the past two decades has become a major player in cross-border trade (see Cliff 2009).
16 This goes so far that Dungan groups in Kazakhstan are becoming appropriated by the Chinese state under the diaspora category of 'overseas Chinese national minority' (Jimenez Tovar 2013, 2016), which gives them particularly favourable access to social benefits offered by the Chinese authorities, such as cultural and educational exchange programmes.
17 Interview, Almaty, 28 May 2014.
18 Interview, Almaty, 28 May 2014.
19 Interview, Masanchi, 6 October 2012.
20 Interview, Husey Daurov, Almaty, 9 October 2012.
21 Interview, Husey Daurov, Almaty, 14 May 2014.
22 Interview, Shortobe, 6 October 2012.

References

Agenstvo po statistike RK (2012) Chislennost' naseleniya Respubliki Kazakhstan po otdel'nym etnosam na nachalo 2012 goda [Population of the Republic of Kazakhstan by Ethnic Origin in the Beginning of 2012]. Astana.

Alff, H. (forthcoming) 'A Sense of Multiple Belonging: Translocal Relations and Narratives of Change within a Dungan Community', in: Mobilities, Boundaries, and Travelling Ideas: Rethinking Translocality Beyond Central Asia and the Caucasus, ed. by Stephan-Emmrich, I. and Schröder, P. Cambridge: Open Book Publishers.

Alff, H. (2014) 'Embracing Chinese Modernity? Articulation and Positioning in China-Kazakhstan Trade and Exchange Processes', Crossroads Asia Working Paper Series No. 21, Bonn. Available at: http://crossroads-asia.de/index.php?eID=tx_nawsecuredl&u=0&g=0&t=1472909716&hash=b03166e-8c1586456065599ab9f58b5a7b39a6a5e&file=fileadmin/user_upload/publications/Crossroads_Asia_Working_Paper_21_Alff_Embracing-Chinese-modernity.pdf (accessed 2 September 2016).

Alff, H. (2016) 'Introduction', Special Section 'Beyond Silkroadism: Contextualizing Social Interaction Along Xinjiang's Borders', Central Asian Survey 35 (3): 327–33.

Beech, N. (2011) 'Liminality and the Practices of Identity Reconstruction', Human Relations 64 (2): 285–302.

Cliff, T.M.J. (2009) 'Neo Oasis: The Xinjiang Bingtuan in the Twenty-first Century', Asian Studies Review 33 (1): 83–106.

Dautcher, J. (2009) Down a Narrow Road: Identity and Masculinity in a Uyghur Community in Xinjiang, China, Cambridge, MA: Harvard University Press.

Davenel, Y.-M. (2012) 'Cultural Mobilization in Post-Soviet Kazakhstan: Views from the State and from Non-titular Nationalities Compared', Central Asian Survey 31 (1): 17–29.

Donnan, H. & Wilson, T.M. (1999) Borders: Frontiers of Identity, Nation and State, Oxford: Berg.

Eilenberg, M. & Wadley, R.L. (2009) 'Borderland Livelihood Strategies: The Socio-economic Significance of Ethnicity in Cross-border Labour Migration, West Kalimantan, Indonesia', Asia Pacific Viewpoint 50 (1): 58–73.

Forbes Kazakhstan (2014) 'Taktika vykurivaniya', Issue No. 29 (January 2014). Available at: http://forbes.kz/process/probing/taktika_vyikurivaniya (accessed 26 August 2016).

Gladney, D. (1991) Muslim Chinese: Ethnic Nationalism in the People's Republic, Cambridge, MA: Harvard University Press.

Gladney, D. (1996) 'Relational Alterity: Constructing Dungan (Hui), Uygur, and Kazakh Identities across China, Central Asia, and Turkey', History and Anthropology 9 (2): 445–77.

Gladney, D. (2004) Dislocating China: Muslims, Minorities, and Other Subaltern Subjects, Chicago: The University of Chicago Press.

Hong, D. (2005) 'A Comparative Study on the Cultures of the Dungan and the Hui peoples', Asian Ethnicity 6 (2): 135–40.

Horstmann, A. & Wadley, R.L. (eds) (2006) Centering the Margin: Agency and Narrative in Southeast Asian Borderlands, Oxford: Berghahn.
Horvath, A., Thomassen, B. and Wydra, H. (2015) 'Introduction: Liminality and the Search of Boundaries', in: Breaking Boundaries: Varieties of Liminality, ed. by Horvath, A., Thomassen, B. and Wydra, H., 1–8. Oxford: Berghahn.
Jimenez Tovar, S. (2013) 'Coming Back (to Which) Home? Kazakhstan Dungans' Migration to China', East-BordNet Working Paper. Available at: www.eastbordnet.org/working_papers/open/relocatingborders/Jimenez_Tovar_%20Coming_back_%28to_which%29_Home_130113.pdf (accessed 25 March 2015).
Jimenez Tovar, S. (2016) 'Limits of Diaspority in Central Asia: Contextualizing Dungan's Multiple Belongings', Central Asian Survey 35 (3): 387–404.
Laruelle, M. & Peyrouse, S. (2012) The Chinese Question in Central Asia: Domestic Order, Social Change, and the Chinese Factor, New York: Columbia University Press.
Megoran, N. (2007) 'On Researching "Ethnic Conflict": Epistemology, Politics, and a Central Asian Boundary Dispute', Europe-Asia Studies 59 (2): 253–77.
Megoran, N. (2013) 'Shared Space, Divided Space: Narrating Ethnic Histories of Osh', Environment and Planning A 45 (4): 892–907.
Reeves, M. (2007) 'Unstable Objects: Corpses, Checkpoints and "Chessboard Borders" in the Ferghana Valley', The Anthropology of East Europe Review 25 (1): 72–84.
Reeves, M. (2014) Border Work: Spatial Lives of the State in Rural Central Asia, Ithaca, NY: Cornell University Press.
Rimsky-Korsakoff Dyer, S. (1978) 'Soviet Dungan Nationalism: A Few Comments on Their Origin and Language', Monumenta Serica 33: 349–62.
Roberts, S. (2007) '"The Dawn of the East": A Portrait of a Uyghur Community between China and Kazakhstan', in: Situating the Uyghurs between China and Central Asia, ed. by Bellér-Hann, I., Cesàro, C., Harris, R. and Smith Finley, J., 203–18. Aldershot: Ashgate.
Sadovskaya, Y. (forthcoming) 'Ethnically Diverse Diasporas and Migrations from China to Central Asia in the Twenty-first Century: Origin and Contemporary Challenges with Special Reference to Kazakhstan', in: China's Rise and the Chinese Overseas, ed. by Wong, B.P. and Tan C.-B., London: Routledge.
Steenberg, R. (2016) 'Embedded Rubber Sandals: Trade and Gifts Across the Sino-Kyrgyz Border', Central Asian Survey 35 (3): 405–20.
Sushanlo, M. (1967) Ocherki istorii sovetskikh dungan [Accounts on the History of Soviet Dungans], Frunze: Ilim.
Turner, S., Bonnin, C. & Michaud, J. (2015) Frontier Livelihoods: Hmong in the Sino-Vietnamese Borderlands, Seattle: Washington University Press.
Turner, V. (1967) The Forests of Symbols: Aspects of Ndembu Ritual, Ithaca, NY: Cornell University Press.
van Schendel, W. & de Maaker, E. (2014) 'Asian Borderlands: Introducing their Permeability, Strategic Uses and Meanings', Journal of Borderlands Studies 29 (1): 3–9.
Vansvanova, M. (2000) Dungane: Lyudi sud'by [Dungans: People-Destinies], Sözdik-Slovar': Almaty
Zhaparov, A. (2009) 'The Issue of Chinese migrants in Kyrgyzstan', China and Eurasia Forum Quarterly 7 (1): 79–91.

11

Ritual and issues of ethnic integration in the borderlands of the State of Rakhine/Arakan (Myanmar)

Alexandra de Mersan

First encounters with Arakanese/Rakhine[1]

The anthropologist Lucien Bernot and his wife, the linguist Denise Bernot, founders of the French "Burma Studies School", started their careers in the Chittagong Hill Tracts of East Pakistan (now Bangladesh) in the 1950s on the recommendation of the famous anthropologist Claude Levi-Strauss. It was at the time a largely unstudied, little-known region with a multiethnic and multilingual population. The couple spent one and a half years undertaking extensive anthropological and linguistic surveys mostly among those who called themselves Marma (or Marama). In brief, the Marma are originally from Arakan, having fled the kingdom after its conquest by the Burmese King Bodawpaya in 1785, if not even a few decades earlier as the nation was already in decline.

Significantly, the title of Lucien Bernot's impressive related monograph (1967) was: *The Arakanese peasants of Eastern Pakistan* with, as its subtitle *the history, their world of vegetable resources and the social organization of* Marma *refugees* (Mog).[2] Unfortunately, neither this work nor the majority of the Bernots' works on the region, written in French, have been translated into English. Indeed, their contribution has suffered from being firstly unknown to most English speakers/readers and scholars, and secondly because it concerns a population living outside Myanmar or Southeast Asia. This misfortune is a clear illustration of how marked this frontier between Burma (Myanmar) and Bangladesh has become, not only on the ground but also in institutional, academic, administrative, and political terms in both the Indian subcontinent and the rest of Southeast Asia.[3]

The title and contents of Lucien Bernot's monograph cover most aspects related to limits and boundaries, whether institutional, academic, ethnic, administrative, or linguistic. His work reflects the idea that social space transcends administrative lines and borders, and at the same time indicates how much ethnic identities, like demarcation lines, are multiple, moving, contextual, and situational. It also reveals his awareness of the need to focus on relationships, exchanges, and links that are maintained among populations despite more or less effective administrative frontiers even before the notion of ethnicity became so determinant in the social sciences, maybe already influenced by Leach (1960). But it also reveals how differences are maintained in a multicultural region, a predominant characteristic of most borderlands in the region, despite these strong inter-relationships (Leach 1960; Lehman 1963; Evrard 2006; Robinne 2008).

From this perspective, Lucien Bernot's work can be used to keep one on track, ensuring caution while addressing Arakanese (Rakhine) in Myanmar, helping to distance oneself – or to decolonize oneself, to follow Sadan's expression (2007) – from questions of identity and ethnicity so predominant in Burma (Myanmar) studies.

Since colonial times, the mode of administration accorded to places or the political context have been quite different on either side of the frontier with, as a logical consequence, the concept of groups and territory evolving differently: while social organization is based on kinship and clan with slash-and-burn cultivation among the Marma, among the Arakanese (Rakhine) it is based on residence and territory with wet-rice growing as their main economic activity (Bernot 1967, 2000). For similar reasons when comparing these two populations, rituals, which reflect their social organization, livelihood, and the respective specific political contexts, are also found to differ. Because they are linked to resources and access to them, territorial cults or spirits cults have been widely documented in Southeast Asia over last few decades (sometimes for even longer), demonstrating practices in which political relationships between groups or within groups feature significantly (Brac de la Perrière 1989, 2002; Tannenbaum and Kammerer 2003; Schlemmer 2012; Sadan 2013). In this chapter, I shall demonstrate it for Arakan. In doing so, I argue, ritual affords an alternative way of thinking about space both in relation to and beyond the nation/state.[4]

The making of a frontier

The region that lies between Chittagong in Bangladesh, and the former Buddhist Kingdom of Arakan that flourished from the 15th to the 18th centuries was the scene of active commercial and cultural exchange. Historians (Leider 2004, 385; Van Galen 2008) have demonstrated the strategic and economic importance of this area for the prosperity of the Kingdom of Arakan which, as a matter of fact, was at its peak when it controlled the port of Chittagong in the 17th century. Many people living in Bengal were captured by the King of Arakan and deported to his kingdom where they worked in the paddyfields, as pagoda slaves, or were sold to the Dutch for their colony. When the Kingdom of Arakan collapsed, some of its inhabitants escaped westwards, while others were deported to the capital of the Burmese King Bodawpaya. Forty years later, after the first Anglo-Burmese war,[5] the region fell under British colonial rule[6] and was integrated into India. The British then encouraged the migration of thousands of Indians to develop the rice industry, working either in the rice paddies or as coolies in the ports. Most were seasonal workers originating from several different parts of India. Those who came to Arakan originated from the Chittagong region and were thus called "Chittagonian" or labelled as being of "Indian race" in British reports. They settled there, mostly in Akyab (Sittwe) and in the adjacent northwestern area, and in a higher proportion than in other parts of Burma (Myanmar), some becoming farmers, merchants, and so on. The idea is still widespread among the Muslims that the prosperity of this colonial port was due to those "Indians" and/or Muslim merchants. Longer standing but less numerous groups,[7] either Muslim or Hindu, became mixed together with the newcomers despite their occasional efforts not to be considered the same (see the 1921 Census, Grantham 1923).[8] Most of today's Muslims in Arakan are descendants of these migrants, who sometimes took a local wife and founded families, but whose children were brought up as

Muslims. This helps to explain why they are considered foreigners associated with colonialism. There were also very few conversions to the Islamic faith.[9]

Anti-Indian rioting broke out in Yangon in 1930 and again in 1938. This occurred in the strained political context of developing nationalism that had been underway in both Burma (Myanmar) and India since the 1910 to 1920 period. "Burma is not India" stated the report from the commission that had been appointed to make recommendations on political evolution in Burma (Myanmar) and its separation from India. Its author also wrote: "The Burmese are as distinct from the Indians in race and language as they are from the British" (Simon Commission Report on India 1930, vol. 1, 77–78). This report pointedly aimed to demonstrate the considerable differences between the two races, but by means of a predominantly Western concept of races or nations. A constitution was promulgated in 1935 (becoming effective in 1937) settling the frontier between the two countries and established the clear separation between Burma (Myanmar) and India. This then obliged those of "Indian" origin to position themselves according to this new political configuration, as underlined by Leider (2015).[10] This differentiation according to "race" would be used after independence, with those labelled as of or affiliated with Indian race coming to be considered as foreigners in the new Burmese nation.

Ever since, this frontier has marked the divide between two wider geopolitical blocs: South Asia (or the Indian subcontinent) and Southeast Asia, two "natural" geopolitical entities long reinforced by the isolation of Myanmar after the Ne Win military coup of 1962.

Creation of the State of Arakan (1974): a colonial racial legacy

The State of Arakan (Rakhine State as it is known today) within the Union of Burma bordering on Bangladesh was created in 1974 at the same time as the Mon State. This gave official recognition to the cultural and historical differences between the Arakanese (Rakhine) and the Burmese; it endorsed the Arakanese (Rakhine) as a specific national race or nationality (*tuin ran sa:*) within the nation and as the most numerous or dominant among others within that eponymous state.

It took time for the Arakanese (Rakhine) to become properly recognized as such in a lengthy process of localization and appropriation of notions of race and nation similar to descriptions of what has taken place elsewhere in Burma (Myanmar).[11] This process of population differentiation at whose conclusion race (as defined by criteria of language and religion) became a decisive aspect of identity started during the colonial era, and has never been subsequently questioned. However, through it the Muslims of Arakan (or *kala* in the vernacular) became progressively marginalized in Burmese social space until they began to incarnate one of the figures – if not *the* figure – of the foreigner in contemporary Burma (Myanmar).

Since that time there have not only been few voices to condemn such territorial-based racial/ethnic divisions, whether by the central government or by the populations concerned, but the opprobrium became particularly reinforced by the 1974 creation of the State of Arakan. This was the consequence of a political struggle led by ethno-nationalist movements or Arakanese (Rakhine) elites against the Burmese drive for a centralized hegemonic power base, and may have been the only way to legitimize political rights.

While it put an official stamp on the cultural and historical differences between the Arakanese (Rakhine) and the Burmese, its effect was only symbolic because it gave no specific power to the Arakanese except reassuring them that they were masters of their own land as this recognition also implied an implicit "autochthony". However, it further encouraged a process by which the Arakanese (Rakhine) scholarly and intellectual elite became actively involved in the preservation and maintenance of their differences from the dominant Burmese, something which became even more marked in Arakan in the 1990s with the religious policy of the then military junta (de Mersan 2005, 2015). This led to the reification of ethnicity, characteristic of movements involved in political and cultural struggle and was accentuated by the specific political context of military authoritarianism (Gravers 2007).

Although this concept of national race is related to the political struggle of the making of a nation, the Arakanese (Rakhine) consider themselves to be a historical, religious, and cultural community that descends directly from their own former Buddhist kingdom, inheritors of this land blessed by the Buddha himself, with a specific duty to maintain the dispensation (*sasana*) (de Mersan 2012). This position has been strongly cultivated ever since the conquest of their kingdom by the Burmese (Leider 2008).

Other populations such as the Mro, Kami, Chin, Marma, Daignat, Sak, and Khaman are also officially recognized as nationalities or national races (*tuin ran sa:*) in Rakhine State. Little if anything is known about them beyond what is written in colonial literature or in official publications (similar to British colonial gazetteers), such as the one published in 1976 after the creation of Rakhine State.[12] However, none of these official or authorized documents makes any mention of Muslim populations or population groups originating from India, whether Muslim or Hindu (with the exception of those known as Kaman),[13] whereas they constitute about one third of the total population now living in the state.[14]

Muslims in Arakan

There are different names for the Muslims in Rakhine State: Rohingya, *kala*, Bengali, and Kaman. The use of these terms and their meaning change according to the period, but there is no doubt that Muslims in Rakhine State cannot be gathered under one single term as a community, a priori, when considering them from a diachronical or synchronical perspective. Even today the denomination of these populations often provokes heated debate.[15]

All Muslims in Rakhine State are known in the international media and to foreign governments and International Non-Governmental Organizations (INGOs) as "Rohingya" as a result of the conflict which emerged in 2012 and if not sometimes because of earlier ones (1978, 1991/92) through international media and organizations working then with refugees from Northern Arakan. Among them were seemingly representatives of the self-referring Rohingya group who fought for an independent or autonomous state at the end of the Second World War until Ne Win's military coup.[16] As far as we know, until 2012, not all Muslims of Arakan identified themselves as Rohingya, but as 'yakaing kala' or 'Arakan Muslim'. But this word was almost unknown to the majority of Buddhist Arakanese (Rakhine) except among the elites or more generally throughout Myanmar and was thus hardly used within the country. In Myanmar people speak of *kala* and since 2012 more often of Bengali.[17] The word *kala* is an ancient generic term and for a long time was used to indicate "people from the west". This could be translated as "Indian" in a broader sense or as "foreigner" (as has often been the case in English translations ever since colonial times), but in doing so it immediately suggests a degree of exteriority that surpasses its inherent one. *Kala* is a vernacular term that belongs to a category of "other", but with different contextual meanings. Those labelled as such were anyhow seen in the pre-colonial period as belonging to the Buddhist socio-cosmos, as they were found among the 101 peoples or groups of laymen inhabiting Jambudipa, the island were humans live in Buddhist cosmology (Candier 2010). The term usually designated people from the west, because of their geographical location, or their language, or their religion and rites. Nowadays, it is usually pejorative, even an insult, and tends to refer only to Muslims. In other words, it has become an expression of radical differentiation. This was not always the case before the 2012 conflict and depended on the context.[18] Although problematic, I continue to use the word as it was a commonly used, a generic term, and frequently encountered in rituals until the conflict. In refering to it and in its use, there is of course no intention to insult or to belittle any group; it moreover frees discussion from any ethnic filter. However, when describing facts I use the religious categories such as Muslims and Buddhists.

Social, religious, and ethnic inter-relationships in Arakan

There are few if any references to *kala* in official or authorized documents such as the publication mentioned earlier (see Official Publications 1976), since no indigenous religious group is recognized as Muslim (except, again, for the Kaman). This is to say that readers of publications written in Burmese since the 1960s/1970s would only have a partial view of the region's social space (quite apart from the fact that these publications were already distorted by those years' implacable censorship). However, there is a real lack of studies of Islam in Myanmar in general, as well as of Muslims in Arakan. By the 2000s, there was also a tendency for even ancient cultural or historical references to India or Bengal to disappear from official publications, as well as from socially controlled narratives such as the more valued ones linked to Buddhism via pagoda (hi) stories no doubt because it has been a field of practices much invested by the elite, by scholars or by the leaders of ethno-nationalist movements.[19] In addition to the former military junta's restrictive policy, tensions between Buddhists and Muslims made it impossible by the end of 1990s and later to conduct any ethnographic study focusing on inter-relationships between different social components within the state.[20] Buddhist and Muslim communities, whether previously living together or not, were also ideologically and/or physically separated. For example, after the Burmese junta decided to promote Mrauk U, the former capital of the Kingdom of Arakan and the Arakanese (Rakhine) cultural and historical heartland, as a tourist destination in the 1990s, houses, which had been built within the ruins of the ancient palace, had to be removed. If the owners were Muslim, they had to move out of town. Muslims also had to leave some nearby villages to go and live near the Bangladeshi border.

However, there were many inter-relationships based on economic and social exchange that depended on such variables as occupation, place of residence, town or village, or social position. These relationships could be qualified as a form of neighbourly interdependence that often acted hierarchically in favour of the Arakanese (Rakhine). Many Muslims were employed by the Buddhist as cleaners, unskilled labourers, or coolies in subaltern, despised, difficult, or dirty jobs. As a matter of fact, after the outbreaks of violence in Sittwe in 2012, the Arakanese (Rakhine) had to recruit workers from the surrounding villages to replace Muslims as labourers, garbage collectors, or water-carriers. These inter-relationships seemingly work better when the livelihood or commodity belong to complementary rather than competitive domains. For example, in a town like Sittwe, fish sold on the market by Buddhists had been caught by Muslim fishermen; Buddhists were growing rice, while Muslims were cultivating vegetables. There also appeared to have existed interdependant relationships between rice-growing peasants and buffalo breeders in some villages around Mrauk U. Muslims were also (and still are) more involved in such activities as ferrying goods and people to and from Bangladesh. There were also many strong interpersonal relationships, even very friendly ones, mostly between those of similar socioeconomic standing, as among certain merchants (some even provided protection for their partners during the violence in 2012).

These factors were not adequately taken into account. Inter-marriages, which had occurred formely (in an unknown proportion) did not take place at that time and belonged to the domain of the unthinkable, at least at a conversational level. Finally, to my knowledge there were no common collective celebrations between members of the two religions. This general picture gives an idea of the climate and its evolution, which are difficult to describe in greater detail, but are to be found in rituals. In the absence of reliable studies and operating in the face of official or social censorship, investigating ritual offers a way of accessing an alternative discourse and has much to do with mutual positioning, with otherness, and centrality.[21]

Spirit cults in Rakhine State

Ritual practice in Rakhine State is poorly documented even by the Arakanese (Rakhine) themselves, as it is usually seen as something marginal and is disregarded by the elite or scholars who often relegate it to the field of superstition.

Spirit cults are above all celebrations of specific localities (de Mersan 2016a). They indicate the importance of territory in the constitution of local groups and reflect the social organization among the Arakanese (Rakhine) as based on residence. A village or town guardian spirit, mostly territorial but also ancestral, exerts a protective power over inhabitants living in its domain. For example, in June 2012, Sittwe was the scene of violent conflict between Buddhists and Muslims. The events happened to coincide with the June/July period preceding the Buddhist Lent, when the inhabitants make spirit offerings. At this moment of continuing high tensions and fear, the ceremony was performed in just one day (instead of the usual three) because of a curfew. Despite the climate of violence and fear, hundreds of people attended as usual, making their offerings to the town spirit, begging for its protection, or expressing their gratitude towards it. Also, many of the Arakanese (Rakhine) inhabitants, whose houses had not caught fire in the course of the confrontations that spread through the town, claimed that the town's guardian spirit had protected them from the flames and from the enemy.

There are a few past references to cults common to the different groups in Sittwe (formerly Akyab) during colonial times (in the 1920s) and, in particular, to the guardian spirit (*nat*) of the town/island, where Buddhists, Hindus, and Muslims performed rituals in a common setting. In the early days of my research into this subject in Rakhine State in the late 1990s, I was expecting to find that inhabitants of a given place (village, quarter, or town) would observe common practices in spirit cults and ritual exchanges, regardless of religion or ethnicity, as is the case, for example, in Southern Thailand. This was not so when I observed these rituals, showing instead that Muslims and Buddhists no longer shared any common ritual language, contrary to Hindus[22] and other Buddhists who attended the celebration. Here and elsewhere, even before the outbreak of violence in 2012, Muslims were not to be found among participants or devotees of these cults. However, it was puzzling to discover the presence of *kala* spirits in some rituals or territorial cults conducted by Arakanese (Rakhine).

The archetypal figure of "the other" in Arakanese (Rakhine) spirits cult or spirit guests of the feast

The Arakanese (Rakhine) pay collective homage to the guardian spirits of their village or place in an annual three-day ceremony (*nat pwe, rwa rhan pwe*) in the course of which they make offerings to the spirit so as to obtain success (for the village football team, for example), for their health, wealth, and gain protection from dangers and enemies. Briefly put, the ceremony consists of inviting and pleasing this tutelary spirit through songs and dances performed by ritual specialists: musicians and mediums. Although dedicated to this spirit, who is considered to be the owner of the village, many others are also invited so as to ensure the ceremony's success; indeed, the more the merrier.

Most are spirits whose domain has been socialized by human activities: rivers, fields, the forest, towns, islands, villages, and so on. Other non-Arakanese (Rakhine) spirits are also invited: mostly *kala*, Burmese (*bama nat*), and Chin (*khyan: nat*). These guest spirits are like figures of archetypal others characterized by a place or domain, or some other feature that the Arakanese (Rakhine) hold important.[23] When these *nat* are invited, the mediums change clothes and attire, dance specific dances, and even change their tone of voice. The "ethnic" denomination signifies a spirit whose domain is supposed to be inhabited mostly by *kala*, Burmese, or Chin. The domains of most *kala* spirits are situated to the west, somewhere near the actual border, or in Bengal or even India. Burmese guest spirits are said to have their homes in Burmese cultural and historical regions like Pagan, while Chin spirits are linked to the upper reaches of the main rivers of Arakan. Religion associated with the *kala nat* might be evoked by a title indicating a higher rank such as *raja* or *pacha*, respectively Hindu and Muslim.

The denomination or ethnic label also sometimes indicates the distinction between a territorial or ancestral spirit. Territorial spirits, the most common, refer to a process by which the local or place-related force was transformed into a tutelary spirit, a precondition for any human settlement. In this case, the foundation seems to refer to an initial clearing of the forest. The ancestral nature focuses on the founder of the place or domain, as the fact that founders were sometimes *kala*, Burmese, or Chin becomes apparent. It should be noted that in the performance of an Arakanese-centric ritual, there is no Arakanese (Rakhine) labelled *nat* as that is self-evident.

In the Mrauk U region, another kind of *kala* spirit plays a central role in a final sequence at the end of the three-day ceremony, representing the sacrifice of a goat. This spirit is like a ritual performer (*punna*), like those of "Indian" origin who at one time officiated at the King of Arakan's court. The ceremony's success depends on this final sequence.

The invitation to all the guest spirits to attend the annual ceremony means that they honour and pay homage to the village's tutelary spirit. But above all it means they represent those groups with whom the Arakanese (Rakhine) interact most frequently in daily life. So it is about sustaining relationships of a more or less neighbourly type.

Central and peripheral power

As the ceremony progresses, the chanting of songs invites the spirits to appear one by one. These incantations, part of the rich repertory of oral literature, describe the spirits' "physical" appearance as Lords or more often as Ladies, or the characteristics of their domain, and sometimes even mentions their journey to attend the ceremony. I call these recitations "mental maps of Arakanese social space". While describing and exalting the land (*prañ*) as specific places and their natural resources, they also evoke the geography of Arakan country, even its doors or entrance points, but these do not correspond to the Arakanese (Rakhine) state's actual administrative frontiers. Incantations are much more than that though; they are celebrations of specific localities through every feature that constitutes and characterizes them according to specific historical, social, and polical contexts. These include the land and its resources, topography, and soil, but also values, history, relationships, economic activities, and so on. Here is one of the main reasons why rituals are always changing, and also why differences are to be found from one place to another.

Its status as the former royal capital is one of Mrauk U's most characteristic aspects and is expressed in various ways: the spirits of the town's ancient quarters indicate a royal cult as the centre of the kingdom, and the spirits' domain is similar to the administrative units of the former kingdom. The kingdom is also represented as a politically controlled domain with the network of relationships or spheres of influence of the Buddhist monarch over populations whether conquered or not, a configuration of the former kingdom that corresponds more closely to that of the 17th century, its golden age. Another feature that characterizes the Mrauk U region as a former capital is to be found in the ritual's closing sequence with the presence of a *kala* spirit representing a ritual specialist. No *kala nat* was invited to the ritual ceremony dedicated to the guardian spirit observed near Mrauk U in 2013. The tension caused by the social and political situation in Rakhine State affected everything. Ever since the outbreaks of violence in 2012, *kala* were identified as the enemy from the west.

For the ceremony's final sequence a *kala nat* was still invited to participate, but when questioned about it one of the ritual officiants told me that it was as a servant of the village guardian spirit. In other words it had been relegated to the lowest class. Meanwhile a new spirit guest appeared; named "*doppa nat*" and physically handicapped because of a misdeed during its former life (he ate a monk's food), it was a way of underlining the Law of Kamma and demonstrating what happens when Buddhism is mistreated.

Conclusion

Before June 2012, Muslims in Arakan had become scarcely visible but pervasive figures in official narratives. However, rituals like territorial cults embody a discourse at the margins of society, which while not directly opposing, at least challenge socially dominant narratives within Arakanese (Rakhine) society. These rituals, which represent group values at the local level, are lasting evidence of a network of relationships between different social components for commodities and livelihoods. In these spirit cults, assigning an identity to a third party is a manner of recognizing their presence and role both in daily interactions and in transcending boundaries.

Acknowledgement

I wish to thank Ma Thandar for her valuable help on several occasions and in particular in 2012 for her fieldwork. I also thank B. Brac de la Perrière and Chris Fisher for their reading and comments on this chapter. However contents and analysis expressed in this article are my sole expression and engage only myself.

Notes

1. In this chapter I will use "Rakhine State" or "Arakan" or "Rakhine/Arakan" to refer to the region and Arakanese or Rakhine interchangeably when referring to the people.
2. My emphasis. Mog (Mag, Mug) is the derogative term by which Marma or Arakanese (Rakhine) are called by the Bengalis.
3. For a similar point of view, see van Schendel (2002).
4. Most data were collected during several fieldwork sessions that took place between 1999 and 2016 in Rakhine State, mainly in Mrauk U, Sittwe, and on Rambye Island.
5. The Kingdom of Burma was colonized in three stages: in 1824/1825 with the annexing of Arakan, Tenasserim, Assam, Martaban, and Rangoon; in 1853/4 adding Lower Burma (Pegu); and in 1885/1886 Upper Burma.
6. It first became part property of the East India Company until 1830 and then was part of the British Raj.
7. The generic and most common term by which these populations were known is "kala". See note 18 and de Mersan (2015). Other words are found in pre-colonial sources such as "rohingya", "mola", and "atumara" about which little is known, but there is no racial idea of groups; see Leider (2015). Rohingya probably referred to a socio-professional group linked to the Arakanese (Rakhine) kingship.
8. Just before World War II, there are mentions of "Indigenous Mahomedans" or "Indigenous Hindus" in colonial administrative reports distinguishing them (known and called '*yakain* [i.e., Rakhine]-*kala*') from "newcomer" migrants. However, in independent Burma (Myanmar) they received no official

recognition as special religious communities and even less as an indigenous race and thus no legal existence in the constitution.
9 These data mostly come from reports and should be considered with care or cross-checked with other sources.
10 It would explain why the first reference found on "Rohingya" in colonial writings dates from this period.
11 See de Mersan (2016b). For a demonstration of the process in other places of Myanmar, see several examples in Gravers (2007).
12 See Official Publications (1976).
13 Kaman are Muslims who sought refuge in the Kingdom of Arakan in the 17th century, and are considered to be fully "arakanized". They were, however, also attacked after the outbreak of violence in Arakan in June 2012.
14 The 2014 census was the first to cover the whole country for decades. The total population of the state was 3.2 million inhabitants (including an estimated 1.09 million inhabitants who were not officially accounted for, mostly if not all, Muslim).
15 In June 2016, Myanmar State Counsellor, Aung San Suu Kyi said he was in favour of using "Muslim community in Arakan State", instead of the term "Rohingya" (much preferred and used by foreign governments and NGOs) or "Bengali" (as did the former President Thein Sein) in order to encourage "mutual trust" between the Buddhist and Muslim communities in Arakan State, but both disagreed.
16 Although ancient, the word "Rohingya" emerged in the 1950s through some Muslim organizations from Northern Arakan who initially fought to get a separate/independent state in Myanmar or struggled for a special political status in the country. For more details see Leider (2013: 212–215, 235–237). The international community brings strong pressure to bear on former and current governments to recognize them as Rohingya, that is, as a national race. Conflicts or tensions occurred throughout the 20th century whenever a new constitution was drafted or when elections were held, thus at moments of political reconfiguration.
17 For a detailed approach concerning the word and its evolution, see de Mersan (2016b) and Leider (2015).
18 Adequate evidence of this may be found in commonly used words in Burmese language, which refer to *kala* without any such connotation as for example *kalatuin* for chair or a brand name of a famous masala known as 'The Little *kala*'. For more details see de Mersan (2016b) and Nyi Nyi Kyaw (2015).
19 See de Mersan (2015) for a detailed approach of culture as political contest in Arakan.
20 Contrary to examples elsewhere; see for example Robinne (2000) for his work on Inle Lake region in Shan State of Myanmar or Evrard (2007). Also there is nothing comparable with southern Thailand where large Muslim communities are living among the Buddhists, and which have been well documented for several decades. In addition to Bernot's (2000) work undertaken from Bangladesh in this borderland, see van Schendel (2005, 2006) or Than Tun (2015) on the circulation and dynamics of social and ethnic interactions.
21 There are numerous examples concerning Burma (Myanmar), or other places in Southeast Asia. Reference to the Burmese Cult of the Thirty Seven Lords and spirit cults in general among the Burmese is to be found in Brac de la Perrière's works on the subject. See among others, Brac de la Perrière (1989, 2002, 2009). See also Sadan (2013) in Kachin State for the "Kachin" point of view or Boutry (2011). Elsewhere, in Southern Thailand, Buddhist and Muslim communities share common ancestral spirits, cults, and cultural practices, for example see Horstmann (2011). See also Hayashi (2003) on the borderlands of Northeast Thailand.
22 Hindus, less numerous than the Muslims, are seen today as a specific ethnic group/race and similar to the Buddhists, maybe because when there are mixed marriages between Hindus and Buddhists, the children are Hindu and/or Buddhist. It also means that there is no need for religious conversion.
23 For the Burmese, see Brac de la Perrière (2002).

References

Bernot, Lucien. 1967. Les paysans arakanais du Pakistan Oriental: l'histoire, le monde végétal et l'organisation sociale des réfugiés Marma (Mog). 2 vols. Paris, La Haye: Editions Mouton & Co., Ecole Pratique des Hautes Etudes.
Bernot, Lucien. 2000. Voyage dans les sciences humaines. Qui sont les autres? Paris: Presses de l'Université de Paris-Sorbonne, collection Asie.

Boutry, Maxime. 2011. "The "Moving" Frontiers of Burma". Moussons 11: 15–23.
Brac de la Perrière, Bénédicte. 1989. Les rituels de Possession en Birmanie: du Culte d'état aux Cérémonies Privées [Possession Rituals in Burma: from State Cult to Private Ceremony]. Paris: Editions Recherches sur les Civilisations.
Brac de la Perrière, Bénédicte. 2002. "Sibling Relationships in the Nat Stories of the Burmese Cult to the 'Thirty-seven.'" Moussons 5: 31–48.
Brac de la Perrière, Bénédicte. 2009. "An Overview of the Field of Religion in Burmese Studies." Asian Ethnology 68, no. 2: 185–210.
Candier, Aurore. 2010. "Convergences conceptuelles en Birmanie: La Transition du xixe Siècle." [Conceptual Convergences in Burma: The 19th Century Period of Transition]. Moussons 16: 81–101.
de Mersan, Alexandra. 2005. "L'expression du particularisme arakanais dans la Birmanie contemporaine." Moussons 8: 117–141.
de Mersan, Alexandra. 2012. "The 'Land of the Great Image' and the Test of Time. The Making of a Buddha Image in Arakan (Burma/Myanmar)." In The Spirit of Things: Materiality in the Age of Religious Diversity in Southeast Asia, edited by Julius Bautista, 95–110. Ithaca, NY: Southeast Asia Program Publications.
de Mersan, Alexandra. 2015. "The 2010 Election and the Making of a Parliamentary Representative." In Metamorphosis: Studies in Social and Political Change in Myanmar, edited by Renaud Egreteau and François Robinne, 43–68. Singapore: NUS Press/IRASEC.
de Mersan, Alexandra. 2016a. "Ritual and the Other in Rakhine Spirits Cults." In Myanmar's Mountain and Maritime Borderscapes. Local Practices, Boundary-Making and Figured Worlds, edited by Su-Ann Oh, 121–145. Singapore: ISEAS Press.
de Mersan, Alexandra. 2016b. "Comment les musulmans d'Arakan sont-ils devenus étrangers à l'Arakan (Birmanie/Myanmar)?" [How Muslims in Arakan became Arakan's Foreigners]. Moussons 28: 123–146.
Evrard, Olivier. 2006. Chronique des cendres: anthropologie des sociétés khmou et des dynamiques interethniques du Nord-Laos. Paris: IRD.
Evrard, Olivier. 2007. "Interethnic systems and localized identities: The Khmu subgroups in North-West Laos." In Social Dynamics in the Highlands of Southeast Asia. Reconsidering Political Systems of Highland Burma by E.R Leach, edited by François Robinne and Mandy Sadan, 127–159. Leiden: Brill.
Grantham, S. G. 1923. Census of India – 1921, vol X, Burma, Part I, Report, Rangoon: Office of the Superintendent, Government Printing.
Gravers, Mikael, ed. 2007. Exploring Ethnic Diversity in Burma, Copenhague: NIAS Studies in Asian Topics, no. 39. Copenhagen: NIAS Press.
Hayashi, Yukio. 2003. "Reconfiguration of Village Guardian Spirits among the Thai-Lao in Northeast Thailand." In Founders' Cults in Southeast Asia: Ancestors, Polity, and Identity (Monograph 52), edited by Nicola Tannenbaum and Cornelia Ann Kammerer, 184–209. New Haven, CT: Yale University Southeast Asia Studies.
Horstmann, Alexander. 2011. "Living Together: The Transformation of Multi-Religious Coexistence in Southern Thailand." Journal of Southeast Asian Studies 42, no. 3: 487–510.
Leach, Edmund. 1960. "The Frontiers of 'Burma'." Comparative Studies in Society and History 3, no. 1: 49–68.
Lehman, Frederick K. 1963. The Structure of Chin Society: A Tribal People of Burma Adapted to a Nonwestern Civilization. Urbana, IL: University of Illinois Press.
Leider, Jacques P. 2004. Le Royaume d'Arakan, Biranie. Son histoire politique entre le début du xve et la fin du xviie siècle [The Kingdom of Arakan, Burma. Its Political History between the Fifteenth and the Beginning of the End of the Seventeenth Century]. Paris: EFEO.
Leider, Jacques P. 2008. "Forging Buddhist Credentials as a Tool of Legitimacy and Ethnic Identity." Journal of the Economic and Social History of the Orient 51: 409–459.
Leider, Jacques P. 2013. Rohingya: The Name, the Movement and the Quest for Identity. Nation Building in Myanmar, Yangon: Myanmar Egress/Myanmar Peace Center, 204–255.
Leider, Jacques P. 2015. "Competing Identities and the Hybridized History of the Rohingyas." In Metamorphosis: Studies in Social and Political Change in Myanmar, edited by Renaud Egreteau and François Robinne, 151–178. Singapore: NUS Press/IRASEC.
Nyi Nyi Kyaw. 2015. "Alienation, Discrimination, and Securitization: Legal Personhood and Cultural Personhood of Muslims in Myanmar". The Review of Faith & International Affairs 13: 50–59.
Official Publications. 1976. Tuin: ran: sa: yañ kye: mhu – rui: ra dha le. thum: cam mya: – rakhuin [Traditional Customs: Indigenous Cultures, the Rakhine]. Rangoon: Myanmar Government.
Robinne, François. 2000. "Fils et maîtres du Lac. Relations interethniques dans l'Etat Shan de Birmanie." Paris: CNRS Editions, Editions de la Maison des Sciences de l'Homme.

Robinne, François. 2008. "Jeux d'échelle et Enjeux: Dynamiques Identitaires des Cérémonies Processionnelles en Birmanie Bouddhique." [Scale Games and Issues: Identity Dynamics of Processional Ceremonies in Buddhist Burma]. Aséanie 22: 121–150.

Sadan, Mandy. 2007. "Constructing and Contesting the Category 'Kachin' in the Colonial ad Post-colonial Burmese State." In Exploring Ethnic Diversity in Burma, edited by Mikael Gravers. Copenhagen: NIAS Studies in Asian Topics, n°39.

Sadan, Mandy. 2013. Becoming Kachin, Oxford: Oxford University Press.

Schlemmer, Grégoire. 2012. "Rituals, Territories and Powers in the Sino-Indian Margins." Moussons 19: 19–31.

Simon Commission Report on India (Indian Statutory Commission). 1988 [1930]. "Vol. XI – Burma" (Memorandum Submitted by the Government of Burma). Delhi: Swati Publications.

Tannenbaum, Nicolas, and Cornelia Ann Kammerer. 2003. Founders' Cults in Southeast Asia: Ancestors, Polity, and Identity (Monograph 52). New Haven, CT: Yale University Southeast Asia Studies.

Than Tun. 2015. "Rakhaing Thungran in Cox's Bazar: Celebrating Buddhist New Year in Southern Bangladesh." PhD diss., The University of Western Australia.

Van Galen, Stephan. 2008. The Rise and Decline of the Mrauk U Kingdom (Burma) from the Fifteenth to the Seventeenth Century AD. Phd dissertation. Leiden: University of Leiden.

van Schendel, Willem. 2002. "Geographies of Knowing, Geographies of Ignorance: Jumping Scale in Southeast Asia." Environment and Planning D, Society and Space 20: 647–668.

van Schendel, Willem. 2005. The Bengal Borderland: Beyond State and Nation in South Asia, London: Anthem.

van Schendel, Willem. 2006. "Guns and Gas in Southeast Asia: Transnational Flows in the Burma Bangladesh Borderland." Kyoto Review of Southeast Asia 7: 1–19.

Part 3
Physical land use and agrarian transformations

Introduction

Jean-François Rousseau

In their introduction to the *Companion of Borderland Studies*, Wilson and Donnan (2012: 1) state that the processes that shape national and international political economies "may be found in borderlands in sharper relief". With this in mind, I argue that the chapters assembled in this part, and their focus on how agricultural change manifests in Asian borderlands, sharpen our understanding of agricultural change in four ways.

First, echoing De Koninck's (1996) argument that peasantries spearhead state territorial projects, the chapters in this part demonstrate that agricultural change transcends the sole agrarian realm. State regimes instrumentalize borderland agricultural ventures to consolidate their territorial peripheries, to expand their clout over their neighbours' portions of the borderlands, or to discourage others to engage in such expansionist projects. Perennial crop plantations are a preferred vehicle to achieve these aims, and the land and labour requirements, along with organizational structure from the plantation economy, have served colonial projects just as well as they serve contemporary "development" or "modernization" agendas (Goldthorpe 1988; Byerlee 2014).

Second, borderland agriculture and livelihoods are shaped by national and global markets for specific crops, non-food commodities, and currency markets. Markets notably drive crop boom cycles that foster state and corporate interests in the borderlands, often framed as the ultimate frontier (Hall 2011). Market influences sometimes yield surprising, if not counterintuitive, outcomes. Such is the case of Indonesia welcoming Malaysian companies to build plantations in order to secure the Indonesian side of the border that both nations share, as Eilenberg's chapter uncovers. The same applies to Ishikawa's finding that Indonesian borderlanders were apt at capitalizing on the Indonesian currency's devaluation by piling up the Malaysian Ringgit. My chapter likewise outlines how market forces and state agendas have propelled plantation schemes, whose proponents did not consider the agrarian potential of targeted lands – or total lack thereof.

Third, the modalities governing access to land uphold key influences upon borderland agricultural developments. The chapters by Ishikawa and Zhou reflect the idea that borderlanders are active "border-crossers" (Chan and Womack 2016: 95), and as such actively benefit from transnational opportunities, including those that pertain to land access. These two chapters further demonstrate that state authorities, whether located on the sending or receiving side of the border, encourage cross-border movements when it serves national geostrategic agendas or creates tax-raising opportunities. Eilenberg's chapter also highlights a pattern whereby real or imagined territorial security threats resulted in the army gaining the authority to control formal access rights over extensive non-titled lands. State decisions have also facilitated the enclosure of non-titled land resources, as discussed in my own chapter. Yet in this case, it was the conclusion that these lands were "wasted" that have made these areas attractive for jatropha developers.

Fourth, although the chapters highlight how frontier livelihoods oftentimes weigh little into how agricultural development unfolds in the borderlands, this part nonetheless provides insight into how rural populations negotiate state predicaments, regardless of whether they are enforced by colonial or authoritarian regimes, or military forces (see Turner et al. 2015). The Sino–Soviet split annihilated transborder opportunities between China and Russia; yet Zhou finds that Chinese peasants were quick to re-exploit these options as soon as geopolitical tensions toned down. The Kalimantan borderlanders at the core of Eilenberg's case study resisted the enclosure of their land, including through their involvement in non-governmental origanization (NGO) campaigns. The same goes for Bornean borderlanders who, as Ishikawa retraces, cumulated centuries of strategies to exploit opportunities on both sides of the Borneo border. As for the Handai people that inform my chapter, they never whole-heartedly embraced state-driven jatropha plantation expansion, and openly doubted that crops could fare well in the barren lands.

The above discussion highlights how this part adds "relief" to how we understand agricultural change. Taken individually, the chapters in this part achieve this just as well. I conclude this introduction by highlighting key aspects from the four chapters.

Settled in the Sino–Russian borderlands, Jiayi Zhou's chapter retraces how evolving Sino–Russian relations have yielded evolving opportunities for Chinese peasants settling in the Russian Far East region. Doing so, she illuminates how Chinese migrants have actively benefited from cross-border opportunities while serving agendas from both the Russian and Chinese governments.

Emphasizing the notion of frontier constellations, Micheal Eilenberg's piece retraces the militarization of Indonesia's West Kalimantan province during the Suharto era, and how the military instrumentalized palm oil plantation expansion to consolidate its presence on Borneo Island after the dictator's fall.

Also set in Borneo, Noburu Ishikawa's chapter revisits state/non-state dichotomies, demonstrating that throughout history, markets for commodities such as timber, rubber, palm oil, and pepper have had much more influence upon transborder movements and flows than the authorities from successive state regimes, regardless of whether these regimes were strong or weak.

Finally, my chapter investigates how numerous Chinese state agendas combined in fostering biofuel plantation experiments that were doomed to fail in the Sino–Vietnamese borderlands. I find that while such failure made no difference for state and corporate actors that promoted jatropha plantation expansion, the outcomes were quite different for local populations.

References

Byerlee, D. 2014. The Fall and Rise Again of Plantations in Tropical Asia: History Repeated? *Land* 3: 574–597.

Chan, Y. W., and B. Womack. 2016. Not Merely a Border: Borderland Governance, Development and Transborder Relations in Asia. *Asian Anthropology* 15 (2): 95–103.

De Koninck, R. 1996. The Peasantry as the Territorial Spearhead of the State in Southeast Asia: The Case of Vietnam. *SOJOURN: Journal of Social Issues in Southeast Asia* 11 (2): 231–258.

Goldthorpe, C. C. 1988. A Definition and Typology of Plantation Agriculture. *Singapore Journal of Tropical Geography* 8 (1): 26–43.

Hall, D. 2011. Land Grabs, Land Control, and Southeast Asian Crop Booms. *The Journal of Peasant Studies* 38 (4): 837–857.

Turner, S., C. Bonnin, and J. Michaud. 2015. *Frontier Livelihoods: Hmong in the Sino-Vietnamese Borderlands.* Seattle: University of Seattle Press.

Wilson, T. M., and H. Donnan. 2012. *A Companion to Border Studies.* Hoboken, NJ: John Wiley & Sons.

12
Genesis of state space
Frontier commodification in Malaysian Borneo

Noboru Ishikawa

Introduction

How is a border recognized, when spatial demarcation is not obvious, both geographically and geomorphologically, and the state apparatus for boundary making is functionally weak? What forces, other than border control measures by the state, are at work to demarcate the line in the mental mapping of borderland peoples? To answer these questions, this chapter looks at the historical process of commodification in the borderland of western Sarawak, Malaysian Borneo as a case in point.

The borderland under study has the following three characteristics. First, it has been centrally located in a web of commodity chains linking resource-rich tropics with international markets. Second, the border is inconspicuous: "altitude" and "distance" from any political center are not the crucial factors that make this borderland a distinctively nonstate space (McKinnon and Michaud 2000; Michaud 2008, 2010; Scott 2009). Third, the borderland is a space where the organizational power of the state is nominal, if not nonexistent.

In the borderlands, commodification represents a process whereby value is added to products as they move across a territorial boundary. While the state attempts to generate revenue from this process, people do so illicitly. This chapter sees the genesis of the state space and boundary making within the context of long-term processes of frontier commodification, recognizing that nontimber forest produce, timber, rubber, and pepper have functioned as critical linkages connecting local society with regional and global market systems.

This chapter concludes with the following findings. First, the more illicit flows of goods and people intensify, the clearer the state boundary becomes. The unintended and paradoxical amalgamation of the state-repelling actions of border communities and the border-making actions of the state apparatus formulates a threshold between state and nonstate space. Second, the genesis of state space lies not in the expansion of state power, but in the transnational and global process of commodification. In other words, the organizational power of the state needs the structural power of global markets in the making of state space.[1]

Borderlands in maritime history

In 1824, a profound spatial divide was inaugurated in maritime Southeast Asia (Map 12.1). The Anglo-Dutch Treaty of that year began transforming unbounded frontiers into the bounded

Genesis of state space

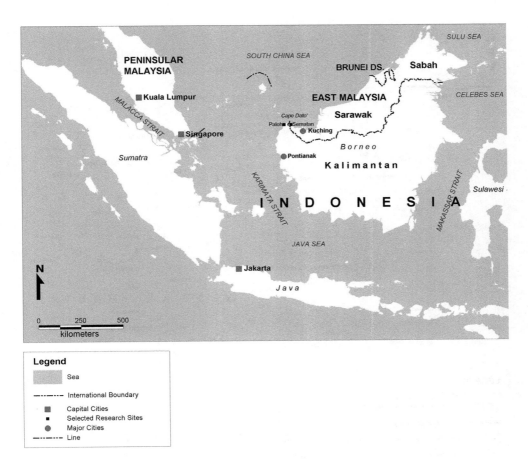

Map 12.1 Malay maritime world
Copyright by NUS Press

territories of two European empires. The transfer of Bencoolen in Sumatra to the Dutch, and of Malacca on the Malay Peninsula to the British divided the region into two domains: one north and one south of Singapore. This division was useful in settling claims in Sumatra and Malaya, but it was of little use on the island of Borneo, where the boundary between local sultanates was zonal. In coastal western Borneo, located at the same latitude as Singapore across the South China Sea, the border between the Sambas and Brunei sultanates was defined by a central mountain range. Following the colonial division after 1824, the British and Dutch territories in this region remained an ambiguous political buffer zone. It was here that a British ex-officer of the East India Company, James Brooke, established his own kingdom in 1841.[2]

Lundu District, located at the western corner of Sarawak and sharing an international border with Dutch East India, was one of the first administrative districts under Brooke rule (Map 12.2). The borderland was divided by the low mountain range that runs from Cape Dato on the coast to the interior. The boundary between Sarawak and Dutch Sambas coincided with that of the Brunei and Sambas sultanates. Cape Dato, at the western edge of Lundu District, was located at the heart of a maritime trading network that linked Singapore, the west coast of Dutch Borneo, Sarawak, and Brunei. The 1869 opening of the Suez Canal further boosted trading activities significantly in the region.

169

Map 12.2 Sarawak and West Kalimantan (Dutch West Borneo)
Copyright by NUS Press

In the Sarawak/Dutch Borneo borderland, policing by state agencies was minimal, and where it did exist, it was largely ineffective. Lundu District at the turn of the century covered an area of 1,870 km^2 and had a population density of fewer than three persons per square kilometer. The borderland lacked physical signs of demarcation such as immigration posts or border gates. Only one European and one native Malay officer administered the district with an 80-km-long border. Most areas of the district were covered by dense primary forest and were inaccessible by sea during the half-year long monsoon season. Officers stationed at Lundu fort had to walk overland to inspect sparsely populated inland communities, a trip that usually took more than a week. It was impossible to put borderland communities under close surveillance.

Transborder swidden practice

During the early period of development of Lundu District, one of the first recorded border disputes between Sarawak and Dutch West Borneo occurred over the affiliation of the Dayaks, who engaged in swidden cultivation.[3] Both governments claimed the Jagoi, a group of Dayak in upper Sarawak, as their subjects, and thus the right to collect a head tax on them. As early as 1874, the Committee of Administration of Sarawak and the Dutch authorities discussed the matter of border crossing by Jagoi Dayak (*Sarawak Gazette*, May 16, 1874: n.p., *Sarawak Gazette*, May 1, 1893: 78) and the demarcation of the colonial boundary (*Sarawak Gazette*, July 24, 1874: n.p.; *Sarawak Gazette*, August 1, 1884: 80).[4] The affiliation and farming practices of the migratory Jagoi remained an issue into the 1930s, and involved negotiations between high-level officials in Kuching and Pontianak, the respective capital cities (*Sarawak Gazette*, December 2, 1935: 228).

From the beginning of Brooke's rule, claiming subjects was crucial, even in the sparsely populated mountain region of southwestern Sarawak, because the head tax contributed substantially to district revenue. In 1892, for example, the Dayak head tax constituted 40 per cent of the total revenue of Lundu District (*Sarawak Gazette*, May 1, 1893: 78). Neither the national affiliation nor the permanent residence of these swidden cultivators was a critical issue for either government. As long as tax was paid, mobile Dayaks were allowed to engage in shifting cultivation of rice in both Sarawak and Dutch West Borneo:

> The Jagoi Land Dayaks are growing very short of land for farming purposes, and are anxious to take up land across the Dutch border, where there is a large area of old jungle available. They were informed that permission for them to do this would have to be obtained from the Netherland Indies authorities, and that in any case, if they farmed over the border, they were liable to find themselves paying two separate sets of taxes.
> (Sarawak Gazette, *April 1, 1935: 51*)

Apart from the payment of head tax, authorities were also indifferent to Dayak mobility because they were not involved in the commercial estates where labour was indispensable and had to be controlled.[5]

Forest products

During the initial period of Brooke colonization, forest products attracted commercial interest. The commodification and taxation of forest products only became possible, however, with the formation of colonial governments on both sides of the Sarawak–Dutch West Borneo border. Products such as *damar, jelutong*, beeswax, *gutta-percha*, and camphor commanded high prices on the Singapore market, and Sarawak inhabitants collected them as far inland as Dutch Sambas territory.[6] In 1876, in response to a complaint from the Sambas Sultan, Charles Brooke, the successor to James Brooke, issued an order discouraging border crossing to gather forest products. The order alerted Sarawak residents that the Sultan would demand 'a payment of 10 per cent on primitive produce... before such produce can be taken out of his country' (*Sarawak Gazette*, June 5, 1876: 3). Even into the 1890s, when a monopoly on forest product collection in Sambas District had been granted to T.W. Kaat of Java, forest exploitation by Sarawak subjects had not stopped, prompting additional complaints and a ban by the Brooke government (*Sarawak Gazette*, October 10, 1890: 125).

Natural resources within Sarawak's territory were similarly attractive to outsiders and provided the state with an opportunity to levy taxes. Because of its proximity to Singapore and such regional commercial centers in Dutch West Borneo as Pontianak, Mempawah, and Sambas, the coastal area of Lundu District was frequented by non-Sarawakian *nakoda* traders who came to cut timber and build *sampan* boats.[7] The Lundu authorities reported enforcing the regulation that '[n]o strangers are permitted to work timber without first obtaining a permit at the Court House,' and in at least one case, 'in lieu of taxation [collected] one boat out of ten…' (*Sarawak Gazette*, February 1, 1893: 26).

In 1894, Charles Brooke ordered his officials in Lundu to open up forestland in Sematan on the east coast of the district to facilitate logging by anyone wishing to do so (*Sarawak Gazette*, December 1, 1894: 208; *Sarawak Gazette*, August 1, 1895: 144). Consequently, officials in the Lundu District Office were kept busy collecting export duties as the volume of exports from Lundu and the Sematan coast increased. They kept an eye on incoming and outgoing vessels to ensure the legal traffic of goods and devised ways to improve surveillance (*Sarawak Gazette*, September 1, 1900: 175). As the timber market expanded in Singapore and Java in the latter half of the century, a substantial number of traders extracted timber on the coast. These traders were not regarded as foreign intruders, but rather welcomed as long as they paid duties on the exported timber. It is intriguing that despite the government's open policy welcoming natural resource exploiters from outside the territory, a Malay *engkabang* tree owner asked Brooke officials to protect his interests against foreign intruders from across the border:[8]

> Tan Ahmat begged that persons from other districts should be forbidden to collect engkabang fruit in this district and the Court Writer at Simatan wrote in asking whether permission to collect this fruits might be refused to natives of Sambas and a notice to that effect might be sent to him.
>
> (Sarawak Gazette, *February 1, 1912: 33*)

State–society symbiosis

In the first five decades of colonization under the Brooke Government, physical demarcation of the Dutch–Sarawak boundary itself did not exist, let alone effective regulations that prevented the illicit flows of commodities. Following the enactment of regulations during the reign of the second Rajah, Charles Brooke (1868–1917), the *Sarawak Gazette* and the Lundu District Monthly Report recorded numerous reports on border crossing and control issued to outstation officers. Such records reflect the will of the colonial state to determine the affiliation of peoples as well as the origin of natural and cultivated biomass in Sarawak, yet attests to their failure to do so. During this period state–society relations were not explicitly antagonistic. Rather, the colonial state of Sarawak and local society of Lundu were in a symbiotic relationship of mutual engagement, constitution, and transformation. These relations embodied specific representations of the colonial world in an incubator stage at the margins.

Enforcement and violation of border regulations took place repeatedly. Measures implemented by the Charles Brooke administration to counter recurrent problems were ad hoc and inconsistent. It was only after specific "border problems" were reported that new regulations were written and notification made to administrative officers. Laws were rarely announced directly to inhabitants of the borderland; instead they were published in government gazettes and official reports. Even where prohibitions were announced, certain violations, such as border trespassing, exploitation of banned forest products, and cross-border swidden cultivation, never ceased. Such cases were reported to the capital, which led to the issuing of almost identical regulations or orders, as the cat-and-mouse game between administrators and "untamed" locals continued. State–society relations at the periphery of Sarawak were contentious—albeit at a low intensity—and in a sense, complementary. Officials reported cases of offence and nominal punishment ensued. Yet despite the state's repeated intent to enclose a national space, locals never really stopped maneuvers for personal profit. State and society formed a reflexive relationship in which a dialectical process between state policing and the adaptive strategies of local society contributed to the gradual formation of a national space.

Rubber smuggling

Colonial management of commodity flows, however, drastically changed with the advent of rubber production in western Borneo in the 1920s. With the arrival of rubber, an early form of a nationally singular economic space emerged. The rubber trade in the boom periods necessitated the demarcation of the colonial boundary between Sarawak and Dutch Borneo to ensure revenue flowed to the respective governments. As we see in the following, rubber smuggling from Dutch West Borneo into Sarawak Kingdom exhibits a departure from the previous mode of transnational flows of commodities.

The advent of rubber cultivation in western Borneo marked a new era for the borderland. Rubber tied the periphery of the European colony directly to the international commodity market. Signficantly, the focus of commodification shifted from forest produce to cash crops during the 1920s. This gave rise to a rampant smuggling economy in the borderland. During the interwar period, demand for rubber rose as supply was first restricted by the Stevenson Scheme in 1922–1928.[9] The temporary price recovery peaked in 1925 before declining toward the end of the decade. Thereafter, the Great Depression resulted in a prolonged slump in the market and rubber production and export. Rubber-producing colonies concluded the International Rubber Agreement (INRA) of 1934 to maintain a minimum rubber market price after the Great Depression. All new planting was forbidden and state-wide tapping holidays were declared every fourth month. An imperial quota system for the production of rubber created a price difference between the two colonies and swiftly generated cross-border flows of raw rubber from the Dutch territory to Sarawak.[10] The difference in demand as well as price created by the international production scheme therefore became an instrument for the formation of difference in a borderland located between two opposing imperial market domains, the British and the Dutch. Locals engaged in transnational *smokel* (smuggling) of rubber were also keenly aware of the price difference between the two colonies. Regulation of cultivation and export through a national quota system resulted in tighter control of the cross-border movement of rubber. Smuggling was conducted both overland and by sea. Smugglers' boats came around Cape Dato to bring rubber sheets to Kuching by sea. Two Malay villages located near the cape functioned as transit points. Smugglers also carried the bulky sheets across the border on foot, entering Sarawak in places such as Biawak and Serikin (see Map 12.2). By land or by sea, local peasants brought rubber sheets to transit points, and Chinese merchants shipped them to Kuching and Singapore. At the same time as this transnational smuggling of rubber began to flourish, peasants began to smuggle other commodities from Dutch colonial territory and sell them to Chinese *taukay* in Sarawak.[11]

By the 1930s, Lundu District had been incorporated into the state-led commodity production system. Hinterland peasants and merchants swiftly established transnational networks of a corresponding scale to evade border control measures imposed by the state. The production quota presented both new limitations and opportunities for the locals; smuggling of rubber and other dutiable commodities between Dutch West Borneo and Sarawak was their strategic response. It should be noted here that rubber cultivation had started earlier in Dutch West Borneo than in Sarawak, and yields were considerably higher, as Dutch Borneo trees were more mature. In Sambas District of Dutch Borneo adjacent to the Sarawakian border, rubber production was mostly undertaken by Malay peasants along the major rivers and by Dayaks along the border in the interior (*Sarawak Gazette*, April 1, 1936: 86; *Sarawak Gazette*, May 1, 1936: 107).

The emergence of a smuggling economy coincided with the development of a national and supra-national order. For the first time in history, the Sarawak colony became recognized as a full-fledged territorial state, because of its incorporation into the world-wide rubber production system and rubber restriction schemes. Its participation in rubber quotas gave Sarawak internationally recognized status as an independent economic unit required to control the production and distribution of an important commodity.

The hinterland of Lundu District, adjacent to the border, remained in curious isolation at the periphery of the colonial space during the heyday of smuggling. Over the course of the 1950s and early 1960s, the economy of Lundu became dependent on smuggling. With the Kuching-based distribution network far away, bazaars in the frontier district continued to obtain Indonesian goods from smugglers and redistributed them to local merchandizing networks. Many peasant communities adjacent to the border gave up planting commercial crops and chose the more profitable smuggling business (*LDR*[12] 2nd Half Year 1959). The "aversion" to agrarian production and the frequent changes of livelihood strategies have remained a hallmark of these borderlands until this day.

Non-agrarian characteristics

Both under Brooke rule and within the modern nation state of Malaysia (the State of Sarawak), the borderlands have never witnessed the rise of a sedentary peasantry that undertakes agrarian production, despite state interventions and corporate enterprise initiatives.[13] Border communities have maintained multifaceted livelihood strategies, combining various modes of subsistence rather than solely depending on perennial cropping regimes. Locals have, at different points in time, engaged in swidden cultivation, foraging, forest produce extraction and trade, crop cultivation during boom periods, cross-border smuggling of dutiable commodities, wage labor (albeit to a limited extent), and so forth. Through such diversified economic portfolios, borderland communities have upheld a distinctive non-agrarian character.

These strategies are made possible by extremely low population pressure, high biodiversity, and abundant biomass of both fauna and flora. The need to produce and store resources via settled agriculture has never been acute. In addition, linkage to international commodity chains has secured diversified income sources. Forest produce such as natural rubber for submarine cable insulation, latex used in foods as a clouding or glazing agent, iron wood for roofing and construction materials, and rattan for furniture, handicrafts and even grenade basket cases, just to name a few, are all items highly valued in the global commodity market (Jayl and Ishikawa 2017). Borderland society has thus been primarily based on flows and exchanges of such items rather than sedentary agrarian production.

Even with the advent of the oil palm plantation system and the arrival of economies of scale to the frontier, a substantial part of contemporary Sarawak's borderlands has retained its non-agrarian character. Unlike neighboring Kalimantan of the Indonesian frontier, where oil palm cultivation has rapidly expanded with corporate capital investment and the active participation of smallholders, the Sarawak borderlands still lack basic infrastructure, most importantly a road network that links the interior with downstream markets. Because of the peculiar nature of the oxidation-prone oil palm, fresh fruit bunches need to be processed within 24 hours after harvest to be marketed as an industrial commodity. Although larger roads now connect major cities and towns, the insufficient road network in Sarawak's frontier has discouraged the development of large-scale plantations as well as the engagement of local smallholders.

Other regions in Sarawak are currently witnessing both corporate and smallholding expansion of oil palm cultivation on a massive scale. Oil palm now accounts for about 8 per cent of the total land area and 70 per cent of the area used for agricultural crops in the state of Sarawak. Almost half (46 per cent) of the area planted with oil palm trees is located on a flat-to-undulating coastal belt. Over the past decade, oil palm tree cultivation has expanded in every administrative division of the state, from downstream to Sarawak's extensive peatlands and further into the hilly interior (Cramb 2013: 1). While Sarawak has experienced a more than 40-fold increase in oil palm cultivation since 1980, the boom has yet to reach the borderlands.

Osmotic pressure between states

Just as osmotic pressure is determined by the difference in the concentration of a liquid between two organs, the difference between two national economies determines the direction of the movement of people and goods across borders. The widening economic gap between post-independence Indonesia and Malaysia accelerated movements of natural resources and agricultural commodities from Indonesian Kalimantan to East Malaysia. In response, the two countries strengthened the international border with official immigration posts and customs houses, which eventually gave further impetus to illicit flows of traded goods and undocumented laborers. The Cross Border Agreement of 1984 proposed the opening of 10 points of entry and exit, known as *Pos Lintas Batas*, along the Kalimantan–East Malaysia border. These were: Paloh, Sanjingan, Sungai Aruk, Saparan, Jagoi Babang, Sidding, Bantan, Merakai Panjang, Nanga Badau, and Entikong (Map 12.3). On October 1, 1989, the completion of the first sealed road linking Kuching with Pontianak via the border towns of Tebudu in Sarawak and Entikong in West Kalimantan created a new entry–exit point where border trade has since increased tremendously.

As hubs for local cross-border traffic were transformed into official entry–exit points under the supervision of postcolonial nation states, the small paths traditionally called *jalan tikus*, or rat paths, used for informal border crossing, were replaced by larger roads to facilitate increasing traffic. Some of the paths through which raw rubber sheets were illicitly brought to Sarawak during the rubber boom were upgraded to major corridors connecting the state capitals of Pontianak and Kuching. Traditional *jalan tikus* became *jalan gajah*, or elephant roads, connecting border towns not only to Pontianak and Kuching, but to other major towns in Kalimantan and East Malaysia.

Although the border-crossing inspection post of Entikong functions as a crucial commercial hub between the two countries, the development of the Entikong–Tebudu trade route at first yielded more economic benefit to West Kalimantan than to Sarawak. In 1998, West Kalimantan's trade surplus reached US$3 million due to the depreciation of the Indonesian *rupiah*. Many traders in Entikong came to depend on the weak Indonesian *rupiah*. The outflow of commodities from Indonesian territory continued as long as the depreciated Indonesian *rupiah* rendered profits to locals who were marginalized from the Pontianak-based commercial network. The opening of the Entikong post did not therefore eliminate illicit cross-border trade. The most commonly smuggled goods were cigarettes, rice, bird's nests, clothing, household items, and hewn timber (Fariastuti 2000, 2002; Riwanto and Haba 2005).

The downturn of the Indonesian economy during the last phase of President Soeharto's rule in the late 1990s was regarded as a favorable opportunity not only by traders engaged in commercial activities at frontier marketplaces, but also by peasants and Indonesian traders at the margin of the national territory. Weak Indonesian currency meant a stronger Malaysian *ringgit*, which, as residents of the borderland, they could readily access. Saving cash in *ringgit* rather than *rupiah* was safer and more profitable for many in the borderland villages of West Kalimantan.

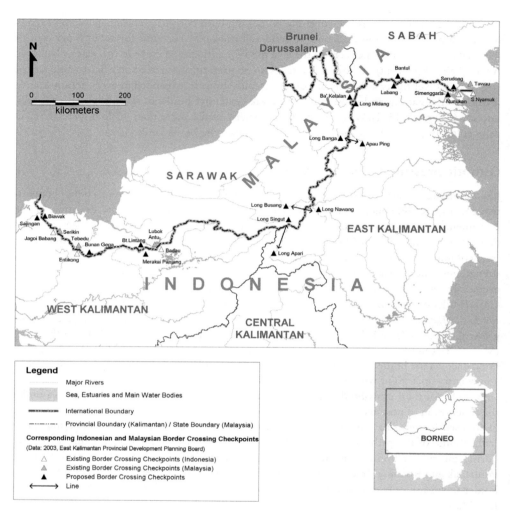

Map 12.3 Borneo border checkpoints
Copyright by NUS Press

The dramatic depreciation of the *rupiah* after the economic crisis of 1997 transformed the lives of cultivators of commercial crops, especially pepper. For instance, an Indonesian pepper producer living near Cape Dato made a substantial profit from selling his pepper seeds to Malaysian middlemen who came from across the border. He had previously sold pepper to Malaysian middlemen at exchange rates in the range of Rp (*rupiah*) 750 (1992) and Rp 1,200 (1994) to one *ringgit*. When the exchange rate surged to Rp 3,500 in 1997, he sold his pepper at a value 4.7 times higher than that of five years before.

State–society reflexivity

An analysis of the century-long formation of the western Borneo borderland suggests that the state-repelling actions of the frontier community, and its acknowledgement and strategic usage of the state boundary, have not always been contradictory or irreconcilable. On the contrary, the seemingly opposing dynamics have constantly co-existed, gradually bridging the territorialization of the state, the global forces of capitalism, and daily life on the border, to form a resonance of sorts. What is observable at this periphery of the state territory is not the counterpoising of state and society—an assertion of a "strong" society versus a "weak" state or vice versa. The dynamics of state and nonstate spaces is not entirely a story of state power extending to the periphery, nor of the decline of the power of local elites, traders, and peasants. While the state may have been weak, the local society was also not strong enough to form its own collective social organizations. Social groups such as corporate descent groups, domestic business networks, rigid patron–client dyads, and ethnically mobilized interest groups were all missing from this border space.

The maritime border area under study illuminates the local dynamics of a borderland transitioning from nonstate to state space where the synergy and resonance between state policy implementation and cross-border flows of people and things are at work in the realization of state territoriality. The historical analysis shows how both the state and local society contributed, in a slow and gradual process, to the making of the state boundary in a type of call and response resonance rather than an antithetical relationship. The historical evidence suggests that in the borderland area of western Sarawak, the more illicit flows of goods and people intensified, the clearer the state boundary became. This seemingly paradoxical relation does not comfortably comply with the zero sum perspective, where one or more player's gain or loss equals the loss or gain of others. The state and the borderland communities are more symbiotic rather than two separate and dichotomous, or conflicting, entities. State and society thus responded to each other in turn, eventually engraving a borderline in a collective enterprise of boundary making.[14]

Workings of global forces

The Bornean borderlands in this study are located in a maritime frontier densely incorporated into international commodity chains. What sets this particular territorial margin apart from others is its maritime accessibility to both coastal and regional trading hubs, making it particularly susceptible to global forces of market expansion. The existence of navigable rivers that connect the coast with the inland and allow for the collection of forest produce enabled frequent contact between local communities and traders from afar.

These borderlands therefore differed from counterparts in mainland Southeast Asia where distance and elevation separate hills (highland) and plains (lowland), and such terrestrial factors therefore mattered far less in the process of boundary making. Rather, global market forces connected to regional commodity chains have played a transformational role in establishing a marker that separates identities of people and commodities on both sides of the porous border. These forces included the imperial quota system for the production of rubber in the interwar period and the economic gap between Malaysia and Indonesia manifested in the 1992 monetary crisis. The structural forces toward the genesis of the boundary have not been the expansion of state power, but the connectivity between the borderlands and commodity markets. This illustrates that where the state machinery is weak, the global forces of capitalism are instrumental in making state space, particularly in the mental mapping of borderland peoples.

Notes

1. For a detailed account of the transformation of the borderlands in southwestern Sarawak, see Ishikawa (2010).
2. As a reward for helping the Sultanate of Brunei fight insurgency, James Brooke was granted the landmass of Sarawak in 1841. The Brooke family then established a monarchy, referred to as the White Rajahs of Sarawak Kingdom, which lasted for the next 100 years. The White Rajahs' dynasty continued

through Brooke's nephew and grandnephew, the latter of whom ceded his rights to the United Kingdom in 1946. For a comprehensive analysis of colonial policies under James Brooke (1841–1868) and Charles Brooke (1868–1917), see Ishikawa (1998) and Reece (1988).
3. Dayak refers to a member of an indigenous group of peoples, including the Iban, the Orang Ulu, and the Land Dayak.
4. Charles Brooke created a gazette in 1871 to transmit his official proclamations, internal appointments, and any important news. The *Sarawak Gazette* is a unique resource, featuring detailed reports made by officers stationed in outstations.
5. For the development of Lundu plantation economy, see Ishikawa (2010).
6. *Damar*, obtained from the *Dipterocarpaceae* family of trees, is used in incense, varnish, and other products. *Jelutong* (*Dyera costulata*) is best known for its use in latex production in the manufacture of chewing gum. *Gutta-percha* latex is biologically inert, resilient, and is a good electrical insulator with a high dielectric strength. It served as the insulating material for some of the earliest undersea telegraph cables, including the first transatlantic telegraph cable.
7. *Nakoda* means ship captain in Malay, and generally refers to Muslim traders. On the activity of *nakoda* in colonial southwestern Sarawak, see N. Ishikawa (1999) and M. Ishikawa (2005).
8. *Engkabang*, the oil-bearing nuts of the forest tree species *Shorea spp.*, is used in confectionery industries, especially for chocolate manufacturing.
9. In accordance with a strict export quota, the British colony banned new rubber planting, controlled harvesting, and regulated the number of rubber sheets circulating through domestic trade networks. It is important to note that this was not the case in the Dutch territory where there was no such policy (Drabble 1973: 192).
10. A coupon system regulated the number of rubber trees planted and the quantity of rubber sheets sold to local dealers. Both rubber producers and dealers were issued government coupons, which authorized them to market an approved quantity of rubber.
11. *Taukay* is a common word of Hokkien origin, meaning the head of a firm or shop.
12. Short for: Lundu District Report (The Sarawak Museum).
13. Vast tracts of uncultivated land regarded as "no man's land" were redistributed to the "Sarawak" subjects for agricultural production. For the general process of spatial configuration by the state, see Greenblatt (1991). For the detailed description of Sarawak land administration, see Porter (1967).
14. Theory generated from the state–society relationship in the "outer islands" of maritime Southeast Asia necessarily differs from that of the irrigated lowlands of mainland Southeast Asia or densely populated Java. This study has thus sought a new way of locating society and the state in locally specific history (cf. Warren 1981; Tagliacozzo 2005; Lumenta 2010).

References

Cramb, R. 2013. A Malaysian Land Grab?: The Political Economy of Large-scale Oil Palm Development in Sarawak. The Hague: The Land Deal Politics Initiative.
Drabble, J. 1973. Rubber in Malaya 1876–1922: The Genesis of the Industry. Kuala Lumpur: Oxford University Press.
Fariastuti. 2000. "West Kalimantan and Sarawak Trade Relation." In Borneo 2000: Language, Management, and Tourism, ed. Michael Leigh. Kuching: Universiti Malaysia Sarawak and Sarawak Development Institute.
Fariastuti. 2002. "Mobility of People and Goods Across the Border of West Kalimantan and Sarawak." Antropologi Indonesia 67: 94–104.
Greenblatt, S. 1991. Marvelous Possessions: The Wonder of the New World. Chicago: The University of Chicago Press.
Ishikawa, M. 2005. "The Story of Nakoda Hitam: Her Life and Ventures at Maritime Crossroads at the Turn of the 20th Century." The Sarawak Museum Journal 61(82) (New Series): 247–62.
Ishikawa, N. 1998. "A Benevolent Protector or Failed Exploiter?: Local Response to Agro-economic Policies Under the Second White Rajah, Charles Brooke (1868–1917) of Sarawak." In Japanese Anthropologists, Malaysian Society: Contribution to Malaysian Ethnography, eds. A.B. Shamsul and T. Uesugi. Osaka: National Museum of Ethnology.
Ishikawa, N. 1999. "The Social History of Coconuts in Sematan, Southwestern Sarawak." The Sarawak Museum Journal 54(75): 239–51.

Ishikawa, N. 2010. Between Frontiers: Nation and Identity in a Southeast Asian Borderland. Singapore; Athens; Copenhagen: NUS Press; Ohio University Press; NIAS Press.

Jayl, L. and Ishikawa, N. 2017. "Community, River and Basin: Watersheds in Northern Sarawak as a Social Linkage." In Borneo Studies in History, Society and Culture, eds. Victor T. King, Zawai Ibrahim, and Noor Hasharina Hassan. Singapore: Springer.

Lumenta, D. 2010. "Changing Spaces and Border Regimes: A Central Borneo Trajectory of 'Globalisation'." Jurnal Kajian Wilayah 1(2): 190–202.

McKinnon, J. and Michaud, J. 2000. "Presentation: Montagnard Domain in the South-east Asian Massif." In Turbulent Times and Enduring Peoples: The Mountain Minorities of the South-east Asian Massif, Richmond, ed. J. Michaud, 1–25. Surrey: Curzon Press.

Michaud, J. 2008. "Economic Transformation in a Hmong Village of Thailand." Human Organization 56(2): 222–32.

Michaud, J. 2010. "Editorial: Zomia and Beyond." Journal of Global History 5(2): 187–214.

Porter, A. 1967. Land Administration in Sarawak: An Account of the Development of Land Administration in Sarawak from the Rule of Rajah Brooke to the Present Time (1841–1967). Kuching: Government Printing Office.

Reece, R.H.W. 1988. "Economic Development under the Brookes." In Sarawak: Historical and Contemporary Perspectives, eds. R.A. Cramb and R.H.W. Reece. Monash Paper on Southeast Asia No.17, Center of Southeast Asian Studies, Monash University.

Riwanto, T. and Haba, J., eds. 2005. Dari Entikong Sampai Nunukan: Dinamika Daerah Perbatasan Kalimantan Malaysia Timur (Sarawak-Sabah). Jakarta: Pustaka Sinar Harapan.

Sarawak Gazette. 1870–. Sarawak Museum, microfilm edition, Originally published: Kuching: [S.M.].

Scott, J. 2009. The Art of Not Being Governed: An Anarchist History of Upland Southeast Asia. New Haven, CT: Yale University Press.

Tagliacozzo, E. 2005. Secret Trades, Porous Borders: Smuggling and States Along a Southeast Asian Frontier, 1865–1915. New Haven, CT; London and Singapore: Yale University Press; NUS Press.

Warren, J.F. 1981. The Sulu Zone 1768–1898: The Dynamics of External Trade, Slavery, and Ethnicity in the Transformation of a Southeast Asian Maritime State. Singapore: NUS Press.

13

Frontier constellations

Agrarian expansion and sovereignty on the Indonesian–Malaysian border

Michael Eilenberg

Introduction: between borders and frontiers[1]

In 2011, the Indonesian Agency for Border Management released a national regulation named the 'Grand Design' (BNPP 2011). The 'Grand Design' stipulated a 15-year master plan for economic development, defense, and security along the country's neglected borders. The country's border regions were to become Indonesia's new centers of economic growth with large-scale plantation development as the main economic driver (Perpres 2010). Besides economic development, it was highlighted how such large-scale agrarian initiatives would enhance territorial sovereignty and increase the state's presence along the country's porous borders (Perpres 2010). One of the eight targeted regions was the district of Kapuas Hulu in the province of West Kalimantan, bordering the Malaysian state of Sarawak (*Jakarta Post* 2011).

With the introduction of the border regulations, the Indonesian government plan was to boost economic development and security in the 'remote and underdeveloped' borderlands through large-scale investments in infrastructure, mining, and agricultural expansion, carried out in cooperation with the private sector and the military (BNPP 2011). According to the director general of plantations at the Ministry of Agriculture, the only way to create a 'prosperous border region is to establish oil palm plantations' (Media Perkebunan 2011). 'Wastelands' along the border should be reintegrated into the sovereign nation state and local populations nationalized through the allocation of private oil palm concessions and firm military intervention (BNPP 2011). In line with the government plan, the Indonesian Armed Forces publicly announced that they would increase their presence in the border regions by establishing new military commands and infantry divisions in order to take control of the 'lawless' borderlands and protect abundant natural resources from foreign (Malaysian) intrusion (*Jakarta Post* 2010). By focusing on these processes of remilitarization along the border, I show how the Indonesian military repositioned themselves in the lucrative role of protectors of national sovereignty, working in tandem with private transnational capital.

The increased government focus on border development is the latest chapter in a long and contested history of resource exploitation and militarization in the Indonesian border regions since the early 1960s. It illustrates the intimate linkages between policy regimes of national development and discourses of territorial sovereignty and security. This chapter investigates these linkages and their contested nature and highlights how processes of agricultural expansion in the West Kalimantan borderlands are repeatedly justified through government discourses of national sovereignty, security, and powerful notions of 'wild' and unexploited resource frontiers.

Military involvement in resource extraction and population resettlement in Indonesia and Southeast Asia as a whole is not a novel phenomenon and can be traced back to the counter-insurgencies of the Cold War era, when many of the burgeoning Southeast Asian nation states were plunged into violent conflict. The rugged and forested borderlands often became insurgent hideouts and thus key battlefields in the war against communism and communist regimes (Jones 2002; Tuck 2004), instigating processes of violent resettlement, resource exploitation, and firm military control (De Koninck 2006). As argued by Nancy Peluso and Peter Vandergeest (2011), counterinsurgency measures in forest frontiers in Southeast Asia (especially along national borders) have played a crucial role in state territorialization of forest resources. Many of these forestlands have since been under various forms of military control and have become zones for economic exploitation, generating revenue for the military budgets (Peluso 2008; Eilenberg 2011). Despite the fact that many of these resource-rich borderlands are increasingly being targeted for large-scale development schemes and territorial control in a way that resembles past government strategies of securitization (Geiger 2008), so far only a few studies have critically engaged with the intricate links between emerging agricultural expansion and militarization in the borderlands (see, for example, Ito et al. 2011; Woods 2011; Laungaramsri 2012).

In an attempt to trace the linkages between agrarian expansion, sovereignty, and securitization along the Indonesian–Malaysian border, I will introduce the notion of '*frontier constellations*' as an analytical starting point and highlight the multiple meanings and notions associated with regions where resource frontiers and national borders interlock. I argue that such frontier constellations in Southeast Asia are distinctive social, economic, and political formations with multiple meanings, such as: (a) political borderlines separating two or more nation states; (b) areas physically separate from state cores; and (c) zones between allegedly settled and unsettled land, accentuating underdevelopment, remoteness, and dense forest landscapes. I argue that scrutinizing this specific frontier constellation provides insight into state-led notions of development and sovereignty. As expressed by Nils Fold and Philip Hirsch, 'The frontier is thus in part a metaphor for national development in its material and ideological senses, as well as in terms of spatial expansion and delimitation' (Fold and Hirsch 2009: 95).

According to Danilo Geiger, frontier spaces are not necessarily situated along national borders, but when they are, 'we are dealing with a special constellation rather than a definitional criterion for "frontierness"' (2008: 95). Building on work that conceptualizes frontiers as 'myth, analytical framework and material reality' (Redclift 2006: viii), I argue that the frontier imaginary becomes especially powerful and potent in regions where resource frontiers and national borders interlock. This is especially so as these zones of immense natural resources and sparse populations play an important role as the territorial and economic spearhead of many Southeast Asian states. In other words, by bringing together the issues of frontiers, borderlands, and agrarian expansion and grounding them in extensive empirical research I wish to direct attention to novel forms of state making and securitization in Southeast Asia and contribute to debates on agrarian change at the margins of developing states (De Koninck 2006; Barney 2009; Woods 2011).

Security and sovereignty through frontier colonization in West Kalimantan

The Indonesian province of West Kalimantan on the island of Borneo shares 966 kilometers of its land border with the Malaysian state of Sarawak; about 25,168 square kilometers or 16 percent of the total landmass of the province. In 2011, the total population of the West Kalimantan borderlands was estimated to be about 180,000, with an average population density of seven people per square kilometer (Bappenas 2011). The indigenous inhabitants of the West Kalimantan border hills are a mixture of ethnic Dayak groups, primarily practicing swidden agriculture supplemented with small-scale rubber tapping and circular labor migration across the border with Sarawak (Eilenberg and Wadley 2009). Apart from the main border avenues, for example between Nanga Badau (Indonesia) and Lubok Antu (Sarawak, Malaysia), which locals have used for centuries, the low-lying hills along the border are easily crossed and constitute no physical barrier. It is estimated that there are more than 50 small back roads into Sarawak.

The sparsely populated borderlands are widely forested and contain large patches of land classified in government policy narratives as 'sleeping', 'waste', or 'idle', waiting to be colonized and exploited for agricultural development and security reasons (*Jakarta Post* 2005b; Potter 2009; Wakker 2006). Subsequently, the popular 'image' of the borderlands, as seen by outside influences such as government officials and plantation companies, is of a thinly populated resource frontier, separating civilization from 'wilderness', inhabited by an underdeveloped and 'uncivilized' population (Kepmenhut 2004). Underdevelopment and poor infrastructure along the border with Malaysia, together with the increase in illegal logging and smuggling, have long been considered a national security problem by the central state.

Since the early 1960s, the Indonesian state has struggled to assert control over its national border with Malaysia and its natural resources, presenting arguments of national security and development promotion to the 'estranged and backward' frontier inhabitants (Eilenberg 2012a). In 1963, the Kalimantan borderlands became heavily militarized as a result of an armed confrontation (*Konfrontasi*) between Indonesia and Malaysia, which was later followed by a communist insurgency in the mid-1960s and the 1970s (Jones 2002; Eilenberg 2011). Ever since, border development and security has been a dominant state discourse and until the early 1990s the forested borderlands were categorized as a 'safety belt' or security buffer zone facing neighboring Malaysia (Soemadi 1974). Access for civilians not residing in the borderland region was largely restricted, and access permits from military and police were needed. Consequently, the Indonesian state purposely delayed infrastructural and other kinds of development (Wadley 1998). More to the point, successive Indonesian governments have since allocated large-scale timber and plantation concessions along its resource-rich national border to military entrepreneurs, local elites, and private companies as part of a pragmatic frontier colonization and resource extraction strategy (Davidson and Kammen 2002; Potter 2009). The allocation of concessions was thus part of a nationwide policy of 'nationalizing' ethnic customary lands in unruly forest frontiers. In the case of the Indonesian–Malaysian border, the appropriation of land was an additional tool for imposing territorial sovereignty and displaying state authority (Peluso and Vandergeest 2011). Additionally, in return for awarding the military this opportunity for economic gain, President Suharto received military support in ensuring strict conformity to his New Order politics in the outer regions of the nation (Brown 1999; Human Rights Watch 2006).

So-called 'development' often became an excuse for large-scale resource extraction. For example, in 1967 former President Suharto allocated concession rights to a huge tract of land, covering more than 1 million hectares, to a foundation created by the Indonesian Armed Forces, named 'Yayasan Maju Kerja' or Yamaker. In West Kalimantan, Yamaker combined economic exploitation with national security concerns, and its operations encompassed a stretch of border from Tanjung Datu, the westernmost tip of the province on the coast, to the upper part of the Embaloh River to the far east, about 843,500 hectares and 400 kilometers in length. The foundation's main activity was logging to generate income for the armed forces. In return for the concessions, though, the foundation was officially required to improve the socioeconomic welfare of the border communities by promoting various rural development programs.[2] Yamaker did not fulfill its promises of developing the area and providing local jobs, and repeatedly blocked access to the land on the pretext of security. For local communities the benefits were few. Today, most people still recall the Yamaker logging operations with resentment.

Decades later, in 1994, President Suharto issued the first official presidential decree on development initiatives in the border areas of Kalimantan (Keppres 1994). According to the decree, border development was imperative for national security, and the approach taken should therefore involve a system of defense and security. The 1994 decree appointed a special 'Agency for the Implementation and Control of Development in the Border Area'.[3] This agency involved various ministries, but – tellingly – was mainly headed by the Ministry of Defense and Security (Dephankam). Although grand development plans for the border area, including opening the area to transmigration settlements, mining, and plantations were put forward, any genuine commitment to the noble cause quickly died away. The only processes that took place in the borderlands were large-scale forest resource extraction, of which local communities benefited little (Wadley 1998).

Agricultural corridor and security buffer zone

According to government reports, the only way to guarantee sovereignty, territorial integrity, and national security was to improve the welfare of people in the border region (Bappenas 2003). The main strategy for attaining this goal, as noted in several reports, was to create a large agricultural region or corridor along the border (*Kawasan Agropolitan*) and thereby create local prosperity, reorient the border population's large economic dependence on neighboring Malaysia, and prevent separatism and illegal activities, especially illegal logging (Bappenas 2003). Large-scale oil palm monocropping was highlighted as the primary driver of significant agricultural expansion along the border, which fed into a larger national strategy of development through agrarian expansion. As the global demand for palm oil increases, Indonesia has been allocating large tracts of land for plantations throughout the country and continues to pursue new agricultural frontiers (Ahmad et al. 2009; McCarthy and Cramb 2009; De Koninck et al. 2011).

Following the numerous and vaguely defined border plans previously outlined, and despite the lack of an overall legal framework, in May 2005 the Minister of Agriculture publicly announced the formation of a 2000-kilometer-long plantation corridor that was to span the entire length of the border with Malaysia. The initial goal of this grand plan was to create the world's largest oil palm plantation – 1.8 million hectares – in a 5 to 10-kilometer band along the border (*Jakarta Post* 2005b). The minister claimed that the plantation would create more than half a million jobs, both locally and through the movement of unemployed surplus workers from densely populated provinces to the sparsely populated border area as part of a large transmigration project. This would secure 'empty' state edges by filling them up with loyal citizens, as a high-ranking military officer told me during a visit in 2005. The main investors in the plantation project would be the Chinese government and Malaysian companies, with US$567 million in projected initial capital being invested over the next five years (Wakker 2006; Potter 2009).

Ironically, the Indonesian government did not seem to believe that the act of giving land concessions to foreign companies (Malaysian) and opening up for transnational investment (Malaysian and Chinese) along the border would weaken its territorial sovereignty (Hall 2012). More strikingly, many of the Chinese Malaysian entrepreneurs (locally known as *tukei's*) who had worked the borderland 'illegally' during the previous timber boom, now have reoriented their investment into cross-border oil palm plantation development. Several of these entrepreneurs were on the provincial police's 'most wanted' list for their previous illegal engagements in the borderlands (Eilenberg 2012b). However, in the news media, the government continued to portray Malaysia as a potent threat to its territorial sovereignty, an image that fits well with public national emotions condemning Malaysia as a modern age 'colonizer' (*Jakarta Post* 2005b). This discrepancy clearly shows how the state discourse of territorial sovereignty and security is used strategically to manipulate and win the hearts and minds of the public and, thus, justify larger military budgets and open new land to state–private investment triggered by Chinese and Malaysian capital, as seen elsewhere in Southeast Asia (Geiger 2008; Barney 2009; Woods 2011).

However, in July 2005 the government-owned plantation cooperative Perkebunan Pusantara (PTPN) informally released a rather hasty and poorly thought out report showing that the proposed oil palm plantation scheme would run straight through and overlap with several large national parks and hilly areas completely unsuitable for oil palm cultivation (Persero 2005). The extensive planning proposal was quickly turned down by the minister of forestry, who said that his ministry would stop any new conversion of forest into plantations and instead recommended the use of abandoned and deforested land in the border area for such developments (*Jakarta Post* 2005a). The minister of agriculture later acknowledged that only 180,000 hectares, not 1.8 million hectares, along the border were actually suitable for oil palm plantations (Kompas 2006).

Contestations over land access

In the months after the release of the PTPN report, the overall plantation plan received much attention from national and worldwide media (*The Wall Street Journal* 2005; *Jakarta Post* 2005b). The plan also received much criticism from various national and international non-governmental organizations (NGOs) and the Regional Representatives Council for its potential impact on the natural and human environment. A major concern of local and international NGOs was that the development of large-scale plantations would prioritize the interests of big business over community-based development. Such projects, if not carefully implemented, were expected to intensify the conflict over land and resources in the resource-rich area along Indonesia's international border with Malaysia, leading to the further impoverishment of local communities and the destruction of the remaining natural resources (Down to Earth 2005; WWF 2005; Arang 2006). In particular, the World Wildelife Fund (WWF) initiated intensive public relations work against the government because of fears that it would destroy the WWF's 'Heart of Borneo' initiative. Launched in 2004, the WWF initiative seeks to establish a 225,000 square kilometer conservation corridor along the entire Indonesian–Malaysian border (Persoon and Osseweijer 2008).

Upon receiving much attention and criticism from other countries, the Indonesian government immediately began downplaying and modifying the grand plantation plans. However, the president never publicly denounced the grand plan, and although the initial plan was called off and not implemented in its original form, the Indonesian–Malaysian agricultural corridor along the border was still high on the government agenda (Bappenas 2008; Departemen Pertanian 2009).

Enclosures of customary lands

A few years after the grand plantation plan had disappeared from the radar screen of the national and international media, the first plantation companies entered the borderlands with approval from district governments and supported by regional police and the military (Ahmad et al. 2009). In 2007, several subsidiaries of the Sinar Mas Group, Indonesia's largest palm oil producer, had begun land surveying in the remote Kapuas Hulu district along the border with Sarawak, and some had already initiated large-scale land clearing and planting. Before initiating the process, the companies, accompanied by the regional police, military, and district officials, had invited villagers to 'socialization' meetings, where the villagers were 'persuaded' to allocate their land for palm oil cultivation. Without formal land certificates, most farmers had little chance of resisting such persuasive demands. The process of acquiring official land certificates is an expensive and complicated affair that requires a well-established network within local government, something few Dayak farmers have. However, since 2006 many district officials and local elites had bought up large parcels of land along the border and had official certificates made – readily awaiting the oil palm boom.

During a 2010 trip to the Kapuas Hulu borderlands, the chief of police in West Kalimantan visited the Sinar Mas subsidiary PT. Buana Tunas Sejahtera in Badau. He met with local police and military commanders, community heads, and company personnel and stated that 'Oil palm can open up access to remote areas and help create an investment climate that is conducive to smooth development.' He later encouraged all parties to support the development of oil palm plantations, refrain from acts of vigilantism, and resolve any disputes quietly – if not, the law would deal with the culprits (*Equator News* 2010). By 2011, large patches of land along the border in Kapuas Hulu were under oil palm cultivation; the first crop was harvested in 2012.

It is significant that government, military, and plantation companies readily justify the enclosure of customary lands for large-scale plantation development by drawing on the discourse of national sovereignty. They stress the national security advantages of an ordered landscape of monocrop plantations and accompanying infrastructure along the border. With headlines like 'Malaysia violates Kalimantan border', Indonesian news media and military spokespersons have occasionally accused Malaysian plantation companies of moving border poles several meters into Indonesian territory in order to gain access to more land and timber (Tempo 2011). The Indonesian military even claims that 50 poles have gone missing altogether. For example, in 2009 and again in 2011 the military command in Pontianak destroyed several Malaysian oil palm plots on the border that were said to 'illegally' encroach on Indonesian territory (*Jakarta Post* 2009; Kompas 2011). Ironically, the provincial government has directly encouraged Sarawak companies to invest in the West Kalimantan border region (*The Star* 2010), and it was estimated that about 70 percent of oil palm companies in the province are already Malaysian majority owned (Colchester 2011).

Critics observe that the military focus on the discourses of national sovereignty and security is manufactured in order to justify larger military budgets. Several commentators claim that the military build-up in the border area is more about reclaiming a share of the revenues lost after the fall of Suharto from further timber harvesting and oil palm plantations than dealing with illegal activities threatening national security (WALHI 2007). It could be argued that the military needs a 'good cause' to prove the continued need for a strong military establishment in post-Suharto Indonesia. For example, the Indonesian military has begun calling for increased funds to provide sufficient border patrols and create new border posts and military checkpoints (*Jakarta Globe* 2010). However, according to the military its role is not only to defend the country against outside aggression; it also believes it has an educational role. Military personnel stationed on the border have recently become teaching assistants in rural schools, where they teach 'lessons in nationalism' in order to implement a 'sense of nationalism' among the 'autonomous tribal communities' (Antara 2012).

These initiatives feed into the TMMD program – an acronym for the 'Indonesian National Armed Forces United in Village Development'. In the district of Kapuas Hulu, the TMMD program was introduced by the military in 2010, and its main rationale was to improve 'backward villages' along the border and maintain a sense of national unity, which involved instructions in 'village defense' and 'mental development' (appropriate lifestyle, family planning, religious guidance, and nationalism) supplemented with the construction of physical infrastructure like roads, bridges, and schools.

The senior segment of the border population interviewed in 2011 views the TMMD program with caution and mixed emotions. The program conjures memories of forced labor, indoctrination, and resettlement during the 1970–80s counterinsurgency programs (see Peluso 2008; Eilenberg 2011). In the 1980s, the Suharto government introduced an official program of direct military development intervention called AMD (Indonesian Armed Forces Enter the Village). In the border area, the AMD programs involved military personnel, who were involved in teaching projects and the development of rice production schemes. Although development was the official rhetoric of the AMD programs, they were primarily an attempt to take control of the region's immense natural resources and to prevent 'unreliable' border communities from being influenced by foreign (communist) ideologies (Eilenberg 2011). The processes of militarization that have taken place in the West Kalimantan borderlands in many ways resemble what Kevin Woods in his study of the China–Burma borderlands has called 'military territorialization' (i.e. 'military-state agencies and officers exhibiting power and authority over land and populations') (Woods 2011: 748). However, compared to the case of Burma, the Indonesian military actors' economic incitements and cooperation with private capital along the border are less conspicuous. They mostly work behind the scenes and receive 'fees' by lending out personnel as plantation guards and keeping up steady pressure on local communities to conform to plantation company demands.

The military presence and authority in the border area have waxed and waned over time, from being extremely conspicuous during the Suharto era to being less noticeable since the decentralization reforms in 1999 (Mietzner 2009). The political role of the military was greatly reduced after the fall of Suharto, as the new reform governments initiated a restructuring of the institution. Although it has lost ground in civil politics, the military has largely maintained its role in the business sector (Human Rights Watch 2006).

Conclusions

In this chapter I have discussed how the rapid agrarian transformations taking place in the Indonesian borderlands, with palm oil as the boom crop, involve a complex interplay of forces. These forces range from discourses about territorial sovereignty to regional attempts to promote plantation development as the main economic savior and revenue provider in impoverished border regions. Through extensive development plans that involve allocating private land concessions and increasing military authority, the Indonesian government has once again accentuated the perceived importance of strengthening state presence and sovereignty along its borders with Malaysia. The case of the Indonesian–Malaysian border reveals that powerful discourses of security and territorial sovereignty play a major role in state-led processes of land colonization, legitimizing resettlement, and dispossession. However, the case also reveals the flipside of the imagined 'sovereign state' when, for example, the national military publicly condemns Malaysian intrusions into Indonesian territory and simultaneously serves as security for Malaysian extractive companies along the border.

Today, the militarist rhetoric of the former Suharto regime is echoed in terms such as 'security buffer zones' and 'security belts', while population resettlements and agricultural expansion along Indonesia's territorial borders are widely used and often evoke past failures. Hence, one major consequence of the renewed interest of the Indonesian government and private capital in the border region is a new era of top-down development. The remilitarization of the borderlands thus indicates the beginning of another chapter in the waxing and waning of military power on the border. Moving away from its role of protector of internal unity by quelling internal separatist movements during Suharto's New Order regime, the military now wants the lucrative role of protector of national sovereignty, working in tandem with private transnational capital.

Returning to the case of the world's largest oil palm plantation and its consequent failure to materialize in the envisioned form, we can see how grand schemes are often undermined by the numerous and, at times, contradictory agendas of various state agents and agencies. This is a vivid example of frontier imagery with its utopian promises of 'unoccupied' lands, unlimited economic advancement, and instant riches. The frontier then becomes a kind of *tabula rasa*, a blank page on which the implementation of developmental agendas can be written or from which resources can be extracted (McCarthy and Cramb 2009: 113).

Notes

1 This chapter is a shortened version of a paper that appeared originally in the *Journal of Peasant Studies* (Vol. 41, No. 2, 2014, pp. 157–182) and is republished with permission. Data presented in this study were collected during 25 months of field research in the West Kalimantan borderlands in the period 2002 to 2012. Interviews were conducted with a wide array of local and national actors ranging from state officials, politicians, NGOs, entrepreneurs, and local elites (community heads and tribal heads), to local peasants and plantation workers. The field research was academically sponsored by Tanjungpura University, Pontianak, with permission from the Indonesian Institute of Sciences (LIPI) and the Indonesian Ministry of Research and Technology (RISTEK), Jakarta. The conclusions drawn here are not necessarily those of the above agencies; the author alone is responsible.
2 Surat Keterangan (certificate), Dewan Pengerus Yayasan Maju Kerja, No. 165/Kep/P.Y/X/1980.
3 Badan Pengendali Pelaksanaan Pembangunan Wilayah Perbatasan.

References

Ahmad, Nurhanudin, W. Wagiman and T. Bawor. 2009. Pembangunan Perkebunan Sawit Di Perbatasan Indonesia-Malaysia: Diskriminasi Rasial Terhadap Masyarakat Adat. Bogor: Tim Advokasi Sawit Perbatasan.
Antara. 2012. Personel Tni Di Perbatasan Jadi Guru Bantu. Antara News Agency, 25 Jan.
Arang, L. 2006. Kelapa Sawit Sang Primadona: Suatu Analysis Pembangunan Perkebunan Kelapa Sawit Di Kabupaten Wilayah Perbatasan Indonesia-Malaysia, Provinsi Kalimantan Barat. WWF Indonesia, Forest Conversion Initiative Program.
Bappenas. 2003. Strategi Dan Model Pengembangan Wilayah Perbatasan Kalimantan. Jakarta: Kementerian Perencanaan Pembangunan Nasional, Badan Perencanaan Pembangunan Nasional.
Bappenas. 2008. Bahan Diskusi: Rencana Pembangunan Jangka Menengah Pengembangan Kawasan Perbatasan Tahun 2010–2014. Jakarta: Kementerian Perencanaan Pembangunan Nasional, Badan Perencanaan Pembangunan Nasional.
Bappenas. 2011. Profil Wilayah Perbatasan Negara Di Provinci Kalimantan Barat. Jakarta: Kementerian Perencanaan Pembangunan Nasional, Badan Perencanaan Pembangunan Nasional.
Barney, K. 2009. Laos and the Making of a 'Relational' Resource Frontier. The Geographical Journal, 175(2): 146–159.
BNPP. 2011. Desain Besar Pengelolaan Batas Wilayah Negara Dan Kawasan Perbatasan Tahun 2011–2025. Jakarta: Kementerian Perencanaan Pembangunan Nasional, Badan Nasional Pengelola Perbatasan.
Brown, D.W. 1999. Addicted to Rent: Corporate and Spatial Distribution of Forest Resources in Indonesia; Implications for Forest Sustainability and Government Policy. Jakarta: Indonesia UK Tropical Forestry Mangement Programme.
Colchester, M. 2011. Palm Oil and Indigenous Peoples in South East Asia. Rome: International Land Coalition (ILC).
Davidson, J.S. and D. Kammen. 2002. Indonesia's Unknown War and the Lineages of Violence in West Kalimantan, Indonesia. Indonesia, 73(April): 53–87.

De Koninck, R. 2006. On the Geopolitics of Land Colonization: Order and Disorder on the Frontiers of Vietnam and Indonesia. Moussons, 9(10): 33–59.

De Koninck R. et al. 2011. Borneo Transformed: Agricultural Expansion on the Southeast Asian Frontier. Singapore: NUS Press.

Departemen Pertanian. 2009. Pedoman Teknis Pengendalian Lahan Pertanian Di Wilayah Perbatasan. Jakarta: Direktorat Pengelolaan Lahan, Diirektorat Jenderal Pengelolaan Lahan Dan Air, Departemen Pertanian.

Down to Earth. 2005. Oil Palm Expansion Will Bring More Conflict. Down to Earth, 66: 1–16.

Eilenberg, M. 2011. Straddling the Border: A Marginal History of Guerrilla Warfare and 'Counter-Insurgency' in the Indonesian Borderlands. Modern Asian Studies, 45(6): 1423–1463.

Eilenberg, M. 2012a. At the Edges of States: Dynamics of State Formation in the Indonesian Borderlands. Leiden: KITLV Press.

Eilenberg, M. 2012b. The Confession of a Timber Baron: Patterns of Patronage on the Indonesian-Malaysian Border. Identities: Global Studies in Culture and Power, 9: 149–167.

Eilenberg, M. and R.L. Wadley. 2009. Borderland Livelihood Strategies: The Socio-Economic Significance of Ethnicity in Cross-Border Labour Migration, West Kalimantan, Indonesia. Asia Pacific Viewpoint, 50(1): 58–73.

Equator News. 2010. Kapolda Kunjungi Pt Buana Tunas Sejahtera. Equator News, 28 Jan.

Fold, N. and P. Hirsch. 2009. Re-Thinking Frontiers in Southeast Asia: Editorial. The Geographical Journal, 175(2): 95–97.

Geiger, D. 2008. Frontier Encounters: Indigenous Communities and Settlers in Asia and Latin America. Copenhagen: IWGIA.

Hall, D. 2012. Land. Cambridge: Polity Press.

Human Rights Watch. 2006. Too High a Price: The Human Rights Cost of Indonesian Military's Economic Activities. Human Rights Watch, 18(5 (C)).

Ito, T., N.F. Rachman and A.L. Savitri. 2011. Naturalizing Land Dispossession: A Policy Discourse Analysis of the Merauke Integrated Food and Energy Estate. Paper presented at the International Conference on Global Land Grabbing. Land Deals Politics Initiative (LDPI), University of Sussex.

Jakarta Globe. 2010. Military to Boost Presence in Papua, Kalimantan Border Zones This Year. Jakarta Globe, 30 Mar.

Jakarta Post. 2005a. Forest Conversion on Kalimantan Border Halted. Jakarta Post, 12 Sep.

Jakarta Post. 2005b. Government Plans World's Largest Oil Palm Plantation. Jakarta Post, 18 Jun.

Jakarta Post. 2009. Malaysia Moves Border Poles into Ri's Land for Oil Palm Plantations. Jakarta Post, 4 Mar.

Jakarta Post. 2010. New Military Command in Kalimantan to Guard Border Areas. Jakarta Post, 31 Jan.

Jakarta Post. 2011. Government to Develop Border Areas before 2014. Jakarta Post, 27 Dec.

Jones, M. 2002. Conflict and Confrontation in South East Asia, 1961–1965. Cambridge: Cambridge University Press.

Kepmenhut. 2004. Rencana Stratejik Pengelolaan Kawasan Hutan Wilayah Perbatasan Ri-Malaysia Di Kalimantan. Jakarta: Keputusan Menteri Kehutanan, No. SK.55.

Keppres. 1994. Badan Pengendali Pembangunan Kawasan Perbatasan. Jakarta: Keputusan Presiden Republik Indonesia, No. 44.

Kompas. 2006. Deptan Hanya Izinkan 180.000 Hektar Di Perbatasan. Kompas, 6 May.

Kompas. 2011. Perusahaan Sawit Malaysia Serobot Tanah Perbatasan Indonesia. Kompas, 8 Nov.

Laungaramsri, P. 2012. Frontier Capitalism and the Expansion of Rubber Plantations in Southern Laos. Journal of Southeast Asian Studies, 43(3): 463–477.

McCarthy, J.F. and R.A. Cramb. 2009. Policy Narratives, Landholder Engagement, and Oil Palm Expansion on the Malaysian and Indonesian Frontiers. The Geographical Journal, 175(2): 112–123.

Media Perkebunan. 2011. Sawit Solusi Mensejahterakan Daerah Perbatasan. Media Perkebunan, 20 Nov.

Mietzner, M. 2009. Military Politics, Islam, and the State in Indonesia: From Turbulent Transition to Democratic Consolidation. Singapore: Institute of Southeast Asian Studies.

Peluso, N.L. 2008. A Political Ecology of Violence and Territory in West Kalimantan. Asia Pacific Viewpoint, 49(1): 48–67.

Peluso, N.L. and P. Vandergeest. 2011. Political Ecologies of War and Forests: Counterinsurgencies and the Making of National Natures. Annals of the Association of American Geographers, 101(3): 587–608.

Perpres. 2010. Rencana Pembangunan Janka Menengah National (Rpjmn). Tahun 2010–2014. Peraturan Presiden Republik Indonesia, No. 5.

Persero. 2005. Pembangunan Kawasan Perbatasan Melalui Pembangunan Perkebunan Kelapa Sawit Di Propinsi Kalimantan Barat. Jakarta: PT Perkebunan Nusantara 1-XIV (Persero).
Persoon, G.A. and M. Osseweijer. 2008. Reflections on the Heart of Borneo. Wageningen, The Netherlands: Tropenbos International.
Potter, L. 2009. Resource Periphery, Corridor, Heartland: Contesting Land Use in the Kalimantan/Malaysia Borderlands. Asia Pacific Viewpoint, 50(1): 88–106.
Redclift, M.R. 2006. Frontiers: Histories of Civil Society and Nature. Cambridge, MA: MIT Press.
Soemadi. 1974. Peranan Kalimantan Barat Dalam Menghadapi Subversi Komunis Asia Tenggara: Suatu Tinjauan Internasional Terhadap Gerakan Komunis Dari Sudut Pertahanan Wilayah Khususnya Kalimantan Barat. Pontianak: Yayasan Tanjungpura.
Tempo. 2011. Malaysia Violates Kalimantan Border. Tempo Interactive, 11 Oct.
The Star. 2010. Sarawakians urged to invest in West Kalimantan border projects. The Star, 14 Apr.
The Wall Street Journal. 2005. Jobs Vs. Jungle in Borneo. The Wall Street Journal, 4–6 Nov.
Tuck, C. 2004. Borneo 1963–66: Counter-Insurgency Operations and War Termination. Small Wars and Insurgencies, 15(3): 89–111.
Wadley, R.L. 1998. The Road to Change in the Kapuas Hulu Borderlands: Jalan Lintas Utara. Borneo Research Bulletin, 29: 71–94.
Wakker, E. 2006. The Kalimantan Border Oil Palm Mega-Project. Amsterdam: AIDEnvironment.
WALHI. 2007. There is Still Military in the Forest. Indonesian Forum for Environment (WALHI), 27 Jun.
Woods, K. 2011. Ceasefire Capitalism: Military-Private Partnerships, Resource Concessions and Military-State Building in the Burma-China Borderlands. Journal of Peasant Studies, 38(4): 747–770.
WWF. 2005. World's Largest Oil Palm Plantation Could Spell Disaster for Upland Forests of Indonesian Borneo. Gland, Switzerland: World Wildlife Fund.

14
Beyond 'natural' pressures
Chinese agriculture in the Russian Far East

Jiayi Zhou

Introduction

China and Russia share a border of over 4,000 km along Heilongjiang, Jilin, and Inner Mongolia provinces in Northeast China, and the five southernmost provinces of Russia's Far East Federal District (RFE): Amur Oblast, Primorsky Krai, Khabarosky Krai, the Jewish Autonomous Oblast, and Zabaikalsky Krai (see Map 14.1). Although the RFE constitutes one-third of Russia's total territory, it comprises only about 2 percent of the country's arable land, virtually all of which is concentrated within these five border provinces. At present, Chinese land acquisitions, directly or indirectly through joint ventures with Russian companies, now cover more than 20 percent of the region's arable land. Chinese agricultural engagement in this part of Russia dates back to the late 1850s, when the region was first annexed by Tsarist Russia. In certain respects, farming by the Chinese in this part of Russian territory today is a continuation of older historical dynamics. However, there are also a number of ways in which current dynamics and processes are also specific to contemporary actors and institutional arrangements.

Chinese migration and economic activity in this borderland region is often described rather simplistically as stemming from 'natural' pressures such as population density and resource availability. But beyond these basic structural conditions there are also sociopolitical and economic factors that need to be taken into account. A deeper unpacking of the political economy of this borderland region is thus required. This chapter briefly traces the evolution of Chinese farming in the RFE from its historical roots, to the early phase of border liberalization and the farming boom in the 1990s, and finally to the period of the mid-2000s, characterized by much more capital-intensive Chinese activities in the area. Following this historical sketch, this chapter analyses the contemporary political economy of the region, in particular some of the push factors in Heilongjiang province, from where most of the Chinese farmers hail. Based primarily on Chinese media and governmental sources, it shows the significance of market drivers, but also links Chinese land acquisitions to the state-promoted export of Chinese surplus labor, as well as to China's increased policy focus on scaling-up and 'modernizing' agriculture. Policies in Russia are, of course, also significant, but

Beyond 'natural' pressures

Map 14.1 Map of the relevant areas in Northeast China and the Russian Far East
Map by Christian Dietrich

for reasons of space and coherence, this chapter does not address the Russian perspective on these issues.

Background: a century of Chinese farming in the RFE

Throughout the late 19th and early 20th century, tens of thousands of Chinese were active in the RFE's agrarian economy as seasonal migrants, employed by Russian settlers to compensate for the lack of local labor. Their contributions to the local economy were substantial. As Shkurkin (2002: 76) writes about this period:

> The vegetables grown by Chinese included potatoes, cabbages, turnips, beets, carrots, onions, garlic, string beans, tomatoes and herbs, while the fields were usually sown with corn, wheat, oats, beans, hemp, tobacco and poppy. Chinese agriculture played an important role in supplying the Far East's population with agricultural produce. In the South Ussuri region, one Chinese peasant fed 25–26 Russian inhabitants. Vegetables were sold at greengrocers', in the streets and delivered to houses, including on credit…In addition to their own land, the Chinese rented land from Russian Cossacks and peasants. With this, relations between the Russian as landowner and the Chinese as tenant or hired worker changed. The Chinese became the actual owner of the land, with the Russian owning it only nominally.

Chinese presence within the RFE diminished after the 1917 revolution and was affected further by Stalin's border and nationality policies in the 1930s. The Sino–Soviet split in the early 1960s led thereafter to a full closure of the border. Following the political rapprochement and border liberalization between the two countries in the 1980s, however, the flow of farmers and farm laborers across the Amur River resumed in much the same form that it had a century before. Soviet *kolkhozes* and *sovkhozes* (collective and state farms), privatized in the early 1990s, hired Chinese laborers to compensate for labor that had previously been drafted from the demographically declining urban centers of the RFE (Minakir 1996). One of the first instances of this was in 1988, when the Baranovsky state farm in Siberia contracted the municipal government of Suifeihe, a Chinese city bordering Primorsky Krai, to provide agricultural labor to assist with vegetable production (Liu 2011). In other cases, Russian collective and state farms – or their privatized successors – also directly leased their land to production teams from China (Chazan 2006).

Stemming from these interactions, Chinese farm workers and entrepreneurs soon began to rent land independently from Russian landholders and former collective farms, sometimes under sharecropping or similar contractual arrangements, which allowed them the use of agricultural machinery, transportation, and other services. The rural agricultural backgrounds and expertise of the Chinese laborers proved useful in accelerating the local production of vegetables and other high-value crops. These products were sold back onto the RFE market, including some which were new to the markets of the RFE – for instance, watermelons (Alexseev 2003). Though never systematically calculated, estimates put the Chinese share of the RFE's market for fresh produce at anywhere from one half to 90 percent (Shkurkin 2002; Tencent Network 2006). Parallels to the situation a century earlier are quite stark.

These Chinese agricultural laborers and farmers capitalized on a market characterized by rural decline, low land rental costs, and lack of local vegetable production. In doing so, they were able to make substantially higher profits than on the more saturated Chinese market. Rumours about the RFE's profit potential then led to what has been termed a 'farming rush' by the Chinese media, which was marked by more robust networks of Chinese migrant farmers and farm workers being recruited into developing Russian agricultural land. Newly recruited workers often came from rural northeast villages, following migration chains and existing networks. And as more Chinese farmers began to develop larger production areas over the years, they increasingly hired wage laborers for their own expanding scale of activities.

This relatively small-scale farming by peasants and agricultural laborers in the 1990s took place largely in a 'private (*minjian*), loose, and disorderly' fashion. However, the Chinese presence in Russia has since become more regularized, with more institutional, state-affiliated corporate actors now acquiring and developing much larger agricultural land concessions (Li et al. 2013:

104). This shift took place in conjunction with a number of high-level policy changes. New legislation passed by the Russian Parliament in 2002 allowed foreigners to lease Russian agricultural land for up to 49 years, and ownership by Russian-majority shareholder companies (Russian Federation 2002). Concurrently, the Chinese government also began to push enterprises to invest in foreign markets with a variety of financial and political incentives, in a 'Going Out' strategy that precipitated a major uptick in China's overseas foreign direct investment (Ministry of Commerce of the PRC, n.d.).

Since the early 2000s, larger Chinese companies and agribusinesses have acquired production bases in Russia amounting to thousands of hectares of land. Both private corporations and state-owned farms are involved. Indeed, China's first foreign agricultural park was set up in Primorsky Krai with the initiative of a Chinese private enterprise. Large-scale land acquisitions sometimes take place in joint ventures with Russians, although such joint ventures account for only about one in five Chinese agricultural projects in the RFE (Zhang 2016). Production patterns have shifted from labor-intensive high-value crops and vegetable greenhouses to more land-intensive mechanized grain and pulse crops production. Livestock breeding and dairy farming have also expanded and industrial agroprocessing activities that require greater upfront capital have also increased. In some cases, cooperative arrangements have developed whereby a private corporation leases the land and state-affiliated actors provide the labor. Arrangements of this type, as well as 'contract farming' between Chinese actors, have also become prevalent (Liu 2011).

Over the years, the predominant share of Chinese production has remained within the RFE market, due to higher local market demand and profitability, as well as physical transportation and policy barriers for importing to China. This is changing somewhat: one of the first shipments of soybean imported from Chinese production bases in Russia took place in 2014, and the total amount of such exports rose from around 80,000 tons that year, to around half a million tons the next (eFeedLink 2014; Ministry of Commerce of the PRC 2016). This is likely to increase with time, as certain policy bottlenecks have already been resolved (Heilongjiang Government 2013). Cross-border vertical integration, with movement up into agroindustrial processing is also accelerating. Major actors now also go beyond Heilongjiang Province. National-level enterprises such as the China National Cereals, Oils and Foodstuffs Corporation (COFCO) have announced plans to invest in grain storage facilities. In addition, agricultural investment and cooperation has been the subject of national-level investment cooperation agreements, including a joint agricultural investment fund of US$2 billion announced as part of President Xi Jinping's May 2015 state visit to Moscow (Yap 2015).

As for the scale of Chinese agricultural involvement in the RFE, there is in China unfortunately no systematic or centralized monitoring of such activities, much of which takes at a private or local level. However, according to the government of Heilongjiang, the estimated amount of land under development by actors from the province was 667,000 ha in 2016 (Ministry of Commerce of the PRC 2016). This amount represents 20 percent of the RFE's total arable land, and is an amount that by Chinese projections is expected to increase over the next years.

Driving factors: beyond demography

Writers and analysts have tended to portray the dynamics of labor migration and economic integration between the two sides of the border as a matter of structural drivers, describing them as 'natural' pressures or 'natural' economic forces – pointing to differences in population density, land availability, and labor supply. Indeed, although aggregate arable land is almost identical in the two countries, arable land per capita is among the world's lowest in China (0.08 ha) and among the world's highest in Russia (0.85 ha) (World Bank 2014). These regional differences have been

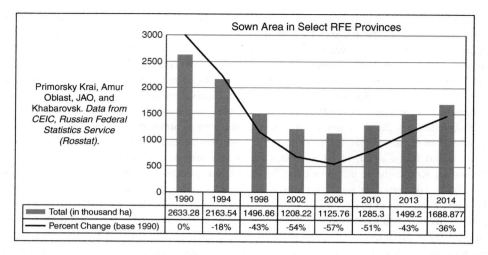

Figure 14.1 Changes in sown area in RFE provinces between 1990 and 2014, in absolute hectare and percentage terms

Photo by Jiayi Zhou

only exacerbated by economic and demographic decline in the RFE. Within a decade after Soviet collapse, the RFE's economy contracted by about 50 percent, and suffered a nearly 20 percent decline in population over the next two decades (Motrich and Naiden 2009: 554). By contrast, on the Chinese side of the border, the population size in Liaoning, Jilin, and Heilongjiang has increased by about 10 percent since 1990 (National Bureau of Statistics 2014). Figures 14.1 and 14.2 illustrate some of these contrasts, specifically in sown areas in both Northeast China and in the RFE.[1] Notably, Chinese farming has been an important part of what limited agricultural revival can be seen in the RFE figures.

While structural factors are important, using simple numbers or imagery on demography and geography, as is typically the case in popular discourse, tends to obscure much more than it reveals in terms of the complex processes, actors, and push–pull factors at work. Population density should not itself be seen as a primary indicator of migration pressure. For instance, cross-border traffic through Blagoveshchensk, a major border town in Amur Oblast, has throughout the years been higher for Russian citizens going to China than the opposite. And of the Chinese migrants staying in Russia, relatively few are interested in long-term relocation, permanent residency or citizenship (Prosvirnov 2009; Balzer and Repnikova 2010: 12).

Chinese farming in the RFE is indeed linked to economic liberalization, the 'freeing' of the markets for labor, land, and capital, and the removal of certain trade barriers. It is economic factors such as wage differentials and profit opportunities that have most fundamentally driven Chinese labor movements (Lotspeich 2010). At the same time, it is also important to place these flows within the social and political systems in which they take place. In addition to the bureaucratic role that local Russian and Chinese state officials play in regulating cross-border migration, they also have agendas of accumulation and securitization that heavily influence these flows – sometimes constraining and sometimes facilitating them. In Russia, the competing imperatives of economic growth, for which external labor resources are necessary, and securing the region against perceived or actual foreign encroachment – have resulted in highly fickle policies toward Chinese investment and labor migration over the past decades. On the Chinese side, the state's

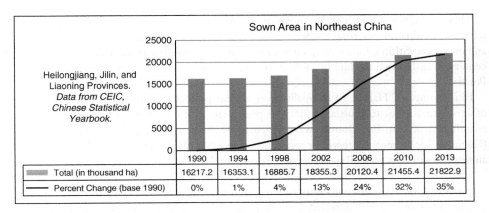

Figure 14.2 Changes in sown area in Northeast China between 1990 and 2013, in absolute hectare and percentage terms
Photo by Jiayi Zhou

accumulation imperative plays a crucial role. The following sections examine Chinese farming in Russia through a number of these angles, focusing on the Chinese side.

Economic differentials

Russia's internal market collapsed during the 1990s in the absence of the central regulatory regime on which the economy had been dependent. The RFE was particularly affected, as a remote region that was more highly dependent on the center for subsidies, and on other parts of the country for consumer items – including agricultural products. The RFE had never been particularly food self-sufficient, and fresh produce became an even more valuable commodity in the region after Soviet disintegration. Traders from China took advantage of this market demand, shuttling vegetables across the border into the RFE and Siberia. But there were also Chinese farmers operating on Russian soil itself. Situated in peri-urban areas, producing greenhouse vegetables and other high-value crops, such migrant farmers were best positioned to capitalize on this situation. And the profits they made were such that reports heralded hundreds of new 'peasant millionaires' (China Russia Information Network 2012a).

In all public profiles and media interviews with Chinese laborers and farmers on Russian soil, they described their primary motivations as being related to economic opportunity and higher income. Throughout the 1990s, Russia still remained far more attractive than China in terms of wages. A survey of two villages in Heilongjiang, one of which borders Russia directly, found that the daily wages in 1998 during harvest amounted to a mere 14–19 yuan (Wang et al. 2000: 98). Even nearly two decades of sustained growth in China versus decline in Russia, per capita income in Russia in 2005 was still more than twice that of urban residents in China, and over six times that of rural residents (Lotspeich 2010). Factor inputs were also much cheaper in Russia. Agricultural land in Russia costs only a fraction of the cost compared to China – in some cases 10 times lower, with 'symbolic' rental costs of 10 to 100 yuan a hectare annually. Even accounting for the hefty costs to obtain a work permit, and the investment required to start a farm in Russia, Chinese rural residents have reportedly been able to earn several times more than they would working at home (Hu 2009; China Russia Information Network 2012b).

These conditions are changing, however. In recent years Russia has become a much less attractive destination for rural residents from Northeast China. Better economic opportunities and prospects within China – coupled with loosened restrictions on internal migration to urban centers – has led to a decline of interest by Chinese in becoming farm laborers or farmers in Russia.

Bin County of Harbin Municipality was at one point the leading county-level exporter of agricultural labor to Russia. In 2005, its peak year of labor export to Russia, the per capita monthly income in Bin County was 854 yuan. By 2012, that figure had more than doubled (Cheng 2013). In recent interviews conducted in its labor market, all individuals asked expressed an unwillingness to go to Russia to farm. As one rural resident explained,

> working [in Russia] for 15 hours a day, making about 5–6,000 yuan a month... now here in Bin County, with farming plus (migrant) laboring, you make also about 40–50,000 a year. The difference is not that big, so who would be willing to go there just to suffer punishment?

Indeed, for those Chinese working in Russia, incomes have dropped precipitously since 2014. By 2016, average monthly salaries in Heilongjiang Province were $US667, compared to $US563 in the bordering Primorye, and average salaries in Russia on the whole are now lower than in China (*The Moscow Times* 2016; Repnikova and Gabuev 2017).

Labor export and rural surplus

While economic motivations drove many individuals' decisions to invest or engage in Russian farming, government policies have also played a role. Throughout the initial market liberalization process in China, the state played a highly active role in shaping economic flows, particularly at the local level. Since decentralization of the fiscal system starting in 1980, local governments have had a vested interest in economic growth and production as a means of increasing their own revenue. This was particularly noticeable at the township and village level. Even after township and village enterprises (TVEs) became privatized and local officials stepped out of a direct managerial role, local governments continued to play an instrumental role in shaping economic flows by 'removing barriers and uncertainty, in planning, providing information, linking into product and factor markets and gaining access to finances' (Cuddy and Qian 2007: 180).

Far from being a neutral actor, the local 'developmental state' also had political and economic mandates to increase rural incomes, and to create off-farm employment opportunities to help solve the issue of surplus agricultural labor. Decollectivization and rural liberalization in the late 1970s had led to a release of peasants from the land; by the 1980s, this surplus labor was estimated to account for about 30 percent of the countryside's labor force (Cai 2012). Some of this surplus was absorbed into TVEs, but loosening policies on internal migration as well as the internationalization of China's economy provided other outlets.

Labor export has been one of the outlets for China's surplus rural workforce, serving as a form of foreign economic cooperation loosely overseen by state authorities (Wang 1995: 430). Throughout the 1980s and 1990s, province- and prefecture-level authorities set targets for labor export, which were implemented by county labor bureaus. Chinese local authorities were and continue to be very proactive in this regard, facilitating, if not directly organizing outmigration through local state-affiliated migration brokers and export labor corporations. This was also the case for labor export to Russia after the Soviet collapse. The number of Chinese workers in the Russian Federation tripled between 1990 and 1992, after which Russia and China signed an agreement that outlined the general principles of their labor cooperation (Minakir 1996; Kim 1994).

The involvement of Chinese local state actors in this regard was strong. Bin County's labor export peak year in 2005 coincided with the highest levels of local government support for migration through a rural development policy goal of shifting peasants into wage-work elsewhere. The policy was of – *zhuanyi wugong yiban, liusheng wunong yiban* – 'transferring half as wage laborers, leaving half (in the countryside) to engage in agriculture.' Those rural residents willing to work in Russia received financial incentives through tax breaks, received free vocational training from the local Labor Bureau, and other benefits. Speaking to the level of governmental involvement, the Deputy Director of the Labor Bureau of Bin himself served directly as a migration broker. In 2006, approximately 6,000 of the county's rural residents traveled to Russia to farm, some two-thirds of which went through him (Tencent Network 2006). Note that the boundaries between private and public office in China are often blurred: one study of labor export in three counties of China found that private, profit-making labor exporters were operating under the auspices of all three county government labor bureaus (Murphy 2002). Besides Harbin, other cities most notable for farm labor export to Russia are located at the border: Heihe, Mudanjiang, Jiamusi, and Jixi, in Heilongjiang Province (Xu et al. 2014: 76).

The problem of rural surplus labor was, and to a more limited extent continues to be, 'a top priority for all levels of the [Heilongjiang provincial] government' (Tencent Network 2006). State-owned farms in Heilongjiang and Northeast China are also actively involved in this kind of surplus labor transfer and encourage their farm employees to go abroad. Beyond direct support of labor export, the state also provides other services that promote and lubricate these market interactions, including establishing information service centers about laboring abroad (Xu et al. 2014: 78).

Of course, this occurs in tandem with private migration chains and networks stemming from rural northeast villages. As Chinese migrants began to develop their own larger-scale farms or production areas in the RFE over the years, they hired more wage laborers from China in order to support this. There are also labor migration networks and channels that operate on a more informal and illegal basis – side-stepping the costly and time-consuming bureaucratic procedures required in formal channels of labor cooperation (Xu et al. 2014: 77). In addition, it is local Russian authorities who hold the right to distribute licenses to domestic enterprises to hire foreign labor, and this is subject to strict quota regulations in terms of Chinese. These barriers have in fact increased the attraction and hiring of more migrant laborers from Central Asia and the South Caucasus in recent years. Nevertheless, enterprises and employers have in a number of media sources attribute enterprises and employers continuing to hire Chinese agricultural labor to their comparatively higher work ethic, and that fact they may be easier to manage than local Russians. This latter view may also be related to the lack of standards to which Chinese overseas labor groups are held in terms of workers' rights.

Agricultural internationalization and modernization

Most of Chinese agricultural activities in the RFE have been driven by local dynamics in Northeast China, with less direction coming from national-strategic actors until recently. China's 'Going Out' policy of supporting overseas investment has been much more limited in the agricultural sector than in others. In contrast to international alarmism about China's food demands necessitating state-led land and agricultural acquisitions abroad, there has in fact been little strategic coordination of agricultural investment at the national level. In addition, production from Chinese foreign agricultural bases have largely been sold on local markets, including in the RFE. Strict import quotas, domestic tariffs, and trade barriers have hindered all but the largest state-owned enterprises from exporting back to China (Cheng and Zhang 2014). Indeed, with 98 percent national self-sufficiency in edible staple grains, China remains food secure on the whole (Lockett 2015). However, imports of soybeans – the one agricultural commodity for which China depends on international markets to fulfill the majority of its demand – have rapidly increased since the 2000s. China is now the world's largest importer, accounting for nearly two-thirds of the international market supply (World Grain News 2015). This dependency will likely only grow, due to pressures from environmental degradation as well growing consumption needs.

Though 'rational' use of international markets for ensuring food security in a limited number of agricultural commodities has been a state policy since at least 2008, vertical integration and control over a global supply chain has become increasingly prominent. In 2013, the State Council stressed, 'utilizing international markets and overseas resources in a way that ensures a dominant role for Chinese companies in the supply chain for imported commodities' (Gale et al. 2015: 19). Indeed, some large-scale exports of soybeans produced by Chinese actors in Russia, back into to the Chinese market, have taken place. This is likely to increase with time, as certain policy bottlenecks have already been resolved, and investments in vertical cross-border integration schemes have also increased in recent years (Heilongjiang Government 2013).

Nevertheless, China's land deals and agricultural activity in Russia have on the whole, and as in most parts of the world, been driven by investment opportunities and the profit potential of untapped markets, rather than food security motives (Cotula et al. 2009). This is the case both for Chinese public and private sector enterprises, large-scale capital-intensive as well as smaller-scale counterparts (Zhou 2017). Instead, agricultural investments abroad are connected to larger processes of market liberalization – capital accumulation and the profit potential of relatively untapped markets abroad. The state serves a shaping role in this regard – in its promotion of what we could call agricultural modernization writ large. As Deng Xiaoping announced in 1990, decollectivization was to be followed by the second 'great leap' in rural development, to be marked by a shift in China from traditional to modern agriculture; from uncoordinated small-scale operations, to coordinated operations, which are 'commercialized,' 'specialized,' 'scaled-up,' 'standardized,' and 'internationalized' (Zhang 2008: 29). Agricultural modernization through government policy and financial support to 'dragon-head' enterprises,[2] farmer cooperatives and so-called modern 'family farms,' have encouraged deeper financialization of production, consolidation of value chains through vertical integration, and economies of scale (Yan and Chen 2015) – both domestically and internationally. Chinese activity on Russian soil, which is marked by prevalent use of wage labor, mechanized large-scale grain and crop production, commodification of all production – has the hallmarks of the type of modern and capitalistic agriculture the national government is promoting, even if driven largely by provincial state or private sector actors (Zhou 2017).

Concurrently, institutional constraints within China also encourage this outward investment. Agriculture has in fact lagged behind other production sectors in China in terms of privatization; the Household Responsibility System (HRS) put in place since decollectivization provides for collective villages rather than individual ownership rights to agricultural land. This lack of a free rural land market means that to the extent that agribusinesses would like to acquire bases to engage directly in agricultural production, land abroad is often a more viable option than land within China itself for the processes and goals of capital accumulation and globalization that the state is actively promoting.

Conclusions

The factors outlined above, whether related to local state imperatives, or economic opportunity driven migration, are all connected to a wider system of post-socialist transformation in China. It perhaps goes without saying that as China's actors and its capital becomes more mobile and globalized, they are transforming regional and global economic orders; the question of China's agrarian trajectory therefore increasingly implicates land systems and markets outside its own borders.

As this chapter shows, simple 'natural' pressures have insufficient explanatory power to describe the phenomenon of Chinese farming in the RFE. Rather, drivers need to be understood in terms of the broader economic as well as political processes within which they are embedded. Land availability and demographic figures do not account for the degree to which it is land-poor China that has boosted food security in the RFE, rather than the other way around. Moreover, while economic drivers are extremely important, China's state-level interests, politics, and strategies also need to be taken into account as direct or indirect drivers.

Economic and migration flows are neither purely one-sided nor are they static. Shifting economic dynamics as well as political dyanmics will continue to play a role in the future of Chinese agriculture in Russia. But, suffice to say that under conditions of liberalization and globalization, the agrarian trajectories in both countries of this borderland will continue to be intertwined and interlinked.

Notes

1. Inner Mongolia is less relevant and excluded from the calculations for the Northeast, as its population centers are clustered farther from the border, as is its border neighbor Zaibaikalsky Krai in the RFE.
2. Dragon-head enterprises are agribusinesses that are targets of state support for their role (vertically) integrating, scaling up, and expanding agricultural production processes.

References

Alexseev, M. (2003). "Chinese Migration in the Russian Far East: Security Threats and Incentives for Cooperation in Primorskii Krai," in Thornton, Judith and Ziegler, Charles E. (eds.), *Russia's Far East: A Region at Risk*, Seattle: University of Washington Press.

Balzer, H. and Repnikova, M. (2010). "Migration between China and Russia." *Post-Soviet Affairs* 26(19).

Cai, F. (2012). "Reform of the Hukou System and Unification of Rural–Urban Social Welfare," in Cai, F. (ed.), *The Chinese Academy of Social Sciences Yearbooks: Population and Labor Volume 3*, Beijing: Social Sciences Academic Press.

Chazan, G. (2006). "Giant Neighbors Russia, China See Fault Lines Begin to Appear." *The Wall Street Journal*, 14 November 2006.

Cheng, J. (2013). "黑龙江民工在俄打工被殴不实 钱被扣想逃回家 [Heilongjiang Peasants Working in Russia Getting Beaten Is Not True; Their Wages Withheld, They Fled Home]." *Sina News*, 14 July 2013, available at: http://dailynews.sina.com/bg/chn/chnpolitics/sinacn/20130714/22314746258.html [accessed: 8 August 2016].

Cheng, G. and Zhang, H. (2014). "China's Global Agricultural Strategy: An Open System to Safeguard the Country's Food Security," RSIS Working Paper.

China Russia Information Network (2012a). "赴俄务农村"造就数百个百万富翁：收成比打工翻好几倍 [Villages of Chinese laborers in Russia Have Created Several Hundred Peasant Millionaires]." *China-Russia News*, 15 June 2012, available at: www.chinaru.info/huarenhuashang/eluosihuaren/14615.shtml [accessed: 8 August 2016].

China Russia Information Network. (2012b). "从落魄小子到俄罗斯地主—东北人在俄罗斯种地 [From a Down-and-out Guy to a Russian Landlord: A Northeasterner Farming in Russia]." 15 February 2012, available at: www.chinaru.info/huarenhuashang/eluosihuaren/11642_2.shtml [accessed: 8 August 2016].

Cotula, L., Vermeulen, S., Leonard, R. and Keely, J. (2009). *Land Grab or Development Opportunity?* Rome: Food and Agriculture Organization (FAO), International Institute for Environment and Development (IIED), and International Fund for Agricultural Development (IFAD).

Cuddy, M. and Qian, L. (2007). "The Rural Economy in China and Russia: What is Different? Is there a Lesson for Russia?" *Economic Change and Restructuring* 40(1).

eFeedLink. (2014). "China Ships Back First Batch of Chinese Soy Produced in Russia," 31 October 2014, available at: www.efeedlink.com/contents/10-31-2014/59e2e46e-48bb-462a-852b-96183b05d750-b171.html [accessed: 1 February 2017].

Gale, F., Hansen, J. and Jewison, M. (2015). *China's Growing Demand for Agricultural Imports*. Economic Research Service, United States Department of Agriculture.

Heilongjiang Government. (2013). "牡丹江市东宁县成为我国最大俄罗斯进口粮食集散地 [Mudanjiang's Dongning County Has Become the Nation's Largest Distribution Center for Russian Grain Imports]." 31 December 2013, available at: www.mofcom.gov.cn/article/resume/n/201312/20131200446395.shtml [accessed: 8 August 2016].

Hu, J. (2009). "海外种地渐热 [Overseas Farming Getting Hot]." *Panorama Network*, 26 February 2009, available at: www.p5w.net/news/cjxw/200902/t2189425.htm [accessed: 1 June 2016].

Kim, W. B. (1994). "Sino-Russian Relations and Chinese Workers in the Russian Far East: A Porous Border." *Asian Survey* 34(12).

Li, P., Song, X. and Song, K. (2013). "中俄农业和食品工业合作 [China-Russia Agricultural and Food Industrial Cooperation]." *Eurasian Economy* 4.

Liu, J. (2011). "中国农民赴俄罗斯种地淘金调查 [Investigation of Chinese Peasants' 'Farm Rush' in Russia]." China Times 华夏时报, available at: http://wenku.baidu.com/view/f88e0de49b89680203d8251f.html [accessed: 1 January 2015].

Lockett, H. (2015). "China's Grain Self-Sufficiency Policy Lives on After Its Official Demise." *China Economic Review*, 7 April 2015, available at: www.chinaeconomicreview.com/cereal-dysfunction [accessed: 8 August 2016].

Lotspeich, R. (2010). "Economic Integration of China and Russia in the Post-Soviet Era," in Bellacquia, J.A. (ed.), *The Future of China-Russia Relations*. Lexington: University Press of Kentucky.

Minakir, P.A. (1996). "Chinese Immigration in the Russian Far East: Regional, National, and International Dimensions," in Asrael, J.R. and Payin, E.A. (eds.), *Cooperation and Conflict in the Former Soviet Union: Implications for Migration*, Santa Monica, CA: RAND Corporation.

Ministry of Commerce of the PRC. (2016). "黑龙江对俄境外农业开发面积今年将达850万亩 [Heilongjiang Agricultural Development in Russia to Reach 8.5 Million Mu This Year]." 3 April 2016, available at: www.mofcom.gov.cn/article/resume/n/201603/20160301268361.shtml [accessed: 8 August 2016].

Ministry of Commerce of the PRC. (n.d.). "中国企业"走出去"发展战略 [China's Going Out Development Strategy]." Available at: http://history.mofcom.gov.cn/?newchina=%E4%B8%AD%E5%9B%BD%E4%BC%81%E4%B8%9A%E8%B5%B0%E5%87%BA%E5%8E%BB%E5%8F%91%E5%B1%95%E6%88%98%E7%95%A5 [accessed: 16 March 2017].

The Moscow Times. (2016). "Sberbank Says Average Russian Salary Lower Than Chinese." *The Moscow Times*, 19 May 2016.

Motrich, E. and Naiden, S. (2009). "The Social-Demographic Situation and Labor Migration: the Far Eastern Sector." *Studies on Russian Economic Development* 20(5).

Murphy, R. (2002). *How Migration Labor is Changing Rural China*, Cambridge: Cambridge University Press.

National Bureau of Statistics. (2014). *China Statistical Yearbook 2014*, available at: www.stats.gov.cn/tjsj/ndsj/2014/indexeh.htm [accessed: 5 February 2017].

Prosvirnov, S. (2009). "Migration between the Amur Region and China at the turn of the 21st Century." *Far Eastern Affairs* 37(2).

Repnikova, M. and Gabuev, A., "Why Forecasts of a Chinese Takeover of the Russian Far East Are Just a Dramatic Myth." *South China Morning Post*, 14 July 2017.

Russian Federation. (2002). "Федеральный закон об обороте земель сельскохозяйственного назначения [Federal Law (No. 101-FZ) on Turnover of Agricultural Land]." 26 July 2002.

Shkurkin, A.M. (2002). "Chinese in the Labour Market of the Russian Far East: Past, Present, Future," in Nyiri, P. and Savelev, I. (eds.), *Globalizing Chinese Migration*, Burlington: Ashgate Publishing Company.

Tencent Network. (2006). "到俄罗斯种菜去!中国农民握远东90%菜市 [Going to Russia to Plant Vegetables! Chinese Peasants Capture 90% of the Far East Vegetable Market]." 18 August 2006, available at: http://finance.qq.com/a/20060818/000287.htm [accessed: 1 March 2014].

Wang, S. (1995). "China's Export of Labor and Its Management." *Asian and Pacific Migration Journal* 4(2–3).
Wang, T., Maruyama, A. and Kikuchi, M. (2000). "Rural–Urban Migration and Labor Markets in China: A Case Study in a Northeastern Province." *The Developing Economies* 38 (1).
World Bank. (2014). "Arable Land (Hectares per Person)," available at: http://data.worldbank.org/indicator/AG.LND.ARBL.HA.PC [accessed: 8 August 2016].
World Grain News. (2015). "China Soybean Imports to Continue to Grow." 13 March 2015, available at: www.world-grain.com/articles/news_home/World_Grain_News/2015/03/China_soybean_imports_to_conti.aspx?ID=%7B713B31ED-C95F-4199-856A-6E644DBB613E%7D [accessed: 5 February 2017].
Xu, H., Wang, L. and Feng, Z. (2014). "Farmer Labor Service Export from Heilongjiang Province to Russia." *Journal of Northeast Agricultural University* 21(2).
Yan, H. and Chen, Y. (2015). "Agrarian Capitalization without Capitalism? Capitalist Dynamics from Above and Below in China." *Journal of Agrarian Change* 15(3).
Yap, C. (2015). "China, Russia Prepare $2 Billion Agricultural Investment Fund." *The Wall Street Journal*, 8 May 2015, available at: www.wsj.com/articles/china-russia-prepare-2-billion-agricultural-investment-fund-1431080535 [accessed: 8 August 2016].
Zhang. G. (2016). "黑龙江省对俄农业合作硕果满枝头 农业"走出去 [Heilongjiang Province and Russia Agricultural Cooperation Fruitful Over the Branches of Agriculture, 'going out']." *Heilongjiang Times*, 7 April, 2016.
Zhang, Q. (2008). "The Rise of Agrarian Capitalism with Chinese Characteristics: Agricultural Modernization, Agribusiness and Collective Land Rights." *The China Journal* 60.
Zhou, J. (2017). "Chinese Agrarian Capitalism in the Russian Far East." *Third World Thematics: A TWQ Journal* 1(5).

15
A failed market experiment and ignored livelihoods
Jatropha expansion in the Sino–Vietnamese borderlands

Jean-François Rousseau

The areas of China's Yunnan Province bordering Myanmar, Laos, and Vietnam underwent rapid development over the past decade. Large-scale infrastructure schemes proliferated at an unprecedented pace and fuelled rapid state-led expansion of a capitalist economy into Southwest China's mountainous frontier, overcoming 'friction of terrain' (Scott 2009; see also Turner et al. 2015).

These developments occurred in response to a series of state policies enacted in the Yunnan borderlands since the mid-2000s. Some of these policies supplement national programmes such as the Go West campaign, which officially promotes infrastructure development as a means to address development imbalances between 'poor' but resource-rich western areas such as Yunnan and wealthier eastern provinces. Go West also fosters the expansion of the capitalist economy and a central state-endorsed modernisation programme into ethnic minority societies (Goodman 2004; Sturgeon 2009; Yeh 2009). At the same time, externally oriented state policies are aiming to make Yunnan a core node, or a 'bridgehead', within an expanding China–Southeast Asia international transport corridor (Su 2013; Ptak and Hommel 2016; Summers 2016).

Within the policies resulting from this double opening process, specific provisions are made for peripheral borderland areas in an attempt to overcome the geographical characteristics that have long created insurmountable challenges to state and business ventures (Summers 2016; Yao 2009). Specific measures are also dedicated to integrating borderland ethnic minority populations and the assets and strategies upon which their livelihoods rely into the realm of the state.[1] Energy projects are central to these ventures in the Yunnan borderlands (Ptak and Hommel 2016).

In this chapter, I retrace how in Honghe Prefecture along the Vietnam border the political reframing of vast tracts of sloping lands as 'wastelands' has opened up new development opportunities for state-backed corporate actors and energy development schemes. I investigate how this new tenure regime and the ensuing expansion of a plantation dominated by a single perennial crop contrasts with how local Handai ethnic minority populations customarily understood and utilised this land for grazing buffalo, collecting non-timber forest products (NTFP), and as cemeteries. I also unpack the livelihood consequences of landscape changes associated with such land use change for Handai households established along the Red River floodplain in Honghe

Prefecture. I build my interpretations from a case study of a failed energy crop plantation scheme implemented on sloping land areas of Honghe Prefecture, which aimed to produce biofuels from the oil contained in the seeds of *jatropha curcas* trees in the mid-2000s.

I argue that the 'development push' in the Yunnan frontier has justified development experiments on the sole basis that their potential success might contribute to a series of state policy priorities for border regions. Such potential outputs have led to particular arrangements between the state and corporate actors that implement policy-sponsored projects in exchange for subsidies, quick profit opportunities, and access to both credit lines and cheap land resources. I argue that this outlook overshadows all other criteria typically utilised for evaluating the feasibility of a development project, including its actual potential for success and foreseeable livelihood consequences. This outlook is further consolidated by the fact that the failure of the jatropha project investigated here came at no cost to local authorities or other state and corporate proponents. The outcome, however, was different for local Handai farmers, who were well aware of the low agrarian potential of the targeted sloping lands and anticipated plantation failure from the outset. Though no one ever asked them for their input, it is these individuals who are now forced to endure the consequences that the plantations have had upon their livelihoods.

I argue that the Sino–Vietnamese borderlands have become a laboratory for development experiments that the state permits, subsidises, and promotes as long as they are framed as fostering specific state priorities, including some that do not relate to the targeted borderlands whatsoever. I demonstrate how this facilitates development schemes that are doomed to fail and I unpack the wide-ranging livelihood consequences that arise from one such failure. Though earlier borderland scholarship provides rich insight into how ethnic minorities from the China–Southeast Asia borderlands experience the livelihood consequences of development schemes (see Michaud and Forsyth 2011; Turner et al. 2015), the impacts of jatropha expansion have yet to be documented in the Southwest China frontier.

The evidence I build upon was gathered over the course of repeated long-term ethnographic fieldwork journeys to Handai settlements in Honghe Prefecture in 2011–2012 and 2015 (Map 15.1). With the help of a Handai research assistant, my methods included participant observation, conversational interviews, and livelihood surveys. I concentrated most of my inquiries on jatropha expansion in one settlement I refer to as Gaotong Cun,[2] with 33 households and 145 individuals, where an important jatropha model plantation scheme was developed.

The 'gift' of jatropha plantation expansion

As Yeh (2013) demonstrates for Tibet, landscape transformations have shaped China's territorial project since the 1950s. She highlights key material transformations characterising many successive state development projects, the latest of which epitomises the neoliberal ideology of the current post-reforms economic climate. To Yeh (2013), urbanisation and the concrete that fuels it exemplify this latest state endeavour in the Tibetan frontier. Her conclusion, I argue, also holds for Honghe Prefecture in the Sino–Vietnamese borderlands.

In the last decade, hundreds of kilometres of expressways, overpasses, and tunnels have been built in the remote and mountainous landscape of Honghe. Road travel from Kunming to the Vietnamese border at Hekou now takes only five hours or so, half the time it took in the late 2000s. A new railway line was opened in 2013 connecting Kunming to Mengzi in just over four hours; the line was extended to the border at Hekou one year later.[3] Sustained transportation infrastructure development has fostered socioeconomic change in rural borderland areas, as renovated or newly built 'Fourth Grade' highways now connect all of Honghe's neighbouring county-level

Jean-François Rousseau

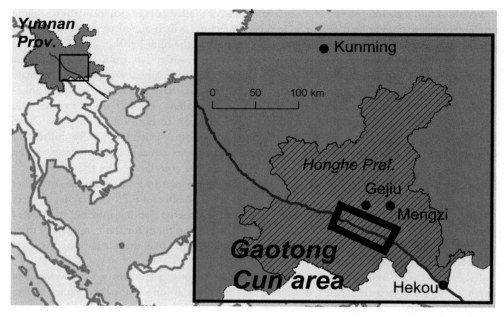

Map 15.1 Approximate location of Gaotong Cun
Source: Redrawn from Rousseau 2014b

cities.[4] In James Scott's (2009: 166) words, these developments exemplify the expansion of 'distance-demolishing technologies' that simultaneously allow rural borderland populations to access new markets, both national and international, while increasing state control over ethnic minorities and the resources they build their livelihoods around (Rigg 2002; Trincsi et al. 2014). Yet as Rigg (2002: 625) explains: 'Roads not only give opportunities for local people to get out and access new opportunities, but also for outsiders to get in.'

Diminished 'friction of terrain' and state incentives have indeed convinced some outsiders to enter Honghe Prefecture and attempt to exploit a very unlikely commodity in this area: jatropha biodiesel produced in plantations on sloping lands. Jatropha was deemed the 'green gold of the desert' (Campa 2012: v) in the mid-2000s owing to its capacity to survive in dry environments and poor soil. The global biofuel industry was then facing criticism regarding the impacts of biofuel plantation expansion on food safety and had high ambitions for jatropha. The Chinese government banned the expansion of grain energy crop plantations in 2006 in order to avoid biofuel plantations infringing on the country's food security (Weyerhaeuser et al. 2007; Yang et al. 2012). Since then, only non-grain energy crops such as jatropha have been tolerated, and their expansion is restricted to areas designated as 'wastelands'.

This latest attempt at valorising 'wastelands' came after the interruption of the so-called wasteland auction policy of the 1990s, which had allowed individuals and companies to secure access rights to communal sloping lands. Though officially promoted as simultaneously fostering afforestation and economic development priorities, the policy often led to clearcut logging, monocrop plantation expansion, and the loss of resource access for farmer communities. In addition, it allowed many local cadres overseeing land auctions to embezzle money destined for the communes (Grinspoon 2002; Sturgeon 2005).

Though the specific sloping lands discussed here were not auctioned, similar environmental and development rhetoric following vague territorialisation criteria formed the foundation for the

A failed market experiment

biofuel expansion in Gaotong Cun.[5] As an informant with close ties to the Yunnan Forestry Bureau explained:

> Wasteland classification rests on the weak prospects that these lands hold for commercial agriculture development based on eight criteria, namely land use, elevation, slope, precipitation, temperature, soil type, alkalisation and effective soil depth. There are no precise benchmarks for these aspects, though.
>
> *(Kunming NGO worker 2011)*

While restricting where biofuel expansion could occur, China adopted very ambitious objectives for the biofuel sector with the aim of addressing environmental and energy security priorities. These objectives state that biofuel products should fulfil 15 per cent of the transport sector's energy needs by 2020, compared with 6 per cent in 2006 (National Development and Reform Commission 2007). In parallel, other development programmes including the Go West campaign, reforestation efforts targeting sloping lands such as the Sloping Land Conversion Programme (SCLP),[6] and the 'Bridgehead' programme have supported national biofuel guidelines. In areas such as Honghe, with large tracts of sloping – and allegedly waste – lands, these factors have combined to create a thriving biofuel market. In addition, as jatropha grows wild in Honghe,[7] local and provincial authorities were proactive in framing it as the latest 'miracle crop' that would allow the prefecture to overcome socioeconomic backwardness (Sturgeon 2010). Great portions of the Sino–Vietnamese borderlands were thereby promoted as potential grounds for jatropha expansion.

By the late 2000s, 'wastelands' identified for potential jatropha expansion totalled 675,000 ha in Yunnan, with 22.5 per cent of the area located in Honghe alone (Wang et al. 2010).[8] Indeed, the two main plantation schemes initiated in the province were both located in Honghe Prefecture (Yang et al. 2012). These sites include a 20,000 ha project overseen by a Sino–British joint venture called Sunshine Technology. The first step in the implementation of this project was the creation, from 2006 onwards, of a 250 ha 'jatropha demonstration site' on the communal lands of Gaotong Cun along with the construction of a seed crusher.

Provincial and prefecture authorities offered the 'gift' of jatropha plantation development to borderland ethnic minorities, including the Handai farmers from Gaotong Cun. Yet, as was often the case in the jatropha boom and more widely in other Chinese crop bubbles, no institutional arrangements were implemented to ensure the long-term development of the jatropha sector (Sturgeon 2010; Li et al. 2014). For instance, a 3,000 RMB (US$455) subsidy offered to Sunshine Technology per hectare converted to jatropha plantation was paid in a lump sum, with no measure put in place to ensure that the plantations would be taken care of after the subsidies were paid (Kunming scholar 2011). Further, by the time jatropha bushes sown in the mid-2000s yielded their first harvest in the early 2010s, market prospects for jatropha had all but vanished due to lower than expected yields, falling oil prices, and failure to adopt national biofuel blending guidelines, among other issues (see Li et al. 2014; Rousseau 2014b). Sunshine Technology was long gone by then, even if the plantation remained.

The 'green gold of the desert' rhetoric failed to acknowledge that farming jatropha is a water-, work-, and chemical input-intensive venture. This has led to the commercial failure of a great many jatropha plantation schemes implemented over the last decade, both in China and elsewhere (Ariza-Montobbio and Lele 2010; Li et al. 2014; Singh et al. 2014). However, jatropha can indeed survive on its own in harsh environments such as the Honghe borderlands, and a large portion of the bushes sown in the mid-2000s remains alive a decade later (Figure 15.1).

Jean-François Rousseau

Figure 15.1 Abandoned jatropha plantation in Gaotong Cun
Taken from Rousseau 2014b

But now that the plantations have been developed, the targeted 'wastelands' have been reclassified as 'economic forest' and peasants are not allowed to cut the bushes. This has had a significant impact upon the capacity of Handai populations to access a series of customary livelihood assets and opportunities in the sloping lands. I delve into these aspects below, but first I introduce the borderland ethnic group at the core of this research.

Aspects of Handai livelihoods

The people informing this research self-identify as Handai, although they officially belong to the Dai minority nationality, one of 56 ethnic groups officially recognised in the People's Republic of China. Similar to other Dai societies, Handai customarily dwell along lowland floodplains adjacent to the Southeast Asian Massif's waterways. Such environments have traditionally allowed them to grow wet rice on the same land perennially, intercropped with maize and all sorts of greens (see, for instance, Berlie 1991; Henin and Flaherty 1994; Zheng 2007). Yet, as is the case for many ethnic groups in the Southeast Asian Massif,[9] Handai informants reckon that they share more ethnocultural traits with Tay groups based in neighbouring northern Vietnam than with many other Dai societies from Yunnan, most of which inhabit Xishuangbanna and Dehong Prefectures. Since the ethnic classification campaign undertaken in China in the early 1950s first and foremost emphasised linguistic criteria, and as Handai and other Dai dialects are to some degree mutually intelligible, Handai were de facto included in the Dai category (see Mullaney 2011).

When asked what distinguishes Handai from other Dai groups, villager informants mentioned that their language is different and that they do not have an orthography, that their houses are different and have flat rooftops, that they practice a local/animist (*bendi*) cult and that they are not Buddhist, and that they never had a king. These aspects are important to this jatropha case study as they exemplify the central government's long history of enacting policies that do not account for local characteristics. Among these is the livelihood importance of sloping lands adjacent to the river valleys where Dai groups are settled. The bungled founding of a jatropha plantation in Gaotong Cun and the long-term livelihood consequences of Sunshine Technology's failure demonstrate how much the sloping lands did indeed matter.

The not-so-wasted 'wastelands'

Similar to authorities' distinction between 'wasteland' and other land categories, Gaotong Cun villagers see the sloping lands adjacent to their village as areas where conditions are inadequate for growing rice or cash crops intensively. Yet the villagers insist that this setting fulfils important livelihood functions that complement those of intensive riverside farming systems.

About half of the households surveyed used to grow cassava and/or sesame on portions of the sloping lands where jatropha expansion occurred. Through cultivating these areas year after year, these households had acquired usufruct rights over portions of these communal lands. While they invested relatively little time and energy into these ventures, extensive cassava and sesame cultivation nonetheless provided the farmers with both food and supplementary income. It also supported farmers' capacity to cope with harvest failure, and, more recently, drops in the market prices of the main cash crops grown intensively along the floodplain, such as banana, mango, and papaya, which provided villagers with 85 per cent of their average annual household income in 2012.

Handai farmers also used to utilise the sloping lands adjacent to their village for grazing water buffalo. While buffalo were originally used to till rice fields along the floodplain, with their dung used as fertiliser, hand tractors and chemical farm inputs have displaced buffalo in the village over the past decade. Nonetheless, buffalo have retained their cultural significance and, along with their meat, are still required for weddings, funerals, and shamanistic rites for healing the sick or keeping malevolent ghosts at a distance. Therefore, as all of Gaotong Cun households used to raise buffalo prior to jatropha plantation expansion in the mid-2000s, access to grazing grounds located close to their houses was deemed a vital livelihood asset.

Similar to buffalo grazing, the sloping lands targeted for jatropha expansion used to fulfil other livelihood functions that pertained to food safety and/or held important cultural significance. The sloping lands, for instance, allowed for firewood collection. Firewood stoves remain widely used by all surveyed villagers in Gaotong Cun, especially when large gatherings occur. Firewood stoves are deemed better for cooking than electric or gas stoves, and food cooked the traditional way is preferred. Half of the surveyed villagers used to collect a wide range of non-timber forest products, including edible roots, grasses, leaves, flowers, and mushrooms in the sloping lands. Village elders recall that in the past, villagers relied upon such NTFPs when food shortages occurred in the wake of political campaigns and/or bad climatic conditions. Nowadays, villagers and outsiders value these products as aspects of the 'Handai taste' (*handai fengwei*), and many local NTFPs fetch high prices in neighbouring urban centres. Last but not least, the sloping lands host the tombs of deceased villagers, which endows this setting with a unique cultural significance.

The now wasted sloping lands

Most Gaotong Cun informants first learned about the planned jatropha plantation development after the communal land rental agreement had already been settled by the local village committee, the county forest bureau, and Sunshine Technology. The villagers welcomed this news with both enthusiasm and scepticism. On the one hand, many initially saw this large-scale project as an opportunity to increase household incomes – which averaged 10,470 RMB (US$1,600) in 2012 – without having to leave the village. Work migration had become an increasingly frequent, although widely unpopular, livelihood strategy for Handai farmers.

On the other hand, however, villagers doubted that jatropha would grow well in the barren lands, even with mechanical irrigation systems. They knew that the soil layer was particularly thin and poor in this setting and doubted that any intensive farming activity could be undertaken in the hills. Some also raised doubts early on about the developers' real intentions. While the scale of the buildings on Sunshine Technology's compound impressed the villagers, it also made them speculate that 'the company was more interested in the government subsidies than in long-term jatropha exploitation' (Gaotong Cun villager 2015).

As jatropha planting began, the villagers quickly came to realise that the livelihood functions the barren hills used to fulfil were now ruled out and that they would not be compensated for this. Those who had long grown cassava and sesame in the targeted areas were barred from their land, and besides a small 200 RMB (US$30) annual payment offered to all of Gaotong Cun's households until Sunshine Technology went bankrupt, they received no further financial compensation for their loss. As grass does not grow well under jatropha trees, the area is no longer suitable for grazing buffalo; and as the journey to proper grazing lands is now much longer than before, rearing buffalo has become a more labour-intensive activity, contributing to about one-third of the surveyed households abandoning buffalo grazing altogether.

Jatropha plantation development also forced the villagers to relocate their firewood and NTFP collection activities in areas further from the village. First, jatropha wood does not burn well, and even if it did, the villagers would not be able to harvest it since the sloping lands are now zoned as economic forests. Second, none of the NTFPs that Handai villagers used to harvest grow in the monocrop plantations. Consequently, customary harvesting activities have now been widely abandoned, depriving villagers of cherished food and a potential supplementary income. Finally, while they had no choice but to accept jatropha trees alongside their graveyards, the villagers deplore this intrusion.

As their early enthusiasm towards the potential economic opportunities of jatropha development suggests, the farmers could have tolerated the above trade-offs if they had been compensated with job and/or income opportunities. However, the plantation in the end brought fewer work opportunities than people had hoped for. Members of only two-thirds of surveyed households had ever worked for Sunshine Technology, and in most cases they had done so for a few days a year during the 2007 to 2009 period, earning just 30 RMB (US$4.50) a day.

Hence, by 2012, early enthusiasm towards jatropha had all but vanished; 90 per cent of surveyed households argued that the jatropha plantation would bring them no financial benefits whatsoever in the future, while a similar proportion thought that plantation development had stopped for good. As jatropha still grows in large portions of the abandoned plantation, Gaotong Cun's villagers will most likely be deprived of the erstwhile livelihood functions that this land used to fulfil for the foreseeable future.

A failed market experiment and ignored livelihoods

Commenting on the Go West campaign, Holbig (2004: 345) argued that '[the] State Environmental Protection Agency (SEPA) was conspicuously absent (and still is today), a fact which might result from this agency's early critical assessments of the ecological damage that could be caused by an irrational development craze'. As this chapter focusing on development-induced livelihood damage demonstrates, Sunshine Technology's jatropha plantation scheme exemplifies an outcome of this ongoing craze in the Sino–Vietnamese borderlands.

A range of policies and development programmes supplement the Go West campaign in facilitating development projects in the borderlands. Jatropha development in Honghe indeed occurred due to converging government policies that encouraged and subsidised a specific market niche (biofuel development in 'wasteland' areas) in a specific setting (border regions) inhabited by a specific category of Chinese citizens (ethnic minorities). These policies themselves unleashed economic forces that allowed jatropha promoters to gain almost free access to land and generous state subsidies that came with credit lines. Such a neat alignment of public and private interests obscured the actual (minimal) potential of intensive jatropha planting on communal sloping lands, along with the market prospects of jatropha-based biofuels.

This also ensured that local livelihood consequences were entirely ignored in the planning of the jatropha plantation. To the state, Gaotong Cun's sloping lands, lacking intensive agricultural activities, were considered 'wasted' regardless of the livelihood functions they fulfilled for Handai farmers. Mandated to modernise this landscape, Sunshine Technology had no reason or motivation to be sensitive to these aspects. The livelihood importance of the barren lands was therefore not taken into consideration before, during, or after jatropha development.

Furthermore, Handai borderland farmers were never invited to participate in development decisions targeting the communal lands adjacent to their villages. They have not been allowed to obtain appropriate financial compensation for loss of access, nor have they been offered a share of potential future profits. Although they were initially committed to the success of the plantation, which they foresaw as an opportunity to enhance their livelihoods, it made no difference to the villagers in the end whether the plantation turned a profit or not. The subsidy regime further sealed the fate of the project, as Sunshine Technology had no incentive to continue investing in the project after it had received the bulk of the state subsidies (Kunming scholar 2011).

Given these facts, none of the villagers interviewed for this research had anything positive to say about jatropha or Sunshine Technology. To them, jatropha is a most useless crop, and the plantation excluded them from culturally meaningful lands that used to fulfil important livelihood functions. The villagers also claim that corrupt managers from Sunshine Technology were the only ones that ever benefited from the plantation. With regards to direct financial benefits, this claim appears justified (although, given widespread corruption, it is also possible that authorities at various levels benefited as well). However, the plantation has also driven more subtle outcomes, to which I will now turn.

In some ways, the development of the Sunshine Technology jatropha plantation in Honghe has served various objectives that state policies promote in the Sino–Vietnamese borderlands. First, as the barren lands are now covered with neatly aligned jatropha bushes, 'forest cover' has increased along with the area of Honghe Prefecture's economic forest. From the state's point of view, this is considered more desirable than earlier less green and less modern landscapes, regardless of the greater livelihood outcomes they used to fulfil for Handai farmers.

Second, the development of the plantation was part of a wave of increased investment in the Sino–Vietnamese borderlands. Expanding the capitalist economy is a central priority of the development model that currently prevails in China, and Yunnan's provincial authorities have been eager to promote development projects that are especially large-scale and outward-oriented compared to other western provinces (Donaldson 2011). The failure of the jatropha plantation does not conflict with these objectives whatsoever. Typically, local authorities and corporate actors involved in Chinese development experiments are not held accountable for project failure (Heilmann 2008). Specifically addressing how this manifests in campaigns promoting specific cash crops, Sturgeon (2010) points out that the blame most often falls on local farmers rather than on state agents. Yet, as there was so little farmer involvement in jatropha expansion, no one ended up being blamed for Sunshine Technology's failure. The authorities derive substantial benefits when economic growth does occur – growth being the most important criteria regulating cadre promotion – or when they oversee a successful experiment that translates into wider policy outcomes. Given these factors, this jatropha expansion experiment came at no risk for the local authorities and corporate stakeholders who promoted it and benefited from extensive subsidisation by the central government.

Third, the policies that encouraged jatropha plantation expansion have led to land resource governance changes that themselves have driven wider social changes aligning with state policy objectives. Deprived of their access to livelihood functions previously fulfilled in the sloping lands, Handai farmers were convinced to become further involved in activities that the state promotes in the borderlands, including commercial and input-intensive agriculture. The same goes for the new exclusion from firewood harvesting, a practice that the state discourages as it allegedly conflicts with forest cover expansion objectives. Eroding customary livelihood assets has further convinced increasing numbers of villagers to engage in work migration, a decision that most Handai villagers make reluctantly, but that nonetheless fuels the urbanisation spree at the core of the China's current development model. All these aspects are reminders that the governance of natural resources and the governance of people are closely interlinked. This is particularly the case for borderland societies such as the Handai, whose livelihoods are built around both customary and 'modern' assets and activities. Yet, as the state becomes increasingly involved in borderland natural resource governance, aspects of customary livelihoods are either becoming less common or undergoing forced hybridisation processes. The presence of old tombstones in the remains of the modern jatropha plantations near Gaotong Cun is a stark reminder of this. The tombstones could well outlive the trees.

Notes

1 In China, the 'state' encompasses a broad coalition of actors, many of whom hold differing priorities (see Lieberthal and Oksenberg 1988). Here I use the 'state' to refer to the central and Yunnan provincial governments, which corresponds to how the villagers informing this research generally understand this notion.
2 A pseudonym.
3 This new railway follows a route that Tonkin-based colonial authorities first envisioned in the early 20th century for the French-built Hanoi–Kunming railway. It was first supposed to travel through Mengzi, already an important trading centre 100 years ago. However, technical challenges convinced French authorities to adopt a different itinerary bypassing Mengzi (Rousseau 2014a). More recently, Mengzi became the seat of Honghe Prefecture's government in 2003, due to expansion constraints in the former capital of Gejiu.
4 For details on China's road grading system, see Chen et al. (2016).
5 Nalepa and Bauer (2012) demonstrate that such vague territorialisation criteria are frequently used when biofuel expansion occurs in the Global South.
6 The SCLP provides grain, cash, and saplings to farmers who convert sloping land fields into forest plantations or grasslands (see Xu et al. 2004; Yeh 2009). The jatropha project discussed was not part of the SCLP per se. However, it led to increased forest cover in the barren lands, thereby abiding by the spirit of this campaign.
7 Ethnic minority farmers have traditionally used jatropha to fence their fields and house gardens, as the fruit and leaves from jatropha bushes are toxic to cattle.
8 Honghe's area represents some 9 per cent of the provincial total.
9 The Southeast Asian Massif is a regional ensemble spanning areas of Southwest China and mainland Southeast Asia. The Massif is home to a mosaic of transnational ethnic minorities whose territorial distribution antedated modern state boundaries (see Michaud 2006).

References

Ariza-Montobbio, P. and Lele, S. (2010) Jatropha Plantations for Biodiesel in Tamil Nadu, India: Viability, Livelihood Trade-Offs, and Latent Conflict. *Ecological Economics* 70(2):189–195.
Berlie, J. (1991) Les dai de Chine. *Péninsule* 1(22):1–132.
Campa, C. (2012) Preface. In *Jatropha, Challenges for a New Energy Crop, Volume 1: Farming, Economics and Biofuel*, eds. Carels, N., Sujatha, M. and Bahadur, B., V–VI. New York: Springer.

Chen, J., Chen, J., Miao, Y., Song, M. and Fan, Y. (2016) Unbalanced Development of Inter-Provincial High-Grade Highway in China: Decomposing the Gini Coefficient. *Transportation Research Part D: Transport and Environment* 48:499–510.

Donaldson, J. A. (2011) *Small Works: Poverty and Economic Development in Southwestern China*. Ithaca, NY: Cornell University Press.

Goodman, D. S. G. (2004) The Campaign to 'Open Up the West': National, Provincial-Level and Local Perspectives. *The China Quarterly* 178:317–334.

Grinspoon, E. J. (2002) *Socialist Wasteland Auction: Collective Forest Land in China's Economic Transition*, PhD thesis. Berkeley: University of California Berkeley.

Heilmann, S. (2008) From Local Experiments to National Policy: The Origins of China's Distinctive Policy Process. *The China Journal* 59:1–30.

Henin, B. and Flaherty, M. (1994) Ethnicity, Culture, and Natural Resource Use – Forces of Change on Dai Society, Xishuangbanna, Southwest China. *Journal of Developing Societies* X:219–235.

Holbig, H. (2004) The Emergence of the Campaign to Open up the West: Ideological Formation, Central Decision-Making and the Role of the Provinces. *The China Quarterly* 178:335–357.

Li, J., Bluemling, B., Mol, A. P. J. and Herzfeld, T. (2014). Stagnating Jatropha Biofuel Development in Southwest China: An Institutional Approach. *Sustainability* 6(6):3192–3212.

Lieberthal, K. and Oksenberg, M. (1988) *Policy Making in China: Leaders, Structures, and Processes*. Princeton, NJ: Princeton University Press.

Michaud, J. (2006) *Historical Dictionary of the Peoples of the Southeast Asian Massif*. Lanham, MD: Scarecrow Press.

Michaud, J. and Forsyth, T. (2011) *Moving Mountains: Ethnicity and Livelihoods in Highland China, Vietnam, and Laos*. Vancouver: UBC Press.

Mullaney, T. S. (2011) *Coming to Terms with the Nation: Ethnic Classification in Modern China*. Berkeley: University of California Press.

Nalepa, R. A. and Bauer, D. M. (2012) Marginal Lands: The Role of Remote Sensing in Constructing Landscapes for Agrofuel Development. *The Journal of Peasant Studies* 39(2):403–422.

National Development and Reform Commission (NDRC) (2007) 可再生能源中长期发展规划 – Medium and Long Term Development Plan for Renewable Energies, 32. Beijing.

Ptak, T. and Hommel, D. (2016) The Trans-Political Nature of Southwest China's Energy Conduit, Yunnan Province. *Geopolitics* 1–23:556–578.

Rigg, J. (2002) Roads, Marketization and Social Exclusion in Southeast Asia. What do Roads do to People? *Bijdragen tot de Taal-, Land- en Volkenkunde* 158(4):619–636.

Rousseau, J.-F. (2014a) An Imperial Railway Failure: the Indochina-Yunnan Railway, 1898–1941. *The Journal of Transport History* 35(1):1–17.

Rousseau, J.-F. (2014b) *Green Energies the Socialist Way, Hydropower, Energy Crops and Handai Livelihoods in the Red River Valley, Yunnan Province, China*, PhD thesis. Montreal: McGill University.

Scott, J. C. (2009) *The Art of Not Being Governed: An Anarchist History of Upland Southeast Asia*. New Haven, CT: Yale University Press.

Singh, K., Singh, B., Verma, S. K. and Patra, D. D. (2014) Jatropha Curcas: A Ten Year Story from Hope to Despair. *Renewable and Sustainable Energy Reviews* 35:356–360.

Sturgeon, J. C. (2005) *Border Landscapes: The Politics of Akha Land Use in China and Thailand*. Seattle: University of Washington Press.

Sturgeon, J. C. (2009) Quality Control: Resource Access and Local Village Elections in Rural China. *Modern Asian Studies* 4(2):481–509.

Sturgeon, J. C. (2010) Governing Minorities and Development in Xishuangbanna, China: Akha and Dai Rubber Farmers as Entrepreneurs. *Geoforum* 41(2):318–328.

Su, X. (2013) From Frontier to Bridgehead: Cross-border Regions and the Experience of Yunnan, China. *International Journal of Urban and Regional Research* 37(4):1213–1232.

Summers, T. (2016) China's 'New Silk Roads': Sub-National Regions and Networks of Global Political Economy. *Third World Quarterly* 37:1628–1643.

Trincsi, K., Pham, T.-T.-H. and Turner, S. (2014) Mapping Mountain Diversity: Ethnic Minorities and Land Use Land Cover Change in Vietnam's Borderlands. *Land Use Policy* 41:484–497.

Turner, S., Bonnin, C. and Michaud, J. (2015) *Frontier Livelihoods: Hmong in the Sino-Vietnamese Borderlands*. Seattle: University of Seattle Press.

Wang, Z., Lu, Y. and Li, S. (2010) *Producing Biodiesel from Jatropha Curcas L. in Yunnan, China: Life-Cycle Environmental, Economic and Energy Performance*. Singapore: IDRC.

Weyerhaeuser, H., Tennigkeit, T., Su, Y. and Kahrl, F. (2007) *Biofuels in China: An Analysis of the Opportunities and Challenges of Jatropha Curcas in Southwest China*. Kunming: ICRAF China.

Xu, Z., Bennett, M. T., Tao, R. and Xu, J. (2004) China's Sloping Land Conversion Programme Four Years on: Current Situation, Pending Issues. *International Forestry Review* 6(3–4):317–326.

Yang, C.-Y., Fang, Z., Li, B. and Long, Y.-F. (2012) Review and Prospects of Jatropha Biodiesel Industry in China. *Renewable and Sustainable Energy Reviews* 16(4):2178–2190.

Yao, Y. (2009) The Political Economy of Government Policies Toward Regional Inequality in China. In *Reshaping Economic Geography in East Asia*, eds. Huang, Y. and Bocchi, A. M., 218–240. Washington, DC: World Bank.

Yeh, E. T. (2009) Greening Western China: A Critical View. *Geoforum* 40(5):884–894.

Yeh, E. T. (2013) *Taming Tibet: Landscape Transformation and the Gift of Chinese Development*. Ithaca, NY: Cornell University Press.

Zheng, X. (2007) Water Culture as an Ethnic Tradition and Sustainable Development of the Tai People of China. *Tai Culture* 20:97–108.

Part 4
Borders and boundaries of the state, governance, and the production of statelessness

Part 4

Introduction

Karin Dean

Over time, society has become associated with a territorial state delimited by boundaries, and our everyday lives embroiled with state institutions and governance. Accordingly, the state has emerged as the subject matter of numerous disciplines and as one of the most defined and discussed entities in social and political sciences. Two main features have been common to all definitions of state: exercising power through a set of political institutions and clearly delineated territory it governs (Agnew and Corbridge 1995). Alongside the shifting configurations within state power, increasingly seen as embroiled in assemblages of a widening assortment of political agents, dynamics, and scales, it is common to assert that territorial boundaries of states are no longer commensurate with political authority and absolute control. In a lot of the world this has never been the case as state boundaries and the subsequent invention of new nations were imposed onto places and people where the entire idea was baffling or unacceptable. The border worlds that emerged in many parts of Asia embroiled in multiple, competing, and contesting regimes of governance, state-making, and state-evading: the subject matter of this part. The "messy" realities, continuously adapting to and negotiating with ever changing conditions, opportunities, and relationships pinned down in this part, are those in Northern Myanmar (Dean and Viirand), Eastern Nepal (Bennike), the former Bangladesh–India enclaves (Ferdoush and Jones), the border worlds of the Thai–Myanmar land border (Saltsman), and littorals (Boutry and Ivanoff). What emerges as a common theme in all these complex realities is resistance to the governance of the nation state designed and imposed from faraway offices and thus confronted by various degrees and styles of state-evading, which objectives and outcomes, however, diverge.

In Northern Myanmar and Eastern Nepal, alternative regimes of governance compete with the state in the form of, respectively, the Kachin Independence Organization (KIO) and the Limbus' "sub-national" movement. Both political movements have territorial claims as both are seeking autonomy in a federal union, seen as a better arrangement for safeguarding local concerns. Both replicate state-like practices. The KIO de facto governs the territorial enclaves under its control, including sections of the Sino–Myanmar border, and is currently engaged in an armed struggle with the Myanmar government. The Limbu elites used the time when federal restructuring of Nepal was high on the political agenda, and established claims to Limbuwan with ancient connections, issued documents, publications and political symbols, and manifested the Limbu territoriality with signs at borders. In analyzing the situation in northern Myanmar, Dean and Viirand examine bordering as a process by studying the enactment, neglect or transgression of different Kachin borders, which they argue reflect the wider political developments that order the society. Bennike (this volume: p. 232) uses "territory as a governmental technique employed both by the national state and by 'subnational' groups," arguing that while the Limbus' movement is ostensibly mobilized against the centralized nation state, it in fact supports the national territorialization of the borderland. Territoriality, borders and the processes of bordering in both cases are central to understanding the socio-political developments, while also underlining the importance of taking seriously the "sub-national"—or non-state actors'—attempts to re-territorialize the nation state in a more acceptable way.

State-evading at the Bangladeshi–Indian border enclaves and the (re-)making of state space in the wake of the 2015 exchange of the 162 enclaves between the two countries are the outcomes of historical and geopolitical contingencies. Ferdoush and Jones discuss the enclave residents' decisions after having been granted the option to move to their "home countries"—in the context where less than two percent moved regardless of India's generous resettlement package to its "citizens" in enclaves in Bangladesh. Interviews with the people who had been de facto "stateless" their entire lives and with the different local government officials raise important questions on practical and theoretical meanings of statelessness, citizenship, state governance, and the making of state space.

Multiple regimes of control, or in Saltsman's words, the diversity of orders, is also the case at the Thai–Myanmar border world of refugees and low-wage migrants in the environs of the Thai border town Mae Sot. Alternative regimes of governance are embodied by the Karen National Union and the transnational political social and religious networks that make use of the ambiguity of the borderlands. However, as Saltsman shows, these are rather subjected to the more pervasive power of the Thai state to exercise exclusion and marginalization, but also arbitrary interpretation of regulations, and to the neoliberal logics of the production zone connected to global markets. Multiple sovereignties and boundaries thus shatter the border zone into "dozens of imbricated discontinuous shards" (Saltsman, this volume: p. 252)

The inclusion of maritime boundaries makes up a much needed contribution to borderland studies, demonstrating that littorals are dynamic and contested spaces of multiple governance, state-making and state-evading. Boutry focuses on littorals as zones of production of ethnic identities and struggle over the positionality connected to identities and livelihoods. He examines the strategies by various populations along the Andaman coasts such as the sea-nomadic Moken, the insular Bamar-Moken society, the Rohingya, and the ethnically diverse migrant labourer communities in the Southern Thai coastal provinces. He argues that certain favourable positionalities in the intricate social, ethnic, political, and economic relations is what the borderlanders need in order to survive. Ivanoff focuses on the state-evading practices of the Moken representing a wider nomadic culture of Austronesian origin scattered across the Mergui Archipelago at the peripheries of nation states, but also of dominant groups. He describes a panel of ethnic responses to the encroaching of the state and dominant peoples such as deliberate diversion strategies involving adaptation, mobilities, and self-reinvention in a new place, or splitting of groups to survive—all that enables the Moken to maintain basic social dynamics and ways of living.

In this part, boundaries become the privileged sites that help to unbundle and theorize crucial socio-political processes, the restructuring and transformation of space, spatial practices, and social relations. The chapters show that the political maps with brightly coloured blocks displaying neatly divided state spaces, adorned by the capital city as the seat of power, present a highly deceptive image of stability and order. On the ground, there is a continuous contested struggle to redefine space, belonging, and specific identity units triggered by the often prescriptive state-making across much of Asia.

Reference

Agnew, J. and Corbridge, S. (1995). *Mastering Space: Hegemony, Territory and International Political Economy*. London & New York: Routledge.

16
Multiple borders and bordering processes in Kachin State

Karin Dean and Mart Viirand

Introduction

Border scholars have deployed borders conceptually from territories' edges to a wide range of locations in the midst of our everyday lives, giving rise to the idea of *bordering* as a continuously evolving multisited process, driven by competing political actors (Paasi 1999; van Houtum 2002; Newman 2006). Bordering as a socio-political practice shapes human territoriality and political maps, and is employed in political discourses, institutions, media representations, school textbooks, and everyday forms of transnationalism (Kolossov and Scott 2013: 3–4). Many scholars study bordering in policing and surveillance or document ordinary people doing daily "borderwork" (Rumford 2011). This is while territorial edges remain relevant to scholars, but also to policymakers and the wider public, mostly because territory and borders continue to matter to states (Wilson 2014: 105).

Territory and borders definitely matter at the contested edges of contemporary Myanmar, where disputes over territory and sovereignty extend back to the ways the area was governed during the British colonial era, and to the contested ways the nation state has been imagined and performed since the establishment of the Union of Burma in 1948. Political fragmentation has galvanized in protracted armed resistance, fought over territorial control of spaces and populations in all Myanmar's ethnic states. Kachin State, bordering India and China, and inhabited by an ethnically diverse population, saw the predominantly Christian Kachin mobilize into the Kachin Independence Organization (KIO) in 1961 to fight against what was perceived as central state's politics of marginalization and discrimination. The KIO demands greater regional autonomy for Kachin State, with a population of nearly 1.7 million, according to the principles set in the country's founding document, the Panglong Agreement, in 1947. This counters the Myanmar government's vision of a unitary state since the end of 1950s.

At the heart of the violent political, economic, and cultural confrontations in Kachin State are three types of borders (see Map 16.1). First is the Sino–Myanmar boundary (international boundary on Map 16.1)—the internationally recognized line between two sovereign countries. It is the most visible and institutionalized border, determining the internationally recognized sovereign territory of the Republic of the Union of Myanmar. Second, less visible but deeply felt, are the borders that separate the de facto sovereign enclaves controlled by the KIO from the rest of the country (not depicted on Map 16.1 due to lack of reliable data). The KIO-controlled diminutive and disjointed enclaves span Kachin and Shan States, with stretches of the Sino–Myanmar boundary also under the control of this non-state armed group. This blurs the nominal understanding of an international border while creating new borders not marked on most maps. The third type of borders are state level administrative boundaries (township and state/region boundary on Map 16.1). These borders are relevant for their symbolic meaning in contemporary ethno-national politics, and for their bureaucratic influence. For example, borders of individual townships have been enacted by the central government in efforts to exclude certain populations from the census and voting. Importantly, territorial bordering in Northern Myanmar is not limited to these sets of territorial boundaries. Other, often highly politicized borders abound, such as those around church parishes, mining zones, nature parks, military bases, or territories controlled by other armed opposition groups. In this chapter, however, we limit our discussion to the Sino–Myanmar border, the lines between the KIO and the Myanmar

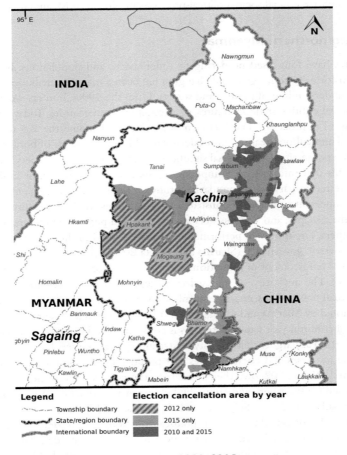

Map 16.1 Election cancellation in Kachin State 2010–2015
Source: Adapted from Myanmar Information Management Unit 2015, www.themimu.info

government, and Kachin State administrative boundaries, treating these as the "*central ordering devices* at the core of societies both in symbolic and material terms" (Popescu 2015: 49, *emphasis added*).

We demonstrate how these borders are enacted—or not—by competing state and non-state actors. We ask why and how particular borders are performed at certain socio-spatial contexts and not in others. We study "bordering", emphasizing the process of border enactment, neglect, or transgression, and bring local contexts and perspectives into scholarly debates around power topologies. We demonstrate that enactment, navigation, or circumvention of borders in Northern Myanmar are deeply embedded in wider political developments. By analyzing bordering practices across these borders, we focus on how the audiences of the repetitive performance of bordering react, and how such a spectacle "shapes audiences' ideas about the translocal nature of the state and their relationship to … [state power]" (Sharma and Gupta 2006: 13). This responds to recent critiques that border studies scholarship has been unduly limited to the so-called international boundaries (Piliavsky 2013). We build on this, demonstrating that an international border may also emerge deep inside the state, far from the "true" international boundary line, while the latter can be enacted less vigorously than expected. For us, borders are privileged sites that help to theorize crucial socio-political processes in Northern Myanmar.

(B)ordering northern Myanmar

Modern states have long used bordering to order spaces and populations. Recognizing that borders are historically contingent and changing has been a major contribution of border studies to wider understanding of politics and society. Until the 1990s, borders were largely seen as mere ontological entities, static structures, or geographic demarcations. Today, they are increasingly scrutinized as processes. The focus on bordering has become the key for understanding socio-political and cultural realities in modern states. "It is the process of bordering, rather than the border line per se, that has universal significance in the ordering of society" (Newman 2003: 15). Within this dynamic process, competing actors assert, appropriate, or evade the regimes of control invested in particular boundaries. Studying their varied investments is highly informative. It is important to ask who constructs and maintains the borders, how borders acquire and change their shapes, and why borders are enacted and performed in certain circumstances and not in others. The model of performativity has been used in the context of state power to explore bureaucratic governance (Sharma and Gupta 2006), spectacles of state violence (Taylor 1997), as well as enforcement of migration laws and "spaces of exception" around state borders (Mountz 2010). The authority of state actors is dependent upon repetitive re-enactments of their institutional power. Thus, enactment imbues power with structure that allows it to be recognized. As noted by Sharma and Gupta (2006: 13), "it is through these re-enactments that the coherence and continuity of state institutions is constituted and sometimes destabilized".

Popescu (2012: 152) argues that "twenty-first-century state borders have to be understood in relation to the processes and circumstances that produce them". Southeast Asian states, which emerged from 1945 to 2002, owe their borders to the complex interactions between colonial powers, local and central rulers, and culturally heterogeneous societies (Winichakul 1997; Tagliacozzo 2005; Sadan 2013; van Schendel and de Maaker 2014). State-centric models treating borders in their ahistorical administrative-political functions, as if separate from social and cultural realms, are insufficient. Discussing mainland Southeast Asian borders, Grundy-Warr (1998: 33) maintains that the past political and socio-spatial arrangements hold very contemporary meanings for the political agencies, actors, functionaries, activists and others, and these must be taken into account when interpreting present political maps. This critique has been followed by diversification of topics and methodologies in border studies, recognizing the complexity of power dynamics governing most Asian borderlands.

Historically, areas of contemporary Kachin State were inhabited by various clan-based and linguistically-related tribal populations. Tribes that later became the "Kachin" were also dominant in the northern parts of Shan State, contemporary Dai-Jingpo Autonomous Prefecture in China, and parts of Assam and Arunachal Pradesh of India. The heart of Kachinland (*Jinghpaw Wunpawng Mungdan*) is generally placed in the triangular area north of the confluence of two rivers, N'Mai and Mali Hka, that subsequently form the Irrawaddy in Myanmar. The evolution of the Kachin ethno-nationalist ideology and geographical imagination has been influenced by larger historical processes such as the British colonial rule, World War II, and Burma's independence movement (see Sadan 2013).

The British colonial administration exercised significant influence over the Frontier Areas without ever attempting to territorialize the population as it had done in India or Lower Burma. While supporting the Allied forces against the Japanese occupation (1942–1945), the areas were largely self-governing until the end of World War II. In 1947, General Aung San and the political representatives from major ethnic nationalities, including the "Kachin", signed the Panglong Agreement to establish the Union of Burma. The proceedings suggest that the Kachin elites were considering greater political integration while leaving open the possibility of eventual autonomy (Maran La Raw 1967). However, the legal device of the agreement proved short-lived after General Aung San's assassination in 1947, six months before Burmese independence from Britain. Attempts to secure political autonomy of Kachin State in the nominally federal Burma continued throughout the uneasy years of Burmese parliamentary democracy (1947–1962), while Rangoon embarked on building a unitary state instead, and was actively marginalizing the political aspirations of the local non-Bamar elites.[1]

After difficult negotiations, the Sino–Burmese border was settled between Beijing and Rangoon on 28th January, 1960. As part of Burma's concessions, three Kachin speaking villages were ceded to China, serving as one of the triggers for the armed resistance initiated by the Kachin Independence Army (KIA) in 1962. Owing to local perceptions of forced Burmanization of Kachinland, the KIO and its armed wing, the KIA, grew quickly in popularity, and consolidated its territorial control. Only the urbanized centres, such as Myitkyina and Bhamo, together with the railway line connecting towns and villages across an impenetrable jungle, remained under Rangoon's control.[2] Despite significant military superiority, the central government of Burma/Myanmar have failed to establish full sovereignty over KIO territories. Central state legitimacy among the Kachin population remains as tenuous as its bureaucratic reach into the mountainous rural Kachinland, where it has largely been experienced through violent governance by Myanmar Army, or *tatmadaw*. A defining feature of this militarized landscape are the fronts of armed conflict. Tense even during the ceasefire (1994–2011), these dangerous and shifting fronts have seen constant fighting since 2011.

The KIO enclaves, and especially its control over parts of the Sino–Myanmar boundary, challenge the sovereignty of Myanmar. Taylor (1995: 6) uses the term "internal sovereignty" to signify "effective control of a territory". He says that "external sovereignty"—recognition by other state actors—is the basis on which a state is considered sovereign in international law. By implication, states do not necessarily need internal sovereignty for international recognition. Indeed, de facto sovereign enclaves, such as those controlled by the KIO, are what the realist approaches prefer to ignore. With their "existence undertheorized and their achievements under-reported", it is assumed such enclaves will ultimately be defeated (McConnell 2009: 344). It is tempting to treat this fragmented territoriality and the corresponding borders as a temporary dysfunction. Yet doing so overlooks the fact that it is not only the Kachin communities who lend the KIO a degree of legitimacy. The government of Myanmar have also recognized the organization as an important political actor—by signing the formal agreement in 1994, inviting the KIO to its constitution drafting process, and consorting with the KIO official representation in Kachin State capital Myitkyina throughout the ceasefire era. China has authenticated the KIO by exercising diplomatic relations with the organization at its borders, including bilateral meetings and agreements, or occasionally hosting the ongoing peace talks between the Myanmar government and ethnic armed forces. In all cases, performance of territoriality and borders has been central to political relations. As the second strongest armed opposition in Myanmar, the KIO has certain leverage on Nay Pyi Daw's nationwide peace process that has been the policy priority of both, President Thein Sein's cabinet (2011–2015) and the National League for Democracy (NLD) led government since 2016.

To conclude, the state-within-state nexus with ongoing multiple bordering should not be dismissed as mere "dysfunctions", but as actual political complexes demonstrating the contested nature of state-building in Northern Myanmar. They affect everyday life and politics both locally and nationally, drawing attention to the relevance of bordering processes. We will now discuss the aforementioned three sets of boundaries, and highlight how studying their performance offers insights to Myanmar's complex territorialities.

Bordering at the international Sino–Myanmar border

One expects international borders to be visible almost by definition. However, the 2,190-kilometre-long Sino–Myanmar border cuts through areas of sparse habitation and mountainous jungle. It constitutes some of the wildest, roughest, and remotest landmass in Asia distant from larger regional centres. For the most part, it has no manifest audience. The physical visibility of such borders, even if militarized, is often saturated around limited crossing points while the supposed line blends into the surrounding landscape elsewhere. Even the presence of territorial contestants such as the KIO, *tatmadaw*, and NDA-K[3] on one side of the border, and the Chinese on the other, largely accompanies the extent of human settlements. The general thesis suggests that in many borderlands of upland Asia, the state has only slowly and very recently made its presence felt (Scott 2010). Yet why do some areas experience greater state presence than others? Why do border enactments change both temporally and spatially?

The dynamics of the Sino–Myanmar border can partly be explained by resilient trade. Despite the presence of armed conflicts, these borderlands have long supported a complex cross-border entrepreneurship. The 1994 ceasefire intensified the pre-existing commerce, opening new areas for logging, mining, and monocrop cultivation. Woods (2011) has described the resulting dynamics as "ceasefire capitalism", referring to competitive resource acquisition in the post-1994 political environment. This was partly driven by the Chinese entrepreneurs tapping into the largely unregulated and lucrative border economy. But the cross-border trade was also underpinned by extensive, historically-rooted kin and trade networks between Kachin/Jingpo living on both sides of the border. Traditional practices such as five-day markets rotating between villages of different ethnic compositions did not cease after the demarcation of the border in 1960. In fact, better infrastructure and communications that have been developed on the Chinese side since the end of 1980s, together with the supply of manufactured goods and foodstuffs have only intensified cross-border trading.

In recent years, Kachin landholders have been renting out their borderland fields for cash-cropping and tree nurseries for the Chinese *renminbi*—a currency used alongside Burmese *kyat* in the KIO border enclaves. Chinese entrepreneurs have established themselves in the KIO towns of Mai Ja Yang and Laiza, or at Myanmar government-controlled border towns such as Lweje, attracted by the opportunities for providing goods and services. China's unwavering demand for resources has been met by local elites facilitating trade in timber, precious minerals, fruits, or opium products. Large trading towns such as Ruili, district centres such as Yingjiang, or smaller border villages in China are connected via lucrative economic networks to towns, mines, and forests in Myanmar, crossing or circumventing the border. This resilient border trade may have perpetuated armed conflicts since the shadow economy disproportionately benefits certain politico-economic elites.

The way in which the international border with China was formed during the ceasefire (1994–2011) influenced wider political developments. For example, the KIO's capital Laiza emerged in the 1980s, but has since grown into a regional trade and population centre. The KIO has built state-like institutions such as ministries and offices (of public relations, liaisons, foreign affairs, etc.). Together with Mai Ja Yang near the KIA 3rd brigade headquarters, Laiza acts as an important locus for KIO statecraft and social projects such as health and education. These border towns have also nurtured the Kachin grassroots organizations with international connections who operate in "networked ways across space", transgressing the territorial containers of state (Agnew 2015: 47). The development of international networks was facilitated by an easy access to China's internet and mobile services from the early 2000s, when the rest of Myanmar had neither publicly viable telecom networks nor 24-hour power supply. Routing communication through China helped activists and political agents to evade state surveillance in Myanmar. The relaxed Sino–KIO border regime allowed foreign journalists and academics to access the Kachin communities otherwise silenced by Myanmar's military regime.

Renewed hostilities since 2011 have reduced and altered cross-border dynamics. These have caused displacement for tens of thousands of civilians, most of whom seek refuge in the KIO-controlled territories near the Sino–Myanmar border. These have also generated politics of aid of highly spatial design. Concerns over the inflow of refugees and spread of conflict to its territories have led China to enact the border, emphasizing its sovereignty, expanding military presence, and monitoring flows of people and goods more aggressively.

Despite the above, the local populace continues to negotiate and traverse the boundary and find ways to exploit economic and political opportunities. Tacit arrangements are struck between the local populace, traders, and governing authorities on both sides, with mutual gain ultimately depending on mutual efforts. Temporary passes issued to the local populace to allow limited cross-border stays constitute one notable mechanism for navigation. This involves three sets of authorities on both sides—the representatives of the Myanmar state, the KIO, and Chinese provincial districts. The role of the Sino–Myanmar border in China's foreign policy plus the local economic interdependence have arguably underpinned the pragmatism of Chinese authorities towards their neighbours, including informal acceptance of armed groups such as the KIO and NDA-K.[4] Relevant to the power topologies are also the strong cross-border social ties—epitomized in the protest by 1,500 Chinese Jingpo in 2013 in a Chinese town across the border from Laiza, demanding a ceasefire and promising to cross the border to help the Kachin unless a ceasefire was agreed (Ma Ning 2013).

The international boundary is recognized in the everyday utterances of the border dwellers referring to the "China side" (or "China gate") and to the Kachin (or Myanmar) side or gate. However, the border is enacted at certain times and in certain interactions, while not in others. People cross the border for shopping, markets, and other commercial interactions such as leasing land or subscribing to mobile and internet services with relative ease, using the currencies of both states. Yet the border's role in differentiating other economic and social spaces remains. Politically, it remains the line for enforcing China's sovereignty, enacted, for example, to stop the flow of refugees.

Bordering between the KIO and the Myanmar government

We now turn to borders separating the KIO enclaves from the rest of Myanmar. In the Kachin perceptions, these mark the extent to which the state of Myanmar has managed to "invade" Kachinland. The "unofficial" lines separating distinctive administrative regimes and opposing ideologies are primarily enforced through confronting armies. During the ceasefire period, these boundaries-cum-frontiers enjoyed a measure of stability—they generally kept the Myanmar military out, while the rest of Kachin State was subject to "military territorialization" by the *tatmadaw* and other armed groups setting up extractive industries and selling off concessions to Chinese entrepreneurs (Woods 2011). "Ceasefire capitalism" (Woods 2011) was also pursued by the KIO elites in its enclaves—a reason why many Kachin perceive the ceasefire years as a continuation of economic dispossession and plunder of natural resources. Provocative encroachments by *tatmadaw* into the enclaves in the KIO's possession led to the renewal of fighting in 2011.[5]

Although absent from official political or administrative maps, the bounds between the territories controlled by the KIO and the Myanmar government constitute truly inter-national borders. Their crossings separate two sovereign regimes, actively enacted at both sides. During the ceasefire, separate national flags were flown above the uniformed guards at checkpoints. Personal documents, belongings, and articles of merchandise were inspected or taxed at both sides. These de facto boundaries have generally been more guarded, and more conspicuously performed, than the Sino–Myanmar boundary. People travelling between the competing sovereign domains of the KIO and Myanmar must either subject themselves to these militarized checkpoints or else attempt to evade them through perilous jungle routes. While locals generally know how to navigate this terrain, they are often subjected to martial laws or, since the breakup of the ceasefire, caught up in sporadic clashes. These complexities illustrate how the region defies normative assumptions of statehood in international discourse. *Formally*, Kachin State belongs to Myanmar, yet Nay Pyi Daw's sovereignty is but one among many that are daily enacted or experienced.

Another example of bordering between the KIO and the Myanmar government can be drawn from the bureaucracy of schooling. While less conspicuous than armed violence, the enactment of borders through educational qualifications carries long-term social consequences. The main provider of formal schooling in Kachin State is the Myanmar government. Yet access to its services is territorially limited, especially for students from rural areas and the KIO enclaves. As one alternative, the KIO started an independent system of schooling in the 1970s. Today, it runs hundreds of primary schools, several middle and high schools throughout its territories, and a number of higher educational establishments such as the Teachers Training College in Mai Ja Yang and Law Academy in Laiza. Yet these are lacking international credibility and recognition outside the Kachin community, rendering its graduates' ensuing admittance into international higher educational establishments problematic. Throughout the ceasefire period, a tacit arrangement allowed students from the KIO areas to sit their high school matriculation exams in Myanmar government schools, which certificate allowed enrolling at colleges throughout the country and abroad. This arrangement depended upon a spoken agreement between the ministries of education in the KIO capital Laiza and Nay Pyi Daw. The onset of war in 2011 voided this arrangement, re-establishing the bureaucratic boundaries barring the KIO students from higher education in Myanmar or abroad.

Another example of bordering between the KIO and the Myanmar government since the war is the highly territorialized politics of aid to over 100,000 Kachin displaced by the fighting and settled at refugee camps in both the KIO and Myanmar government controlled areas. For crossing into the KIO controlled territories, the United Nations (UN) aid convoys assembled in Myitkyina need government authorization—a permission often withheld or delayed because of "security concerns".[6] The internally displaced persons (IDPs) in the KIO enclaves have had to rely on support by the KIO and the Kachin volunteer aid organizations. The latter rely on funds raised by the Kachin diaspora and, occasionally, international organizations such as the Danish Refugee Council. The IDP camps in the government controlled areas have benefitted from aid provided regularly by the United Nations High Commissioner for Refugees (UNHCR), the World Food Program (WFP), and other UN agencies since 2012. Civil society organizations in Myanmar have organized concerts and other fundraisers in distant cities such as Yangon. Thanks to extensive church networks, only Kachin Christian organizations have access to most IDP camps, and have provided a significant portion of humanitarian relief.

Enactment of the border is also experienced through military conscription by both the KIA and *tatmadaw*; through media images depicting frontline fighting that feed discussions on social media, at church congregations, within families or workplaces; or through Nay Pyi Daw's cease-fire negotiations with the ethnic armed groups. Most populated areas under KIO control are commonly perceived as potential frontlines threatened by invasion. At the same time, the KIO is perceived by the majority of the Kachin as the legitimate political authority that expresses common Kachin demands for political autonomy, carries out politically justified armed resistance, offers basic social services such as education and healthcare, and takes care of IDPs within its capacity.

The examples above resonate with Piliavsky's claim that "processes observed around national borders are also present deep inside the territories of states" (2013: 41). Writing of rural India, Piliavsky has shown how the techniques of power usually associated with national borders are manifest at local police jurisdictions. Viewing borders as key structuring mechanisms, there is little difference in kind between the national borders and the boundaries of provinces, administrative blocs, and police jurisdictions. In response to Piliavsky's critique, the case of the KIO–Myanmar borders shows that *inter-national borders* themselves can be deep inside state territories that international relations discourses treat as undivided wholes.

Kachin State administrative boundaries

Scholars have long recognized that borders work as "meaning-making and meaning-carrying" entities, charged with political sentiments (Donnan and Wilson 1999: 4). Piliavsky's suggestion of the similarities between bordering mechanisms at international and intra-state administrative borders is also insightful in its more literal meaning when looking at how administrative boundaries are performed in Northern Myanmar. It must be stressed that the administrative boundaries in question have long been embedded in larger political contests. While certainly drawn and enforced by states, these boundaries cannot be reduced to either colonial or Burmese inventions. Contemporary notions of Kachin State trace their origins to colonial Burma where Kachin Hills designated the vast areas traditionally inhabited by peoples speaking various dialects and ruled by local clan chieftains. However, those "Hills" were only a small part of contemporary Kachin State. Multi-ethnic areas around the regional administrative centres of Myitkyina and Bhamo were initially categorized as "plains" and separated administratively from "the Hills" by the British colonial "ecological essentialism" (Sadan 2013: 276–277). Sadan (2013) describes how these were subsequently included in Kachin State through negotiations with the Kachin elites, who saw this as the only territorially viable stake in the future Union. The inclusion of "plains" was expected to make Kachin State territorially sustainable, while opening the Kachin areas to the presumed financial and developmental support of new state structures (Sadan 2013). The construction of Kachin State across larger areas than originally designated by the British administrators was premised upon the "complex, sophisticated understanding of the periphery's new relationship with the centre and of new political challenges" by the Kachin political elites (Sadan 2013: 277).

In contemporary Kachin political imaginations, it is this Kachin State—and not the diminutive KIO enclaves—that is the target of the territorial aspirations for autonomy. Administrative boundaries are thus charged with political sentiment. Against the background of perceived Burmanization in language policy, education, and religious affairs, and the conspicuous rise of in-migration to Myitkyina and other towns by workers from Lower Burma, Kachin State boundaries remain an acute political, social, and cultural issue since the number of ethnic Kachin these contain matters hugely in the Kachin political aspirations. The immediate prospect of the "Other" outnumbering the Kachin in Kachin State is seen as affecting policy decisions at every level. Existential concerns are evident in the local opposition to the controversial 2008 constitution that has left open the possibility of changing the existing names of States. Many Kachin fear that the renaming, which may erase the toponymic link of territory to ethnicity, would undermine the "legitimate" Kachin claims to autonomy set out in the 1947 Panglong Agreement (see Kiik 2016).

Conversely, Nay Pyi Daw's electoral policies illustrate how the state enacts administrative boundaries to consolidate its power. Under the 2008 constitution, the state governments consist of a partially elected unicameral parliament called *hluttaw*, an executive led by a Chief Minister and cabinet of state ministers, and judicial institutions. The *hluttaw* is composed of two elected members per township, representatives for "national races", and appointed military representatives who can form up to one third of the total. The Chief Minister is selected by the President from among elected or unelected *hluttaw* members. In the charged ethnic politics of Kachin State, historically situated existential concerns assume contemporary reality when administrative boundaries are enacted in the election process. Many Kachin were excluded from voting in the 2010 elections, the 2012 by-elections, and the 2010 and 2015 general elections, as the Union Election Commission designated certain constituencies in Kachin State, many in the KIO controlled areas, as "unsafe" due to "active conflict" (see Map 16.1).

Conclusion

We have argued that the enactment of territorial boundaries in and around Kachin State is central to wider political processes, and spatial and social ordering. Militarized bordering across Myanmar exposes the violent forces of statecraft, often concealed from wider international attention. What conceals such militarized bordering is not merely their geographical location in areas of limited access. Dominating discourses of sovereignty, territorial integrity, and orderly international boundaries are all narrative devices through which methodological nationalism mis-represents local realities and silences competing perspectives. We have drawn attention to the complex practices of bordering in Kachin State by looking at junctures at which three types of borders are enacted. Focusing on whether, how, and by whom borders are performed offers a more nuanced understanding of the borders and regions in question. Beyond the immediate borderlands, however, our analysis places boundaries within the larger political, economic, and social complexes to which they necessarily belong. Borders can thus be explored as privileged sites for understanding the dynamics of power in the wider society.

In the Kachin context, administrative boundaries within Kachin State, and those between the KIO's enclaves and the Myanmar government controlled territory are actively enacted by these competing political actors, often through violence. The most obvious has been the territorial confrontation between the KIA and Myanmar Army (*tatmadaw*) that creates tense militarized borders. What results are parallel territories where sovereignty is often performed through displays of force, symbols of state, and the monitoring or taxing of the movement of people and goods for political, economic, or opportunistic purposes. Violence and threat with which these borders-cum-frontiers are enacted speaks of long-standing political grievances and the pressure of resource economy.

The central government in Nay Pyi Daw has further sought to order space and society by selectively enacting township boundaries in electoral politics. The enactment of existing township boundaries to exclude ethnic populations from the census or electoral lists—thus marginalizing and suppressing their political agency—illustrates the wider dynamics of power in contemporary Myanmar. However, even under these tense conditions, creative or contingent agreements can be stuck, bridging territorial and ideological divides, such as allowing students from the KIO controlled territory to continue their formal education in state-run schools. This is a rare example where specific practices of bordering have been temporarily suspended by state authorities.

The borders between the KIO enclaves and China are illustrative of different dynamics, deeply embedded in their historical context. Together with supra-local kinship networks, economic pragmatism has created conditions under which the Sino–Myanmar border remains relatively unrestricted. At the local level—to which regional district administrators and security forces inevitably belong—there has been little motivation to perform the boundary. This was particularly evident throughout the 1994–2011 ceasefire that witnessed high volumes of natural resources crossing between the Dai-Jingpo Autonomous Prefecture and the KIO, the NDA-K or the Myanmar government controlled territories. Complex local allegiances, often involving state officials, allowed resourceful entrepreneurs to circumvent state control even further. Apart from obvious revenues for the local elites, this period helped the KIO to develop its territories, while the Kachin civil society organizations were able to establish crucial international networks. From the perspective of this chapter, the changes to the Chinese border policies following 2011 are highly illustrative. Growing volumes of Kachin refugees seeking to cross into Yunnan led to China enacting its borders with increasing visibility and bureaucratic scrutiny. Movement of border dwellers came to be monitored more closely than before and refugee groups deemed illegal were evicted. Alleged border violations by the Myanmar Army drew loud critique from Beijing vocally asserting its territorial sovereignty. Within the changing geopolitical context, borders are continuously undergoing transformations, their enactment and retraction being a litmus test for statecraft and regional relations.

Acknowledgements

A part of the research leading to this chapter (by Karin Dean), was funded by the Estonian Research Agency grant IUT 3-2 "Culturescapes in transformation: Towards an integrated theory of meaning making".

Notes

1. Rangoon (renamed Yangon in 1989), about 1,000 km south from Kachin state capital Myitkyina, was the capital of Burma/Myanmar between 1885 and 2005. In 2005, the ruling junta moved the capital to Nay Pyi Daw, 640 km south from Myitkyina.
2. The dynamics of the civil war and the KIO's internal politics are complex. Sadan (2013), South (2008), Smith (1991), and Lintner (1996, 1997) have written on various aspects of the Kachin historical, political, and armed struggle.
3. New Democratic Army-Kachin (NDA-K) was a former splinter group of the KIA that in 2009 merged with *tatmadaw*'s controversial Border Guard Force (BGF).

4   The wider strategy of China's Yunnan province to keep up with the coastal provinces is that of becoming a "bridgehead" to Myanmar. Supporting development in the following four areas is prioritized: oil and gas pipelines to Yunnan, extension of the Trans-Asia Railway, re-opening of the old Ledo Road to India, and establishment of hydro-electric power plants along Myanmar's rivers. Good relations with non-state armed groups as these control parts of the Myanmar border are essential (Transnational Institute 2016).

5   This view is largely shared by international observers and foreign media, while Nay Pyi Daw cites security concerns over its territories as the cause for the breakup of the ceasefire. Tense relations between *tatmadaw* and KIO deteriorated further in 2009 when the KIO refused to join the government's Border Guard Force scheme. The latter attempted to absorb various ethnic armed groups into the Myanmar Army. In exchange for keeping most of their arms and territories, the groups would be subordinated to the command of Myanmar Army. There was little space for meaningful political dialogue or guarantees offered by the Army. The KIO was one of the groups to turn down the offer indefinitely.

6   While the fighting started in June 2011, the first UN aid convoy was allowed into the KIO controlled territory in December 2011. The next mission was only allowed in, in September 2013. The UN agencies (UNICEF (The United Nations Children's Fund) and UNHCR) were then allowed to deliver aid three times a month on average until aid was again stopped in September 2014. At the same time, China's national Red Cross Society has also sent humanitarian assistance to Kachin IDPs, both in the government and the KIO-controlled territories across its border with Myanmar.

References

Agnew, J. (2015) "Revisiting the Territorial Trap", *Nordia Geographical Publications*, vol. 44:4, pp. 43–48.

Donnan, H. and Wilson, T. (1999) *Borders: Frontiers of Identity, Nation and State*, London: Bloomsbury Academic.

Grundy-Warr, C. (1998) "Turning the Political Map Inside Out: A View of Mainland Southeast Asia", in Savage, V. R., Kong, L. and Neville, W (eds.) *The Naga Awakens: Growth and Change in Southeast Asia*, Singapore: Times Academic Press.

Kiik, L. (2016) "Conspiracy, God's Plan, and National Emergency: Kachin Popular Analyses of the Ceasefire Era and Its Resource Grabs", in Mandy S. (ed.) *War and Peace in the Borderlands of Myanmar: The Kachin Ceasefire, 1994–2011*, Singapore: NIAS Press.

Kolossov, V. and Scott, J. (2013) "Selected Conceptual Issues in Border Studies", *Belgeo*, vol. 1, pp. 2–15.

Lintner, B. (1996) *Land of Jade: A Journey from India through Northern Burma to China*, Bangkok: White Orchid Press.

Lintner, B. (1997) *The Kachin: Lords of Burma's Northern Frontier*, Chiang Mai: Teak House.

Ma Ning. (2013) "China Urges End to Kachin Violence Amid Border Shelling", *The Myanmar Times*, January 21. Available at: www.mmtimes.com/index.php/national-news/3853-china-urges-kachin-ceasefire-complains-over-border-shelling.html

Maran La Raw. (1967) "Towards a Basis for Understanding the Minorities of Burma: The Kachin Example", in Peter, K. (ed.) *Southeast Asian Tribes, Minorities, and Nations*. Vol. 1, Princeton, NJ: Princeton University Press.

McConnell, F. (2009) "De Facto, Displaced, Tacit: The Sovereign Articulations of the Tibetan Government-in-Exile", *Political Geography*, vol. 28, pp. 343–352.

Mountz, A. (2010) *Seeking Asylum: Human Smuggling and Bureaucracy at the Border*, Minneapolis: University of Minnesota Press.

Newman, D. (2003) "On Borders and Power: A Theoretical Framework", *Journal of Borderlands Studies*, vol. 18:1, pp. 13–25.

Newman, D. (2006) "The Lines that Continue to Separate Us: Borders in our Borderless World", *Progress in Human Geography*, vol. 30:2, pp. 143–161.

Paasi, A. (1999) "Boundaries as Social Process: Territoriality in the World of Flows", in Newman, D. (ed.) *Boundaries, Territory and Postmodernity*, London: Frank Cass.

Piliavsky, A. (2013) "Borders Without Borderlands. On the Social Reproduction of State Demarcation in Rajasthan" in Gellner, D. (ed.) *Borderland Lives in Northern South Asia*, London: Duke University Press.

Popescu, G. (2012) *Bordering and Ordering the Twenty-first Century: Understanding Borders*, London: Rowman & Littlefield.

Popescu, G. (2015) "Topological Imagination, Digital Determinism and the Mobile Border Paradigm", *Nordia Geographical Publications*, vol. 44:4, pp. 49–55.

Rumford, C. (2011) "Seeing Like a Border", *Political Geography*, vol. 30:2, pp. 39–54.
Sadan, M. (2013) *Being and Becoming Kachin: Histories Beyond the State in the Borderlands of Burma*, Oxford: Oxford University Press.
Scott, J. (2010) *The Art of Not Being Governed: An Anarchist History of Upland Southeast Asia*, New Haven, CT: Yale University Press.
Sharma, A. and Gupta, A. (2006) "Introduction", in Sharma, A. and Gupta, A. (eds.) *The Anthropology of the State*, London: Blackwell.
Smith, M. (1991) *Burma: Insurgency and the Politics of Ethnicity*, London: Zed Books.
South, A. (2008) *Ethnic Politics in Burma: States of Conflict*, London: Routledge.
Tagliacozzo, E. (2005) *Secret Trades, Porous Borders: Smuggling and States Along a Southeast Asian Frontier, 1865–1915*, New Haven, CT: Yale University Press.
Taylor, D. (1997) *Disappearing Acts: Spectacles of Gender and Nationalism in Argentina's "Dirty War"*, Durham, NC: Duke University Press.
Taylor, P. J. (1995) "Beyond Containers: Internationality, Interstatedness, Interterritoriality", *Progress in Human Geography*, vol. 19:1, pp. 1–15.
Transnational Institute. (2016) "China's Engagement in Myanmar: From Malacca Dilemma to Transition Dilemma", *Myanmar Policy Briefing*, July 19. Available at: www.tni.org/files/publication-downloads/chinas_engagement_in_myanmar-final.pdf
van Houtum, H. (2002) "Borders, Strangers, Doors and Bridges", *Space and Polity*, vol. 6:2, pp. 141–146.
van Schendel, W. and de Maaker, E. (2014) "Asian Borderlands: Introducing their Permeability, Strategic Use and Meanings: Special Issue on Asian Borderlands", *Journal of Borderland Studies*, vol. 29:1, pp. 3–10.
Wilson, T. M. (2014) "Borders: Cities, Boundaries, and Frontiers", in Nonini, D.M. (ed.) *A Companion to Urban Anthropology*, Oxford: John Wiley & Sons.
Winichakul, T. (1997) *Siam Mapped: A History of the Geo-body of a Nation*, Honolulu: University of Hawaii Press.
Woods, K. (2011) "Ceasefire Capitalism: Military–Private Partnerships, Resource Concessions and Military–State Building in the Burma–China Borderlands", *The Journal of Peasant Studies*, vol. 38:4, pp. 747–770.

17
Turning your back to the border
Federalism, territory, and claims for autonomy in the Nepal–India borderland

Rune Bennike

Introduction

On 20 September 2015, Nepal adopted a new constitution – the first ever drafted by a democratically elected constituent assembly. Hurriedly finalised in the aftermath of the major earthquakes that shook the Himalayas in spring 2015, the constitution did not meet the expectations of Nepal's marginal population groups. Whereas many had looked at the past decade of prolonged constitutional negotiations with high hopes of a devolution of power in the centralised Himalayan state, the constitution failed to deliver. Widespread and contentious discussions of a future federal organisation of the state were silenced with a proposal that was widely regarded as centralistic and elitist.

In the present chapter, I take a look at some of the conjunctural politics that emerged before this bitter end – at a time when federal restructuring of the Nepali nation was high on the political agenda and the country's 'social contract' was to an unprecedented degree open for discussion. Based on fieldwork conducted in 2010 and 2011, I explore demands for a Limbuwan state in Nepal's eastern borderland to Indian Darjeeling. I focus on the multiple ways in which the Limbuwan movement seeks to establish territorial authority of a Limbuwan state in the context of a major national transition. The movement, I argue, describes a balancing act of political mobilisation between an indigeneity-oriented *politics of culture* and a state-oriented and state-emulating *culture of politics*. These two dimensions operate at different scales. While the former connects the movement to pre-national histories and global narratives of ethnic belonging, the latter ties the movement thoroughly back into the territorialised politics of the Nepali nation state. Counterintuitively, the political practice of this movement for local autonomy ends up supporting a national territorialisation of the borderland.

The borderland: normative landscapes and national territories

As long as you appear South Asian, the border between Nepal and India is open. Nepalese and Indian citizens are free to cross the border and many borderland citizens do so on a daily basis. In the borderland of eastern Nepal and Darjeeling, school buses take Nepali children to Indian schools that enjoy a better reputation than their Nepali counterparts; relations of kin span the border and many are said to (illegally) hold dual citizenship and own property on both sides; green leaf tea is brought across from Nepal on the backs of mules to be processed in (and probably labelled as) Darjeeling; Nepalese noodles and Chinese shoes and garments are transported across the border and onto Indian markets while cooking gas (subsidised in India) is smuggled back into Nepali kitchens.

In a different sense, however, the border is closed. The political movements for local autonomy on either side of the border – movements with shared roots in the same population groups – turn their attention towards the national centres: Kathmandu, Calcutta, and Delhi. In doing so, they turn their backs to each other. Speaking to activists on both sides of the border, I was met with clear distinctions about what can cross and what cannot. While relations of kin and 'culture' were widely assumed to criss-cross the border, all political relations were denied. In the anxiety-ridden politics of belonging in Darjeeling, all connections to Nepal were severed in fear of being labelled as 'foreigners' and 'Maoists' (Middleton 2013). And on the Nepali side of the border, political activists persistently framed their demands within the already bordered notions of an emerging federal state. Seen in this light, the story of the Limbuwan movement that I provide in this chapter, is telling for the ways in which borderland politics is territorialised. It illustrates that borderland territorialisation is not only determined by the hard government of fences, border posts and jurisdictional divisions, but just as much by the vectors of actual political practice. We begin with an illustrative encounter on the Indian side of the border, in Darjeeling.

'What democracy you have in Nepal, you made an Indian president!' the keeper of the bookstore told Narayan. This was not the first time my friend had received this sort of half joking, half baffled comment while assisting me during my fieldwork in Darjeeling. As a 'Nepalese Nepali' among the 'Indian Nepalis' of Darjeeling, my friend easily attracted such off-the-cuff evaluations of the political changes taking place across the border. The 'Indian president' in question was Ram Baran Yadav, the President of Nepal since the country's official declaration as a Republic in 2008. For Darjeeling residents, such as the keeper of the bookstore, Yadav's supposed Indianness obviously stemmed from his origin in Nepal's southern plains. To them, Yadav's Nepali citizenship, his mainstream political career in the Nepali Congress Party, or his earlier ministerial positions in Nepali governments, did not matter. The president's loyalties were seen as determined by his originating landscape – the plains. And notwithstanding the eager commentator's own Indian citizenship, and everyday life in a North Indian town, the 'Indian' loyalties of the Nepali president seemed to offend their political sensibilities. What was this plains-dweller doing heading the former 'Himalayan kingdom' across the border?

We live in a world where politics is usually imagined in a language of spatially organised disjuncture (Gupta & Ferguson 1992). The 'maps in our mind' largely reflect the image of a school atlas (Ludden 2003): a jigsaw puzzle of truncated spaces, neatly coloured and sharply bordered pieces, flat areas with no bleeding boundaries, shared borders with no in-betweens. In Narayan's encounters, this 'national order of things' (Malkki 1992) that constitute the *borderland* unravelled for a moment providing a glimpse of an underlying and much more fluid normative *landscape*. Here, the topographical map of *plains* and *hills* suddenly takes precedence over the political distinctions of the school atlas. Indian citizens of Nepali origin living in the Indian hills of Darjeeling criticise the election of a Nepali plains-dweller as the first Nepali president due to his supposed alienness to the erstwhile Himalayan kingdom. My friend Narayan's experience, thus, illustrates a tension between the bordered national territories of India and Nepal, on the one hand, and this cross-border normative landscape, on the other.

The present chapter deals with this tension, exploring its articulation in relation to the politics of belonging of the Limbus in eastern Nepal. What significance does the open, fluid border of a transitional, fragile state hold in relation to claims for recognition, belonging, and local autonomy in its periphery? What does this border actually border and what is allowed to cross? And what do the vectors and orientations of local political practice tell us about the territorialisation of the Nepali nation state in a period of fundamental political transformation?

In order to answer these questions, I approach territory as a governmental technique employed both by the national state and by 'subnational' groups. Territory here indicates a political space that is 'owned, distributed, mapped, calculated, bordered and controlled' and is, in fact, 'nothing else but the effect, the profile, the mobile shape of a perpetual territorialisation' (Elden 2010: 804–8, 10; Elden 2013: 14). While a number of studies have analysed this process in the context of the nation state (Thongchai 1994; Goswami 2002, 2004; Ramaswamy 2010; Bennike 2015), much less attention has been given to the territoriality of 'subnational' political movements. Supposedly monopolised by the modern state, territory has – it seems – largely been deemed an irrelevant category to employ in the analysis of such movement (van Schendel and Abraham 2005). However, this study shows how territorialisation and the distinctly state-like practices that it relies upon are also employed by subnational groups in the borderlands of national territory. And it illustrates connections between such 'subnational' forms of territorialisation and the wider national project.

History, mobility, and contentious territorialisation in the borderland

As Narayan's story indicates, territorialisation does not take place in a vacuum but operates on a landscape already provided by history: the ostensibly uniform, bordered territory of the nation state is only one among several modes of authorising and legitimising centralised rule that have a bearing on contemporary politics of place. Historically, the Himalayas and their foothills constituted an area that was relatively impenetrable by the imperial formations in the Indian plains and the Tibetan plateau. For some, this space represented the uncivilised and savage. For others it provided a zone of refuge from imperial exploitation on either side. Over time, however, empire was superimposed even upon the challenging terrain of the Himalayan hills. In the mid-18th century, Prithvi Narayan Shah expanded the Gorkha kingdom eastwards across the hills subduing dozens of small polities. Around the turn of the century, this empire stretched all the way across the central Himalayas. However, merely a decade later the Anglo-Gorkha war stopped the Gorkha expansion. In 1816, with the Treaty of Sugauli, the Gorkha kingdom was forced to relinquish parts of the newly conquered territory and the eastern border of what is present-day Nepal was delineated and marked with stone pillars that still stand today. What used to be a zone of refuge from imperial expansion had thus, by the mid-19th century, been superimposed by imperial territory.

Before the 1816 Sugauli treaty, the borders of the young Gorkha kingdom were a relatively fluid construction dependent de facto on the maintenance of taxation. Those who paid taxes to the vassals of the Gorkha king were effectively his subjects and their lands included in the territory of the Gorkha kingdom. As fiscal allegiances shifted between the Gorkha kingdom, the British East India Company and the waning Mughal empire, so did territorial borders (Michael 1999, 2012; Rupakheti 2016). In the east, the Gorkha kingdom extended across the contemporary border and well into the Darjeeling district of present-day India for a short spell between 1783 and 1816. Eastward migration was probably a common occurrence even before the Anglo-Gurkha war and from the mid-1800s people migrated on a large scale. A combination of increasing marginalisation within the Gorkha kingdom and new opportunities opening up in the emerging British tea gardens of Darjeeling led many from the eastern Tibeto-Burman groups to cross the new border (Mullard 2013; Warner 2014a, 2014b: Bennike 2017). By 1881, the British judged that 88,000 people living in the Darjeeling area had been born in Nepal (O'Malley 1907: 43–4). The vast majority of these were from ethnic groups that resided in the eastern part of present-day Nepal.[1]

Within the Gorkha territory, successive rulers chose to manage vast ethnic differences through a Hindu hierarchy of purity and pollution (Rupakheti 2016). The different 'countries' conquered by Shah and his successors were recast as different castes within a unified national hierarchy and thus detached from their territorial significance (Burghart 1984; Bennike 2015). While more orthodox Hindu groups such as *Brahmins* and *Chhetris* were placed at the top of this hierarchy, Tibeto-Burman 'alcohol-drinkers' (*matwali*) were inserted at inferior levels (Pradhan 2002; Höfer 2004). This happened to the Limbus and other ethnic groups in eastern Nepal, although their significant resistance to conquest had granted them certain privileges in terms of rights to land and local government, delaying their full incorporation into the kingdom for some time (Pradhan 2009 [1991]). Gradually, however, a state-encouraged migration and settlement of Hindu caste groups eastwards along the Himalayan foothills simultaneously incorporated and marginalised the eastern ethnic groups (Burghart 1984; Caplan 2000; Lecomte-Tilouine 2010).

Following Indian independence, the border remained in place and open – re-confirmed by the 1950 'Indo Nepal Treaty of Peace and Friendship' – all the while national territorialisation picked up momentum under the royalist *panchayat* regime. From 1960 to 1990, Nepali development policies – including a massive extension of national schooling – territorialised Nepali nation space to an unprecedented degree. Papering over former hierarchies and inequalities, these policies created an ostensibly more uniform national space legitimised as the world's 'last Hindu kingdom'. However, the application of Hindu ideals as the blueprint for national identity perpetuated extensive marginalisation below the surface of national unity and national development policies themselves created new peripheries within a highly centralised state (Bennike 2015). At the eastern margin, the nationalist policies of the centre led to periodic bouts of resistance – especially in relation to the gradual erosion of the ethnic, communal form of land ownership *kipat* (Caplan 2000: 174–212; Lawoti 2007: 32). Nevertheless, through a slow extension of cadastral surveying and the ensuing possibilities for centralised taxation, national territorialisation proceeded in spite of extensive cross-border mobility (Forbes 1996, 1999; Caplan 2000: 174–212).

National transition and ethnic mobilisation

By 1990, resentment against persistent inequalities within the ostensible national unity of the *panchayat* regime brought revolutionary change to the Himalayan kingdom. The king was ousted and a volatile period of elite-dominated, multiparty democracy ensued. Within a decade, a Maoist insurgency had engulfed large parts of the country fuelled, at least in part, by the resentment of traditionally marginalised groups – plains-people (*madeshi*), low castes (*dalit*), and a host of different ethnic groups (*adhivasi janajati*). By 2001, the country was in a state of civil war and in 2005 the king, closely allied with the army, utilised this 'emergency' to take over central government once again. Widely unpopular, this move prompted a peace agreement between the Maoist insurgents and the mainstream political parties who, together, led a second revolutionary people's movement that ousted the king the following year. Subsequently, the central political parties and the Maoists initiated a peace process and the formulation of a new constitution through an elected constituent assembly (CA). As discussions before and during the constituent assembly developed, Nepal was declared a republic. The king was removed from his palace in central Kathmandu and stripped of his title. With increasing pressure from a variety of organisations representing formerly marginalised ethnic and caste groups, it was also decided that Nepal was to become a federation. In the interim constitution that was promulgated to provide the temporary framework for government until the CA had finished a new constitution, Nepal was thus refashioned as a 'Federal, Democratic, Republican State' (UNDP 2009: 56).

With the prospect of Nepal becoming a federal state, the ethnic politics that had been picking up pace since 1990 took a decisively territorial turn. From the early 1990s onwards, the discursive intervention of a broad range of 'ethnic' organisations had contributed to a refashioning of the former *matwali jat* ('alcohol-drinking sub-castes') as *adivasi janajati* (indigenous nationalities) connecting these groups to globalised notions of indigeneity (Onta 2006: 311, 2011). Beginning with the 1991 census, these groups were counted separately and by 2002 increased state recognition of Nepal's multi-ethnic setup resulted in the official designation of 59 state-recognised ethnic groups as a basis for affirmative action policies. At the same time, the national development programmes of the *panchayat* period were increasingly superseded by internationally supported programmes of 'targeted development' directed at the country's formerly marginalised groups. As a result, a new 'classificatory moment' emerged in which the pursuit of visibility and recognition in the eyes of the state became the order of the day for many ethnic groups increasingly supplementing or replacing earlier strategies of evasion and resistance (Shneiderman 2013). When federalism arrived at the national political agenda, ethnic organisations were quick to connect demands for autonomy to prospects of federal statehood (Adhikari & Gellner 2016).

One of the most insistently vocalised demands for ethnicity-based federal statehood to emerge in the constitution-writing process was the demand for a Limbuwan state in the eastern borderland of the country (The Carter Center 2010). As I began doctoral fieldwork in Nepal in 2010, the Limbu organisation leaders I met with were deeply engaged in presenting a viable, legitimate, and authoritative sketch of a future Limbuwan state to the world. As I discuss in detail below, these efforts are telling for the specific 'terms of recognition' operating at the time (Appadurai 2002; Shneiderman 2010) and – ultimately – how this 'fragile' moment in national politics counterintuitively supported a continued national territorialisation.

Claiming Limbuwan

On the basis of this brief historical sketch, I now turn to the political strategies employed by a spectrum of Limbu organisations and individuals in authorising and legitimising their claims. This involves a *politics of culture* that situates the Limbus as indigenous people with an ancient connection to the land of Limbuwan – a strategy that is well-known in South Asia and beyond. However, it also involves an engagement with an emerging *culture of politics* that directs attention towards the state and involves much more state-like practices: while the movement had to establish exclusive linkages to a specific area, it also needed to display the politically correct inclusiveness of cultural diversity that has become the hallmark of *Naya Nepal* (new Nepal); and while the movement needed to continue performing as a popular movement with unmet demands, it also had to provide credibility to the federal state project by acting, already, in a state-like manner.

Politics of culture: academic texts and indigenous belonging

> Nepal was a federal country in history. …So, what we are going towards now, federalisation of Nepal, is not actually new to Nepal. …[In] 1780-something, the Gorkha king's army and Limbuwan's army fought on the bank of the Arun River and the war was equal and, at final, a treaty was done between Limbuwan and the Gorkha king … in the treaty, the main condition was for Limbuwan to stay [an] autonomous region, autonomous state. …around

1960–65, the late king Gyanendra's father, Mahendra, he captured all power and dismissed the treaty of Limbuwan and Nepal. Then, finally Limbuwan was 'uniterised' and that is just 40 years ago. So, in the blood of the Limbuwani people, they feel: we are different people from Nepal because we have the specific history, unconquerable or undefeated history... I feel, in my blood, this my blood is federal blood, because we have a long history of federalism and Limbuwan, our blood is undefeated blood – so, we are fighting for not 'free Limbuwan', but 'autonomous state Limbuwan', inside Nepal.

This long reference to 18th century Nepali history was given to me by Kumar Lingden, the young leader of Federal Limbuwan State Council (FLSC), a Limbu political party, in September 2011. Although I had asked Lingden about the most recent developments in the parliamentary politics of federalism, he immediately chose to delve deeply into history. Using the political vocabulary of federalism and autonomy in vogue at the time, he described the history of Limbuwan in a way that resonated clearly with contemporary claims to federal statehood: Nepal was historically a 'federal country' and Limbuwan an 'autonomous state'. To support this claim, Lingden and many other Limbu activists relied heavily on the academic authority of history and ethnography.

Another vignette: when my initial interest in eastern Nepal began some years ago, I read the British anthropologist Lionel Caplan's classical book *Land and Social Change in East Nepal: A Study of Hindu-Tribal Relations* (1970). At that time, I did not expect that this 40-year-old book would turn up again much later, during my doctoral fieldwork in the area. The next encounter was in eastern Nepal in 2010, during an interview with Mohan – a local leader of the Limbu indigenous peoples' organisation Kirat Yakthum Chumlung (KYC). Interviewing Mohan about the present-day movement for a Limbuwan federal state, I became aware, first, of numerous historical references going as far back as to the official 'birth' of Nepal with Prithvi Narayan Shah's conquests in the later 18th century, and then, of the similarities between his perspective on the history of Limbuwan and the one presented in Caplan's book. Further into the conversation, Mohan made direct references to Caplan's book and by the end of the interview, he showed me numerous copies of the book – in Nepali translation – piled up in the back of his small shop.

The experience took me by surprise. I somehow expected such academic discourse to be situated 'at home' separated from the empirical, political reality of 'the field'. Suddenly, this separation seemed untenable as I was being fed back the same academic discourse that shaped my initial perspectives on the social and political situation of eastern Nepal. Later, my surprise subsided. The mobilisation of academic texts in support of a Limbuwan state that I experienced in fact closely resembles experiences across the South Asian subcontinent. Often relying on colonial ethnographies, this 'found anthropology' appears disconcertingly essentialist when approached with modern anthropological sensibilities, but it nonetheless holds a vibrant social life in contemporary *politics of culture* (Middleton 2010, 2011).

Treated in detail in Caplan's book, one of the central notions in this academic discourse of Limbu indigenous belonging is the specific land tenure arrangement called *kipat*. *Kipat* is typically described as a 'communal' form of land tenure practiced until the land reforms in the late 1960s. The practice is seen as 'communal' in the sense that *kipat* land is regarded as inalienable from the local 'indigenous' community. Only members of this community can own *kipat* land, although they can give the land in lease to other groups in exchange for loans. As opposed to other forms of land tenure, the tax paid on *kipat* to the central state is based on landholding households rather than the actual area of usable land (see e.g. Caplan 1970, 1991, 2000; Regmi 1978; Forbes 1996). As a 'head-tax' rather than a 'land-tax', *kipat* thus exemplifies the limited reach of central control over the territory in eastern Nepal until well into the 20th century (cf. Scott 1998, 2009).

In the contemporary politics of culture, however, *kipat* goes beyond simply signifying a specific relationship of tenure and taxation between the rulers in central Nepal and the people living in the eastern periphery (see e.g. Forbes 1996: 40). The notion of *kipat* is taken to root the Limbus deeply in the soil of Limbuwan while connecting their struggle to 'indigenous' communities across the globe. Caplan states that:

> the Limbus shared a conception of land as held by countless indigenous or tribal peoples around the world, for whom membership in the community generates an attitude to the land which is antecedent to the working of it …. Kipat was thus more than a system of land tenure; it was the basis of Limbu identity as a people.
>
> *(Caplan 1991: 312–13)*

More recently, similar global connections of indigeneity have been emphasised in relation to the global environmental crisis. Here, scholars and activists present the link between Limbus and Limbuwan soil associated with *kipat* as an 'indigenous system of sustainable conservation' (Mishra 2003: 125), imbuing the recognition of indigenous rights to land with a strong environmental imperative (Chettri et al. 2008; Maden et al. 2009).

This emphasis on a global, indigenous dimension in the recent discourse of *kipat* is politically significant, as notions of indigeneity have increasingly informed Nepali politics since 1990. *Kipat* now fits perfectly, not only with globalised notions of indigeneity in general, but also with the Nepali state definition of those who are indigenous (*janajāti*). Here, indigenous communities are defined as those: 'who have a separate collective cultural identity; … are traditionally located in particular geographic regions; [and] who do not have [an] influential role in the modern politics and state governance of Nepal' (cited in Onta 2006: 311–12). In one national definition of indigeneity, *kipat* has even slipped in as a possible defining criteria (Onta 2006: 311). The academically legitimated politics of culture thus contributes to the making of Limbuwan as an 'indigenous' place, which in turn is seen as justifying Limbuwan's claim as a future federal state. However, the Limbuwan movement is balancing this globally and historically oriented grassroots politics of culture against a much more state-emulating culture of politics.

Culture of politics: looking and speaking like a state

'I've heard they even have their own number plates out there, now', said my friend Deependra. We were sitting in a bar in Kathmandu, talking about my plans of going to Ilam on fieldwork. A few days later, I was going from the plains of Jhapa district into the hills of Ilam. Though the young taxi driver taking us there was driving at a nerve-racking speed, my friend managed to catch a glimpse of a big roadside signpost among the blur of green hills flying by: 'You are now entering Limbuwan State' it read. A few weeks later, visiting Pashupatinagar, the border town between Indian Darjeeling and Nepali Ilam, another similar sign struck our eyes, attached to the very top of the arch marking the entry into Nepal from the no-man's land of the border. Here, the Limbu wing of the Maoist party (Limbuwan Rastriya Mukti Morcha) made visitors aware that going through the gate not only means entering Nepal, but also entering 'Limbuwan'. Though at the national level, the political question of federalism was far from settled, my stay in eastern Nepal in 2010 was rife with examples of this sort of 'insurgent' federalism. Although they

Turning your back to the border

did not have 'their own number plates' as Deependra had foreseen, a large part of the vehicles had 'Limbuwan' and 'State' written on the bumper on either side of the number plate. And in the neighbouring district of Panchhtar the gate to the district headquarters was decorated not only with the words 'Limbuwan State' and the common Limbu symbol of the drum, but also with a map showing the nine existing districts that many Limbu organisations define as Limbuwan (see Figure 17.1).

These sporadic field observations illustrate the precarious positioning of Limbuwan between a demand still to be met and an already established fact. Arguing for a federal restructuring along ethnic lines, the Maoist party, already in 2009, declared a Limbuwan state to be in existence (Adhikari 2009). As evident from the signs around the area, this reality did have a certain social life. What is interesting about this as a political strategy for authorising territory is the way in which these signs replicate state practices. Allocated at the international border, a district headquarters and repeated relatively uniformly across car bumpers the signs seem to signal an official origin.

The same indications of state-like order are replicated in some of the Limbuwan publications. In 2008, Kirat Yakthung Chumlung (KYC), a Limbu indigenous people's organisation, produced and distributed the lobbying document 'Limbuwan Autonomous State: A Proposed Sketch'. Organised and phrased in the language of a constitution, the document seeks to address all the issues supposedly needed for statehood including even a section on national 'anthem, music, flower, color, animal, bird, game etc.'. Living up to politically pertinent notions of inclusive

Figure 17.1 Gate at Panchhtar district headquarters
Photo by Rune Bennike 2010

democracy, the document furthermore stipulates arrangements for separate, autonomous regions for no less than 13 non-Limbu groups within a future Limbuwan. As Arjun Limbu, the president of KYC, explained to me in 2010 they had three groups of people they needed to convince: the indigenous people who were not from Limbuwan, but had migrated there; the non-indigenous people who would not be granted a homeland in a future of ethnic federalism; and the smaller indigenous groups who would need such measures of 'autonomy within autonomy'.

Like the visual signs I encountered across eastern Nepal, the KYC discourse attempts to project an image of a responsible, rights-ensuring proto-state. In sharp distinction to the notions of Limbu indigeneity revisited above, the strategies employed here are clearly state-emulating. Looking and speaking like a state is obviously seen as a step to becoming one.

Bordering Limbuwan

The two elements in Limbuwan claims making – an indigeneity-oriented politics of culture and a state-emulating culture of politics – were joined at times in the territorial political practice of Limbu organisations. The sketch of an 'Autonomous Limbuwan State' mentioned above clearly establishes the northern, southern, eastern, and western borders of Limbuwan: the Arun River, the mountains of Tibet, and the international borders with Bihar, Sikkim, and West Bengal. Multiple informants connected these borders with the notion of a historical Limbu territory deeply founded in indigenous cultural tradition. One Limbu representative referred to Limbu oral tradition:

> we use these terms during our funeral rites. We say we have brought this water from Tista and Arun [rivers] and the mountain and the sea and give this [to the soul of deceased].... we can proudly claim the historical boundaries [of Limbuwan] by referring to these chants.[2]

Here, the concrete and presumably lasting character of the Teesta and Arun/Dudhkoshi river valleys provides a substance to the bordering of Limbuwan that cuts across time and connects distant – even mythical – history with present-day politics. However, in the 'sketch', these natural eastern and southern borders have been seamlessly replaced with the current international borders with India on Nepal's southern and eastern flanks. Although grounded in references to a pre-national past, the bordering of Limbuwan is thus circumscribed by the contemporary nation.

At the western end of the proposed territory, the FLSC organised a range of marches that trace out specific lines in the landscape of Limbuwan.[3] One march led to the Koshi River barrage on Nepal's southern border to India. Here the FLSC marked out the southeastern corner of Limbuwan territory by placing flags on the barrage structure. Connections to the contemporary territorial politics were emphasised with the burning of symbols of the 'unitary state' by the river. The march was furthermore supplemented by the orchestration of simultaneous torch rallies in all of the nine districts of Limbuwan. While the discursive delineation of Limbuwan's borders draw directly on narratives of an ancient, indigenous territory, these political practices imply some of the same histories less directly. The march to the Koshi barrage makes sense only when understood in the light of claims to past territory. Only then, this place is transformed from a random border point between Nepal and India, to a historically significant place on the southwestern edge of Limbuwan. In concert with this, a much more state-emulating practice seems at play in the torch rally which seeks, it seems, to tie the area together in an almost Andersonian sense through bordered and uniform experience of the embryonic state (Anderson 2006; Roy 2007).

Conclusion: the territorialisation of borderland politics

In this chapter, I have explored the movement for a Limbuwan federal state in Nepal's eastern borderland. I have analysed the movement as engaged in a balancing act of political mobilisation between an indigeneity-oriented *politics of culture* and a state-oriented and state-emulating *culture of politics*. When I returned to the Pashupatinagar border-crossing in 2011, a new police constable had arrived and with him a stricter national regime. On his command, the banner declaring that one was entering Limbuwan State had been removed and replaced with an advertisement for a bank. Four years later, the promulgation of Nepal's new constitution extended this symbolic deferral of the demand for a Limbuwan state to the national level – at least for the time being.

Nonetheless, the conjunctural politics of the Limbuwan movement tells us good deal about territorialisation of Nepal's eastern borderland, and maybe borderlands more broadly. The Limbuwan movement illustrates how a 'sub-national' movement for local autonomy ostensibly mobilised against the centralised nation state employs a range of the same territorialising techniques as the central state. More importantly, however, it also tells a story about how national territorialisation can be infused in the vectors of actual political practice even of 'sub-national' groups just as much as in the hard government of fences, border posts, and jurisdictional divisions. Although the borderland is open to almost all forms of mobility, the state-oriented and state-emulating dimensions of the Limbuwan movement ensures that it turns its back to potential allies across the border. In effect, Limbu activists direct their political practice on a course that ultimately supports the national territorialisation of the borderland they inhabit.

Notes

1. Kumar Pradhan estimates that 12–15 per cent of the total *Kirant (Rai, Limbu, Sunuwar)* population of Nepal emigrated between 1840 and 1860 (Pradhan 2009 [1991]: 211).
2. Interview with KYC member and historian, Ilam, September 2010.
3. My description of these marches relies on information and pictures received from Kumar Lingden, the leader of FLSC whom I interviewed in Kathmandu in the autumn of 2011.

References

Adhikari, K. P., & Gellner, D. N. (2016) New Identity Politics and the 2012 Collapse of Nepal's Constituent Assembly: When the Dominant Becomes 'Other'. *Modern Asian Studies, CJO2016*, 1–32.

Adhikari, R. (2009, 11 December). Maoists declare Kochila, Limbuwan 'states'. *Republica*. Retrieved from: http://archives.myrepublica.com/portal/index.php?action=news_details&news_id=12775

Anderson, B. (2006) *Imagined Communities: Reflections on the Origin and Spread of Nationalism* (revised ed.). London: Verso.

Appadurai, A. (2002) Grassroots Globalization and the Research Imagination. In J. Vincent (Ed.), *The Anthropology of Politics: A Reader in Ethnography, Theory, and Critique*. London: Blackwell.

Bennike, R. B. (2015) Textbook Difference: Spatial History and National Education in Panchayat and Present Day Nepal. *Indian Economic and Social History Review*, 52(1), 53–78.

Bennike, R. B. (2017) Frontier Commodification: Governing Land, Labour and Leisure in Darjeeling. *South Asia: Journal of South Asian Studies*, 40(2), 256–71.

Burghart, R. (1984) The Formation of the Concept of Nation-State in Nepal. *The Journal of Asian Studies*, 44(1), 101–25.

Caplan, L. (1970) *Land and Social Change in East Nepal: A Study of Hindu-Tribal Relations*. London: Routledge.

Caplan, L. (1991) From Tribe to Peasant – The Limbus and the Nepalese State. *Journal of Peasant Studies*, 18(2), 305–21.

Caplan, L. (2000) *Land and Social Change in East Nepal: A Study of Hindu-Tribal Relations* (2nd ed. with a postscript. ed.). Lalitpur, Nepal: Himal Books.

Chettri, N., Shakya, B., & Sharma, E. (2008) *Biodiversity Conservation in the Kangchenjunga Landscape*. Kathmandu, Nepal: ICIMOD.

Elden, S. (2010) Land, Terrain, Territory. *Progress in Human Geography, 34*(6), 799–817.
Elden, S. (2013). How Should We Do the History of Territory?. *Territory, Politics, Governance, 1*(1), 5–20.
Forbes, A. A. (1996) The Discourse and Practice of Kipat. *Kailash, 18*(1–2), 39–80.
Forbes, A. A. (1999) Mapping Power: Disputing Claims to Kipat Lands in Northeastern Nepal. *American Ethnologist, 26*(1), 114–38.
Goswami, M. (2002) Rethinking the Modular Nation Form: Toward a Sociohistorical Conception of Nationalism. *Comparative Studies in Society and History, 44*(4), 770–99.
Goswami, M. (2004) *Producing India: From Colonial Economy to National Space.* Chicago: University of Chicago Press.
Gupta, A., & Ferguson, J. (1992) Beyond Culture – Space, Identity, and the Politics of Difference. *Cultural Anthropology, 7*(1), 6–23.
Höfer, A. (2004) *The Caste Hierarchy and the State in Nepal: A Study of the Muluki Ain of 1854.* Kathmandu, Nepal: Himal Books.
Lawoti, M. (2007) *Contentious Politics and Democratization in Nepal.* Thousand Oaks, CA; London: SAGE.
Lecomte-Tilouine, M. (2010) To Be More Natural Than Others: Indigenous Self-Determination and Hinduism in the Himalayas. In M. Lecomte-Tilouine (Ed.), *Nature, Culture and Religion at the Crossroads of Asia* (pp. 118–55). Delhi: Social Science Press.
Ludden, D. (2003) Presidential Address: Maps in the Mind and the Mobility of Asia. *Journal of Asian Studies, 62*(4), 1057–78.
Maden, K., Kongren, R., & Limbu, T. M. (2009) *Documentation of Indigenous Knowledge, Skill and Practices of Kirata Nationalities with Special Focus on Biological Resources.* Retrieved from www.digitalhimalaya.com/collections/rarebooks/
Malkki, L. (1992) National Geographic: The Rooting of Peoples and the Territorialization of National Identity among Scholars and Refugees. *Cultural Anthropology, 7*(1), 24–44.
Michael, B. A. (1999) Statemaking and Space on the Margins of Empire: Rethinking the Anglo-Gorkha War of 1814–1816. *Studies in Nepali History and Society, 4*(2), 247–94.
Michael, B. A. (2012) *Statemaking and Territory in South Asia : Lessons from the Anglo-Gorkha War (1814–1816).* New York: Anthem Press.
Middleton, T. (2010) *Beyond Recognition: Ethnology, Belonging, and the Refashioning of the Ethnic Subject in Darjeeling, India.* PhD Dissertation, Cornell University.
Middleton, T. (2011) Ethno-Logics: Paradigms of Modern Identity. In S. Dube (Ed.), *Modern Makeovers: Handbook of Modernity in South Asia* (pp. 200–13). Oxford: Oxford University Press.
Middleton, T. (2013) Anxious Belongings: Anxiety and the Politics of Belonging in Subnationalist Darjeeling. *American Anthropologist, 115*(4), 608–21.
Mishra, P. N. (2003) Conservation of the Nature and Natural Resources in Nepal: Traditional Versus Modern Approaches and Management Issues in Protected Areas. *Journal of the National Science Foundation of Sri Lanka, 31*(1–2), 125–37.
Mullard, S. (2013) Negotiating Power in 19th Century Sikkim: The 1830 Covenant on Tax Exiles and Sikkimese Border Regions. In C. Ramble, P. Schwieger, & A. Travers (Eds.), *Tibetans Who Escaped the Historian's Net: Studies in the Social History of Tibetan Societies* (pp. 179–208). Kathmandu, Nepal: Vajra Books.
O'Malley, L. L. S. (1907). *Bengal District Gazetteers: Darjeeling.* Retrieved from Bengal Secretariat Book Depot.
Onta, P. (2006) The Growth of the Adivasi Janajati Movement in Nepal after 1990: The Non-Political Institutional Agents. *Studies in Nepali History and Society, 11*(2), 303–54.
Onta, P. (2011, 29 July). Adivasi/Janajati: Definitional Politics of the Past and the Future. *República*.
Pradhan, K. (2009 [1991]) *The Gorkha Conquests: Process and Consequences of the Unification of Nepal, with Particular Reference to Eastern Nepal.* Lalitpur: Himal Books.
Pradhan, R. (2002) Ethnicity, Caste and a Pluralist Society. In K. M. Dixit & S. Ramachandaran (Eds.), *State of Nepal* (pp. 1–21). Kathmandu, Nepal: Himal Books.
Ramaswamy, S. (2010) *The Goddess and the Nation: Mapping Mother India.* Durham, NC: Duke University Press.
Regmi, M. C. (1978) *Land Tenure and Taxation in Nepal* (2nd edn). Kathmandu, Nepal: Ratna Pustak Bhandar.
Roy, S. (2007) *Beyond Belief: India and the Politics of Postcolonial Nationalism.* Durham, NC: Duke University Press.
Rupakheti, S. (2016) Reconsidering State-Society Relations in South Asia: A Himalayan Case Study. *Himalaya, the Journal of the Association for Nepal and Himalayan Studies, 35*(2), 11.

Scott, J. C. (1998) *Seeing Like a State: How Certain Schemes to Improve the Human Condition Have Failed.* New Haven, CT & London: Yale University Press.

Scott, J. C. (2009) *The Art of Not Being Governed: An Anarchist History of Upland Southeast Asia.* New Haven, CT: Yale University Press.

Shneiderman, S. (2010) Are the Central Himalayas in Zomia? Some Scholarly and Political Considerations Across Time and Space. *Journal of Global History, 5*(2), 289–312.

Shneiderman, S. (2013) Developing a Culture of Marginality: Nepal's Current Classificatory Moment. *Focaal, 2013*(65), 42–55.

The Carter Center. (2010) *Federalism and Constitutional Issues in Nepal: Perspectives from the Local Level.* Kathmandu, Nepal: Carter Center.

Thongchai, W. (1994) *Siam Mapped: A History of the Geo-Body of a Nation.* Honolulu: University of Hawaii Press.

UNDP. (2009) *The Interim Constitution of Nepal, 2063 (2007): As Amended by the First to Sixth Amendments.* Retrieved from Kathmandu, Nepal: UNDP.

van Schendel, W., & Abraham, I. (2005) *Illicit Flows and Criminal Things: States, Borders, and the Other Side of Globalization.* Bloomington: Indiana University Press.

Warner, C. (2014a) Flighty Subjects: Sovereignty, Shifting Cultivators, and the State in Darjeeling, 1830–1856. *Himalaya, the Journal of the Association for Nepal and Himalayan Studies, 34*(1), 8.

Warner, C. (2014b) *Shifting States: Mobile Subjects, Markets, and Sovereignty in the India-Nepal Borderland, 1780–1930.* PhD Dissertation, University of Washington.

18

A proliferation of border interfaces

Ordering insecurity for migrants in the Thai–Burmese borderlands

Adam Saltsman

Introduction

Like many of Asia's borderlands, the space between Myanmar and Thailand is rife with apparent tension and contradiction. The place is at once bucolic and industrial as it is simultaneously remote and plugged into global production networks. The border is both a site of refuge and opportunity for Burmese migrants to leave their country, as well as a space defined by the exploitation and lack of rights many of those migrants face. It is also as much Burmese as it is Thai, as it is neither of the two.

These contrasts reflect what Etienne Balibar (2002) refers to as the polysemic nature of borders: spaces defined, imagined, and materialized in different ways by different actors and various practices, contingent on intersections of discourse and relationality. In part, the multiple characterizations of the Thai–Burmese borderlands correspond to state and global imaginings of a Southeast Asian "region" interlinked through transport corridors and supply chains that streamline productive power and consolidate a consumer base (Arnold 2012). This manifestation of globalized capitalism renders borders central in regional and global development and investment plans, as sites of free-flowing cross-border trade and low-wage labor (Sidaway 2007). But this kind of reterritorialization is in tension with narratives of periphery, security, and marginality regarding the Thai–Burmese borderlands, narratives that are and have been central to a dominant sense of what it means to be Thai and to the articulation of the edges to that Thai-ness (Thongchai 2000). At the heart of both of these at times contradictory imaginaries are the Burmese migrant and highland populations that inhabit and move through the borderscape and that see it simultaneously as a site of possibility and repression, as home and as a space of exclusion and as fixed and yet permeable. Migrants are a linchpin in political economic visions for the region, the promise of low-wage labor that can undercut the Thai labor force (Piya 2007). And yet they are the threatening alien others in the nation state accounts of belonging and exclusion. As migrants navigate their rather insecure place in the borderlands, their experiences and ways of ordering their lives both confound and accommodate the dominant narratives of free trade and national security. However, it is, I suggest, the interplay between these narratives and migrants' practices of everyday life that contribute to the diverse sets of actions and orders which give meaning to this border space.

This chapter asks how the diverse sets of discourses, practices, and relations present in the Thai–Burmese borderlands coalesce as an assemblage of power which performatively produces and reproduces an insecure border space that Burmese migrants must navigate. However, instead of searching for the combination of factors that produce *a* border space, the chapter considers how the intersection of situated as well as broader political and economic flows, nation state spatial narratives and cosmologies, and the lived experiences of migrants manifests itself in multiple *border interfaces*. This concept builds on what Mezzadra and Neilson (2013) call a "proliferation of borders," as different populations experience territory, sovereignty, and governance in varying ways, encountering disparate manifestations of law and different assemblages of economic, social, and political power. By looking at what it means to experience governance in the varying interfaces of the Thai–Burmese borderlands for migrants, it becomes possible to untangle, at least a little bit, the complex threads of imbricated relations and discourses that converge to performatively constitute a diversity of political subjectivities and interpretations of border space.

This analysis expands an awareness of how borderlands in Southeast Asia lie at the "center" of contemporary social, political, cultural, and economic struggles over issues of sovereignty and subjectivity there (Horstmann and Wadley 2006). Emphasizing the role of "assemblages" and performativity, this chapter speaks to an interpretation of the relationship between power and space in which order and the experience of order manifests through the intersection of heterogeneous forces of practice, relations, and discourse at particular moments in time (Deleuze and Guattari 1987). Rather than focusing on formal institutions of governance, Allen and Cochrane (2007: 1171) suggest we concentrate on the "*interplay* of forces where a range of actors mobilize, enroll, translate, channel, broker and bridge in ways that make different kinds of government possible" (author's emphasis). I posit that the unique assemblages that enact the borderlands allow for a kind of legal pluralism—or at least a pluralism of social orders—which play a role in governing practice. This chapter, then, deepens an understanding of how borderlands materialize at the interface of the political meanings attributed to them and their inhabitants, the lived experience of order there and the physical transformations that reshape borderlands' landscape, and the practices that are possible there.

To address these questions and assertions, this chapter weaves together some of the forces that coalesce on the Thai–Burmese border to understand the opportunities and constraints for Burmese displaced or in transit there. To further elucidate the conceptual framework buttressing this chapter, in the following section, I explicate the notion of border interfaces in relation to space and politics on the Thai–Burmese border. In subsequent sections and subsections, I offer snapshots of three overlapping interfaces at which sets of actors, discourses, and processes intersect to produce a certain fragmented borderland with diverse yet imbricated social orders. First, I consider how the Thai state's immigration policies and designation of its borders as geographic zones of productive economic power are rooted in, and yet at tension with, ideals of center and periphery which derive from Thailand's own history of defining its geo-body via hierarchies of exclusion (Thongchai 1994). Second, I point to the ways in which these ideals and policies translate to a heterogeneity in the regimes of order that Burmese migrants must navigate in a state of "liminal legality," to use Menjívar's term (2006). Moving to the third interface, I illustrate how this heterogeneity of orders, in turn, interacts with translocal political, social, and religious networks that span the Thailand–Myanmar state boundary and play an important role in daily governance and social support. In this latter section, I provide concrete examples of cross-border political networks that practice forms of order-making which draw on "religious custom" as well as scattered references to the laws of Thailand, Myanmar, and Karen ethno-political legal systems.

This chapter is based on two years of research in the Thai town of Mae Sot and the nearby rural district Phob Phra, both on the border with Myanmar's Kayin State (see Map 18.1). My

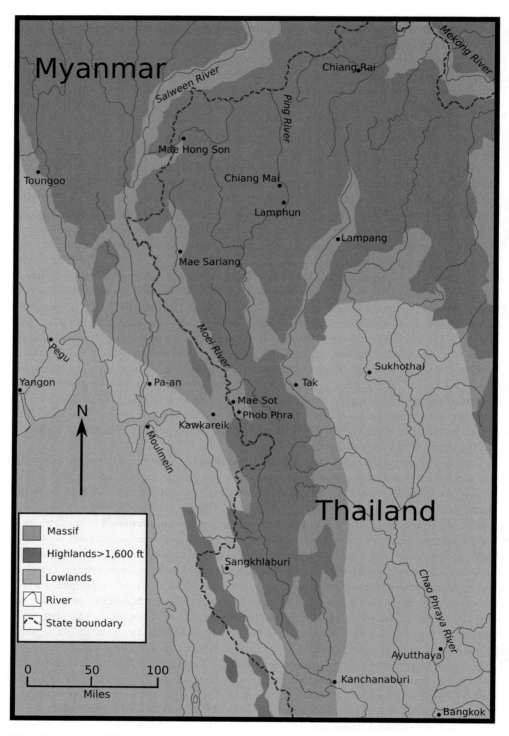

Map 18.1 Map of Thai–Burmese borderlands highlighting mainland Southeast Asia Massif
Map by Adam Saltsman (adapted from Keyes 1979)

research was primarily qualitative and focused on the various contours of order-making in Mae Sot's migrant neighborhoods and Phob Phra's labor camps. Mae Sot itself is a lively border town that embodies many of the tensions highlighted above; it is a hub for Burmese migrants entering Thailand in search of refuge and/or work, and the town is located nearby the largest camp on the border housing predominately Karen refugees. As well, Mae Sot is home to hundreds of formal and informal garment and textile factories where tens of thousands of Burmese migrants are employed, many without legal status in Thailand and earning far below the national minimum wage. In Phob Phra, on the other hand, migrants are dispersed in hundreds of agricultural labor camps and private homes, working as farm hands and domestic workers. This chapter's focus on assemblages of order is especially relevant in this context where, as I will show, traditional interpretations of institutional power break down.

A proliferation of border interfaces

I deploy the term border interfaces in this chapter in order to convey the importance of relationality and the interplay between the material and the representational in the production and reproduction of border spaces and the subjectivities that inhabit or transit through them. Both the material encounter of borders and the diverse social practices in such spaces are significant in the defining and redefining of borderlands.

The border, and other spatial edges, emerge "out of the material transformation of space and how it is refracted off of common social categories used to describe space and social relations" (Harms 2011: 35). In other words, borders materialize at the point where territorial markers of difference merge with other lines of social and political hierarchy. Ludden (2011: 136) reminds us that temporal frontiers play an important role here as well, as "imperial histories mingle in borderlands," and haunt contemporary notions of belonging and exclusion. This interplay between the relational and the material enables social groups in the same territory to encounter and embody varied representations of the state, rights, and space (e.g. Balibar 2002). As Mezzadra and Neilson (2013: 64) suggest, this confounds a Manichaean demarcation of the world into so-called "third-world" and "first-world" hierarchies, enabling spatial analyses of how certain sectors, corridors, or groups may be left out of circuits of development and political and economic inclusion, and may thus experience conditions of insecurity and precarity. At the same time, these authors write, "in former so-called third-world countries those areas and sectors that are integrated into global networks tend to exist alongside other areas and sectors that experience extreme privation and dispossession."

Nation state borders in Southeast Asia invoke a multitude of physical and social boundaries. They are important zones of flow, exchange, and identity, where states tend to amass their energies of securitization and evaluation, and where the "everyday politics" (Kerkvliet 2009) of border-crossers and borderland inhabitants constitute transgressions of conventional notions of sovereignty. They also reflect hierarchies and divisions that have accumulated and shifted over time in ways that haunt the present. Amidst such a diversity of orders, migrants must equip themselves with the skills to traverse a variegated terrain that shifts constantly, contingent on space as well as social relations.

It makes sense, then, to consider borders as fragmented and proliferated. I describe the Thai–Burmese borderlands as a multitude of interfaces at which diverse assemblages gather in space and time to offer certain perceptions and possibilities while foreclosing others. These interfaces do not only converge on state-controlled spaces or locales which lie on geographical boundary lines. Rather, spaces materialize as borders for those who encounter social and physical barriers or hierarchies (Mountz 2010). Material border spaces might include a river that needs to be crossed in order to enter a new country, a checkpoint, the backroom of a police station where officers exact bribes or negotiate migrants' access to their rights, or a welfare office in an urban center where caseworkers exercise discretion upon migrants in a way that reminds them that they do not belong. As well, border spaces are those where economic arrangements manifest themselves in material terms that suggest periphery, as a political economic concept: labor camps that are "off the grid," squatter settlements housing non-citizens or citizens deemed unworthy of basic rights to housing and sanitation, or a home set up with sewing machines operating informally as a factory that pays migrants a quarter of the minimum wage.

Such bordering translates not only to varied conditions and life experiences, but to vastly different relationships between subjects and the law as different spatial arrangements correspond to different legal subjectivities. Thus, this chapter regards the law as performatively constituted through interactions and discourse among a diversity of power brokers to show that the law is alive, "growing out of fragmented social institutions" (Teubner 1997: 7). Burmese migrants in this context do not only find themselves subject to a heterogeneity of social orders in the borderlands. Their precarious position, especially for those who are undocumented in Thailand, grossly inflates the discretion with which employers and authorities may interpret Thai law in their interactions. Such discretion engenders further insecurity for migrants who cannot be sure whether, at any given encounter, they are beyond the law, subject to its harshest interpretations, or whether an authority acting as patron may bend the law to protect them. This discretion is one manifestation of a border interface, bringing together relations and perceptions in ways that define the space for different migrants at different moments in space and time.

Three border interfaces

I turn now to the three overlapping interfaces at which assemblages of actors, relations, practices and discourses coalesce to produce social order and a border space defined by insecurity and limited possibility for Burmese migrants. As noted earlier, I start with the interface between an ever-evolving ethno-geographic sense of Thai-ness and Thai immigration policies. Building on this, I then reflect on the heterogeneity of orders that pervades the Thai–Burmese borderlands for migrants there. And finally, I analyze the interaction between this variegated terrain of governance and the translocal networks which link ideals and practices in Myanmar and Thailand. This latter part draws on case studies from organized cross-border networks.

Temporary asylum, semi-legal labor, and producing the Thai periphery

The efforts of the Thai government and local industries to render the border zone profitable has played a significant role in shaping the social landscape of the Thai–Burmese borderlands. These strategies, however, also reinforce the space's status as peripheral and "other." That is, the Thai–Burmese frontier space represents much more than the boundary between two neighboring countries; it reflects a history of transit, exchange, mapping, and margins-making (e.g. Scott 2009). Part of the great massif of mainland Southeast Asia, scholars have documented how, during the 19th century, the mountainous territory between Thailand and British colonial Burma developed as an increasingly mapped boundary attracting traders and timber operations, and dividing the area's inhabitants into the imaginaries of Siam and the British empire (Thongchai 1994). As Thongchai argues, the establishment of the border as such reflects a nexus between mapping during an era of imperial expansion and a developing sense of national spatial identity; that is, territorial agreements about where one state begins and one ends were bound up with questions of identity and belonging. Deeply embedded in both territorial and social concepts of nation in Thailand (then Siam) has been the idea of center and periphery such that the former suggests political power, city, organized territory, Thai identity, and inclusion while the latter connotes a less familiar undeveloped frontier, the forest, alien others, and the limits of state sovereignty (Renard 2000; Turton 2000). It is from within this framework that dominant lowland centers of power in Siam and Burma discursively imposed notions of ethnic identity onto the communities inhabiting this highland edge space (Pinkaew 2003). Such constructions have been simultaneously embedded in the production of state borders as well as nationalistic and racialized narratives of belonging (Thongchai 2005). As Pinkaew (2003: 32) writes, "migratory behaviour, opium growing, and shifting cultivation were marked as the three most dangerous threats posed by 'hill tribes'—all needing to be urgently controlled and suppressed in order to maintain the security of the entire nation."

The ethnic embodiment of "otherness" and periphery that pervades the highland spaces of the Thai–Burmese borderlands has manifested itself in a regime of citizenship that allows for partial membership in Thai society and a continued sense of marginality (e.g. Pitch 2007). While this refers primarily to Thailand's many ethnic minority groups who have had to navigate a variety of unequal citizenship categories over the last decades, the linkage between legality and periphery also forms a foundation for border inclusion and exclusion policies in Thailand. The notion of "border as ethnic other" has been an implicit—or sometimes explicit—voice in determining policy for hundreds of thousands of displaced Karen seeking refuge on the Thai side of the border, who the Thai public tends to see as the same ethnicity as some of those highland communities in Thailand who the government has long-treated as "outsiders." Indeed, a national security lens has largely dictated the government's policy towards refugees, considering them an embodiment of the conflict and political instabilities that spilled over the border from Myanmar (Lang 2002). Despite many among this encamped refugee population having lived in Thailand for upwards of 20 years, the government has refused to integrate them as legal members of the national community, instead giving them (semi-permanent) temporary permission to avoid deportation, and raising the specter of mass repatriation to Myanmar with some regularity.

Exclusion and insecurity also lie at the heart of Thailand's schemes to register the estimated 2–3 million migrant workers who come from neighboring Myanmar, Cambodia, and Laos. Since Thailand's period of economic liberalization began in the mid-1980s (and, relatedly, since larger numbers of migrants arrived to work in labor-intensive sectors), the government has issued cabinet resolutions that grant amnesties to employers and their undocumented migrant employees who come forward and sign up for work permits, which granted the workers, who had violated Thailand's immigration laws by entering the country illegally, the right to work *pending* deportation. Importantly, each of these resolutions initially came with geographic and sector eligibility; that is, only migrants living in particular parts of the country and working in particular sectors could regularize, while the rest would remain undocumented (see, e.g. Kritaya 2010). Then, starting in 2006, in addition to requiring migrant workers to have work permits, the Thai government deemed it necessary to verify the nationality of every migrant worker from neighboring countries, initiating bilateral agreements to provide this population with temporary passports, valid for six years at a time.

This set of policies toward migrant workers, built on the two pillars of national security and the maintenance of a low-wage labor population, might appear as equivocal and disorganized, with nearly annual cabinet resolutions that frequently changed the terms of eligibility and the convoluted path to registration, including deadlines and expiration dates. However, it provides the Thai state a release valve for their economy and renders an alien/other population into a flexible labor force; that is, migrants that can be deported at any time (Chang 2009). In those

Thai territories bordering Cambodia, and especially Myanmar, labor practices and the conditions in which migrants live epitomize this dynamic of exclusionary inclusion because, as entry points to Thailand, there are higher concentrations of undocumented migrants, many of whom take low-paying labor-intensive jobs as an initial step towards more stable employment elsewhere in the country.

In fact, these border spaces have thrived as sites for low-cost labor specifically because of their role as periphery or frontier within national imaginaries (Maneepong and Wu 2004). Decha (2015) writes about this dynamic as an "illegality-alterity nexus," with vulnerability at the center. The borderlands embody the duality between a national security concern among Thai government representatives toward the presence of historically alienated foreigners and the priorities of industries interested in keeping wages low to better enable firms to remain regionally competitive in labor-intensive industries, such as garment manufacturing. As Arnold and Pickles (2011) explain in relation to the Thai–Burmese border, this duality is key to distinguishing the latter as a zone in which precarious Burmese migrants endure "Third World" conditions and pay, while other parts of Thailand can excel towards "First World" conditions. The ethnicized notions of otherness that are bound up in the borderlands are part of this dynamic, suggest Arnold and Pickles (2011: 1615), because it provides "easy justification of intolerable conditions."

For documented and undocumented migrants, the border zone, then, is defined, at least in part, by insecurity, and reflects what Menjívar (2006) calls "liminal legality," an extended uncertainty about one's status from one year to the next, affecting their mobility, family life, and ability to plan for the future. Compounding this is the social boundary that most Burmese migrants, especially those who are undocumented, sense in relation to all the various institutions of the Thai state and their representatives, including courts, schools, and health facilities. This is not only true for the encamped refugees who are effectively living in a parallel system of governance, as discussed by McConnachie (2014) (and see below), but also in varying degrees for those Burmese living outside the camps and working in garment factories, on farms, in the service industry, or as waste pickers.

"Border economic zones" as spaces of heterogeneous governance

The maintenance and reproduction of a flexible migrant worker class on the Thai–Burmese border, and especially in the town of Mae Sot, reflects an assemblage of governance that draws on the power/authority of the state and employers/managers alike. While migrants are not in a complete "state of exception," and outside the state's law enforcement mechanisms (e.g. Agamben 2005; Ong 2006), the law materializes differently for them in order to enforce their precarious position. As highlighted above, part of this relates to the production of a permanently liminal legal class of migrant workers, in which some are temporarily registered and others remain completely undocumented. Precarious legality is itself a mechanism of governance, imposing a sense of what De Genova (2002) calls "deportability"; the internalization that one can be deported at any moment. Such a mechanism reminds migrants that they are in a state of exclusion, that they do not belong, and that they are not free to move about and access public spaces and services in the same way as others.

In addition, local decrees in border areas over the years that drastically restrict migrants' movement has led to different sets of rights for migrants in different parts of the country. In the name of national security, provincial governors in Phang Nga, Phuket, Ranong, Rayong, and Surat Thani have issued curfews for migrants and proscriptions on their right to own mobile phones, motorbikes, or cars (Human Rights Watch 2010; Supapong 2014). These local policies are in response to discursive constructions of migrants as criminal others among politicians and certain media arenas. But in addition, such local directives are useful in maintaining a geographically fixed reserve of low-wage labor in a space constructed as peripheral. In 2012, in response to complaints from employers about migrants leaving Mae Sot for more central parts of Thailand offering higher wages and more job security, the police began turning migrants back at checkpoints on the way out of town, even those migrants with registration (Lawi Weng 2012). Such maneuvers help to maintain the fiction that Burmese migrants are coalesced on the border and willing to work for a fraction of the minimum wage, while, in reality, it only manages to curtail their mobility via formal channels, pushing them more frequently into dangerous smuggling networks (Gjerdingen 2009). These various local policies and law enforcement practices are central to what makes these borderlands attractive for distinction as Special Economic Zones; without them, argues Arnold (2012), low-wage labor-intensive industries on the border would not survive.

Complementing these governmental strategies to enforce a flexible and informal workforce are the tactics on which firms rely to maintain a profitable edge. Confident that they can continue to exploit the migrant population without losing their workers, employers in Mae Sot's garment industry are effectively free to engage in labor practices that violate Thailand's Labour Protection Act (1998) and Factory Act (1992). This includes rapid downsizing without paying worker compensation, outsourcing work to informal factories/home workshops, exorbitant deductions from wages to cover room and board, and restrictions on employee mobility (see, for example MAP Foundation & Clean Clothes Campaign 2014).

Such state tactics and factory regulations work together to engender a heterogeneity of governance for Burmese migrants in the borderlands. While their place before Thai security officials renders them neither beyond nor within the legal framework of the state, the nearly absolute authority of employers over their workers in this context fragments and multiplies order into the various worksites. With extreme limits on their mobility, it is as if each worksite engenders its own borderscape for migrants, with widely varying experiences of order.

As the next section shows, the dynamic of (dis)order and governance in the borderlands is far more complex than a state-market dyad. The messy assemblage of non-governmental organizations (NGOs), individual power brokers, and survival strategies that provides a kind of constantly shifting order to life for migrants is both born from the precarious conditions in which Burmese find themselves on the border, and also relates to intersecting transnational political and social networks.

Forging transnational social and political networks

For both the encamped refugee population and those Burmese living in towns and rural parts of the borderlands, transnational political, social, and religious networks that extend across the Thai–Burmese border play a key role in governance and social support (Horstmann 2015). In most of the refugee camps, the Karen National Union (KNU), the political wing of the predominant Karen movement for self-determination in Myanmar, is the primary source of order, having installed the camps' governance apparatus "in accordance with templates of governance already operating in KNU-controlled areas inside Burma" (McConnachie 2014: 12). Their work, however, is indirect via religious organizations and civilian departments focused on health, education, camp administration, security, and youth and women's welfare (Horstmann 2011). This, writes Horstmann, is part of the KNU's efforts to cultivate a national Karen identity; a project that involved the performative privileging of certain political, cultural, and religious narratives and the subordination of others.

One cannot, however, simply point to the refugee camps as reproductions of an existing system in KNU-controlled territory in Myanmar. For camp residents, law and order materialize at the intersection of their exclusion from Thai society and normative jurisprudence, the state-making projects of the KNU and the involvement of the humanitarian sector. Not fully absent yet content to let the camps operate as a semi-autonomous space, the Thai authorities have engaged with the camps from primarily a security perspective, with army and paramilitary checkpoints set up on the camps' perimeters, monitoring entry and exit. This position, which derives at least in part from the perception of the Karen and their camps as an alien but "temporary" space in the already peripheral borderlands, left room for the KNU (and Karenni political groups in the northernmost two camps) to take part in everyday order-making. Nevertheless, since the late 1990s, when the Thai government allowed the UN refugee agency (UNHCR) to work with the refugee population, humanitarian NGOs have taken on roles related to education, healthcare, and advising everyday governance. In the last decade, NGOs and UNHCR have made efforts to fold what has been called the "customary law" of the camps within the Thai legal system, though this has, for the most part, led to its own articulations of law and legal plurality, with agency or NGO staff acting a sort of authority in the form of intermediaries between what are, at best, partial systems of governance.

Thus, on the one hand, the Thai–Burmese borderlands as a site of refuge and humanitarian action constitutes a space for the invigoration of Karen nationalist politics as well as governance that might not otherwise flourish in the ways it has (Horstmann 2014). On the other hand, though, the borderlands is itself a productive force that not only allows the KNU to exert an influence, but intersects the latter with transnational humanitarian notions of refugee management and the Thai state's policies of exclusion and securitization.

For the Burmese population living outside the refugee camps—those who are more likely to be found in factories, farms, or on the streets of border towns—transnational political, social, and religious networks continue to have an important influence on the performative production and reproduction of order. Effectively, such networks step in to fill the vacuum created by migrants' de facto exclusion from the Thai state. But, rather than seeing this as a transnational network assuming the role of the sovereign over the migrant population in the complete absence of any official authority, the lived reality more closely reflects a constantly shifting assemblage of power (Allen and Cochrane 2007) in which transnational networks interact with Thai security officials, employers, and other actors to produce and reproduce a semblance of order.

Networks, like those affiliated with the KNU, expand, move, and contract based as much on relationships with local authorities and personalities and capacities of power brokers as those networks' particular geographies and histories on the border. For example, there are villages and migrant worker settlements in rural areas along the border where Karen set up Baptist churches or Buddhist monasteries in the 1980s or where individuals affiliated with the KNU "settled," and continue to maintain some influence. Other places bear the mark of Thailand's internal conflict between the late 1960s and early 1980s, including *Romklao Sahamit* villages (translating to "under the protection of the king") the Thai government established along the border to settle Chinese Kuomintang and Burmese and Thai highland groups (such as the Akha, Lahu, Lisu, and Yao) and displace or outnumber Hmong groups perceived as opium cultivators and communists (Schmid and Jongman 2005). These histories of Cold War and postcolonial struggle helped to reshape the borderlands, infusing them with identities and relations that are transnational in nature, and that engender different modes of local governance.

One iteration of this network is called the Kaw Moo Raw Karen Youth Organization, which considers itself an affiliate of the KNU's armed wing, the Karen National Liberation Army (KNLA), and which was mandated to "organize" Karen people displaced in Thailand, but outside refugee camps. Beyond the KNU apparatus, the People's Volunteer Association is a group established by a former member of the All Burma Student Democratic Front (ABSDF), an armed organization formed by students involved in the 1988 mass protests in Yangon (then Rangoon). Both groups operate as loosely connected networks of mediators, local leaders, and community organizers united by the mission to provide an element of security in the lives of displaced Burmese who have limited or no fair access to the official court system. They both rely on a transnational identity to legitimize their authority to migrants, Thai government officials, and employers. On a discursive level, this means referring to their work as "customary" or "traditional" Burmese methods that are most fitting for a Burmese population. This also involves citing centuries-old Burmese texts to solve intimate partner violence or the inclusion of religious doctrine, whether Christian, Buddhist, or Muslim, to explain decisions or rules. (For example, the People's Volunteer Association works closely with the Islamic Association of Tak Province to resolve disputes that involve Burmese Muslim parties.) On a practical level, these groups can draw on relationships on both sides of the border to facilitate the movement of individuals and to track and apprehend those who perpetrate crimes in one country and then flee to the other. The former tactic complements an informal perception among Thai authorities that an "alien" population needs their "alien" law to keep order, while the latter assuages these authorities' observations that violence and impunity on the frontier stems from the ease with which criminals slip across the border.

Beyond this, such networks' ability to govern on some level relies to a certain extent on the long-term presence of their network on both sides of the border. It is also rooted in informal agreements with local Thai authorities reluctant to get involved in crimes involving Burmese and ethnic minority groups, as well as on their ability to speak multiple languages, especially Burmese, Karen, and Thai, and employers' and landlords' familiarity with them as a group that can maintain order and settle conflicts. Networks only take on the meaning they have because of the influence of those who affiliate themselves with them. Outside the formal system of governance, largely excluded from state institutions, and with migrants heavily reliant on employers for mobility and security, it becomes necessary to envision governance on the border as stemming from a multitude of groups, many operative only in one cluster of houses, one labor camp, or in two or three villages, though, in some cases, still symbolically affiliated with transnational networks and the political, religious, and social narratives that come with them.

Such sources of order are often not in concert with one another. Indeed, everyday manifestations of and encounters with law and order are effectively mediated by "strongmen" and can be interpreted through the lens of patron–client relationships, that is, both a much-needed source of security and a source of potentially intimidating authority for migrant workers. These strongmen include but extend beyond transnational networks, and they might be local level village heads, Thai or Burmese Karen men with political capital, line managers from factories, employers, landlords, religious leaders, Thai police officers acting off-duty, or staff from NGOs or grassroots organizations. Each of these groups or individuals might wield power in a particular site or series of locations, which varies according to a range of factors, including shifting local understandings of where certain neighborhoods end and others begin and the parameters of farm compounds, factory dormitories, or a landlord's property.

Conclusion

The Thai–Burmese borderlands reflect a space of both destruction and creativity in governance. Exclusion and the maintenance of a liminal refugee population and a flexible migrant worker regime are forms of violence involved in the work of affixing a people to an idea of periphery and margins, and the work of maintaining a securitized notion of state boundaries. And yet this same violence and exclusion facilitate an innovation of order-making processes.

While it is clear that borderlands do not necessarily signify an erosion of state power, in Thailand as elsewhere, state actors are more likely to engage with populations deemed illegal or peripheral from primarily a national security stance or from the perspective that the population is disposable. Moreover, their interpretation and application of the law for the Burmese forced migrant population produces and reproduces this marginality, infusing the order of everyday life with a level of insecurity. This insecurity represents an important manifestation of governance in the lives of Burmese migrants in so far as it regulates mobility, relationships, and decisions about the future. The exclusionary or demeaning tactics of local authorities is part of what creates space for the involvement of multiple other modes of governance and order-making, which do not necessarily correspond to the restrictions of state boundaries, but which step in where the state has designated a population as external to the legal space afforded to those within its territory.

Market-oriented forms of discipline, such as those found in factory regulations aimed at maximizing worker productivity, are a significant source of governance in these borderlands. And yet, it would be erroneous to assume that borderlands are merely the site for contestations between state power and neoliberal logics. In fact, these two seem to function in concert here, and are intertwined with and stem from histories and geographies that are rooted in transnational borderland identities as well as in national imaginaries of belonging and exclusion, center and periphery.

What this means is that order as well as the lived experience of the border is made and remade at interfaces which are, by definition, fleeting and heterogeneous. To the extent to which law is an element of sovereignty, the movement in and out of jurisdictions, some of which are state-centered and others transnational and non-state, is indicative of a certain permeability and flexibility to the quality of state boundaries. However, rather than implying that migrants move in an out of legality with ease, they are more likely further constrained as sovereignty and boundaries have proliferated and shattered the border's geography into dozens of imbricated discontinuous shards. Periphery, otherness, and exclusion act as forces *in concert* with the mobility of people and political networks to produce environments in which the production of multiple orders signifies the production of multiple borders that migrants must navigate in an effort to survive.

References

Agamben, G. 2005. *State of Exception*. Translated by K. Attell. Chicago: The University of Chicago Press.
Allen, J. and Cochrane, A. 2007. Beyond the Territorial Fix: Regional Assemblages, Politics and Power. *Regional Studies*. 41(9), pp. 1161–1175.
Arnold, D. 2012. Spatial Practices and Border SEZs in Mekong Southeast Asia. *Geography Compass*. 6(12), pp. 740–751.
Arnold, D. and Pickles, J. 2011. Global Work, Surplus Labour, and the Precarious Economies of the Border. *Antipode*. 43(5), pp. 1598–1624.
Balibar, E. 2002. *Politics and the Other Scene*. Translated by Christine Jones, James Swenson, and Chris Turner. London: Verso.
Chang, D. 2009. Informalising Labour in Asia's Global Factory. *Journal of Contemporary Asia*. 39(2), pp. 161–179.
Decha, T. 2015. Illegality and Alterity: Preliminary Notes on SEZ, Civil Society, and the Thai-Burmese Borderland. *Journal of Territorial and Maritime Studies*. 2(2), pp. 53–72.
De Genova, N. 2002. Migrant "Illegality" and Deportability in Everyday Life. *Annual Review of Anthropology*. 31, pp. 419–447.
Deleuze, G. and Guattari, F. 1987. *A Thousand Plateaus: Capitalism and Schizophrenia*. Minneapolis: University of Minnesota Press.
Gjerdingen, E. 2009. Suffocation Inside a Cold Storage Truck and Other Problems with Trafficking as Exploitation and Smuggling as Choice along the Thai-Burmese Border. *Arizona Journal of International & Comparative Law*. 26, p. 699.

Harms, E. 2011. *Saigon's Edge: On the Margins of Ho Chi Minh City*. Minneapolis: University of Minnesota Press.
Horstmann, A. 2011. Sacred Networks and Struggles among the Karen Baptists across the Thailand-Burma Border. *Moussons*. 17(1), pp. 85–104.
Horstmann, A. 2014. Stretching the Border: Confinement, Mobility and the Refugee Public Among Karen Refugees in Thailand and Burma. *Journal of Borderlands Studies*. 29(1), pp. 47–61.
Horstmann, A. 2015. Uneasy Pairs: Revitalizations of Karen Ethno-nationalism and Civil Society across the Thai-Burmese Border. *Journal of Territorial and Maritime Studies*. 2(2), pp. 33–52.
Horstmann, A. and Wadley, R.L. 2006. *Centering the Margin: Agency and Narrative in Southeast Asian Borderlands*. New York: Berghan Books.
Human Rights Watch. 2010. *From the Tiger and the Crocodile: Abuse of Migrant Workers in Thailand*. New York: Human Rights Watch.
Kerkvliet, B. 2009. Everyday Politics in Peasant Societies (and Ours). *Journal of Peasant Studies*. 36(1), pp. 227–243.
Keyes, C.F. (ed.) 1979. *Ethnic Adaptation and Identity: The Karen on the Thai Frontier with Burma*. Philadelphia: Institute for the Study of Human Issues.
Kritaya, A. 2010. *Thai State Policy to Manage Irregular Migration from Neighboring Countries*. Bangkok: Institute for Population and Social Research.
Lang, H. 2002. *Fear and Sanctuary: Burmese Refugees in Thailand*. Ithaca, NY: Southeast Asia Program Publications.
Lawi Weng. 2012. "Rights Groups Say Migrants Blocked from Leaving Mae Sot." *The Irrawaddy*, [online] 2 October. Available at: www.irrawaddy.com/news/burma/rights-groups-say-migrants-blocked-from-leaving-mae-sot.html [Accessed 11 January 2017].
Ludden, D. 2011. The Process of Empire: Frontiers and Borderlands. In: P.F. Bang and C.A. Bayly, eds. *Tributary Empires in Global History*. London: Palgrave/Macmillon. pp. 132–150.
Maneepong, C. and Wu, C. 2004. Comparative Borderland Developments in Thailand. *ASEAN Economic Bulletin*. 21(2), pp. 135–166.
MAP Foundation and Clean Clothes Campaign. 2014. *Migrant Workers in Thailand's Garment Factories*. Bangkok.
McConnachie, K. 2014. *Governing Refugees: Justice, Order and Legal Pluralism*. Abingdon: Routledge.
Menjívar, C. 2006. Liminal Legality: Salvadoran and Guatemalan Immigrants' Lives in the United States. *American Journal of Sociology*. 111, pp. 999–1037.
Mezzadra, S. and Neilson, B. 2013. *Border as Method, or, the Multiplication of Labour*. Durham, NC: Duke University Press.
Mountz, A. 2010. *Seeking Asylum: Human Smuggling and Bureaucracy at the Border*. Minneapolis: University of Minnesota Press.
Ong, A. 2006. *Neoliberalism as Exception: Mutations in Citizenship and Sovereignty*. Durham, NC: Duke University Press.
Pinkaew, L. 2003. Constructing Marginality: The "Hill Tribe" Karen and Their Shifting Locations Within THAI State and Public Perspectives. In: C.O. Delang, ed. *Living at the Edge of Thai Society*. London: Routledge. pp. 21–42.
Pitch, P. 2007. Border Partial Citizenship, Border Towns, and Thai-Myanmar Cross-Border Development: Case Studies at the Thai Border Towns. PhD thesis, University of California, Berkeley.
Piya, P. 2007. *Textures of Struggle: The Emergence of Resistance among Garment Workers in Thailand*. Ithaca, NY: Cornell University Press.
Renard, R.D. 2000. The Differential Integration of Hill People into the Thai State. In: A. Turton, ed. *Civility and Savagery: Social Identity in Tai States*. Richmond: Curzon Press. pp. 63–83.
Schmid, A.P. and Jongman, A.J. 2005. *Political Terrorism: A New Guide to Authors, Actors, Concepts, Data Bases, Theories, and Literature*. 2nd ed. New Brunswick, NJ: Transaction Publishers.
Scott, J.C. 2009. *The Art of Not Being Governed: An Anarchist History of Upland Southeast Asia*. New Haven, CT: Yale University Press.
Sidaway, J.D. 2007. Spaces of Postdevelopment. *Progress in Human Geography*. 31(3), pp. 345–361.
Supapong, C. 2014. Migrant Workers May Face Island Curfew. *Bangkok Post*, [online] 28 October. Available at: www.bangkokpost.com/news/general/440100/migrant-workers-may-face-island-curfew [Accessed 6 November 2014].
Teubner, G. 1997. Global Bukowina: Legal Pluralism in the World Society. In: G. Teubner, ed. *Global Law without a State*. Brookfield, VT: Dartmouth Publishing. pp. 3–28.

Thongchai W. 1994. *Siam Mapped: A History of the Geo-body of a Nation*. Honolulu: University of Hawaii Press.

Thongchai W. 2000. The Others Within: Travel and Ethno-Spatial Differentiation of Siamese Subjects 1885–1910. In: A. Turton, ed. *Civility and Savagery: Social Identity in Tai States*. Richmond: Curzon Press. pp. 38–62.

Thongchai W. 2005. Trying to Locate Southeast Asia from its Navel: Where is Southeast Asian Studies in Thailand? In: P. Kratoska, R. Raban, and H.S. Nordholt, eds. *Locating Southeast Asia: Geographies of Knowledge and Politics of Space*. Singapore: Singapore University Press. pp.113–133.

Turton, A. 2000. Introduction to *Civility and Savagery*. In: A. Turton, ed. *Civility and Savagery: Social Identity in Tai States*. Richmond: Curzon Press. pp. 3–31.

19

The decision to move

Post-exchange experiences in the former Bangladesh–India border enclaves

Md. Azmeary Ferdoush and Reece Jones

The residents of the enclaves along the Bangladesh–India border spent decades in limbo waiting for the two countries to address their precarious existence. When the exchange finally happened in the summer of 2015, many people were unsure of what to do next. When asked about future plans, a 33-year-old farmer in the Dohola Khagrabari enclave in Bangladesh, who had decided to relocate to India, answered:

> Plan? I don't have any plan. India has taken the responsibility of us. They are going to give us money, give us food, give us home. They are going to take care of our children, pay for their education and health. India took care of millions of Bangladeshis during the 71 war; we are now only 400–500 families. Are they going to throw us out? No, they will take care of us.

The enclave residents had long dreamed of the moment of exchange, but since it remained elusive for decades, many had not thought about what would happen if the exchange actually happened. They were now facing a dilemma. They could remain in their homes and become citizens of a new country as the enclaves were folded into the surrounding state or they could leave their homes, friends, and livelihoods and move across the border to the country of their citizenship, but a place that many of them had never even visited. The governments of India and Bangladesh expected large numbers to opt to move, but the enclave dwellers were more conflicted and in the end less than 2 percent (989 out of 55,000) finally decided to move (Shewly 2016).

The partition of British India in 1947 left the Bengal borderlands with a number of unresolved issues, including a vague and un-demarcated border and mapping errors that led to disputes (van Schendel 2005). However, one problem that started to gain attention in the scholarly world from the late 1980s was almost unnoticed during the partition: the existence of almost 200 political enclaves along the border. Although the first known initiative to exchange the enclaves was embarked on in 1932 by the British administrators, it took 83 more years to finally exchange the enclaves in the summer of 2015.

The chapter begins with a brief history of the enclave formation and the long process that resulted in the exchange of the enclaves. Then the chapter delves into the post-exchange issues for enclave residents of deciding whether to relocate and for state officials of merging these small but characteristically distinct pieces of lands into the state space. In doing so, it argues that a 'subsistence strategy', in addition to religion or ideology, played a particularly significant role for many of the enclave residents in choosing whether to remain in their homes or migrate across the border. It also suggests that the biggest challenge for India and Bangladesh is inscribing the organizing system of the state into these non-state spaces while incorporating the enclave residents into the citizenship regime of the state. Fieldwork for this chapter was conducted in two phases by the authors. The first phase was conducted by the second author during 2006 when there was no apparent possibility of exchanging the enclaves. The second phase was conducted by the first author during June and July of 2015 when the decision to exchange the enclaves was made and all the preparations for the exchange were occurring.[1] The first author conducted interviews with the residents who decided to stay in Bangladesh, those who decided to choose Indian citizenship, and different government officials. He also observed different practices and preparations for the exchange in government offices, including the (re)naming of places and the registration of enclave residents as they decided whether to move or not.

The conclusion considers the theoretical implications of the exchange. In the past, the enclaves were theorized as abandoned spaces and the failure to exchange them as symbolic of territory's allure that prevented states from even giving up land they had never possessed. In post-colonial South Asia, the enclaves' significance as symbol of nationalism overshadowed their role as ungoverned state territories for decades. Although more attention was cast on the dire situation of the residents in recent years, the exchange finally happened as the enclaves became a bargaining chip in negotiations between the two states.

The creation and exchange of the enclaves

An enclave is a portion of one state completely surrounded by the territory of another state (van Schendel 2002). According to Whyte (2002), Bangladesh and India shared 198 of the 256 enclaves worldwide until the enclaves were finally exchanged in 2015. At the India–Bangladesh border there were also counter enclaves (an enclave inside an enclave) and dual enclaves (two separate enclaves that are geographically contiguous with each other). To simplify the exchange, the governments agreed to ignore counter enclaves which means a counter enclave will automatically be merged and exchanged with the enclave. Additionally, in the 1974 Land Boundary Agreement (LBA), India and Bangladesh had already agreed not to exchange the dual Bangladeshi enclaves of Dahagram–Angorpota, which were the only enclaves that had actually been administered by their home state due to their close proximity to Bangladesh through a narrow corridor. This resulted in the exchange of a total of 162 enclaves in 2015 (Shewly 2013b; Ghosh 2015; MEA 2015). The total exchangeable land area of these enclaves was 98.5 km^2. Bangladesh and India respectively hosted 69.5 km^2 and 29.0 km^2 of these lands (Jones 2010). According to a census conducted by both governments from 14 to 17 July 2011, the total population of the enclaves was 51,549 among which Bangladesh and India respectively hosted 37,334 and 14,215 people (MEA 2015). Another count was carried out before the exchange from 6 to 16 July 2015 to remove the names of people who died and add babies born since the 2011 census. Three thousand more people were registered, most of whom were either newborn or newly married, making the total population almost 55,000 at the time of the exchange (*The Daily Star* 17 July 2015).

For years, several myths have circulated about the formation of the enclaves including outlandish stories of late night gambling and spilled ink on a map at the time of partition. However, historically the enclaves came into existence after the treaty between the Mughals and the

Maharaja of Cooch Behar in 1713 (Whyte 2002; Jones 2010). The treaty allowed both parties to retain the pieces of lands they controlled at the time of the treaty even if they were surrounded by enemy territory. The British came to the subcontinent and started to gain control over territories in the mid-18th century and the first proper demarcation of the enclaves took place between 1937 and 1938 (Whyte 2002; Jones 2010). As the enclaves were kept unchanged, the Mughal enclaves ended up in the British territories (as the British were controlling the formerly Mughal territories) and the Cooch Behar enclaves were administered by the Kingdom of Cooch Behar. Prior to the partition of India in 1947, the existence of the enclaves was a local administrative issue which merely meant that some areas were administered by Cooch Behar while others by Rangpur. Without a formal border, the administrative distinction had little impact on the lives of residents.

The first attempt to exchange the enclaves was in August 1932 when the Director of the Land Records for Bengal requested that the Revenue Department exchange the enclaves between Cooch Behar and British India in order to simplify tax collection. Since Cooch Behar was an independent kingdom, this was the easiest practical solution. However, in March 1934, he was told that it was not possible because of protests from the enclave dwellers (Whyte 2002). This is the only known proposal of exchange before partition, and surprisingly the opinion of the enclave dwellers was taken into account.

The border created with the partition of India went through the area of the enclaves but the enclaves were not addressed in the original partition documents because the princely states, like Cooch Behar, were given the choice of whether to join India or Pakistan. When the princely state of Cooch Behar eventually decided to join India in 1949, the odd administrative enclaves became political enclaves, little islands of India and Pakistan completely surrounded by the territory of the other country (Whyte 2002).

After the partition, the first initiative to exchange the border enclaves was taken in 1953. The Pakistani Prime Minister Mohammed Ali hosted the Indian Prime Minister Jawaharlal Nehru in Karachi at the end of July 1953 and paid Nehru a return visit from 17 to 20 August. At these meetings, an agreement was reached to exchange the Cooch Behar enclaves, but several internal political issues in both states, as well as deteriorating bilateral relations between the countries, made things more complicated and the exchange could not be executed (Whyte 2002). Nevertheless, Nehru seemed to be very keen on resolving the enclave issue when he said on 4 June 1958 that 'Any two reasonable persons on behalf of the two Governments could sit together and decide them in a day or two' (quoted in Whyte 2002: 91; Cons 2014: 4). In the same year, the Prime Minister of Pakistan, Firoz Khan Noon, visited Nehru in Delhi from 9 to 11 September. In this visit, they agreed to exchange the enclaves without compensation for the net territorial loss to West Bengal. They also decided to divide the disputed Berubari Union in half. Berubari was an area near the enclaves that had been mistakenly depicted as part of both countries on different documents produced during the partition (Whyte 2002).

The Nehru–Noon Agreement attracted immense criticism both in India and Pakistan. Nehru was criticized because he agreed to transfer half of Berubari and did not ask for any compensation for the territorial loss. The agreement was challenged in several court cases that dragged on for 13 years. The Indian Supreme Court finally decided that the exchange could proceed on 29 March 1971, but by that point East Pakistan (Bangladesh) had already declared independence from Pakistan three days earlier on 26 March 1971. On 16 December 1971, East Pakistan won its independence and became Bangladesh. The first Prime Minister of the country, Sheikh Mujibur Rahman, had a friendly relationship with Indira Gandhi, the Prime Minister of India. Mujib visited New Delhi from 12 to 16 May 1974 to discuss many political and economic issues. On the last day, they reached an agreement based on the Nehru–Noon Agreement to exchange the enclaves and solve the land boundary issues between India and Bangladesh. This is known as Indira–Mujib Pact, the Land Boundary Agreement (LBA) or the Delhi Treaty (Whyte 2002; MEA 2015). According to this treaty, Bangladesh gave up its claim on Berubari, and in exchange, Bangladesh was allowed to retain the enclaves of Dahagram–Angorpota, which were only 178 meters away from Bangladesh proper. Bangladesh ratified the LBA on 27 November 1974, with an amendment in its constitution, but India delayed.

A series of political disputes between India and Bangladesh complicated the issue. The assassination of Sheikh Mujib in a military coup on 15 August 1975 created a hostile bilateral relationship. Additionally, the initiative of successive governments in Bangladesh to replace its alliance with the India–Russia bloc with the United States–Pakistan and Islamic world affected the mutual trust between the two governments (Lifshultz 1979). Over the 1980s and 1990s, different issues such as migration from Bangladesh to India, access to the Tin Bigha Corridor that connects the Dahagram–Angorpota enclaves to Bangladesh, India's suspicion that Bangladesh supported terrorists and insurgent groups, and the construction of the Farakka dam in West Bengal worsened the relationship. As a result, the enclave exchange remained overshadowed (Shewly 2012).

In 2009, the Awami League and Indian Congress Party came into power in Bangladesh and India, the same combination of political parties that signed the 1974 LBA. The Prime Minister of Bangladesh, Sheikh Hasina, Sheikh Mujib's daughter, visited India in January 2010 and expressed the desire to reach a final solution to the long-standing problem of border issues in the spirit of 1974 LBA (MEA 2015). All disputes over the un-demarcated sections of the border were resolved within a year of the visit (Shewly 2012). In September 2011, the Prime Minister of India, Manmohan Singh, was scheduled to visit Bangladesh. During this visit different bilateral treaties were to be signed, including the enclave exchange agreement, but at the last minute, the West Bengal state government convinced Singh not to sign the water sharing and border agreements. Hence, only a protocol was signed approving the exchange of enclaves, but the document lacked a fixed deadline (Shewly 2013a).

The lack of a fixed timeframe created dissatisfaction among the enclave dwellers on both sides and led to a sustained protest movement. For example, on 21 August 2011, residents of enclaves in India held a protest in the Metro Channel of Dharmatala, Kolkata demanding the exchange of the enclaves (Saha 2011). Enclave dwellers from both countries decided to turn off all the lights in the enclaves from 11 September to 12 September 2011 to demand a specific date of exchange (*The Daily Prothom Alo* 13 September 2011). The biggest and most serious strike took place in March 2012 in Putimari, an enclave of India situated in Panchagar district of Bangladesh. They began a hunger strike for an indefinite period with a three-point demand that called for the immediate implementation of the 1974 LBA as well as a definitive timeframe for the enclave exchange. The strike went on from 18 March until 11 April 2012 and only ended with a promise from the government of Bangladesh to press the issue with the Indian government (*The Daily Star* 11 April 2012).

The protocol, not surprisingly, was opposed in India again. On 18 December 2013, a bill was introduced in Indian Parliament for the implementation of 1974 LBA. The Bharatia Janata Party (BJP), the Asom Gana Parishad (AGP), and the Trinamool Congress Party protested the bill. Trinamool MP Derek O'Brian termed it as a 'Bangladesh Giveaway Bill' and Mamata Banarjee, West Bengal's Chief Minister and head of the Trinamool Congress, posted on her Facebook page 'We are not accepting, not accepting and not accepting [the agreement]. The state government will not implement it' (Cons 2014: 2). As time passed, the bilateral relations between the two states improved as they signed several smaller agreements that permitted India to use

Bangladesh's sea port and established a road transit route through the country. These concessions from Bangladesh influenced the political leaders in India, including Mamata, to accept the implementation bill and it was finally passed on 6 May 2015, with a unanimous vote for the exchange (*The Daily Prothom Alo* 7 May 2015). The newly elected BJP Prime Minister of India, Narendra Modi, visited Bangladesh and signed the exchange treaty on 7 June 2015. At midnight on 31 July, the enclaves were formally exchanged between the two countries leaving Dahagram–Angorpota as the only remaining enclave.

After the exchange

After decades of waiting, the actual exchange happened quickly and smoothly. Both countries were keen to know the population of the enclaves and the number of people who wanted to stay and leave. The enclave residents were given two choices: stay in the country of residence and accept a change of citizenship or move to their 'home country' and retain their original 'official' citizenship there. Home country and official citizenship are in quotes because in practice none of the residents had contact with these home countries and had received no services from them for decades. They had lived in a de facto stateless existence for many years. While Bangladesh offered no incentives for residents of Bangladeshi enclaves in India to move to Bangladesh, India came up with a resettlement package for the people from Indian enclaves in Bangladesh to encourage them to move to India. The package included 500,000 (US$7,500) rupees per family, dry food for two years, kitchen utensils, animal feed, temporary camp in Cooch Behar, drinking water, medicine, healthcare, education, and eventually a house or flat (*The Daily Prothom Alo* 26 July 2015). At first, 1,006 enclave dwellers in Bangladesh opted to relocate to India while none of the enclave dwellers in India opted to move to Bangladesh (*The Daily Star* 17 July 2015). However, a few decided not to move later, making the number 989 (Rahman 2015). Scholarly work had predicted that most residents would want to stay in their homes, but it came as a surprise to both governments that so few decided to move (*The Daily Prothom Alo* 26 July 2015).

Although the relocation of the enclave dwellers was supposed to begin on 31 July 2015, it was postponed based on the complaints that some who had opted to move were threatened by others. After this, an observational period was introduced until 31 October when the enclave dwellers were issued a travel pass and could visit the place where they would be relocated in India (Ali 2015). In the end, a few changed their minds and 989 made the move to India by 30 November 2015.

The enclave dwellers reported numerous factors that shaped their decision whether to relocate. Choosing citizenship was not exclusively a matter of ideology or a sense of belonging for many of the residents. Critical factors were India's resettlement package and India's 'image' as a more economically solvent country than Bangladesh. For those that decided to leave, there were several significant factors including kinship ties, religion, and maintaining connections to both countries as a hedge against future problems. A 27-year-old farmer in the Dohola Khagrabari enclave in Bangladesh who decided to move to India explained:

> Look, it was not an easy decision. But I have to take care of my family and think about their future. I don't have anything here [Bangladesh]. I work in other's lands and struggle to make my ends meet… I have heard that they [India] will give us money, home, and everything. The Indian government will also provide education for my daughter, and I have heard that it is easy to get a job there. So why shouldn't I move there?

Although religion was a significant factor, these other subsistence issues had more weight for many. A 31-year-old farmer from the same enclave, who also decided to move to India, when asked why, answered:

> I'm a Hindu, and I have struggled a lot here. I always feel insecure. India is *Hindustan* [the land of Hindus], and I belong there. My mother's brother lives there. Also, you know, India has offered money and support for us.

The Indian resettlement package was extremely generous, and many enclave dwellers had never had that much money and other facilities in their entire lives. Additionally, the enclave dwellers perceived that India was a place with new economic opportunities and numerous life chances.

Although they did not have a clear idea of what they would do once they moved to India, they were very optimistic and were depending wholly on the Indian government to help them settle in and start a new life. A 38-year-old farmer who decided to move from the same enclave expressed his plans as follows:

> Aaa....I have not thought about it yet. But I heard that India will take care of us, they will give us money, give us jobs, take care of our children. ....Look I have struggled a lot in my life so far. I am not anxious about struggling more. I am struggling here, it does not make a difference if I have to struggle there.

From his perspective, it was worth taking the risk on India's generous offer rather than remaining as a religious minority in Bangladesh.

Existing kinship ties in India was another important factor behind the decision to move for many. Most of the enclave dwellers have some relatives or immediate family members living in India. They had settled in India during different periods of time; for instance, during the partition in 1947, during the liberation war in 1971, and so forth. In most cases, families or individuals who were left behind either did not have enough resources to move and settle in India or did not want to. The resettlement package came as a boost for them to rethink their decision and join their relatives across the border.

A 48-year-old small shop owner from the Dohola Khagrabari enclave explained why he had decided to move:

> Look, most of my family members had moved there long before, and they are doing well over there. My uncle was the first to move there right after liberation (1971). He got married and settled there. Then my sister got married there. I am the only person living this side. I wanted to move but never had enough money and did not know what to do. Now, since India is taking us and also helping us to go there, I have decided to move with my family.

Not only had the enclave dwellers developed kinship ties in India, but many also made kinship ties outside the enclaves in Bangladesh. It is very common among the enclave dwellers to get married outside the enclave. As a result, the majority of the families living in the enclaves were already absorbed, to some extent, as regular citizens of Bangladesh.

For a few families, this allowed for a strategic decision to settle some family members in India and some in Bangladesh. Members who had already been regularized as Bangladeshi citizens decided to stay in Bangladesh and those who were still living in the enclaves decided to move to India. The idea is that if things get worse in Bangladesh, people living in India will help their counterpart in Bangladesh to move to India and vice versa. A large number of families were being split to execute this plan from different enclaves. For example, a mother from Dohola Khagrabari decided to move to India while her son was staying in Bangladesh. When asked why they had chosen to split, the son replied:

> I have a brother living on that side from the last 13 years. I have my own family here, my house, my land. I can't leave all these. But my mother wanted to go to India. So we thought, as my brother is already there, my mother can easily go and settle in. …Also, two brothers will be on two sides, if any one of us face problem on one side, the other one can take care and help to move in and out.

Religious identity also played a role in deciding citizenship, but not for all the enclave dwellers. The enclave dwellers who decided to move to India were almost all Hindu and they were following what has been a constant migration of Hindus from Bangladesh to India since 1971 (Samaddar 1999). The enclave dwellers who were interviewed thought that they should go to India because that's where they belong. As a Hindu, they should be in India, and they would feel more comfortable there. But this simple explanation does not account for the complexity of the situation. There were other Hindu enclave dwellers who decided to stay in Bangladesh and not a single Muslim enclave resident from India decided to move to Bangladesh. For many, it was not only the sense of religious belonging, but additionally the feeling of insecurity and other subsistence strategies that drove the decision to migrate or not. A 45-year-old enclave dweller in Dohola Khagrabari explains when he was asked if his religious identity had anything to do with his decision to move:

> Yes, of course. I am a Hindu, and I belong to India. India is the land of Hindus. Being a Hindu, I always felt insecure here. Now, after the exchange I feel more insecure. If I were a Muslim, I would not have taken this decision. But I think I will, at least, feel secure being a Hindu in India. Even if I can't make three meals a day there, I will be happy.

The most surprising result of the exchange is that not a single resident of the Bangladeshi enclaves in India decided to return to Bangladesh. The lack of a resettlement package from Bangladesh played a significant role in the decision. Furthermore, Bangladesh does not have as strong an economy as India has. Without a clear promise of assistance from the Bangladesh government, the move would have been very risky.

The decision to move was a calculated trade-off, a survival strategy rather than an ideological or emotional decision. For the 98 percent of the enclave residents who did not move, the sense of stability and belonging in their current situation outweighed any potential benefits of moving to an unfamiliar country, even if it was officially their home country all along.

Making state space

Local administrators were given the responsibility of executing the exchange with the help of other government agencies such as the police, magistrates, and border guards, but the planning was done at the highest level of the administration. For the officials of the state, the challenge of the exchange revolved around questions of legibility (Scott 1998, 2009). The former enclaves of India and Bangladesh used to be the non-state spaces within a state space where these two modern states could not extend their control. Scott (1998) argues that a state's attempt to make a society legible includes steps such as taxation, conscription, and prevention of rebellion. Moreover, he clearly demonstrates how non-state spaces become a headache for the state since these can be a 'zone of refuge' where people who want to avoid the state can go to escape the ordering systems of the states (Scott 2009). The enclaves long served as such a refuge because the police and courts of the surrounding states did not have jurisdiction in the enclaves and some criminals used that protection to evade the laws of the state.

The process of turning these newly incorporated lands into legible state territories had been the primary task of government officials in the post-exchange period. For example, none of these enclaves had any formal documentation of land records. The documents they had were obsolete because they were issued by the British Empire, the other country across the border, or locally made in an attempt to document ownership. The Land Record Office of Bangladesh did not have any record of these lands. To make these territories legible, both states have to conduct surveys to document what is there and bring it into the administrative space of the state. An Assistant Judge in Panchagar district of Bangladesh described the challenges:

> I think, it would take some time to normalize the situation in the enclaves. They have been living there without any legal and formal support. As a judge, I am expecting a lot of legal issues regarding land. They do not have any legal documents of their lands except the locally made and managed stamps. It will take time to sort all these out… Moreover, these enclave dwellers have been involved with different illegal activities which now should be easy to control by the legal system. You know, when these were not under the control of the state of Bangladesh, we could not do anything formally, and they [the enclave dwellers] have taken that advantage.

A 55-year-old farmer in Garati enclave who decided to stay in Bangladesh expressed his concern when asked about anticipated life after the exchange:

> Ummm…yes. I think there will be different problems too. You know about our land registration system, right? We don't have any state document for our land. We buy and sell our land in our own stamps. Now, for example, there are lots of people from Bangladesh residing around the enclave have bought lands from us. Also, there have been instances where some people have copied a stamp and claimed a land that does not belong to him. Now to registrar the land, if these two parties file a case in the court, who do you think the court will decide for? …Again, take the example of police. They did not used to come to the enclave as this was not Bangladesh. Now, after the exchange, they will have no problem coming in here and arresting us.

While both the judge and the former enclave resident were expecting complexities regarding land registration, taxation, and ownership determination, there were different perspectives on the changing position of the enclaves as a zone of refuge.

Many government officials share the judge's view that these enclaves are breeding zones of crime such as smuggling, selling drugs, and offering refuge to criminals. Since these lands were out of the legal governance of the state, they became safe havens for criminals. However, now that the enclaves have been brought under the sovereignty of the state, the officials thought it would be easier for the state mechanism to govern them. By contrast, the enclave dweller is happy to be a citizen of the state because it will formalize his land registration, but at the same time he is worried about not being treated equally. He had concerns about being a victim of unnecessary hostility and injustice by the state now that the refuge was gone.

Conclusion: theorizing the exchange

The exchange itself opens up an interesting theoretical discussion in relation to the state's desire to hold territory. The persistent problem of exchanging the enclaves has been cited as an example of 'territory's continuing allure' (Murphy 2013) in which the desire to maintain control over land trumps almost any other consideration for the state, even when the state has never even had administrative control over the piece of territory. James Scott (1998, 2009) argues that a major problem of modern statecraft has been the need for legibility: to have calculable knowledge of the people, land, and resources that allowed a territory to be governed. States loathe to have non-state spaces within their jurisdiction, but in the case of the enclaves, neither India nor Bangladesh were keen to extend their control and govern the enclaves. Rather, both states were more interested in upholding these enclaves as symbols of their national integrity and holding onto them without even minimal control over them. As Jason Cons puts it, 'They are spaces that … the center thinks with intense passion, though not necessarily with great care' (Cons 2016: 21). Because of the 'intense passion' these enclaves became *amplified territories* which were transformed into territorial symbols irrespective of their size and strategic use (Cons 2016). In this context, particularly for India, holding onto these small pieces of land for decades was more important than extending control and administration over them.

Consequently, the fact that India and Bangladesh did eventually overcome this obstacle and exchanged the enclaves deserves particular scrutiny. For this, we turn to Evgeny Vinokurov's (2007) theory of enclaves and particularly the various relationships between the mainland, the enclave, and surrounding areas. Vinokurov (2007) argues that the nature of the enclave is determined by these different types of relations and typically the mainland–enclave relations are most significant. But in case of the India–Bangladesh enclaves, except Dahagram–Angorpota, none of the enclaves had any connection or relation with the mainland. Instead, daily life in the enclaves was mostly influenced and shaped by their relations with surrounding areas. Furthermore, they also became a significant pawn in negotiations between the two states that had little to do with the actual conditions in the enclaves. After the 2009 elections in India and Bangladesh, both the governments sowed interest in developing bilateral relations which included solving disputed borders and resolving trade relations. In the end—although there was constant pressure and protests from the enclave dwellers from both sides—the bilateral discussions between India and Bangladesh put very little weight on the conditions on the ground in the enclaves. Finally in 2015, a number of memorandums and protocols were signed between the two states which included Bangladesh sharing its sea port with India and allowing a road transit for Indian vehicles to pass through Bangladesh. Both of these were concessions on the part of Bangladesh and as an inducement India finally agreed to ratify the exchange agreement.

The exchange is both an end and a beginning. It marks the end of the unusual story of the enclaves, but it is only the beginning of the journey for enclave residents, who have to negotiate their new citizenship, and for state officials, who will work to bring the people and the land into the legibility regime of the state. While the exchange of the enclaves will solve many problems for both the former enclave residents and the states, the construction of infrastructure and the extension of the protections such as the citizenship to the former enclave residents will be a long term project on both sides of the border. The distinct geographical location, size, and population in each of the exchanged enclaves will require careful planning and individualized solutions. For now, the burdens of survival in a stateless enclave have been lifted, but much of the hard work of realizing the anticipated benefits of the exchange is still to come.

Acknowledgements

Azmeary would like to acknowledge the partial funding provided by the Graduate Student's Organization of UH Manoa and the East West Center that allowed him to conduct the field work. Also, he thanks Md. Shafiqul Islam and Mr Arifur Rahman for their support and hospitality.

Note

1 The second phase of reseach was conducted in the enclaves of Garati and Dohola Khagrabari under Debiganj subdistrict of Panchagar district. Debiganj subbsidtrict alone hosted 37 percent of the total enclave population in Bangladesh. Garati and Dohola Khagrabari enclaves were two of the biggest enclaves in size, respectively 4 and 11 km^2 (Whyte 2002). Also, they respectively hosted 125 and 255 residents who opted to move out from Bangladesh and settle in India (UNO Office Fieldwork 2015). All the respondents were selected purposively and interviews were recorded with a digital audio recorder with the consent of the interviewees. In the first group, he interviewed five adults from Dohola Khagrabarai and three adults from Garati enclave. In the second group, he interviewed five from Dohola Khagrabari enclave and in the third group he interviewed the Assistant Judge of Debiganj subdistrict and the Union Nirbahi Officer (UNO, the highest ranked administrative officer in a subdistrict).

References

Ali, A., 2015, 'India-Bangladesh land swap: Over 14,000 people await new identities, recognition', The Indian Express, 1 August.
Cons, J., 2014, 'Impasse and opportunity: Reframing postcolonial territory at the India Bangladesh border', South Asia Multidisciplinary Academic Journal, 10. doi:10.4000/samaj.3791
———, 2016, Sensitive spaces: Fragmented territory at the India-Bangladesh border, University of Washington Press, Seattle.
Ghosh, A., 2015, Chhitmahal: The defacto stateless of the Indo-Bangla border. Mahanirban Calcutta Research Group, Kolkata.
Jones, R., 2010, 'The border enclaves of India and Bangladesh: The forgotten lands', In A. C. Diener & J. Hagen (eds.), Borderlines and borderlands: Political oddities at the edge of the nation-state, pp. 15–32, Rowman & Littlefield Publishers, New York.
Lifshultz, L., 1979, Bangladesh: The unfinished revolution, Zed Press, London.
Ministry of External Affairs (MEA), Government of India, 2015, India and Bangladesh Land Boundary Agreement. Available at www.mea.gov.in/Uploads/PublicationDocs/24529_LBA_MEA_Booklet_final.pdf.
Murphy, A., 2013, 'Territory's continuing allure', Annals of the Association of American Geographers, 103, 1212–1226.
Rahman, M., 2015, '39,621 Indian-enclave people seek Bangladeshi citizenship', The New Age, 22 July.
Saha, A., 2011, 'Kolkatai Bangladeshi chhitmoholbashider shomabesh: Abilombe chitmohol binimoyer dabi' (Bangladeshi enclave dwellers meet at Kolkata: Demand immediate exchange of the enclaves). The Daily Prothom Alo, 22 August.
Samaddar, R., 1999, The marginal nation: Transborder migration from Bangladesh to West Bengal, University Press Limited, Dhaka.
Scott, J. C., 1998, Seeing like a state: How certain schemes to improve human conditions have failed, Yale University Press, New Haven, CT.
———, 2009, The art of not being governed: An anarchist history of upland Southeast Asia, Yale University Press, New Haven, CT.
Shewly, H. J., 2012, 'Life, the law and the politics of abandonment: Everyday geographies of the enclaves in India and Bangladesh', Durham University. Retrieved 28 November 2015, from http://etheses.dur.ac.uk/5898/.
———, 2013a, 'Abandoned spaces and bare life in the enclaves of the India-Bangladesh border', Political Geography, 32, 23–31.
———, 2013b, 'Sixty six years saga of Bengal boundary making: A historical expose of Bangladesh-India border', BIIS, 34(3), 205–219.

———, 2016, 'India and Bangladesh swap territory, citizens in landmark enclave exchange', Migration Information Source. Available at www.migrationpolicy.org/article/india-and-bangladesh-swap-territory-citizens-landmark-enclave-exchange.

The Daily Prothom Alo, 2011, 'Chitmohol binmoyer dabite Bharote nishprodip kormoshuchi' (Lights off in Indian enclaves in demand of enclave exchange), 13 September.

———, 2015, 'Shesh hochhe 41 bosorer opekkah' (41 years of wait is going to be over), 7 May.

———, 2015, 'Chitmohol bahsir jonno boraddo komalo Bharot sarkar' (The Indian government reduces budget for the enclave dwellers), 26 July.

The Daily Star, 2012, 'Enclave people call for hunger strike', 11 April.

———, 2015, 'Most opt to remain where they are', 17 July.

van Schendel, W., 2002, 'Stateless in South Asia: The making of the India-Bangladesh enclaves', The Journal of Asian Studies, 61(1), 115–147.

———, 2005, The Bengal borderland: Beyond state and nation in South Asia, Anthem Press, London.

Vinokurov, E., 2007, A theory of enclave, Lexington Books, Lanham, MD.

Whyte, B. R., 2002, Waiting for the esquimo: An historical documentary study on the Coochbehar enclaves of India and Bangladesh. School of Anthropology, Geography and Environmemntal Studies, University of Melbourne, Melbourne, Australia.

20

The backdoors of resistance

Identities in the Malay Peninsula's maritime borderlands

Maxime Boutry

Littorals: utter borderlands?

Since the late 1990s and through the 2000s, Asian borderland studies have been a fertile ground of developing "counter-history", exemplified by Winichakul (2003), van Schendel (2002), and Scott (2009). These works offer a perspective that reverses state-centric analyses of peripheries that often vehicle binomial relationships such as civilized vs. wild, sedentary vs. nomadic, or national ideology vs. ethnicity. However, most studies in this field deal with upland areas and turn a blind eye on the sea and its littorals. This current condition is due to at least two different reasons.

First, in the post-World War II era, defining nation states' borders represents a powerful claim over resources and people located in *territories* that in many cases used to escape state control on the one hand, and link different states on the other. In particular, the pre-World War II geopolitical situation in Southeast Asia (SEA) was based on tributes and multi-allegiance systems linking "tribal" areas with state ones. These areas also functioned as a link between different states, most notably through trade of valuable goods (Scott 2009: 330). The avoidance of the state (Scott 2009) in the Southeast Asian uplands relies primarily on their "remoteness": the difficulty of accessing the Zomia "region"[1] allowing societies to remain out of reach from the mainstream lowland civilizations, while developing distinctive ethnic features. From that perspective, littorals, on the contrary, have been easily accessible, apart from the noteworthy exception of deltas[2] and archipelagos[3] that offer insular mazes in which to hide. Besides, Scott (2009: xiv) acknowledges that the many sea-gypsy populations of insular SEA "are clearly a seagoing, archipelago-hopping variant of swiddeners dwelling in mountain fastnesses", and here we may add that not only those, but many littoral societies may escape state control, but also dominant cultural models. Indeed, the second, often unspoken reason for downplaying the importance of littorals in the production of resisters and ethnicity is that in most Asian cultures – and interestingly in Western ones as well – the sea is seen as a frontier separating the world of humans from non-humans (Geistdoerfer 2004). Littorals are in this sense a cultural borderland as such, for the mainstream SEA lowland societies and their scholars alike.

Since the institutionalization of international borders and borderlands in the modern context of sovereign nation states (Paasi 1999), a question arises whether there is any space left to resist the state at the margins of SEA. Uplands have been "pacified" and are being "developed" through drug eradication and crop substitution programmes (Goudineau and Vienne 2001) and anti-communist wars (Lohmann 1993). Upland societies, although resisting integration in many instances (Bourdier et al. 2015), are progressively subjected to state intervention.

In this context, this chapter aims to show that littorals – and the closely associated action of proceeding to the sea – can be seen as increasingly important places of resistance against the state, along with ethnic genesis. Indeed, finding a space of cultural expression and socioeconomic reproduction on littorals often entails the re-processing of identity especially for mainland SEA societies for whom the marine environment represents a cultural border. This idea is further developed moving from the example of Bamar[4] fishermen who came to settle in the Myeik Archipelago[5] stretching along the eastern coast of the Andaman Sea in Southern Myanmar. While borderlands have already been described as places of continuous ethnic genesis (Scott 2009; Bourdier et al. 2015), this chapter emphasizes in particular the concept of "positionality" in analysing the socio-political hierarchy that structures interactions between different populations in the borderlands.[6] I explore this idea through the dynamics of migrant labour management in the Southern Myanmar–Thai borderland. Finally, I look to the case of the Rohingya[7] people whose migration lead them to the Malay Peninsula. I argue that to be true "resisters", littorals and the sea have to be an integral part of identity building, enabling populations to construct a positionality vis-à-vis the state, otherwise they incur the risk of becoming modern state "slaves".

The Myeik Archipelago: from buffer zone to borderland

The Tenasserim region (including South Myanmar and South Thailand littorals), to which the Myeik Archipelago belongs, makes the case of a "watery Zomia" (Scott 2009: xiv). Geographically, ecologically (White 1922), and culturally speaking it is best defined as a transition between insular and continental SEA. Historically, even if the Tenasserim region was successively claimed and conquered by both the Thai (Siam) and Burmese kingdoms, it was never a place that attained actual integration within these "states", but rather represented a buffer zone between them – a theatre of regular plunder for military enlistment, and a resource for recruiting a workforce to serve the surrounding agrarian monarchies.[8] The archipelago itself, a maze of hundreds of islands and islets, served as a refuge for Malay "pirates" (Warren 2002), but the only long-term inhabitants found there are the Moken, sea nomads representing the northernmost edge of Austronesian migrations (Ivanoff 2004). While their presence in the Myeik Archipelago can be traced back to the 17th century, their founding myth clearly links the Moken identity to the flight from lowlands' paddy cultivator societies, Islam, and slave raids perpetuated by the Malays in order to farm their sparsely populated land (Ivanoff 2004: 97; Scott 2009: 49). While Boutry et al. (2015; Ivanoff this volume, Chapter 21) already provided countless similarities between Moken – and most Austronesian Sea people – and any other "anarchic" society of the Southeast Asian Massif, the Myeik Archipelago's function as an escape from state domination does not end, as Scott (2009: xii) suggests about Zomia, with World War II. The border between Burma (later Myanmar) and Siam (later Thailand), was drawn up by the British in the middle of the 19th century (Winichakul 1994), but became an administrative reality only after independence, and only really took effect once the Burmese military seized power in 1962. Even then the border remained very porous, and population movement and economic exchange between the two countries remained fairly unrestricted until the 1990s. It was not until then that a real enforcement of the administrative border took shape, transforming what used to be unrestricted, local trade into more formalized international trade between the two countries. This move also induced Myanmar's development of marine fisheries, a sector previously led by Thailand.[9] The archipelago then became an "economic haven" for the Burmese. Dozens of Karen, another ethnic group of Myanmar, already participated in the development of compressor-diving fishing activities, competing with the Moken for similar resources: sea cucumbers, mother of pearl, and later lobsters. Together with a developing Burmese fishing industry, it led to the depletion of resources usually traded by the Moken. Through the 1980s and 1990s, the Moken took their turn at compressor-diving fishing, a dangerous activity (often leading to lethal decompression sickness) and where drug addiction is almost compulsory.[10] It resulted in a deficit of Moken men, which in turn led a number of Moken women to marry Bamar men.[11] Indeed, a massive migration of hundreds and then thousands of Burmese (mostly Bamar, but also Mon and Karen) fleeing the political and economic crisis in Myanmar has taken place since 1988 (Bourdier et al. 2015). A large number of students crossed the border to Ranong to take refuge in Thailand in the wake of the 1988 repressions. The Tenasserim and the hundreds of islands of the Myeik Archipelago in particular, far from the grip of the central state, were appropriate places to hide and full of resources to exploit. This period also sees the transformation of the Tenasserim region from a buffer zone between Myanmar and Thailand into a borderland, through complementary policies aiming at a better control of resources and people on the Myanmar and Thai sides. From 1988 to 1991, the Thai prime minister adopted a new political orientation toward Myanmar (Chachavalpongpun 2005: 65). It favoured loose forms of control over the border, since the Myanmar government was in negotiation with its Thai counterpart to profit from this resource-laden region. On the one hand, it helped to settle Myanmar's internal political matters. For instance, some Myanmar students who fled to southern Thailand after taking part in the 1988 demonstrations were "traded" by Thai officials in order to obtain marine concessions in the Myeik Archipelago. On the other hand, the economic opening led by General Khin Nyunt resulted in the privatization of fisheries in Myanmar, in order to foster this sector nationally and provide the government with a secure share[12] of the archipelago's resources, mostly fished by Thai fleets until this period. Although these measures effectively led to the development of the Myanmar fleet operating from the littoral (principally Dawei, Myeik, and later Kawthaung ports) and a market (with ice factories and fish export companies) operating through the Thai–Myanmar border, the islands remained far from any administrative control. There, an insular Burmese society could blossom, just as the Moken developed their nomadic identity when they reached the Myeik Archipelago.

The Burmese insular society: between social segmentation and ethnic creation

Evading the state is as much a choice as a response to a particular context, yet such choice comes with a "price". Some of the Burmese living in the islands often say: "we have a debt toward the Moken from a previous life, that is why we are here". Even without more elaboration, these words set the beginning of a differentiation, a rationale for having embraced a way of life that is the exact opposite of the Bamar sedentary, cultural ideal. Through the 1990s, some Burmese pioneers (mostly Bamar) ventured into the islands, taking on the role of the Moken flotillas' intermediaries (*tokè*[13]) both to exchange their valuable products (particularly sea cucumbers) and to develop island-based fishing activities of their own. On their journey with the nomads, they learned the waves, the places to hide from both pirates and militaries (Boutry 2015a), where to find fresh water, currents, how to read the sky's colours to forecast weather, and so on. They also developed a symbolic world of their own, imprinted by Moken mermaids, populated by "water-ghosts" (*yei thaye*) and marine "witches" (*pinle son*) (Boutry 2015a). When the mixed Moken–Bamar communities finally settled into permanent villages, the first mixed race children were born, eventually creating a new Bamar-Moken (*bama-hsaloun"*) category of "race" in the local census along with Bamar and Moken households. Although penetration of the state in the islands (through administrative authorities) and the *burmanization* of this 'territory' (Boutry 2015b) seemed inevitable, a new society of "Sons of the Islands" (*kyun" tha"*), as insular Bamar identify themselves, was born. Eventually, these Burmese pioneers, by protecting their own niche built on ethnic interactions, that is, their "debt" towards the Moken, hence protecting their space of resistance, also shelter the Moken from a mainstream *burmanization* process.

Identities, exclusiveness, and inclusiveness in the development of South Thailand

Although the purpose of this chapter is not to discuss the validity of Scott's theory about Zomia, looking at littoral borderlands as long-lasting places of resistance brings us to this critique:

> "It's too easy for [Scott] to say that his argument doesn't apply to the 20th and 21st centuries," [Clunan] says, "because if it did, it would incorporate a whole bunch of pretty nasty actors," among them insurgents, human traffickers, and terrorists.
>
> *(Hammond 2011)*

Yet, it is this very dimension of "contemporary Zomia(s)" that is of interest to us, especially when dealing with Burmese migration into Southern Thailand. The organization of labour and human trafficking networks across the Myanmar–Thailand–Malaysia borderlands is not a chaotic social space. On the contrary, ethnic and sociocultural belongings structure the dynamics of inclusion and exclusion regarding migrants' access to labour opportunities, their involvement in traffickers' networks, and "security" vis-à-vis the state.

The economy of Southern Thailand has been developed essentially by migrants. Successive waves of migration (Chinese, Isaarn from Northeastern Thailand, and finally Burmese) are related to the exploitation of different types of resources: tin, then rubber, and later fisheries (Fournier 1983). The enforcement of the Myanmar–Thailand border throughout the 1990s had two paradoxical consequences on the Thai side. Until the 1980s, crossing the border was easy, allowing economic exchange and the existence of a pool of labour for seasonal work in Thailand. Although mobility was greater, the flux of migrant workers was less than it is at present. The reinforcement of the border accelerated different levels of economic development in the region between Myanmar and Thailand. Former transborder workers were forced to settle permanently on the Thai side if they wanted to continue working in Thai industries. In addition, the fisheries sector in Thailand was still developing in the 1990s, requiring increasing amounts of cheap labour. The Thais do not belong to a seafaring culture, leaving an unoccupied economic niche for migrant workers. Indeed, in Thailand, immigrants (mainly from Myanmar and Cambodia) represent 90 per cent of the maritime industry (UNDCP et al. 1997: 36). The Bamar, who had already developed their maritime culture through the colonization of Tenasserim and the Myeik Archipelago, went to occupy the economic niche of Southern Thailand's fishing industry. Thus, the administrative border stimulated Burmese migration into Southern Thailand, and led to interactions with the regional pattern of social, cultural, and ethnic relationships at the Malay Peninsula.

Within the ethnic pattern of the Malay Peninsula, defined by the shaping of interethnic relations in its politico-religious organization (Ivanoff 2011), the Burmese (*Phamar* in Thai) became an ill-defined ethnic group. One could even state that the use of the appellation *Phamar* can be considered as an exonym to encompass the interlocking of ethnic, geographic, and social boundaries constituting an "intermediary social space" (Ivanoff 2010). For instance, the increasing role that some Bamar (mostly of Dawei origin) of Southern Thailand take in the yearly tenth month ceremony (*ngan bun duean sip* in Thai), reveals their pursuit of a possible integration within the ethnic framework of the region. The tenth month ceremony recalls the complex links between minorities (sea nomads) and recently arrived dominant groups (Thai, Chinese, and Malay) and is one of the region's main expressions of "ethno-regionalism" (Ferrari 2012). Some Burmese migrants participating in the ceremony take on the same role as the sea nomads, receiving gifts from the dominant population, while others declare commonality with the dominant groups and donate to the nomads. Although the implications of the Burmese role in this ritual remains to be studied more thoroughly, it already emphasizes their quest for a "positionality" (Scott 2009: 261) vis-à-vis the dominant populations and the state. This positionality is not a "given", but is shaped by claims and attributions that individuals make about their position in the social order of things, their views of where and to what they belong (and do not belong), as well as an understanding of the broader social relations that constitute and are constituted in this process (Anthias 2002). Positionality is notably achieved by building a conjunction of ecological and occupational niches and ethnic boundaries (Godelier 2007: 37; Scott 2009: 261) differentiating, identifying, and situating the different Myanmar populations of Southern Thailand among the complex ethnic diversity of the region.[14] Indeed, within the Southern Thai borderland, the Burmese migrants organize access to resources and society through different categorizations, recreating hierarchies from mixed ethnic and social origins. Their position in this socioethnic hierarchy defines their capacity to defy national territories and their boundaries (inclusion in borderland's livelihoods) or to fall to the lowest strata of statehood, that is, modern slavery through exploitation orchestrated by traffickers *and* the state (Boutry et al. 2017).

The local expression of Myanmar's centre–peripheries relationships in the Malay Peninsula borderland

Many Thai–Burmese (mostly *Bamar* of Dawei origin) middlemen doing transborder business have both Thai and Myanmar identity cards (Bourdier et al. 2015), as do people in communities living on both sides of the Thai–Malay border (Horstmann 2002). As these populations became de facto borderlanders through the course of the 20th century, dual citizenship became an endemic part of their "post-national belonging" (Horstmann 2002). However, the enforcement of mutually exclusive national borders also propelled the development of borderland economies, the "capital" of which is migrants (Boutry and Ivanoff 2009). Much like the "manpower-starved states of mainland Southeast Asia" in pre-modern times (Scott 2009: 336), contemporary nation states still need cheap, often illegal, labour, both to control and develop their borderlands and the state's economy. From rubber plantations to fisheries and construction work, Myanmar migrants represent the main resource for the development of Southern Thailand. However, access to borderland's livelihoods depends much on a hierarchy imposed by the reshaping and segmentation of identities among the different ethnic and regional groups of Myanmar's migrants across the border. The concept of "translocational positionality" (Anthias 2008) is helpful in considering how the imposition of a national border impacts on migrants' identities. Translocational positionality "addresses issues of identity in terms of locations which are not fixed but are context, meaning and time related and which therefore involve shifts and contradictions" (Anthias 2008: 5). For instance, for Mon migrants coming from Myanmar, the administrative border, instead of being restrictive, embodies a cultural interface with the Thais. The Mon are considered by the Myanmar government to be an ethnic minority who thus have a lower status in the explicitly stated ethnic hierarchy of the state (where Bamar ethnicity is placed above all), and this has been accompanied by decades of oppression from the central government (South 2003). However, the

Mon from Myanmar identify themselves as ethnically closer to the Thai who, in return, consider them closer than the Bamar for historical and cultural reasons.[15] As a direct socioeconomic consequence, Thai patrons trust Mon migrants more than those of a different ethnic background so that in the fishing industry they win the envied position of foreman and are in control of the Bamar crew (their salary, behaviour on board, and employment). The relationship between centre (Bamar) and periphery (ethnic minorities) prevailing in Myanmar is thus reversed, as Mon often act as smugglers (*pueza*) and recruiters for Bamar trafficked on fishing boats. The latter may stay months or years at sea, sold from one boat to another, and often dying at sea in tragic circumstances (Boutry and Ivanoff 2009). A different transborder population consists of the Bamar coming from Dawei (identified as Tavoyans in colonial literature), who mostly migrate to Ranong and other fishing ports in the south. Coming from the south of Myanmar, they distinguish themselves by their singular dialect (mostly incomprehensible to the Bamar from the centre of the country) and their skilled fishing practices. This particularity "naturally" pushes them along migration routes leading to the fishing ports of Thailand (see Map 20.1). Their predominance among the fishing crews (under the supervision of Mon foremen) is the product of an identity built upon their mastery of the sea, itself matching an economic niche within the borderland's economy. The same particularity situates them at the fringes of the historical construction of a Bamar identity where the sea is seen as a cultural as much as a physical border. Dawei people's affinity to the sea, which may put them at the lowest level of Myanmar social hierarchy, proves to be an asset when they settle in Thailand. Many of them, at least in the main 'Burmanized' border town of Ranong, have married other migrants, giving birth to a new generation of Thai-born children that the local Thai government cannot ignore, torn between the desire to refuse the integration of Burmese children, the necessity to inculcate them with "moral values", and the still growing demand for cheap, illegal labour.

To summarize, the difference between national (Bamar migrants from the centre of Myanmar) and transborder belongings (Mon and Dawei migrants) frame access to the borderland's livelihoods. The Mon, an oppressed minority in Myanmar, and the Dawei people find a way to escape a state-shaped oppression in the economy of the borderland. The Mon and the Dawei people are even able to bend the Thai state's policies to their benefit, acquiring greater security through gaining some rights such as schooling. On the other hand, the Bamar coming from the centre of Myanmar find themselves trapped in modern slavery fuelled by the need for a cheap workforce – with men mostly trafficked onto fishing boats and women for prostitution (Boutry and Ivanoff 2009) – even though the Thai government has taken new measures to tackle the problem since 2014 (Marschke and Vandergeest 2016). The affinity to the borderland – hence the capacity to resist the state – is itself greatly shaped by the affinity developed through history between these different categories of migrants and the sea. Both Mon and Dawei are sea-faring people, building a positionality linked to the sea that, in Southern Thailand's economy which greatly depends on fisheries, enables them to exploit an economic and cultural niche at the margins of continental Southeast Asia's states.

Rohingya: an attempt to internationalize borderlands and ethnicity by sea

In the terms presented above, the characteristics of "Zomia" as a place of resistance relate less to the geographical features (remoteness) of a particular zone, than to the capacity the population has in constructing an identity that relies on ecological and occupational "niches" and is structured on the relationship with surrounding populations and ethnicities. The case of the Muslim community of Arakan, now internationally known as Rohingya, helps to better understand the

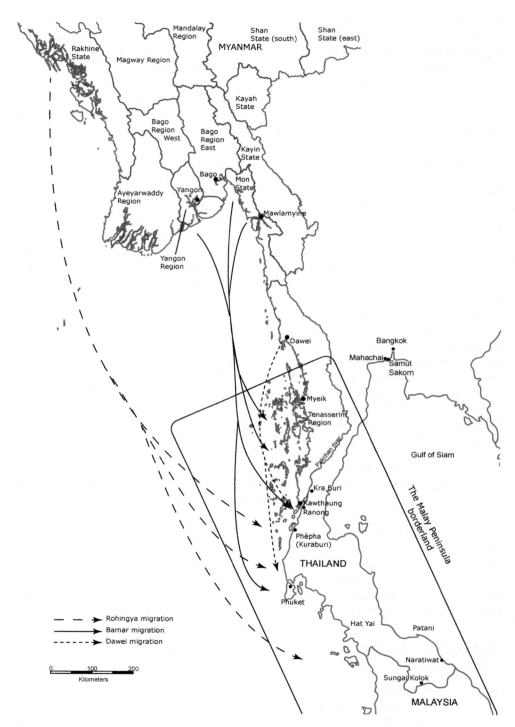

Map 20.1 Burmese migrations to the Malay Peninsula
Map by Maxime Boutry 2017

necessity to articulate together these three dimensions (identity, ecological-occupational niche, and integration in a multi-ethnic construct) in the process of identity construction.

While the historical legitimacy of the term Rohingya is debatable, the fact that it became an ethnic claim for the Muslim community of Arakan within the Myanmar borders is now a reality. It is, however, necessary to better understand the ground on which this claim is acknowledged and spread. One important thing to underline is the shift initiated by the communal unrest in 2012 between Rakhine Buddhists and Muslims of Arakan. While before most of the Muslims living in Arakan made little use of the term Rohingya to identify themselves,[16] the author witnessed its wide use from 2012 onward – from intellectuals and farmers alike. The massive exodus of Muslims from Arakan took a new shape in the late 1990s and throughout the 2000s, following the interdiction of travelling in Myanmar outside Arakan and greater control of the border with adjacent Bangladesh. Taking to the sea became the main route for escaping the Myanmar state, where the Rohingya are "stateless".

A search in English on scholarly databases[17] shows no articles until 2008 (whether from the general or scientific press) associating in its title the words "Rohingya" and "stateless". From 2009 onwards, however, the same query produces more than 300 results. This clearly denotes a shift in representations from the international community that followed the massive exodus by sea of Muslims from Myanmar, revealed in 2009. Their citizenship – and more precisely their lack of citizenship – had not in fact changed since the 1970s. What actually changed is the Arakan Muslim's pattern of migration. First bouncing back and forth between Myanmar and Bangladesh (Loescher 2001), the closing of the national borders led them to seek new ways to escape, mostly by sea. The status of "statelessness" became an identity marker for international watchers. "Living at sea" is not a form of statehood in any way, but rather living in an "empty space", a watery Zomia. It is since this shift of migration pattern that the sea became part of an *exogenous* process of ethnogenesis. Indeed, Leider (2016) underlined the competing narratives between Rohingya activists instilling a positivist discourse in the historical legitimacy of Rohingya identity in Arakan and, on the contrary, the international recognition of Rohingya ethnicity which is based on oppression by the Myanmar state and their quality as victims. As explained above, the emigration pattern taking sea routes has greatly contributed to this international, exogenous identity creation of the Rohingya. But, contrarily to the populations of the Malay Peninsula described earlier, the Rohingya's relationship to the sea in this case is not part of an identity creation process that builds upon the occupation of an economic or cultural niche.

"Statelessness" vs. positionality? The eternal fight for freedom in the Malay Peninsula borderland

Most Rohingya, to be sure, may end their journey by sea in the hands of Thai smugglers (Oh 2013) in the Malay Peninsula borderland described throughout this chapter. These smugglers and traffickers are indeed part of the new resisters – as suggested by Clunan (Hammond 2011) – actually working with the state's apparatus.[18]

In the contemporary international framework where all land, resources, and population have been integrated into national territories, "statelessness" may seem to describe "resisters" to the state. This chapter argues that this is not necessarily the case. Actual statelessness and resistance do not necessarily pertain to the lack of citizenship. Examples throughout this chapter show that borderlanders often hold dual citizenship. On the contrary, statelessness becomes the trigger for bringing populations into the state's framework and threatens these resisters and their identities. Because Moken are "stateless at sea", they are subsequently perceived as "vulnerable" (Chambless 2015: 5–6) and in need for integration by the state. The Thai government attempted to address the issue of illegal Myanmar migrants to Thailand through different policies, for example, by implementing a Memorandum of Understanding with bordering countries. However, the relative success of legalization not only underlines a cumbersome and sometimes expensive process, but also a form of resistance from migrants willing to retain mobility and flexibility for employment opportunities (Carden 2014: 56). It also reveals the nature of borderlands' economy that develops based upon informality and mobility, as in the case of the fishing sector. One may argue that the international conceptualization of statelessness concerning the Rohingya brought their "case" to more recognition. Nonetheless, it did very little, or rather nothing, to improve the situation in Arakan,[19] but merely reinforced their exogenous status in the eyes of the Myanmar population. Indeed, amidst strong criticism by Rohingya activists, the cartoon published in the Irrawaddy magazine depicting them through an individual wearing a sign "boat-people" hanging on his back and cutting in front of a queue of Myanmar ethnic minority groups[20] exemplifies this representation.

Resistance is a matter of identity creation resulting in a positionality vis-à-vis the modern states that are, to a great extent, the result of hegemonic claims by dominant populations over a territory – for instance the Bamar in Myanmar and the central Thai populations in Thailand. Such positionality implies a relationship, hence a kind of continuity, between these populations and the centres (Bourdier et al. 2015). On the contrary, "statelessness" is only the expression of a kind of exclusion that makes the Rohingya easier prey for traffickers. Sea-oriented livelihoods and identity processing (translocational positionality) provide populations of the Malay Peninsula with means to occupy an "empty space" with little interference from modern states. These resisters' positionality is nonetheless negotiated at the margins of the states for whom they help by feeding the labour-starved dominant economies.

Notes

1. Scott (2009: ix) identifies Zomia as "the largest remaining region of the world whose peoples have not yet been fully incorporated into nation-states". Though the scholars who have imagined Zomia – Zomia is a geographical term coined first by van Schendel (2002) – differ over its precise boundaries, Scott includes all the lands at altitudes above 300 metres stretching from the Central Highlands of Vietnam to northeastern India.
2. See, for example, the Baga in the mangroves of the coastal region of Republic of Guinea.
3. The Myeik Archipelago, stretched across south Myanmar and South Thailand, is where Moken hid from Malay slave raids.
4. Throughout this chapter, "Bamar" refers to the ethnic majority population (*bha-ma*) of Myanmar, itself composed of many ethnic groups. Burmese is used as a generic term to designate Myanmar citizens as a whole.
5. Building on the author's PhD thesis fieldwork between 2003 and 2007, followed by yearly visits to the region.
6. Based on a study by the author and Jacques Ivanoff of human trafficking networks in South Thailand in 2008–2009 (see Boutry and Ivanoff 2009).
7. Based on fieldwork in Sittwe, Maungtaw, and Buthidaung townships of Rakhine in 2013 and 2014.
8. See Labbé (1985), Reid (1988), and Ivanoff (2004).
9. Until the 1990s, the Myanmar government had little control of its resources-laden southern sea. Following the privatization of fisheries in 1994 and the enforcement of the Myanmar–Thai maritime border, the entry of foreign vessels into Myanmar's waters was closely monitored and traded through licences issued by the Myanmar government. From that time, Myanmar-based fishing companies (often supported by Thai and Singaporean interests) started to operate from the Tenasserim littoral.
10. Patrons of compressor-diving fishing provide drugs to the divers to bond them, but also to make the Karen and Burmese overcome their fear of the underwater world which is closely associated with dangerous mythical figures.
11. The Moken, due to their small number (about 3,000 individuals in the archipelago), have long tolerated marriages with outsiders as necessary for the renewal of their population. Traditionally, the most

northerly and southerly subgroups are the first subjects of inter-ethnic marriage, the rule of exogamy being moderated by the prohibition of marrying into too distant subgroups (Ivanoff 2004).

12 Fisheries is a sector that in most cases, as seen throughout the world, can hardly be handled by the public sector, for its particularity, unlike most production, is that the ownership and increase of means of production do not necessarily equal to increased production, notably due to the underwater resource's invisibility and mobility (Geistdoerfer, 1997). For these reasons, the Myanmar government opted for the privatization of fisheries and a tax of 10 per cent on exports.
13 *Tòkè* is a term of Chinese origin employed from south Myanmar to Indonesia, including Thailand and Malaysia, which designates a patron–entrepreneur. Traditionally, the *tòkè* has been central to the preservation of the Moken nomadic way of life. The relationship between the *tòkè* and his Moken group lies in the necessity of the nomads to acquire rice, the staple food and the paradox of an insular population that only cultivates the cereal for ritual.
14 It reminds us of the Burmese living in the islands of the Myeik Archipelago, whose positionality can be found in the ecological and economical niche developed together with the Moken, giving rise to the *kyun" tha"* (Sons of the Islands) identity.
15 Notably, the Mon fled the Burmese kingdoms in the late 18th and 19th centuries to Siam where they sought refuge and even obtained positions of high rank within the Siamese administration.
16 See, for example, Tréhondart (2002).
17 See: http://biblioshs.inist.fr (regrouping different databases such as JSTOR) consulted on 25 June 2016.
18 See, for example, Boutry and Ivanoff (2009) as well as Szep and Grudgings (2013).
19 More than 100,000 Muslims are still living in camps with no or little possibility of wandering outside.
20 See: https://asiancorrespondent.com/2016/05/offensive-boat-people-magazine-cartoon-slammed-rohingya-activist-dangerous/, consulted 25 June 2016.

References

Anthias, F. (2002), "Where Do I Belong?: Narrating Collective Identity and Translocational Positionality", *Ethnicities*, Vol. 2, No. 4, pp. 491–514.
Anthias, F. (2008), "Thinking through the Lens of Translocational Positionality: An Intersectionality Frame for Understanding Identity and Belonging", *Translocations: Migration and Social Change*, Vol. 4, No. 1, pp. 5–20.
Bourdier, F., Boutry, M., Ferrari, O. and Ivanoff, J. (2015), *From Padi States to Commercial States: Reflections on Identity and the Social Construction of Space in the Borderlands of Cambodia, Vietnam, Thailand and Myanmar*, Amsterdam University Press, Amsterdam.
Boutry, M. (2015a), *Trajectoires Littorales de L'hégémonie Birmane (Irrawaddy, Tenasserim, Sud Thaïlande)*, IRASEC/Les Indes Savantes, Paris.
Boutry, M. (2015b), "How far from national identity? Dealing with the concealed diversity of Myanmar", in Robinne, F. and Egreteau, R. (Eds.), *Metamorphosis: Studies in Social and Political Change in Myanmar*, NUS Press, Singapore, pp. 103–126.
Boutry, M. and Ivanoff, J. (2009), *La Monnaie Des Frontières: Migration Birmanes Dans Le Sud de La Thaïlande, Réseaux et Internationalisation Des Frontières*, IRASEC, Bangkok.
Boutry, M., Ivanoff, J. and Chantavanich, S. (2017), "L'esclavage en Asie du Sud-Est ; une vielle histoire. Adaptation et résiliences des pratiques esclavagistes en Thaïlande et en Birmanie", *Anthropologie et Sociétés*, Vol. 41, No. 1, pp. 29–49.
Carden, R. J. (2014), *Smuggling of Female Migrant Workers from Myanmar to Thailand*, Degree of Master of Arts in International Development Studies, Chulalongkorn University, Bangkok.
Chachavalpongpun, P. (2005), *A Plastic Nation. The Curse of Thainess in Thai-Burmese Relations*, University Press of America, Lanham, MD.
Chambless, D. (2015), *Stateless at Sea: The Moken of Burma and Thailand*, Human Rights Watch, New York.
Ferrari, O. (2012), "Duean sip, théâtre de l'ethnorégionalisme Sud. Les nomades de la mer et le cycle rituel du dixième mois dans la province de Phang Nga (Sud de la Thaïlande)", *Moussons, Recherche En Sciences Humaines Sur l'Asie Du Sud-Est*, Vol. 20, pp. 101–120.
Fournier, J.-B. (1983), "Le Sud péninsulaire de la Thaïlande. 'Pak Tai': la terre entre les deux mers", *ASEMI (Asie Du Sud-Est et Monde Insulindien)*, Vol. 14, No. 3–4, pp. 29–46.
Geistdoerfer, A. (1997), "La mer coule dans leurs veines. Les marins pêcheurs, de la race des insoumis", *Bulletin de Psychologie*, Vol. 50, No. 432, pp. 651–668.
Geistdoerfer, A. (2004), "De l'origine des marins. La genèse mythique d'une spécialisation technique", *Techniques et Culture*, Vol. 43–44, pp. 217–234.

Godelier, M. (2007), *Au Fondement Des Sociétés Humaines: Ce Que Nous Apprend L'anthropologie/Maurice Godelier*, Albin Michel, Paris.

Goudineau, Y. and Vienne, B. (2001), "L' Etat et les minorités ethniques: la place des populations montagnardes (chao Khao) dans l'espace national", in Dovert, S. (Ed.), *Thaïlande contemporaine*, L'Harmattan, Paris, pp. 143–172.

Hammond, R. (2011), "The battle over Zomia", *The Chronicle Review*, available at: chronicle.com/article/The-Battle-Over-Zomia/128845/ (accessed 19 August 2012).

Horstmann, A. (2002), "Dual ethnic minorities and the local reworking of citizenship at the Thailand-Malaysian border", CIBR Working Papers in Border Studies, available at: www.qub.ac.uk/research-centres/CentreforInternationalBordersResearch/Publications/WorkingPapers/CIBRWorkingPapers/Filetoupload,174412,en.pdf (accessed 4 August 2016).

Ivanoff, J. (2004), *Les Naufragés de l'Histoire. Les Jalons épiques de L'identité Moken*, Les Indes savantes, Paris.

Ivanoff, J. (2010), *The Cultural Roots of Violence in Malay Southern Thailand: Comparative Mythology: Soul of Rice*, Vol. 1, White Lotus Press, Bangkok.

Ivanoff, J. (2011), "Une modernisation sans développement. Construction ethnique et ethnorégionalisme en Thaïlande", in Dovert, S. and Ivanoff, J. (Eds.), *Thaïlande Contemporaine*, Les Indes Savantes/IRASEC, Bangkok, pp. 473–516.

Labbé, A. J. (1985), *Ban Chiang: Art and Prehistory of Northeast Thailand*, Bowers Museum, Santa Ana, CA.

Leider, J. (2016), "Competing identities and the hybridized history of the Rohingyas", in Egreteau, R. and Robinne, F. (Eds.), *Metamorphosis: Studies in Social and Political Change in Myanmar*, NUS Press in association with IRASEC, Singapore, pp. 151–178.

Loescher, G. (2001), "The UNHCR and World Politics: State Interests vs. Institutional Autonomy", *International Migration Review*, Spring, pp. 33–56.

Lohmann, L. (1993), "Land, Power and Forest Colonization in Thailand", *Global Ecology and Biogeography Letters*, Vol. 3, No. 4/6, pp. 180–191.

Marschke, M. and Vandergeest, P. (2016), "Slavery Scandals: Unpacking Labour Challenges and Policy Responses Within the Off-shore Fisheries Sector", *Marine Policy*, Vol. 68, pp. 39–46.

Oh, S.-A. (2013), *Rohingya Boat Arrivals in Thailand: From the Frying Pan into the Fire*, ISEAS Publishing, Singapore.

Paasi, A. (1999), "The political geography of boundaries at the end of the millennium: Challenges of the de-territorializing world", in Eskelinen, H., Liikanen, I., and Oksa, J. (Eds.), *Curtains of Iron and Gold: Reconstructing Borders and Scales of Interaction*, Ashgate, Aldershot, pp. 9–24.

Reid, A. (1988), *Southeast Asia in the Age of Commerce, 1450–1680*, Vol. 1, Yale University Press, New Haven, CT.

Scott, J. C. (2009), *The Art of Not Being Governed: An Anarchist History of Upland Southeast Asia*, Yale University Press, New Haven, CT.

South, A. (2003), *Mon Nationalism and Civil War in Burma: The Golden Sheldrake*, Routledge Curzon, New York.

Szep, J. and Grudgings, S. (2013), "Authorities implicated in Rohingya smuggling networks", *Reuters*, p. 11.

Tréhondart, A. (2002), *Enquête Socio-économique Au North Rakhine State*, Unpublished report, GRET, p. 73.

UNDCP, Thailand Seafarers Research Team and Ministry of Public Health. (1997), *Rapid Assessment of Seafarers in Cambodia, Myanmar, Thailand and Vietnam. A Sub-National Study: Profiling the Maritime Industry and Responses to HIV and Drug Use among Seafarers in Ranong, Thailand*, Bangkok.

van Schendel, W. (2002), "Geographies of Knowing, Geographies of Ignorance: Jumping Scale in Southeast Asia", *Environment and Planning. D, Society & Space*, Vol. 20, pp. 647–668.

Warren, J. F. (2002), *Iranun and Balangingi: Globalization, Maritime Raiding and the Birth of Ethnicity*, Singapore University Press, Singapore.

White, W. G. (1922), *The Sea Gypsies of Malaya; an Account of the Nomadic Mawken People of the Mergui Archipelago with a Description of Their Ways of Living, Customs, Habits, Boats, Occupations, Etc. ...*, Seeley, Service & Co., London.

Winichakul, T. (1994), *Siam Mapped a History of the Geo-Body of a Nation*, University of Hawaii Press, Honolulu.

Winichakul, T. (2003), "Writing at the interstices. Southeast Asian hisorians and postnational histories in Southeast Asia", in Ahmad, A. T. and Tan, L. E (Eds.), *New Terrains in Southeast Asian History*, Singapore University Press, Singapore, pp. 3–29.

21

Ethnic reconstruction and Austronesian strategies at the borders

The Moken social space in Burma

Jacques Ivanoff

Borderlands or maritime Zomia?

The Moken, sea nomads living mostly in the Burmese part of the Mergui Archipelago, have been moving up the western coast of the Malay Peninsula since the 16th century, leaving the Moklen behind them in Thailand.[1] They have crossed the borders of Indonesia, Singapore, Malaysia, Thailand, and Myanmar. While it can be argued that the region's borders were more porous in the past than they are today, as the most widely adopted socio-political system was traditionally based on the mandala model (Hall 1968), these nomads, importantly, had to cross cultural borders (i.e. Islam and Buddhism) and thus developed relevant strategies.

Sea nomads tend to adapt to the different environments they encounter, as the Moklen have done in the mangroves, the Orang Kuala ("men of the estuaries") along the mouth of the rivers of Malaysia, the Urak Lawoi ("men of the sea" in their language) on the islands of Thailand, and the Moken throughout the Burmese Mergui Archipelago. They encounter the peoples of the "centres" by trading sea and forest products, while trying to maintain their lifestyle and practices. Their engagement in trading activities is under the domination of the *taukay* (trading middleman), resulting in unequal forms of exchange, as the nomads become indebted in exchanges for protection, rice, clothing, motors, and petrol. However, this practice creates a point of contact with the wider world and guarantees their own survival. The coastline is woven together with these cross-border nomad groups, each linked to the other, with the Moken representing the apex of a wider nomadic culture. The *kabang*, the Moken boat, is their flagship item.

Up until the 1980s, the Moken considered the 800 islands of the Mergui Archipelago as the "natural" territory of their nomadic livelihood. This archipelagic Eldorado permitted the distribution of gathering areas where Moken collect food on the strand or seashells in the sea between five mother islands (in Moken: Chadiak, Nyawi, Lebi, Jait, and Dung; see, e.g. Map 21.1). Each island community of the Moken can be divided into flotillas: 7 to 10 boats collect various products (sandworms, yams for meals or for trade, sea slugs and seashells) and hunt (mostly wild boars and turtles) in defined territories during the rainy season. This division

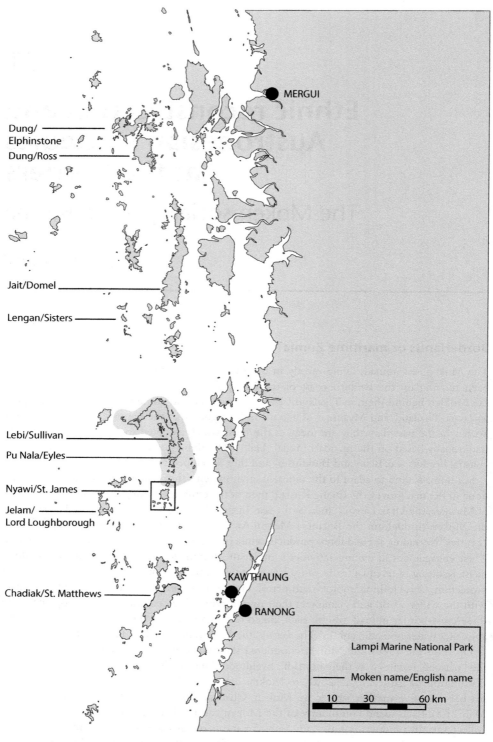

Map 21.1 Distribution of Moken groups in the Mergui Archipelago
Map by Jacques Ivanoff

into subgroups helps to maintain a demographic balance of about 5,000 individuals. Indeed, the Mergui Archipelago was far from the grip of surrounding civilizations (Siamese, Burmese, and Malay) until the annexation of the Tenasserim region by the British in 1826. Moken ideology and nomadism were at their climax in the late 1980s, when thousands of Burmese began to migrate to the islands, fleeing political unrest and economic distress in Central and Lower Burma. Moken ideology (such as non-accumulation and non-violence) is based on strategies (dissimilation, mobility, symbolic technology, etc.) which blossom from "ethnic latencies" (cultural, technical, and social experiences accumulated during their migration). Within a specific group, latencies can either be developed or not – for instance, notch out boats representing a human being were not developed by the Moklen. Yet, all of the sea gypsies shared these latencies and have the same historical places of gathering (Riaw and Phuket for instance), creating a line of communication between all groups. This chapter argues that this is made possible by the pivot system, which allows a specific group to separate from its matrix and go further north to continue its migration while part of the group remains within the dominant nation encompassing its social space, like the Moklen and the Moken.

Zomia versus borders

The sea nomads are often thought of as groups located at the peripheries of nation states, living in what Scott (2009) calls Zomia: places where distance and terrain have provided freedom from the dominant states. This concept can be applied to the sea nomads as they live at the peripheries by choice. In this context national borders have not existed until recently, and in fact the history of these nomads largely predates the emergence of nation states. In other words, sea nomads were not always Zomians, but became so following the rise of nationalism. While, argued by Scott, the Zomian territory disappeared with the post-World War II emergence of nation states and "distance-demolishing technologies" such as all-weather roads and railways, borders emerged as geographical lines, replacing frontier zones between "interpenetrating political systems" (Leach 1960: 50). In the era of nation states, borders create geographic units, forging new differences between social, cultural, ethnic, and national entities in the borderlands, even where these dimensions have traditionally overlapped. The post-colonial process of nationalization generated new national spaces, changing the character of borderlands on both sides, and thus Zomia re-emerged within the states. Every category, social space, or "interstice" (Winichakul 2005) offers a new opportunity for the rewriting of identity. The term "Zomians", in other words, is "de-territorialized", going from being representative of the inhabitants of Scott's Zomia, to that of "inner Zomians", that is, cast-out migrants, modern resisters within ethno-national borders (Bourdier et al. 2015).

Scott's Zomia provides a reversal account of the notions of hierarchy in the analysis of minorities, state relationships, and the translation of cultural choices into conscious objectives. This displaces research that works from the centre towards peripheries, an example emphasized by Scott, when writing about the creation of "fictional" territories. Scott described Zomia as a zone of refuge, bordering fixed centres with ideologies based on the notion that the farther you are from the centre the more "savage" you are. This marginal system has been present since the emergence of states in Southeast Asia and even before. Indeed, it could be argued that there can be no state without nomadic or peripheral populations functioning as necessary "others", given their ability to develop new ideologies to survive as ethnic groups and to find solutions in times when they are cut off from "national" affairs (Brun and de Miroschedji 2001). In fact, the techniques that the nomads used (slash-and-burn agriculture, for example), the ideologies they have developed (non-accumulation, egalitarianism), and the strategies they have devised, all aim to avoid the centre. Such strategies include dissimulation (Benjamin and Chou 2002), cultural exogamy (Boutry and Ivanoff 2008), and enslavement (Condominas 1998), to name only a few.

When nations asserted themselves and borders appeared, historical places of nomad regroupment such as Riaw, Langkawi, and Phuket remained transborder landmarks. It can be observed that even when the sea nomads of southern Thailand and Myanmar, namely, the Urak Lawoi, Moklen, and Moken, are confronted with borders or dominant Buddhist and Muslim populations, they do not seem to consider borders as an obstacle. They had already devised strategies to defuse the "danger" posed by major religions by staying close to their practitioners, even if it means remaining under their submission. In fact, thanks to their diversion strategy, they exclude any belief system in one unique god by keeping seemingly contradictory external aspects which they eventually use to reinforce their own beliefs – or what I have called "art of diversion" (Ivanoff 2014). Thus, the Moken, for instance, believe that there are three spirits aboard their boats: Adam, Eve, and their daughter. As for the Moklen, given their historical past as temple slaves for Siamese Buddhists, their system of beliefs includes myths based on this period, showing marked syncretism with Siamese beliefs that define their movements and integrations (Ivanoff 2001). Both the British missionaries (White 1922) and the Karen missionaries have been unsuccessful in getting the nomads to sedentarize, despite efforts spanning over several decades. There is thus a nomad history that is independent from the histories of the centres and of the major religions, and which does not pay attention to borders but chooses a way to penetrate the national ideology whenever a new border is created. Even when groups of people from the centre come to colonize the last pioneering frontiers in nomad territory, such as the Burmese fishermen did in the 1990s, the nomads find ways to become Inner Zomians – ethnic or even social groups that emerge from within a different dominant group. As it will become clear throughout this chapter, this process often implies, for the sea nomads, sacrificing part of their territory and leaving some of their nomad siblings behind. Yet even before they became Inner Zomians, which only occurred as a result of their encounters with the Other, it is important to stress that they already had strategies in place to overcome specific obstacles such as new borders or religions. To be sure, leaving behind an integrated part of their own people is what enables them to move forward in their journey. This is how a series of front posts and rear guards took shape from Riaw to Mergui: to enable the nomads to communicate with and find each other later.

The pivot practice

One of these practices is what I shall call the pivot, which demonstrates how nomadic culture has spread throughout the few thousand kilometres from Riaw to Mergui, while making the dominant peoples assume that integration has succeeded. In fact, the pivot constitutes the dynamics of the migratory group as it reinvents itself farther away within a new social space, beyond the borders (such as in the case of the Moklen and Moken) or within the same country. Thus, from the north of Malaysia to Mergui, the nomads, being Urak Lawoi or Moklen or Moken, all consider themselves as being close to the Moken, while the Moken call all of them Moken collectively. Borders do not seem to have a major impact on ethnicity and identity constructions, although the nomads obviously have to deal with them in certain ways. Their border, to put it in a different way, is a social space that can be displaced and migrate with them into their new territories.

The cultural markers the sea nomads use – non-accumulation, life aboard boats, gathering, non-violence, non-integration, myths and stories that give meaning to their nomadic ideology (Ivanoff 2004) – are sometimes interchangeable, and are variable because it is necessary to show different facets of their society depending on the groups with whom the Moken interact. These multiple facets of the same ethnicity, perceived differently by the outside world according to what the Moken want to reveal, are the result of a strategy that allows the same group to split into two to survive, a strategy that most often follows a historical shock (e.g. separation from the Moken following temple slavery in the case of the Moklen).

The institution of the Myanmar–Thai border that the Moken have traversed without any problem has nevertheless had an impact. Since the 1990s, citizenship and the crossing of borders have become important issues for the national agencies responsible for the integration of "non-Thai". The Moken who did not want to return to Myanmar became Thai citizens, but at the great cost of abandoning their social organization into different flotillas. The rituals (like the "spirit poles ceremony" which brings back the flotilla of each subgroup to one island before the rainy season) remained, but were fixed by the authorities on certain dates. In Myanmar, boats and flotillas managed to survive for about 20 more years, but the decreasing demographics of the Moken forced them to engage in inter-ethnic marriage with the Burmese newcomers. What took place was a process of "natural" social transformation – without state intervention – which allowed the Moken to perpetuate their traditions. In Thailand, on the other hand, this was no longer possible because the state had quickly taken an active stance on the integration issue.

The Moken of Myanmar have adapted to the new social dynamics, allowing the Burmese husbands (no Burmese women choose to marry Moken men) to use their boats for fishing (the Moken are hunters, not fishermen). With families no longer living on boats, the latter eventually disappeared. Just when one would think that the ideal nomad has disappeared, this could not be farther from the truth. Resiliency is strong and the group expects their shamans to take action with the world beyond and the Burmese invading their space to find new social adjustments. Moken have always believed that shamans could give the group a new direction; for example, new gathering areas where flotillas can collect food and new marketable products. Today, they are being reconstructed with the new *taukay* and the great rituals have finally returned since the situation has stabilized. With borders now being fixed, it is no longer possible for the Moken to leave for new countries: they have to invent their social space within the country in which they live. It is thus these Inner Zomians who practise the pivot strategy – adapting to new political and social conditions – as the next section will describe in more detail.

Burmese colonization and the renewal of the Moken ceremonies

With the arrival of diving compressors in the 1990s together with the first Karen encroachers, and ahead of the Burmese state-driven fishermen intrusion, dozens of young Moken people died due to their lack of knowledge of decompression stops and other diving techniques. They were replaced by Karen fishermen who depleted the Moken traditional trade resources (sea slugs, turbo and trochus snails). Furthermore, the foreshore had also by then been depleted, forest games had been decimated by Burmese firearms, and the best trees had been cut down to build fishing boats. As Moken still need to fish to survive, these developments pushed them into the arms of Burmese fishermen/entrepreneurs. As the *kabang* was disappearing, the Moken were using small secondary *sampan* boats to fish for squid.

The Moken are a permeable society for obvious demographic reasons. The widows were the first to marry Burmese men while girls, not being able to go on boats with their families, became increasingly attracted to the "modernity" of Burmese life in the villages of the islands. This inter-ethnic mixing did not prevent a group of Moken migrants, known as the "People of Jait" (Domel Island), from keeping their traditions and even imposing their resiliency strategy onto other Moken.

Centuries of interactions (Hogan 1972; Hinshiranan 1996; Benjamin and Chou 2002) with other populations along the shores of Malaysia provided the Moken with a stock of cultural and technical knowledge (or "latencies") which they could express and adapt to their environment. The archipelagic environment offered relative tranquillity from the mainland civilizations, so the Moken could test some of these "latencies". This is how Moken culture blossomed, with the *kabang* that represents a microcosm of their society, and with the emergence of the great ceremony *bo lobung*, "making the spirit poles", which takes place when the nomadic season transitions to the settled lifestyle of the rainy season. This ritual is of primary importance and preserves the history of Moken society, divided into phases, remembering for example the cultural "Malay" past and the Siamese "slavery" past, and also marking the birth of contemporary borders. It also enabled the expression of their ideology: sea and land hunting, non-accumulation, non-violence, egalitarianism, the refusal to learn and thus to attend school.

During the ceremony, the Moken renew the spiritual contract made between humans and their ancestors. Communication becomes "vertical", from the piece of land around the spirit poles, through the spirit poles, and upwards to the world of spirits and ancestors. The "sacred men" are at the foot of the spirit poles to welcome the spirits, giving them offerings. The Moken then make a new deal after "reimbursing their debt" to the ancestors who protected them from evil spirits during the dry season. Conversely, if the ancestors did not fulfil their role, the Moken may not please them with offerings and may not perform the *bo lobung* ceremony during which a specific space is designed and closed off with a symbolic door, and sometimes even a real one (made of pandanus and bamboo).

The Domel "refugees" subsequently colonized other subgroups within their own families and thus helped to link the remains of the "Moken" archipelago back together according to Moken coordinates. The greatest shaman, Gatcha, is from this group of "refugees", and he leads the Moken towards their uncertain future. While he refuses to perform the shamanic journey that would have them all agree on a common future, as practised in the old days, he still continues to ensure that rituals are performed in the Moken nomadic area (Nyawi, Pu Nala-Lebi, Lengan, and Busby) and has become the spiritual leader. Everyone expects him to renegotiate with the ancestors (about gathering, moving safely around their islands, finding a way to live as nomads even with the Burmese fishermen, and all this in exchange for offerings) and bring society back to its nomadic pace.

Not everyone accepts the absence of the shamanic voyage being performed, even if the intention behind it is to focus on building a solid socioeconomic position among the Burmese, thus providing opportunities for the future of Moken society. In fact, Gatcha sacrificed himself to allow the Moken forces to focus on a clear goal: the shaman's function will only be reactivated once the situation allows it. The process is ongoing. As for some shamans who seem less powerful in appearance, the wait is no longer possible and rituals that had supposedly disappeared 10 or 20 years ago are being revived according to their agenda. In fact, nothing had disappeared; it was merely hidden. For instance Ibling, the shaman of Nyawi (St. James, e.g. Map 21.2), the southernmost subgroup within the new configuration, located outside Lampi National Park "transferred" the role of shaman to his sister after the death of his wife and children. He became a timid and frail old man. Yet it was he, in 2016, who offered to perform the first three-day ritual that had not been held for several decades. For once, this ritual was performed with respect to the ritual calendar, so it took place on the rising moon of the fifth month of the waxing moon of the ancient Thai calendar.

Nowadays, Nyawi is not the centre of Moken cultural life. Rather Lampi, where we find various subgroups mixed together (Moken flotilla were chased away from the Domel Islands after the Japanese took control of pearl farming in the 1980s) and where the Burmese installed

The Moken social space in Burma

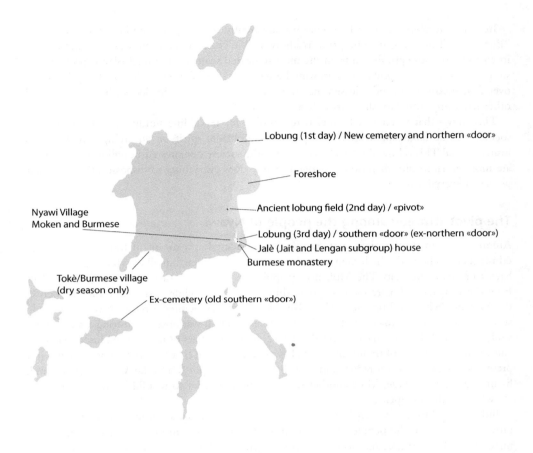

Moken symbolic territory of Nyawi Islands

Map 21.2 The pivot system in action (Nyawi subgroup)

Map by Jacques Ivanoff

their Marine National Park, has become such a place. The Burmese consider Lampi Island as the geographical centre of the archipelago and part of the Moken sphere, and various initiatives were imposed on the local communities: a "Moken Village" (2000), an "Ideal Village" (2002), a "Selung Festival" (2004), and even the consolidation of each subgroup into specific "streets" (1998). When the army forced the Moken to settle in these "villages", they all ran away and embarked on 43 *kabang*, hidden in the mangroves, fleeing from the soldiers who in the end were only trying to "help" them. The Moken know there are limits to adaptation, and even the army cannot manage to make the Moken submit to them. It was a time of misunderstanding and tension which only stopped once the ritual of "the spirit poles" was over. The Burmese have now understood that the situation is not stable and that the Moken have to be left to their own devices.

In 2013, the old shaman of Lebi who was apparently "off duty" (living in the middle of the "Burmese village"), regained his pride as a holy man in charge of communicating with the spirits by using the strength drawn from the most respected shaman of Domel Island and bringing some of his siblings to Lebi. He performed a dazzling show for which he erected spirit poles over four metres high, and released into the sea a miniature boat, loaded with evil spirits and other bad things (military ships, army helicopters, etc.).

This shows that Gatcha of Domel is responsible for rebuilding flotillas and redrawing the socioeconomic landscape which re-imposed the nomadic spirit on an archipelago that was losing its soul. This is how this "egalitarian" nomadic society operates. Although some holy men are more equal to him than others, Moken society does everything to dispossess them of their power in everyday life.

The pivot strategy among the people of Nyawi

Among sea nomads, the pivot strategy may be considered as a means of forging variables of ethnic markers behind which their true identity remains hidden, but all of which can be traced back to a single ethnicity. The Moken may apply this strategy in order to separate themselves from the Burmese who are increasingly pushing them aside, while at the same time accepting the Moken's beliefs and practices. These Burmese "invaders" ignited a reaction within a single space that was getting smaller and smaller. This phenomenon was observed during a recent field study in April 2016, after having witnessed 12 consecutive years of integration, inter-marriage, and the disappearance of traditional boats. It was an indication that this strategy is still alive and presently at work, however reduced in scale. In this way, one portion of the Moken stays behind, living with the Burmese, while another separates itself in order to rebuild its own social space elsewhere in the archipelago.

Indeed, the Moken's internal dynamics, driven and organized according to external forces, provoked splits, and the people of Nyawi started to move away from their village, which had mixed with the Burmese, and from their former cemetery, both under Burmese "control". And so they went towards the beach, leaving the south of the island. They still perform the ritual, but the sacred "doors" (*pétao*) have been relocated. This entrance is now three and a half kilometres north of the former one, the latter of which has been left as the Moken moved northwards, where there is still a place to live, gather, fish, or at least be left alone. The door that "closes" the ritual is located in the village, indicating the new limit of the Moken social space. The end of the ritual takes place in the village: the new pivot. The Burmese leave them to perform their ritual and the spirit poles are in the village. Even though the village represents the "closing door", it is through this "door" that the spirits of the sea – dolphins and others – can come for the offerings, symbolizing the union between the sea and the forest. This reconstruction of the territory is physically embodied by these sacred doors, which welcome the spirits while simultaneously drawing the limits of the sacred space. The mixed village henceforth serves no other purpose than to act as a pivot in the inexorable advance of the Moken groups towards places that are freer from constraints. These few kilometres north, a short hop on the nomadic scale, operates as a pivot that helps them to show many facets that can disorient outsiders in the conjectures over the "meaning" of Moken ethnicity. Indeed, Moken direct these outsiders to wherever they want to lead them, thus hiding another facet (such as the other nomads fleeing north). A rearguard action is thus created to maintain ties with the dominant people and to enable others to continue to build, or at least preserve, their Moken identity. The "entrance" door that was relocated to the north in the new ritual "field" is thus a gateway (the new area of Moken ritual and domination), with the "closing door" ending the Moken social space in the village itself. This is how the Moken proceed in advancing their migration.

Nyawi has thus become one of the limits of the Moken social space in Burma. Everything that lies southwards is not really part of the social space that has been reconstructed for their survival. The Chadiak Moken have been condemned to acculturation (when military stations or pagoda are built on Moken islands, as in Jelam), and extinction, as the cross-border Moken of Surin have become Thai citizens and traditionalists for mere tourism purposes. The Moken dynamic is thus confined to a space defined by the three groups designated by Gatcha.

Notwithstanding differences in scales (time and space), this pattern can be compared to that which united and disunited the Moken and the Moklen, and, from a larger perspective, to the one that allowed the spread of Austronesian populations across Southeast Asia (Bellwood 1985; Sather 1993a).

The pivot system: a binomial organization in the making

The cultural markers the Moken use are variable as it is often necessary for them to show different facets of their society depending on the groups with whom they are interacting, for example the Burmese, so that the latter can accept them. These multiple facets of the same ethnicity, perceived differently by the outside world according to what the Moken want to reveal, are the result of a strategy that allows the same group to split into two to survive, a strategy that most often follows a historical shock. It was, for instance, temple slavery that initiated the first split between the Moklen and the Moken, yet both groups have always maintained links to each other through cultural practices, rituals, and various habitats, even through cultural borders (mainly religious ones, Buddhist and Islamic), "cultural landscapes" (separating social space of the Dawei people and Moken), and more recently administrative ones. Triggering the pivot strategy thus results in a split, with all the concerned groups retaining links to the previously inhabited places where part of the group remains to ensure continuity in the line of communication and exchange between nomads on the one hand, and "dominant peoples" on the other. Beyond practices, beliefs, and habitats, there is a shared identity between "Austronesian nomads", separated from the "mother-culture", farming or fishing within their politically dominant Austronesian matrix, which have often become Islamic nation states. These men of the sea constitute the strategic outposts of Austronesian migration, but appear as "savages" within their own group. Since they are always on the "outside", they may also be considered as the inhabitants of a maritime Zomia. They are pioneers; they "surf" ahead of the wave of Islamization (Moken); they adapt to Buddhist cosmology (Moklen) through specific local Buddhist rituals; they integrate commercial island networks (Urak Lawoi); and they maintain links with the littoral as far as the Riaw-Lingga Archipelago (Benjamin and Chou 2002; Ivanoff 2004). Thus, the Moken are linked to the Moklen, who in turn are related to the Urak Lawoi who are close to the Orang Kuala of Malaysia. This dynamic of splitting into groups and the creation of differential markers in no way affects the uniqueness of their shared nomadic ideology, even though cultural differences are considerable.

The Moken's belonging to the Austronesian groups is known from language reconstruction. For instance, the sea Bajau and the Sama who are sea nomads living in Indonesia, possess social structures similar to the Moken's. Evidence (e.g. archaeological findings, Bellina 2006; linguistic discoveries, Blust 1995; and social structure, Sather 1993a) also points to a long familiarity with farming, iron-forging, pottery-making, and weaving, though each group has encountered different people, thus adapting, learning, or rejecting different techniques. Their knowledge of the sea is more intimate than what they knew of the land; the early Sama were a population made up entirely of boat nomads and fishermen. However, their marine orientation coexisted with "a significant and coherent tradition of land-oriented activity" (Pallesen 1985: 255), "indicating the presence, [...] already at this [time of pre-dispersion of] a divergence of orientation between the land and the coastal strands" (Pallesen 1985: 117). Reflecting this divergence, different Sama groups from the beginning appear to have pursued, much as they do today, various permutations of this "dual orientation", some focusing on the land and others on the strand or sea, with communities of sea nomads forming only one of a multitude of economically diverse groups.

Through this system of procurement, the shore-based Sama provided their local patrons with services, artisans, and labourers, including skilled seamen, boat builders, smiths, artisans, mat makers, potters, fishermen, and inter-island carriers and traders, while the most prestigious and independent of these groups, such as the Balangingi Sama, supplied maritime raiders and procured slaves for the Tausug markets of Jolo (Warren 1978, 1981). Sather (1984, 1993b) described this system in its "binomial" form, explaining how sea nomads and/or coastal populations split into two, with one group living on land in order to pursue spiritual and material negotiations with the dominant sedentary peoples, thus allowing the other group to continue on its quest. Like the Moklen, they may integrate a new livelihood (living on the littoral, in the mangrove, or in the rubber plantations) or the ethnicity of the dominant people into their social space. Seemingly, the Moken/Moklen difference manifests itself through a choice between fishing and hunting, yet it is based on the choice to adapt – or refuse to do so – following a historical push factor (slavery) that led to the split. Within their own nomadic social space, the Moklen create ethnic borders based on specific techniques (slash-and-burn cultivation, boat building, social dissimilation, access to mangroves resources, and so on), linguistics, and mobility. They enlarge their territory and knowledge by doing so, and maintain contact through inter-marriage. Thus the Moklen feel at ease with both nomads and sedentary peoples. This "pivot", the core of the nomad people, thus creates an illusion when it comes to envisioning a linear development needed for the state and still represents a landmark for their kin who went farther afield.

The segmentation process can be repeated or replicated infinitely, even in the case of a breaking point, especially a demographic one. The people from Nyawi have shown us that it is indeed possible; the elders of Pu Nala-Lebi performed a great ritual complete with a turtle sacrifice and the launch of a miniature boat into the sea (reviving the tradition of Koh Sireh in Phuket, Thailand, a "historic" meeting point for nomads); the northern Moken created ritual frescoes and mosaics, and have gone back to building *kabang* (Ivanoff 2014). It is therefore obvious that ethnic forces are still at work, that transmission is still occurring, and that the Moken still live according to their notion of nomadic time which allows them to wait 10 years, or even 100 years, before setting out to conquer new territories, despite being dispersed over hundreds of square kilometres.

Conclusion: the pivot strategy in a partitioned world

The example of the Moklen, who separated from the Moken as a result of slavery, leading to the sea-oriented Moken of the islands and the coast-oriented Moklen, and the ethnographic observations of the Nyawi separating themselves from the "centre" (the mixed Burmese–Moken village) to rebuild another social space of their own, suggest that these nomadic groups share a unique pivot strategy. This suggests a dynamic that goes beyond the Moken that is a part of the unravelling of Austronesian history in the long term.

In Burma, as in Thailand, the *kabang* disappeared, notably because of the Moken's interactions with the Burmese through inter-marriage and fishing activities. The difference is that, in Burma, in the absence of state involvement, "natural interactions" are still at work, leaving the Moken to find their own way to cope with the modern world according to their own ideology. Dispersal, dissimilation, adapted technology, non-accumulation, and living on the fringes of the dominant populations are the strategies that make the Moken true Zomians. In this regard, their use of the pivot strategy provides them with the ability to move away from oppression and find ways to continue their migration and maintain their knowledge.

Note

1   The 3,000 Moklen are a semi-nomadic population on the west coast of Thailand, inhabiting areas between the Moken (to the north) and the Urak Lawoi (to the south). While they are considered the maritime nomadic populations of Thailand, they practice slash-and-burn cultivation, rubber plantation, fishing, and collect crabs in the mangroves. Their villages, scattered among the other littoral communities within walking distance, are strongly related to each other by inter-marriage, as well as by a complex calendar of shared elements of rituality and oral literature (Ivanoff 2001).

References

Bellina, B. (2006). The Archaeology of Prehistoric Trans-Asiatic Exchange: Technological and Settlement Evidence from Khao Sam Kaeo. *Bulletin de l'Ecole Française d'Extrême-Orient* 93: 249–255.
Bellwood, P. (1985). *Prehistory of the Indo-Malaysian Archipelago*. Sydney: Academic Press.
Benjamin, G. and Chou, C. (2002). *Tribal Communities in the Malay World: Historical, Cultural and Social Perspectives*. Singapore: ISEAS/IIAS.
Blust, R. (1995). The Prehistory of the Austronesian-speaking Peoples: A View from Language. *Journal of World Prehistory* 9: 453–510.
Bourdier, F., Boutry, M. and Ivanoff, J. (2015). *From Padi States to Commercial States. Reflections on Identity and the Social Construction of Space in the Borderlands of Cambodia, Vietnam, Thailand and Myanmar*. Amsterdam: Amsterdam University Press.
Boutry, M. and Ivanoff, J. (2008). De la segmentation sociale à l'ethnicité dans les suds péninsulaires? Réflexions sur les constructions identitaires et les jalons ethniques à partir de l'exemple des pêcheurs birmans du Tenasserim. Bangkok, Centre d'Anthropologie Sirindhorn. *Aséanie* 22: 11–46.
Brun, P. and de Miroschedji, P. (2001) Avant-propos au thème 2. *Cahier des thèmes transversaux ArScAn*, I, 1998/1999, Nanterre: UMR 7041, 49–52.
Condominas, G. (1998). *Formes extrêmes de dépendance en Asie du Sud-Est. Contributions à l'étude de l'esclavage*. (Coll "Civilisations et Sociétés" 96), éditions de l'Ecole des Hautes Etudes en Sciences Sociales.
Hall, D. G. (1968). *A History of South-East Asia*. Houndmills, Basingstoke, Hampshire/London: Macmillan Education.
Hinshiranan, N. (1996). The Analysis of Moken Opportunistic Foragers's Intragroup and Intergroup Relation. Unpublished PhD thesis, Hawai'i University.
Hogan, D. (1972). Men of the sea: Coastal tribes of Thailand's west coast. *Journal of the Siam Society* 60(1): 205–235.
Ivanoff, J. (2001). *Rings of Coral. Moken Folktales*. Bangkok: White Lotus Press.
Ivanoff, J. (2004). *Les naufragés de l'histoire. Les jalons épiques de l'identité moken*. Paris. Les Indes Savantes.
Ivanoff, J. (2014). L'art, vecteur de l'identité chez les Moken. La continuité de l'adaptation rituelle et artistique chez les Moken. In: *Ethnocentrisme et Création*, A. Dupuis and J. Ivanoff (eds). Paris: éditions de la Maison des Sciences de l'Homme (FMSH), 297–321.
Leach, E. (1960). The Frontiers of Burma. *Comparative Studies in Society and History* 3(1): 49–68.
Pallesen, A. (1985). *Culture Contact and Language Convergences*. Manila: Linguistic Society of the Philippines.
Sather, C. (1984). Sea and Shore People: Ethnicity and Ethnic Interaction in Southeastern Sabah. *Contributions to Southeast Asian Ethnography* 3: 3–27.
Sather, C. (1993a). Bajau. In: *Encyclopedia of World Cultures*, D. Levinson (ed.), Vol. 5. New Haven, CT: Human Relations Area Files Press, 30–35.
Sather, C. (1993b). Samal. In: *Encyclopedia of World Cultures*, D. Levinson (ed.), Vol. 5. New Haven, CT: Human Relations Area Files Press, 217–221.
Scott, J. (2009). *The Art of Not Being Governed: An Anarchist History of Southeast Asia*. New Haven, CT: Yale University Press.

Warren, J. (1978). Who Were the Balangingi Samal? Slave Raiding and Ethnogenesis in Nineteenth-century Sulu. *Journal of Asian Studies* 3: 477–490.

Warren, J. (1981). *The Sulu Zone, 1768–1989*. Singapore. Singapore University Press.

White, W. (1922). *The Sea Gypsies of Malaya: An Account of the Nomadic Mawken of the Mergui Archipelago with a Description of Their Ways of Living, Customs, Habits, Boats, Occupations, etc.* London: Seeley Service & Co.

Winichakul, T. (2005) Writing at the Interstices: Southeast Asian Historians and Postnational Histories. In: *New Terrains in Southeast Asian History*, Center for International Studies, Ohio University, 3–29.

Part 5
It's all about relations: re-conceptualizing trade and the economy in the borderlands

Introduction

Caroline Grillot

At the turn of the last decade of the 20th century, Asia experienced some tremendous changes in its politic arenas. In 1991, the Soviet Union collapsed and a number of Central Asian republics subsequently emerged as independent entities, driven by political and socioeconomic reforms meant to bring out the best of their potential to eventually play their own role in the development of the region. Whereas exchanges with China slowly resumed in the Russian Far-East, Deng Xiaoping gave a significant impulse to the structural changes that had taken place during the post-Maoist era. In 1992, he launched the reforms that brought a distinctively Chinese version of liberalism to the country's economy, which triggered remarkable developments in Mainland China and led it to eventually become one of the major economies in the world. In the meantime, China re-established a diplomatic relationship with Vietnam, which contributed to the development of special economic zones along their shared border and to the opening of an economic corridor with the purpose of disseminating Chinese goods, people, knowledge, and commercial influence in Southeast Asia. In the Indian subcontinent, the development of Nepal and the opening of its Mustang Kingdom to foreigners in 1992 provided opportunities for new international roads and a new role as a node linking Nepal with China through the Tibetan plateau.

One of the immediate consequences of all these internal structural changes was a renewed attention to borderlands across Asia, now deemed as gates to new perspectives and exchanges with regional neighbours. The opening of borders, although restricted at first, has offered those citizens living in the borderlands new opportunities and the prospects of an accelerated access to modernity – a "disruptive and contradictory process" (Murton, this volume) manifested in infrastructure development, embodied by Chinese commodities influx, and brought by international tourism.

Drawing upon five case studies, this part brings us to Asian border towns in Kyrgyzstan, Nepal, Vietnam, and Russia, where ordinary people from various socioeconomic backgrounds endeavour to make a living from border trade. The contributions all describe the everyday experiences of native residents and new immigrants of the borderlands in adjusting and reinventing their livelihood under new conditions brought about by a new political order, infrastructure projects, and the involvement of innovative economic agents. The authors propose to use "borderland modernity", "sovereignty", "trust/distrust", "predatoriness", and "follow-the-thing" approaches to conceptualize the upheavals of border practices and trade-related human activities.

The authors offer us three main viewpoints to understand relationships in the light of borderland economies and more specifically border trade since China's rising economy has accelerated commercial exchanges with its neighbours. They discuss relations among borderlanders within the frontiers of a particular country, cross-border relations between traders, and relations between border traders and the state in general. Within these frames, each contribution highlights the tremendous importance of networks, rooted in kinship, ethnicity, or religion; problematic state governance in remote regions; and the impact of increasing access to modern infrastructures, be they roads or Internet facilities.

Focusing on the cases of the Uyghur and the Hmong[1], two politically marginalized ethnic groups in Vietnam and China, respectively, Steenberg and Bonnin demonstrate how kinship, ethnic, and religious networks enable mobility, and hence trading activities across borders. While cultural and linguistic competences have offered traders an easier access to markets beyond their countries' borders (despite its spatial limit in the Hmong case), they make use of their strong ethnic connections in order to investigate the newly opened border economies, and rely strongly on their long-established networks to venture into cross-border trade and invest in specific businesses, thanks to their pioneering skills in market niches. In the meantime, Hmong and Uyghur entrepreneurs are aware of the inherent limits of their social networks when they consider extending their business and sustaining partnerships with the main dominant ethnic groups (respectively the Kinh, the Kyrgyz, and the Han) who have greater access to structural facilities enabling them to contemplate more ambitious plans.

In their case studies, Grillot and Ryzhova examine smuggling and invisible networks. Chinese and Russian entrepreneurs manage to rely on newly built and more adventurous relationships with local partners, eager to participate in new business deals with potentially experienced traders. Imaginative and with better financial means, the Chinese find in Vietnam and Russia great channels to sell manufactured commodities of all kinds, according to customers' needs, and to search for natural resources, whether controversial or not. On the Himalayan front, Murton explores the impact of border trade on the local institution of *nyetsang*, a ritual friendship and kinship network that used to facilitate mobility within Mustang, but which came under pressure with motorized mobility and the extension of one's activities outside familiar territories.

The relationships among traders participating in the same commercial chain are another core subject addressed in this part. Both Steenberg and Grillot discuss the delicate issue of trust in the establishment of sustainable trading partnerships across borders. In the Uyghur case, Steenberg found that the establishment of trustful relationships among partners across the border is sometimes more meaningful and precious than the actual profit made in a particular business, thus emphasizing how social capital is seen as a long-term investment, and a way of pooling resources along generations. Whereas in the case of Chinese traders in Vietnam, the regular occurrence of risky deals for short-term profits reveal the lack of trust that often mars their relationships. This is the result of previous failures in business partnerships or from excessive cautiousness nourished by stories of mutual cheating in the trade realm. Overall, regardless of their financial power, trust emerges as the most difficult social asset to build and maintain between partners whose purpose is constantly questioned.

Hierarchy among border traders is another emerging topic in the case studies discussed in this part. While Bonnin shows the dependency that still exists between ethnic groups of the same countries who play different roles in the commercial chain, Ryzhova emphasizes how technology and individual experience with China creates a hierarchy among Russians at the border, and enables those with social connections and knowledge to invest in e-commerce and to act as retailers of Chinese goods for their peers. Steenberg shows how access to formal infrastructure has gradually excluded Uyghur businessmen from trade with Kyrgyzstan for the benefit of the formally-established Han and Kyrgyz businesses, themselves being dependent on the political context underlying the ups and downs of commercial exchanges.

Murton approaches the issue of state intervention by analyzing the transformations of the Himalayan border between China and Nepal and their impact on people's mobility versus containment. He shows how new infrastructures and central/global investments orchestrated by state development policies disrupt the local social equilibrium, hence revealing the ambivalent nature of a border space as one that both separates locals yet unites neighbours. Building on the development of Sino–Russian border trade, Ryzhova also examines traders' interactions with state officers using the concepts of predatoriness and invisibility. In her case, traders have learned from experience how to navigate the state-imposed system of border governance, be it tax regimes or import–export restrictions.

All chapters focus on remote spaces once left aside and that are now reshaped by the state's visions of development. They address the issue of state governance from the perspective of rules and regulations related to quantity, nature, and mode of transportation; tax collection; and people's ways of navigating the interstices of laws precisely to evade tariffs, and to avoid further involvement in unsatisfactory procedures that have attempted to formalize commercial activities in border zones so far. Drawing on ethnographic materials, the authors vividly describe the incredible inventiveness of people living in the borderlands in taking advantage of an ever-changing economic environment. Their case studies all highlight the fundamental role of social networks in these pioneering ventures. However, these entrepreneurs often engage in border trade without knowing much about their neighbours and potential business partners, and thus must overcome suspicion and build trust. Without much experience – most of the case studies evoke cross-border trade as a re-emerging activity after decades of interruption – traders must start from their obvious and precious social capital – namely family, co-ethnic and co-religious peers – before being able to expand their network geographically. Traders in these regions all complement each other, but they also need to expand their network according to an increasing diversity among border-trade actors, a diversity that is embedded in ethnic or national concealed competition over wealth, and the controversial means of state intervention over cross-border trade profits.

Note

1 One of the larger upland ethnic minority groups in the Southeast Asian borderlands spread over China, Vietnam, Laos, Thailand, and Burma. At present, the Chinese state does not formally acknowledge the Hmong as an individual ethnic group, and has categorized them along with others under the larger umbrella "Miao". The majority of Hmong in these borderlands live in rural areas with livelihood practices based on semi-subsistence agriculture involving a blend of permanent and temporary farming centred on household production.

22
Accumulating trust
Uyghur traders in the Sino–Kyrgyz border trade after 1991

Rune Steenberg

Introduction

This chapter tells two entangled stories. The framing story is the reinvigoration of the cross-border trade between Kyrgyzstan and Xinjiang after the collapse of the Soviet Union. It traces the border trade's trajectory from the reopening of the borders in the 1990s, over the surge in trade and vastly expanding bazaars in the early 2000s, to its gradual decline after 2010. The second story, embedded within the first one, is that of Uyghur traders from the villages around Atush, a town 40 kilometres north of Kashgar in southwestern Xinjiang, taking part in the cross-border trade. These traders rose to prominence and prosperity in the risky early phase of the border trade in the 1990s and early 2000s, but struggled as the trade's conditions and infrastructure became more formalised. When I visited a group in 2013, they were finding themselves faced with increasing competition and in a marginal position in relation to both the Kyrgyz and the Chinese authorities. Developments, development policies, and economic schemes limited their opportunities. Many were on the brink of moving on to other markets and other types of business. When I revisited them in 2016, virtually all of them had made this move.

Within this uncertain business environment and marginalised in structures of the state and formal markets, the Uyghur traders rely heavily on social networks. Their economic activities and social relations are intimately linked within institutions of exchange and mutual support. At the heart of these institutions, often expressed in terms of kinship (*tughqandarchiliq*), friendship (*dostluq*), and neighbouring (*qoshundarchiliq*), are gift-giving relations that are upheld at life cycle rituals and in daily interactions. Commonly given gifts include business support, job provisions, and money transactions. These gift-giving relations are the primary institutions in their business endeavours, while at the same time these endeavours provide opportunities to expand and strengthen networks.

The stories presented here show cross-border trade as a meandering business, the profitability and success of which is heavily dependent on rapidly shifting macro-political factors and on access to state resources. Such volatile trade environments offer business fields for marginalised groups and minorities with little access to formal economic opportunities, employment, education, and government resources. These groups, not permeated by bureaucratic institutions to the same extent as those that are more formally integrated, are typically organised in closely knit social networks. These networks – and not any particular contract or education – are the traders' main assets and are meticulously maintained. This allows them to quickly and flexibly access new niches in high-risk environments of less developed infrastructure before more stable, formal institutions make them attractive to better integrated actors.

Border trade

In 1992, the newly independent Kyrgyz Republic and the Peoples' Republic of China (PRC) took up diplomatic relations after decades of interruption. Border trade again began to develop across the Torugart pass between Xinjiang and Kyrgyzstan (Alff 2016: 5). Initial transactions were local and restricted, but soon cheap Chinese products began to saturate the markets in Central Asia. Kyrgyzstan, just west of Xinjiang, claiming low import duties and featuring a more than porous border control, quickly became a main hub for re-exports to the markets of neighbouring countries. By 1996, the Dordoi market, which had been established on an empty field north of the Kyrgyz capital Bishkek only 12 km from the Kazakh border a few years earlier, had 3,500 trading places. Ten years later it featured 6,000–7,000 containers[1] with up to 20,000 people working at the market (Spector 2008: 162). In 2013, the number of containers had increased to 15,000 with at least 40,000 people working there (Alff 2014: 76–79, 2016: 2).

Uyghur traders were involved from the outset. They were well equipped, having the advantage of 10 years of experience in Deng Xiaoping's reformist Chinese economy, a long trading tradition, and extended social networks across the region (Clark and Kamalov 2004; Brophy 2016). Uyghurs from Xinjiang's southern oases found themselves in a particularly favourable position after the border crossing at Irkeshtam, on the road between Osh and Kashgar, re-opened in 1999 after about 60 years of closure. This shifted the gravitational centre of business away from Bishkek towards Osh and the nearby former kolchoz bazaar of Karasuu, a small town very close to a main Uzbek–Kyrgyz border crossing in the south of Kyrgyzstan.[2] Many Uyghur traders began to frequent the rapidly growing market in Karasuu (Angermann 2006: 62–70; Ibraimov 2009: 49). By 2006, the bazaar featured 3,000–6,000 containers, a total of 10,000 trading places and about US$150,000–450,000 in daily turnover (Spector 2008: 168). The bazaar's trade volume continued to increase until 2010 when, following violent clashes in Osh, frequent and prolonged border closings with Uzbekistan severely limited access to the bazaar for the approximately 70–80 per cent of its customers that came from Uzbekistan (Spector 2008: 168). This initiated a slow decline of Karasuu bazaar.

In the summer of 2013, I visited a group of Uyghur traders from Atush at their trading location in southern Kyrgyzstan. At this time, the re-exports of Chinese goods through Bishkek into Kazakhstan was still thriving, while Karasuu in the south of Kyrgyzstan had lost much of its transit potential. Instead of crossing the officially sanctioned border posts, many goods were now making their way informally across the heavily guarded but still porous border cross-cutting the Ferghana Valley (Megoran 2004; Bichsel 2009; Reeves 2014). One such place was Kadamjay in Batken, Kyrgyzstan's southernmost region, near a long stretch of Kyrgyz–Uzbek border in a barren, but easily negotiable terrain. A group of Uyghur traders from Atush had moved their business here from Karasuu. They were selling clothes, fabric, and shoes, and lived nearby in rented rooms of Uzbek families' courtyard houses.

Accumulation and relation

The Atush traders conduct their business in groups of three to five people from one to a few closely related households (Laruelle and Peyrouse 2009: 101; Steenberg 2016: 409). Typically, businesses are set up around a group of siblings and their spouses, with one or two households doing the actual trading and the others contributing funds and other support. Gheyretjan, a retired government cadre from Kashgar, explained to me how he and his siblings had supported and encouraged their younger brother to first enter the trade and then move on to the restaurant business. He now runs successful restaurants in Bishkek and Osh. Gheyretjan saw this as the result of a deliberate strategy: within the family, they would collectively invest in one person to help him grow, he said. Then, once this person succeeded, he in turn would lift the rest of the family along with him and provide the others with opportunities to succeed as well. The pioneer's success benefits all and stabilises the family and its networks. Gheyretjan had used his good government connections to provide his brother with the required documents, while other relatives had contributed funds. The trick was, he went on, to give each brother or brother-in-law the feeling that they were succeeding on their own account, but at the same time keep their loyalties bound to the family. That was his task, he declared, as the eldest brother.

Such accumulation of capital gives leverage to a given individual's business potential. It multiplies the groups' chances for success and disperses risk. The capital accumulated is both money and what Bourdieu (1986) calls social capital, that is, relations and connections. This accumulation of social capital extends the number of people whose resources can be drawn on, but more importantly it also exponentially increases the number of people strongly interested in the success of the endeavour – people whose support and help, or at least goodwill, can be relied upon. Therefore, capital accumulation not only promotes the group; it also, in a sense, defines it and positions it within wider social networks. These groups are not business or investment cooperatives that get together for one given business endeavour. They are long-term groups of relatives and close friends that are, not unlike in a marriage, meant and hoped to last for a lifetime, even if this cannot always be sustained. They constitute the main hubs in wider social networks, which also include further kin, in-laws of in-laws, close friends, former classmates, neighbours, and fellow villagers. These networks connect groups and individuals that conduct their own trade alongside each other but share infrastructure, information, and business channels. Traders become introduced to the business through such connections and retain close cooperation with others in their networks, despite structurally competing with them for the same market niches. They draw on each other for essential services including money transfer and lending, as well as logistics, housing, and cooking.

While the traders certainly aim at making a profit, this is not their only goal, and sometimes not even the main one. After 2010, the profit margin of Uyghur traders dropped drastically. Atush traders were aware that prospects for earning good money in the border trade looked rather bleak in 2013, but they nevertheless kept undertaking the exhausting trips to Kyrgyzstan (Steenberg 2016). As Madeleine Reeves (2012) argues for Kyrgyz labour migration to Russia, there is clearly a minimum level of profit below which the trade is not embarked on anymore. For most of the Uyghur traders from Atush trading in Karasuu and Kadamjay, this threshold was reached in 2016, but not in 2013. Besides money, the traders were pursuing relative independence from the Chinese state, more religious freedom, and social status as international traders. But for many Atush traders it was and is as much about social integration and the upkeep of their networks. Having knowledge, resources, and connections, and therefore being able to offer opportunities to relatives and friends, is a prerequisite for integration into social networks. A position in the local administration with access to government resources can offer this; or, less controversially, being part of strong trading networks. This logic is consciously pursued by Uyghur traders. In 2013, many went less for the profit and more for the networks. In 2016, the Uyghur traders I knew had abandoned their stalls in the bazaars of Kyrgyzstan. They now employed the very same social networks they had used and cultivated in the border trade to conduct other business in new fields.

The local economy in southern Xinjiang and Kyrgyzstan is not merely oriented around formal markets, state bureaucracies, and other anonymous structures, but also strongly embedded in social networks. Therefore, social ties are not compromised but rather strengthened by being put to economic use. As such, trading is not unlike playing pool with one's peers on sunny afternoons and inviting each other for lunch in restaurants despite the family cooking at home: it keeps up social relations, which are to many a main asset and resource far more important than any particular, singular business undertaking or short-term profit.

Credit and trust

The Atush traders' customers in the bazaars of Kadamjay in southern Kyrgyzstan in 2013 were mainly female small-scale traders from Uzbekistan. They crossed the border on foot to purchase small amounts of clothes and footwear for their village markets. The goods were smuggled back wrapped in tablecloths, camouflaged as gifts for a wedding, or by bribing the border guards. These women usually did not pay for their purchases right away, but only after they had sold the commodities. In the meantime, the sale was noted as debt by both seller and buyer. Each would sign in the other's ledger. The two entries would later be compared and annulled by another two signatures after the final payment. This arrangement is called *nési* (credit, delayed payment) and is based on trust between seller and buyer. This trust depends on the transaction's embeddedness within the social relations of the collective of traders on each side of the border. Uyghur traders have no means of legal sanctions against a customer who runs off with a stock of commodities without paying. They cannot cross the border into Uzbekistan without a costly visa and, even so, would most likely not be able to locate the perpetrator anyway, much less have local police take action against her. Yet, according to the Uyghur traders, defaulting occurs extremely rarely. The sanctioning powers are not with the seller or police, but with the buyer's own peers who are interested in avoiding disturbances to their own business. Any breach of contract lessens the trust relations between the two groups, making it more difficult for others to obtain goods on credit in the future. A breach of trust that went unsanctioned by the guilty party's peers would be seen as a collective, not an individual violation. Serious violations could even result in the Uyghur traders abandoning the location. The trade is crucial for many household's meagre incomes, and this collective interest of maintaining the trade sanctions irresponsible individual profit seeking.

To label this as "relations of trust", is, while not wrong, slightly misleading, given Western cultural connotations of the concept of trust that understand it as being about a benevolent relationship between two free, righteous individuals of mutual goodwill. The trust between the traders in the case at hand is not primarily about individual judgements or personal qualities. Rather, trust is embedded in the social networks that the traders on both sides are involved in and depend on for their business conduct. It is trust, not in any particular individual, but rather in the system of social relations (Luhmann 2000; Steenberg 2014: 8). The atmosphere of trust established within the network provides the structural conditions to make default a rare occurrence. This atmosphere is constituted by the long-term relationships and interdependencies of the trader's households, as well as by their personal friendships and by the traders' self-understanding as being righteous. These elements are invoked perfomatively through the use of certain symbols. Some of these are closely tied to giving and sharing, especially of food. Eating together and inviting each other for meals (*mehman qilish*) carry a uniting force. Other practices of symbolic value are explicitly Islamic in content. Going to the mosque, praying regularly, using religious phrases and idioms, and strict adherence to Muslim food prohibitions symbolise trustworthiness. This is often formulated in the idiom "fear of God" (*xudadin qorqash*) and is connected to many traders' genuine striving to be good moral persons through exploring their religion more deeply outside the restrictions of the PRC.

Their networks, here too, are a main and constant factor for the traders, as their agency is tied to them. Other conditions of the border trade shift on short notice, mostly due to macro-economic and macro-political changes beyond their influence. We will now proceed to examine the connection between the workings of these social networks, family and trust relations, and the wider political and economic context. For this, we need to look more closely at the circumstances under which the trade was conducted and the historical trajectory it is part of. Changes in these circumstances altered the conditions for trade and influenced the life of the traders in a way that points to an intimate relation between marginalisation from formal structures and the certain kind of network maintenance and trust generation described here. In order to draw up this connection, the next section traces the history of the Sino–Kyrgyz cross-border trade in more detail and from the perspective of Uyghur traders.

A history of Sino–Kyrgyz cross-border trade

Preamble

The route across the Pamir mountain pass at Irkeshtam, from Kashgar at the western edge of the Tarim Basin to Osh in the eastern Ferghana Valley, was for centuries a main artery in the ancient network of trading routes popularly known as the Silk Road (Hansen 2012). Up until the 1930s, the cross-border trade westwards from Kashgar was economically important, and taxation of the trade was among the main means and aims of political control over the region (Brophy 2016: 9–10). Following the disquiet surrounding the establishment and dismantling of the first Eastern Turkestan Republic in 1933–1934, border trade via Irkeshtam came to a standstill. Due to international political tension, it did not see a revival in the decades that followed (Kreutzmann 1998: 292). It was only after the Sino–Soviet political freeze ended in the 1980s that trade slowly started to recover. Uyghurs from Atush and Kashgar were amongst the earliest cross-border traders. The breakdown of the Soviet Union and independence of the Central Asian republics provided them with new markets, which they, on the basis of their close geographical proximity, cultural and linguistic competences, and extended social networks, were well equipped to exploit. The experience of trade in Kyrgyzstan varied over the following two and a half decades in ways strongly influenced by political events, trends, and government programmes in both China and Kyrgyzstan.

1991–2005

During the presidential reign of Askar Akaev in Kyrgyzstan (1991–2005), Uyghur traders dominated much of the border trade and experienced little competition. Profits were high, but so were the risks; government regulation was loose regarding import fees, taxes, licences and, indeed, security. According to Uyghur traders living in Bishkek and Osh in the early 2000s, the Kyrgyz had little understanding of prices, haggling, or trade in general, and this allowed large profits for the apt and the cunning. On the other hand, in the absence of proper policing and with widespread poverty, violence was experienced as a daily threat. Many stories of robberies and even killings still circulate from those early days. The traders were generally defenceless. In 2002, the Uyghur bazaar in Bishkek, consisting of small wooden stalls and huts, burned down in one night. The traders were convinced that the fire had been laid by envious local competitors. Miraculously, no one was seriously hurt, but many lost their entire stock of goods. The bazaar was never rebuilt, but trading continued in other markets, the largest and most well-known of which were the Dordoi and Madina bazaars in Bishkek and the Karasuu bazaar near Osh.

A rather insignificant kolchoz[3] market in the 1980s, Karasuu bazaar grew to become one of Central Asia's largest markets in the 2000s (Angermann 2006: 62–70). Its close proximity to Osh and the Uzbek border made it a perfect transfer place for Chinese goods into Uzbekistan. Tursun-aka, a moderately wealthy farmer from rural Atush was in his 40s when he started trading in Kyrgyzstan in the mid-2000s. He was helped by other men from his village who had established themselves in Karasuu after having traded in Bishkek for several years. Tursun-aka was a late starter, but managed to become very successful within only a few years. His eldest son, Abduwéli, who spoke acceptable Mandarin, took it upon himself to travel to Tianjin, Wenzhou, and Yiwu in eastern China to buy stock and have it shipped to Ürümchi. There, his wife's younger brother had it repackaged and sent on via Kashgar to Osh and Karasuu. By 2011, Tursun-aka was one of the wealthiest men in his village. He used a part of his private fortune to pave all the main paths of the village with cement, taking over infrastructural obligations that the state did not provide. By this time the conditions of trade had changed. Both risk and profits had fallen owing to shifts in Kyrgyzstan's political environment. Akaev was ousted in a popular uprising in 2005 and Kurmanbek Bakiev took his place.

2005–2010

During the presidency of Bakiev (2005–2010), stricter enforcement of laws and regulations was implemented. The security situation improved and armed robbery was no longer a daily concern. However, taxes and trade licence fees multiplied. Often, tax collectors demanded substantial additional bribes from foreign traders, not least Uyghurs who were seen as wealthy and largely unprotected by either the Kyrgyz or Chinese authorities. The cost of trade surged: the monthly taxes demanded from Uyghur traders in Karasuu rose from 2,000 Kyrgyz Som (about US$46) under Akaev to 8,000 Som (about US$194) in the early years of Bakiev's rule. During my stay in the summer of 2013, taxes rose to over 15,000 Som (about US$320). Bribes rose as well. One Uyghur trader said that whereas before they had feared lawless gangs, now it was the police who performed the same robbery in uniform. Uyghur traders' anxieties shifted from concerns with criminals to state authorities in the late 2000s. In 2013, telephone chains had been set up to warn against tax collectors and police raids at the bazaars. A friend of mine from Kashgar who worked as a chef in a Uyghur restaurant, sneaked out of the bazaar through side exits and secret paths each day after work to avoid harassment and bribe extractions by the bazaar guards. Likewise, the border crossing at Irkeshtam involved prolonged searches of traders' baggage and on the Kyrgyz side standardised bribes that varied according to ethnicity and origin. The stronger integration of society and the state that arguably took place under Bakiev provided local Kyrgyz traders with advantages as the government openly supported trade enterprises. In addition, the cultural shame connected to trading was decreasing and local authorities clearly favoured Kyrgyz traders. As a result, Uyghur traders were faced with much stronger local competition than before.

At the same time, competition was increasing from another side as well. In 2000, the Chinese government had launched their large-scale Western Development scheme (西部大开发) to help counter the country's vast regional disparities. In several phases and programmes, this strategy has seen billions of dollars invested into Xinjiang alone (Shan and Weng 2010: 61). The flow of money into Xinjiang accelerated the region's economic growth and benefitted a part of the local population, including traders who profited from improved infrastructure. Yet, it benefitted the Han-Chinese disproportionately more than Uyghurs and favoured eastern Chinese, Han-owned export companies with good direct links to the government and large funds. The latter claimed an ever larger share of the export to Kyrgyzstan in the late 2000s, while Uyghur small-scale traders saw themselves increasingly marginalised (Laruelle and Peyrouse 2009). Their condition became even more difficult as Bakiev's presidency ended in 2010.

2010–2013

Kyrgyz President Bakiev was ousted in a popular uprising in April 2010. A few months later, violence erupted in Osh. Uzbek shops and restaurants were targeted in particular, causing dozens, or possibly even hundreds of deaths (cf. Matveeva et al. 2012). This again changed the conditions for trade. In the months and years after the killings, the Kyrgyz–Uzbek border was often closed, as Uzbek authorities feared the spread of violence into their part of the Ferghana Valley. Business in Karasuu slumped and many small traders failed to sustain profitability. The Uyghur traders I met in Karasuu in 2013 who had managed to retain their foothold were able to do so by not being dependent on the day-to-day small market transactions. They had established stable business connections and conducted wholesale trade with Russia and Uzbekistan. One trader, Qare from Atush city, had developed his own brand and logo, which he had printed onto mass-produced speakers and other cheap hifi devices at a factory in eastern China. For a majority of the Uyghur traders selling small quantities of fabric, clothes, or cheap plastic products, Karasuu no longer offered any profitable market in 2013. Some moved to Bishkek to trade on the Medina and Dordoi markets, the major hubs of re-export of Chinese goods into Kazakhstan. Others saw opportunities in Tajikistan. A group of traders from Atush, with whom I was in close contact, moved to Kadamjay in the southernmost region of Batken. Here I met with Tursun-aka's youngest son. His father, who three years earlier had used his earnings from trade to pave the streets of their village, had retired, leaving his son with a stock of almost unsellable rubber sandals (Steenberg 2016). He had moved from Karasuu to Kadamjay, but faced with further difficulties and painfully slow sales, he now considered a trip to Bishkek's Madina or Dordoi bazaars to sell off his stock there. A few months later, he returned to Atush to marry, and the following year the family moved their business to Ürümchi. They were among the many Uyghurs who quit trade into Kyrgyzstan after 2013 as conditions continued to worsen and the remaining customers' purchasing power declined.

2014–2016

In the following years, Central Asia experienced severe financial difficulties, not least due to falling oil prices and the crises of the Russian economy. When I arrived in Karasuu in the summer of 2016, the picture was rather bleak. The adjacent wings of the bazaar were almost completely empty and within the main market several areas were only sparsely occupied. This included the part that had been full of Uyghur fabric traders in 2010 and 2013. Within three years, this large international bazaar had been reduced to one much smaller and more local scale. Local Kyrgyz and Uzbeks dominated the remaining stalls; Uyghurs and Han-Chinese were hardly to be found. A young Han-Chinese merchant from Fujian told me that for most Han traders the prospects for a healthy profit had dwindled as the fees and taxes had continued to rise while the customer base had been continuously reduced over the last few years. According to his estimates, the Han-Chinese in Karasuu had been decimated from almost 2,000 in 2014 to only 200–300 in 2016. None of my Uyghur friends and acquaintances from Atush was still in Karasuu in 2016, and people told me that the bazaars in Kadamjay had been all but abandoned.

The window of opportunity in Karasuu had closed for the Uyghur traders from Atush. This was a set-back, but not devastating, nor, indeed, exceptional. Most of them had already been engaged in several different more or less successful business endeavours or ran other businesses in parallel. As the border trade declined, they moved on to other fields of business. Some were concentrating on the trade between East China and Xinjiang. Tursunjan's small family business had shifted from rubber sandals in south Kyrgyzstan to women's trousers in Ürümchi. Other traders had likewise been engaged elsewhere. One group of young men, all cousins or in-laws, focused their efforts on agriculture. They had combined their funds to rent newly opened, government-irrigated land from Chinese migrants near Kashgar to grow cabbages, melons, and pumpkins for the local markets. In their new businesses, all these people retained and drew on their main assets that they had both utilised and cultivated in the trade: their social networks and interconnectedness with their fellow villagers, relatives, and friends.

Conclusion

This chapter tells two related stories; that of the Sino–Kyrgyz border trade from 1991 to 2016 and, within this frame, that of a group of Uyghur traders from Atush benefitting from, struggling in, and finally leaving the business. Both of these stories are influenced by global and local developments. The Sino–Kyrgyz border trade has over centuries fluctuated strongly, depending much on the wider economic circumstances and political environment. After border trade had been an important economic and political playing field in the region in the 19th and early 20th centuries, the 1930s brought it to an almost complete halt that lasted until the late 1980s. When trade was reinvigorated in the 1990s, Uyghurs from Atush and other oases pioneered the new markets. Drawing on tightly knit social networks, they dominated trade in the early phases, which were marked by uncertainty, insecurity, and a barely established formal infrastructure. As formalisation increased in the 2000s, Kyrgyz traders and larger Han-Chinese owned export companies with close ties to state institutions and the formal banking system began to outcompete the Uyghurs. Around 2015, most traders from Atush left the Sino–Kyrgyz border trade to invest their efforts and money elsewhere. Besides knowledge, skill, and capital, their resources prominently included their social networks. These have been constructed, formed, and maintained, at least in part, through cooperation and interaction around the border trade and continue to be crucial for the households as they venture into new businesses elsewhere. The story of the border trade has by no means ended – nor, probably, has that of Atush traders' involvement in it. This is not the first time the border trade has flourished or declined in accordance with shifting political circumstances, nor is it likely to be the last. Whether or not Atush traders will once more be at its forefront very much depends on keeping up their networks, that is, the continuation or transformation of local social organisation.

While the material conditions of the business environment undergo rapid changes and opportunities open and close quickly, the social networks and the trust they entail remain more consistent, though by no means static. This, under the given circumstances, makes them more important to local actors than either short-term profit or engagement in formal structures. Any particular business opportunity provides only a limited time slot to profit economically, but if it is used to consolidate social connections too, the invested effort and resources may pay off in multiple ways over the years to come. The window for this never really closes and is not so dependent on political events or economic trends beyond people's experience and control. Thus, the choice to invest in social networks instead of trusting the formal structures is a way for these marginalised groups to claim both security and ownership of one's own destiny.

Stepping back from the particularities of the Uyghur traders' story, a more general point arises. This chapter's analysis suggests a strong structural relation between the marginalised position of groups like the Uyghurs; their limited access to state resources, security, infrastructure, education, and formal markets; their strong social networks; and their engagement in high-risk, pioneering business undertakings. Wherever state institutions and other formal structures cannot be relied upon, it is particularly sensible to invest into social networks and to value their construction and upkeep over short-term profit making – and also over efforts of integration with formal systems, including formal education. This makes it rational and sensible to spend days (albeit not every day) playing pool with one's peers rather than going to school or seeking low wage formal employment, for example. It also makes it sensible to invest large amounts of money in elaborate life cycle celebrations, and to help a neighbour become established in one's own business niche. The reliance on social networks instead of anonymous formal structures of the modern state and markets makes high-risk, high-profit marginal business niches with little formalisation or state involvement a logical field of business pursuit for such marginalised groups. They have an advantage in such pioneering fields, as they, in a sense, carry along their own infrastructure and security mechanisms in the form of social relations. This turns to disadvantage when these fields become acquired by established formal structures.

Notes

1. Standard shipping containers employed on large freight ships and trains are used as shops and storage rooms at bazaars all over Central Asia. They provide good protection against both thieves and rain, and are widely accessible, as many goods arrive in them but the empty containers are very expensive for the logistics companies to return.
2. The road through Torugart leads over Naryn to Bishkek whereas the road over Irkeshtam goes to Osh. The crossing at Irkesham was the main port of entry between the Russian and Qing empires, and later the Soviet Union and the Chinese Republic.
3. A large state-run farm collective during Soviet times.

References

Alff, Henryk (2014): "Post-Soviet Positionalities: Relations, Flows and the Transformation of Bishkek's Dordoy Bazaar." In H. Alff and A. Benz (eds): *Tracing Connections: Explorations of Spaces and Places in Asian Contexts*. WVB, Berlin, 71–90.

Alff, Henryk (2016): "Flowing Goods, Hardening Borders? China's Commercial Expansion into Kyrgyzstan Re-examined." *Eurasian Geography and Economics* 57(1), 1–24.

Angermann, Matthias (2006): *Zwischen "Autozug" und "Drahtseilakt". Grenzueberschreitendes wirtschaftliches Handeln in Zentralasien dargestellt am Transithandelsmarkt Kara-Suu im Ferghanatal*. Unpublished MA thesis, Zentralasienseminar, Humbold University, Berlin.

Bichsel, Christine (2009): *Conflict Transformation in Central Asia: Irrigation Disputes in the Ferghana Valley*. Routledge, London and New York.

Bourdieu, Pierre (1986): "The Forms of Capital." In J. G. Richardson (ed): *Handbook of Theory and Research for the Sociology of Education*. Greenwood Press, New York, 241–258.

Brophy, David (2016): *Uyghur Nation: Reform and Revolution on the Russia-China Frontier*. Harvard University Press, Cambridge, MA.

Clark, William and Ablet Kamalov (2004): "Uighur Migration Across Central Asian Frontiers." *Central Asian Survey* 23(2), 167–182.

Hansen, Valerie (2012): *The Silk Road: A New History*. Oxford University Press, Oxford.

Ibraimov, S. (2009): "China-Central Asia Trade Relations: Economic and Social Patterns." *China and Eurasia Forum Quarterly* 7(1), 47–59.

Kreutzmann, Hermann (1998): "The Chitral Triangle." *Asien Afrika Lateinamerika* 26, 289–327.

Laruelle, Marlene and Sebastién Peyrouse (2009): "Cross-border Minorities as Cultural and Economic Mediators between China and Central Asia." *China and Eurasia Forum Quarterly* 7(1), 93–119.

Luhmann, Niklas (2000): *Vertrauen. Ein Mechanismus der Reduktion sozialer Komplexität*. Lucius & Lucius, Stuttgart.
Matveeva, Anna, Igor Savin and Bahrom Faizullaev (2012): *Kyrgyzstan: Tragedy in the South*, Ethnopolitics Papers 17.
Megoran, Nick (2004): "The Critical Geopolitics of the Uzbekistan–Kyrgyzstan Ferghana Valley Boundary Dispute, 1999–2000." *Political Geography* 23(6), 731–764.
Reeves, Madeleine (2012): "Black Work, Green Money: Remittances, Ritual, and Domestic Economies in Southern Kyrgyzstan." *Slavic Review* 71(1), 108–134.
Reeves, Madeleine (2014): *Border Work: Spatial Lives of the State in Rural Central Asia*. Cornell University Press, Ithaca, NY.
Shan, Wei and Weng Cuifen (2010): "China's New Policy in Xinjiang and its Challenges." *East Asian Policy* 2(3), 58–66.
Spector, Regine (2008): "Securing Property in Contemporary Kyrgyzstan." *Post-Soviet Affairs* 24(2), 149–176.
Steenberg, Rune (2014): "Network or Community? Two Tropes for Analysing Social Relations among Uyghur Traders in Kyrgyzstan." Crossroads Asia Working Paper Series 18. Competence Network Crossroads Asia, Berlin/Bonn.
Steenberg, Rune (2016): "Embedded Rubber Sandals: Trade and Gifts Across the Sino–Kyrgyz Border." *Central Asian Survey* 35(3), 405–420.

23
The "leech plot"
Discourses on alleged deception strategies among traders in the Sino–Vietnamese borderlands

Caroline Grillot

The "leech plot"

In early November 2013 in the border city of Móng Cái (Quảng Ninh province, Vietnam), my research assistant and I had a late dinner at a small family-run restaurant. We were enjoying chicken soup and a glass of corn juice when a Vietnamese customer appeared and started a conversation with the owner. We silently listened in and learned about what later appeared to be an actual event. The man, the owner of a boat building company, complained about the Chinese:

> These Chinese are trying to destroy our economy! They are cheating us, but so many people still believe in partnerships with them. After the leech plot, how can we trust them? These people are *thâm như tàu* [insidious like Chinese].

Even though the man was not directly involved in the affair he was mentioning, he seemed to have given it some thought, and his viewpoint captured the complicated position of two economic partners engaged in an often denounced and uneven trade cooperation. What was this "leech plot"?

According to Vietnamese media,[1] the business of selling leeches started around 2009 and boomed from 2011 to 2012, despite a ban issued by the Vietnamese Ministry of Agriculture and Rural Development against breeding these dangerous invertebrates. Several Chinese traders appeared in southern Vietnam at first and started to buy leeches from farmers at an unusually high price and in large quantities. Feeling that this was a rare opportunity to earn money from a widely available natural resource – not to mention an annoying creature – many Vietnamese farmers ventured into this strange trade. When they could not meet the demand by simply collecting leeches in local ponds and fields, they started breeding them in family-owned ponds until they reached a good enough weight to be sold. Rumour had it that the leeches were used in traditional medicine in China,[2] but no one apparently seriously checked whether the species they found in their ponds were indeed medicinal leeches[3] or not. During the year of 2013, however, leech suppliers experienced a sudden wake-up call when Chinese purchasers suddenly disappeared, leaving behind stocks of unsold leeches, indebted suppliers, and uninformed collectors. Early that year, a Vietnam TV special report[4] had established that, in reality, the business was mere speculation with no other purpose than to earn large amounts of money on the backs of farmers' naivety. According to the report, the leeches did not even leave Vietnam. They were collected for a good rate on farms, and then resold at an inflated price to collectors in different locations, owing to rumours of bottomless demand in China. Stocks grew, and when collectors tried to sell their leeches to local agents of Chinese companies, they found that, in several cases, the companies had simply vanished and abandoned existing stocks, leaving their local intermediaries with environmental damage and without further instructions.

This episode of "leech fever" became widely regarded as a plague, not only because the creatures invaded the ecosystem and populations grew uncontrollably, but also because it ruined many people involved and left behind economic hardship in regions that were once dedicated to farming. The Vietnamese media rendered this phenomenon as one of the many examples of how unscrupulous Chinese traders were cheating, breaking promises, and simply disappearing with nothing left behind except ecological disaster and farmers in despair. Years later, nourished by other similar episodes of failed business collaborations, the local discourse developed even further and branded Chinese business people as mere speculators, who aimed to undermine Vietnam's economy. Their actual goal, so the allegations went, was to exploit Vietnam's natural resources, grow fat with impunity, and eventually ruin Vietnam's economy from inside. In other words, local discourse blamed the Chinese for wanting to suck Vietnam's blood like leeches do.

The very nature of the leech is dualistic. Although the creature can harm, it can also cure, as recorded throughout medical history (Whitaker et al. 2004). In this chapter, I associate the intriguing characteristics of the symbiotic relationship between the leech and other organisms with the frustrating collaboration between Chinese and Vietnamese traders, in order to explore cross-border trading activities and relationships in Móng Cái. I draw on empirical materials collected between 2013 and 2014 in the border city's market spaces, and focus specifically on the logistic and management practices of the small-scale, mostly extra-legal border trade of manufactured commodities and natural products. I collected small-scale Chinese traders' accounts of their difficulties and their perplexity towards the practices of Vietnamese state agents and business partners. These accounts suggest that they were subject to unscrupulous and controlling economic partners. On the Vietnamese side of the border, however, a different set of narratives and stories, such as the leech plot, revealed the grievances of Vietnamese traders, who face Chinese economic and commercial power over Vietnam and, in particular, its natural resources.

After a short introduction about the trading centre of Móng Cái, I offer traders' perspectives on the financial bonds that sustain their activities. I then turn to the pressure that states impose on them, before analyzing the interdependent dynamism that animates various levels of the border economy's actors, who are regarded as "leeches", whether in their parasitic form or as symbiotic elements of trade cooperation. I argue that owing to a lack of reliable information and trust, both the Chinese and Vietnamese sides struggle with distorted understandings of their business partners' strategies while having their own agendas. These agendas maintain invisible yet tacit control over the other side.

Móng Cái: a node of border trade economy

Separated from the bustling city of Dongxing (Guangxi, China) by the Beilun River, Móng Cái is a growing border city in the northern province of Quảng Ninh and the busiest border crossing between China and Vietnam. According to recent official reports, trade with China now accounts for 85 percent of Vietnam's total border trade.[5]

Wholesale markets and dozens of shops that sell an incredibly large range of commodities have invaded the city centre. Market No. 2 and Market No. 3 are increasingly run-down due to a lack of care. However, there is a plan to renovate them. Most of the shopkeepers are Vietnamese, but a few Chinese-run shops are also present. Similar to these two markets, Togi Market is hosted in a concrete building that also looks old and is emptying slowly; here, Vietnamese and Chinese are equally present. Móng Cái Plaza and Vinh Co Market are privately-owned modern buildings mainly occupied by Chinese shopkeepers. Finally, Móng Cái Centre Market, the most notorious and visible market, is a modern, hexagonal, four-storey building with mostly Chinese and some Vietnamese traders. Market No. 1, as it is informally called, faces Kalong port and is well equipped with underground warehouses and storage spaces. Trucks and transporters can easily access the building. Built jointly by the Vietnamese state and a private Chinese company, it was state-run but is now privately owned. This has resulted in some changes, since each shop now belongs to private individuals, and a quite confusing management system. Today, some of the shopkeepers own their own shops. However, many are just renting spaces at rates that have dramatically dropped since 2012 owing to a decline in China's economic growth and general difficulties encountered in cross-border trade since the hardening of the diplomatic crisis between China and Vietnam over the issue of sovereignty in the South China Sea. It is within this dense and active setting that most small trade operations take place, where traders come and go, and where success meets failure on a daily basis. It is here that constant tensions are articulated in recurrent discourses about the "other" and the anxiety attached to the unpredictability of the market.

Perspective on financial pressure: seeing suppliers/customers as "parasites"

The leech is an annoying and unpredictable organism[6] that drains others of their resources, energy, and means until it feels satisfied. It then changes its target and leaves the assaulted host exhausted and anxious about his or her ability to recover. A leech and the metabolism to which it is attached, are intertwined: the host must wait until the leech is full and detaches itself. Forced detachment will make the host suffer even more as it can cause the wound to tear. This archetypal parasitic relationship serves as a metaphor that captures the complex principles governing the dynamic between the three main actors in this borderland economy: the state authority, the Chinese traders, and the Vietnamese traders. The modalities of collaboration between Chinese and Vietnamese traders operating in the borderlands are the arena in which this exhausting relationship evolves, and where the tensions between business partners are rendered visible. One of these tensions concerns the financial pressures of the practices of "returning goods" and "outstanding debt". The issue of debt repayment is a frequent bone of contention for traders that ties into this parasitic metaphor, as it leaves debtors with the feeling of having been drained of their financial capacity and puts traders' economic survival in this competitive commercial environment at risk (Grillot 2016).

Thuy, a young Vietnamese woman and her Chinese husband Lin have managed a flourishing business over the last decade. Starting from a modest shop selling basic decoration materials in the early 2000s to managing two shops specializing in high quality tiles, their reputation in Móng Cái's Vinh Co market has guaranteed them a regular clientele. However, the couple keeps complaining about the uncertainties of their trade given the payment method their Vietnamese customers persist in using. Lin summarizes his feeling of being controlled by the Vietnamese:

> We've become passive, they are the active ones. We must follow their rules: first we deliver the goods, then they pay. But they often don't pay according to what was initially agreed

on, that is to say: in one go. They pay in several instalments, make extra orders, and they sometimes even forget to finish paying the whole bill. That's how we lose a lot of money. We don't make any profit; they actually have a strong hold on us.

Lin speaks out about what almost all Chinese traders doing business in Vietnam complained about when asked about their experiences. They call it *laizhang*: to repudiate debt and backpedal on agreements by employing subtle tactics to maintain such a system and bind two parties together in a perpetual debt relationship. The reason why so many Chinese traders keep pursuing their business interests despite such tactics is because they have invested a lot of money at the outset, which is how business is conducted in China. For instance, many of the small-scale Chinese traders interviewed in Móng Cái admitted that they knew almost nothing about Vietnam and border trade before starting their business there. At best, they had made some preliminary investigations on the market possibilities, relying on their acquaintances to provide them with relevant information and advice on how to tap into Vietnamese market needs. However, in searching for economic opportunities and easy money, many inexperienced traders coming from China's interior provinces found themselves insufficiently prepared. They were poorly informed about the real commercial demands of Vietnam, reliant on wide-spread stereotypes about Vietnamese, and believed firmly in the superiority of Chinese products and trading talents. As such, many of them quickly faced the harsh reality of dealing with Vietnamese customers. Not only did many come to realize that they had invested their entire savings in what turned out to be an unreliable and ultra-competitive business, but they also found themselves trapped in the difficulties of recovering their investment, getting out, and moving on. Many Chinese traders assumed that they would be participating in a booming Chinese borderland economy and a developing Vietnamese market. In a way, these traders initially acted as "medicinal leeches" – "curing" the "backwardness" of Vietnam's economy by providing the market with commodities and, in return, feeding off of Vietnam's resources. However, they experienced that the situation was out of their control. Disoriented by the way their Vietnamese customers, associates, and business partners managed their financial resources, Chinese investors and traders had no other choice than to continue bearing what they felt were abusive Vietnamese business practices, much like the passive host of a leech attack.

As I have demonstrated elsewhere, judgemental comments on the tactics of business partners and the general discourse on divergent national trade ethics mostly emerge from common misunderstandings of "culturally marked approaches to capital management" (Grillot 2016: 184) and asymmetries in access to investment. Moreover, Chinese entrepreneurs' harsh judgement of their Vietnamese "others" also serves as justification for questionable business practices that would not be acceptable in China. In a foreign environment where control over commodities, transportation, and financial flows is by and large managed through informal channels, Chinese traders avoid admitting that they allow themselves some moral flexibility in their own practices. To maximize profit, they develop commercial strategies that embrace irregularities and thus enhance the mutual feeling of mistrust.

Who is the host and who is the leech?

Roles remain contested and dependent on mutual othering. However, the leech plot does not just need leeches, but also plotters. The controversial quality of many commodities produced in China and introduced into Vietnamese markets since the opening of cross-border trade (Zhang 2016) provides an accurate example of the contradiction at hand. While Chinese wholesalers blame their Vietnamese retailers for returning goods that they could not sell, they forget to mention the low quality of their commodities and assume that they are sufficient to meet the market demands of an "economically backward country". Vietnamese television reports regularly point out the poor quality of Chinese clothes and household appliances, products beyond their expiration date, and traditional medicines of questionable authenticity and safety. This fuels Vietnamese consumers' general suspicion. As some Vietnamese informants explain it: "many so-called famous Chinese teas are made from low-quality Vietnamese leaves that are processed in China, flavoured, and then re-imported to Vietnam"; "there are so many chemicals on Chinese apples that children get sick if they eat them"; "shipping is not properly controlled at the border gate, so bad quality commodities invade the Vietnamese market"; "Chinese get rid of their old fashions by selling them to the Vietnamese"; and, so forth.

Such allegations go hand in hand with anti-Chinese propaganda in the context of rising tensions in the South China Sea. They reflect the contradictory feelings Vietnamese have of both respect and annoyance towards China's economic superiority and arrogance in the commercial realm. They also point out the need to remain cautious of unfair practices that are deemed as attempts to ruin long-term partnerships. As Endres noticed,

> Vietnamese traders often perceived their Chinese business partners as not stressing *tình cảm* (sentiment) as much as the Vietnamese did… [they] considered this highly valued and constitutive element of Vietnamese social relationships lacking not only in Chinese business relations but also in Chinese society as a whole.
>
> *(Endres 2015: 727–8)*

To explain this, the strict pragmatism of Chinese business culture might be one interpretation. Chinese business people are not totally ignorant of these problems. Mr Xiang, a Chinese garments seller in Móng Cái's Market No.1, for example, mentioned the grim agenda of some small-scale Chinese businesses in Vietnam that contradicts the harmonious and sustainable partnership promoted by the Chinese and Vietnamese states:

> You wonder why some people don't want to talk to you? It's because many Chinese here prefer to remain inconspicuous about their purpose. They do not care so much about making long-term profits or building relationships. They come to Vietnam for money laundering – they rent a shop, buy a stock of substandard clothes from a factory, sell them here to make some money, and then they go. They have no scruples.

The standard of quality of the goods that Chinese traders select for export are often interpreted by Vietnamese to be signs that the Chinese are exploiting Vietnam under the guise of contributing to the development of its economy. The prevalence of Chinese low quality goods on Vietnamese markets casts doubt on China's true agenda and gives rise to protective measures.

The entrepreneurs, the state, and its border trade "therapists"

In the tangled realm of cross-border trade, the art of negotiating illicit commerce and the mechanism for smuggling are part of the game. Cross-border trade does not only involve traders and customers. It also requires complicity and negotiation with a state that uses various governance tools and rules to regulate the demanding process of building and smoothing sustainable partnerships. Enforcement, here again, is perceived as an invading agent causing financial haemophilia. When Vietnamese traders and their Chinese counterparts are not complaining about each other's business practices, they constantly refer to the uneven nature of their working environment to explain the difficulties of conducting successful business. Their weariness and helplessness towards state policies and enforcement practices also mirror the established bond between the leech and host organism. The systemic corruption that drives the Vietnamese socialist-oriented market economy is an overwhelming and unavoidable feature of the trading environment. Traders from both sides feel that their benefits get "sucked up" by state agents, who intervene at different stages of the business chain to "make the law" (Endres 2014). State agents impose fines or bribes on top of official fees in order to exert control over commodity flows, to "manage" traders, and to supplement their low salaries.

Mr Zhu, for example, was selling blue jeans on the ground floor of Móng Cái's Central Market. In 2013, he was attracted to Móng Cái by a family member, who had already established a business there and convinced him to give it a try. Inexperienced and unaware of the realities of Vietnam's culture, market rules, and trade environment, he came only with the intention of making money. Now, his business is not going well. While patiently waiting for new faces to show up at his shop's doorstep, he complained:

> I don't get it. Vietnam is backward, its economy is weak, and it's undeveloped. There is no industry in the region, so people need Chinese goods. What they produce is not of good quality. So, they should welcome us and provide us with basic protection and encouraging policies here. At least the market management should take care of this place. It's the centre of the city. Instead, they pressure us with taxes and try to squeeze more money out of us. We pay a low rent to the shop owners because business is not good and they can't find people to fill up the market, but the management board is different. They work for the government. They still request us to pay high taxes. It's unfair. Look how empty the market is! What is the point of ripping us off? If we all leave, what will they do? Well, actually, if we leave we lose our investment because many of us have many unpaid bills…

The art of negotiating with state agents around strict rules and laws and making illicit arrangements for the cross-border shipment of goods is a difficult and challenging skill to acquire. However, it has become essential in the tangled realm of cross-border trade. Mr Fan, a middle-aged shopkeeper in the Central Market provided me with ample detail about the fees he needed to pay on a daily basis in order to do business in Móng Cái, on top of the taxes collected by the market's management board. While he acknowledged that he would pay even more for a similar shop in China, he nevertheless emphasized the dubious regulations behind many of the taxes that Vietnamese state agents claim in the market as well as at the border gate, which he crosses daily to bring in his commodities. Like many of his fellow Chinese, Mr Fan adopted a "DIY import" method, a practice designed to avoid steep tariffs of large-quantity imports through official channels. Each person crossing the border is allowed to carry one bag of commodities for sale in Vietnam (see Figure 23.1). Although this practice is legal and not officially considered to be smuggling because each bag is taxed according to its content, size, and weight, it is still deemed to be informal trade.

Mr Fan's account provides us with a glimpse of the numerous layers of income created by the authorities' tolerance of DIY import:

> When I come to Vietnam every morning, I must pay 10,000 VNĐ[7] to the Vietnamese border officer for each pack I carry (newcomers are often asked to pay 50,000), and every evening I need to pay 15,000 just to return to China. Then, there is the health department

Figure 23.1 Móng Cái, Chinese traders carrying their load at the border gate with Vietnam
Photo by Caroline Grillot 2014

that controls the contents of the bags. The first time I had to pay 100 yuan because I could not provide any documents or receipt for the commodities I was carrying. In principle, you pay this tax only once, but since they do not give you any receipt, the officers in charge regularly claim it again. This is the case both for going in and out the country. Most of the time, they don't even bother to check your bags. As for the visa, they also have a strategy. You must pay 30 yuan for a 10-day multi-entry visa. But they like to stamp it on different pages of the border-pass to waste space so that very soon, there is no space anymore and you must buy another pass and another visa as well. If you forget to get your pass stamped, it's another 100 yuan fine. There are so many people every morning that things must go fast. There is no time to bargain or complain, so you pay. These are small sums but regular ones, and these border administrators make lots of money off our backs!

Many small-scale traders carry their goods across the official border gate while other traders smuggle goods using private inland navigation channels. Although bigger cross-border businesses transport goods by freight trucks and use the official border crossing on a regular basis, they can also be involved in illegal practices. Some of these traders have learned to master strategies that misuse Chinese state subsidies, which were initially meant to encourage the import–export economy. Thus, they generate revenue without producing anything. The small-scale traders who operate in Móng Cái's markets clearly express their disagreement with such practices, branding them as a form of official corruption that threatens the long-term health of national business – like a leech regularly sucking the blood of another organism.

Nevertheless, despite incoherencies and the obvious unevenness between policies and their enforcement, border trade needs state governance to regulate flows and avoid chaos, similar to how hirudotherapy uses medicinal leeches to treat health disorders, in particular vascular congestion (Bennett-Marsden 2014). State agents act as "therapists", who regulate border activities according to the informal rules of the corruption game played by officers (Endres 2014). They fine those traders who avoid paying taxes, while also collecting informal taxes. In addition, border patrol agents stand at night on the shores of the river separating Vietnam from China, and accept bribes on the spot from traders who evade law enforcement. However, by rendering these practices systemic to handling the border economy, state agents expose the inefficiency of state governance and help to enhance the very market uncertainties that traders tend to blame on their neighbours.

Leech anxieties in border trade

The "leech plot" and its analogical power reveal the complex motivations sustaining the continuity of trade dynamics between China and Vietnam as experienced by actors on the ground and as monitored by state agents. Like other episodes that regularly occur in the realm of cross-border commercial exchanges, this incident, in particular, highlights two main issues: the fierce market competition that leads to hazardous speculation; and, the feeling of anxiety and suspicion that underlies the relationship between competitors, who cannot see themselves as *merely* traders.

Chinese and Vietnamese traders' activities sustain the economic development of the borderlands in two countries that, over the last 50 years successively or simultaneously, have been socialist brothers and/or military aggressors, and whose citizens have been soldiers, refugees – the Hoa[8] who flew from Vietnam in the late 1970s – and/or commercial partners. They are bound by economic necessity and scrutinized by omnipresent state authorities represented by lax agents. As Zhang noticed during a 2007 Trade Fair that exposed the fragility of cross-border trade politics,

> the façade of amicable relations and friendships is kept until the moment when the unexpected happens. When the normalcy of interactions is disrupted abruptly, the familiar social relations and practiced norms break down and prove to be inadequate and fragile.
>
> *(Zhang 2016: 218)*

Although small-scale Chinese traders suffer from the challenging context in which their commercial activities take place, many still manage to adjust to Vietnamese governance of cross-border trade and to their partners' business ethics.

With its inherent instability, border trade does not necessarily attract long-term planning. Borderlands are often the sites of business experiments, such as the promotional selling of innovative products, factory-stock liquidation, the import of illicit items, and all sorts of trade that is not allowed in China, but is permitted or tolerated in Vietnam. Chinese traders rely on their knowledge of the current market needs, on their creativity, and on the management of a trust capital that they build with local partners who are working for them. Some traders go beyond the borderlands to endeavour to expand their commercial activities with what Vietnam has to offer, that is to say, its natural resources. However, a large part of those Chinese involved in cross-border trade are migrants, who must operate through intermediaries because of their lack of language skills and limited access to inland Vietnam (due to a lack of documentation and discriminatory visa procedures). This is especially the case when they become part of long-distance business chains in Vietnam over which they have no direct control and that can only be supervised by locals. However, the intermediaries are in a position to exploit the ignorance and the business agenda of various parties involved in a deal. They are also often part of multiple business chains. Therefore, traders' trust and reliance in them can lead to unexpected changes in their business plans, depending on how the intermediaries navigate the market.

China's clear strategic move towards Vietnam's natural resources that are scarce or costly in China, and the anxiety resulting from a lack of mutual understanding in each other's motivations and business agendas underlies their mutual suspicion. Turner et al. (2015), who have conducted extensive research on Hmong people's involvement in cross-border trade in the upland borderlands, provide one instance of a Chinese demand driven trade that puts Vietnamese suppliers (in their case, the Hmong living in Lào Cai province) in a subordinate and dependent position. Their description of trade in cardamom (another ingredient in traditional Chinese medicine) and woven textiles shows how "the irregularities of these trade connections and the large geographical distances between trade participants at different nodes in the networks mean that trade ties are often weak" (Turner et al. 2015: 143). As a consequence, the absence of a direct bond between suppliers and buyers creates misunderstandings that play as important a role in raising anxiety as market competition or potential speculation. This situation forces both sides to take considerable risks in the hopes of winning the competition, resulting in further misunderstandings and causing financial bankruptcy or environmental upheaval.

When the state and the economic system are corrupt (Endres 2014) and unreliable, especially during crises, when most small-scale trade contracts are informal and ineligible for legal protection, personal networks are the only grounds on which business deals, operations, and resolutions to problems become possible (Grillot 2016; Zhang 2016). However, it is a fragile ground, involving knowledge, perceptions, trust, experience, time, and compromise. Under such conditions, conspiracy theories offer justifications for traders' business strategies that aim at protecting personal as well as national economic interests, and serve as an explanation for traders whose projects fail. In analyzing the occurrence of the word "eat" in the formulation of exploitative relationships in Malaysia, Scott notes that "the metaphor is used not only by the poor to describe what is done to them by the powerful but is used also by the rich to describe the demands for loans and charity pressed on them by the poor" (Scott 1987: 187). This clearly echoes the leech analogy that serves to describe Chinese and Vietnamese traders' complaints about the difficulties they encounter in their collaborations and the uneasiness they generate.

However, Zhang (2011, 2016) has also emphasized in her work that the anxiety and mistrust that is palpable in the realm of border trade, and the difficulty of adopting various business codes, prove to be more constructive than destructive. As a matter of fact, traders need to become creative in order to compete, so they will try anything to make money, including making risky investments, taking out accumulative loans, and entering uncertain associations. Most Chinese and Vietnamese entrepreneurs come to the borderlands confident that they will succeed by seizing on commercial opportunities that border trade claims to offer. They invest their savings in a business that they believe, no matter how and under what conditions, will provide them with a minimum level of profit; at least they must get some reward for their efforts, before moving on to new strategies or a different place.

Conclusion: a parasitic or a symbiotic relationship?

Was the "leech episode" a sign of a Sino–Vietnamese cross-border trade crisis? Who benefits from whom? To what extent does state intervention or non-intervention impact trade development at the Sino–Vietnamese border? What effect do locally spread interpretations of unfair practices in informal trade have on business that already occurs in an unstable environment? These are questions left open to speculation on both sides of the border, but this chapter has attempted to provide one interpretation. Navigating market niches is common to any free market environment. However, this becomes an unsustainable business strategy in a border trade environment that often relies on unpredictable networks. The resulting priority is given to short-term, opportunistic, and fast-income-generating deals, such as the trade in cardamom, Hmong textiles, or leeches.

The leech needs blood to grow and is demanding. It finds a suitable creature to feed on, develop, and grow bigger, until it then detaches and departs. Building on the metaphor of the leech, and informed by viewpoints from Chinese entrepreneurs and their Vietnamese counterparts, this chapter has explored articulations of the lively experience of trading in this Sino–Vietnamese border space. It has argued that complaints about partners' failures and questionable methods that emerge from both objective empirical knowledge and scarce reliable information, articulate anxiety over the global economy's uncertainties and create mutual dependence. However, this anxiety has little to do with the actual facts that partners blame each other for.

As mentioned earlier, the leech is paradoxical: it can harm and it can also cure. If we sustain the analogy, we should also give some credit to the beneficial aspect of the "leech-like" relationship between Chinese and Vietnamese traders, as well as between traders and states. However, the flexibility that borderlands offer comes with a price. The pressure felt on each side of the commercial chain and the impediments embedded in maintaining each party's position in the realm of border trade – namely, mutual dependence, mutual exploitation, and negotiated flexibility – also remain powerful drivers for innovative commercial strategies. Despite structural hindrances and personal grievances, these strategies eventually manage to enhance economic collaboration and develop the border economy.

Acknowledgments

The research presented in this article was funded by the Minerva Program of the Max Planck Institute for Social Research (Germany).

The author would like to thank this volume's editors, as well as Naomi Hellman for their meticulous and valuable editing of this chapter.

Notes

1 See: www.thanhniennews.com/society/vietnam-in-leech-scare-as-trade-to-china-goes-uncontrolled-9431.html (last consulted on 18 March 2016).
2 See: www.chineseherbshealing.com/medicinal-leeches/ (last consulted on 10 October 2017).
3 *Hirudo medicinalis.*
4 See: http://tuoitrenews.vn/business/11820/print?undefined (last consulted on 18 March 2016).
5 See: http://english.gov.cn/news/international_exchanges/2016/01/06/content_281475267268764.htm (last consulted on 3 October 2016).
6 Among the hundreds of species, only some are parasite.
7 About half a US$.
8 The Hoa are overseas Chinese living in Vietnam and categorized as a national minority. Many escaped persecution in 1978–1979 and flew to China. After the re-establishment of diplomatic relations between the two countries in 1991, some returned to Vietnam and engaged in border trade. Although Chinese by origin, the Hoa have deep roots in Vietnam and are still regarded by borderlanders as different from Mainland Chinese, partly because many of the Hoa who chose to remain settled in China still hold refugee status, and those who returned to Vietnam show ambivalent loyalty towards China.

References

Bennett-Marsden, Michael. 2014. "Hirudotherapy: A Guide to Using Leeches to Drain Blood from Tissue." *Clinical Pharmacist* 6 (3): 69.
Endres, Kirsten W. 2014. "Making Law: Small-Scale Trade and Corrupt Exceptions at the Vietnam-China Border." *American Anthropologist* 116 (3): 611–25.
Endres, Kirsten W. 2015. "Constructing the Neighbourly 'Other': Trade Relations and Mutual Perceptions Across the Vietnam – China Border." *Journal of Social Issues in Southeast Asia* 30 (3): 710–41.
Grillot, Caroline. 2016. "'Trust Facilitates Business But May Also Ruin It': The Hazardous Facets of Sino-Vietnamese Border Trade." *Asian Anthropology* 15 (2): 169–85.
Scott, James C. 1987. *The Weapons of the Weak. Everyday Forms of Peasant Resistance*. New Haven, CT & London: Yale University Press.
Turner, Sarah, Christine Bonnin and Jean Michaud. 2015. *Frontier Livelihoods Hmong in the Sino-Vietnamese Borderlands*. Washington: University of Washington Press.
Whitaker, Iain S., J. Rao, D. Izadi, and P. E. Butler. 2004. "Historical Article: Hirudo Medicinalis: Ancient Origins Of, and Trends in the Use of Medicinal Leeches throughout History." *British Journal of Oral and Maxillofacial Surgery* 42 (2): 133–7.
Zhang, Juan. 2011. *Border Opened Up: Everyday Business in a China-Vietnam Frontier*. Macquarie University, PhD dissertation.
Zhang, Juan. 2016. "Neighbouring in Anxiety along the China-Vietnam Border" in Martin Saxer and Juan Zhang (eds.), *The Art of Neighbouring. Making Relations Across China's Borders*. Amsterdam: Amsterdam University Press: 203–22.

24

Nobody stops and stays anymore

Motor roads, uneven mobilities, and conceptualizing borderland modernity in highland Nepal

Galen Murton

One summer morning, sitting in the private family quarters of the oldest guesthouse in Kagbeni, Nepal, I asked how new road systems affect everyday life in Mustang District today. Drolma,[1] sipping her morning tea, told me matter of factly: "nobody stops and stays anymore"! Wanting to know more, I asked how could this be, as Kagbeni is strategically located at the intersection of two major rivers, a sacred *pitha* place for Hindu pilgrims, a key junction of the region's most popular trekking route, and the base for government checkposts and a conservation area office that supervise tourism into Nepal's northern restricted zone of Upper Mustang. Kagbeni has long been a point of rest for regional travelers, and *kag* means "stop" in Tibetan.

While visitors to Kagbeni travel according to various agendas, Drolma's point transcends demographic differences. Unlike historical tradition, when locals and foreigners alike would routinely stay overnight in Kagbeni, new road networks to the north, south, and east of Kagbeni have all but eliminated the need to break one's journey in town. Near Drolma's guesthouse, the owner of a small shop, Jigme, echoed his neighbor, emphasizing that few Mustangis stop in Kagbeni anymore, and international visitors tend to do so only to complete bureaucratic formalities. Exaggeration aside – as the town remains home to no less than two dozen guesthouses, restaurants, and supply stores, and foreigners traveling to Upper Mustang are required to stop at the government checkpost – Jigme's comments signal a disruption of traditional cultural practices in this borderland region as a result of new transport networks.

Beyond the fact that motorcycles, jeeps, and buses facilitate faster modes of travel and obviate the need for routine rest stops, Drolma and Jigme reveal more nuanced, cultural dimensions of social transformation in Mustang affected by new transborder road infrastructures that increasingly connect Nepal's northern districts with both China and central Nepal. Specifically, the development of transborder as well as domestic road infrastructure through Mustang has facilitated new configurations of mobility and containment at local, regional, and transnational levels that both disrupt and reinforce sociocultural legacies established with Mustang's location along trans-Himalayan trade routes. In order to better understand these transformations and place them in a context of borderland modernity, this chapter uses a dialectical framework of mobility and containment to examine how new infrastructures at the Nepal–China borderlands

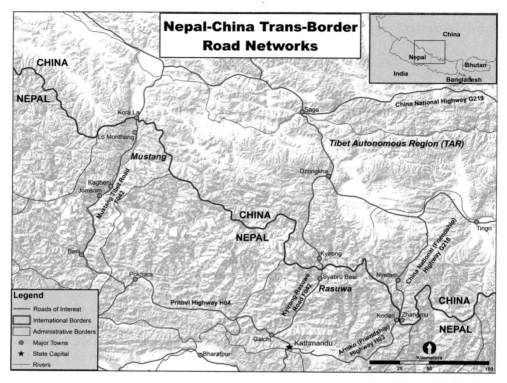

Map 24.1 Nepal–China transborder road networks
Map by Galen Murton

both reconfigure and reinforce social relations and political economies at a key intersection of geopolitical and global capital circulations.

On the basis of ethnographic, multi-site fieldwork in the borderlands of both Nepal and Tibet,[2] this study looks specifically at the expansion of motor roads in Nepal's northern borderland district of Mustang to understand how access and exclusion to new mobilities reinscribe social hierarchies in borderland spaces (Map 24.1). While I focus the study on the shifting cultural practices of trans-Himalayan *nyetsang*[3] social systems and expanding tourism sector in Mustang, I suggest this case represents a broader dynamic of social change reflected in wider experiences with infrastructure development, state formation, and forces of capital across the Asian borderlands. To advance this analysis, I introduce borderland modernity as a rapidly expanding and internationalized experience with globalization in highland Asia, accelerated by road infrastructure and characterized by new consumer practices, capital circulations, and state bureaucracy and in non-urban places.

Contextualizing mobility, containment, and modernity in the Nepal borderlands

For the purposes of this chapter, I put *mobility* – or the ability of people, goods, and ideas to move across spaces and between places – in productive tension with *containment* – or the limits placed upon mobility through particular social and institutional restrictions. I conceptualize containment as a process and experience of distinct state intervention and territorialization. Containment is similar to but distinct from Harris's (2013) theorization of fixity, or a socially situated condition that places limits on mobility on the basis of road access (and exclusion). In Mustang and across wider Nepal, containment includes structural entities such as fences and tax policies that comprise new border regimes as well as limits on social mobility that are conditioned by new road infrastructures. Together, these processes of mobility and containment have converged in borderland spaces such as Mustang to make local populations increasingly legible (Scott 1999) to the Kathmandu center and subjects of a modernizing Himalayan state. As roads, border posts, trade fairs, and guest lodges mediate social relations between populations in Mustang and communities in Chinese Tibet as well as central Nepal, it is at these points of convergence that the Nepali state increasingly and conspicuously takes shape in the form of institutional bodies that function to expand commerce, tax trade, regulate transport, and cultivate tourism. Bearing in mind ongoing oscillations between mobility and containment, this chapter argues that local experiences with new mobilities at once transform social and economic relations across trans-Himalayan spaces and undergird material practices that produce space for both markets and the Nepali state to take shape through new mechanisms of containment.

Everyday experiences in Mustang take place at and are strongly conditioned by the dialectical intersections of mobility and containment. Roads and border infrastructures are synthetic forms produced by a convergence of mobility (thesis) with containment (antithesis). Mobility implies a centrifugal force (Kristof 1959) and refers to the ability of both goods and people to move across landscapes (both borderland and domestic spaces) as well as a historical practice formative to place-based identities (Cresswell & Merriman 2012; Cresswell 2016). Aspects of mobility include: Mustang's place along the historical trans-Himalayan Salt Trade; the provenance, cultivation, and legacy of Tibetan Buddhist monastic institutions across the district; Mustang's key position in Nepal's Strategic Road Network development program; the current proliferation of private and motorized vehicle systems in Mustang; and the dynamics of transborder trade and commerce that connect Mustang's villages with Chinese manufacturing centers as well as international remittance economies. Conversely, containment is the processes of bordering and delimitations of exclusion that made Mustang into an exceptional borderland space; containment is essentially centripetal, and refers to the ways in which mobilities are foreclosed. Local experiences with the state in Mustang have long been characterized by containment: suzerainty over the Kingdom of Mustang (Lo) by the region and state's successive regimes of rule; Nepal–China bordering policies of the 1960s; prohibition of foreigners in Mustang until 1992; Chinese fencing of the border in 1999 to 2000; and complex Sino–Nepali regulations over trade between Mustang and Tibet.

Modernity constitutes a disruptive and contradictory process rather than a state of being or a reified "thing". Specifically, modernity is an uneven experience punctuated by shifting moments of order and chaos, categorization and fragmentation, rationality and bewilderment, legibility and disunity (Berman 1983). This conceptualization makes modernity especially useful for engaging with the disorienting and dislocating experiences brought about by technological change, particularly with respect to the transformative force of roads and vehicles in Mustang. New technologies, and the social spaces they create, constitute crucibles of change. It is within such spaces that transformations of everyday life take place (de Certeau 2011), reflected in the reorientation of material practices that characterize key moments of the modern experience (Hetherington 2007). Though critical scholarship often looks to the city when observing the modern experience (Lefebvre 2003), a view to the margins and into rural and non-urban space reveals similar patterns of bewilderment and uneven development with forces of modernization.

Whither the *nyetsang:* roads, social change, and uneven development

Road infrastructure development is a fundamental project of national state making and the impacts of roads are both heightened and complicated in borderland regions. Amidst large, national imaginaries and policy agendas of development and modernity that motivate road construction in Nepal – such as ambitious plans to lay thousands of kilometers of new highways in the next five years and visions of linking Sino–Indian commerce via Nepal (*Kathmandu Post* 2016; Ministry of Transportation 2016) – the reality of transportation infrastructure development and its effect on local communities is far more complex and nuanced. The most obvious of these factors include the discrepancies of where roads do and do not go as well as the burdens of building and maintaining transportation infrastructures across seismically active and monsoon-affected landscapes.

For example, Nepal's Strategic Road Network is vigorously promoted as one of the great new routes to economic prosperity and human development across the country (Department of Roads 2014).[4] In particular, and despite chronic problems with maintenance, new roads through Mustang remain key components of this national agenda (Ministry of Transportation 2016). However, the Mustang road's contribution to the broader Strategic Road Network depends upon its connection with central Nepal via a newer division of roads that link Mustang's cultural center of Lo Monthang with the district capital of Jomsom as well as Jomsom with Nepal's larger, southern-central cities of Beni and Pokhara. While this road network between Lo Monthang and Pokhara remains punctuated by broken sections due to monsoonal landslides, missing bridges, and general obstacles to maintenance, it is now possible (at certain times outside the monsoon season) for both people and goods to make in just two days what 20 years ago was a two week journey. But as expectations and dependencies upon the road grow steadily greater, hardships become magnified when the road becomes inoperable, leaving social systems and traditional modes of transport suspended by new reliance on vehicles. Jigme succinctly explained this reality to me during one of our conversations in Kagbeni: "If you are poor, the road makes you (feel) poorer".

Today in Mustang, as in countless places around the world, road developments are at once promoted as great equalizers while they in fact reinforce long-standing social and economic stratifications. Public buses, shared jeeps, and chartered vehicles now operate along the new roads in Mustang. But as a man without the means to own a private vehicle, and without the cash liquidity to charter a jeep to carry goods to his store from bazaars in southern Tibet or central Nepal, Jigme has become increasingly dependent on public transportation networks that do not keep reliable schedules. In addition to creating new costs that he formerly avoided by walking with his goods loaded onto mules and relying on his *nyetsang* network, Jigme finds that new roads have made life harder in Mustang. While cargo costs are ultimately lower for truck transport than for mule caravans, the unpredictability of road travel adds additional hardship to what was previously a more dependable journey. "Before (when we walked), you knew how long a trip to Beni or Pokhara would take, and you planned for that (10–12 days). Today, it might take you two days, or it might take you two weeks. We never know."

For centuries across the Mustang–Tibet borderlands, inter-village travel depended on the cultural institution of *nyetsang*. A social practice predicated on common cultural ground and maintained across distant mountain spaces, *nyetsang* represents and maintains a lived experience of trans-Himalayan mobility. From village-level social commitments to broader networks of the trans-Himalayan Salt Trade, *nyetsang* comprises unique mobility practices that are situated in and across place(s). In villages throughout Mustang, an individual could depend upon his/her *nyetsang* to ease the burden of travel and provide local knowledge alongside a bed and a meal. Because traditional modes of travel – by foot or horse – also required the adequate feeding of pack animals, *nyetsang* kin also took responsibility for provisioning the hay and fodder necessary for travelers' livestock. An ancient cultural institution common across the trans-Himalaya, the *nyetsang* tradition upheld social connections throughout Mustang's villages and furthermore between Mustang's households and those in Tibet as well as neighboring districts of highland Nepal, such as Dolpo and Manang. A common sociocultural practice for the sparsely populated environments of High Asia, the legacies and practices of *nyetsang* have long shaped transborder geographical imaginaries and mobility practices between Mustang and Tibet.

The historical function of *nyetsang* resonates with a central claim behind Sheller and Urry's (2006) "new mobilities paradigm" – that mobile life, rather than sedentary life, is endemic to society and that mobility should be considered fundamental instead of exceptional to humanity. In the case of Mustang, legacies of *nyetsang* challenge long-standing (and erroneous) depictions of the erstwhile Himalaya Kingdom and modern-day district of Nepal as isolated and remote. Rather than a self-contained and bordered territory, Mustang – as with the greater Himalayan region – is in fact a cultural arena into and through which social, economic, and political relationships have long been forged and maintained. Therefore, instead of barriers to movement and deterministic "containers" that divide spaces of South Asia from the rarified expanses of the Tibetan Plateau, Mustang and the Himalaya can be better thought of as geographical corridors of sociocultural and political economic exchange.

Upon the advent of road travel in Mustang, *nyetsang* systems began to collapse, and with them many other long-standing social structures have shifted. Another Mustangi friend, Pasang, told me, "the system is in the process of vanishing – because of development of infrastructures, [but also because] people started to not disturb their *nyetsang*". Today, travel throughout much of Mustang is made almost entirely by motorized vehicle. As the pace of travel has increased, the regularity of visits with *nyetsang* has decreased. A consequence of this inverse relationship is that families within a *nyetsang* unit have lost familiarity with one another. As Pasang further explained to me, "lacking of going to each other's villages often make the excuses of getting distance [i.e. becoming separated]". Instead of encouraging one to call upon his *nyetsang* during the course of travel, this unfamiliarity instead dissuades participation in the network.

There are many reasons why the *nyetsang* system started to collapse with the arrival of vehicular travel in Mustang. At the ground level, grass fodder is no longer sought as the primary fuel for travel, but rather gasoline. With widespread outmigration to Kathmandu as well as abroad – especially New York City[5] – overall populations have significantly declined as well. Homes are empty for much of the day while residents tend their shops and guesthouses or work the fields. As villages depopulate, travelers lack familiarity with the few who are there. Compounding these shifting social and economic dynamics, and owing to faster rates of travel, villages where one's *nyetsang* network was traditionally strong are frequently bypassed in favor of destinations down the road. Pasang explained:

> Now that everyone is busy on their own [livelihood], so people try not to disturb their *nyetsang*. However, in the past, there was no road – so people [*would*] take at least a few days to reach their home ... now we have road access where we can reach Lo Monthang [*in*] eight hours from Jomsom. So people don't go to [*their*] nyetsang [*and instead pass through other villages*] – so they are skipping nyetsang; slowly such systems are declining.[6]

Journeying further in a single day and no longer reliant on *nyetsang* support, travelers in Mustang increasingly turn toward new, roadside lodges instead of traditional forms of reciprocal household hospitality. Particularly for Mustangi travelers for whom time has become more valuable than money (and indeed for others who now live outside the district), lodges offer a degree of convenience, informality, and autonomy – distinct trappings of modernity – that contrast with *nyetsang* experiences. The decline of the *nyetsang* is just one example of the powerful effects of modern transport mobilities on everyday life in Mustang, and, by extension, to broader social dynamics of the trans-Himalaya.

Access to and the utility of Mustang's new roads remains highly uneven. Transportation requires cash, and for communities historically dependent on subsistence agriculture and regional trade, access to transport requires connections to capital, and those connections are largely predicated on the tourism industry and remittance economies. Jigme and Pasang's points are that motorized transport tests – and at times steals – one's agency. When a truck breaks down, and you have no other means of travel, nor *nyetsang* relations in a nearby village, you have little recourse than to pay for lodging until another vehicle comes by, and that may be in three hours or three days' time. Thus, "if you are poor", road travel makes everything more difficult, and thereby makes you (feel) poorer. Conversely, however, if you own your own vehicle, or have the means to charter a private jeep, or at least sufficient disposable income to pay for lodging when necessary, motorized transport is perceived and lived very differently. That is, the roads are convenient and economical for some, and debilitating and marginalizing for others. In an ironic twist, however, when talking about tourism economies or other business ventures, critiques of the roads are often loud from more historically established and wealthier class populations – that is, from those who own the vehicles, guest lodges, and cash reserves to utilize and benefit from the roads.[7] Despite these elite grievances, however, road travel and associated mobilities ultimately reinforce rather than recalibrate social and economic hierarchies in Mustang today.

Cash circulations, tourism, and state formation

In addition to disrupting social institutions like *nyetsang*, new road networks, mobility practices, and border regimes have strongly accelerated an ongoing shift from barter-oriented to monetized commercial trade relations in the Mustang–Tibet borderlands. Central to this change is the predominance of cash and its influence as a medium of exchange and a factor of accumulation, both of which strongly affect consumer practices and systems of value across the region. This is not to say that trans-Himalayan trade was not monetized with national currencies before the 21st century. In fact, trade across the Himalaya has been monetized to some degree for centuries (Bishop 1990; van Spengen 2000), represented by the circulation – first sparingly, then more widely – of silver Indian rupees, Tibetan coins, and both Nepali and Chinese paper currencies. However, up until the 1950–60s and the occupation of Tibet by China, the majority of trade between Mustang and Tibet remained predominantly barter-oriented (Fürer-Haimendorf 1988). The Tibetan guerilla resistance movement based in Mustang motivated Beijing to close the border in the early 1960s and this was an initial disruption to regional trade relations, including the suspension of person-to-person trade and the semi-annual trade fairs, or *tsongra*. Although the easement of border regulations in the 1970s enabled a renewal of barter-based trade relations, many informants claim it was at this time that money became increasingly central to transborder transactions between Mustang and Tibet.

Commodity exchange in Mustang, as elsewhere in the world, has never been defined exclusively as *either* a barter-based *or* a money-mediated relationship. Although barter is indeed "a special form of commodity exchange", this is not to say, as Appadurai claims, that barter remains a relationship between people and things in which "money plays either no role or a very indirect role (as a mere unit of account)" (Appadurai 2013: 17). Arguing against anthropological tropes that romanticize barter and condemn monetized relations, Hart (2005) notes that the two forms of exchange have never been mutually exclusive and in fact historically work together. Hart points out that money mediates and stabilizes highly complex forms of exchange and, as such, is as useful for trade and barter-oriented societies as it is for 21st century global finance. "So money is the common measure of value uniting all the independent acts of exchange, stabilizing the volatile world of commodity exchange" (Hart 2005: 9). Hart goes on to argue that money, and the control of it, quickly became fundamental to both state and merchant practices, such that the state gains and utilizes tax revenues on trade as a symbol and mechanism of power just as merchants cooperate with state policies in order to gain legal protection and maintain public standards. This underscores how the barter of commodities and the exchange of money have long worked hand in hand, in Mustang and across the trans-Himalaya.

A dramatic shift to cash-based economic relations in Mustang occurred in the 1990s with the advent of a highly regulated and uniquely expensive tourism industry for Upper Mustang. In a break from the long-standing, state-imposed isolation of Upper Mustang, in 1992 the Government of Nepal "opened" Mustang to international visitors according to a closely managed, low quota policy. Jumping at the opportunity to travel to a region that had almost always been closed to the outside world, foreign adventurers quickly lined up to pay upwards of US$1,000 per week (far more than the annual income for an average citizen in Nepal) for the privilege to visit a place sold as the Himalaya's "Last Forbidden Kingdom" (Matthiessen & Laird 1996). Early visitors to Mustang were obligated to visit the district through guided tours run by trekking companies established in Kathmandu. These groups were required to be self-sufficient, such that all shelter, provisions, and sundries were carried for 10 to 14-day treks through the district. Elite families in Mustang with economic and social capital quickly joined the action by forming their own trekking companies that operated both in concert and in competition with more established tour operators based in Kathmandu. The strict state regulations requiring self-sufficiency and limiting visitor numbers were ostensibly intended to protect Mustang's fragile alpine landscape as well as what Nepal's Tourism Board advertised as the "unique and pre-modern" cultural traditions of Mustang. While these dynamics brought about new experiences with and perceptions of the global marketplace to residents of the district, a more powerful effect of new tourism policies was the consolidation of capital and uneven distribution of revenues collected from new business enterprises. Sidelining the majority of Mustang's population, this process asymmetrically privileged the Mustang elite (as well as established tour operators in Kathmandu) and transformed many locals into objects of cultural consumption according to capital logics embedded in national and international tourism economies (Minca & Oakes 2006).

After 10 years of highly regulated and lucrative tourism to Mustang, state policies again changed in the mid-2000s. The easing of requirements for self-sufficiency translated into the establishment of guesthouses and restaurants for tourists along Mustang's more popular trekking routes. These small businesses introduced new and unprecedented opportunities for capital accumulation to Mustang and relied upon a cash medium of exchange. Although Mustang's elite families were – and still are – at the forefront of tourism entrepreneurship, community members from other class and caste groups quickly joined the fray. This nascent political economy based on tourism subsequently gained momentum through incremental policy changes such as higher quotas for foreign visitors, further relaxations on the requirements for self-sufficiency, and formal incorporation and coordination with Nepal's major tourism industry. More recently, high numbers of domestic Nepali tourists – adventurous trekkers and teenage motorcyclists alike – have generated yet another profile and political economic dynamic for Mustang's tourism sector.

The expansion of the tourism industry in Mustang coupled with pervasive outmigration and associated remittance incomes has generated a purchasing power that shapes new terms and scales of cash-based relations for trans-Himalayan borderland populations. Initially accelerated by tourism and cash injections from outside the district, and now fueled by an unprecedented consumption of foreign manufactured commodities throughout the trans-Himalaya, cash flows across the region have deepened as a result of new road infrastructures and state policies that collectively encourage and facilitate greater trade growth between Chinese Tibet and highland Nepal. This convergence of trans-Himalayan borderland roads and mobility practices with new cash-based political economies and consumer practices has led to unprecedented institutionalizations of the Nepali state in Mustang.

Higher volume cash flows connected to both the tourism sector and large-scale commodity imports from China and India have produced new space for the state to take shape in order to generate tax revenue and regulate international and domestic mobilities alike. Across Mustang, these institutionalizations include the first Government of Nepal Border Commissioner to maintain residence in Lo Monthang as well as new assignments for regional tax officers. Beyond bureaucracy, new physical infrastructures include plans to upgrade the Government of Nepal Customs and Quarantine Houses in Mustang as well as the construction of barracks below the Nepal–China Kora La borderpost for new regiments of Nepal's paramilitary Armed Police Force (Post Report 2016). Further pointing toward an international agenda to make Mustang the newest trade corridor between China and Nepal, feasibility studies also commenced in 2015 for the construction of a major dry port in Upper Mustang. Located in a place once and long considered peripheral to the Kathmandu state center, these projects situate Mustang as increasingly central to visions and strategies of a more modern Nepal. Alongside new road-based mobilities, cash-based trade relations, and political economies based on tourism, remittances, and international commodity circulations, bureaucratic forms of state making are fundamental aspects of borderland modernity in the trans-Himalaya.

Conclusion: borderland modernity in Mustang

Everyday life along new roads in Mustang makes infrastructure development and the concomitant dynamics of mobility and containment a productive starting point for analyzing borderland modernity in Asia today. The paradox of modernity is illustrated through its internal contradiction as both a spatialized ordering principle and a state of chaos and bewilderment. Peter Taylor notes,

> modern people and institutions devise projects which aspire to order their world but without fully appreciating that the modern world is the antithesis of order. Modernity, therefore, is a perpetual battle between makers of order and the incessant change which is the condition of modernity.
>
> *(2013: 17)*

As expressed by many citizens of Mustang as they navigate new road networks amidst the decline of *nyetsang* systems, modern technologies of mobility present "standardized" (if unreliable) means of transport that routinely leave travelers adrift on the roadsides, bewildered by a wait for vehicles that rarely arrive on time. As some citizens enthusiastically welcome the new roads, and benefit from accelerating cash circulations, others complain that such infrastructures have done little more than remarginalize residents already on social, economic, and geographic peripheries. Alongside the reinforcement of established hierarchies, processes of modernity generate new forms of symmetry, structure, and control by which the state organizes a population so as to wield power over it – and thus make it legible (Scott 1999). By imposing order upon the disorganized and chaotic "margins", the center strives to rationalize and hence prevail over the periphery.

Across the trans-Himalaya today, borderland modernity presents a new terrain of inquiry for studies of modernity as a non-urban experience facilitated by distinct translocal infrastructures, linked to global social media and financial networks, and subject to both broad and situated conditions of geopolitics shaped by the forces of international capital. Transforming those "subjected to development" into "subjects of development" (Sivaramakrishnan & Agrawal 2003: 5), new transport infrastructures in Mustang beget more development interventions, from village solar projects and tourist lodges to customs offices, dry-port stations, and army barracks. Advancing Sivaramakrishnan and Agrawal's argument for "regional modernities" as "place-specific accounts of development to disrupt universalizing, homogenous interpretations of development", I call for a distinctly *borderland* critique of modernity to extend focus on the "multifaceted relationships of development to modernity" from urban South Asia to the trans-Himalayan borderlands (Sivaramakrishnan & Agrawal 2003: 2–5).

Modernity in rural highlands and borderlands is different from modernity in urban centers. As areas historically marked as "peripheral" and differentially ignored by and intentionally resistant to central state control (Scott 2009), Asian borderlands are increasingly enrolled within the ordering principles of expansive state institutions. Border regimes, road networks, and tax systems present powerful techniques by which the state effectively territorializes land and creates legible citizen subjects. Although these processes are not necessarily unique to highland regions alone – as they are widely experienced in urban and peri-urban contexts as well – they take shape in distinctly *internationalist* forms in borderland spaces. As this chapter shows, the Mustang–Tibet borderlands are both a political crossroads between Nepal and China as well as an area increasingly subject to the forces of capital, mobility, and containment generated not only from Kathmandu, but also Beijing.

This study analyzed the ways in which cultural practices, social hierarchies, and the Nepali state are (re)configured in Mustang as a result of road infrastructure and how everyday life in Mustang is conditioned by new experiences with mobility and containment between Nepal and China. By examining local experiences with motorized transport and asking what constitutes the modern experience for communities across Mustang today, I argue that the development of road infrastructure in Mustang has facilitated new mobilities that both reinforce and disrupt historical, social hierarchies and produce new space for the state to take shape in an Asian borderland. With a focus on new political economies circulated by roads, tourism, and cash, I show how infrastructural systems affect socio-spatial and territorial processes where local actors and the Nepali state struggle for control and access across borderland spaces. In a perpetual tension between mobility and containment, the development of new roads, economies, and institutions is rapidly expanding the everyday conditions of borderland modernity in Mustang and across wider Asian borderlands.

Notes

1. All names have been changed unless otherwise noted.
2. Data for this study were generated through international, participatory fieldwork in 20 villages in Upper Mustang in spring–summer 2015, both on and off the main road through the district (Nepal Road F042). Methods were actively mobile and a key approach to participatory observation included travel by motorcycle, jeep, truck, horse, and foot throughout Upper and Lower Mustang; this enabled grounded experiences with and observations of new vehicle road systems on the material and social life of multiple Mustang communities. Building upon these mobile insights, qualitative and ethnographic data were produced from semi-structured interviews ($n = 100$) and survey questionnaires ($n = 60$) and research informants were identified through both random and snowball sampling.
3. *Nyetsang* is an extra-familial social network that established and maintained reciprocal support systems for travelers to receive food and lodging from non-kin relations when moving across trans-Himalayan

landscapes. Similar sociocultural traditions throughout the region include practices such as *miteri*, *drobo*, and *ngoshes*.
4 Personal communication with Hari Bashyal, Consul General of Nepal to China (Lhasa, Tibet; November 25, 2014).
5 New York City is now where the largest community of Mustang's population resides outside Nepal. This New York-based population is so large that virtually every family in Mustang has a relative in Queens, NY and when a visitor to Mustang now asks "where are all the 18–30-year-old men and women, a typical answer is "they are in New York!" A local impact of this migration pattern is that Mustang now maintains a robust remittance economy sourced not from Gulf countries or Southeast Asia, much like the rest of Nepal, but instead from New York City.
6 *Parenthetical italics* inserted by author for interpretation.
7 Despite the conveniences of road transport for many business owners – widely referenced as reduced shipping costs – wealthier hotel owners frequently criticize the roads because of their negative effects on trekking tourism. This criticism largely echoes the grievances voiced by foreign tourists who are decidedly unhappy about walking on dusty motor roads in Mustang's grand, alpine landscape. And yet, tourist numbers to Mustang – foreign and especially domestic – continue to climb annually.

References

Appadurai, A., 2013. *The Future as Cultural Fact*, London: Verso.
Berman, M., 1983. *All That is Solid Melts Into Air*, London: Verso.
Bishop, B.C., 1990. *Karnali Under Stress*, Chicago, Illinois: University of Chicago.
Cresswell, T., 2016. *Geographies of Mobilities: Practices, Spaces, Subjects*, London: Routledge.
Cresswell, T. & Merriman, P., 2012. *Geographies of Mobilities*, Farnham: Ashgate Publishing, Ltd.
de Certeau, M., 2011. *The Practice of Everyday Life*, Berkeley, California: University of California Press.
Department of Roads, 2014. *Strategic Road Network 2013_14 Map*, Kathmandu: Government of Nepal.
Fürer-Haimendorf, von, C., 1988. *Himalayan Traders*, Delhi: Time Books International.
Harris, T., 2013. *Geographical Diversions*, Athens, Georgia: University of Georgia Press.
Hart, K., 2005. *Notes Towards an Anthropology of Money*, London: Kritikos, 2 (June).
Hetherington, K., 2007. *Capitalism's Eye*, London: Routledge.
Kathmandu Post, 2016. Roads to China border top budget priority. Available at: http://kathmandupost.ekantipur.com/news/2016-05-04/roads-to-china-border-top-budget-priority.html [Accessed May 23, 2016].
Kristof, L.K.D., 1959. The Nature of Frontiers and Boundaries. *Annals of the Association of American Geographers*, 49(3), pp. 269–282.
Lefebvre, H., 2003. *The Urban Revolution*, Minneapolis, Minnesota: University of Minnesota Press.
Matthiessen, P. & Laird, T., 1996. *East of Lo Monthang: In the Land of Mustang*, London: Shambhala.
Minca, C. & Oakes, T., 2006. *Travels in Paradox*, Lanham, Maryland: Rowman & Littlefield.
Ministry of Transportation, 2016. *5 Year Plan for Transportation Infrastructure Development*, Kathmandu: Government of Nepal.
Post Report, 2016. Government begins preparation to set up army barrack at Korala border point. *The Kathmandu Post*. Available at: http://kathmandupost.ekantipur.com/news/2016-07-07/govt-begins-preparation-to-set-up-army-barrack-at-korala-border-point.html [Accessed July 7, 2016].
Scott, J.C., 1999. *Seeing Like a State: How Certain Schemes to Improve the Human Condition Have Failed*, New Haven, Connecticut: Yale University Press.
Scott, J.C., 2009. *The Art of Not Being Governed: An Anarchist History of Upland Southeast Asia*, New Haven, Connecticut: Yale University Press.
Sheller, M. & Urry, J., 2006. The New Mobilities Paradigm. *Environment and Planning A*, 38(2), pp. 207–226.
Sivaramakrishnan, K. & Agrawal, A., 2003. *Regional Modernities: The Cultural Politics of Development in India*, Palo Alto, California: Stanford University Press.
Taylor, P.J., 2013. *Modernities*, London: John Wiley & Sons.
van Spengen, W., 2000. *Tibetan Border Worlds*, London: Routledge.

25

Cultivating consumer markets

Ethnic minority traders and the refashioning of cultural commodities in the Sino–Vietnamese border uplands

Christine Bonnin

Introduction: the journey of one textile design

In the remote upland border commune of Pha Long, in Lào Cai province, northern Vietnam, it is 6 am and Paj, a 60-year-old Hmong woman, gets ready to set off once again on a 10-day trade route of well over 150 kilometers. A few days earlier, she had made a day trip into Yunnan province, China, along with her husband Chue, to purchase trade supplies and visit relatives. Crossing at the small local border gate at the edge of the commune, several other Hmong from Pha Long also made this journey because it was Wednesday, the day of the Lau Kha periodic market in Ma Guan, Yunnan, located around 5 kilometers from this border entry. For Paj it is easy to make this trip to China because of her status as a border resident, which lets her purchase a renewable permit so she may cross freely for a period of six months. Furthermore, Paj is bilingual. While Hmong is her mother tongue, she is also fluent in the local borderland dialect of Mandarin. This means she communicates easily with Hmong as well as Han traders selling in the Chinese market. Through her kinship networks in China, Paj has made many market contacts.

In the late 1990s, Paj started to notice new products turning up in China's Lau Kha border market. These were decorative materials, synthetic cloths, and manufactured clothes used by Hmong women as customary dress. At first, Paj imported these goods in small quantities to sell at her home market. But competition soon grew as more cross-border and other petty textile traders from both Vietnam and China arrived on the scene. So, Paj and her husband decided to explore the possibility of trading at a Vietnam market more distant from the border; one where these new Hmong commodities had yet to arrive. As they had kinship connections in the neighboring province of Yên Bái, they visited a central market there and found they could do well as traders.

Paj travels by public bus to Yên Bái's daily market. There, she rents out a market stall from a contact she made through her uncle who is a local resident. Hmong residents of Yên Bái province live far from the Vietnam–China border and number more than 80,000, creating a significant demand for customary textiles. Paj proudly claims she is one of the first traders to introduce these new, Hmong-oriented "cultural commodities" from China into this area of

Vietnam. Since that time, these goods have caught on dramatically. While Paj sells a variety of lightweight items that she can easily transport, her biggest seller is manufactured Hmong skirts, which are highly sought after by local Hmong women, especially for the summer when traditional hemp-woven skirts are heavy and hot for working in the rice fields.

After remaining in Yên Bái for a week, Paj will return to Pha Long. However, on her way home, she makes a stop at the tourist center of Sapa in Lào Cai province. Sapa, a former hill station during the French colonial period and home to a number of ethnic minority communities, rose to fame in the late 1990s as an ethnic tourism destination for international and, increasingly, domestic visitors. In particular, Hmong clothing and textiles – most notably women's attire – are often among the most striking impressions made upon visitors to Sapa and serve as the basis for a vibrant tourist-oriented handicraft trade.

In the past, Paj also used to sell handicrafts in the Sapa town market before it became oversaturated with traders like her, but she still has friends working there. While in Sapa, Paj trades some second-hand traditional embroidered skirts made from hemp that she has collected from Hmong in Yên Bái. She typically barters these used skirts in exchange for the new synthetic Hmong skirts. She then sells the worn skirts to Hmong friends in the Sapa marketplace who make them into a variety of ethnic handicrafts. These handicrafts then enter Sapa's tourist market, with some moving much further afield to global markets.

This chapter is about Paj and other upland petty textile traders like her – "peripheral traders" in a number of different senses: they operate in places situated on the margins of the national economy; they engage in trade activities that would not be regarded as yielding profits of great economic significance; and as upland ethnic minorities, they are often viewed and treated as marginal citizens. Yet, as Paj's story shows, this group of traders – many of whom are women – are nonetheless influential agents who play a key role in cultivating consumer aesthetics and seeking out new markets in the borderlands and beyond. Their trade networks knit together a variety of contacts and mechanisms of exchange and span vast geographical distances. Although the livelihoods of only a small percentage of Hmong in the Sino–Vietnamese borderlands are directly linked to these trade networks, their cultural influence is much greater, owing to the enduring significance of clothing in Hmong society.

In these borderlands, customary clothing, textiles, batik, and embroidery worn by Hmong upland ethnic minorities, especially women, remain a crucial element of ethnic belonging, representation, and understandings of gender. However, such "traditional" apparel is far from static and draws on a multiplicity of designs and technologies of production, resulting in ever shifting styles, fashions, and materials. The roles played by Hmong individuals within the trade networks that have developed around these textiles highlight the enduring nature of Hmong fabrics as dynamic cultural and economic phenomena. These commodity flows have also been influenced by tourism, cross-border networks, trade opportunities in the commoditization of textiles, innovations in textile production, and new consumption patterns.

Analyzing the implications of such changes requires examining the shifting exchange values and processes of commoditization, as well as the social and cultural dynamics underpinning these transformations. This objective can be most fruitfully achieved as Appadurai (1986) has contended, by paying attention to the "things in motion" themselves, as a vital analytical and methodological entry point for revealing the human and social contexts within which material objects flow and transform. Human geographers have drawn insights from such anthropological perspectives on the social life of commodities through the conceptualization of a "follow-the-thing approach" to commodity chains (e.g. Cook and Harrison 2007; Cook 2004). This framework "humanizes" commodity chains by incorporating a more multi-dimensional, culturally-based understanding of material objects' movements. Unlike the sequential stages of global commodity chains, analysts do not focus on beginning or terminal points and rather than pre-given as fixed, each "site" is constructed and changing (Jackson et al. 2006: 132). Commodities interrelate with other things as they move, and as such, social relations, cultural meanings, economic power, and geographical knowledges are continually (re)shaped (Leslie and Reimer 1999: 402, 406). The task, therefore, is to focus on how these complex culturally-inflected dynamics combine and work to interlink circuits of production, distribution, and consumption.

Utilizing such a "follow-the-thing" approach to the geographies of commodities, I explore a complex cross-border textile system, involving Hmong clothing moving between China and Vietnam. Focusing on the trajectories of these things in motion, but also giving consideration to their forms and uses, provides "a means of exploring negotiations of culture, questions of mobility, translocal commercial networks, and the complex connections between places" (Pfaff 2010: 345). In this case study, objects formerly interpreted for their use value alone are increasingly being (re)assessed in terms of their monetary worth. Hmong textiles enter new regimes of value as markets are emerging for a diversity of forms of these items, destined for local as well as external markets.

I showcase the key role of Hmong petty traders in the diffusion of new manufactured Hmong fabrics throughout the borderlands. Elsewhere, such as in the case of African countries and imported Chinese-manufactured "African cloth," the influx of Chinese "copies" of traditional fabrics are often viewed as threats to local markets (Sylvanus 2016: xi). Yet in this case, the emergence of new technologies of production has rather enlivened, strengthened, and diversified the use and trade of Hmong textiles: synthetics and "hybrids" alike. Moreover, for Hmong borderlanders – for those living on the Vietnam side at least – these new Hmong-oriented commodities sit alongside or even merge into customary practices of clothing production.

This chapter is based on more than 17 months of ethnographic fieldwork on small-scale trade and marketplaces in a stretch of the Sino–Vietnamese borderlands. Data collection methods included semi-structured and informal conversational interviews with textile traders, shopkeepers, customers, and state officials in Vietnam and China, as well as participant observation in upland and border marketplaces. This fieldwork was carried out primarily in the border districts of Lào Cai province, Vietnam between 2006 and 2011, as well as two months of follow-up research in 2012. I also made several field trips to border markets, market towns, and Hmong villages in the directly adjacent border area in China: Ma Guan county, Yunnan province.

Hmong textile production and cultural meanings

Throughout Southeast Asia, textile production and knowledge is customarily women's domain. For Hmong in the Sino–Vietnamese borderlands, the production of customary textiles is a female responsibility and remains important to women throughout their lives. In upland Vietnam, women and girls undertake the entire time- and labor-intensive process of making clothes, from growing hemp for cloth to cutting and processing hemp stalks and producing thread. They weave the thread into cloth, and then sew it into garments that are adorned with fine embroidery or batik designs. These traditional techniques are highly-valued, gendered skills.

Hmong customary clothing and textiles play a vital role in ethnocultural identities and gender roles and the transmission of history and ideologies (Lee and Tapp 2010: 137). As Hmong do not have an indigenous script, oral histories and textiles have been a key means of communicating historical information, stories, spiritual beliefs, and cultural practices (Feng 2007: 18). The geometric motifs and designs used in textile embroidery often describe historical events, mythologies, and spiritual practices, or represent objects significant to Hmong life-worlds and livelihoods. For instance, members of the Hmong diaspora from Laos retell stories of their flight from their homeland in the 1970s through "story cloth'" embroideries (Lee and Tapp 2010: 140). Even the pleating characteristic of many Hmong women's skirts is reported to symbolize the hills and valleys associated with Hmong creation myths (Tran Thi Thu Thuy 2007).

While clothing has been used as a complex endogenous and exogenous marker of Hmong local ethnic identity for centuries, it is women's traditional dress that is the most elaborate of Hmong garments and which is perceived as the quintessential cultural dress. Nevertheless, these dress styles have continuously transformed over time and space through interaction with other minority and majority groups and with access to new materials, production technologies, and information about Hmong fashions elsewhere (Tran Thi Thu Thuy 2007). Hmong textiles, especially hemp fabric, have retained their significance in life-cycle events (weddings, childbirth, and funerals), as well as for healing and shaman rituals, at important Lunar New Year festivities, and at everyday social gatherings such as market day. For Hmong on both sides of the Sino–Vietnamese border, hemp has historically been an important fiber for producing cloth and is embedded in various spiritual and sociocultural practices. Although, as we will see, Hmong in some areas of Vietnam have started wearing factory-made Hmong clothing imported from China for daily use, it is important to emphasize that this has not replaced the domestic production of handmade textiles which still remains essential.

Dress is an important and conspicuous way to convey ethnic belonging in the multi-ethnic space of the Sino–Vietnamese borderlands. Interviewees in Vietnam and Yunnan explain that clothing helps to identify someone as Hmong, and local Hmong residents can distinguish what specific locality another Hmong person comes from, as styles, colors, and patterns differ between localities as much as between Hmong subgroups. For example, Ly, a young woman from Sa Pa, Vietnam, spent eight months in Yunnan. She explained how when observing a stranger in Yunnan, "I knew that she was Hmong because of the skirt she was wearing. Without the skirt I would never have known." She went on to say, "I think there are many Hmong people living in China, but I couldn't tell if they were Hmong or not because they were dressed like the Chinese." Unlike in Vietnam, Hmong living in neighboring China and Laos as well as Thailand are increasingly adopting the Western-style clothing associated with their respective lowland, majority populations, and with notions of modernity.

However, in northern upland Vietnam, the majority of Hmong women still tend to prefer wearing their customary clothing on a daily basis, whether it be handmade or factory-made. Paradoxically, Hmong women in Lào Cai also regard the emerging new forms of "traditional" clothing as "modern," as evidenced by the growing popularity of factory-made Hmong apparel and accessories imported from China. Many young women embrace these as fashionable, alternative symbols of modernity that are still seen very much as "Hmong."

Hmong manufactured textiles in the Sino–Vietnamese borderlands emerge

In Yunnan Province, new cultural commodities produced from industrially-manufactured materials are oriented entirely toward Hmong consumer markets on both sides of the border and beyond. Since the late 1990s, thanks to new technologies, high levels of production and low-cost, factory-made Hmong textiles in China have significantly influenced Hmong customary dress. This industry produces synthetic or blended cloth printed with Hmong batik and embroidery designs, as well as synthetic decorations. A range of ready-made apparel mimicking Hmong styles and patterns is also available, from skirts and shirts for everyday wear to ornate wedding dresses. So far, no similar industry in factory-made Hmong clothing has started up in Vietnam.

As such, the spread of these commodities into Vietnam has occurred exclusively through small-scale, cross-border imports, activities undertaken by petty market traders and generally through remote, local-level border crossings. The development of this market was facilitated by the official reopening of the Vietnam/China land border in 1988, after an almost 10-year closure following the Sino–Vietnamese war (Turner et al. 2015: 36). Since the 2000s, a vibrant cross-border trade in Hmong textiles has flourished, with the emergence of several new opportunities for differently situated groups. Borderland residents – mainly Hmong residents of both Vietnam and China as well as Han Chinese traders – play an instrumental role within these trade networks and in stimulating consumer demand as they transmit new materials and styles throughout the wider borderlands and uplands of Vietnam.

The development of synthetic Hmong fabrics partly relates to a hemp cultivation ban imposed in Yunnan by the Chinese state in the 2000s. This has affected clothing practices for large numbers of Hmong, triggering demand for replacement materials (Clarke 1999; GSO Vietnam 2009; Miao Yun 2010). While the widespread practice of Hmong growing hemp for cloth-weaving was affected with the introduction of manufactured Western-style clothing in the 1980s, this declined much more still after the hemp prohibition. Even though small-scale hemp growing for personal use seems tolerated by the state in practice, the official suppression has greatly affected the customary practice of domestic clothing production. Other observers have suggested that the industrial production of Hmong clothing has likewise been fueled by the Hmong diaspora in the United States (over 220,000 persons), who rely on enterprises in China to provide them with traditional clothes for festivals and ceremonies (Miao Yun 2010). Indeed, Schein (2004: 282) observed, the sale of Hmong clothing is one of the few ways this group in China "are making money from the renewal of transnational ethnic ties. As the longing for the homeland becomes displayed on the migrant's body, those at home simultaneously find a means by which to commodify their culture for commercial gain."

Cultivating new borderland consumer preferences

Hmong residents of the Sino–Vietnamese borderlands, and particularly young women, prefer these new synthetic clothes and fabrics manufactured in China over traditionally-made versions for everyday wear. These include both ready-to-wear garments as well as factory-made materials that Hmong sew into various items of clothing. Ready-made Hmong garments free women from time-consuming clothes-making, allowing them to engage in other activities, while the synthetic materials now used to make Hmong clothes are also less laborious to work with. What is more, these new forms of clothes and textiles are quite affordable. Such considerations make it more feasible for women to own a larger set of dress – as opposed to only one or two handmade ones as was always the norm before. And in addition to being lightweight, interviewees explain that the new materials are easier to wash and maintain than handmade clothes.

Another perspective expressed by some Hmong women is that the synthetic garments and cloth are "more beautiful." This is because there are a wide range of designs and also because the industrial dyes produce different, more vibrant colors from the traditional, plant-based ones. Hmong borderland consumers of these new clothes and materials reflect a "diversification of tastes being pushed in numerous directions…turning local consumers into arbiters of stylistic innovations" (Hansen 2004: 373). These findings in the Sino–Vietnamese borderlands link to studies in other regions addressing similar transformations of "ethnic clothing," and highlight the emergence of new aesthetics with the creation of hybrid designs – as well as how this shifting of fashions is linked to gender and ethnic identity politics (Niessen et al. 2003).

Clothes-making out of the synthetic decorations – cloth, ribbons, thread, and yarn – is facilitating the development of new Hmong fashions, allowing women to express their creativity and innovativeness, as fresh styles and designs can be more easily achieved than by customary production methods.

While some Hmong in Lào Cai province purchase clothing from China as ready-to-wear items, others adapt the synthetic materials into their own particular clothing designs. In many parts of Lào Cai, Hmong women use the imported materials to make lower cost, less time-consuming versions of dress, while these still resemble their own local styles. Place-based elements of clothing design in the borderlands are therefore retained – while adapted with the new input materials. Likewise, some Hmong traders like Paj, whom we met at the start, have arranged to have Vietnam-based local Hmong designs printed onto these synthetic fabrics which are transformed into "copies" of the traditional skirts. These examples illustrate how the manufactured materials and clothes are not entirely replacing or eroding older, customary styles. Rather, "traditional" and "modern" elements are actively and creatively combined by Hmong women to suit their desires and practical needs. Indeed, there exists a vast spectrum of Hmong factory-made clothing and synthetic materials being imported into Vietnam from China.

Changing consumer tastes are also manifesting in terms of generational differences, with older and younger Hmong women providing different reasons as to why they appreciate these new synthetic clothes. For example, Hmong traders explained how younger women are at a stage in their lives where they tend to be more preoccupied with their physical appearance and are more fashion conscious and interested in the latest trends and materials. Middle-aged and elder Hmong women in turn, tended to say that they were concerned with their practicality and ease of wear.

Cross-border trade networks in Hmong manufactured textiles

Today, manufactured Hmong clothing is found for sale widely in every small town market in the border prefectures of Yunnan, and in larger shops in the central towns. For example, in Maguan Town, 20 kilometers from the Vietnam border, more than 10 primarily wholesale shops specialize in Hmong dress, cloth, and accessories. These shops cater to the local demands of Yunnan Hmong people and sell ready-to-wear factory-made clothes, as well as synthetic fabric and accessories. Yu, a Han Chinese woman who runs one of these shops in Ma Guan, grew up in an ethnically-mixed rural community where she learned to speak Hmong. When she moved to Maguan Town in the mid-1980s, she capitalized on her language skills and started a Hmong apparel business. Yu and her employees produce all of the Hmong garments sold in her shop. She is visited frequently by Hmong traders from Vietnam who cross the border to purchase her skirts. According to Yu, the amount that these traders buy depends on the current "popularity" of a style in Vietnam. She explained that traders like to experiment, buying only a few items at first to test the market back home before returning to buy bigger quantities. These Vietnam-based traders typically cross at local border gates, like Paj's crossing point at Pha Long, sometimes smuggling textiles or disguising them as items for their own personal use. While import fees for these goods at local crossings are not usually very high, traders who wish to carry a large volume may try to avoid or save on these through strategies such as divvying up their goods between different trips or by having friends or relatives import them.

Both Han and Hmong traders interviewed in Yunnan explained that the synthetic cloth, printed with Hmong embroidery and batik designs, comes from Zhejiang. This eastern coastal province over one thousand kilometers away from Yunnan boasts major textile manufacturing industries. Yunnan residents explained that inhabitants of Zhejiang manufacture Hmong textiles because they have a reputation as being entrepreneurial and are skillful at "making good copies." Yu places orders for computer-generated prints of specific local Hmong designs directly with manufacturers in Zhejiang. She often requests prints that traders inform her are selling well in Vietnam, from contacts like Paj at the start of this chapter who access their textile stock from the Sino–Vietnamese border marketplaces. The patterns are printed onto bolts of cloth, which are then mailed to her shop.

Interestingly, at this node in the commodity chain is an interlinkage with the geographically expansive network in Hmong textiles for handicrafts I noted earlier. Illustrating this, Yu had a number of second-hand hemp skirts in her shop when I visited, which she purchased from Hmong traders from Vietnam. Yu was selling these old skirts to collectors who would transport them to distant markets and shops in Xishuangbanna, Yunnan. Some of these used skirts would be exported back across another point in the Chinese border. Eventually, they would end up at points in Thailand and Laos – namely Chiang Mai, Bangkok, Luang Phrabang, and Vientiane – to be reworked there into a number of different tourist handicrafts (Miao Yun 2010). In the past, handicraft intermediaries used to buy the hemp skirts produced by local Hmong in Yunnan. Nowadays, the much smaller volume of hemp grown has shrunk the availability of old traditional skirts in China, and Vietnam has become the new supply source for the global Hmong handicraft industry. The large demand for used Hmong pieces in Thailand originating from Vietnam and China owes to the vast international tourist markets located in the former, combined with the fact that many Hmong in Thailand and Laos no longer wear traditional clothes on a daily basis and have smaller populations than Hmong in China (Miao Yun 2010, personal observations). In China, Hmong handicraft and factory-made textile commodity chains are thus mutually influenced by a number of important factors. The dynamics of these two textile chains are largely shaped by gendered knowledge, ethnicity, and place. These elements feature in the politics of trade and consumption within these very different Hmong textile systems of provision – one for externally-oriented tourist markets and the other for Hmong consumers directly (c.f. Leslie and Reimer 1999). Such dynamics and connections behind the cross-border and global sale of textiles are invisible to consumers at the end of the commodity chain and are only fully revealed when specific trade networks and activities are investigated in their entirety.

To date, it is Han Chinese such as Yu, as well as Hmong residents from China and Vietnam, who are involved in this borderland trade, while Vietnamese lowlanders (ethnic Kinh) are far less so. This is noteworthy given the overall pattern of an ethnicized division in upland trading on the Vietnam side of the border in which Kinh have become a dominant force (Bonnin forthcoming). Kinh traders are often at a greater advantage over ethnic minority traders owing to their upland–lowland social networks, relatively larger financial capital, better ability to communicate with state officials, and greater mobility. As such, Kinh have tended to end up monopolizing upland trade (Bonnin forthcoming; World Bank 2009: 41). Yet, in the case of the Hmong textile trade, at present Kinh face a number of access barriers including a lack of specific language skills (in Hmong), residential status (being usually not registered to live in remote upland localities on the border), necessary cross-border social ties, and knowledge of Hmong consumer preferences. As such, Hmong residents of Vietnam like Paj have remained the dominant players transmitting these new materials and fashions from China. This highlights the important influence of key factors such as ethnicity, language, upland border residency, and gender in creating and expanding these trade networks and markets.

On the Vietnam side, some groups of Hmong from Lào Cai specialize in long-distance trading to other provinces, while others orient their activities around weekly circuits of periodic markets. Their activities have been aided by recent enhancements of connective infrastructure – including improved mountain roads – alongside better public transportation and more Hmong owning private motorbikes. With enhanced mobility and access to local periodic markets in previously hard-to-reach communes, the textile trade has spread far beyond the immediate border area into Vietnam to reach other Hmong communities. These circuit and long distance traders often spend the night with kin, drawing upon geographically expansive kinship-based social networks in order to support their activities. Many of these groups work together as a team of married couples or family members. While Hmong women are highly visible in the textile trade, their travel over distances to work in markets is restricted by cultural gender norms that limit their independent mobility, hence the involvement of other male household members (Bonnin and Turner 2014: 12).

Conclusion

Tracing the different routes of these new commodities reveals borderland trade networks covering a wide spatial range and incorporating trade circuits on local, regional, cross-border, and global scales. At first glance, these networks appear to be separate systems oriented toward very different consumer markets. However, the actors and activities that underpin them are linked into much larger transnational commodity networks encompassing China, Vietnam, Thailand, and Laos, as well as global markets.

These transformations in the production and trade of Hmong textiles present distinctive livelihood opportunities for particular groups of participants, revealing the importance of access – particularly to knowledge, information, and networks – in carving out a trade niche. Conditions shift according to context. Livelihood opportunities and networks open to traders are not static, but depend upon how individuals and households are situated geographically, socially, and economically.

For factory-made textiles, Han and Hmong border residents are best positioned to take advantage of new markets and trade opportunities. However, Chinese nationals (whether Han or Hmong) are limited by state regulations regarding their distance of movement and duration of stay in Vietnam. As such, Hmong border residents of Vietnam are better positioned to take advantage of trading opportunities beyond border markets, though they have yet to move into the large-scale manufacturing of textiles themselves. While Kinh appear to hold the economic upper hand in upland trade on the Vietnam side of the border, in this case they are excluded from entering certain networks and markets. Their insufficient access to markets in China, poor social networks with Hmong and Chinese, and a lack of necessary language skills contribute to this exclusion.

Hmong in the Sino–Vietnamese borderlands are emerging as an important group of consumers supporting the livelihood endeavors of Hmong small-scale textile traders. The development of Hmong manufactured clothing is necessarily dynamic in design and style, serving the consumer preferences of different groups of women while continuing to support the assertion of regional and localized identities. While demand in China may have initially slowed under state pressure to cease hemp production, it now reflects Hmong women's own changing opinions of what they want to wear on a daily basis.

These examples presented here counter the dominant perspective in Vietnam and China that Hmong are inept at trading and lack economic entrepreneurship. Instead, close examination and patient ethnography show that Hmong engagements in the borderland textile trade and in market activities are strategically small-scale pursuits, taking place within and across a wide variety of local and regional settings that remain difficult for outsiders to access and negotiate. This case study also provides a more critical response to common concerns regarding the emergence of manufactured products deemed as a convenient replacement of traditional homemade textiles. Moreover, it challenges the mainstream assumption that changes in material culture are necessarily coming from outsiders or damaging the richness of Hmong clothing in the Sino–Vietnamese borderlands.

References

Appadurai, A. 1986. Introduction: Commodities and the Politics of Value. In: Appadurai, A. (ed.), *The Social Life of Things: Commodities in Cultural Perspective*. Cambridge: Cambridge University Press, pp. 3–91.

Bonnin, C. forthcoming. Grand Designs? State Agendas and the Lived Realities of Market Redevelopment in Upland Northern Vietnam. In: Endres, K.W. and Leshkowich, A.M. (eds.), *Traders in Motion: Networks, Identities, and Contestations in the Vietnamese Marketplace*. Ithaca, NY: Cornell Southeast Asia Program Publications.

Bonnin, C. and Turner, S. 2014. "A Good Wife Stays Home": Gendered Negotiations Over State Agricultural Programmes and Food Security, Upland-Vietnam. *Gender, Place and Culture: A Journal of Feminist Geography*, 21(10): 1302–20.

Clarke, R.C. 1999. Confusion over Cannabis in Yunnan. *Journal of International Hemp Association*, 6(2): 77–80.

Cook, I. 2004. Follow the Thing: Papaya. *Antipode*, 36(4): 642–64.

Cook, I. and Harrison, M. 2007. Follow the Thing: West Indian Hot Pepper Sauce. *Space and Culture*, 10(1): 40–63.

Feng, X. 2007. Gender and Hmong Women's Handicrafts in Fenghuang's "Tourism Great Leap Forward", China. *Anthropology of Work Review*, 28(3): 17–26.

GSO (General Statistics Office) Vietnam. 2009. *The 2009 Vietnam Population and Housing Census: Completed Results*. Hanoi: Central Population and Housing Census Steering Committee.

Hansen, K. 2004. The World in Dress: Anthropological Perspectives on Clothing, Fashion, and Culture. *Annual Review of Anthropology*, 33: 369–392.

Jackson, P., Ward, N. and Russell, P. 2006. Mobilising the Commodity Chain Concept in the Politics of Food and Farming. *Journal of Rural Studies*, 22(2): 129–41.

Lee, G.Y. and Tapp, N. 2010. *Culture and Customs of the Hmong*. Santa Barbara, CA: Greenwood.

Leslie, D. and Reimer, S. 1999. Spatializing Commodity Chains. *Progress in Human Geography*, 23(3): 401–20.

Miao Yun. 2010. *Commercialising Hmong Used Clothing: The Transnational Trade in Hmong Textiles across the Mekong Region*. Chiang Mai: The Regional Centre for Social Science and Sustainable Development, Chiang Mai University.

Niessen, S., Leshkowich, A.M. and Jones, C. (eds.). 2003. *Re-Orienting Fashion: The Globalization of Asian Dress*. Oxford and New York: Berg Publishers.

Pfaff, J. 2010. A Mobile Phone: Mobility, Materiality and Everyday Swahili Trading Practices. *Cultural Geographies*, 17(3): 341–57.

Schein, L. 2004. Hmong/Miao Transnationality: Identity beyond Culture. In: Tapp, N., Michaud, J., Culas, C. and Lee, G.Y. (eds.), *Hmong/Miao in Asia*. Chiang Mai: Silkworm, pp. 273–90.

Sylvanus, N. 2016. *Patterns in Circulation: Cloth, Gender, and Materiality in West Africa*. Chicago, IL: The University of Chicago Press.

Tran Thi Thu Thuy. 2007. Hemp Textiles of the Hmong in Vietnam. In: Hamilton, R.W. and Milgram, B.L. (eds.), *Refashioning Bast and Leaf Fibers in Asia and the Pacific*. Seattle, WA: University of Washington Press, pp. 41–62.

Turner, S., Bonnin, C. and Michaud, J. 2015. *Frontier Livelihoods. Hmong in the Sino-Vietnamese Borderlands*. Seattle, WA: University of Washington Press.

World Bank. 2009. *Country Social Analysis: Ethnicity and Development in Vietnam*. Washington, DC: The World Bank.

26
Invisible trade
Sovereign decisions on the Sino–Russian border

Natalia Ryzhova

Ethnography usually starts with a story of adventure. It allows the author to demonstrate how little he or she knew before fieldwork and how much he or she knows after. In this chapter, I cannot follow such conventional ways. I never "arrived" at the place I am writing about with the purpose of doing research. I faced my "ethnography" before I started thinking as an anthropologist. I was born and raised in Blagoveshchensk, a Russian city on the border with China. I visited Chinese Heihe, situated opposite Blagoveshchensk across the Amur River, many times with various purposes, but not as a researcher. The first time I was there, it was as a tourist, then as a member of an official delegation. After that, I visited Heihe many times as a shuttle trader. During that time – in 1993 – I was a student in one of Saint Petersburg's universities. I needed money and two months of hard work during the summer holidays enabled me to earn quite enough for a year of residence in Saint Petersburg. In that turbulent post-socialist period, many Russian and Chinese locals travelled back and forth between Russia and China, trying to "make money", to start a small business, or to cover, at least, the most urgent daily expenses.

Thus, this chapter is about the practice of trade on the Russian–Chinese border that I have observed in various roles since the 1990s. It is well known that a significant share of cross-border trade in developing countries, and in Asia in particular, is not recorded by official statistics (Womack 2001; Khan et al. 2005; Yukseker 2007). The border between Blagoveshchensk and Heihe is one of the most famous and glaring cases in this respect. It is often referred to as a special place for "informal", "invisible", "shuttle", or "people-to-people" trade. References to invisibility and informality by no means imply, however, that officials would not know about it. In contrast, there is hardly anybody who does not.

In the Russian–Chinese border cities of the 1990s, custom checkpoints became a space for incredible entrepreneurial opportunities and sources of hope, as well as targets for surveillance. While the collapse of the Soviet Union led to huge delays in the payment of salaries, to lost jobs, sky-rocketing inflation, and total instability, people nevertheless believed in a bright, capitalist future. The emerging capitalism seemed inseparable from lawlessness, and the violation of formal (or former) rules was absolutely evident for all Russians.

Locals at the Russian–Chinese border who participated in cross-border trade in the 1990s and, for example, bought bed sheets in Heihe to sell them on the bazaars in Blagoveshchensk, hardly thought about the "illegality" of this business – despite not paying taxes or custom duties and not registering as entrepreneurs. Almost everyone who lived in Blagoveshchensk in the 1990s bought Chinese goods at the street bazaars. Many of them did not find the mess and disorder of street peddling particularly appealing; however, they hardly thought of it in terms of (il)legality. What was evident for all – those who sold and those who bought goods, those who served as border guards, and those who crossed the border to go shopping – is that the former state had suddenly "disappeared" from their lives. This disappearance did not last long. It ended with a kind of rebirth of control, the creation of new rules, and different methods of their enforcement. However, it led people to believe that they could create their own rules and play their own games, in which the state not just could, but had, to be cheated.

Despite ongoing state attempts to stop deception, and tax and duty evasion, this basic conception not only continued to exist into the 2010s, but also developed, matured, and found new forms, including e-commerce based on new technologies. Thus, in this chapter, analyzing ethnographical data on shuttle trade and e-commerce, I consider how "ordinary people" can pay or not pay taxes, obey or violate rules, and hence remain in control and continue to engage in everyday politics.

The phenomenon of post-socialist law violation time and again came into scholars' views and was studied and explained in different ways by representatives of different disciplines (Hendley 1997; Radaev 2000; Frye 2000; Murrell 2001). Anthropologists often underlined that people perceived their societies as being without rules, their states as lacking institutions and laws, and their national communities as bereft of a moral compass (Humphrey 2000; Greenberg 2011). Nonetheless, it was expected that with the end of the "transition period", post-Soviet people would eventually start obeying formal rules, institutions would be created, and moral circumscription would appear. However, although the transition in the Blagoveshchensk–Heihe area started some 30 years ago, attitudes towards the law have hardly changed, at least not towards legalization. Even more, the Soviet legacy of the 1990s encouraged people to think about a specific Soviet morality (not legality) of trade. Now trade is conceived of differently. However, for both the early post-Soviet and the present era, (in)formality and (il)legality as an official discourse is hardly the right anthropological concept. People themselves shifted their interpretations from concerns over morality and ethics towards lawfulness and authority. They do not question whether they can participate in morally dubious "speculation" (as in 1990s), but believe that they have rights to trade in accordance with their own rules. Therefore, I argue that the concept of sovereignty as suggested by Caroline Humphrey (2004) and other anthropologists allows for a better understanding of shuttle trade as practiced by "ordinary people". Thus, in this chapter I am concerned with the question of who makes sovereign decisions regarding the control of movement across borders, the regulation and collection of taxes, and the fixing of the state budget.

Anthropologists engaging with the notion of sovereignty have shown that the dominating international relations concept of sovereignty as a matter for nation states can no longer be taken for granted. According to Chalfin (2006), new forms of sovereignty emerge in the context of transnational commerce, national security threats, and customs policies shaped by the World Trade Organization and the World Customs Organization rather than by the nation state. Alternative indigenous forms of sovereignty and nationhood were studied by Simpson (2014) in her book on the Iroquois societies divided by the US–Canadian border. Studying post-colonial settings in which multiple and contested powers are at work, Ong (2006) emphasizes "fragmented" and "graduated" sovereignty, while Bartelson (2006) highlights the "mixed", and Hansen and Steputat (2006) the "plural" character of sovereignty. All these authors point out that sovereignty is never absolute and requires relationships with other entities that, in turn, can create and maintain their own rules. According to Nordstrom (2004), private military companies, often operating in the shadow of governments and invisible to the public eye, perform various functions that were once the domain of state armies. Following such observations, it must be questioned how a sovereign state can be an independent stand-alone entity, able to draw boundaries between the self and the rest of the world and enforce its own rules. Tying in with this debate, and most relevant for this chapter, are the questions raised by Rutherford (2012) who asks whether citizens, missionaries, competing governmental powers, non-governmental organizations, or the international community are main players in the sovereign games.

In a sense, many anthropological concepts of plural and other forms of sovereignty lie between classical liberal thinkers (e.g. Mill 1985 (1859)) and anarchists (e.g. Stirner 1995 (1907)). Very much like classical liberals, anthropologists see the individual as a sovereign in and of himself/ herself. But, similar to anarchists, anthropologists focus their attention on the liberation of people from repressive state interventions. In contrast to both classical and anarchist views, anthropologists often focus on the *everyday lives of people* who experience projects of state expansion and try to maintain a form of sovereignty. One exciting work in this regard is Scott's book *The Art of Not Being Governed* (2009). It his research, Scott focuses on people who live in relatively "ungovernable" peripheries (mostly in the uplands of Southeast Asia). These people, Scott argues, are best seen as descendants of those who sought refuge from the voracious behaviour of states. Their ways of life and mode of agricultural production have made it difficult for state-predators to control them. Their religions and social structures are the results of continuing attempts to escape from the state with its wars, taxes, and slavery. Only people seeking refuge in the periphery managed to retain sovereignty over themselves.

Although anthropology is traditionally concerned with repressive power and human beings who resist it, the discipline still has not much to say about how sovereign power is experienced and reproduced in day-to-day interactions, how decisions are made and mediated, translated into action, why and how grey zones in law appear, and how are they maintained. I believe that informal trade on the Russian–Chinese border is a good case for suggesting answers to these questions. To do so, I focus on two markers of sovereignty – *predation* and *invisibility* – that are both present in informal trade. Addressing predation, I underline that the state is always eager to collect different forms of taxes while people almost never desire to pay them. The focus on the interplay between taxation and tax evasion allows us to see how both state and popular power is experienced and why grey zones appear. Speaking of shades of grey, using visibility/invisibility as a marker of sovereignty, I take a loan from another of James Scott's books. In *Seeing Like a State* (Scott 1998), he argues that the state always tries to make its population visible for taxation, control, normalization, and simplification. People often effectively resist becoming "legible" (visible) as subjects and choose to subvert control by "illegal" activities, staying to some extent invisible. Invisibility as a marker also enables one to grasp how decisions are made, how politics within and beyond state institutions is produced, and how it might be debunked.

The chapter consists of two sections. The first investigates the evolution of border trade in the light of the notion of predation. I try to shed light on the question of who extracts wealth and how, and how sovereign power is produced, concentrated, and reproduced in day-to-day interactions. The second section discusses recent occurrences of cross-border e-commerce through the lens of invisibility. My purpose in this section is to show that rules are always adapted and changed not only by the state as a sovereign, but also by people who use their creativeness, new niches, and technologies in order to hide from the state, and, in doing so, make their own sovereign decisions. In the conclusion, I bring together these strands and engage with the idea of incoherency.

Predators and prey on the border

The small-scale border trade between Blagoveshchensk and Heihe started in 1987 with the signing of the agreement on cross-border tourism between the local authorities of Blagoveshchensk and Heihe. Russian and Chinese citizens, suffering from a deficit of goods and a lack of money, started relations of exchange as tourists, bartering goods, and trading them on unorganized informal markets along streets or in squares, next to Chinese hotels, and on riverbanks. This form of entrepreneurship was more inadmissible than illegal – it took place *outside* legal rules: one could not get a business registered as there was no agency for registration, and one could not pay tax as there was no authority to collect it. Moreover, the Soviet Union did not have custom houses around the perimeter of the border, and hence, one could not pay duties – there was just no place to do it. Thus, people did not pay any fees, neither when goods crossed the border nor when they were sold. At the beginning of this popular border trade, neither local nor central authorities intended to extract rents from these activities. In contrast, they supported people in their aspirations for self-sufficiency. Although experts and officials saw the positive effects of border trade, many of the traders and customers themselves regarded it as immoral speculation, and hence believed they were predators at this border.

After the Soviet Union's collapse in 1992 and the liberalization of international trade in Russia, cross-border trade increased dramatically and increasingly fewer people perceived it as predatory speculation (Ryzhova and Ioffe 2009; Łopińska 2012). One of the most obvious reasons behind this was that the number of actors multiplied. Teachers, physicians, workers, and students all tried their luck. The most valuable goods included Russian watches and coats, as well as Chinese gym clothes and thermos bottles. In 1993, almost every local family in Amurskaya Oblast[1] had, or dreamed to obtain, a thermos bottle – usually a red one with garish flowers. Every teenager of Blagoveshchensk seemed to wear "Adidas" (or "Abibas", as a Chinese version of the brand was labelled). Despite the prevalence of cross-border trade and its importance for local markets, still nobody paid anything to the state during these early years after the collapse. Even though a customs office was established, traders usually just ignored it. In contrast, they preferred to remain hidden. What was really exciting was that the official discourse on this issue of informal "duty-free" border trade remained rather positive, because it led to a decrease of social tensions and an improvement of the social basis for economic reforms. Thus, the state still did not extract wealth from cross-border traders.

However, nothing lasts forever. The Russian budget deficit of 1994 led to significant changes in both legal regulation and discourse on border trade. Local authorities established official open-air markets and obligated road-side vendors to vacate their improvised shops. New legislation was introduced, intending to make entrepreneurs participating in the small-scale border trade pay customs taxes and duties. Needless to say that those accustomed to zero tariffs did not welcome these changes. Considering that consignments in the popular trade were truly small, trader tourism made economic sense only if the traders managed to pass the border as tourists rather than entrepreneurs and thus avoid paying taxes. Most of the traders involved continued doing so, and were thereby quite creative, claiming successfully that the goods they were carrying were "for personal, not commercial purposes". The maximum amount of goods "for personal use" was constantly revised. To understand the rules, traders had to keep a close eye on them, cross the border regularly, bargain with custom officials, and communicate with other traders. Obviously, immersing oneself in this constantly changing world required time and effort. This caused many to leave the business. As a result, cross-border trade grew from an unofficial part-time activity into a professional but still unofficial employment.

The traders' constant attempts to avoid taxes and duties encouraged custom officials to take part in this game. Traders pretended that they went back and forth every week just to buy something for "personal need" while officials pretended they believed their tales. When credence weakened, officials asked for "support" with some money. Thus, customs officials extracted wealth for the state in the form of taxes and duties as well as for themselves in the form of bribes. The amount payable for a bribe was subject to negotiation. If one was a friend or classmate of an official in charge, one could easily get a better bargain. However, not only established social ties but also skill and wit were required to lower the fees asked for. A proficient negotiator could sometimes secure an even more profitable deal than one who had a preceding arrangement. I remember how a custom officer spared the mother of several children – she wore the medal of the hero mother – and let her pass without any payment at all. When this woman arrived at the customs with her two children the next time, the officer assisted her with not only her baggage, but also with negotiating the amount to be paid. Some officials were known as more friendly and human, while others were branded as strict and selfish, and some were even blamed for outright atrocity. One of the cheating practices consisted of wearing as many clothes as possible and pretending that this was the normal way of dressing. One would, for example, wear a fur coat and pair it with a raincoat, a couple of tuxedos, and a few leather jackets. Of course, officers understood that this was just a game – and a rather uncomfortable one for the wearer. Officers would then prolong the customs procedure to increase the obvious discomfort. Traders would discuss all these tricks and adventures jokingly, but the reality was not pleasant. By the mid-1990s, they no longer thought of themselves as predators. Speculation as a negatively connoted term had faded away. People started to be proud of their hard work and blame others as being the real "predators" – that is, the officials who made their work harder than it should have been.

Crucially, discursive practices helped to construct the public perception of corruption at customs. Both traders and officers believed that the state has the right to require payments. However, when officials acting on behalf of the state used their position to demand payments in order to overcome state rules, they were understood as "normal" predators. That is to say that corruption was understood not as a deviation, but as a habitual way of living. Consider the following analogy. If a fox appears on an island with hundreds of rabbits but no carnivores, it could not be assumed the fox would convert into a rabbit. When one or another rabbit disappears, every islander will understand that the fox needs food. However, if the fox takes more and more rabbits, the island will become perceived as predatory territory. Maybe more and more rabbits will decide to leave the unfriendly island as nobody will assume that the fox can stop eating meat. Similarly, customs, and more broadly the state, were gradually and as expected becoming predators and the locals ("islanders") did not see this as a deviation. In contrast, deals or rumours of deals with corrupt customs officers and the recognition of corruption as part of life, helped people to leave the Soviet state behind and to imagine – adopting Akhil Gupta's (1995) notion – a "discursive construction" of the new Russian state.

Unlike on the imagined island, however, the fox-like officers were not the only predators. Banks and quasi-banks joined them as meat eaters. Neither Chinese traders nor Russian entrepreneurs could transfer money via officially registered banks because none of the actors involved wanted to become "visible". The impossibility of transferring earnings – usually from the Russian bazaars to the Chinese producers – caused unofficial "flying banks" to appear (these practices exist on the different borders – see, for instance, Chakraborty 2009; Grillot 2016). Usually, these services did not include any real transportation of cash across the border; rather, they relied on phone calls instructing the agent on the other side of the border to pay a particular amount to a particular person or company. Official Russian and Chinese banks soon understood the potential of cross-border trade and started to lobby their central banks to find ways to facilitate cross-border transactions outside the usual framework of international money transfers.

Thus, the profits made in cross-border trade attracted different types of new predators, and some of them did have more power to assert their rights than others. The state representatives were clearly more powerful than the traders in the bazaars. The state representatives highlighted their legitimacy by stressing that they served the public good – the schools, hospitals, and the pension system. Hence, the main weapon of the state in the unfolding struggle was the accusation that cross-border trade was not just illegal, but also ethically unjustified. In the course of the debate it was soon forgotten that cross-border trade had directly helped to overcome social problems, allowing people to survive, and state reforms to be implemented. Illegality became the main stigma of small cross-border trade.

What is important for my argument here is that the target of the struggle was never customs and the officers and officials who illegally took bribes, but instead the target was the illegal economic activities of ordinary people and, by implication, these people per se. Despite this ongoing struggle, the state (and its finances) did not win, neither in the 1990s nor today.

When in 1997 customs procedures became much stricter, many former small entrepreneurs left the market. Those who continued working strengthened their positions. Customs officials dealing with more advanced traders also became more advanced in terms of standardizing rules. That is to say that both officials and traders more or less agreed on formal (legal) and informal taxes and duties. When crossing the border, traders would usually only pay formal duties; informal fees were handed over later on special occasions. Bargaining remained possible for the next delivery, and hence, this practice became more commercial and less reliant on personal relations.

One of the results of strengthening the customs regime was that large and medium Chinese suppliers moved to the Russian side. Instead of many small Chinese shuttle traders going back and forth across the border with small consignments, sizeable storehouses were established. The restrictions of Russian law did not give them the possibility of legalizing their activities, which is why Russian straw men started offering legalization procedures, such as the registration of businesses in their names. By doing so, they were able to extract some profits without doing anything. This also enabled municipal budgets to access additional revenue, and non-customs officials new types of administrative rents. The mass media, politicians, and various experts began actively discussing the penetration of Chinese illegal migrants into the Russian Far East and the illegality of the Chinese traders. This led to new restrictions on migration, customs, and fiscal matters.

In 2001, the Russian state adopted new legislation in order to curtail shuttle trade and Chinese migration. However, these restrictions did not lead to the disappearance of both, but rather to an adjustment of procedures. Instead of traders transporting their own goods, new actors started offering organized schemes. Let me describe how this worked. Consider, for example, a trader who needs to transport 100 items from Heihe to Blagoveshchensk. It is difficult for him to pretend that 100 items are for personal use because he travels as a tourist for a short period. He could hire people to take five items and declare them as being for "personal use". To do this, he would have to hire 20 people. However, it is difficult to control such a large number of "smugglers" and it is likely that some items would be "lost" on the way. It thus makes more sense to deal with organized groups of "smugglers", informal firms with supervisors (*brigadir*) and carriers (*phonary*, literally "lamps"), themselves "tourists" who register the items (big bag or *baul*) in their names.

As a result of introducing and strengthening the border regime, such organized smuggling companies emerged as a new type of extractor. At the same time, the state as official extractor also increased its revenue because customs officers had to require declaring at least something officially. The possibility of deciding which part of the delivery is officially tariffed and which one is not gave custom officers their slice of the pie. New restrictions on the amount of goods that can cross the border for personal use were adopted in 2006. They led to an adjustment of extraction practices. If, at the beginning of the 2000s, organized groups planned their activities themselves, in 2006 corrupt officials obtained control over all procedures. Before the implementation of the new rules, the *brigadir* of a smuggler's firm decided how many packages he could deliver on a particular day, and he also could bargain with customs officials. After the implementation of the new rules, the customs officers laid down *their* new rules: henceforth it was them deciding on the fees to be paid and the number of packages allowed for delivery on a particular day. The number of smugglers considerably declined. The new rules and their implementation on the ground almost put an end to small-scale cross-border trade. Many more small entrepreneurs left the market.

In 2008, the Russian Federation adopted and enforced again a set of new rules, this time against the presence of illegal migrants. These rules effectively outlawed the possibility for migrants to trade on bazaars, including the Chinese on Blagoveshchensk's bazaars who, for sure, were among those targeted by these rules. However, they found ways to stay. Often this meant that Chinese traders hired Russians or other front men whom the ban did not affect, such as Kyrgyzstani. Another way to circumvent the strict rules was to upscale the business – switching from retail to wholesale operations. While this was not always possible, it provided an avenue for some. In summary, the implementation of legal restrictions based on the discourse on illegality resulted in enfolding small-scale border trade into larger structures, a concentration of businesses, and a proliferation of extractive rent-seeking by customs officials and other elites.

A quarter of a century ago, in the early 1990s, Russians did not know what predation at customs was, and by no means did they know about the privilege of customs officials to decree their own rules in order to generate income. The discourse on the illegality of everyday economic activities of ordinary people encouraged the legislative establishment to implement new and even more severe laws. These laws led to a gradual exclusion of economic agents in the interest of others, resulting in both the concentration of extraction and predation practices as well as a concentration of rights to make "sovereign" decisions in the hands of more or less the same corrupt officials. The question is whether this meant that *only* officials could decide, while ordinary folks, the people of Blagoveshchensk, lost their power to establish rules and keep a certain degree of local sovereignty. Did all of them "lose their teeth" and become prey, rabbits eyed at by an increasing number of hungry foxes on the metaphorical island? My answer is that even though border trade has gone through significant changes throughout the recent three decades, traders still play games over sovereignty. Similar to Scott's (2009) residents of highland Zomia, the traders of Amur plains introduce their own rules and create their own reality. New technologies – the Internet and online shopping, as I show in the next section – enable people, goods, money, and networks of all of these to effectively resist becoming fully legible.

Endless invisibility of the cross-border trade

Yevgenyi, 27, studied informatics and computer engineering. When we met in 2014, he was the owner of a small business in Blago (as Blagoveshchensk is called locally). He rented a small office of about 15 square metres in one of the business centres in the town where he had Internet access. His business consisted of helping Russian customers find goods on Taobao, a Chinese online market and auction platform similar to eBay, owned by the Alibaba Group. On receiving an order and advance payment, he would pass the money on to his Chinese partner and then organize delivery using the old shuttle method. Yevgenyi's business grew out of three personal aspects of his life: his hobby (he loved spending time on the Internet), his own desire to buy things, and his old contacts in Heihe (as a student back in the 2000s, he had taken part in shuttle deliveries). Like his clients, Yevgenyi started by buying the cheapest and most simple things, only gradually increasing his stake and purchasing more expensive things. He would, for example, buy a pair of reading glasses identical to those in the local shop but 10 times cheaper. When his friends and relatives noticed how clever his purchases were, they started asking him to buy things for them. In this way, a trusted circle of customers formed. Yevgenyi did not sell his services, but instead took part in a complex system of reciprocal exchanges. As a result, his relatives – who in general did not trust the Chinese Internet – trusted him and his experience. The sum they handed over to him for each purchase was in a certain sense a quantitative evaluation of this experience, or a rationalization of the trust placed in him. After six months of this activity, friends began asking Yevgenyi why he did not want to sell his experience for money to other people – not to the usual relatives and friends, but to acquaintances of acquaintances.

The Alibaba Group is an originally Chinese company that is now international, located in Hangzhou (China). It comprises 25 strategic businesses, including Aliexpress (retail and small wholesale trade), Alibaba (an electronic platform for business-to-business trade), Yahoo (search engine), Alipay (a payment platform), Taobao (a consumer-to-consumer trade), and others. Alibaba opened its first official branch in Russia only in 2015. However, "ordinary small entrepreneurs", especially those who live in border zones, have been participating in the process of buying goods on Taobao and selling them in Blagoveshchensk and other Russian cities for quite some time. To do that, various creative tricks and "business schemes" were necessary. This trade with items ordered online and shipped to customers in Russia offered new opportunities to hundreds of small traders on the Russian–Chinese border. The reasons behind this are the following.

As Alibaba, at least in the beginning, had not intended Taobao to cater towards international customers, a Russian purchaser had to have a Chinese mobile telephone number in order to register. This meant that only people with contacts with a Chinese citizen had access to the gigantic virtual bazaar and could actually buy something. It is difficult to say now who first dreamed up the idea of founding a business on this basis – may be there were many such people. Unsurprisingly, however, people like Yevgenyi – online savvy border residents with real contacts on the other side – were among the pioneers of this trade in Russia. In Blagoveshchensk, which is separated from Heihe only by a river, the number of mediators providing access to the Chinese Internet-bazaar has risen exponentially. This was helped by the fact that many locals had Chinese SIM cards anyway, a result of the widespread shuttle trade across the border.

Of course, the fact that mediators had the right mobile phone was not the only reason they were necessary. Another barrier for ordinary consumers was that Alibaba demanded payment by a Chinese credit card – only those who had access to Chinese payment systems could register their accounts and hence buy anything. Then there was the fact that although a Chinese phone number and credit card would enable purchases, it did not help them actually receive goods. For that, a postal system connecting the Chinese producer with the Russian buyer was necessary. *Pochta Rossii*, the state-owned Russian post, even 25 years after the fall of the USSR, is still the same inefficient old "Soviet" postal service. According to law, a private recipient may receive foreign goods duty free only up to a value of 1,000 euros per month and a total of no more than 31 kg. Furthermore, the recipient must guarantee that the goods are for personal use. It is the customs service that has oversight of these regulations. The presence of customs officers right at the sorting station greatly speeds up the procedure; otherwise, goods from abroad are delayed by having to sit in customs warehouses waiting to be cleared before they even go to the post office for sorting. All these complications of delivery from abroad can be avoided in only one way – by the unofficial channels set up by the cross-border shuttle trade.

All of this helped to bring about the emergence of Yevgenyi and many other similar businesses. They gathered all the capabilities in one operation (access to the Taobao website, Internet, phone, credit card, and shuttle delivery), and thus helped the customer to overcome the barriers. Speaking in terms of predation – they help ordinary buyers to obtain goods without paying taxes. They allow people to participate in making sovereign decisions and enable these people and themselves to stay invisible.

It is evident that owing to new technologies this invisibility has a specific nature. In contrast to Scott's (2009) Zomia with its agricultural production well hidden from the state, Yevgenyi's Internet business does not – for the most part – require a contingent hidden territory. Despite technologies of surveillance, the world did not become fully transparent; grey zones continue to exist. What is intriguing here is not only the creativity of Yevgenyi and his peers, but also a self-chosen "blindness" of state authorities prevented the elimination of this niche.

While official discourse usually represents smuggling as the state's enemy, the compliance of state officials in helping goods cross the border is obvious to all parties involved. In the case at hand, every single garment shuttled across the border in the 1990s was visible – or legible – to state representatives. A customs officer could always ask to open a bundle of clothes and be shown every secret little nook of it. Nevertheless, most goods stayed "invisible" in terms of taxation.

This observation, to some extent, contradicts Scott's (1998, 2009) argument of the state's quest for legibility. The quick and standard explanation, of course, is that the state does not manage to rein in its corrupt officials. This, however, does not tell the full story. Regional authorities regularly underline that unorganized bazaar and shuttle traders are a first step towards forthcoming cross-border cooperation. At the same time, they also benefit from the discourse of illegality and the "Chinese threat", as it encourages the political centre to financially support cities on the border. A certain amount of illegibility in the form of statistical uncertainty about the actual size of shuttle trade feeds both the discourse of "illegality" and "forthcoming cooperation" and thereby empowers local officials to continue playing their game of sovereignty.

Conclusion

In economics and sociology, the state tends to be conceptualized as a coherent entity. Even if the notion of the predatory state is employed to explain informality, corruption, and the failure of economic development, the state is still often seen as acting coherently in the interest of elites. Anthropologists after Gupta (1995) have repeatedly debunked the notion of the coherent state, and my ethnography of making sovereign decisions (on duties and taxes, movement across the border) provides additional evidence in this regard. It is by no means possible to imagine that low-level and top-level officials work to serve the interests of each other, and that the flows of corrupt administrative rents are directed from the bottom to the top like taxes. The idea that the official on the ground does exactly what he is meant to do seems naïve in the context of many countries – it certainly is in Russia. More plausible understandings require us to depart from the illusion of coherency and suggest exploring the sometimes conflicting aims, incentives, and strategies of the actors involved.

The point of departure for my argument is that trade and traders, especially on the border, attract predators by trying to feed on the flows of goods, money, and people across the border. When I say predators, I mean all types, including the carriers of goods and money, smugglers, corrupt officials, and the various other agents of the state. Moreover, at the outset of my story, traders themselves identified as predators following the Soviet stigma of seeing trade as immoral speculation. While they gradually freed themselves of this stigma and accepted capitalist ideology, they started being blamed of acting illegally, and hence, once more, were labelled predators by state representatives.

This complex interplay between different predators allows us to see that sovereign decisions – the right of a governing body to control movement across borders, regulate and collect taxes, and fix a state budget – rest in practice not only with the designated authorities, but also with local, regional, and trans-regional agents and, most importantly, with ordinary people.

Note

1   Amurskaya Oblast is located in the Russian Far East. It borders the Sakha Republic in the north, Khabarovsk Kray in the east, Zabaykalsky Krai in the west, and Heilongjiang Province (China) in the south. The region saw the first influx of Russian settlers in the mid-17th century; many more (mostly Cossacks and peasant farmers) came after the signing of the Treaty of Nerchinsk in 1858. Although Amurskaya Oblast has large natural reserves, it is one of the less developed regions in the Russian Federation. After the collapse of the Soviet Union, agricultural as well as industrial production shrank. Proximity to China helped people survive during these most difficult times.

References

Bartelson, J. 2006. The Concept of Sovereignty Revisited. *The European Journal of International Law*. Vol. 17 (2): 463–74.
Chakraborty, M. 2009. Indo-Bangladesh Trade Nexus: India's Security Predicament. *Asia-Pacific Journal of Social Science*. Vol. 1 (1): 19–34.
Chalfin, B. 2006. Global Customs Regimes and the Traffic in Sovereignty. *Current Anthropology*. Vol. 47 (2): 243–76.
Frye, T. 2000. *Brokers and Bureaucrats: Building Market Institutions in Russia*. Ann Arbor, MI: University of Michigan Press.
Greenberg, J. 2011. On the Road to Normal: Negotiating Agency and State Sovereignty in Postsocialist Serbia. *American Anthropologist*. Vol. 113 (1): 88–100.
Grillot, C. 2016. "Trust Facilitates Business, But May Also Ruin It": The Hazardous Facets of Sino-Vietnamese Border Trade. *Asian Anthropology*. Vol. 15 (2): 169–85.
Gupta, A. 1995. Blurred Boundaries: The Discourse of Corruption, the Culture of Politics, and the Imagined State. *American Ethnologist*. Vol. 22 (2): 375–402.
Hansen, T.B. and Steputat, F. 2006. Introduction. In Hansen, T.B. and Steputat, F. (eds.), *Sovereign Bodies: Citizens, Migrants, and States in the Postcolonial World*. Durham, NC: Duke University Press, pp. 1–38.
Hendley, K. 1997. Legal Development in Post-Soviet Russia. *Post-Soviet Affairs*. Vol. 13 (3): 228–51.
Humphrey, C. 2000. Dirty Business, "Normal Life", and the Dream of Law. In Ledeneva, A.V. and Kurkchiyan, M. (eds.), *Economic Crime in Russia*. The Hague: Kluwer Law International, pp. 177–90.
Humphrey, C. 2004. Sovereignty. In Nugent, D. and Vincent, J. (eds.), *A Companion to the Anthropology of Politics*. Oxford: Blackwell, pp. 418–36.
Khan, R., Yusuf, M., Bokhari, S. and Aziz, S. 2005. Quantifying Informal Trade Between Pakistan and India. In Naqvi, Z.F. and Schuler, P. (eds.), *The Challenges and Potential of Pakistan-India Trade*. Washington, DC: World Bank, pp. 87–104.
Łopińska, A. 2012. Russian Far Eastern Border Regions and Chinese Immigration. Historical, Economic and Social Determinants of Cooperation. *Sensus Historiae*. Vol. 4 (1): 181–92.
Mill, J.S. 1985 (1859). On Liberty. Himmelfarb, G. (ed.). London: Penguin.
Murrell, P. 2001. *Assessing the Value of Law in Transition Economies*. Ann Arbor, MI: University of Michigan Press.
Nordstrom, C. 2004. *Global Shadows: Violence, Power, and International Profiteering in the Twenty First Century*. Berkeley, CA: University of California Press.
Ong, A. 2006. *Neoliberalism as Exception: Mutations in Citizenship and Sovereignty*. Durham, NC: Duke University Press Books.

Radaev, V. 2000. Corruption and Violence in Russian Business in the Late 1990s. In Ledeneva. A.V. and Kurkchiyan, M. (eds.), *Economic Crime in Russia*. The Hague: Kluwer Law International, pp. 63–82.

Rutherford, D. 2012. *Laughing at Leviathan. Sovereignty and Audience in West Papua*. Chicago, IL: The University of Chicago Press.

Ryzhova, N. and Ioffe, G. 2009. Trans-border Exchange Between Russia and China: The Case of Blagoveshchensk and Heihe. *Eurasian Geography and Economics*. Vol. 3: 348–64.

Scott, J. 1998. *Seeing Like a State: How Certain Schemes to Improve the Human Condition Have Failed*. New Haven, CT and London: Yale University Press.

Scott, J. 2009. *The Art of Not Being Governed: An Anarchist History of Upland Southeast Asia*. New Haven, CT: Yale University Press.

Simpson, A. 2014. *Mohawk Interruptus: Political Life Across the Borders of Settler States*. Durham, NC: Duke University Press.

Stirner, M. 1995 (1907). *The Ego and Its Own*. Byington, S.T. (trans.). Leopold, D. (intro. and annot. (ed.)). Cambridge, New York, and Melbourne: Cambridge University Press.

Womack, B. 2001. China's Border Trade and its Relationship to the National Political Economy. *American Asian Review*. Vol. 19 (2): 31–48.

Yukseker, D. 2007. Shuttling Goods, Weaving Consumer Tastes: Informal Trade between Turkey and Russia. *International Journal of Urban and Regional Research*. Vol. 31 (1): 60–72.

Part 6
Humanitarians, religion, and NGOs

Part 6

Humanitarian Action
and NGOs

Introduction

Alexander Horstmann

This part explores the arrival of humanitarian grassroots organizations as important players in the borderlands. In the context of violence and natural disaster, humanitarian organizations are becoming increasingly important. Not only do they produce an international truth for international audiences as witnesses of the human rights abuses in violent conflicts (Redfield 2013), but they also rise to hold considerable power in the local context, helping internally displaced people in dangerous borderlands by becoming the sole providers of emergency healthcare, mobile education, food, and clothing.

Religious non-governmental organizations (NGOs), combining an ethos of humanitarianism and development with religion, use their historical integration and religious infrastructure of monasteries, churches, and mosques, clinics and schools, as sanctuaries and safety zones for displaced villagers (Horstmann and Jung 2015: 1–20). These local NGOs partner with international humanitarian organizations who do not have the same privileged access to the most vulnerable populations in conflict zones. Such "glocal" partnerships become arenas where "biopolitical" borders are negotiated and where humanitarianism itself becomes a biopolitical technology to shape and mobilize life.

This part also looks at emotions and affects related to border politics and border struggles, shedding new light on capitalist and humanitarian economies. To this end, Su-Ann Oh employs the concept of the moral economy and gives it a new twist: While the capitalist economy comprises factories located at the border, and the humanitarian economy includes all kinds of international humanitarian and community-based organizations, a moral economy concerning the mobilization of feelings and emotions and setting standards for moral values as well as discourses on social suffering (Fassin 2012: 7–8; Oh 2016) has emerged. Dan Smyer Yü addresses competition and boundary making of ethnic and religious identities and how the negotiation unfolds at the level of both the nation and the body.

The chapter by Alexander Horstmann takes the example of the Free Burma Rangers, a faith-based humanitarian organization based in Chiang Mai, Thailand, that proliferated in the ethnic conflicts of Myanmar's frontier regions. The Free Burma Rangers employ nurses from Karen State, but also from other ethnic minority areas, and provide emergency healthcare to internally displaced people who suffer from military assaults. While other humanitarian organizations register with the Myanmar government, the Free Burma Rangers do not ask for permission – they just go. Walking along and under the protection of ethnic minority armies and using military equipment for communication and detecting the enemy, the Free Burma Rangers' only mandate comes from heaven; the organization is Christian and receives support from American church networks. In order to operate effectively, the organization is secretive about its operations, currently carried out in Northern Shan and Kachin States. Driven by a motivation to help, the Free Burma Rangers may endanger the very people that they are aiming to protect.

Till Mostowlansky's chapter discusses the work of the Aga Khan Development Network (AKDN), the Ismaili Imam's global development organization, in Central Asia. Taking a historical approach, Mostowlansky explores the way that overlapping assemblages consisting of local governments, members of the Islamic missionary grassroots movement Tablighi Jama'at, international organizations, and individual traders have all participated in the reordering of borders in the Pamirian borderlands. Mostowlansky's chapter is similar to Reeves' chapter in that it shows that states are entities in progress and that borders are shifting.

The chapter by Su-Ann Oh takes Fassin's definition of the moral economy as economy of affect and emotion as the starting point to discuss the configuration and landscape of humanitarian aid in Thai–Myanmar borderscapes. She identifies different landscapes or configurations of emotion and affect in the refugee public sphere: the discourse on humanitarian relief propagated by humanitarian organizations and human rights groups; the configuration by the political organizations and ethno-nationalist movements; Christian church networks and Buddhist monastery networks, based on utopian ideas of a religious world without suffering. Su-Ann Oh's work is important in that it suggests that different players in the humanitarian field aim to predominate and to partly instrumentalize emotions of suffering for political purposes.

The chapter in Part 6 by Dan Yü discusses the extension of boundaries to the personal and even intimate level of the body. Yü's chapter innovatively uses the concepts of boundary making to analyze the local conflict caused by the elopement of a Tibetan Buddhist woman with a Muslim Hui man. The extramarital affair of the Tibetan woman with a Hui man was seen as a humiliation not only for the family, but for the community as a whole and the man as a threat to the social cohesion of the Tibetan community and to religion. The whole community was thus involved in searching for and returning the Tibetan woman back home to reinstate social order. More than any other chapter in the Handbook, Yü is able to demonstrate how the boundaries are drawn between the communities and that the boundaries of the state can duplicate and multiply on various levels. In this, Yu's chapter is innovative in the way that he shows how the discussion on borders can be extended to examine boundary making in everyday life and on the personal level.

References

Fassin, Didier 2012. Humanitarian Reason. A History of the Present. Berkeley: University of California Press.
Horstmann, Alexander and Jin-Heon Jung (eds.) 2015. Building Noah's Ark for Migrants, Refugees and Religious Communities. Basingstoke: Palgrave.
Oh, Su-Ann (ed.) 2016. Myanmar's Mountain and Maritime Borderscapes: Local Practices, Boundary-Making and Figured Worlds. Singapore: ISEAS.
Redfield, Peter 2013. Life in Crisis: The Ethical Journey of Doctors without Borders. Berkeley: University of California Press.

27

Humanitarian assistance and Protestant proselytizing in the borderlands of Myanmar

The Free Burma Rangers

Alexander Horstmann

Beginning every interview with a prayer, American missionary and humanitarian worker David Eubank tells us that he is giving himself to God and depends on his guidance. The operations of the humanitarian service organization, the Free Burma Rangers (FBR), that he heads do span continents, helping the wounded with emergency healthcare in the borderlands of Eastern Myanmar, the Nuba mountains in Sudan, and the Kurdish Peshmerga in Iraqi Kurdistan and Syria.

This chapter is based on nine years on-and-off ethnographic fieldwork in the dangerous borderlands of Karen State in Eastern Myanmar and in the refugee camps of Northwestern Thailand, focusing on personal narratives of displacement and emplacement of young Karen villagers (Maps 27.1 and 27.2). I looked at the self-organization and self-governance of Karen in political organizations, civil society, and especially private initiatives and grassroots organizations, providing different types of small-scale, but efficient humanitarian assistance to Karen refugee-migrants (Horstmann 2016). The Free Burma Rangers were one of the religious non-governmental organizations (NGOs) positioning themselves in the domain of healthcare and human rights documentation.[1]

I am mainly interested in finding an answer to the question that the founder of the Free Burma Rangers and his wife ask in a trailer: "What am I doing here" in the dangerous borderlands and conflict zone of Karen State in Eastern Myanmar? This question is directed to the audience to find out why the Free Burma Rangers risk their lives to help displaced Karen villagers. But it is also a question that asks for a mandate for the Free Burma Rangers to carry out their activities, to establish a presence with the Karen, and to save lives. Most notably, the Free Burma Rangers have been asked by the political organizations of the Karen, the Karen National Union, to stay on, and operates under the protection of its armed wing, the Karen National Liberation Army.

Taking up humanism as its constituency: the Free Burma Rangers

In his famous lectures on biopolitics, Michel Foucault showed us how the state introduced new technologies to measure and manage its population (Foucault 2007; Dean 2010: 117–121). Meanwhile, the question of state authority has become more complex, with international organizations

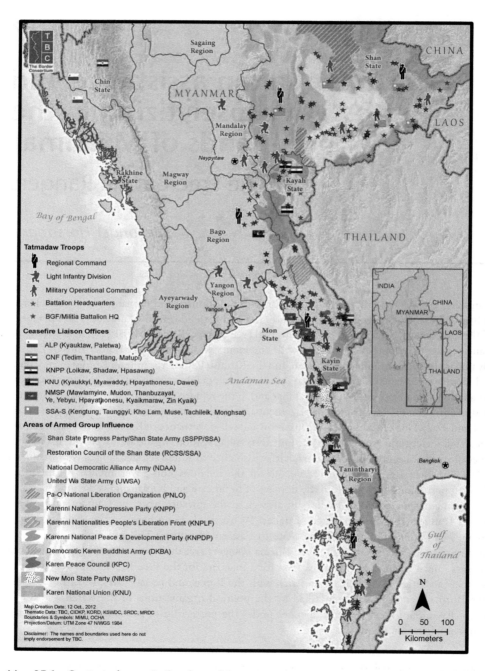

Map 27.1 Contested areas in Southeast Myanmar
Source: Copyright by The Border Consortium (2012), p. 13

Refugee and IDP Camp Populations: December 2016

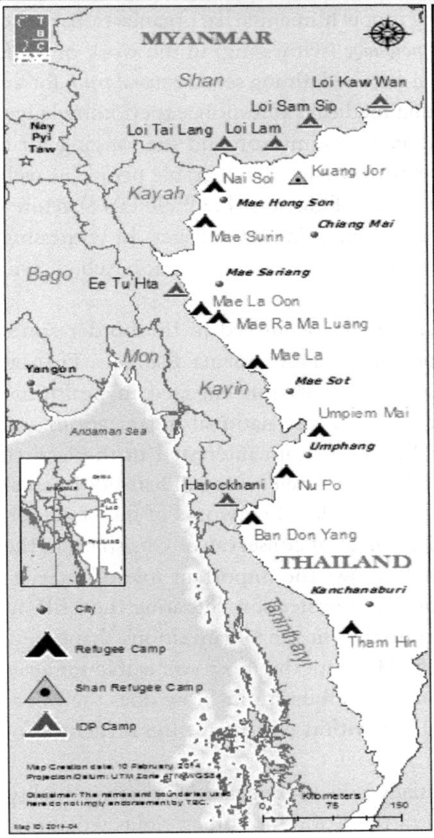

Refugee Camps	TBC Verified Caseload[1]			TBC Assisted Population[2]	MOI/UNHCR Verified Population
Province/Camp	Female	Male	Total	Total	Total
CHIANG MAI					
Kuang Jor[3]	211	205	416	416	
MAE HONG SON					
Ban Mai Nai Soi	5,083	5,339	10,422	10,465	9,994
Ban Mae Surin	1,271	1,247	2,518	2,530	2,406
Mae La Oon	4,641	4,543	9,184	9,183	9,855
Mae Ra Ma Luang	5,145	5,002	10,147	9,809	11,044
Subtotal:	16,140	16,131	32,271	31,987	33,299
TAK					
Mae La	19,005	18,513	37,518	37,302	37,261
Umpiem Mai	5,483	5,380	10,863	11,096	11,971
Nu Po	4,895	4,624	9,519	9,768	11,064
Subtotal:	29,383	28,517	57,900	58,166	60,296
KANCHANBURI					
Ban Don Yang	1,385	1,333	2,718	2,883	2,789
RATCHABURI					
Tham Hin	3,093	2,772	5,865	6,355	6,223
Total Refugees	50,212	48,958	99,170	99,807	102,607

IDP Camps[4]	Female	Male	Total	Refugees by Ethnicity	
Loi Kaw Wan	1,309	1,351	2,660	Karen	79.4%
Loi Sam Sip	148	208	356	Karenni	10.4%
Loi Lam	147	148	295	Burman	3.0%
Loi Tai Lang	1,210	1,159	2,369	Mon	0.7%
Ee Tu Hta	1,547	1,589	3,136	Other	6.4%
Total:	4,361	4,455	8,816		

Notes:
1. The verified caseload includes all persons, registered or not, confirmed living in camp & eligible for rations.
2. The TBC Assisted Population is the number of beneficiaries who collected rations during the previous month. Rations are only provided to those who are physically present at distributions.
3. Access and assistance authorised at the District level.
4. IDP camp population figures are derived from camp committees on a monthly or quarterly basis.
The population of 3,046 people from Halockhani Mon IDP camp is removed in this month since TBC food support is no longer provided.

Map 27.2 Internally displaced people and refugees in Southeast Myanmar
Source: Copyright by UNHCR. The Border Consortium (2016), p. 6.

and NGOs developing alternative structures of governance. Healthcare, for example, is shaped by the World Health Organization, the Red Cross, the Bill Gates Foundation, and many other international organizations and NGOs. Humanitarian organizations such as Médecins sans Frontières (MSF) are constantly confronted with the decision as to whether they should stay on in politically volatile situations. They are confronted with a state of permanent exception. There is no doubt that the organization has become one of the global players in all the regions affected by wars and humanitarian crises. The organization has taken up humanism as its constituency, battling the great killers of humankind in crisis-stricken areas. Such international organizations have become more important in the global politics of health, operating against the authoritarian state in the global South. Crisis, warring, and never-ending suffering propel humanitarian organizations to the forefront of media attention. Examining the use of *témoignage* (witnessing) in the work of MSF, Peter Redfield notes that big NGOs now play a central role in defining secular *moral truth* for an international audience (Redfield 2006: 5–6). Combining medical expression, expert knowledge, public expression, and in the case of the Free Burma Rangers, mission and the longing for a better world, health organizations are able to mobilize both the most vulnerable people as well as substantial financial and moral support from a great field of followers (Redfield 2013). Moreover, the Free Burma Rangers also involve rangers and ethnic minority villagers in witnessing and fact finding, by training them for independent human rights documentation, which will then feed the newsletters of their postings and website.

In the following, I look into emergency healthcare for the wounded in the border zones of Myanmar's ethnic minorities through the example of the Free Burma Rangers. First, as a missionary and armed (for self-defence) humanitarian organization engaged in healthcare and nursing, the FBR represent an expression of the *failure* of international organizations and governments in protecting the most needy villagers. Secondly, I am interested in the lack of mandate of the FBR, who prefer to operate secretly and outside the existing (Thailand–Burma) Border Consortium. The example of the FBR sheds light on global networks of humanitarian organizations and their being embedded into political alliances of conservative Christians in the USA, politicians, and the US Army. Finally, the example shows the important role of international NGOs and their alliances with locals in the politics of protection. Situating the FBR in a larger empirical context, I ask: how do these humanitarian health organizations shape new landscapes of humanitarian assistance and mobilization? How are the most vulnerable refugees situated in this growing field of voluntary intervention and mobilization? How does the insertion into these new assemblages situate the individual self within (Christian) infrastructures of humanitarian aid?

Humanitarian organizations such as MSF substantially add to Foucault's governmentality, establishing alternative networks and actors who monitor the world for human rights violations, making public important evidence of atrocities, bringing them to the attention of the media, and assisting the weakest elements of society, or the bare life. They want more than just to provide medical help; they want to give back dignity and provide a bit of normality in a context of permanent crisis. The FBR crucially not only provide medical assistance, but also solidarity with the refugees, thus echoing Agamben's contribution to the politics of life (Fassin 2007). Revising the Foucauldian theory of biopower, bare life is the remainder of the destroyed political bios. One of the most politically pressing questions raised by *Homo Sacer* is whether emancipatory movements can mobilize bare life itself. The FBR understand themselves as angels sent by God to protect the most vulnerable. However, the organization does not content itself with protection alone. It also forges global alliances with churches, NGOs, and the US Army, as well as local alliances with ethnic militias to go on the offensive. I argue that while the impact of the FBR in Myanmar seems to be minimal; the actual influence over life and death in the local context of violence and the destruction of the social fabric in the village cannot be exaggerated. For a moment, the villagers are subjected to sovereign rangers. As Agamben (1998: 6) writes, "the inclusion of bare life in the political realm constitutes the original nucleus of sovereign power".

I argue that the FBR exercise ideological and practical power, but by taking both rangers and villagers hostage, they are also a node in the establishment of dominating structures of humanitarian and military intervention, all in the name of humanism. Are the FBR an emancipatory force mobilizing bare life? Certainly, the many grassroots initiatives provide a crucial space for violently displaced villagers. Religion, in particular, may provide a sanctuary for villagers on the run. While the violently displaced villagers lose their destroyed homes, the alliance with and patronage from powerful international humanitarian organizations, governments, and Christian churches opens up original opportunities for mobility and political action (cf. Horstmann and Jung 2015).

Religion, however, can also have a confining and disciplinary aspect, and be involved in othering. The most important is that the violently displaced villagers in Syria, Sudan, and Myanmar all become part of a global missionary and humanitarian project in which the FBR are humanitarians, doctors, rangers, soldiers, and missionaries all in one. This self-legitimized project becomes part of a powerful, globally-financed assemblage with its own regime of discipline and its own system of modern biopower. In a state of exception, the FBR participate in the production of a biopolitical body.

Unlike Médecins sans Frontières, the FBR operate secretly in the jungles of Myanmar, protected by the ethnic armies, and use seasoned rangers and military equipment. Walking by night into the conflict zone, the rangers do not wait for permission to help the violently displaced villagers. If the Myanmar Army were to attack the villagers, the FBR will not leave them on their own. The claim of the humanist as its constituency is similar to that of Médecins sans Frontières: the mandate is given to them by their assistance to the most vulnerable. Indeed, the FBR have saved hundreds of lives; however, the FBR are anything but neutral. They perceive themselves as a missionary agency, which brings the rangers themselves, as well as the violently displaced who receive their assistance, to Jesus Christ.

The FBR are an important piece in the process of political community formation in the local arena. They are an American missionary group, but one that is strongly immersed in the local arena of Karen State in Myanmar. Myanmar is represented as the epitome of evil, whereby a ruthless Myanmar Army oppresses innocent villagers. Myanmar thus becomes the centre for the spiritual and financial mobilization of mission groups in the USA and in Europe. The focus on Myanmar is further highlighted by celebrity humanitarianism. The Bush family, and especially the former president's wife, Laura Bush, have developed a keen interest in Myanmar and in the fate of State Counsellor Aung San Suu Kyi. On her trips to Myanmar, Laura Bush also met with the FBR. Since then, the FBR have enjoyed special support from Laura Bush as an ambassador for liberalism and democracy in Myanmar. In this sense, Laura Bush is clearly intervening in local politics and contributing to the emergence of an "American Front" on the side of the democratic opposition as well as the Christianized Karen on the Eastern frontier of Myanmar. Celebrity humanitarianism is further accentuated by regular visits from Hollywood star and special envoy of the UN High Commissioner for Refugees, Angelina Jolie. The Karen are introduced as persecuted Christians, worthy of media attention in the global Christian community. In the global humanitarian field, the FBR and other faith-based groups have succeeded in transforming victimhood into a heroic struggle to assist and liberate persecuted Christians from evil worldwide. In this way, religious solidarity is helping to build a project, mobilized by donations from the local parishes and faith communities, that shrinks distances in a globalized mission.

In my contribution, I highlight the way that displacement and human suffering in Southeastern Myanmar is being used for a missionary calling within a missionary and faith-based humanitarian service group that has provided emergency health services to the wounded in the numerous ethnic conflicts in Myanmar over recent decades. While displacement as involuntary mobility and exodus has only negative connotations, the connection to religion perhaps enables us to think of displacement as a strategy for achieving greater protection. In this more positive light, religion is a tool with which the displaced people rebuild a sense of homeland, belonging, and engagement with other religious spaces. With this tool at hand, displaced Karen can at least attempt to regain control over their lives, and shape and sacralize spaces by placing themselves in and outside the international regime of refugee protection. Sometimes, the benefit of a religious network may make all the difference to physical survival, while in other contexts the benefit may be only spiritual.

The Free Burma Rangers

The FBR is a community-based organization founded by Allan Eubank and his son, David. Allan Eubank is a veteran American missionary based in Chiang Mai, northern Thailand. Before studying mission work, he served as a captain in the US Army during the Korean War. After training as a seminarian and missionary, he settled down in Chiang Mai with his wife Joan to bring God to the Thai and ethnic minority people. Allan and Joan started to convert the Lao Song in Nakhon Pathom (Northeastern Thailand, on the border with Laos), but had to wait 50 long years to earn their first baptisms. In a second project, he also rode elephants to evangelize among the Talako sect in Eastern Myanmar. He is expecting a breakthrough there any time now, with the spiritual leader converting or being prepared for conversion. Building on traditional Thai drama (*lakorn*), he and his wife established a full-time theatre troupe that performs the story of Jesus in Thai villages. His son David used to serve as special envoy of the US Army in the Myanmar–China borderland. Later, he trained as a theologian in a US seminary, when his father called him up as the Wa were looking for a Christian warrior and saw Eubank's picture of David Eubank in a military green uniform.

Seeing the suffering of the Karen, he decided to found the FBR to provide more efficient help. As the Karen have a 200-year history of Christianization, they hold special meaning, as a people, for American Baptist missionaries. The Karen are at the centre of the staffing of the FBR and of protecting their activities through the Karen National Liberation Army troops. David Eubank spends his time in and out of the ethnic conflict zones of Myanmar, in Chiang Mai, and also travels to the USA and Europe to promote the FBR.

The FBR coordinates their activities closely with American Christian groups, especially partners, and also with human rights groups, working in a similar way on human rights documentation. However, being a missionary organization, the FBR work mostly with faith-based groups and missionary churches. There is little contact between the FBR and other international organizations working on similar human rights issues or in the medical domain, and little contact with the Catholic faith. The FBR nonetheless certainly see themselves as part of a democratic front that is bringing the values of freedom, culture, and religion to a vandalized and mismanaged country of the global South.

The intention to save lives through emergency healthcare is, in a sense, an honourable and uncontested one. While the well-known French MSF works on a principle of human rights, the FBR perceive themselves as being in a sacred struggle of good against evil. While the French doctors remain impartial, the FBR take the side of the ethnic minorities and walk with the ethnic armies. While the French doctors are secular, the FBR follow Jesus's call. While the French doctors use only medicine and scalpels, the FBR are armed. While the FBR normally avoid any contact with the Myanmar Army, they are not pacifists and are willing to stand their ground with the displaced villagers, and to defend them if necessary. Positively formulated, the FBR's reason for existence is to assist those marginalized groups most affected by violence. Most significantly, the FBR establish a presence in spaces that are not normally accessible to humanitarians. It is the identity marker and strength of the FBR that they appear in war spaces to demonstrate that the displaced marginalized groups are not alone, and that the FBR will assist them, share time with them, and defend them if necessary. The FBR's leader, David Eubank, does not hide his political viewpoint: showcasing the atrocities of torture, abuse, rape, and brutal killing of civilian populations, he argues that it is our moral obligation to use our physical strength to help the wounded and to take action against the perpetrators. Taking an American, Christian, political standpoint, Eubank risks perpetuating a conflict while ignoring local knowledge, cultural resources, and the ethnic diversity of the Karen and other groups. The military aspect of the FBR is due to the fact that its founder used to work as a special envoy of the US Army while his father, a veteran missionary in Chiang Mai, served as an officer during the Korean War. Strictly speaking, the FBR are a civil society organization, placed within the international church, which draws its mandate from the Lord and its support from donations. Clearly, the FBR's military equipment is only ever used for civilian purposes and never military ones. And yet, if the FBR are forced to use a gun to attack enemy forces, they will do so.

While the French doctors withdraw in political protest at military intimidation, the FBR use military equipment and walk with ethnic minority armies to force their way to the front line. While their engagement for the wounded deserves applause, the fact that the FBR are armed, as well as their close alliance with the ethnic insurgents, positions them as an of enemy of the *Tatmadaw* (Myanmar Army). Their highly-desired presence and medical service may contribute to the insecurity of, and form a potential threat to, extremely vulnerable communities of internally displaced people.

Through this lens, I explore the *religious experience* that is associated with the careers of refugees who become rangers, to help the most vulnerable as well as the mobility of the refugee-migrants. At the centre lies an evangelical expression about the presence of the "saving angels" in a "landscape of evil". The young nurses who serve the FBR are themselves migrants, away from their homes and who understand their job as a service to God and to the Karen people. In this sense, the devotional experience of serving the FBR propels a specific personal trajectory in the mind of the young nurse and places her/him in a global field as a political and ethnic agent as well as a humanitarian one. Most of all, however, it places her/him in a global religious field and a global religious community, as a servant of God. Humanitarian assistance becomes, to put it in Csordas' words, a "portable practice" that dramatically broadens the radius of the participants while taking them hostage in a sort of crusade that brings participating rangers into great danger (Csordas 2009: 4). Indeed, a few rangers have lost their lives in action, as reported by David Eubank online.[2] Yet more have died due to malaria and land mines.

The FBR have become closely associated with the displaced and victimized Karen, being seen as good people who have no responsibility for their fate. The Karen are widely known as Christians, flourishing under the material and spiritual support of the American Baptist missionaries, as are the Kachin. And yet the majority of the Karen are not Christian but Theravada Buddhists, following the Mon-Burmese and Karen cultural traditions as well as resilient spirit beliefs. The hugely popular monk, U Thuzana, for example, may well be a spiritual competitor. Being a staunch Karen nationalist, U Thuzana and his Democratic Karen Buddhist Army are constructing new pagodas in the territory under his influence. In this politically-loaded field, the FBR may well intensify religious tensions. Moreover, while instrumentalist arguments of exchanging humanitarian entitlements for conversion may be avoided, this is precisely what the representatives of an alternative community-based organization in healthcare, the Back Pack Health Worker Team (BPHWT) claim they are doing. Many displaced villagers are definitely not Christian, but this does not stop the FBR from involving the displaced people in Christian prayer, gospel song, and long hours of Bible teaching in the "Good Life Club", organized by Eubank's wife and by the nurses.

I suggest that this expression can best be thought of as a *ritual*, in which the practice of assisting the suffering is ritually confirmed and presented in a variety of social media. The key religious expression is prayer. The prayer is geared to action and personalized to the rangers. The FBR are also part of a prayer group that offers "prayers for Burma" by appointment in Myanmar, Thailand, the USA, and many other places around the world. In a trailer for the FBR, Eubank asks God why he has been sent on this journey and why there is so much suffering in the world. Without any official mandate, they feel that they have a religious commitment of loving kindness and compassion, and they are called by Jesus to help persecuted Christians in Eastern Myanmar.

The FBR do not offer continuity in a new home, but rather a moment of purification, spiritual healing, and conciliation. In this space, people can have a liberating experience through prayer which may even create new hope. David Eubank sees himself as a warrior and crusader who confronts and overcomes evil by saving lives and souls. Instructing and inspiring him as to how to act and pray, the Lord guides him in all his actions. By imposing his prayer on all faith communities in Myanmar, he represents himself as a leader who knows the way out of tyranny and toward the light. My research into humanitarian and Christian missionary practice among the Karen migrant communities emphasizes its political character: humanitarian assistance in the borderland of Thailand and Myanmar is embedded in a much broader picture involving Christian organizations and missionaries, or to paraphrase the words of the missionaries, one of "a struggle between good and evil".

I was also able to watch promotional clips and public relations material. David Eubank promotes the FBR in interviews with charismatic Protestant pastors' churches and US Christian humanitarian organizations such as Compassion International. His team has produced a number of informative and insightful clips on the work and mission of the FBR as well as DVDs. Methodologically speaking, I am interested in the self-declared mandate that the FBR give itself for its intervention in violent conflicts. Participating in an unproclaimed war for humanity and justice, I am interested in the drastically expanded mobility of the Karen who participate in the global operations, but also in the subjectivity of the Karen nurses who become doctors, humanitarians, and missionaries, and in their relations with their Karen patients.

The FBR is a humanitarian organization embedded in a much wider picture of geopolitical factors, situated deeply in the political conflict in Myanmar and, being a global player, connecting the local ethnic Karen and other ethnic minority groups in Myanmar to global formations and communities. It particularly relates the displaced Karen migrants to American and international church congregations who, with their donations, enable the FBR to expand their services, and who are also connected to Karen Christians in manifold networks and webs.

As such, and from a perspective of humanitarianism as everyday practice, the FBR actively participate in what Redfield has called global advocacy (Redfield 2006: 8ff, 2013). In particular, they use the concept of *témoignage* or witnessing to construct the moral truth for an international audience. While the FBR do not have the scale of MSF, they have expanded their operations from Myanmar to many other conflict zones, for example, Kurdistan in Iraq and the Nuba mountains in Sudan. The FBR normally shun media and the Eubank family, in particular, has remained secretive in order to protect its ethical integrity and its informants from possible persecution. The FBR's public relations include presentations and fundraising in evangelical churches in Chiang Mai, Texas, and Prague. In addition, US children prepare Christmas gifts, crafts, and woollen hats for distribution among the needy as part of the activities of the Good Life Club.

This attention to power and coercion is needed in relation to formal, political religion. Informal, private minority religions, especially those related to spirit worship, have not even been recognized or seen as religions, but rather as barbaric and uncivilized. Missionaries argue that ethnic minorities are caught in a climate of fear and have to be liberated and guided to the saviour. In this effort, prayer is a very efficient technology in which the spirits can be harnessed and liberation achieved. The pastoral relationship comes to the fore in the context of humanitarian assistance. Refugee ministries and urban ministries that are organized around the world and work in slums and refugee camps, work among the most vulnerable groups for the Kingdom of God. Missionaries and Christian volunteers organize through outreach campaigns to reach the most disadvantaged populations and offer humanitarian assistance in the form of grassroots education and emergency healthcare. Missionaries specializing in urban mission or refugee mission volunteer in migrant churches, work in train station missions among the homeless, establish shops in red-light districts and pay prostitutes to stay away from sex-work, offer relief to drug addicts, establish their tents alongside garbage collectors, offer shelter to North Korean defectors, offer education and shelter to orphans, and emergency healthcare to the wounded. Christian missionaries have opened hundreds of orphanages in the most crisis-stricken countries affected by natural disaster and violent conflict. Missionaries see themselves as holy warriors who regard Myanmar as a territory in which millions of souls are waiting to be saved. Vulnerable populations now feel pressure to be a part of the imagined community of Christians. They may think that their former cultural traditions are inferior and an expression of their ignorance. Christianity thus exercises a disciplinary effect in which it is positioned as superior, the humanitarian organization regarded as donor, and refugees as passive recipients and helpless "children". In this context, the humanitarian faith organization constitutes a strong case of religious patronage. And yet coercion does not, of course, need to be present in missions, and many of the conversions are not enforced but come about through free will. The mission of a Karen Jesuit priest, for example, helps Karen displaced youth to find sanctuary in a Catholic seminary in Chiang Mai province and to receive trauma therapy and education. Many Karen communities have adjusted Christian doctrines to their traditional utopian and millenarian visions.

Helping the wounded: the Free Burma Rangers in action

In one of the most protracted civil wars, the *Tatmadaw* has inflicted tremendous suffering on the civilian population, resulting in large-scale displacement. The Myanmar Army suspected the villagers of providing food and shelter to the armed wing of the political organization of the Karen, the Karen National Liberation Army. The FBR see the Karen ethnic army as a pro-democratic force and trains and supplies their soldiers and nurses to work for the rangers. It is a dilemma for many international humanitarians that they cannot access or stay in crisis zones. Humanitarians all over the world have become more vulnerable to attack from marauding armies or militias.

The FBR have overcome this problem by deciding for themselves where they go and when they go. This clearly implies a great risk, since the FBR are identified as the enemy. As their presence would also endanger the displaced, the FBR have to move quickly. And yet David Eubank and his team ask the rangers to stay on with the people if they cannot flee. This means, in principle at least, that the rangers must be willing to die in action. This challenge requires hard training in the base camp. More than 350 rangers have been trained in the White Monkey base camp in Chiang Mai province. While the core of its staff is Karen, the FBR today is a multi-ethnic group that incorporates members from other ethnic minority groups as well. In the beginning, there was David and his most loyal Karen followers, often themselves displaced by the violence. Now, there are no less than 70 teams operating in Karen, Kayah, Shan, Kachin, and Chin and Arakan States. Each team consists of four to five rangers: a team leader, a medic, a photographer/videographer, a security specialist to map their route and liaise with rebel armies, and a Good Life Club counsellor, who is in charge of the educational and health needs of village children.

The rangers today operate in many different frontier and conflict zones of Myanmar, especially in Shan, Kachin and Arakan States. Expanding from its model with the Karen, the FBR has trained emergency teams for all ethnic minority groups. Over the years, the FBR has become a force that has gradually increased its activities, working together with other humanitarian organizations, especially with faith-based organization partners (in relief and development), other groups in the Border Consortium, in which international humanitarian organizations coordinate their relief activities, as well as with human rights organizations such as the secular Karen Human Rights Group and Burma Issues. Volunteers and staff often switch between these groups.

Many of the FBR nurses also served in the armed wing of the KNU, the Karen National Liberation Army. Due to their camouflage, the rangers are easily recognized and identified as part of the enemy by the Myanmar Army. The rangers are well equipped, use the latest military tools, provide training and military support in logistics, navigation communications, and satellite technology. They travel into the area by jeep until they reach the conflict zone. From there, they have to walk through the rough forest, avoiding the roads, and at night-time. They make contact with the camps of internally displaced people and begin to work immediately on their arrival. Medics feed children and old people, operate on landmine victims, and help to deliver babies. As the only doctors present, and since the internally displaced villagers basically lack everything, the rangers save numerous lives. Blankets, clothes, medicine, foodstuffs, mosquito repellents, and even radios are distributed. Being constantly in and out of the conflict zones, the rangers document and report tirelessly and in detail on ongoing human rights abuses. While the FBR acts on its own initiative, it is part of an extensive network of community-based organizations in the different ethnic borderlands that are willing to help in dangerous borderlands for religious reasons.

Concluding remarks

While religion is certainly central to community, solidarity, and cohesion, missionization also entails truth claims and involves processes of othering. Religion deals with the construction and disciplining of bodies, the management of churches, and the design of public spaces and communities. More than beliefs, religion mediates the competition over political and economic resources and missionization with competition for the souls of the displaced. Religion can be a conscious strategy and choice, enhancing people in their bare lives and transforming bare into sacred life. To speak of the creative imposition of spatial sacralities in the diasporic space moves the conversation towards a notion of religion as an enabling and constraining force.

The humanitarian and political intervention of the FBR makes it a political force that directly involves itself in the violence in Myanmar. As stated above, the fact that David Eubank is an American missionary does not help to lessen the religious tension present, but may even intensify it. As an armed movement with a clear political message and bias, the FBR may endanger those vulnerable communities they are supposed to protect. The FBR may have saved hundreds of lives, but the way the organization positions itself as an enemy of the Myanmar military is problematic, as is its active involvement and overlap with the ethnic minority armies. The non-state ethnic minority armies are also problematic as they exert pressure on the vulnerable village communities as well, namely in the form of recruitment and taxation. Most problematic, the donations strengthen the FBR and, in part, the ethnic minority armies but not the mutual support and security networks of the ordinary Karen. While the donations enable the FBR to purchase equipment and medical supplies, and to recruit personnel, ordinary Karen villagers have hardly any voice in the rangers' media representations, appearing only as passive and happy recipients of the rangers' generosity. The transition from a victim of the atrocities to a ranger and nurse is introduced as a natural pathway. It is a conversion process in a double sense. The young men and women discussed in this chapter give themselves to Jesus (making a transition from animism) and to the rangers (making a transition from the jungle village). Conversion can be understood in multiple senses: not only conversion to a religion, but also to a lifestyle or an identity. The pressure for individual rangers to convert to Christianity may be subtle, but it is present.

In this sense, the rangers may well be one opportunity for young Karen to find a home, belonging, the spirit of teamwork and, potentially, martyrdom and sacrifice. These young displaced Karen convert to the imagined community of a global Christian ecumene, firmly based in the imagination of the American and Christian political thought that has identified the Karen as worthy of material as well as spiritual support. The FBR are expanding, identifying new enemies and new vulnerable groups that might seek their military and medical assistance, reaching out to places and conflicts around the globe. The young Karen who join the rangers begin a new life on the Thai–Burmese border and find employment with one of the NGOs in the humanitarian economy of Mae Sot or Chiang Mai. Being part of the rangers, they also join a political project and missionary adventure, going on tour to collect donations from church congregations for further dangerous missions with the FBR. However, the rangers also participate in proselytizing activities among the internally displaced. By far, not all displaced Karen or other ethnic minorities are Christian, and villagers belonging to Buddhism or animism may well feel uncomfortable with the powerful Christian message of the rangers. Local cosmologies, cultural traditions and rituals weave powerful emotional "sensescapes" among the minority groups of the Karen, Karenni, and Kayah who resist the pressure of soft missionization in the refugee camps (Dudley 2010). While old Christians welcome the church rebuilding in their communities, internally displaced villagers from animistic communities may feel quite lost amidst the Bible songs of the Good Life Club as they have different visions of a good life or may simply be confused. The FBR constitute an astonishing case of religious mobility and mobilization in the context of a flourishing humanitarianism and the rise of moral ideologies (cf. Fassin 2011) in an increasingly fragile and violent world. The Karen who participate in the missions of the FBR, as well as other humanitarian organizations, become missionaries in their own right who leave their protected environment to go out on dangerous missions as well as doing missionary work in the hills of Eastern Myanmar, in the refugee camps of northwestern Thailand, and as rangers in Myanmar and elsewhere. These Karen cultural ambassadors are not the passive and victimized refugees we know from media images, but home-grown missionaries who use their enhanced mobility to establish religious centres wherever they are.

Notes

1. In writing this chapter, I contacted members of the Free Burma Rangers in Chiang Mai. The rangers all welcomed me with an open heart, especially the members of the Eubank family. I was also able to speak to young Karen nurses who had joined the operations of the Free Burma Rangers on a regular basis after being called in case of need. I would like to express my deep respect for their uncompromising commitment to helping wounded and traumatized villagers. I would especially like to thank veteran and now retired missionary, Allan Eubank, who generously told me the history of his own engagement in Thailand and that of his son, David.
2. See: www.freeburmarangers.org/who-we-are/.

References

Agamben, Giorgio (1998): *Homo Sacer: Sovereign Power and Bare Life*. Stanford, CA: Stanford University Press.
Csordas, Thomas J. (ed.) (2009): *Transnational Transcendence. Essays on Religion and Globalization*. Berkeley, CA: University of California Press.
Dean, Mitchell (2010): *Governmentality. Power and Rule in Modern Society*. London: Sage.
Dudley, Sandra (2010): *Materializing Exile. Material Culture and Embodied Experience among Karenni Refugees in Thailand*. Oxford and New York: Berghahn.

Fassin, Didier (2007): "Humanitarianism as a politics of life," *Public Culture*, 19, 3: 499–520.
Fassin, Didier (2011): *Humanitarian Reason. A Moral History of the Present*. Berkeley, CA: University of California Press.
Foucault, Michel (2007): *Security, Territory, Population: Lectures at the College de France, 1975–1976*. New York: Picador.
Horstmann, Alexander (2016): "The Culture and Landscape of the Humanitarian Economy among the Karen in the Borderland of Southeast Myanmar and Northwest Thailand." In: Su-Ann Oh (ed.): *Myanmar's Mountain and Maritime Borderscapes: Local Practices, Boundary-Making and Figured Worlds*. Singapore: ISEAS, pp. 171–190.
Horstmann, Alexander, & Jin-Heon Jung (eds.) (2015). *Building Noah's Ark for Refugees, Migrants and Religious Communities*. New York, NY: Palgrave Macmillan (Contemporary Anthropology of Religion).
Redfield, Peter (2006): "A less modest witness: Collective advocacy and motivated truth in a medical humanitarian movement," *American Ethnologist*, 33, 1: 3–26.
Redfield, Peter (2013): *Life in Crisis. The Ethical Journey of Doctors without Borders*. Berkeley, LA and London: University of California Press.
The Border Consortium (2012): *Changing Realities, Poverty and Displacement in South East Burma/Myanmar*. Available at www.theborderconsortium.org/media/54376/report-2014-idp-en.pdf.
The Border Consortium (2016): Annual Report. Available at www.theborderconsortium.org/media/80489/2016-annual-report-jan-dec.pdf.

28
The moral economy of the Myawaddy–Mae Sot border

Su-Ann Oh

Introduction

I approach the term "economy" from the much broader perspective of economic sociology and anthropology, as "the production, distribution and consumption of material and immaterial things, which include goods, labour, services, knowledge and myth, names and charms, and so on" (Carrier 2012: 4). In order to make sense of the Myawaddy–Mae Sot border on the Thai–Burmese frontier, we need to analyse the circulation of both material and non-material things. I propose to do this by combining the concept of moral economy as advanced by Thompson (1971), Scott (1979), and Fassin (2009) with the social life of things as formulated by Appadurai (1988).

The core argument is that there is a moral economy that circulates along with the goods and services on this border. Before elaborating on this, I would like to clarify what I mean by moral economy. I use Didier Fassin's conception of the moral economy as "the production, distribution, circulation, and use of moral sentiments, emotions and values, and norms and obligations in social space" (Fassin 2009: 1255).

I believe moral sentiments, values, norms, and affects circulate among the myriad populations in the Myawaddy–Mae Sot border space – refugees, migrants, the internally displaced, Karen villagers, Thai communities of both Tai and other ethnicities, animist and Muslim groups, industrialists, traders and business people – shaping the ideologies and (cross-border) activities of this region. The moral economy at this border, I posit, is configured by international notions of humanitarianism, local understandings of self-help, and political and religious imaginaries. Examining this moral economy, we are able to see how dominant discourses, values, and affects emerge from and are shaped by the local and global context.

I begin by conceptualizing moral economies and their connection with the circulation of objects. This is followed by a discussion of the various identifiable components of the moral economy in the Myawaddy–Mae Sot borderland. In the conclusion, this moral economy is situated within a geographical and historical context, and I provide some reflections on its future configuration are offered.

Su-Ann Oh

Conceptualizing moral economies

Thompson's (1971) fascinating article on the moral economy of the English peasant crowd considers the "social norms and obligations" that governed the workings of the traditional peasant economy. He shows that up until the 18th century, bread and corn were circulated based on a moral economy, one where the price, availability, and sale of these consumables were kept at a certain level to ensure that the poor would be able to afford them. As England entered the 18th century, more market-based types of distribution began replacing and transforming these markets, leading to widespread cases of "riots" as the incompatibilities of these two systems of distribution emerged and adversely affected peasants' ability to afford and obtain these goods. According to Thomson, the "riots" that erupted were actually conducted to defend norms – traditional rights or customs – that were based on certain morals and notions of justice (obligations) regarding the treatment of the poor. In other words, the moral economy corresponded to a set of norms and obligations used to guide judgements and behaviour.

Thomson's conception of a moral economy reminds us that there are other economies besides market-based ones and helps us to understand the moral underpinnings of the humanitarian economy that Horstmann (2016) and I (Oh 2016) have put forward with regard to the Myawaddy–Mae Sot border. The humanitarian economy is defined as an economy because what is produced and distributed is a combination of social services and goods aimed at improving the welfare of people with little or no access to resources and who are caught up in conflict. In addition, the principles of distribution are based on a certain culture of support, suffering, ethno-nationalism, faith-based tenets and notions of democracy, liberation, human rights, and perceived need rather than on market mechanisms (Oh 2016: 194).

In other words, like Thompson's work, there is a certain notion of deservedness underlying the distribution of these goods and services. In this case, this revolves not around society-wide views on the treatment of the poor, but around the suffering of those in exile (in another country or in their own country), and those involved in what is often perceived as an ethnically-motivated and just fight against an abusive state. This is where Scott's (1979) work on Southeast Asian peasants comes into play. His understanding of the moral economy is that peasant communities share a set of normative attitudes concerning the social relations within the local economy, such as the availability of food, the prices of subsistence commodities, and so on. The values and social arrangements are structured in such a way as to respect the subsistence needs of the rural poor, and when these are ruptured by local elites, state authorities, or market forces, peasant communities are provoked to protest. In both Thompson's and Scott's work, moral norms about society and its contract with the poor guide the beliefs and behaviour of poor communities.

Fassin distills the idea of the moral economy even further by claiming that it "corresponds to the system of values that underlie the expression of emotions... There is thus a local world of values that defines the moral economy" (Fassin 2009: 1255). By emphasizing the "moral" in moral economy, he claims that it is not just about norms and obligations, but also about values and emotions. In his opinion, "values arise at least in part from norms, and norms depend partially on values" (Fassin 2009: 1255). The value that Fassin's conception of the moral economy brings to this chapter is the emphasis on the intertwining of emotions, values, and norms and how the moral economy is historically created and destroyed. By expanding the moral economy as a concept that has implications beyond subaltern, subordinated, or scientific communities (Fassin 2009: 1251), Fassin enables us to consider the circulation of moral sentiments in society in general and in specific localities. This is particularly useful when examining the production, distribution, and circulation of affect (e.g. suffering) and values (e.g. self-help and helping others) along with goods, services, and other resources on the Myawaddy–Mae Sot border, given its material and political context, and the macro changes that are occurring on both sides of the border.

Fassin's much more generalized concept of moral economy than that articulated by Thompson and Scott allows us to look beyond the humanitarian economy on the Myawaddy–Mae Sot borderland and to consider the economy of values, sentiments, affect, and so on that circulate therein. Thus, I propose to analyse the connection between the circulation of material and immaterial things by combining the idea of moral economy as an expression of social justice (Thompson 1971; Scott 1979) with that of production, distribution and use of moral sentiments, emotions and values, and norms and obligations (Fassin 2009). Indeed, I believe that the circulation of material and immaterial things is intertwined. As Appadurai writes:

> …we have to follow the things themselves, for their meanings are inscribed in their forms, their uses, their trajectories. It is only through the analysis of these trajectories that we can interpret the human transactions and calculations that enliven things. Thus, even though from a *theoretical* point of view human actors encode things with significance, from a *methodological* point of view it is the things-in-motion that illuminate their human and social context.
> *(Appadurai 1988: 5)*

Appadurai uses the terms "path" and "diversion" to describe the trajectories of objects and how they acquire biographies as they move from place to place (Appadurai 1988: 16–29). For example, the path of rice and fortified flour rations distributed to refugees in the camps on the Thai–Burmese border is set by a consortium of non-governmental organizations (NGOs) (The Border Consortium, TBC). On this path, rice and flour bought from Thai suppliers by the NGOs are meant to be consumed by the camp residents. Their path literally ends when they reach the residents. However, this path is diverted when camp residents use their rations to barter with one another, smuggle them out of the camps, or sell them. The NGOs disapprove of these activities because it transforms refugees from subjects of charity to active consumers or entrepreneurs, and are thus viewed by donors as less worthy of humanitarian aid. As Appadurai observes, "consumption is subject to social control and political redefinition" (1988: 6). The camp residents subvert this power relation when they divert the path of these commodities. In addition, particularly pertinent to the discussion of the moral economy, diversion brings about the transformation of the values, sentiments, and norms attached to these commodities. From unreciprocated gifts to objects of exchange to army rations (food for the Karen National Liberation Army) to welfare (Karen National Union provisions for the internally displaced), the meanings attached to these food items change and in turn they become encoded with other moral sentiments, values, and norms.

Their circulation forms part of the border economy in this region. There is a tendency to think only of trade, industry, and special economic zones when considering the term "border economy" (Kudo 2009, 2013: 188–196, 196–201; Arnold 2010; Wayhu Kuncoro 2014). However, this chapter alerts us to two things. First, there is a whole array of goods and services that circulates on this border but does not fall under the usual administrative trade categories. Second, there are values, norms, and moral sentiments that circulate along with them that are often encoded in or embodied by them. In many ways, the physical movement of these resources resembles that of black markets that span both sides of the border. Similarly, some of the activities that facilitate the distribution of black market goods operate illegally but are perceived as morally justified, or "licit" according to Abraham and van Schendel (2005).

Where the border makes a difference is when it creates differentials in country regulations, policies, costs, security, and resource availability. Border economies differ from "normal" economies not because they take a different form or are based on an alternative philosophy, but because they are spatially situated to exploit these differentials. Operationally, they are no different from the broader global economy in that they operate under similar principles and mechanisms – often market-based ones.

Humanitarianism and the moral economy of the Myawaddy–Mae Sot borderland

The moral economy in the Myawaddy–Mae Sot borderland is made up of several components, some of which have been identified. I shall begin with the humanitarian constituent, which has been more thoroughly investigated and written about than others.

While there has been research conducted on humanitarianism on this border, there has been less of a focus on how it has shaped the local moral economy and vice versa. I believe that this represents a gap in our understanding of the non-material dimension of this border where politics, religion, culture, values, and affects coalesce into a socio-political moral complex that shapes the social landscape and the way in which material goods and services are distributed.

In a previous paper, I wrote about the humanitarian economy in connection with Alexander Horstmann's (2016) work, focusing purely on the types of goods that were being circulated and the mechanisms of distribution (Oh 2016). In this chapter, I would like to refine my thoughts by adding the non-material dimension to this humanitarian economy. I argue that this humanitarian economy forms part of the moral economy in the Myawaddy–Mae Sot borderland. The humanitarian aspect of this moral economy is inflected with local political, cultural, religious, and social norms and codes, and interweaves other moral discourses such as human rights and "contribution to the community". It is also strongly associated with "humanitarian reason", an ideology that dominates the moral economy in the international sphere. As Fassin writes:

> A new moral economy, centered on humanitarian reason, …came into being during the last decades of the twentieth century. We continue to live within it now, in the early twenty-first century. It brings forth new kinds of responses—a humanitarian government—in which particular attention is focused on suffering and misfortune. Whether this shift stems from sincerity or cynicism on the part of the actors involved, whether it manifests a genuine empathy or manipulates compassion, is another question: the point I want to emphasize is that this way of seeing and doing has now come to appear self-evident to us.
>
> *(Fassin 2012: 7–8)*

I begin by situating humanitarianism in the moral economy of this border. David Forsythe defines international humanitarianism as "the transnational concern to help persons in exceptional distress" (Forsythe 2009: 59). This border has been plagued by armed contestation between non-state armed groups in the form of the Communist Party of Burma and Karen-related organizations (the Karen National Union and the Democratic Karen Benevolent Army) and the Burmese Army since at least the 1960s. The counterinsurgency measures – particularly the Four Cuts[1] – taken by the Burmese Army, government efforts aimed at "developing" the border areas, and state neglect have produced what many have described as a landscape of despair, fear, anxiety, and suffering. All across the southeastern border of Myanmar, communities remain subject to multiple authorities, with parallel systems of governance of varying degrees of formality, plagued by confusion and uncertainty. Consequently, they are caught between rival armed groups and beset by multiple governance regimes.

Since the 1980s, humanitarian organizations, both local and international, have established operations to provide aid, first to the refugees who crossed over to Thailand, then to internally displaced persons (IDPs) in eastern Myanmar, and then to migrants residing in the border areas in Thailand.

The international and local dimensions of humanitarianism have crystalized in this space in a form that incorporates other ideologies, including: human rights, social justice, environmental issues, political dissent, religion, cultural rights, and so on[2] (Horstmann 2010, 2011, 2014, 2016; Simpson 2014; Décobert 2016). Global values have been harnessed and reshaped to fit local circumstances, and vice versa, in turn changing the contours of the moral economy of the region. I argue that there are three aspects to this. First, suffering has been constructed in such a way as to legitimize international humanitarian intervention in ethno-nationalist goals and to tie the political fate of the Karen National Union (KNU) to international humanitarian aid. Second, the moral underpinnings of international humanitarianism have been used to provide some sense of political legitimacy in the eyes of the international community to the groups working on this border. Third, while international humanitarianism represents itself as a secular enterprise to appear morally legitimate, local self-help linked to humanitarian efforts draw their moral legitimacy from religious imaginaries.

Self-help, suffering, and humanitarianism

Against the economic–political environment that characterized Myanmar – almost non-existent state welfare, unpredictable currency devaluations, runs on the bank, and great distrust of the government – and the particular circumstances of the border, various groups set up self-help projects to aid themselves and their communities. A whole assortment of civil society organizations (known as community-based organizations) sprouted up to provide badly needed services for these populations. Political organizations were set up by dissidents who fled Myanmar after the turmoil in 1988 (e.g., the National League for Democracy); local and international organizations were established to collect evidence of human rights abuses (e.g., the Karen Human Rights Group, KHRG), and to advocate for the rights of the oppressed and abused (e.g. Burma Project); other organizations provide cross-border aid (e.g., the Back Pack Health Worker Team, Free Burma Rangers, and the Karen Teacher Working Group, KTWG); healthcare and education (e.g., Mae Tao Clinic, Aide Medical Internationale, Curriculum Project); help and advocacy for migrant workers, and so on. While many of them are not strictly humanitarian organizations, they mostly operate with the ethos of service, volunteerism, and self-help.

Interestingly, the culture of self-help appears to be widespread in Myanmar. This became evident when Myanmar individuals and organizations mobilized and organized aid for their communities in the wake of Cyclone Nargis in 2008. This was also observed when natural disasters struck along the border. For example, floods that destroyed houses and businesses in 2012 and 2013 in Mae Sot and Myawaddy prompted local individuals and organizations, both Burmese and Thai, to organize help for the communities affected. This moral sentiment is not confined to instances of disaster. In two separate interviews that I conducted with Myanmar migrants in Mae Sot, the respondents, without prompting, spoke about supporting and contributing to their community. In fact, for certain individuals, border trade was a way in which such high-minded aspirations could be achieved. In addition, the Karen education leadership in the refugee camps have incorporated the ethos of "contributing to the community" in the set of values they hope to inculcate in society through schooling.

My argument is that this moral sentiment of helping others had already been circulating in this borderland and had been a part of its moral economy, but has since been yoked to emotion (suffering) and linked to values that circulate in the moral economy of the international community, in particular humanitarianism.

The "semantic configuration" (Fassin 2012: 23) and visual idiom used to represent certain border residents as suffering, vulnerable, and requiring protection is prevalent. Over the years, there has been a continuous construction and reproduction of this border as a landscape of fear, anxiety, suffering, and vulnerability, through the collection of "victim" narratives and the testimony of humanitarians (both local and international aid workers, advocates, and organizations). Images of this border almost always include photographs of amputees, child soldiers, and displaced people. Unsurprisingly, these "[n]arratives of suffering draw upon surrounding cultural and political codes and are constituted by them" (Wilson and Brown 2009: 25) and contribute to the construction of "secular moral truth for an international audience" (Redfield 2006: 3).

These representations do not come out of thin air. This border space has been plagued by militarization, warfare, structural violence, insurgency, competing governance actors, and competing territorial ploys. Residents have experienced forced relocation and labour, armed violence, confiscation of land and crops, rape, and a host of other abuses at the hands of government forces, non-state armed groups, and militias.

At the same time, natural resource extraction and associated infrastructure projects are becoming more widespread in this locality as the military, militias, and private corporations take advantage of the ceasefire to undertake resource extraction on an even larger scale than before.[3] The consequences of this are that, since the mid-2000s, Myanmar migrants in Thailand have come to be included in this narrative of suffering: the lack of government provision, regulation and protection in employment, and a constant fear of arrest and deportation create a sense of precariousness and vulnerability.

These narratives of suffering are instrumentalized in order to mobilize emotions such as compassion, empathy, and sympathy, to support local forms of self-help and to foster politico-cultural imaginaries of nation. The KNU, for example, represents the Karen as a simple, peace-loving, suffering people. This has both a socializing and political purpose. In interviews conducted with Karen students in refugee camps, I found that many who were considered "inside students" (students who had moved to the camps for the sole purpose of attending school) spoke about the value of camp schooling in teaching them about the political situation faced by the Karen and their suffering, knowledge they were unaware of before coming to camp. In other words, they had to be schooled in recognizing their suffering as a people. Tied in with suffering is self-help – as evidenced by the emergence of "a certain culture of suffering and subsequent [self] help that binds certain people and organizations together in a specific place and geography" (Horstmann 2016: 173–174). This is manifested in schools as well. Refugee camp schools are a means for the production and transmission of these notions of service. One of the post-secondary schools, the English Immersion Programme, offers a year-long intensive course in English, proposal writing, critical thinking, community work and a year-long internship programme with community-based organizations, with the purpose of fostering the ethos of serving the community. In these circumstances, one of the most valued ways of serving the community takes the form of working for civil society organizations and being able to perform and work in the format, framework, and language employed by the international (humanitarian) community (Oh 2016). In a very real sense, this programme is a concrete manifestation of the interweaving of Karen notions of contribution to the community and the ideology and practice of international humanitarianism. When the programme was set up by two foreign volunteer teachers, they were asked by the Karen refugee community to include the ethos of "contribution to the community" as the community was afraid that the students would not justify the efforts of the programme if they left to be resettled. In addition, when the students were asked how they wanted to contribute to their community, they were unable to provide specific ideas despite their intense drive and motivation. Thus, the programme founders incorporated their notions of how the students could contribute to their community by drawing upon their own notions of social justice and the practical framework that was already in place in this locality – that of international NGOs.

Similarly, civil society organizations such as the Back Packer Health Worker Team and the Free Burma Rangers (see Horstmann, this volume), and rights groups such as the Karen Human Rights Group (KHRG) have used textual and visual narratives of suffering to link emotion, values, and international ideologies. Their cross-border work consists of providing medical aid, medical training, first aid, and health and human rights documentation.

The same can be said of enterprises set up by women's organizations, Borderline and WEAVE,[4] which sell crafts produced by refugee and marginalized women under the Fair Trade label, aimed at the ethical consumer market, marketed through organizations such as Oxfam, and purchased by foreign NGO staff, volunteers, and visitors in Mae Sot. Everyday objects such as handwoven Karen sarongs, Karen-style shirts and bags, baskets, and so on have come to embody sentiments of suffering, principles of self-help, ethnic and political identification, and values about helping others.

These various forms of self-help or volunteerism have become tightly linked to the international language, form, and ideology of humanitarianism, human rights, social justice, freedom, and democracy which have in turn been institutionalized in the local organizations involved in the provision of medical care, education, and other services in this borderland (see Décobert 2016: 185).

Political legitimacy through moral legitimacy

This local form of humanitarianism in the moral economy of the border is a highly selective and political one. As Fassin points out "[s]ocial suffering is not just a psychological category: it is also a political construction" (Fassin 2012: 42). Linking humanitarianism to self-help and volunteerism confers moral legitimacy to the activities and causes of actors and their organizations in the international and local sphere. The KNU, other Karen-related organizations, and local organizations have woven these various moral sentiments into their principles, projects, and practices. In fact, Christian Karen perceive a strong link between Western humanitarian aid agencies and their future as a nation (Horstmann 2010).

To a certain extent, the association of the KNU with humanitarian practice has helped to legitimize its claims as the "government" of the Karen in this locality and to circulate "hegemonic" moral sentiments on ethno-nationalism and religion. Between 1990 and 2012, the KNU steadily lost territory to the Burmese Army. This, coupled with other military setbacks and reduced access to border trade, began crippling the KNU and fragmenting its system of governance. The KNU administration began to operate from Thailand while the Karen National Liberation Army (KNLA) brigades acted as administrators in the southeastern border of Myanmar (Smith 1991: 392). At the same time, the refugee camps in Thailand became the formal administrative centre for humanitarian aid, enabling the KNU to sustain itself. From the camps, humanitarian aid steadily spread out to the surrounding areas, formally and informally. This enabled the KNU to appear to provide social services in the refugee camps, which has in turn helped it to gain legitimacy among camp residents.

In contrast, the KNU struggled to provide social services in the areas it governed in Myanmar, even though it was supported by the humanitarian industry on the Thai side of the border.[5] Medical services in KNU-controlled territory were unevenly provided by the Karen

Department for Health and Welfare (KDHW). Consequently, community-based organizations stepped in to fill many of the gaps: the Mae Tao Clinic in Mae Sot, Thailand provides medical services to borderlanders, while Free Burma Rangers and the Back Pack Health Worker Team[6] focus specifically on providing medical and other services to communities on the Myanmar side of the border.

On the educational front, the Karen Education Department (KED), the education arm of the KNU, also provided some basic education in this locality and for the Karen in non-KNU areas. Textbooks developed in the refugee camps in Thailand by Baptist World Aid Australia at the request of the KED and later on by Karen refugees with the help of ZOA Refugee Care, a Dutch relief organization, printed and distributed with donors' funds, have entered schools in KNU-controlled areas under the auspices of the KED. The Karen Teachers Working Group (KTWG), a local border organization, implements KED policies, provides in-service teacher training and distributes education resources in Kayin State.

I argue that the objects distributed and services rendered – medical care, teacher training, textbooks and bibles for example – are vehicles for the circulation of certain sentiments, values, and norms set within a certain political and moral context, in other words, a context-specific moral economy. They are encoded with political, moral, cultural, and other types of significance which transform as they move from the refugee camps to town to Karen villagers in Myanmar. What meanings, values, and affects do beneficiaries attach to these goods and services given that the people who conduct the cross-border work are often accompanied by KNLA soldiers for security reasons, and that there is little knowledge on the part of the recipients about which organizations they represent? Are these goods and services perceived as KNU welfare, humanitarian aid, or something else altogether? If seen as KNU welfare, is the KNU viewed as caring, benevolent, or moral in providing these goods and services?

The association that the KNU and other organizations have with international humanitarianism has brought some political legitimacy to their work in the eyes of the international community and very possibly of the Karen beneficiaries. Unfortunately, deriving political legitimacy from the international humanitarian community is a double-edged sword. As Décobert (2016) describes, the shifting ideologies of donors in the mid- to late-2000s heralded a change in attitudes towards "illegal" but licit cross-border work, and the association of international humanitarians agencies with non-state armed groups, such as the KNU. Donors began to reduce their funding to organizations that were deemed to be working for a non-state armed group. Similarly, in the education sector, the KED was replaced by another non-KNU-linked organization. This was done to cut the links between humanitarian aid funding and organizations seen to threaten the security of the state and the welfare of camp residents (McConnachie 2012; Oh 2017). Thus, while international humanitarianism was able to confer political and moral legitimacy to the work of local organizations, it was also able to take it away.

Moral legitimacy through religious imaginary

International humanitarianism has long derived its moral legitimacy through secular altruism. From the late 19th century onwards, a secular humanitarian sector emerged as a result of the codification of humanitarian principles and law, the institutionalization of humanitarian actors (Calhoun 2008), and increased involvement with intergovernmental structures and government objectives (Thaut 2009). Similarly, many of the international humanitarian organizations on this border (the original group named itself the Christian Consortium of Agencies before changing its name after the inclusion of non-Christian NGOs) operate as secular institutions, fully cognizant that their moral legitimacy in the eyes of the international community is based on their secular policies and discourses.

Local border-based organizations are well aware of this and have often downplayed their Christian tenets when interacting with foreigners. However, their moral legitimacy is intimately tied up with religious missionary work. As Horstmann describes, local organizations such as the Free Burma Rangers, a Christian evangelical cross-border organization, perceive themselves as "soldiers-medics-missionaries" (Horstmann 2015: 134), in the same way that "[t]he heroic behavior of the KNU was underlined by delivering emergency health services and prayer worshipping to the internally displaced in the war zone" (Horstmann 2015: 133). The trinity of nationalism, welfare provision, and religious mission reinforces the moral legitimacy of the KNU (whose leaders are mostly Christian) and local organizations. In fact, "[w]ith the ongoing Christianization of the KNU leadership the nationalist struggle is increasingly regarded as a spiritual struggle… Karen nationalism becomes deeply entangled with and legitimated by Christianity" (Horstmann 2015: 144). This takes place in a transborder network of Christian churches and Christian missionary agencies of various national and international provenances.

This religious component of the moral economy is not confined to Christian groups. Buddhist Karen have created a "transborder religious network of *moral communities* based on the spiritual powers of charismatic monks" (emphasis added) (Gravers 2015: 47) such as U Thuzana, U Vinaya (on the Myanmar side of the border), and Khruba Wong (on the Thai side). These moral communities are built on several factors. First, the Karen monastic lay movement/network is "based on Buddhist cosmological imaginary of moral leadership and moral order" (Gravers 2015: 47). The emphasis is on moral leadership and spiritual politics:

> Leadership has to be morally enchanted and all subjects must strive to acquire knowledge about Buddhist ethics and use their knowledge in practice…A moral order and spiritual politics are preconditions for a righteous rule and establishing a moral community.
> *(Gravers 2015: 50)*

In other words, a moral component undergirds its legitimacy.

Second, these communities combine the sacred (forest monk tradition of meditation and ascetic practice, construction of religious buildings, dissemination of the Buddhist doctrine) with the mundane (helping the poor and internally displaced, offering their monasteries as sanctuaries in the war zones of Kayin State, the construction of roads and schools), creating "a new order based on morality, justice, and prosperity for a suffering population" (Gravers 2015: 46–47) and "manage in some ways to evade state control and form a community close to a non-state space" or even a "'Karen-land' [made of spaces] … which form a network of sanctuaries for refugees, pilgrims, and other persons, and are fields of merits for all followers" (Gravers 2015: 69). Like the Christian Karen, notions of suffering feature prominently. This makes sense in the context of armed conflict where the Karen in Southeast Myanmar are caught between multiple armed groups. However, the construction of suffering differs between the two religious groups. The Christian Karen have drawn upon the idea of Christian persecution and linked protection to humanitarian aid, while Buddhist Karen have tied it to the Buddhist concept of "dhukka" (suffering).

This phenomenon is not usually included in notions of humanitarianism in this borderland. Is there hidden religious favouritism where Christians, disguised as universal humanitarians, prefer to help Christian victims? Or has this to do with the fact that Karen Christian organizations are more aware of the need to appear secular in their work with international humanitarian organizations? One of the pieces to this puzzle is the fact that some monks, such as U Thuzana, do not allow organizations to work in their area and seek personal donations from trusted people with "the right intentions of merit-making" (Gravers 2015: 61). In other words, the moral sentiment here is not one of impartial altruism, but moral enchantment based on Buddhist precepts and the construction of moral communities. Whatever the reasons, it is clear that the moral economy of this borderland is composed partly of what is considered secular humanitarian reason, and religious imaginary concerning visions of a "social order founded on morality" (Gravers 2015: 51) – Christian or Buddhist – set within the context of Karen ethno-nationalist aspirations.

Other components of the moral economy

This brings us to an exploration of the other components of the moral economy of this borderland. Thus far, the focus in this chapter has been on the moral economy on this border in the form of Christian and Buddhist Karen self-help, volunteerism and community organization and creation, and whether or not they are linked to international norms of humanitarianism. This is because these are the most documented phenomena. Refugees and Myanmar migrants have been researched the most, followed by the internally displaced in the southeastern border of Myanmar (particularly the Karen) and Karen villagers on the Thai side of the border. Other populations such as Thai rural and urban communities, animist and Muslim groups, factory owners, traders, business owners, and non-Karen communities, however, have not received as much scholarly attention.

Collecting these data is important because these groups may not have the same sense of moral legitimacy vis-à-vis humanitarian aid as refugees, local migrant organizations, or migrants. For example, humanitarian intervention is viewed by the beneficiaries, associated organizations, multilateral organizations, and commentators in a variety of ways – as a lifeline, as a handout, as a means of creating legitimacy and providing jobs, among others – but they generally agree that it is a good thing. However, local Thai communities perceive aid provided to the refugees as a privilege rather than a need (Yongyuth Chalamwong et al. 2014: 136) because they are not aware of the livelihood and mobility restrictions imposed on camp residents. Many view refugees and migrants as a threat to personal and public health, and as rivals for jobs (Sunpuwan and Niyomsilpa 2012, 2014; Yongyuth Chalamwong et al. 2014: 136). Thus, although it is a significant component of the moral economy, humanitarian reason is not universally viewed in this region as legitimate or moral grounds for providing free goods and services to Myanmar nationals. In this regard, the Buddhist Karen monks seem to provide more justifiable reasons for providing protection and contributing to the welfare of displaced Karen to the non-Christian and Thai communities in this region than the Christian and humanitarian communities. Karen Buddhist monks and their sanctuaries are supported by transborder networks of people who are not just Karen; they also include Thai business people and locals.

Given that religious imaginaries play a significant role in the circulation of non-material goods in this region, it would be worthwhile to examine Muslim and animist communities and the types of moral sentiments and values they regard as important.

In addition, it would be pertinent to go beyond religion-based ideas of values. In particular, examining the values, norms, and the sentiments that traders and factory owners (two sizeable populations that contribute greatly to the economic activity of this region) attach to their goods and services and that guide their business activities and social relations would add significantly to our understanding of the moral economy of this borderland. What moral and normative sentiments circulate among them and does the phenomenon of the border make a difference? Evidently, more research needs to be done to ascertain the different types of norms, values, obligations, and affects that circulate within these communities.

Conclusion

This chapter has identified three components of the moral economy in the Myawaddy–Mae Sot borderland: secular humanitarianism and its focus on compassion and empathy; Christian Karen politico-religious imaginaries entangled with welfare provision, self-help, and contribution to the community; and Buddhist Karen tenets of merit-making and moral order. Other components of the moral economy have yet to be identified and certain avenues for obtaining these data have been suggested.

In this concluding section, I situate the moral economy in its wider geographical and historical context. First, to what extent can we say that the moral sentiments and values identified in this chapter are unique to this border? Second, what are the implications for the moral economy given the macro changes occurring in Myanmar?

To answer the first question, I attempt a comparison of this border with other Myanmar borders, albeit with limited anecdotal data. The two most comparable borders are the Kachin–Chinese and the Rakhine–Bangladesh ones, as they both have sizeable numbers of refugees and international/local NGOs. The Kachin frontier with China continues to be plagued by armed conflict, particularly since the end of the ceasefire in 2011. As with the Karen, there is immense distrust of Burmese government institutions and the military. The lack of adequate government social welfare has also engendered a culture of self-help. However, the circumstances at the border with China are markedly different in that there is less humanitarian aid on both frontiers. In addition, the aid provided is mostly administered through local organizations, including ethnic armed groups, local community organizations, faith-based networks and programmes administered by Chinese health and relief teams, rather than foreign staff of international agencies directly. The main coordinating group in the Kachin and northern Shan States is a community-based Joint Strategy Team comprising nine local humanitarian organizations.[7] The Kachin Independence Organization (KIO) has much more control over the administration of its territory than does the KNU, particularly since the latter has fragmented and disputed territory. Unlike the KNU, the KIO has access to more resources via resource extraction concessions which it can use to fund social welfare activities such as health and education. Like the Karen border (and other parts of Myanmar) the culture of self-help is prevalent, but there has been a less extensive effort on the part of the KIO to tie international humanitarianism to the Kachin political agenda. This is due partly to the fact that most of the NGOs on the border are Chinese teams that do not advertise their links with international humanitarianism so that they may continue their work.

By comparison, up until the end of August 2017, the humanitarian industry at the Bangladeshi border was small even though there were over 33,000 registered Rohingya refugees living in United Nations High Commissioner for Refugees (UNHCR)-managed camps and an estimated 200,000 refugees residing in makeshift settlements within the local community. The Bangladeshi government limited humanitarian access to these populations and only a handful of multilateral organizations and international NGOs operated on this border (for example, the UNHCR, World Food Programme, Action contre la faim, and Médecins Sans Frontières). When the number of camp refugees on the Thai–Bumese border – over 100,000 – is compared to the number of NGOs, it becomes clear that the humanitarian component of the moral economy of the Thai–Burmese border is larger in scale for a decidedly smaller population. As far as I have been able to ascertain, of these three borders, the secular moral sentiments of international humanitarianism have had the most impact on the Thai border.

In terms of the religious underpinnings of moral sentiments, I believe this would be the same in Kachin, Rakhine, and Kayin States, given that it is easier for faith-based organizations to work in Myanmar than for humanitarian ones, because the Myanmar government views the former to be less politically threatening. It is very likely that faith-based forms of service with their respective moral underpinnings operate along the Kachin and Rakhine borders. Although I am unable to present detailed data about the moral economy on these borders, I believe that these broad comparisons provide some valuable observations on the circulation of moral sentiments, their interaction with international moral economies, and their role in the production of political, cultural, and moral legitimacy.

With regards to the historical context of the moral economy at the Myawaddy–Mae Sot border, I believe the moral sentiments of self-help and helping others entwined with religious tenets had already been present at the borders before the international NGOs were officially invited by the Thai government to provide humanitarian aid in 1984. The Karen had already set up transborder and international church networks to provide resources to the internally displaced. The advent of the international NGOs and their presence for over 30 years brought about an added dimension to the moral contours of the borderland. However, changes are afoot. Structural transformations in the sphere of politics and economics occurring in Thailand and Myanmar herald a "changing moral geography" (Fassin 2012: 15). In Myanmar, new socio-political discourses and practices are emerging from ceasefires, peace negotiations, natural resource extraction, development projects, and the transition to democracy helmed by the National League of Democracy (NLD). The change from military to civilian leadership, from dictatorship to democracy, from human rights abuses to contestation over land for development, and from war to post-conflict will undoubtedly have an impact on the moral economy of this border. Similarly, the installation of the military government in Thailand in 2014 has revived long-standing issues of security, which have in turn affected the mobility and lives of Myanmar migrants and refugees.

Now that the KNU has signed a ceasefire agreement with the Myanmar government,[8] active warfare has been reduced to intermittent skirmishes, and the KNU is involved in peace negotiations with the Myanmar government. At the same time, for at least 10 years now, the community-based organizations and international NGOs have had to contend with donor fatigue. Moreover, following the transition to a democratically elected government in 2011 and the landslide victory of the NLD in 2015, aid has been diverted from the border to other regions in the world and to other areas inside Myanmar. When the refugee camps are eventually closed down,[9] the formal centres of humanitarianism will be dismantled. Undoubtedly, other forms of international aid will continue to operate in this region, but the main international humanitarian sector will disappear. This will have repercussions on the work of the local organizations as well as the type of moral legitimacy they can claim in the international sphere.

Concurrent with these structural changes is the construction of economic zones along this border. Plans have been floated to repatriate refugees so as to transform them from recipients of aid to factory labourers in the border industrial zones. In addition, greater access to parts of Kayin State by corporations and the government will bring about even more conflicts pertaining to the control of land. Already, there are innumerable struggles around the acquisition of and compensation for land for natural resource extraction, industry, and "development".

Attention will likely move away from humanitarianism to land and labour rights, and to the legitimization of border welfare infrastructure. Accordingly, the moral dimension will shift away from notions of humanitarianism as the overarching reason for action and towards other moral sentiments. Already, some border humanitarian organizations are shifting from a border-based aid approach (due to severe cuts in aid funding) to that of advocacy within Myanmar. Similarly, the affective landscape – the way in which people interact emotionally with this social space – will transform. Although armed conflict has been largely reduced, the affective landscape is still characterized by uncertainty, anxiety, fear, and distrust (Grundy-Warr and Chin 2016). Nevertheless, the ceasefires enable actors to work on building trust, to move about this area more freely, and to live a life that is not controlled by armed conflict (South 2014). If this continues, and the political and logistical issues are resolved, there will be a shift in the emotional component of the moral economy in this region, and possibly in the values that circulate. In short, political and economic changes, coupled with the withdrawal of border-based international NGOs will bring about substantive changes in the moral fabric of this region.

Acknowledgements

I would like to thank Alexander Horstmann and Martin Saxer for their invaluable comments and editing work.

Notes

1. The Four Cuts is a counter-guerilla warfare strategy that denies insurgents food, funds, recruits, and intelligence.
2. Humanitarianism is usually understood as assistance for those in exceptional distress and most often manifests as emergency relief. It is separate from ideologies and practices relating to human rights, social justice, environmental issues, development, cultural rights, and so on. However, the international humanitarian order includes these other professional fields and communities of practice.
3. See Woods (2011) on large-scale concessions given by the Myanmar to Chinese enterprises during the ceasefire in Kachin State.
4. Borderline is a non-profit collective of women's organizations, artists, and community groups living and working along the Thai–Myanmar border. WEAVE, Women's Education for Advancement and Empowerment, is an organization that aims to empower indigenous women and support their needs and basic human rights.
5. There were, however, accusations of the KNU diverting humanitarian funds from refugee camps towards their own activities and dominating the camp populations (Thawnghmung 2008: 22).
6. The Back Pack Health Worker Team was initiated by Dr Cynthia Maung who founded Mae Tao Clinic.
7. From correspondence with Carine Jacquet and Martin Smith.
8. The KNU signed a ceasefire with the Myanmar government in 2012.
9. No concrete plans for repatriation have been shared, but there is speculation that this will take place in the next few years.

References

Abraham, Itty, and Willem van Schendel. "Introduction: The Making of Illicitness." In *Illicit Flows and Criminal Things: State, Borders and the Other Side of Globalization*, edited by Willem van Schendel and Itty Abraham, pp. 1–37. Bloomington: Indiana University Press, 2005.

Appadurai, Arjun. "Introduction: Commodities and The Politics of Value." In *The Social Life of Things: Commodities in Cultural Perspective*, edited by Arjun Appadurai, pp. 3–64. Cambridge: Cambridge University Press, 1988.

Arnold, Dennis. *Administration, Border Zones and Spatial Practices in the Mekong Subregion*. PhD thesis, University of North Carolina at Chapel Hill, 2010.

Calhoun, Craig. "The Imperative to Reduce Suffering: Charity, Progress, and Emergencies in the Field of Humanitarian Action." In *Humanitarianism in Question: Politics, Power, Ethics*, edited by Michael Barnett and Thomas G. Weiss, pp. 73–97. Ithaca: Cornell University Press, 2008.

Carrier, James, G. "Introduction." In *A Handbook of Economic Anthropology, Second Edition*, edited by James G. Carrier, pp. 1–12. Cheltenham: Edward Elgar, 2012.

Décobert, Anne. *The Politics of Aid to Burma: A Humanitarian Struggle on the Thai-Burmese Border*. Abingdon: Routledge, 2016.

Fassin, Didier. "Moral Economies Revisited." *Annales. Histoire, Sciences Sociales* 6 (2009): 1237–1266.
Fassin, Didier (translated by Rachel Gomme). *Humanitarian Reason: A Moral History of the Present*. Berkeley: University of California Press, 2012.
Forsythe, David P. "Contemporary Humanitarianism: The Global and the Local." In *Humanitarianism and Suffering: The Mobilization of Empathy*, edited by Richard Ashby Wilson and Richard D. Brown, pp. 58–87. Cambridge: Cambridge University Press, 2009.
Gravers, Mikael. "Religious Imaginary as an Alternative Social and Moral Order – Karen Buddhism across the Thai-Burma Border." In *Building Noah's Ark for Migrants, Refugees, and Religious Communities*, edited by Alexander Horstmann and Jin-Heon Jung, pp. 45–76. New York: Palgrave Macmillan, 2015.
Grundy-Warr, Carl and Wei Jun Chin. "Moving On: Spaces of Uncertain Freedom and Engagement in the Kayah – Mae Hong Son Borderland." In *Myanmar's Mountain and Maritime Borderscapes: Local Practices, Boundary-Making and Figured Worlds*, edited by Su-Ann Oh. Singapore: ISEAS Press, 2016.
Horstmann, Alexander. "Confinement and Mobility: Transnational Ties and Religious Networking among Baptist Karen at the Thailand-Burma Border." Max Planck Institute Working Papers WP 10-16, 2010.
Horstmann, Alexander. "Sacred Spaces of Karen Refugees and Humanitarian Aid Across the Thailand-Burma Border." *Austrian Journal of South-East Asian Studies* 4 (2011): 254–272.
Horstmann, Alexander. "Stretching the Border: Confinement, Mobility and the Refugee Public among Karen Refugees in Thailand and Burma." *Journal of Borderlands Studies* 29, no. 1 (2014): 47–61.
Horstmann, Alexander. "Secular and Religious Sanctuaries: Interfaces of Humanitarianism and Self-Government of Karen Refugee-Migrants in Thai-Burmese Border Spaces." In *Building Noah's Ark for Migrants, Refugees, and Religious Communities*, edited by Alexander Horstmann and Jin-Heon Jung, pp. 129–156. New York: Palgrave Macmillan, 2015.
Horstmann, Alexander. "The Culture and Landscape of the Humanitarian Economy among the Karen (Kayin) in the Borderland of Southeast Myanmar and Northwest Thailand." In *Myanmar's Mountain and Maritime Borderscapes: Local Practices, Boundary-Making and Figured Worlds*, edited by Su-Ann Oh, pp. 171–190. Singapore: ISEAS Press, 2016.
Kudo, Toshihiro. *Border Area Development in the GMS: Turning the Periphery into the Center of Growth*. ERIA Discussion Paper Series Area Studies Center, Institute of Developing Economies, Japan, 2009.
Kudo, Toshihiro. "Border Development in Myanmar: The Case of the Myawaddy-Mae Sot Border." In *Border Economies in the Greater Mekong Sub-region*, edited by Masami Ishida, pp. 186–205. London: Palgrave Macmillan, 2013.
McConnachie, Kristen. "Rethinking the 'Refugee Warrior': The Karen National Union and Refugee Protection on the Thai–Burma Border." *Journal of Human Rights Practice* 4, no. 1 (2012): 1–27.
Oh, Su-Ann. "Navigating Learning, Employment and Economies in the Mae Sot-Myawaddy Borderland." In *Myanmar's Mountain and Maritime Borderscapes: Local Practices, Boundary-Making and Figured Worlds*, edited by Su-Ann Oh, pp. 191–214. Singapore: ISEAS Press, 2016.
Oh, Su-Ann. "Working Towards Partnership in Education: Civil Society and NGOs in Refugee Camps in Thailand." In *Educating Marginalized Communities in East Asia: State, Civil Society and NGO Partnerships*, edited by Khun Eng Kuah and Jason Eng Thye Tan. New York: Routledge, 2017.
Redfield, Peter. "A Less Modest Witness: Collective Advocacy and Motivated Truth in a Medical Humanitarian Movement." *American Ethnologist*, 33, no. 1 (2006): 3–26.
Scott, James C. *The Moral Economy of the Peasant: Rebellion and Subsistence in Southeast Asia*. New Haven: Yale University Press, 1979.
Simpson, Adam. *Energy, Governance and Security in Thailand and Myanmar (Burma): A Critical Approach to Environmental Politics in the South*. London and New York: Routledge, 2014.
Smith, Martin. *Burma: Insurgency and the Politics of Ethnicity*. Atlantic Highlands: Zed Books, 1991.
South, Ashley. "Update on the Peace Process." In *Burma/Myanmar: Where Now?* edited by Mikael Gravers and Flemming Ytzen, pp. 250–255. Copenhagen: NIAS Press, 2014.
Sunpuwan, Malee and Sakkarin Niyomsilpa. "Perception and Misperception: Thai Public Opinions on Refugees and Migrants from Myanmar." *Journal of Population and Social Studies*, 21, no. 1 (2012): 47–58.
Sunpuwan, Malee and Sakkarin Niyomsilpa. *The Survey of Thai Public Opinion toward Myanmar Refugees and Migrant Workers: An Overview*. Bangkok, Thailand: The Institute for Population and Social Research, Mahidol University, 2014.
Thaut, Laura C. "The Role of Faith in Christian Faith-Based Humanitarian Agencies: Constructing the Taxonomy." *Voluntas*, 20 (2009): 319–350.
Thawnghmung, Ardeth. *The Karen Revolution in Burma: Diverse Voices, Uncertain Ends*. Singapore: ISEAS Press and East-West Centre, 2008.

Thompson, E. P. "The Moral Economy of the English Crowd in the Eighteenth Century." *Past & Present* 50 (1971): 76–136.

Wahyu Kuncoro. *Burmese-Muslim Social Networks in the Borderland: A Case Study of Islam Bamroong Muslim Community in Mae Sot, Tak Province, Thailand.* Masters Dissertation, Justice, Environmental Issues, Political Dissent, Religion and Cultural Rights, Chiang Mai University, 2014.

Wilson, Richard A. and Richard D. Brown. "Introduction." In *Humanitarianism and Suffering: The Mobilization of Empathy*, edited by Richard Ashby Wilson and Richard D. Brown. New York: Cambridge University Press, 2009.

Woods, Kevin. "Ceasefire Capitalism: Military–Private Partnerships, Resource Concessions and Military–Building in the Burma–China Borderlands." *The Journal of Peasant Studies*, 38, no. 4 (2011): 747–770.

Yongyuth Chalamwong, Naruemon Thabchumpon and Supang Chantavanich (eds). *Temporary Shelters and Surrounding Communities: Livelihood Opportunities, the Labour Market, Social Welfare and Social Security.* SpringerBriefs in Environment, Security, Development and Peace Migration Studies, Volume 15. Cham, Heidelberg, New York, Dordrecht, London: Springer, 2014.

29
Biosocial body of ethno-religious boundaries in a Tibetan marriage

Dan Smyer Yü

Northwest China, as an ethnic borderland, is a region where Han Chinese, Tibetan, Mongolian, and Islamic civilizations, as well as numerous smaller ethnolinguistic communities meet, interact, and continue to retain the region as a site of multiethnic entanglements. Two divergent conceptualizations of the region currently frame the studies of ethnic borderlands inside China, namely the "fault line" and the "middle ground" perspectives. The former employs the metaphor of tectonic plates in complex patterns of faulting and dislocating from one another in order to describe relations between different ethnic groups (Gladney 2004: 26, 2009; Rossabi 2004: 3). This fault line perspective thereby emphasizes the territorial contentions between different ethnic groups. The latter perspective renders the region as a contact zone in which ethnic differences interact with one another and intermittently produce hybrid ethnic groups (Lattimore, 1940: 76–80; Pratt 1991: 33–40; Lipman 1997: xxxiii). Scholars who hold either of these two perspectives make convincing arguments based on the varied emphases of their interpretations of historical and empirical evidence and current interethnic issues. The conceptual common ground of these two divergent perspectives is their macro vision of regional histories and ethnic politics in China, especially socialist China. In many ways, it is cartographical in nature, highlighting the historical and geopolitical placement of each of the ethnic groups concerned.

Based on my fieldwork in the region, I suggest a third perspective to reconceptualize ethnic differences, which don't always occur bound within fixed places such as nations or ethnic communities, but rather as moving borderlines embodied in individual persons of given ethnic origins. In other words, the moving nature of ethnic boundaries is the primary concern of this reconceptualization. The accompanying case study for this conceptual exercise is a set of Tibetan–Hui relations expressed in a near-broken marriage of a young Tibetan family in Northwest China. The storyline of the ethnography I present in this chapter is quite typical for modern married life across human communities: the wife elopes with another man while the husband has an extramarital affair. However, when this abstraction is returned to its regional, ethnic, and familial contexts, it is a story of complex, entangled threads in both tangible and intangible expressions. In this story, religion and ethnicity, two elemental markers of human grouping, are the centerpieces from which my two interrelated conceptual arguments emerge. First, ethnic fault lines or contact zones are not merely fixed to the places of their origins, but are rather moving lines or threads that are crisscrossed, entangled, and knotted together through their routes and points of contact (Ingold 2007: 41). While recognizing the cracks and fractures between different ethnic groups owing to economic, cultural, linguistic, and religious factors, I see both fault lines and contact zones as lines of movement in the moving bodies of the actual persons I am concerned with in this chapter. In other words, wherever the moving body goes, its externally perceived "otherness" goes with it. Second, when inscribed in human consciousness and social behavior, religion and ethnicity are a moving bodily site highlighting the double nature of the human body, namely the biological and the social. In the case of Tibetan–Hui religious encounters, the biosocial nature of body is pronounced in both socially reconceived bloodlines and religiously sanctioned prohibitions.

Ethnographic foregrounds

The protagonists in my ethnography live in a Tibetan and a Muslim settlement of southern Gansu Province respectively. In this chapter, they are fictitiously named Losang, Drolma, and Ma Kui. Losang and Drolma are a married Tibetan couple. Both Losang and Drolma are stigmatized in their village. The former was a monk but returned to lay life, while the latter is stigmatized with two communally alleged accounts – her maternal grandmother ran away with a Muslim man and her paternal bloodline is tainted with what their compatriots call "sidre" (གསེ་དྲི), an undesirable bodily odor. Ma Kui is a Hui businessman who frequents Tibetan villages recruiting seasonal workers for construction and for digging caterpillar fungi.

The story of this near-broken marriage started with Losang's extramarital affair, which caused a series of emotional reactions from Drolma. Ma Kui came onto the scene when Drolma signed up to his caterpillar fungi digging team headed for Golok. Under the circumstances of Drolma's emotional vulnerability, Ma Kui allegedly convinced Drolma to start a new family with him. Enchanted verbally by Ma, she decided to live with him. As soon as they reached his village, Drolma found out that Ma was a married man with two kids and that his wife had left him. In addition to Ma's own marital complications, she found herself suffering from culture shock when she encountered Islam in a lived environment. She wanted to return to her home village, but was afraid of further stigmatization because of her involvement with a Muslim man. She and Ma decided to move to southern China, away from their respective Tibetan and Hui environments, without informing their families.

Meanwhile, Losang began to feel remorseful about his extramarital affair and realized how much Drolma meant to him as companion and mother of their child. The news of Drolma's eloping with a Hui man soon spread through the village. Losang saw himself faced with conflicting voices from his own family members, Drolma's family, and people in the village. The emotional and social pressures were unprecedented in the accounts of the peoples' objection to a Tibetan woman marrying a Hui. Losang's family members were renewing their initial objection to his marriage with Drolma because of the alleged "unclean blood" from her paternal side and of Drolma's parents' fear for the social restigmatization of two of their family members. Drolma's grandmother and now Drolma had eloped with Hui men; however, Losang and Drolma's family determined that they wanted Drolma back from Ma Kui. As soon as everyone in the village confirmed the rumor that Drolma had "run off" with a Hui, finding her for Losang and Drolma's family was no longer just a personal issue, but became a torment for those left in the village, one filled with stigma, shame, and fear, during which Drolma was representative of a lost but ultimately recovered embodiment of a Buddhist Tibet.

The seven-month search for Drolma is laden with multiple ethnographic traces concerning the topics of clean and unclean bloodlines, religious taboos, cultural boundaries set by religious differences, and livelihood choices prescribed by both negative and positive religious sanctions. What stands out amidst this search is that the living human body is a moving site of ethnic, religious, and cultural boundaries. In many ways, the moving body is a line, a thread, or a path that relationally connects cultural differences, ethnic borders, and exclusionary religious sanctions.

Biosocial body of religion and ethnicity

Throughout the drama between Losang, Drolma, and Ma Kui, Drolma's body becomes a body of Tibet, a body of Buddhism, a body of Losang's affinal union with her family, and a body of social stigmatization that calls for purification. Entangled in Tibetan and Hui customary, religious, and economic practices in the context of modern China, Drolma's body is inscribed, intertwined, and embodied with a set of what I refer to as "collective elementals," which embed volitions, motivations, and intentions in the social action of the individual person. In this regard, the human body signifies simultaneously the embodiments of flesh, blood, emotions, learned worldviews, and individual and collective identity. It is mobile and physically independent from other bodies; however, when it is understood in relational terms such as those of bloodline, kinship, ethnicity, and nationality, it no longer appears to be fully independent but is rather one of many in the entangled web of a community, a tribe, an ethnic group, a nation, or a border zone of differences.

In the case of Losang, religion and ethnicity are the two primary collective elementals that influence his body's actions, his expectations of Drolma's actions, and how he relates himself to non-Tibetans in the region. The overlapping of the Buddhist identity with Tibetan ethnic identity is commonly discussed among scholars (Smyer Yü 2011; Makley 2012; Yeh 2013). In this regard, Ma Kui was not the sole cause of Losang's seven-month split from Drolma. There were pre-existing conditions originating from Losang's family, which contributed to the instability of the marriage and became the preconditions of the temporary split. Before Ma Kui came into the picture, Losang's family had objected to the union of Losang and Drolma on two accounts. The first was that, to them, the bloodline of Drolma's mother is not clean because her grandmother ran off with a Hui while she was married to Drolma's grandfather. Although she returned to her family soon after, the bloodline of her children was nevertheless looked upon as questionable. Now, Drolma seemed to be repeating her grandmother's history. This gave more reason to Losang's family to oppose their union. In their view, this historical stigma was obviously being renewed. Losang's parents and siblings thus all wanted him to take the opportunity to end the union after Drolma eloped with Ma Kui.

The second aspect had to do with the community's customary perception of clean and unclean bloodlines, which set the social hierarchy in the past and continued to affect families' choices of marriage alliance. Losang's parents are descendants of a tribal chief in the area. The family's pride in its bloodline showed itself in the selective opinions of Losang's parents about Drolma. Losang's father, who had once been a monk but who was forced to return to lay life in late 1950s, explained why Losang should not marry Drolma. First, in the last three generations, Drolma's family had offspring with sidre (བསེ་དྲི). Sidre refers to offensive body odor and implies a state of uncleanness in the person's family bloodline, especially that of the father's side. Sidre's immediate associative phrases are *regad negpo* (རུས་རྒྱུད་ནག་པོ) and *dsogpa* (བཙོག་པ). The former means "black bones" and the latter literally means the "filthy one," signifying the uncleanness of the former. Both indicate the low social status of the person or the family bloodline.

Sidre is a stigma inscribed in *riba* (རུས་པ) – the bones of both the dead and the living. It is perceived as biologically and socially contagious. If a family has a history of sidre among its ancestors and current members, it is often made known to the entire village through gossip. Drolma's immediate and extended families, especially those from her maternal side, are the subject of such a communal act of containment. On a day-to-day basis, families in the village amiably relate to each other; however, when it comes to possible marriage alliances, checking out each other's "bone history" becomes critical. As the doors to affinal bonds with Drolma's family were mostly shut in the area, Drolma's older sister was married out to an urban Tibetan in the county seat, whose family had no concern about her family's "bone history." Drolma's sister-in-law came from another village, but with the same issue of sidre as Drolma's family. In reality, Drolma does not suffer from body odor and with the exception of one of her maternal granduncles, none of her current family members suffers from it either; and yet, the negative sanction of their community still affects them.

Herein, to interject my anthropological understanding, I see sidre as an issue of what Mary Douglas calls a "pollution conscious culture" (Douglas 1988: vii). It is more social and symbolic than biological, although it is firmly centered upon the human body. I asked Losang's father if the issue of sidre and its association with "bad bones" is a health issue, since people are afraid of it. What he told me only convinces me that containing sidre is a matter of maintaining social order through the language of purity and pollution:

> If someone has sidre, we think his ancestor's bones were unclean and therefore his bones are unclean, too. We don't think he has health problems. This uncleanness is hereditary. Some people's sidre is smelly enough for everyone around him to know. He is obviously unclean. Some people's sidre is not strong but because it is hereditary, we stay away from them and don't marry their children. There is a saying around here about a person with sidre: "If a piece of iron gets stuck in a crack of the wall of his house, it'll be soaked with the odor of sidre!" So, sidre is about the uncleanness of his bloodline.

Losang's father has lived through several radical social transitions since the late 1950s. Yet he seems to have retained the customs of social hierarchy based on the cleanness of one's ancestral bloodline. His vigilant attempt to bar sidre from entering his family bloodline shows that in his view of what is appropriate, the "black bones" (unclean ones) and the "white bones" (རུས་རྒྱུད་དཀར་པོ།, regad garpo) do not mix. Herein, bones are no longer physical but cultural, psychic, and social in nature. They are a social habitus that inscribes the externality of society so that it is internalized on the body (Joyce 2005: 142). This is the double nature of the human body, namely the biological and the social. Douglas writes in *Natural Symbols*, "Two bodies are the self and society: sometimes they are so near as to be almost merged; sometimes they are far apart. The tension between them allows the elaboration of meanings" (Douglas 1973: 112). What I see from the case of sidre is not only the two bodies, as Douglas elaborates, but a third body or an embodiment of both the physical body and the society. Its tangibility is expressed in the moving body of the living person. This moving "bodily site" is the primary concern of Losang's family with the family line being exposed to the socially perceived uncleanness of sidre, the black bones. If Losang formally married Drolma, his family bloodline would be "polluted."

The local cultural consciousness of pollution permitted Losang's family to object to his marriage with Drolma. Since Losang married Drolma, his parents have not yet invited her to their house. Neither is she willing to pay a visit to her in-laws because of the "bone differences" between a family of commoners and a family of a former chiefdom.

In summary, we see that sidre is not a medically-defined illness, but is rather a social "contagion," a perceived pollutant to a family's bloodline and social status. It is socially translated as a stigma. Whoever is "hereditarily" implicated becomes a marginal being who is perceived to emanate danger to others (Douglas 1988: 96–97). This is how Losang's family perceives Drolma's bloodline – as socially inferior due to the perception that it will tarnish Losang's family's association with a historical chieftain. Drolma's entanglement with Ma Kui worsened the existing communal perception of her family. Therefore, the options available to her were that she could either permanently leave Losang and the village or return to both so as to alleviate the shame of both her and Losang's families. In either choice, the religiously sanctioned boundary between cleanness and defilement shows its pressing presence embodied in the body of everyone involved.

Body as an embodied cultural sovereignty

In Losang's quest for the return of Drolma, her body became an embodiment of a "cultural sovereignty" especially in the eye of Losang and his male peers in the village. In this context, her return is not only a return to her family, but also perceptibly a return to Tibet from Ma Kui's Muslim world. This embodied cultural sovereignty signifies "strategies to maintain and develop cultural alterity, as well as assert autonomy from external control" (Bernstein 2012: 266). Embodiment in this gendered, customarily, religiously conditioned case has to be understood not only as a fusion with the biological body, but also a "field defined by perceptual experience and the mode of presence and engagement in the world" and thus the social reality is "inscribed in the body" (Csordas 1993: 135). In other words, external sociocultural conditions embody themselves in the individual body situated in its own cultural environment as well as in the interethnic encounters in the greater region. In many ways, Drolma's situation resembles Joseph Alter's case study of the wrestlers in India, in which the body is "a complex, multilayered indivisible synthesis of psychic, somatic, emotional, sensory, cognitive, and chemical forces" (Alter 1993: 49). In addition, such a living complex is a biosocial body, microcosmic in nature, embodying collective elementals such as religion and ethnicity.

Within the multilayered contexts of the intracultural sense of purity and defilement, and the social conditions of ethnic relations in Northwest China, the body is thus "a public space" (Strathern 2004: 1) regulated by collective worldviews and values. It can be seen as a surface on which the biology of the person and the sociology of his or her culture entwine with one another. Not limited to the anatomy of flesh, bones, organs, and other biologically defining elements of *Homo sapiens*, the body is "the point of articulation between an interior self and an exterior society" (Joyce 2005: 144). Here, I would add that the body, as a public space or a point of social connectivity, simultaneously internalizes the external society and externalizes its individualized understanding and perception of the society. In this regard, the body is biosocial in nature, in which the social order of things can determine thought patterns and bodily acts.

In the empirical world of Tibetan–Hui interactions in contemporary Northwest China, religious and ethnic boundaries are not geographically determined, but entail moving borderlines mostly manifested in the economic relations between the two most populous ethnic groups in the region. The moving nature of the ethnic boundaries is animated by the movement of bodies of Tibetans and Hui in and out of each other's ethnic communities, be it as entrepreneurs, vendors, contractors, or civil servants. Thus the interethnic tensions do not take place behind lines of separation but are interwoven into traditionally recognized ethnic territories and social acts of individuals. In this sense, the ethnic borderlines between Tibetans and Hui are not physically demarcated but are porous, yet felt, perceived, crisscrossed, and emotionally charged. Seen from the perspective of Ingold's idea of line, they are "ghostly" or invisible in nature but produce "very real consequences for people's movements" (Ingold 2007: 49).

In Robert Ekvall's account of his fieldwork in the 1930s, he characterized the Tibetan–Hui relationship as a host–guest relationship. Hui willingly adopted Tibetan language and customs for their trading purposes among Tibetans in Amdo (Ekvall 1939: 48). Owing to a lack of modern means of transportation, the duration of their stays in Tibetan settlements was often long, meaning that they were highly dependent upon local Tibetans and thus had increased exposure to Tibetan culture. The early Hui merchants in Amdo were willing to maintain a viable host–guest relationship for their commercial interest (Ekvall 1939: 53). Many Hui settled down in Tibetan communities and adopted a Tibetan lifestyle. Tibetans refer to this group of Tibetanized Hui and their descendants as *bokhache* (བོད་ཁ་ཆེ་) or "Tibetan Muslims." However, since the early 1990s, the Tibetanized Hui settlements in Tibetan borderlands have undergone a process of de-Tibetanization by reinforcement of their Islamic faith. Along with their compatriots in the greater region, they have reassumed their commercial role as the intermediaries between Tibetans and the greater Han Chinese society.

Recent studies show that the Hui have inherited not only the trading routes and marketing infrastructure built up by their forefathers, but are also expanding them further into Tibetan regions. Hui's alleged economic success is currently known as "the Hui economy" (Yang 2011: 139) shown in the trading of staple foods, fresh produce, livestock, meat, fuel, and construction materials. My recent ethnographic findings are similar to the scholarly assessments since the early 2000s. A few scholars in China take a step further to regard the Hui as the economic monopolizers of the region (Tsering Gyal 2008: 36). The latest ethnic demographic statistics appear to support this claim. In Qinghai, for instance, 90% of the Hui in all Tibetan regions live in proximity with 25% of the total Tibetan population. In nearly every county in this region, Tibetans and Muslims are co-residents. There are also mixed spaces for Tibetans and Muslims in many townships and villages. In 2012, Xinhua Net released official figures showing that 330,000 Hui from Linxia, Gansu Province, work in Tibetan regions and the livelihoods of over 100,000 Hui residents of Linxia depend on making products catering to Tibetans, such as rock sugar, carpets, tents, and boots (Chen and Bo 2012). The total Hui population in Linxia is 610,000 (SEAC 2013). These demographic figures suggest the Hui's alleged economic monopolization appears to be a type of economic dependency on Tibet as both a source of raw materials and as a consumer market.

In his studies, Andrew Fischer also notices that the growing economic dominance of the Hui is triggering Tibetan resentment toward the Hui, as shown, for example, in Tibetans' intermittently boycotting Hui businesses in Amdo since the mid-1990s (Fischer 2005: 12). His findings coincide with those of Tsering Gyal, and Chen and Bo, emphasizing the increasing number of Hui migrants into Tibetan regions. Fischer builds a causal link between the economic "exclusionary force" of the Chinese state with ethnic tensions in the region, especially between Tibetans and Hui, suggesting that the Chinese state is the primary player causing the tensions while the Hui are being scapegoated (Fischer 2005: 12, 21). According to Fischer, this situation permits Tibetans "to justify their cautiously racist characterisations of Muslims as naturally violent, tricky and cheating, thereby explaining the reasons for Muslim success in the Tibetan economy as well as the reasons for Tibetan insecurity" (Fischer 2005: 22). Fischer's assessment underpins his historical understanding of Qinghai and Gansu as "the nerve center for Tibetan-Muslim relations throughout the centuries" (Fischer 2005: 7). Tibetans in Qinghai and Gansu in particular are now bringing forth a new public discussion on the Islamization of Northwest China.

Fischer's macro perspective is well acknowledged; however, the exclusionary force does not only come from the Chinese state's economic policy implementation in the region. It also comes from religion-based practices of exclusion and inclusion in both Hui and Tibetan communities.

While the policy prescriptions could visibly set ethnic communities apart in uneven economic relations, ethnic boundary lines in the practices of Islam and Buddhism play a significant role in determining the economic success of Hui and the disadvantage of the Tibetans.

Ethnic borderlines as a meshwork of entangled threads

From an ethnographical viewpoint, Tibetans and Hui retain their customary exclusionary behaviors as prescribed by their respective religions. Like Buddhists in other countries, Tibetans also hold the view of non-Buddhists as "outsiders" (ཕྱི་པ, *phyipa*) and Buddhists as "insiders" (ནང་པ, *nangpa*). This could be seen as a dividing line separating Buddhists from non-Buddhists; however, as Buddhist teachings require a Buddhist to treat a non-Buddhist as his or her equal, it is not as strictly maintained as that of Islam, which refers to non-Muslims as the kafir, who are doctrinally sanctioned against unless they are willing to convert to Islam. What, then, are the religious factors that contribute to Tibetans' economic disadvantage in relation to the alleged success of Hui economy?

It is the pollution consciousness of Tibetans, as discussed earlier, that excludes many Tibetans from participation in economic activities that are necessities, but are deemed socially low-status or unclean. The Hui have prospered in these occupations and services, such as blacksmithing, livestock trading, and livestock slaughtering, which Tibetans are reluctant to pursue. In the Buddhist customary practices of Tibetans, the "low" and "high," and "clean" and "unclean" professions are determined by their religious values centered upon the Buddhist reservations against killing or acts related to killing. For instance, livestock traders, butchers, and blacksmiths are traditionally looked upon as *dsogpa* (བཙོག་པ) or "filthy." The communal prejudice toward these professions becomes visible when people do not eat with them and do not marry their children (Shu 1964: 42).

As this traditional perception of the "undesirable" professions persists among contemporary Tibetans, and in China there is a growing consumer market for yak meat, the killing-related jobs are being made more available for non-Tibetans. Hui-owned slaughterhouses in Tibetan borderlands are currently perceived as sites of one-sided economic prosperity favoring the Hui and of heightened debates concerning Buddhist life ethics and ethnic identity among Tibetans. Since the 1990s, many lamas have continually raised funds from their lay constituencies to rescue the yaks from the death rows of these slaughterhouses. In recent years, these Tibetan Buddhist "rescue missions" have also led to the burgeoning intra-Tibetan questioning of why Tibetans have to sell their livestock to the Hui to start with and of how the yak rescue actions become economic transactions favoring the growth of the Hui economy, because the donated funds from Tibetans themselves pour into the slaughterhouses to redeem the yaks above the rates of the meat market. Nearly all Tibetan–Hui tensions and conflicts from the turn of the century to now have taken place in Tibetan areas following the trails of the Hui businesses (Tsering Gyal 2008: 37). Tibetan cultural elites characterize the Hui as "a commercial people" to whom "friendship does not exist when business is absent" (Tsering Gyal 2008: 38); however, Tibetans also characterize themselves as being from a culture that "belittles economics but emphasizes spirituality" (Tsering Gyal 2008: 36). Allegedly, the Hui are the ultimate winners of the market economy in the region at the expense of Tibetans. Outspoken urban Tibetans began to build a causal linkage between the Hui's economic dominance in the region and an increase in the incidence of Hui entrepreneurs being accused of seducing or abducting young Tibetan women into marriages with promises of wealth (Tsering Gyal 2008: 37).

In the greater socioeconomic context of Tibetan–Hui relations, Ma Kui follows the same business practices of his ancestors in the region, to be a middleman between Tibetans and Han

Chinese while retaining his Islamic faith and practice wherever he goes. Drolma temporarily joined Ma Kui in an attempt to restart a family with him; however, her own family's perception of her being with Ma Kui was not that she was simply undertaking a fresh start, but that she was in "danger" of becoming a Muslim. Losang, under the intracultural pressures, felt strongly that Drolma had transgressed the expectation that Tibetans do not marry Hui out of principle. Each individual in this case is both a point of connectivity and a thread of multiple entanglements. It connects itself with multiple others and moves its own alterity into communities of others.

Losang, Drolma, and Ma Kui are all caught in the meshwork of the entangled threads of economic activities, religious practices, and ethnic inclusions and exclusions in the region. Entanglement and disentanglement, and conjoinment and disjointment take place simultaneously. A one-sided religious or customary exclusion becomes an economic disadvantage to one ethnic group and success to another group. An individual interethnic sexual relationship is no longer a personal affair, but is subject to culturally judgmental perceptions from all sides. One's bodily contact with that of another person of different ethnic origins can intensify an intraethnic sense of purity and defilement and presents itself as an opportunity for religious reconversion from the standpoint of another ethnoreligious group. The physical movement of an individual can weave in and out of ethnic, religious, and economic differences, but one's ethnic constituency often looks upon the body of the individual as a property of one's ethnicity and religious tradition. In the seven-month long story of Losang's effort to get Drolma back, I see the social materiality of Northwest China as a multi-frontiered surface on which fault lines, points of connectivity, and entangled threads of religion and ethnicity are concurrently meshed together.

References

Alter, Joseph 1993. "The Body of One Color: Indian Wrestling, the Indian State, and Utopian Somatics." *Cultural Anthropology* 8(1): 49–72.
Bernstein, Anya 2012. "A More Alive Than All the Living: Sovereign Bodies and Cosmic Politics in Buddhist Siberia." *Cultural Anthropology* 27(2): 261–285.
Chen, Jun and Wang Bo 2012. "China's 'Little Mecca': The Hot Hui-Tibetan Economy in Linxia, Gansu." [online Xinhua Net]. Available at: http://sp.chinadaily.com.cn/staple/20120926/63516.html (accessed July 11, 2013).
Csordas, Thomas 1993. "Somatic Modes of Attention." *Cultural Anthropology* 8(2): 135–156.
Douglas, Mary 1973. *Natural Symbols*. Middlesex: Penguin Books.
———— 1988. *Purity and Danger: An Analysis of the Concepts of Pollution and Taboo*. London: Ark Paperbacks.
Ekvall, Robert 1939. *Cultural Relations on the Kansu-Tibetan Border*. Chicago: The University of Chicago Press.
Fischer, Andrew 2005. "Close Encounters of Co-existence and Conflict in Tibet, Past and Present." Crisis States Programme Working Papers Series, No. 1.
Gladney, Dru 2004. *Dislocating China: Reflections on Muslims, Minorities, and Other Subaltern Subjects*. Chicago: The University of Chicago Press.
———— 2009. "China's Ethnic Fault Lines: Rising tensions and resistance to Beijing's control challenge China's 'harmonious' society." *The Wall Street Journal*, July 16, 2009, available at: http://online.wsj.com/article/SB10001424052970203547904574279952210843672.html (accessed July 11, 2013).
Ingold, Tim 2007. *Lines: A Brief History*. London: Routledge.
Joyce, Rosemary A. 2005. "Archaeology of the Body." *Annual Review of Anthropology* 34: 139–158.
Lattimore, Owen 1940. *Inner Asian Frontiers of China*. Boston: Beacon Press.
Lipman, Jonathan 1997. *Familiar Strangers: A History of Muslims in Northwest China*. Seattle: University of Washington Press.
Makley, Charlene 2012. *The Political Lives of Dead Bodies. Fieldsights – Hot Spots, Cultural Anthropology Online*, April 8, available at: http://culanth.org/fieldsights/93-self-immolation-as-protest-in-tibet (accessed March 15, 2013).
Pratt, Mary Louise 1991. "Arts of the Contact Zone." *Profession*. Modern Language Association, 33–40, doi:10.2307/25595469.

Rossabi, Morris 2004. "Introduction," in M. Rossabi, ed. *Governing China's Multiethnic Frontiers*. Seattle: University of Washington Press, pp. 3–18.

The State Ethnic Affairs Commission of PRC (SEAC) 2013. "Regional Autonomy." Available at: www.seac.gov.cn/gjmw/zzdf/2004-07-13/1165370092777277.htm (accessed October 4, 2013).

Shu, Jiexun 1964. *Research Materials Concerning Nang-she-ling Area*. Beijing: Institute of Ethnological Research, Chinese Science Academy.

Smyer Yü, Dan 2011. *The Spread of Tibetan Buddhism in China: Charisma, Money, Enlightenment*. London: Routledge.

Strathern, Marilyn 2004. "The Whole Person and Its Artifacts." *Annual Review of Anthropology* 33: 1–19.

Tsering Gyal 2008. "How to Construct a Harmonious Hui-Tibetan Relation." *Journal of Northwest Minzu University* 147(02): 34–41.

Yang, Huaizhong 2011. *Hui Economy* 《回族经济研究》. Ningxia: Ningxia People's Press 宁夏人民出版社.

Yeh, Emily T. 2013. *Emily Taming Tibet: Landscape Transformation and the Gift of Chinese Development*. Ithaca: Cornell University Press.

30
Development institutions and religious networks in the Pamirian borderlands

Till Mostowlansky

Introduction[1]

The geographical intersection where Afghanistan, China, Pakistan, and Tajikistan meet has long served as a crossroads of different ethnic, linguistic, and religious groups. The Pamirian borderlands – as I call this high-altitude crossroads, with reference to the Pamir mountain range in the area[2] – has only recently become divided by militarized political boundaries, first between the British and the Russian empires at the end of the 19th century and then, in the course of the 20th century, between socialist, post-colonial, and post-socialist nation states. In public as well as academic discourse, this relatively young history of division, often expressed through a focus on one nation state,[3] tends to overshadow the legacy of historical relationships and the salience of contemporary connections between different parts of the Pamirian borderlands and other parts of the world. This chapter makes a case for the study of such connections and their historical genealogies. It does so by focusing on connections that have resulted from the concurrence of development institutions and religious networks and which – in the Pamirian borderlands – have largely been established and maintained by the work of Ismaili Muslim institutions. Under the patronage of the Ismaili imamate, these institutions have introduced material and social change, as well as religious reform, to various parts of the Pamirian borderlands since the second half of the 20th century. They have thereby both catered to and been transformed by a borderland population that, despite being predominantly Ismaili, nevertheless remains quite diverse. In this chapter, I propose that looking at the interplay of development and religious networks in the Pamirian borderlands provides insights into rarely considered processes of globalization whose effects range from economics and international development to politics and religion.

This chapter is based on a review of published material on the work of Ismaili institutions in the Pamirian borderlands, as well as on data from my ongoing anthropological research in Tajikistan (since 2008) and Pakistan (since 2012). Given the constraints of space, I will limit the scope of the chapter to places in Gilgit-Baltistan in Pakistan (formerly known as the Northern Areas) and Gorno-Badakhshan in Tajikistan. Both Gilgit-Baltistan and Gorno-Badakhshan are administrative units that have been subject to major development interventions and social change in the course of the 20th century and in the context of several different imperial and

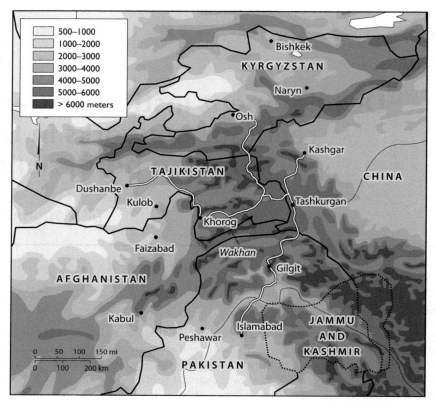

Map 30.1 Map of the Pamirian borderlands
Map by Till Mostowlansky

nation state formations (the Russian and British empires, the Soviet Union, Pakistan, and Tajikistan). The Pamirian borderlands' smaller areas in Afghanistan (Wakhan) and China (Tashkurgan Tajik Autonomous County) have hitherto received less attention in the literature, and the presence of Ismaili development institutions is either a more recent phenomenon, as is the case in post-Taliban Afghanistan (Callahan 2013), or, in the case of China, is discouraged by the state (Kreutzmann 2015: 384–396).

The chapter is organized chronologically. First I introduce early efforts to establish Ismaili development in northern Pakistan and use the region as testing ground for the Aga Khan Development Network in the Pamirian borderlands. I then discuss how an Ismaili political theology of development has emerged through the entanglement of the legacy of British colonial rule in India, 20th-century developmental discourse, and the continuous reinterpretation of Islamic teachings. Finally, I discuss how Ismaili development encounters in Tajikistan's part of the Pamirian borderlands have altered this configuration from the 1990s to the present day (Map 30.1).

Reaching out to the frontier

In 1923 Pir Sabzali, missionary and envoy of Sir Sultan Muhammed Shah Aga Khan III – the 48th imam of the Shia Ismaili community – travelled from India to the Pamirs. In the course of his journey he visited the Aga Khan's followers in areas that are now part of Afghanistan, China, Pakistan, and Tajikistan.[4] Pir Sabzali's visit was meant to gain more knowledge about the Central Asian communities of Ismailis that seemed remote and distant from Bombay, then the Aga Khan's place of residence. Pir Sabzali's journey was also the last visit of an official Ismaili representative to the Pamirs that included all parts of the region. While Soviet and Chinese border closures prevented such visits in the second half of the 20th century, even today – more than 25 years after the collapse of the Soviet Union – China's Xinjiang region remains relatively inaccessible, and international borders throughout the region are difficult to cross.

As a result of these Cold War processes and the incorporation of the Pamirs into different political units, certain places in today's northern Pakistan came to the attention of Ismaili institutions in the course of the 20th century. Hunza, a princedom with a predominantly Ismaili population ruled by a *mir* (aristocratic leader) until 1974, attracted particular attention. In 1940, the Aga Khan III addressed his "spiritual children" in the Northern Frontiers of India, such as Chitral, Hunza, Gilgit and Badakhshan via Delhi Radio and called on them to educate the youth and "to learn European languages and the English language" (Hunzai 2004: 157). In the effort to introduce educational institutions in the region, the establishment of the Diamond Jubilee Investment Trust proved to be central. For the Aga Khan III's diamond jubilee in 1946 celebrating 60 years of his imamate, his followers in Africa and on the Indian subcontinent literally donated the weight of their leader in diamonds. These funds then provided the material base for investments in Ismaili communities, including Hunza (Benz 2013: 126). In the first year following the jubilee alone, 18 Diamond Jubilee schools were constructed in Hunza, followed by another 60 such schools by 1973 (Kreutzmann 1989: 163). This educational enterprise was embedded in far-reaching geographical connections. School projects on the subcontinent followed the example of schools that had been built in Ismaili villages in Khorasan in Reza Shah's Iran starting in 1932 (Kreutzmann 1996: 307 n. 153; Daftary 2007: 493).[5]

The establishment of schools and access to education were an early part of broader development interventions that have continued to transform everyday life in Hunza to the present day. In this respect, the construction of transportation infrastructure, particularly the Karakoram Highway connecting Pakistan and China, has been of utmost importance. The road was built between 1966 and 1978 and is still regularly reconstructed and upgraded. The opening of the road for regular traffic between Pakistan and China in 1982 (Kreutzmann 1989: 35) provided Hunza with road access to both the Pakistani lowlands and nearby Xinjiang. It is precisely this point in time that many of my interlocutors in Hunza associate with the term "development" (Urdu *tarraqi*) and with widespread education, infrastructural improvements, international tourism, and improved access to neighbouring towns, down-country Pakistan and, eventually, other parts of the world (Hussain 2015).

Several of the people I interviewed called the period prior to the road and the emergence of *tarraqi* "medieval". They thereby not only juxtaposed living conditions and infrastructure in Hunza in the past with those of the present, but they were also implicitly referring to an increasing number of institutions attributed to Prince Shah Karim Al Hussaini Aga Khan IV, the 49th Ismaili imam and grandson of Sir Sultan Muhammed Shah. These institutions, situated at the nexus of religious administration and international development, are tightly linked to Pakistan's and China's bilateral road construction projects because they have sprung up along the various branches of the newly established transport network (Kreutzmann 2009: 25). In 1982, the same year the road to China was opened to regular traffic, the Aga Khan Foundation, administered from Geneva and part of the Aga Khan Development Network (Ruthven 2011), brought into being the Aga Khan Rural Support Programme, which has been operating ever since in Gilgit-Baltistan and Chitral with projects in infrastructure, education, health, micro-finance, and agriculture.[6]

Till Mostowlansky

A political theology of development

In conversations that I have had in Hunza during fieldwork since 2012, many middle-aged and elderly men and women described the changes brought about by state-sponsored road construction and Ismaili development projects as having dissected various fields of their lives. Importantly, they described *tarraqi* – in the sense of "development", "progress", and "advancement" – as a large complex of changes in which the material transformation of the environment through road construction and agricultural innovation, education, healthcare, and new sources of income went hand in hand with changes in religious practices. These interlocutors located the source of change in the Ismaili institutions, chaired by the Aga Khan IV, which aimed at the improvement of their lives but also – as a man by the name of Nizam put it – at making them "rational". For Nizam, the English term "rational" had a positive connotation and referred as much to economic matters as to changes in religious rituals, prayers, and theological interpretations that the Aga Khan IV has fostered since the last quarter of the 20th century (Steinberg 2011; Mostowlansky 2016).

This view of development, which conflates all aspects of institutional Ismaili presence, is widespread and popular in Hunza. However, for planners and administrators working within the Aga Khan Development Network to whom I talked in the course of my research – from offices in Geneva to local branches in the villages of Hunza – such a conflation is deeply problematic. It is part of the network's official policy to be "non-denominational" (AKDN 2017). This entails a differentiation between institutions that pursue development projects and others, such as the Ismaili Tariqah and Religious Education Board (Steinberg 2011: 144), which cover questions of religious practice and ensure communication between the Aga Khan and local communities by means of "edicts", "decrees", and "pronouncements" (all subsumed under the general rubric *farman*). In this regard, the Aga Khan Development Network, which is a recognized partner of the world's largest donor agencies, conforms to the dominant discourse of international development whereby religious actors and faith-based NGOs are framed as undesirable "others" and ostracized (Fountain 2013). It is important to acknowledge these conflicting aspects if one wants to understand why and how Ismaili institutions have managed to continuously introduce material and social change to different parts of the Pamirian borderlands. On the one hand, the secular positioning within the broader world of diplomacy and development organizations has allowed Ismaili institutions to avoid the stain of partisanship that an openly religious genealogy might cause (Benthall 2016; Bolotta forthcoming). On the other hand, the nimbus surrounding the Ismaili imamate and the all-encompassing figure of the Aga Khan IV – and the legitimacy to continuously adapt theological frameworks to the changing spatial and temporal conditions that these confer – have fostered local perceptions of Ismailism as transcending the boundaries of religion, development, and political form.

Given that today a large part of the population in the area identifies as Ismaili, one might expect explanations of why Ismaili institutions have even bothered to pay particular attention to the Pamirian borderlands to be rather straightforward. And indeed, published depictions of contemporary Ismailis circulate widely within translocal Ismaili networks and tend to "naturalize" ties between the institutions and the local populations (Daftary 2007, 2011). This view is based on the assumption that all Ismailis worldwide are part of one dispersed yet interconnected Muslim denomination that, assembled around the unifying figure of the Aga Khan, has historically developed as a branch of early Shia Islam. But it also reflects how many Ismailis in the Pamirian borderlands and beyond have to overcome and normalize the inherent tension between a purported global community of Ismailis (*Jamat*) and the many ethnically and linguistically distinct local *jamats*. Other scholars of Ismailism have not assumed such a natural connection, focusing instead on the relatively recent history of Ismaili institutions and the dynamics of power and geopolitics that have allowed them to reach out into the Pamirian borderlands. For instance, Steinberg (2011: 15) describes the Ismaili "complex" as a global assemblage consisting of perceived borderlands that are continuously brought into the fold of the imamate. Ismaili institutions communicate to these borderland populations that they *are* Ismaili and teach them *how* to behave accordingly. The bureaucratic apparatus that supports this process, uniting development institutions and religious administration, works towards centralization, the standardization of religious and communal practices, and the transmission of "modern ideas and ideologies" that are seen as being at the heart of global Ismailism (Steinberg 2011: 15; see also Maertens 2017). Devji (2009) argues that the roots of this bureaucratic apparatus are located in British colonial law and the concept of indirect rule. In 1866, the Bombay High Court gave the first Aga Khan authority over the property and customary law of the Ismaili community (Purohit 2012), which was then locally constituted of Khojas, a trading caste that navigated along networks across the Indian Ocean.[7] Since then, Khojas, now largely situated in North America and Europe, have become a predominant faction within Ismaili institutions and have acted as administrators in the community's borderlands in the Pamirs and elsewhere.

Neither depictions of benign and naturalized interactions between Ismailis around the world nor studies of the historical and contemporary power struggles defining contemporary Ismailism have placed much emphasis on the profoundly ambivalent effects that development interventions in the Pamirian borderlands have brought about. Many of the people with whom I spoke in Pakistan and Tajikistan express tremendous affection for and devotion to the Ismaili imam as the representative of the eternal imamate and kinship with other Ismailis around the globe as mediated through him. At the same time, they also frequently express suspicion of Ismaili institutions and their motives as political and economic actors.

This coming together of cosmology, politics, and theological authority ties in with Asad's (2003) and Fassin's (2012) claim that modern secular formations are inherently and genealogically based on principles from religious pasts. From their perspective, secular nation states (Asad) and humanitarianism (Fassin) draw on the legacy of Western Christianity gone global. In contrast, the presence of Ismaili institutions in the Pamirian borderlands considerably complicates the linearity of such a genealogical take: while Ismaili development is clearly positioned against the backdrop of a Shia Muslim past, the power of the Ismaili imamate emerged just as much from the legal infrastructure and political legacy of the British Empire. In the process of global expansion, Ismaili institutions have also engaged with a range of political forms, including socialism. In the following sections, I look at the case of Tajikistan's section of the Pamirian borderlands to argue that the entanglement of these different genealogical strands has had formative effects on the ways Ismaili institutions took root in the region.

Looking for a master

In Tajikistan, the disintegration of the USSR in 1991 marked the beginning of the Tajik civil war, which ravaged the country from 1992 to 1997 (Nourzhanov and Bleuer 2013: 323–335; Epkenhans 2016). In the winter of 1992–1993, the Gorno-Badakhshan region, with about 180,000 inhabitants and several tens of thousands of refugees, was cut off from other parts of Tajikistan (Bliss 2006: 4; Middleton 2016). Facing starvation following the collapse of the Soviet system of provisioning, people became dependent on alternate supply lines from the outside (Keshavjee 1998, 2014). The first and most important actor that entered the region at that stage was the Aga Khan Foundation, which was able to relate to Gorno-Badakhshan on the basis of both common Ismaili ties and its existing development work in northern Pakistan. Reports of the Aga Khan Foundation's early impressions of Gorno-Badakhshan in 1993 show that the experience in northern Pakistan initially informed perceptions of the broader region as "culturally" and "topographically" uniform (Bliss 2006: 312). It therefore seemed possible simply to replicate the Aga Khan Rural Development Programme, which was considered the "most successful" programme of the Aga Khan Foundation. However, it soon became clear that 70 years of Soviet modernization and an even longer history under Russian rule had significantly shaped Gorno-Badakhshan's infrastructure, social organization, and people's expectations regarding living standards and mobility (Bliss 2006: 4; Mostowlansky 2017a, b).

Soviet efforts to secure Gorno-Badakhshan's border with Afghanistan and China from the 1930s onwards were marked by the establishment of distinction. The separation between "socialist" and "capitalist" realms (Shaw 2011) was not meant to be limited to ideology and economy; it also materialized in the form of border infrastructure and general social and infrastructural development (*razvitie, taraqqiyot*). These efforts included the construction of roads, hospitals and schools, the promotion of gender equality, access to privileged provisioning of basic goods, educational opportunities, and mobility within the Soviet Union.[8] In Gorno-Badakhshan, as in similar places in the former Soviet Union, people still refer to this process as "Moscow provisioning" (*Moskovskoe obespechenie*), a semi-official term denoting Soviet attempts to create "centers in the periphery" (Reeves 2014: 114) in strategically selected places all over the Union. Remtilla (2012: 82) calls the resulting relationship between the paternalistic Soviet state and the people of Gorno-Badakhshan an "economy of grace" in which citizens received provisions in excess of anything they could realistically have been expected to repay. In the context of independent Tajikistan, Remtilla observes that this relationship of "grace" has shifted away from a link between the state and its citizens and towards an emerging bond between Ismaili institutions and the people of Gorno-Badakhshan in which the Aga Khan, representing the Ismaili imamate, features as a new "master" (*soheb*).

With the exception of younger children and teenagers, a clear majority of the people I have encountered during my fieldwork in Gorno-Badakhshan since 2008 recall the Aga Khan IV's early messages to and physical appearances in Gorno-Badakhshan as auspicious and memorable events. For instance, his visit to Moscow in January 1995 and a related "pronouncement" (*farman*) to his followers remains a well-remembered occasion. This first visit of the Aga Khan IV to Russia involved encounters with various political actors, including members of the Russian government, as well as a meeting (*mulaqat*) with his followers (*murid*) from the former Soviet Union. The meeting in Moscow's Olympic Stadium was, as the Aga Khan IV announced, "the first time, in centuries, that the Imam has been physically present with his Jamat in Central Asia" (Al Hussaini 2009: 921). He then outlined the importance of "intellect and faith" to cope with the radical changes that the dissolution of the Soviet Union and the end of the Cold War had brought with them:

> [Y]ou and your families are living at a historical time of very, very deep change. You and your children will need to prepare yourselves for this new world of change which is ahead, and you must have the principles on which to use your intellect to prepare for the future. And the first principle is to use your intellect within the parameters of the ethics of the faith. But do not fear using your intellect to prepare yourselves for the future, because the future will be a meritocratic future where individuals, institutions, countries, will find their position in world society according to the competence with which they govern their lives, their institutions, their countries. The second principle that Hazrat Ali emphasized, but which is part of the interpretation of Islam around the world, is the principle of generosity,

of kindness, of caring, of forgiveness, that is, of searching to serve those in need, forgiving those who may have made a mistake or harmed you, because it is that forgiveness which will strengthen you and which will give them respect for your behaviour, and it will encourage them to follow your behaviour.

(Al Hussaini 2009: 921–922)

The Aga Khan IV then asked his *murid*s to convey his message to their families and communities back home, in Tajikistan, and other places in the former Soviet Union. He also repeated central elements of this pronouncement – the virtues of meritocracy, care, and forgiveness – in visits to Tajikistan in the course of 1995 and thereby set a framework for the development interventions that succeeded humanitarian aid after the end of the civil war in 1997. The idea of meritocracy – in other words, the retraining of socialist minds to be able to compete as individuals in order to meet the challenges of a liberal order – was complemented by an interpretation of Islam as based on humanitarian principles, which in Gorno-Badakhshan still takes the form of donations, micro-finance loans, and volunteer work. Finally, the notion of forgiveness that the Aga Khan IV promoted in this early *farman* was a subtle call for reconciliation in the context of the Tajik civil war, during which the people of Gorno-Badakhshan – because of their ethnicity and religious identity – were both victims and perpetrators of violence.

In contrast to Hunza, where state-sponsored development and the emergence of Ismaili institutions coincided temporally, Gorno-Badakhshan provided the Aga Khan Development Network with the legacy of Soviet infrastructure and provisioning. The use of this infrastructure, starting with the delivery of humanitarian aid in Soviet lorries driven by Soviet drivers, left many people with the expectation that Ismaili institutions would simply replace Soviet ones. As Shahriyor, an elderly engineer, told me during a conversation in 2013, he and his family saw the Aga Khan IV as "a kind of president without a country". On that matter, people to this day envisage Ismaili institutions as performing acts of statecraft – such as the provision of energy, healthcare, and infrastructure – that the Soviet state used to deliver and which the Tajik state is incapable of providing (Mostowlansky 2017a). Nevertheless, the principle of meritocracy as promoted by the Aga Khan IV from day one in Gorno-Badakhshan seeks a form of excellence brought about through competition. This entails economic effort and entrepreneurial spirit on the individual and institutional levels. In Gorno-Badakhshan this means that post-Soviet provisioning now comes at a monetary cost: electricity is sold by Pamir Energy, a company founded by the Aga Khan Fund for Economic Development; healthcare is not free; and the construction of infrastructure is supposed to cater to entrepreneurial activities. In addition, and just as in Hunza previously, since the 1990s Ismaili institutions have also continuously worked towards transforming and standardizing religious practices, a move that affects marriage ceremonies, burial rites, and the customary ways of praying in the region (Lashkariev 2016).

Many of my interlocutors in Gorno-Badakhshan have experienced the convergence of humanitarian aid, religious reform, free-market economy, expectations of statecraft, and development encounters as an ambivalent and sometimes painfully transformative process. Conversely, Ismaili institutions have had to face the legacy of the Soviet "economy of grace" (Remtilla 2012) to which they – as I observed on various occasions – have adapted in manifold ways. The distribution of gifts outside the principle of meritocracy did not stop with humanitarian aid during the civil war, but continues to take place today in the form of, for example, raffles for solar panels and free-of-cost disaster-prevention trainings. In this sense, it is not only Tajikistan's part of the Pamirian borderlands that has been continuously shaped by the presence of Ismaili institutions since the end of the Cold War; by virtue of their specific socio-political past, people in Gorno-Badakhshan have just as actively set out to fit these institutions into the Soviet genealogy with which they are familiar.

Conclusion

One of the by now classical assumptions in the field of borderland studies is that a view from the fringes allows for an alternate outlook on centre and periphery. In this regard, Baud and van Schendel (1997: 235) famously called for an examination of "how borderlands have dealt with their states" rather than vice-versa. In this framework, the examination of transnational connections linking borderlands to other parts of the world has become the norm. Yet even if borderlands have come into the focus as centres of gravity and a category in their own right – "marginalized", "connected", and "cosmopolitan" – they often remain defined as borderlands by virtue of their status within a nation state. The convergence of religious networks and development institutions in the Pamirs adds another dimension to this perspective: while the frontier status of the Pamirian borderlands – in colonial, Cold War, and post-Cold War nation state contexts – has been variously noted, Ismaili institutions have also long regarded the area as one of the borderlands that make up the global Ismaili community. Against this backdrop and going beyond a focus on the nation state, this chapter suggests looking more generally at interrelations between borderland populations and territories, on the one hand, and those political entities, institutions and people who lay claim to them on the other.

The Ismaili institutions' ambivalent positioning vis-à-vis statehood, their entanglement with political, economic, theological, and development discourse, and the unclear boundaries of their global outreach are thought-provoking on many levels. In this chapter, I have restricted the discussion to processes of change in the Pamirian borderlands that have come about as a result of the intersection of development work and religious reform. I have argued that the two spheres are intricately interlinked and cater to a discourse in which integration and progress in the worldwide Ismaili community are ends in and of themselves. The universal claims of the Ismaili imamate build the political–theological foundation for this discourse.

Finally, I have emphasized the non-linear genealogy of Ismaili development work in the Pamirian borderlands. In this respect, I have argued that the very foundation of modern Ismailism is shaped by the entanglement of the legacy of the political and legal infrastructure of the British Empire, international development discourse, a continuous reinterpretation of Islamic teachings, and – in the case of Tajikistan – an engagement with socialist statecraft. If Asad (2003) and Fassin (2012) identified the religious pasts of contemporary political formations, Ismaili institutions in the Pamirian borderlands provide us with a complex, alternative genealogical picture: looking at the transformation that these institutions underwent in Tajikistan in the process of adapting to the earlier Soviet "economy of grace", we might speak of a religious present with a socialist genealogy. Through this lens we can observe how the inhabitants of the Pamirian borderlands have – in the past as well as in the present – dealt with those who claimed them as such.

Acknowledgements

I am grateful to the people of the Pamirian borderlands who – through their openness and hospitality – have made possible my research in the region over the past decade.

For critical feedback on earlier versions of the chapter I am indebted to the editors – Alexander Horstmann and Martin Saxer – Brook Bolander, Brian Donahoe, and to the members of the cluster "Religion and Globalisation" at the Asia Research Institute, National University of Singapore. In particular, I would like to express my gratitude to Giuseppe Bolotta for his detailed comments.

Notes

1 Throughout this chapter, I have used pseudonyms to refer to the people of the Pamirian borderlands.
2 For the purposes of this chapter, I use the "Pamir mountains"/"Pamirs" as a generic category. Geographically speaking, the Pamir range does not completely encompass the borderlands of Afghanistan, China, Pakistan, and Tajikistan that are the subject of this chapter. However, there is no single, generally accepted way to describe this area in geographical terms. Other terms, such as "greater Badakhshan" (Beben 2015: 38), have been suggested, but they likewise suffer from geographical imprecision.
3 See, e.g., Haines (2012), Hussain (2015), and Mostowlansky (2017a).
4 On Pir Sabzali see, in particular, Remtilla (2012: 46), Steinberg (2011: 53), and Tajddin Sadik Ali (2001).
5 On the development and effects of today's Ismaili educational networks on students' mobility to schools, training programmes, and universities around the world, see, e.g., Bolander (2016, 2017), and Steinberg (2011).
6 See Khan (2009) and Wood et al. (2006). In addition to these transnationally organized institutions, there are also local NGOs that interact with, but are only loosely connected to, the larger network (Beg 2009, 2010). These local NGOs often focus on individual settlements, valleys, or ethnic communities in northern Pakistan.
7 See, e.g., Akhtar (2014), Green (2011), and Mukherjee (2015).
8 See, e.g., Bliss (2006), Kraudzun (2016), Mostowlansky (2017a), and Remtilla (2012).

References

AKDN. 2017. "Frequently Asked Questions." www.akdn.org/about-us/frequently-asked-questions (last visited 10 March 2017).
Akhtar, Iqbal S. 2014. "Religious Citizenship: The Case of the Globalised Khojas." *African Sociological Review* 18(1), 27–48.
Al Hussaini, Noor Mawlana Shah Karim. 2009. *Kalam-e Imam-e Zaman: Farmans 1957–2009, Golden Edition*. Canada.
Asad, Talal. 2003. *Formations of the Secular: Christianity, Islam, Modernity*. Stanford: Stanford University Press.
Baud, Michiel & Willem van Schendel. 1997. "Towards a Comparative History of Borderlands." *Journal of World History* 8(2), 211–242.
Beben, Daniel. 2015. "The Legendary Biographies of Nasir-i Khusraw: Memory and Texualization in Early Modern Persian Isma'ilism." PhD dissertation, Indiana University.
Beg, Fazal Amin. 2009. "Societal Development & Change in the Hunza Valley: A Study of Ghulkin, Part 1." *Karakoram Knowledge Highways* 1(4), 47–63.
Beg, Fazal Amin. 2010. "Societal Development & Change in the Hunza Valley: A Study of Ghulkin, Part 2." *Karakoram Knowledge Highways*, 1, 29–46.
Benthall, Jonathan. 2016. "Puripetal Forces in the Charitable Field." *Asian Ethnology* 75(1), 29–51.
Benz, Andreas. 2013. "Education and Development in the Karakorum: Educational Expansion and Its Impact in Gilgit-Baltistan, Pakistan." *Erdkunde* 67(2), 123–136.
Bliss, Frank. 2006. *Social and Economic Change in the Pamirs (Gorno-Badakhshan, Tajikistan)*. London and New York: Routledge.
Bolander, Brook. 2016. "English and the Transnational Ismaili Muslim Community: Identity, the Aga Khan and Infrastructure." *Language and Society* 45, 583–604.
Bolander, Brook. 2017. "English, Motility and Ismaili Transnationalism." *International Journal of the Sociology of Language* 247, 77–88.
Bolotta, Giuseppe. Forthcoming. "'Development Missionaries' in the Slums of Bangkok: From the Thaification to the De-Thaification of Catholicism." In: Catherine Scheer, Philip Fountain and Michael Feener (eds.). *The Mission of Development: Techno-Politics of Religion in Asia*. Leiden: Brill.
Callahan, Edward M. Jr. 2013. "To Rule the Roof of the World: Power and Patronage in Afghan Kyrgyz Society". PhD dissertation, Boston University.
Daftary, Farhad. 2007. *The Isma'ilis: Their History and Doctrines*. Cambridge: Cambridge University Press.
Daftary, Farhad (ed.). 2011. *A Modern History of the Ismailis: Continuity and Change in a Muslim Community*. London: Tauris.
Devji, Faisal. 2009. "Preface." In: Marc van Grondelle. *The Ismailis in the Colonial Era: Modernity, Empire and Islam*. London: Hurst & Company, ix–xvi.

Epkenhans, Tim. 2016. *The Origins of the Civil War in Tajikistan: Nationalism, Islamism, and Violent Conflict in Post-Soviet Space*. Lanham: Rowman & Littlefield.

Fassin, Didier. 2012. *Humanitarian Reason: A Moral History of the Present*. Berkeley: University of California Press.

Fountain, Philip. 2013. "The Myth of Religious NGOs: Development Studies and the Return of Religion." *International Development Policy* 4, 9–30.

Green, Nile. 2011. *Bombay Islam: The Religious Economy of the Western Indian Ocean, 1840–1915*. Cambridge: Cambridge University Press.

Haines, Chad. 2012. *Nation, Territory, and Globalization in Pakistan: Traversing the Margins*. London and New York: Routledge.

Hunzai, Faquir Muhammad. 2004. "A Living Branch of Islam: Ismailis of the Mountains of Hunza." *Oriente Moderno* 84, 147–160.

Hussain, Shafqat. 2015. *Remoteness and Modernity: Transformation and Continuity in Northern Pakistan*. New Haven: Yale University Press.

Keshavjee, Salmaan. 1998. "Medicines and Transitions: The Political Economy of Health and Social Change in Post-Soviet Badakhshan, Tajikistan." PhD dissertation, Harvard University.

Keshavjee, Salmaan. 2014. *Blind Spot: How Neoliberalism Infiltrated Global Health*. Oakland: University of California Press.

Khan, Shoaib Sultan. 2009. *The Agha Khan Rural Support Programme: A Journey Through Grassroots Development*. Oxford: Oxford University Press.

Kraudzun, Tobias. 2016. "External Support and Local Agency: Uncertain Transformations of Livelihoods in the Pamirian Borderland of Tajikistan." In: Hermann Kreutzmann and Teiji Watanabe (eds.). *Mapping Transition in the Pamirs: Changing Human-Environmental Landscapes*. Springer: Dordrecht, 159–179.

Kreutzmann, Hermann. 1989. *Hunza: Ländliche Entwicklung im Karakorum*. Berlin: Dietrich Reimer Verlag.

Kreutzmann, Hermann. 1996. *Ethnizität im Entwicklungsprozess: Die Wakhi in Hochasien*. Berlin: Dietrich Reimer Verlag.

Kreutzmann, Hermann. 2009. "The Karakoram Highway as a Prime Exchange Corridor Between Pakistan and China." In: Hermann Kreutzmann, Ghulam Amin Beg, Lu Zhaohui and Jürgen Richter (eds). *Proceedings of the Regional Workshop Integrated Tourism Concepts to Contribute to Sustainable Development in Mountain Regions Gilgit/Pakistan – Kashgar/P.R. China, 8–14 October, 2008*. InWEnt: Bonn, 13–36.

Kreutzmann, Hermann. 2015. *Pamirian Crossroads: Kirgiz and Wakhi of High Asia*. Wiesbaden: Harrassowitz.

Lashkariev, Amrisho. 2016. *The Construction of Boundaries and Identity through Ritual Performance by a Small Ismaili Community of Gorno-Badakhshan*. Bonn: Politischer Arbeitskreis Schulen e.V.

Maertens, Carolin. 2017. "'No Debt, No Business': The Personalisation of Market Exchange in Gorno-Badakhshan, Tajikistan." In: Roland Hardenberg (ed.). *Approaching Ritual Economy: Socio-Cosmic Fields in Globalized Contexts*. Tübingen: RessourcenKulturen, 159–192.

Middleton, Robert. 2016. "History of the Development of the Pamir Region of Tajikistan (Gorno-Badakhshan." In: Hermann Kreutzmann and Teiji Watanabe (eds.). *Mapping Transition in the Pamirs: Changing Human-Environmental Landscapes*. Dordrecht: Springer, 245–265.

Mostowlansky, Till. 2016. "Humanitarianism Across Mountain Valleys: 'Shia Aid' and Development Encounters in Northern Pakistan and Eastern Tajikistan." In: Hermann Kreutzmann and Teiji Watanabe (eds.). *Mapping Transition in the Pamirs: Changing Human-Environmental Landscapes*. Dordrecht: Springer, 229–244.

Mostowlansky, Till. 2017a. *Azan on the Moon: Entangling Modernity along Tajikistan's Pamir Highway*. Pittsburgh: Pittsburgh University Press.

Mostowlansky, Till. 2017b. "Building Bridges across the Oxus: Language, Development and Globalization at the Tajik-Afghan Frontier." *International Journal of the Sociology of Language* 247, 49–70.

Mukherjee, Soumen. 2015. "Universalising Aspirations: Community and Social Service in the Isma'ili Imagination in Twentieth-century South Asia and East Africa." In: Justin Jones and Ali Usman Qasmi (ed.). *The Shi'a in Modern South Asia: Religion, History and Politics*. Delhi: Cambridge University Press, 105–130.

Nourzhanov, Kirill and Christian Bleuer. 2013. *Tajikistan: A Social and Political History*. Canberra: ANU E Press.

Purohit, Teena. 2012. *The Aga Khan Case: Religion and Identity in Colonial India*. Cambridge, MA and London: Harvard University Press.

Reeves, Madeleine. 2014. *Border Work: Spatial Lives of the State in Rural Central Asia*. Ithaca, NY: Cornell University Press.

Remtilla, Aliaa. 2012. "Re-Producing Social Relations: Political and Economic Change and Islam in Post-Soviet Tajik Ishkashim." PhD dissertation, University of Manchester.

Ruthven, Malise. 2011. "The Aga Khan Development Network and Institutions." In: Farhad Daftary (ed.). *A Modern History of the Ismailis: Continuity and Change in a Muslim Community*. London: Tauris, 189–220.

Shaw, Charles. 2011. "Friendship Under Lock and Key: The Soviet Central Asian Border, 1918–34." *Central Asian Survey* 30(3–4), 331–348.

Steinberg, Jonah. 2011. *Isma'ili Modern: Globalization and Identity in a Muslim Community*. Chapel Hill: North Carolina Press.

Tajddin Sadik Ali, Mumtaz Ali. 2001. "Voyage of Pir Sabzali in Central Asia." *Ismaili.net*. Accessed 10 March 2017, www.ismaili.net/heritage/node/1627

Wood, Geoff, Abdul Malik and Samina Sagheer (eds). 2006. *Valleys in Transition: Twenty Years of AKRSP's Experience in Northern Pakistan*. Oxford: Oxford University Press.

Part 7
Militarization of borderlands

Introduction

Swargajyoti Gohain

Sovereignty, control, and militarization

We live in a world of military metaphors. Military images, symbols, and technologies have invaded all aspects of public life and consumption practices. War-time terminology such as "collateral damage" and "engage the enemy" have entered popular jargon (Van Dongen 2015).[1] Security technologies such as surveillance cameras and metal detectors are now used by prisons as well as schools, shopping malls, and the tourist industry. Popular culture plays on military-themed entertainment and patriotic images (Weaver 2011: 684; Schepher-Hughes 2014: 645).

With the increasing normalization of military presence in our lives, we often tend to overlook the close functional links between militarization, sovereignty, and state control, and especially the effects on those who experience it most intimately. This part focuses on these questions by looking at militarization in spaces where state power is tenuous and, hence, enforced even more directly and forcefully. Most of the chapters in this part are empirical studies of militarized borderlands and conflict zones, and all of them, in a way, speak about the everydayness of militarization, and the routine encounters that shape or blur relations between civilian and military practices and populations.

Militarization of everyday life

Conventionally, militarization is assumed to be a natural process of securitization, somehow independent of political interest. That is, militarization is perceived to be a natural consequence for societies at war, whether internal or external. However, to recapitulate Michel Foucault's (1982, 2007) argument: sovereignty, discipline, and security are different economies of power that are exercised over different types of spaces with the intent of maximizing efficient state control. That is why militarization can exist even when there are no external or internal security threats.

For militarization is more than the aggregation of military forces in a territory. It is simultaneously a discursive process, involving a shift in general societal beliefs and values in ways necessary to legitimate the use of force and the organization of large standing armies. It has powerful spatial and ideological effects, changing the visual landscape, the language and social norms, and the local and global economy.[2]

In the context of neoliberalization, the role and scope of the military have become more ubiquitous. Michael Schwartz (2011) draws a connection between neoliberal policies of free trade, privatization, and deregulation on the one hand, and humanitarian crisis and military intervention on the other. Peace-building and peace-keeping were originally humanitarian interventions in violent zones, where United Nations (UN) military personnel would insert themselves between warring parties in an attempt to create a neutral territory. The end of the Cold War brought about a shift by heralding an era of new forms of military intervention. US militarization was justified in the post-Cold War period by moving the military into areas once considered civilian functions (Lutz 2002; Schwartz 2011). By expanding the frontiers of military intervention and deploying military troops in evacuation operations, disaster relief, famine relief, and other such activities, the military and its industries were saved from decimation. In the 1990s, after the fall of Soviet Union, in yet another shift, the UN sanctioned military intervention as a form of humanitarian intervention by codifying it as "Responsibility to Protect", that is, when sovereign states are unable to bear the responsibility of protecting their own citizens, it must be borne by the larger community of states, leading to new forms of military interventions nationally and globally.

Tisaranee Gunasekara (2014) shows how similar militarization in Sri Lanka today is aided through the "humanitarian" discourse. Following the military ouster of the rebel outfit, the Liberation Tigers of Tamil Eelam (LTTE), from their stronghold in Northeast Sri Lanka in 2009, the then president Mahinda Rajapaksa increased military presence in these areas. While during the period of internecine war, the image of the Sri Lankan military as a good, efficient, and law-abiding entity was necessary to sustain the myth of a "humanitarian" operation with "zero civilian casualties", after the war this image was maintained to justify the continued militarization of society. Sri Lanka was turned into a garrison state in order to serve the interests of a national government, despite the absence of an external or internal enemy.

In the same vein, Duschinski (2009) in her work on Kashmir argues how with the spread of neoliberal economics, national security states are increasingly using linked strategies of militarization and penalization to exercise control over populations. She ties militarization to social exclusion, whereby certain communities living in cultural or geographical border zones are represented as marginal, dangerous, worthless, and are subjected to military control. The discourse of militarization serves to mask the real suffering of particular communities at the receiving end of state-sanctioned violence in the name of national security. The Armed Forces (Special Powers) Act or AFSPA, a controversial act, originally introduced in 1958 in India's Northeast region, and later extended to other areas of India defined as "disturbed areas", most notably in Jammu and Kashmir through the AFSPA of 1990, grants the armed forces extraordinary powers, including the power to arrest, enter property without a warrant, and shoot to kill any person thought to be acting against the law.[3] This has enabled routine violence by military and paramilitary forces in everyday "encounters" – a euphemistic term used to define extrajudicial killings – with people suspected of harbouring antinational intentions. Militarization of everyday life in countries accustomed to war is further perpetuated by a "continuum of violence" in which the tactics of war and war crimes gradually seep into quotidian life. Metaphors such as war on crime and war on drugs attest to the routinization of military action in everyday life (Schepher-Hughes 2014: 641).

The nation state project

It is clear that the military has to be seen as an appendage of the state and an apparatus of rule, and not an extension of a disinterested executive. The project of the nation state is to shape territorial subjectivities in conformity with the national geography, and the military, as an agent of the state, is directly involved in the process of constituting national subjects.

According to John Torpey, "Modern states and the international state system of which they are a part have expropriated from individuals and private entities 'the legitimate means of movement' particularly though by no means exclusively across national boundaries" (Torpey 2000: 4). Border crossing reinforces our social and political status through a documentary regime consisting of passports, visas, and so on and border-crossing rituals such as the performance of going through security checks and other spaces of border control. Border rituals reproduce the meaning of the state system, while those who transgress rituals are exposed to death, detention, or deportation (Khosravi 2007).

Two of the chapters in this part deal with how the act of crossing the border itself serves to reinforce the border. Pradeep Jeganathan shows how the checkpoint, in which the encounter with the military takes the form of a border-crossing ritual, has penetrated into everyday spaces in contemporary Sri Lanka. As he expressively argues, the checkpoint is necessary for the interrogation of biopolitical identity, but by the same token, it can produce vulnerability, as the body becomes a mobile border. In this sense, some borders are no longer situated at the borders at all in geographical or political senses; undesirable persons are not expelled by the border, they are forced to *be border*.

In some cases, people seek to defy/cross the border for economic and commercial gain, often through the complicity of border guards (Van Schendel 2005). Rano Turaeva's chapter affords a glimpse into how this works in practice by showing that state management of population movement creates grey zones and shady effects as both customs officials and border crossers seek to manipulate the rituals of crossing to their best advantage. Through a fascinating autoethnography, Turaeva shows how there is a border regime with rules of crossing, but there is also a regime of uncertainty generated both by the distance and unfamiliarity of the location for border crossers and the deliberate creation of disorder by border personnel; eventually however, both those in power and those without power take advantage of the disorder to undo the rigidity of the border order.

Adam Cathcart's chapter on different forms of evasion in the Chinese–North Korean border shows up the border as a site of transgression as well as creation. Border security forces who jump the border from the North Korean to the Chinese side defy the restriction, while other border crossers creatively remake their identities through the act of crossing, eventually revealing hybrid identities. Cathcart shows us through empirical studies of a border that is commonly inaccessible for anthropological study – not least because there is a dearth of information (made) available on it – how evasion is a strategy used by both state actors and border crossers.

The other two chapters in this part look at strategies of adaptation of people in militarized borderlands, and how they can range from the poetic to the practical to the political. In militarized borderlands, military settlements and technologies of surveillance, such as border fences and security cameras, materially reorder space as well as reify the border in people's minds and lives through psychosociological processes. Swargajyoti Gohain's chapter looks at the politics of the Monpas, a Tibetan Buddhist ethnic minority in Northeast India, who occupy a border region that is disputed between India and China. Previously subjects of the Tibetan state, the Monpas have to balance their transnational allegiances with their present political existence within India.

Masaya Shishikura's chapter shows how on the military island base of Ogasawara, people creatively defy the statist appropriation of the border and injunctions on cross-border settlement by fusing musical practices divided by history and territory. Hybridity is not metaphorical, but a lived experience here.

Notes

1 Collateral damage means to kill or wound innocent people and destroy their property; engage the enemy means to kill suspected terrorists.
2 See: http://tinyurl.com/afgj-intro.
3 In April 2015, the Indian government extended the AFSPA to Arunachal Pradesh (Northeast India) citing political unrest in the eastern parts of the state. This has been opposed by several sections of the public and political leaders who protested the unilateral imposition of the act in a region which is relatively peaceful. This action on the part of the Indian government is increasingly seen as an attempt to better monitor a border region that is also claimed by China. "India extends AFSPA in Arunachal Pradesh", *Reuters*, 8 April 2015: http://tinyurl.com/arunachal-afspa; see also "Arunachal complains that it was not even consulted on AFSPA notification", *Scroll.in*, 11 April 2015: http://tinyurl.com/arunachal-complains – both accessed 11 April 2015.

References

Duschinski, Haley. 2009. "Destiny Effects: Militarization, State Power, and Punitive Containment in Kashmir Valley", *Anthropological Quarterly* 82 (3): 691–717.
Foucault, M. 1982. "Subject and Power", *Critical Inquiry* 8 (4): 777–795.
Foucault, M. 2007. *Security, Territory, Population*, Basingstoke: Palgrave Macmillan.
Gunasekara, T. 2014. "A Garrison State", *Himal SouthAsian*, 13 October 2014.
Khosravi, Shahram. 2007. "The Illegal Traveller: An 'Auto-ethnography' of Borders", *Social Anthropology* 15 (3): 321–334.
Lutz, C. 2002. "Making War at Home in the United States: Militarization and the Current Crisis", *American Anthropologist* 104 (3): 723–735.
Schepher-Hughes, Nancy. 2014. "The Militarization and Madness of Everyday Life", *South Atlantic Quarterly* 113 (3): 640–655.
Schwartz, Michael. 2011. "Military Neoliberalism: Endless War and Humanitarian Crisis in the Twenty-First Century", *Societies without Borders* 6 (3): 190–303.
Torpey, John. 2000. *Invention of the Passport: Surveillance, Citizenship and the State*, Cambridge: Cambridge University Press.
Van Dongen, Teun. 2015. "Drone Strikes and the Sanitisation of Violence", *Foreign Policy in Focus*, 12 February, available at: http://fpif.org/drone-strikes-sanitization-violence/. Accessed October 2016.
Van Schendel, Willem. 2005. *The Bengal Borderland*, London: Anthem.
Weaver, Adam. 2011. "Tourism and the Military: Pleasure and the War Economy", *Annals of Tourism Research* 38 (2): 672–689.

31
Border, checkpoint, bodies[1]

Pradeep Jeganathan

Introduction

The argument of this chapter is that a "checkpoint" is a particular axis of a militarized border that deserves attention and elaboration. By a checkpoint – to attempt an initial definition which I will expand on later – I mean the now ubiquitous governmental or para/shadow governmental apparatus[2] that blocks passage between two points, while imposing criteria – often the checking of "identity" through the examination of documents and bodies – for passage through the checkpoint (Jeganathan 2004; cf. Kelly 2006). While my ethnographic material is drawn from Sri Lanka, I suggest that the general claims of this chapter exceed their ethnological location.

I begin by elaborating the sense in which the terms "militarization" and "border" are related to my conception of the "checkpoint." Militarization, I argue, indexes or points to the presence or possibility of violence in a given space or location. Checkpoints, on the other hand, are nodes that mediate between two imaginative modes of the presence of violence in a space or location: recollection and anticipation. Recollection moves back in time, remaking past time as present, which, in turn, may catalyze anticipation that imagines future time.

It follows that a checkpoint is always adjacent to a putative target, for maps of putative targets are a product of both recollection and anticipation. The idea of the target is the *raison d'être* of the apparatus of the checkpoint: the check is proposed to make the target safe or safer for non-perpetrators, and dangerous for perpetrators. Reported targets are identified, as I suggest, through the crosshatch of the modes of recollection and anticipation of violence. For example, if an airport has been attacked by militants in the past, in either one location or another, airports in other locations, even those that have never been attacked, may have adjacent checkpoints. Indeed, we find this is the case across the globe. It is important to note that since my conceptualization of "violence" may be both recalled and anticipated, it takes on an imaginative quality; it is latent, not always materialized.

A checkpoint, in the sense in which I define it, is one manifestation of a "border." A border produces a particularly inflected unity of that which may be otherwise separate, and separates that which may be unified. I take this co-constitution of unity and separation of the border to be the great insight of Simmel's (1994) classic account of distinctions between the road, the bridge, and the door. In each case, unity and separation are co-constituted by differently inflected borders; in one sense a checkpoint may be thought of as a door in Simmel's sense, but as we will see later, the checkpoint may itself, become mobile.

To elaborate on this understanding of the "checkpoint" we have to move to its operation. A checkpoint is constitutive of a particular logic of the border; the interrogation of biopolitical identity (Foucault 2008).[3] The question, "who are you?" is usually answered with recourse to the materiality of papers certifying identity, such as photo encoded cards or passports, which in turn depend upon a biopolitical availability of the person to the apparatus. This kind of documentary regime commanded by the checkpoint depends on a reading of the body in question – photographs, fingerprints, retina scans, and the final authenticity of the interrogation of the checkpoint rests upon the biopolitical body. Usually, as I have described elsewhere (Jeganathan 2004), identification is requested, examined, and perhaps a short conversation is had. For someone not carrying a bag or dressed in a single garment, there is hardly anything else to check, and indeed, both checker and checked remain uncertain as to the point of it all. If the check is successful from the point of view of a checkpoint, the body is allowed through, creating a unifying flow. If the checked body is apprehended as dangerous, then it is not allowed passage. The dual processes of unity and separation are thus realized in the checkpoint.

The second point to note is the foreshortening of the spatio-temporal distance between targets, checkpoints, and mobile bodies. We see this if we return to our airport example. Given that airport checkpoints are somewhat effective, or are seen as such, there is a foreshortening of the spatio-temporal space between checkpoint and target; airport checkpoints themselves become targets. Clear examples would be the Brussels and Istanbul airport attacks in 2016. When a checkpoint becomes a target, it can no longer check effectively; what must be checked becomes the mobile body, before it reaches the checkpoint. The border itself then permeates outwards, through the logic of the failing checkpoint, and the body becomes a mobile border.

The rest of this chapter will present Sri Lankan ethnological material, in an ethnographic modality, to elaborate on and deepen these general claims.

Ethno-historical framework

Let me provide some historical and ethnological detail as an explanatory lead. Between 1983 and 2009, Sri Lanka was gripped by a civil war between elected Sinhala majority regimes of differing political hues, from right-wing to center-left, and Tamil militant groups, which after an initial period of multiplicity coalesced into one group, the Liberation Tigers of Tamil Eelam (LTTE). The contours of this long period of violence are far too complex to be entered into here (see Hoole and Thiranagama 2001, for a narrative account), but for the purposes of my argument, it is important to understand the following:

1. Sinhala and Tamil are both distinct languages, and ethnic groups. However, apart from signs that mark the social skin, such as adornments, ornaments, and garments, there is no secure way to tell a Sinhala apart from a Tamil through commonsensical phenotypical distinctions.
2. The northern and eastern provinces of the island are largely populated by Tamils, as are some districts of the central hills. Before the onset of the civil war, many Tamils were attacked by groups of Sinhala men in civilian-directed riots and pogroms, leading to an increased concentration of Tamil populations in the north. However, as the war intensified, civilian Tamil populations began to travel south for shelter from the fighting, and to attempt to migrate overseas. So by the mid-1990s, Colombo, the capital city, once again had large Tamil population pockets residing among the Sinhala.
3. "Set-piece" battles that involved infantry, engineers, snipers, and artillery directed against Tamils, laid the grounds for, but did not exhaust the terrain of the long, drawn out civil war.[4]

From 1985 onwards, the LTTE, in response to Sri Lankan Army attacks on Tamil civilians, retaliated with wide-spread massacre of Sinhala civilians. In 1987, the LTTE also began suicide bombings, directed at military targets, state institutions, and prominent political figures, perhaps pioneering and perfecting the deadly art.

By 1996, the LTTE had carried out 24 attacks, succeeding in assassinating both the former Indian Prime Minister Rajiv Gandhi and the sitting President of Sri Lanka Ranasinghe Premadasa, among other political figures, destroyed the towering office of the Central Bank of Sri Lanka, and a major military complex, the Joint Operations Command.[5]

The checkpoint: arrestability

On July 4th, 1996, a bomb detonated on Stanley Road, Jaffna in Northern Sri Lanka, just as a minister of the then government was to inaugurate a new building. At that time, Jaffna, a large, distributed semi-urban Tamil majority settlement of about 700,000 people in the northern peninsula of Sri Lanka, was under the control of the Sri Lankan Army which had wrested it from the LTTE the previous year. Yet, as the bombing itself demonstrated, Jaffna was by no means "secure" in military parlance.

While there were many checkpoints, both mobile and stationary, surrounding the gathering in which the minister was present, the human bomber, a young woman, managed to get close enough to explode the device. While the minister was not hurt, the army commander of Jaffna, a high ranking army officer, was killed, as were many others. In the aftermath of the bombing, checkpoints, ubiquitous in Jaffna, intensified in operation, becoming in some instances sites of violent reprisal as well. In the ethnographic vignette that follows, I turn to an extremely distressing and brutal instance of such reprisals, illuminating the operation of the checkpoint from the vantage point of the soldiers that staff it.

To do so, I must underline that the checkpoint has an enormous range. In times of war, strange to say, the spatio-temporal logic of recollection and anticipation can wax and wane. In the Tamil-populated north, the intensity of checkpoints, always high, pulsated in relation to this logic of anticipation. Although never normal, passing through a checkpoint can become ordinary, part of the everyday that one learns to live with given the ever present possibility of violence. In the wake of the Stanley Road Bomb incident of 1996, the checkpoint became "vigilant" and the force of the "check" intensified. During this time, the Sri Lankan Army in Jaffna began to use checkpoints as zones of extrajudicial arrest and subsequent execution following a logic that purported to see "enemies" of the state everywhere.

On September 7th, 1996, Krishanti Kumaraswamy, an 18-year-old school girl, was stopped at the Chemmani checkpoint – where the ostensible target was the adjacent army camp, a few kilometers east of Jaffna town. She had been cycling back home after finishing one of her school leaving exams and then attending the wake of a friend killed in a vehicular collision a few days earlier. By all accounts, she was a model student and not connected in any way to the LTTE, who were active, albeit underground, in the area. Furthermore, as a resident and not a stranger she would have crossed this checkpoint regularly, perhaps daily, to and from school. It is evident that she would have been recognized by the soldiers as a resident, as she must have been on previous days. Yet, on this day, she was stopped, detained in an underground bunker adjacent to the checkpoint for many hours, repeatedly raped by a number of military personnel, and then killed. Her mother, brother and neighbors who came in search of her, were also subsequently killed.

In an exception where the tattered rule of law appeared momentarily in this conflict, there was a high profile investigation, subsequent arrests, and a trial in a civil court, leading to convictions.[6]

As such, a fair amount of evidence is available, which, even though not answering every question, suggests that a low-ranking, commissioned officer, senior to the men at the checkpoint, may have ordered her detention and execution, since she was a witness to the vehicular collision in which her classmate had died, and in which the army had been involved. While the will to rape may have motivated some of the soldiers concerned, one cannot be certain that this was the reason for Krishanti's detention on that particular day. If indeed we allow some credence to the idea that the motive was one of silencing testimony, the most absorbing observation for me was the imbrication of the checkpoint with illegal detention. Certainly, in Sri Lanka's civil wars, it has not been unusual for military personnel to arrive at someone's doorstep to execute an illegal arrest. Even though such an option existed, it seems that the checkpoint suggested itself more plainly to the lower-level army personnel concerned, as a "natural" or better put, "legitimate" site of arrest than a doorstep, which would lead to less scrutiny. One must pause to wonder why this would be the case, and I suggest that the answer may lie in the availability of the biopolitical body for checking and interrogation that makes it always already arrestable at a checkpoint.

The checkpoint as target

I now move forward a decade to consider the checkpoint in relation to the suicide bomber.

In November 2007, a bomb exploded in the office of a Sri Lankan cabinet minister in Colombo. The minister in question, Douglas Devananda, was a complex sign in the ongoing civil war. He had been a leading figure of Tamil militancy two decades earlier, but then led a breakaway faction, which joined several coalitions of ruling Sinhala majority regimes. He was thus perceived as a bad example; a Tamil traitor and a target of many assassination attempts by the LTTE. In this particular attempt, what drew attention, apart from the death and destruction that followed, is the position of the bomb in relation to the female suicide bomber's body, and her overall location in relation to her target.

The bomber had arrived on the minister's "meet-the-public" day, which in this context was an uneasy confluence that made for public vulnerability. The minister was located in an office, in the interior of the building. Members of the public who wished to see him first showed identity documents at an outside window, went through a preliminary check by guards, then sat down with one of his aides to clarify the reason for their visit, and then, finally, reached the doors of the inner office, where they were body checked. Note of course, the intersection of the checked body and documents here – as pointed out earlier. In this kind of situation, common in Sri Lanka during the war, an entire building becomes a checkpoint, or a border if you like, between, in this case – constituent and legislator, or in the register of violence, bomber and target. But in this case, any kind of ethnic profiling becomes moot, for the target – Devananda and most of his constituent visitors, were Tamil. It was only after meeting the aide – and my understanding of this event is drawn from both field work, and CCTV footage – but before the full body check, that the bomber exploded her device, which seemed to have been strapped to her chest. Several people in the office were killed, but not the intended target. Government and media observers began to call the perpetrator, the "bra bomber" (Gunesekere 2007), in an attempt, no doubt, to delineate and inscribe the boundary between public service and danger, life and death, on a private place in the female body (cf. Singh 2008: 383; Rajan 2011: 102).

The attempted assassination of an army commander in May 2006 had many similar features. Again, the perpetrator was female and gave the appearance of being pregnant. Even final reports do not offer clarity on her condition, but some evidence indicates that she was indeed pregnant, even though the explosive device itself was concealed as part of the distention of her belly. The attack took place inside the Army Headquarters, a complex of buildings in the heart of the city, which as we may imagine was well bounded by a complicated series of overlapping checkpoints. But in a holdover from another era, the headquarters complex also included within its bounds a hospital for the treatment of wounded "war heroes" and/or their kin. In a carefully planned operation that spanned months, the LTTE introduced a woman cadre, who spoke enough Sinhala to pass as one, into the line of regular maternity patients, and she established her *bona fides* by undergoing body checks. After some months when she became a known "friend" of the personnel at the checkpoint, she arrived for her appointment with a strapped explosive prosthetic, and then, with the help of others who provided temporal information for synchronicity via a mobile phone, exploded herself against the side of the official car of the commander, which was taking him home for lunch inside the Army Headquarters. Many died; he survived, but required complicated surgery.

Here again, we see the body as a sort of boundary between safety and danger, life and death. We also see a hidden, private place of the body as being the purported site of a bomb that explodes on the target. These are both ethnographic examples of the increasing proximity of the checkpoint and target, the efficacy of the checkpoint being undone, as it becomes a target. In both cases, the body explodes before it is fully checked, because the body cannot be fully checked owing to the placement of the bomb in a private place in the body, or because in the explosion comes before the "check" of the body in the temporal logic of checking. To elaborate, in the case of the Devananda "bra bomber," the private body was to be checked after the documentary record was examined; in the case of Army Headquarters bomb, it seemed that the body was not checked, as the woman's swollen belly passed as "natural."

In these instances, checkpoints, which were effective perhaps in other ways, seem to fail as their effectivity intensifies; the explosion is especially proximate to the checkpoint, which has now become a target. Ominously, if one were to follow the logic of the checkpoint, it will turn out that for "security" to be realized, our bodies must be always already "checked"; checking them at a materialized point does not prevent explosions. I will attempt an elaboration of this point in the next section.

The mobile checkpoint

Sandwiched in time between these two checkpoint bombings was yet another dark episode, which allows me to offer further evidence of a fresh triangulation of targets; checkpoints and bodies.

Given there were more than 15 high-intensity suicide attacks in the capital city between 2006 and 2007, the security apparatus began pre-dawn "cordon-and-search" house-to-house checks. The checks were first carried out in particular Tamil enclaves in the city, sometimes limited to a few lanes or inexpensive hostels patronized by visitors from the north on various bureaucratic errands. Then, given a Supreme Court warning that warrantless searches were illegal, the security administration fell back on an older, colonial law that allowed for searches of entire wards of the city. During such a search, and I experienced several, soldiers would cordon off an area, enter homes asking for identification of all residents, and note down any resident whose address in the identity document did not match his or her current place of abode. Having done this a number of times, security forces, on June 7th, 2007, identified 376 Tamils in the city whose identity documents did not match their current address, and whose reasons for visiting the city for a length of time were deemed implausible (for example, X had been in the city for 30 days to obtain a passport that could be obtained in 24 hours). These persons were detained and then bussed back to the north. The next day, the Supreme Court issued a writ quashing these "deportations" on the grounds that they violated several provisions of fundamental rights in the

Constitution, the government apologized and transported back those who wanted to return to Colombo (Gardner 2007).

While there are a variety of ways we can probe this incident analytically, my aim here is to underline the fresh triangulation between target, checkpoint, and body. In effect, what happens here is the development of the mobile, dispersed checkpoint. As we have seen in the examples in the previous section, in theory, at least, effective checkpoints protect targets, but upon closer examination, we see that effective checkpoints also collapse the distance between checkpoint and target, making checkpoints themselves targets. Paradoxically, this seriously degrades the effectivity of a checkpoint; the perpetrator's body now must be checked before it reaches the checkpoint. Yet there is nothing on the surface of body, its prosthetics, or in its proximity that yields results. The 376 persons detained and deported by the military apparatus were all such instances; for example, if there was evidence of an explosive vest, explosives, triggers or any other such putative weapon, then a straightforward arrest that would have been upheld in the courts could have been made. In other words, the inability of the apparatus of the mobile checkpoint to discern signs of danger on the material body, incites extreme biopolitical apprehension; the "Tamil" body which is "out of place" is seized. Yet, this creates a problem for the logic of liberal government, and such a body's position is subject to law.

This is a fundamental contradiction of the checkpoint, and it is my claim that the Sri Lankan deportations and court orders of 2007 are an exemplar of this. I also claim that this example exceeds the context from which it is derived. Now, it is certainly possible to argue in response that Sri Lanka is a weak democracy that has been unable to separate the essential functions of judiciary, civilian executive authority, and military operations. Indeed, this is the case. But I suggest that the problem exceeds an easy reading of "Third Worlding," for we see similar processes unfolding in states that have much stronger democratic traditions, and have institutionalized the separation of powers in supposedly robust ways.

There is a resemblance between operations in Western Europe and the United States post-9/11 directed at putatively dangerous bodies, read as a biopolitical modality and those of the Sri Lankan Army, even though the conditions of threat and attack in the former are less than that of Colombo between 2006 and 2007. In both, we find the triangulation between target, checkpoint, and body, where the checkpoint is no longer fixed in a material location. To elaborate, it seems clear that given the anticipation of "terror" attacks in the USA and Europe, there is a move to identify "dangerous bodies," before they arrive at checkpoints and targets. The increasing focus on the forestalling of immigration of certain countries to the United States, and the emphasis on the possible deportation of even settled immigrants from European countries are indications of this direction. If we understand the checkpoint to have a material location, for example in an airport, it also becomes clear that material location becomes inadequate to the task; thus checking disperses. The surveillance of bodies begins long before they reach the checkpoint and just like in Sri Lanka, straightforward ethnic profiling begins to be used, before the body reaches the supposed target, leading of course to legal challenges, which only underline the fundamental nature of the contradiction.

The flesh: beyond the checkpoint

The Sri Lankan civil war ended on May 19th, 2009 in the sense that overt fighting came to an end. But absence of explicit violence should not be mistaken for the absence of latent violence, or indeed the cessation of conflict. It is true that 18 months from that date, and continuously after, checkpoints began to disappear. Certainly, there are residual checkpoints, for example at the airport, but even there the intensity of the everyday check has receded. Yet, the body remains available to be checked and reports of arrests at the airport of former LTTE cadres returning to the country continue to surface. Clearly, even as the intensity of the violence has receded, the checkpoint seems to have moved back from the street to the international border. While the international airport is a border, and is also a checkpoint, which apprehends bodies as they move from overseas to Sri Lanka, the border itself seems to have dispersed greatly.

Consider the case of 36-year-old Velauthapillai Renukaruban, a British subject of Sri Lankan Tamil descent who, on returning to Sri Lanka to enter into marriage with his fiancée, found himself arrested, not at the airport but in his familial home in Jaffna. He was subsequently charged with what appears to be an imaginary crime that was dismissed in court. Although he was later allowed to return to Britain, he alleged, with medical evidence, that he was severely tortured after his warrantless and illegal arrest. He did admit, however, that he was involved with LTTE militant activities prior to his immigration to Britain, and one can speculate that he may have been involved in separatist activity at some level in Britain as well.[7] In light of my argument, this case is an exemplar of the body as border. To understand this, we must remember that thousands upon thousands of Sri Lankan Tamils domiciled abroad in Western Europe and North America travel to Sri Lanka and back, usually without hindrance. Yet, in my perception, the arrest and torture of Renukaruban demonstrates the continuing way that bodies remain under surveillance, their very mobility making militarized borders proliferate.

The checkpoint and its logic, I wish to suggest, is more central to the contemporary lived world than might be at once apparent. Its fluid mobility suggests that its dense material manifestation, which once absorbed me, may be receding. Its ubiquitous proliferation suggests that it cannot settle accounts with a body, taken as a biopolitical one. In its effort to turn the body inside out, to apprehend the possibility of violence that putatively lies within it, it seeks to grasp the ungraspable, not the body but what I will tentatively call the "flesh," a vicious density that is unavailable to any apparatus of apprehension.[8] Hence, torture; or put another way, torture seeks the flesh that is invisible to a biopolitical apprehension, which can only make a particular aspect of the body visible.[9]

To understand this point more fully, dwelling on the "checked" body may be helpful. As I have suggested here, and as I have detailed elsewhere, what is "checked" at a materialized checkpoint, or a mobile, dispersed one, is the biopolitical body and its manifested materiality. The body is made available to the checker through a photograph, a set of fingerprints, or retina scans. And its material manifestation: its surface, its prosthetics, its accoutrements, its apparel. Perhaps even its orifices. In its usual logic, what is sought is a correspondence between the "clean," (non-dangerous) manifest material body at the checkpoint, and this biopolitical record, which may be part of a document, which is then indexed in an archival file, that is available at the checkpoint. This aspect of the "check" seems to be inadequate now, to state authorities. If it were adequate, then there would be little point in arresting and torturing Renukaruban after he was allowed to pass through an airport. Similarly, there would be little point of a discussion barring entry of persons from some countries to the USA, or a discussion of deportations of immigrants from European countries in those contexts.

Furthermore, the logic of this dispersed check is not limited to an ethnic profile. It seems increasingly apparent that emails, WhatsApp messages, social media posts, and so on generated by anyone are subject to scrutiny; so much so that there continues to be legal arguments of what kind of privacy is permissible.

The checkpoint, then, is perhaps no longer only at a place like an airport – a materialized international border – and no longer adjacent to the target, but lodged in the flesh itself. This articulation of apparatus and flesh becomes a border, which is as mobile and distributed as the person.

Notes

1 Earlier versions of this chapter were presented at the workshop, "Territories of Social Justice: Violence, Ruptures, and the Mapping of New Spatial Claims," held at the Radcliffe Institute for Advanced Studies, Harvard University in November 2016, and the Warwick-SNU Sociology Global Partnership workshop, "Order and Disorder: Self and Society," held at Shiv Nadar University, in May 2017. I thank Diane Davis and Daniel Hoffman (at Harvard), Sarah Hodges, Mekhala Krishnamurthy, and especially Deepak Mehta (at SNU) for their sustained engagements. In addition, I am grateful to Swargajyoti Gohain for her editorial comments.
2 "by the term apparatus I mean a kind of formation, so to speak, that at a given historical moment, has as its major function the response to an urgency. The apparatus there has a dominant strategic function" Michele Foucault quoted in Gerogio Agamben (2009: 2).
3 In this context, a "biopolitical" identity is one which is secured and read, by a formation of practiced knowledges, which depend upon a scientized body, its surfaces (fingerprints), cavities (retinas), attachments (concealed weapons), and its "recognizable" face (matching a photograph).
4 "Set-piece" battles are military engagements in a choreographed, mechanized theater of war. See Monash (1920 [2014]:226–7), for a classic discussion.
5 For chronological lists of attacks, see the South Asia Terrorism Portal, (SATP) at www.satp.org.
6 For extensive details, see UTHR (1999).
7 See: www.ceylonews.com/2016/04/tid-arrests-another-tamil-man-on-return-from-abroad-video.
8 My notion of the *flesh*, is inspired by Merleau-Ponty and Lefort (1968: 130–55), but I have reversed their terms of perception; it is the formation of practiced knowledge – the apparatus – which (fails) to apprehend (perceive).
9 In the TV Series *Homeland* (Season 1, Showtime, International Cable Television) for example, Carrie Matheson's inability to fully apprehend Nicholas Brody, through say a biopolitical apparatus such as a lie detector, leads to the possibilities of torture and/or erotic love, that both seek to reach the invisible flesh.

References

Agamben, Giorgio. *"What is An Apparatus?" And Other Essays*. (Stanford: Stanford University Press, 2009.)
Foucault, Michel. *The Birth of Bio Politics: Lectures at the Collège de France, 1978–1979*. (London: Palgrave Macmillan, 2008.)
Gardner, Simon. "Sri Lanka court blocks state deportation of Tamils" Reuters News Port, June 8th, 2007. Available at: www.reuters.com/article/us-srilanka-idUSSP4209420070608. Accessed 2/24/2017.
Gunesekere, Mel. "Tamil bra bomber targets Sri Lanka minister: military" (AFP News Report, 2007). Available at: http://ftp.lankabusinessonline.com/news/sri-lankan-tamil-tiger-bra-bomber-targets-minister/923407657. Accessed 2/24/2017.
Hoole, Rajan, and Rajani Thiranagama. *Sri Lanka: The Arrogance of Power: Myths, Decadence & Murder*. (Colombo: University Teachers for Human Rights (Jaffna), 2001.)
Jeganathan, Pradeep. "Checkpoint: anthropology, identity, and the state." *Anthropology in the Margins of the State*, Veena Das & Deborah Poole (eds) (Santa Fe: School of American Research, 2004): 67–80.
Kelly, Tobias. "Documented lives: fear and the uncertainties of law during the second Palestinian intifada." *Journal of the Royal Anthropological Institute* 12.1 (2006): 89–107.
Merleau-Ponty, Maurice, and Claude Lefort. *The Visible and the Invisible: Followed by Working Notes*. (Evanston: Northwestern University Press, 1968.)
Monash, Lieutenant-General Sir John. *The Australian Victories in France in 1918* [Illustrated Edition]. (London: Pickle Partners Publishing, [1920] 2014.)
Rajan, VG Julie. *Women Suicide Bombers: Narratives of Violence*. (London: Routledge, 2011.)
Simmel, Georg. "Bridge and door." *Theory, Culture & Society* 11.1 (1994): 5–10.
Singh, Colonel Harjeet. *South Asia Defence and Strategic Year Book*. (New Delhi: Pentagon Press, 2008.)
UTHR (University Teachers for Human Rights, Jaffna). "Gaps in the Krishanthy Kumarasamy case: disappearances & accountability" (Jaffna, 1999). Available at: www.uthr.org/SpecialReports/spreport12.htm. Accessed 2/24/2017.

32

Musical crossings over the militarised borderland

A case study of the Ogasawara Islands

Masaya Shishikura

Imagined boundaries, militarised borderlands

As Benedict Anderson (1991) suggests, national borders are imagined constructs and fundamentally exist on a metaphysical level. National boundaries are often originally dynamic spaces, where multiple crossings and interactions of people occur. Nevertheless, the imagined lines defined by the nation state eventually create tangible boundaries that are secured with a military objective, through fences, walls, lookouts, and security gates. Militarised borders regulate people's crossing and mobility, and further limit our mental horizons with a conceptual veil. However, in this chapter, I propose to recognise the local practices that overcome the manipulation of borderlands. The human spirit's defiance against constraints creates various activities and connections that transcend enclosing boundaries. This chapter explores an alternative way of seeing the borderland through the musical activities of the Ogasawara Islands. At a national level of political discourse, performing arts are often considered insignificant, meaningless, and not worthy of serious attention. However, this chapter shows how music and dance can be a vital medium to reconsider people and society beyond imagined boundaries. It explicates a "view from the islands" that transcends the borderlines framed by nation states.

Here, I refer to the innovative concept, "view from the frontier", proposed by historian Tessa Morris-Suzuki (2000). In her study of *ainu* people, located between Japan and Russia, Morris-Suzuki problematises the conventional historiography based on such conceptions as civilisation or nation. This type of history is often authoritative and exclusive, and eventually marginalises minor and regional memories from its narrative. Morris-Suzuki proposes the "view from the frontier" as a transposed approach to see a place, region, and the nation. The frontier here is not a national border or a line that must be protected by the law, acts, and forces. Rather, the frontier is a spatial designation that preserves its own dynamic locus with living and moving people. Because it is not a definite space enclosed by a line, the frontier expands to many other places and peoples. The view from the frontier allows us to have an alternative vision of the borderlands that are characterised by human movements and interactions.

The Ogasawara Islands have been utilised as a defence line and thus have been a militarised borderland for many years; even today, a major military base of Japan's Self-Defense Forces remains stationed there. From the point of view of the state, it is crucial for the military to secure these islands, which lie on the edge of Japanese territory. However, in the view from the frontier, Ogasawara has never been located at the periphery of one single nation, instead preserving its own expanding locus to other places and peoples. To demonstrate this view from the islands, this chapter utilises music and dance, and illustrates human bonds that transcend national and political boundaries. Ogasawara musical culture represents the plurality of the islands' history and culture that contests singular and exclusive discourses of the nation state. Music and dance emancipate the island people from the confined mentality caused by war, military activities, and state politics. Immigrants from different countries and travelling islanders around the Pacific Ocean have provided a variety of musical genres, which attests to the crossings and transborder networks in this frontier community.

Colonial and militarised history of Ogasawara

Located in the Pacific Ocean to the south of Japan, the Ogasawara Islands (or "Bonin Islands" in English) had a tangled colonial history under different political regimes. These islands were virtually uninhabited, except for some castaways who had accidentally arrived there, until the early 19th century.[1] The first attempt to colonise Ogasawara was made in 1827, when British naval officer Captain Frederick William Beechey directed the warship HMS *Blossom* around the Pacific Ocean near Japan and discovered the islands. Beechey landed on one of the islands for exploration, named it Peel Island (now Chichi Jima), and stuck a copperplate on a tree declaring British annexation of the islands under the name of George IV (Beechey 1831, cited in Tanaka 1997: 28).[2] In 1830, the first planned migration occurred. An American by the name of Nathaniel Savory and four other Westerners, together with some 20 people from Hawai'i,[3] departed O'ahu in May, voyaged around the Pacific Ocean searching the scattered islands, and finally arrived in Chichi Jima of Ogasawara on 26 June (Cholmondeley 1915: 17).[4] Since then, and until today, Savory's descendants have sustained his lineage on the islands. After this first migration, there were some more voluntary migrants from Western countries as well as Micronesia. Amongst these migrants, Maria del los Santos y Castro (commonly known as Maria Dilessanto), from Guam, later became the wife of Nathaniel Savory and is now recognised as "the mother of Ogasawara", to whom almost all Western descendants are related (Long and Inaba 2004: 14). These early settlers retained a small autonomous colony, though they have experienced plots of murder, attacks by pirates, and betrayal among the immigrants in this isolated community (Cholmondeley 1915; Ishihara 2007). In 1853, on his way to Japan, Matthew Calbraith Perry Commodore of the US Navy sailed around Ogasawara, visited and explored Peel Island, appointed Nathaniel Savory as the governor of the island,[5] and later travelled southward, declaring the colonisation of Haha Jima Islands of Ogasawara (Hawks 1856).

Following the British and American trials of occupation, Japanese colonialism extended to the Bonin Islands from the 1860s onward. In 1862, the Tokugawa shogunate first attempted to colonise the islands as Ogasawara of Japan; the shogunate sent an envoy to the island and compelled Nathaniel Savory and other inhabitants to accept its governance. To establish its occupation, the government brought more than 30 migrants to Ogasawara, mostly from neighbouring Hachijō Island, which is still more than 700 km away from Chichi Jima. However, this first scheme by Japan to colonise Ogasawara failed due to the political conflicts with the British Empire: the Namamugi Incident (14 September 1862),[6] and the subsequent Anglo-Satsuma War, known also as the Bombardment of Kagoshima (15–17 August 1863) (Tanaka 1997: 182–208). The shogunate abandoned Ogasawara in 1863 in order to avoid creating unnecessary international hostilities that could be caused by occupying these small islands.

More than a decade later, in 1875, the newly formed Meiji government of Japan again sent an envoy to Ogasawara. The British Consul Russell Robertson soon detected the Japanese plot, followed the Japanese lighthouse tender *Meiji Maru*, but arrived in Ogasawara two days later. During this delay, the Japanese emissary Obana Sakusuke compelled the islanders to sign a written pledge: "We, the Chichi Jima residents, request protection from the Japanese government and observe the law to be effective on this island" (Ministry of Foreign Affairs 1940: 489, cited in Ishihara 2007: 238–39). The envoy also conducted a "recovery" ceremony to mark the return of Ogasawara to the Japanese administration (Tanaka 1997: 245–46). Robertson reports that Nathaniel's widow Maria Dilessanto and other residents, numbering 69 on Chichi Jima and three on Haha Jima, preferred to be recognised as the "Bonin Islanders" rather than belong to any specific nation to which they would owe tax obligations (Robertson 1876: 137–39). Notwithstanding this, the Japanese colonisation scheme of the Ogasawara Islands commenced again from the following year of 1876.

The Meiji government recruited immigrants to this new territory by providing salaries and subsidies for settlement. The majority of early migrants were again from Hachijō Island, yet the compensations for settlement attracted some people from mainland Japan as well. Thereafter, the island population drastically increased from about 30 Japanese settlers in 1877, to 999 inhabitants in 1887, and 4,360 in 1897 (Ishii 1967: 21). Under the Japanese colonisation scheme, the Westerner/Pacific Islander settlers and their descendants were identified as "naturalised people [*kikajin*]" and forced to be *shinmin* (obedient citizens) of Japan. Along with the growth of Japanese imperialism and corresponding international conflicts, the gaze towards the "naturalised people" had shifted to seeing them as strange, suspicious, disloyal, dangerous, and threatening. With their physical appearance and behaviour associated with something "foreign", these people were often called *ijin* (literally "different people", but with the connotation of "aliens"), and identified as hazardous elements. Antagonism between the "naturalised people" and "Japanese migrants" also arose in the days before the Pacific War. Already in 1929, Japanese military police [*kenpei*] began inspecting the "naturalised people" and patrolling the houses of "possible spies" almost every day. Later, the army headquarters of Chichi Jima excluded English from the Ogasawara school curriculum, and restricted the use of this enemy's language [*tekisei go*] (but the native language of many naturalised families) even at home (Shepardson 1977; Ishihara 2007). Such marginalisation and discrimination eventually created a sense of displacement among the Westerner/Pacific Islander residents, and provoked their mass emigration to the island of Guam under American administration; the "naturalised people" of Ogasawara, once numbering more than 120, decreased to 79 in 1913 (Office of the Chief of Naval Operations, Navy Department 1944: 36, cited in Ishihara 2007: 304).

Following the occupation of Ogasawara, the Empire of Japan expanded its territory through several wars and battles such as the first Sino–Japanese War (1894–1895), the Russo-Japanese War (1904–1905), and World War I (1914–1918). The Empire acquired Taiwan after the Treaty of Shimonoseki (1895), South Sakhalin after the Treaty of Portsmouth (1905), and Korea after the Japan–Korea Treaty of Annexation (1910).[7] After the Treaty of Versailles (1919), the Japanese government was also granted a League of Nations Mandate over German territories in Micronesia and constituted the Nanyō Chō (South Seas Bureau) in Koror on Palau (1922).

Japanese aggression in international affairs eventually resulted in the Pacific War (1941–1945), in which different peoples around the frontiers of Japan, including Okinawans, Koreans, Taiwanese, and Micronesians, were implicated and experienced hardship. In the last stage of the war, the Ogasawara Islands were located on the frontline and became a battlefield;[8] all the residents were forced to evacuate to mainland Japan where many of them had almost no affiliations. For those "Japanese settlers", this was the beginning of an exile that lasted for more than 20 years.

When Japanese rule of Ogasawara was terminated with Japan's defeat in the Pacific War, the USA appropriated the islands as a military base and allowed only "Westerner descendants" to reside there. "Former Japanese settlers" were evicted from their homes and became refugees on the mainland, where they often had no relatives or friends, so that they were forced to reside in a temple or school, and lived desperate hand-to-mouth existences (Ishii 1967: 30–2). During this period, opposing Japan's non-nuclear policy, the US Navy deployed nuclear weapons on the islands of Chichi Jima and Iwo Tō (Norris et al. 2000). For national security reasons, the navy segregated Ogasawara and severely restricted the islanders' activities, such as leaving the island without permission and preventing them from communicating with families and friends overseas. For more than 20 years, around 300 island residents (including navy officers and their families) led lives disconnected from the rest of the world.

In 1968, the islands were returned to Japan. American diplomat U. Alexis Johnson utilised the opportunity to secure US bases in Okinawa in return for giving up Ogasawara (Eldridge 2002: 264–68). The reversion of Ogasawara again brought trouble for the "Westerner descendants" who experienced difficulties and discrimination within the newly introduced social system. For instance, the Japanese administration excluded English from all public services and enforced employment contracts and school education in Japanese only. As a result, about 30 per cent of "Westerner descendants" discarded Japanese citizenship and left their home of Ogasawara within two years (Ishihara 2007: 413–25).[9] In 2018, Ogasawara village, under the Tokyo Metropolitan Government, will celebrate the 50th anniversary of reversion, but this complex history continues to cast a shadow over the island community today.

The arbitrary politics of nation states created entangled social conditions in these islands placed at the borderland. For instance, as suggested above, three types of residents are conventionally identified in Ogasawara: "Westerner descendants [*ōbeikei tōmin*]" and "former Japanese settlers [*kyū tōmin*]", both of whom are minorities as compared to the majority of "newcomers [*shin tōmin*]", who moved to Ogasawara after the reversion.[10] However, it should be noted that most of the "Westerner descendants" have Japanese lineage, as well as ancestors from the Pacific Islands, such as Hawai'i and Micronesia. Further, just like "newcomers", many of the so-called "former Japanese settlers" were born and raised on the mainland and then moved to Ogasawara after the reversion, although their families can trace lineage back to Ogasawara before the Pacific War. These terms are thus not only discriminatory but also ambiguous and uncertain, yet, they are still used customarily in Ogasawara today.

Ogasawara remains a fringe locality in the larger mapping of the nation state. Significantly, these scattered islands of Ogasawara preserve an extensive part of Japan's exclusive economic zone in the Pacific Ocean, measured from the shoreline of permanent terrestrial features under the United Nations Convention on the Law of the Sea. Located in the borderland, the island people live in an in-between state, awkwardly administered as part of Tokyo Metropolis. A boat trip of 24 hours from Tokyo metropolitan area is the only public transportation to Ogasawara, where less than 2,500 people reside today in relative isolation. Out of 30-odd tropical and subtropical islands, only two are inhabited: Chichi Jima and Haha Jima. There are about 2,000 people on Chichi Jima, and less than 500 people reside on the other inhabited island of Haha Jima. The rest of the islands are currently uninhabited, although more than 1,000 people had lived on the island of Iwo Tō (known as "Iwo Jima" in English) before the Pacific War. In spite of repeated petitions for repatriation, residence on Iwo Tō is still prohibited. Now, the island is exclusively occupied for military and other national interest purposes, and some employees of government institutions, such as the Japan Self-Defense Forces and Japan Coast Guard, are stationed there. More than 70 years have already passed since the forced evacuation, and the hope of return to Iwo Tō is fading as the evacuees of 1944 are dying one after another.

Musical crossings over the militarised borderland

As shown above, the Ogasawara Islands have been subject to different systems of colonialism, militarism, and segregation. Despite such a complex history, various musical crossings have occurred in this frontier community, transcending national and militarised boundaries—as if to prove that the frontier preserves its own space, expanding outward to many other places and peoples. A good example is a dance form transmitted from Micronesia, called *Nanyō odori* (literally "South Pacific dance").[11] This dance was introduced in Ogasawara because of Japan's colonial and military expansion towards Micronesia, and retained great popularity in Ogasawara until the forced evacuation in 1944, as I shall explore below.[12]

Along with Japan's colonial scheme towards the south, many Japanese nationals, including Okinawans, Koreans, and Taiwanese, sought job opportunities and a better quality of life in the newly acquired territory of the Nanyō (South Pacific). In 1921, a national strategic company, the Nanyō Kōhatsu (South Pacific Enterprise), was established in accordance with a national policy *nanshin ron* (southward advance doctrine).[13] Under this policy, nearly 100,000 Japanese migrated to the area called Nanyō Guntō (literally "South Sea Islands" that covered Japanese territories of Micronesia).[14] An increasing number of Ogasawara Islanders also travelled to Nanyō Guntō (Tsuji 1995: 265). Josiah Gonzales, a clergyman at St George's Church of Chichi Jima, was such a migrant to the new territory. Josiah moved to Saipan in Micronesia to work for Nanyō Kōhatsu, where his sister's husband was a branch manager. While working for the company, Josiah became acquainted with the local people and learnt their songs and dances. On returning to Chichi Jima, Josiah began teaching Micronesian dance (now called *Nanyō odori*) at St George's Church (Interview with his son Aisaku Ogasawara 2009;[15] see also Kitaguni 2002: 134–5). This was one of the most significant musical crossings throughout the history of Ogasawara. The dance attracted many people of different religious beliefs and ethnicity; it was also disseminated to the islands of Haha Jima and Iwo Tō, and attained great popularity in Ogasawara.

After the autumn of 1941, the Imperial Japanese Navy established a military base and facilities in Ogasawara, and stationed a battalion of migrant soldiers there. However, despite raised feelings of insecurity due to the imminent war, the islanders retained their enthusiasm for music and dance activities. In his self-compiled booklet, *The Performing Arts of Pre-war Okimura, Haha Jima* (2003), a former Haha Jima resident, Mineo Wakazawa, presents interesting accounts of musical activities of Ogasawara. He vividly describes how Haha Jima people entertained the soldiers with their performances of music and dance. For instance, on the day of the shrine festival, the soldiers often enjoyed watching and dancing *Nanyō odori*, the highlight of the programme. For this purpose, the navy extended the curfew of soldiers to 9 pm and asked the villagers to present the dance earlier in the programme. Also, the military headquarters sometimes invited the villagers to present the *Nanyō odori* dance in the army base to dispel the loneliness experienced by soldiers on the remote island.

In addition to such official performances, the villagers also performed *Nanyō odori* at alumni parties, family reunions, or just gatherings around the pier under the moonlight. The dance also featured as an interlude of *kabuki* and other theatrical shows, and further provided the scenario for an original theatrical piece, titled "Towards the South [Minami e]". The play recounted the story of a young Japanese boy who yearned for and travelled to the South, and where he fell in love with a beautiful local Chamorro girl (Kitaguni 2002: 136–7; Interviews 2009).

Although the *Nanyō odori* was one of the most popular performing arts in Ogasawara, it disappeared from the islands and was never performed during the US Navy era, when many of the islanders were forcibly evacuated to the mainland. However, defying borders and state controls over mobility, Ogasawara people revived the *Nanyō odori* after more than 20 years of interruption of its performance. Since the reversion of 1968, Japanese people began migrating to Ogasawara again, and the population of Ogasawara gradually increased. Amongst them, a "former Japanese settler" named Masayoshi Asanuma took an important role in the revival of *Nanyō odori*. With growing numbers of fellow islanders, including "Westerner descendants" and many "newcomers", Masayoshi began sharing his dance experience that he had learnt when participating in a youth association [*seinen dan*] in Ogasawara before the Pacific War. It was a male only performance during the pre-war time, but the revival movement demolished such a restriction and recruited all, regardless of gender, ethnicity, or religion. Indeed, everyone on this small community, including visitors, was expected to participate in the activities. For instance, when the boat from Tokyo arrived at Futami Port, the islanders would gather around the pier and welcome the passengers with the dance performance. They would say to the visitors: "Thank you for taking the long voyage to visit us. This is the dance you must learn upon landing on this island!" (Kitaguni 2002: 138; Interviews 2010).

Today, *Nanyō odori* is recognised as part of the cultural heritage of Ogasawara and is performed on various occasions, including the New Year's event, the island summer festival, farewell parties for visitors, and to send off the boat to mainland Tokyo. The islanders also provide dance workshops for visitors, just like the past practice when visitors were asked to learn *Nanyō odori* upon arrival. In 2004, the Ogasawara Islanders participated in the 9th Festival of Pacific Arts held in Palau, and presented *Nanyō odori*, together with some Micronesian songs (Konishi 2005).[16] In 2008, on the occasion of the 40th anniversary of reversion, Ogasawara village hosted dancers from Palau to symbolise the mixed heritage of *Nanyō odori*. After more than 20 years of disruption caused by the war and militarisation of the islands, Ogasawara now celebrates this musical tradition inherited from Micronesia to affirm its own expansive locus beyond geopolitical boundaries.

In addition to *Nanyō odori*, a variety of musical crossings has occurred in the Ogasawara Islands that cannot be accommodated within this chapter. However, I shall here introduce the story of an island singer, Edith Washington, and her composition titled, "Dance-Song of Reversion [*Henkan Ondo*]". It provides an extraordinary vision of musical passage in the militarised islands. Edith Washington was born and raised in Chichi Jima before the Pacific War. Her father was the grandson of the New Englander Nathaniel Savory, and her mother was a Japanese who migrated from Enoshima of Kanagawa Prefecture. After graduating from a school in Ogasawara, Edith voluntarily migrated to mainland Japan for a few years, returned to Chichi Jima in her early 20s, and then experienced forcible evacuation in 1944. After the war, as a "Westerner descendant", she received a special return permit jointly signed by Supreme Commander of the Allied Powers and the Ministry of Foreign Affairs, Japan. But this was the beginning of a long period of segregation from other places in the world. During the US Navy era, Edith could neither leave the island nor communicate with her friends in Japan. Thus, she was extremely delighted when she heard about the reversion, and wrote the "Dance-Song of Reversion" to express her happiness. Thereafter, she collaborated with returnees and greatly contributed to the island's musical activities, including the revival of *Nanyō odori*. Today, she is more than 90 years old, yet still participates in various cultural activities, providing stories in public, and singing songs on stage.

During interviews with me (2009, 2010), Edith described herself as *monozuki* (a person who loves trying out things). She recalled her youth when she learnt "Dance-Song of Susaki [*Susaki Ondo*]" from a migrant military worker. In 1932, the Imperial Japanese Navy began constructing an airport base in the area called Susaki, Chichi Jima. Edith, then aged about 16 years old, worked there in conditions close to those of forced labour—carrying a heavy straw basket [*mokkō*] filled with stones. Upon the completion of the airport,[17] Edith and other workers were invited for a clam digging party [*shiohigari*], hosted by the supervisor of the construction. From this supervisor, Edith learnt the "Dance-Song of Susaki", probably composed by the supervisor himself, and they sang the song together at the party. She was quite impressed with the song that describes stories set against the beauty of Susaki, such as "thinking about a girl viewing shaded moonlight under the leaves of coconut trees", "riding in a canoe with my husband in the rough ocean", and "a pleasant assignation in a *tamana* (*Calophyllum inophyllum*) bush under the cloudy moonlight". Although the beautiful landscape was lost owing to the airport construction, the song was inscribed on Edith's heart, and later she applied its melody to her own composition, "Dance-Song of Reversion".

As is evident from the above descriptions, there was some amount of fun and entertainment in Ogasawara under the imperial and military administration. But, as a "Westerner descendant", Edith's life was certainly entangled with the politics of nation states. She experienced evacuation from home, was forced to work at an arsenal during the Pacific War, and then lived in segregation under the US Navy for more than 20 years. It was a period of loneliness for Edith; with fewer than 300 residents, there was no *matsuri* festival, *bon* dance, *kabuki* theatre, nor even *Nanyō odori* performance on the islands during this time.

Living separated from the rest of the world, it was a radio, a gift from her husband Ned who worked away in Guam, that connected Edith to other places. It was a small and simple radio, but captured Japan's NHK broadcasts well.[18] Edith listened to a programme called "Radio Melodies [*Rajio Kayō*]" every day from 4 pm while cooking dinner. Through the radio programme, she picked up many Japanese songs, such as "Tokyo Boogie Woogie" (1947) that was her most favourite.[19] However, she had difficulty catching the lyrics of the song, as she told me: "On the radio, you didn't know when it would be played again." What helped her to learn the lyrics was a typhoon. After the storm, when several Japanese fishing boats took refuge at Futami Port in Chichi Jima, Edith visited the fishermen and learnt the lyrics of "Tokyo Boogie Woogie". But this was a rare case, as most of the time, Edith hummed the latest Japanese songs without complete lyrics.

Another time, when the reversion was about to be realised, Edith received "a bundle of songs [*uta no taba*]" from a temporary Japanese visitor who came to the islands with special permission to help conduct worship for ancestors' graves [*bosan*]. The bundle included many local song lyrics transcribed by Kikuo Takasaki, who had been evacuated to the mainland after the war. The song lyrics, forgotten for many years, allowed Edith to recollect old melodies and increased her nostalgia for a past Ogasawara. When she heard the news of reversion, Edith was exceedingly delighted: "Everyone is coming back and we can live together again." She was filled with deep emotion and described it in the following verses:

> The wish is granted and the reversion is coming
> Everyone indeed, everyone must be joyful indeed
> Joyful, joyful
> Everyone must be joyful indeed
> It was long, days and months, more than twenty years
> Getting older together, getting older together, but don't forget
> Don't forget, don't forget
> Getting older together, but don't forget
> Even a travelling swallow eventually comes home
> Towards the beloved and yearned for, beloved and yearned for home
> Towards home, towards home
> Towards the beloved and yearned for home
> Come, come soon, the crowd of swallows

> Waiting for the day of reunion, the day of reunion
> Waiting, waiting
> Waiting for the day of reunion
> (Excerpt, translation my own)

It is ironical that she applied the melody of "Dance-Song of Susaki", written by a military worker, to the lyrics. The song made her remember difficult days under the imperial and military administration. But Edith reincarnated the song as "Dance-Song of Reversion" that now emancipates her confined emotion and mentality from the segregation, isolation, and militarisation.

As anticipated in the lyrics, the reversion was realised after "days and months, more than twenty years" and since then, along with the growing number of returnees and newcomers, the islands have been gradually animated with music and dance activities. However, it should be noted that the reversion was also the beginning of another disruption for the "Westerner descendants". Edith particularly extends her sentiments to her eldest son Rance, who experienced true hardship. Even though Rance spoke Japanese fluently (it was the language of family communication), he was still discriminated against mainly because of his insufficiency in writing Japanese characters. When he realised the inerasable bias against "Westerner descendants", Rance eventually left Ogasawara and became an American citizen.[20] Just like Rance, as mentioned before, about 30 per cent of "Westerner descendants" left Ogasawara within two years of the reversion.

Edith Washington herself certainly survived a troubled life, including political harassment as a naturalised islander, forcible evacuation from home, compulsory labour at an arsenal, and extended segregation under the US Navy. However, in the interviews with me, Edith was reserved in describing her life experiences: "It is not only us who suffered from the war; there were many others who experienced further hardship." She recalled her fellow forced labourers who were also abused in the arsenal during wartime, including schoolchildren, apprentices from poor hamlets, and naturalised ethnic Koreans. Likewise, in the "Dance-Song of Reversion", Edith conflates her sentiments with those of refugees living away from the islands, and emphasises that Ogasawara is the beloved home of all despite the imputed categorisations of "Westerner descendants", "former Japanese settlers", and "newcomers". The song embraces the stories of many different peoples, beyond the 23 years of separation, and now overcomes the politics implicated in the militarised borderland.

Conclusion

Today, the islands of Ogasawara are basically safe and at peace, but some social problems owing to their fringe status remain unresolved. The major armed forces are still stationed on the islands, and change the look of the landscape with warships, helicopters, and military personnel. The marginalisation and militarisation of Ogasawara are also noticeable in the politics of memory, as is evident in the case of Iwo Tō. Since the Pacific War, a substantial number of records about the Battle of Iwo Jima have been collected, including detailed statistics of the tactical situation and strategies against the US military campaign. In the same way, as exemplified by the film *Letters from Iwo Jima* (2006), books, photos, and movies repeatedly feature stories around the battle, and reinforce the collective memory of Iwo Tō with emphasis on military activities. But little is known today about daily life on the island before the war. There were certainly rich and diverse cultural activities, including *bon* dance conventions during summertime, *sumo* wrestling tournaments dedicated to the Iwo Tō shrine, film viewing in the elementary school's courtyard, and dance events derived from Micronesia where many Iwo Tō islanders worked before the

Pacific War. Former Iwo Tō residents, who currently live in Chichi Jima, revealed these facts during interviews with me (2009, 2010), yet their stories were often fragmented and uncertain; they all confessed to finding it difficult to recollect past stories away from home, and without friends and family who constitute the missing link in their narratives. Today, the airbase of the Japan Self-Defense Forces occupies most of the past Motoyama district, which was previously the largest residential area, in ironic representation of how the politics of memory acts.

In addition to the cases presented in this chapter, various musical crossings have occurred in this frontier community, despite arbitrary politics and militarisation of the islands. The Ogasawara Islands are filled with a diversity of performing arts that typically represents Ogasawara's expanding locus to other places and peoples. The islanders perform *taiko* drumming, *bon* dance, and shrine festival music, and imagine the days before the Pacific War, when the people enriched their life with Japanese music and dance in this place of isolation and solitude. The *Nanyō odori* allows the current residents of Ogasawara to extend their sentiments towards Micronesia where past islanders travelled and encountered local music and dance. The summer rock music festival Jammin' is a legacy of the US Navy period, as the so-called "Western descendants" play rock 'n' roll and country music influenced by American popular culture. The current Ogasawara residents also enjoy performing hula, in which they embrace nostalgia for the early Hawaiian migrants who brought cultural practices that still remain on the islands today.[21] In the plurality of musical activities, the Ogasawara Islanders preserve gratitude and affinity to many peoples, who created a community in the middle of nowhere, sustained life in this remote place, survived colonial and international politics, and crossed boundaries to bring a wide diversity of musical culture to their home of Ogasawara. Without these multiple crossings and interactions, Ogasawara musical culture would never appear as it does today. In the plurality of history and culture, Ogasawara people find sympathy and rapport with many others and identify themselves beyond the politics of borderlands and their militarisation.

As the case of the Ogasawara Islands shows, people living in the borderlands indeed thrive beyond imagined boundaries. They may not be able to escape appropriation by the wider discourses and ideology of the nation state. Nonetheless, the local practices of music/culture often attempt to overcome the conventional gaze regulated by the nation states. The view from the islands allows us to see the borderlands in an alternative way in which musical crossings and human interactions flourish beyond fences, walls, and militarisation.

Acknowledgements

Very many thanks to Stephen Wild and Swargajyoti Gohain for their advice and generous support in preparation of this chapter.

Notes

1. For instance, in 1670, a Japanese boat transporting oranges was driven out to sea and carried to a beach in what is now Oki Port of Haha Jima after 72 days of drifting. The captain died soon after the arrival, but six other men constructed a small boat with materials available on the island, voyaged northwards, probably through the islands of Chichi Jima and Muko Jima, and finally survived by reaching the inhabited island of Hachijō (Tanaka 1997: 2–7).
2. Beechey's experiences on the island are described in *Narrative of a Voyage to the Pacific and Bering Strait* (1831).
3. The other four Westerners included Mateo Mozaro (Matthew Mazarro) from Croatia; Alden (Aldin) B. Chapin from the United States; Richard Millichamp (John Millinchamp) from England; and Carl Johnsen from Denmark (Quin 1856: 232–35). There is no specific record of the migrants from Hawai'i.
4. They were seeking lucrative business with whalers and traders.

5 Following this exploration of Peel Island, Perry visited Uraga of Japan, known as *Kurofune Raikō* (Black Ships Visit). Later, he compelled the Tokugawa shogunate to abandon the restricted seclusion policy [*sakoku*].
6 The incident happened at Namamugi village of Musashi Province (now Tsurumi District of Kanagawa Prefecture). Japanese *samurai* (the military nobility) from Satsuma Province (now the western half of Kagoshima Prefecture), during their procession to the Edo capital (Tokyo), attacked English merchants Charles Lennox Richardson, Woodthorpe Charles Clark, William Marshall, and Marshall's cousin Margaret Watson Borradail; these foreigners did not make way for the procession—probably without knowing the customary rule in such a case. Richardson was killed and three others were also injured.
7 This resulted from the Treaty of Shimonoseki, which recognised the independence of Korea from China, but also meant free Japanese interference in Korea towards colonisation that eventually happened in 1910.
8 American victory in the Battle of Saipan (15 June–9 July 1944) was followed by the Battle of Iwo Jima (19 February–26 March 1945) in the Ogasawara Islands.
9 It should be noted that the "Westerner descendants" remained Japanese citizens during the US Navy era, although they were under the control of the US and could not travel to mainland Japan, nor any other places, without special permission (Ishihara 2007: 406–7).
10 These terms are literally translated as "European/American lineage islanders", "old islanders", and "new islanders" respectively.
11 The dance was actually called *dojin odori* (kanaka dance) in Ogasawara before the Pacific War. After the reversion, the islanders renamed the dance *Nanyō odori*, because the word *dojin* is considered an ethnic slur in Japan today.
12 Besides, Japanese migrants had also provided such performing arts as *taiko* drumming (mainly from the Hachijō Island), *bon* dance, and *kabuki* theatre in this small frontier community. They also retained great popularity in Ogasawara before the Pacific War.
13 The *nanshin ron* policy had already been proposed in the 1880s. See Yano (1975, 1979) for more details on the *nanshin ron*.
14 In 1920, there were only 3,671 Japanese (including people from Okinawa, Korea, and Taiwan) in the Nanyō Guntō. Afterwards, the number continued to increase and reached 96,670, about 65 per cent of total residents of the Nanyō Guntō, in 1943 (Tamaki 2002).
15 Aisaku Ogasawara (Isaac Gonzales) now serves as the clergyman of St George's Church.
16 Several Micronesian songs are also preserved as part of the cultural heritage in Ogasawara. See Shishikura (2014) for details.
17 After rigorous work on its construction and much environmental destruction, the airport was not useful after all due to strong airflows around the area and an inadequately short runaway (Matsuki 1998: 92–93).
18 NHK is abbreviated from Nippon Hōsō Kyōkai [Japan Broadcasting Corporation]. It is the national broadcasting organisation of Japan.
19 Lyrics by Masaru Suzuki (biographical data unknown), music by Ryoichi Hattori (1907–1993), and first released by Shizuko Kasagi (1914–1985). The song retained great popularity on mainland Japan from the late 1940s to early 1950s.
20 After his father Ned passed away, Rance returned to Ogasawara and now manages a music bar named "Yankeetown".
21 For instance, a famous island cuisine *pīmaka*, which is vinegared *sasayo* fish [*Kyphosus pacificus*], was probably brought by Hawaiian migrants; the word *pīmaka* corresponds to a Hawaiian word *pinika* (vinegar) (Long and Hashimoto 2005: 261).

References

Anderson, Benedict. 1991. Imagined Communities: Reflections on the Origin and Spread of Nationalism. New York: Verso.
Beechey, Frederick William. 1831. Narrative of a Voyage to the Pacific and Bering Strait. London: Henry Colburn and Richard Bentley.
Cholmondeley, Lionel Berners. 1915. The History of the Bonin Islands. London: Constable.
Eldridge, Robert D. 2002. "Ogasawara to Nichi-Bei Kankei, 1945–1968 (Ogasawara and US-Japan Relations, 1945–1968)". In Ogasawara Gaku Koto-hajime (The Introduction of Ogasawara Studies), ed. Daniel Long, 245–70. Kagoshima: Nanpō Shinsha.

Hawks, Francis L. 1856. Narrative of the Expedition of an American Squadron to the China Seas and Japan, Performed in the Years 1852, 1853, and 1854, under the Command of Commodore M. C. Perry, United States Navy (published by order of The Congress of the United States).
Ishihara, Shun. 2007. Kindai Nihon to Ogasawara Shotō: Idō-min no Shima-jima to Teikoku (The Japanese Empire and the Ogasawara/Bonin Islands: Socio-historical Studies on the Naturalized People's Encounters with Sovereign Powers). Tokyo: Heibon Sha.
Ishii, Michinori. 1967. Ogasawara Shotō Gaishi, Sono Ichi (A General History of the Ogasawara Islands, Vol. 1). Tokyo: Ogasawara Kyōkai.
Kitaguni, Yu. 2002. "Ogasawara Shotō no Minyō no Juyō to Henyō: Sono Koto-hajime (Adaptation and Change of the Folksongs of the Ogasawara Islands: An Introduction)". In Ogasawara Gaku Koto-hajime (The Introduction of Ogasawara Studies), ed. Daniel Long, 129–60. Kagoshima: Nanpō Shinsha.
Konishi, Junko. 2005. "Ogasawaran Dancers' Encounter with Pacific Dancers: A Report from the 9th Pacific Festival of Arts in Palau". In Refereed Papers from the 1st International Small Island Cultures Conference, ed. Mike Evans, 99–107. Sydney: The Small Island Cultures Research Initiative.
Long, Daniel and Inaba Makoto, eds. 2004. Ogasawara Handobukku (Ogasawara Handbook). Kagoshima: Nanpō Shinsha.
Long, Daniel and Naoyuki Hashimoto, eds. 2005. Ogasawara Ktoba Shaberu Jiten (Ogasawara Spoken Language Dictionary). Kagoshima: Nanpō Shinsha.
Matsuki, Kazumasa. 1998. Chōki Taizaisha no Tame no Ogasawara Kankō Gaido (Ogasawara Tourist Guide for Long-term Visitors). Tokyo: Yamamogura.
Ministry of Foreign Affairs. 1940. Dainippon Gaikō Bunsho (Documents of Japanese Diplomacy). Tokyo: Nippon Kokusai Kyōkai.
Morris-Suzuki, Tessa. 2000. Henkyō kara Nagameru: Ainu ga Keiken Suru Kindai (The View from the Frontier: The Modern Experiences of Ainu), trans. Okawa Masahiko. Tokyo: Misuzu Shobō.
Norris, Robert S., William M. Arkin, and William Burr. 2000. "How Much Did Japan Know?" Bulletin of the Atomic Scientists 56/1: 11–13, 78–9.
Office of the Chief of Naval Operations, Navy Department. 1944. Civil Affairs Handbook: Izu and Bonin Islands. Washington, DC: Office of the Chief of Naval Operations, Navy Department.
Quin, Michael. 1856. "Notes on the Bonin Islands." Journal of the Royal Geographical Society of London 26: 232–5.
Robertson, Russell. 1876. "The Bonin Islands". Transactions of the Asiatic Society of Japan 4: 111–43.
Shepardson, Mary. 1977. "Pawns of Power: The Bonin Islanders". In The Anthropology of Power: Ethnographic Studies from Asia, Oceania, and the New World, eds. Raymond D. Fogelson and Richard N. Adams, 99–114. New York: Academic Press.
Shishikura, Masaya. 2014. "Wanting Memories: Histories, Remembrances and Sentiments Inscribed in Music and Dance of the Ogasawara Islands". PhD thesis, The Australian National University.
Tamaki, Takeshi. 2002. "Nanyō Dekasegi Imin no Sensō Taiken (The War Experiences of South Pacific Migrants)". In Yomitan Son Shi, Dai Go Kan Shiryō Hen 4, "Senji Kiroku" Jō Kan (The History of Yomitan Village, Volume 5, Appendix 4, "The Wartime Record" 1). Yomitan Village, Okinawa: Yomitan Son Shi Henshū Shitsu. www.yomitan.jp/sonsi/vol05a/chap02/sec05/cont00/docu148.htm (accessed 7 June 2012).
Tanaka, Hiroyuki. 1997. Bakumatsu no Ogasawara: Ōbei no Hogei Sen de Sakaeta Midori no Shima (Ogasawara at the End of Shogunate: The Green Islands Flourished with Whaling Boats from the West). Tokyo: Chūō Kōron Shinsha.
Tsuji, Tomoe. 1995. Ogasawara Shotō Rekishi Nikki, Jō Kan (The Historical Diary of the Ogasawara Islands, Vol. 1). Tokyo: Kindai Bungei Sha.
Wakazawa, Mineo. 2003. Senzen Haha Jima Okimura no Minzoku Geinō (The Performing Arts of Pre-war Okimura, Haha Jima) (self-compiled booklet).
Yano, Toru. 1975. "Nanshin" no Keifu (The Genealogy of "Southward"). Tokyo: Chūō Kōron Shinsha.
———. 1979. Nihon no Nanyō Shikan (Japanese Historical View of the South Pacific). Tokyo: Chūō Kōron Shinsha.

33
Evaded states
Security and control in the Sino–North Korean border region

Adam Cathcart

Introduction

The Chinese–Korean border county of Changbai comprises part of the easternmost frontier of the People's Republic of China, and of Jilin province. Changbai means 'ever-white,' a nod to Chanbaishan ('ever-white mountain'), the symbolically loaded and active volcanic peak a few rural hours' drive to the north and east from the county centre. Here, the waters of the Yalu River are cold and narrow, and North Korea is a stone's throw, or a lusty shout, away. While there are certain spiritual energies shared with the Koreans across the river, on its northern bank the Chinese do not appear to acknowledge that the Koreans have different names for the mountain (Paektu) and the river (Amnok) than do the Chinese. Such overlapping linguistic maps can play to the advantage of local tourism officials in Changbai, who would prefer the county to be known best as a launching-point for expensive junkets by South Korean tourists up to Changbaishan (Mount Paektu). But Changbai's placement on the mental map of most external observers is decidedly more dark, due to its twin city across the river – Hyesan, a city known best for its export of methamphetamines, illegal border crossers, and rogue North Korean border guards.

Hyesan is on the physical periphery of Democratic People's Republic of Korea (DPRK) Ryanggang province. But in the North Korean context, Hyesan is more powerful than its geography might indicate: it is the political, cultural, and economic centre of Ryanggang province (Kim Jong-il 1968). It is therefore the focal point of state security, trade relations, and is a hub of Korean People's Army (KPA) activity. There may not be a great deal of trust in Chinese comrades across the Yalu River, and there is certainly official encouragement from Pyongyang to inculcate perceptions of the danger posed by China as a source of ideological and cultural contamination of North Korean youth (Korean Central News Agency 2017).

More measurably, there may also be a dearth of food for the KPA and border guards around the city. On 18 September 2015, reports emerged of a Chinese smuggler or individual shot at from across the border by a KPA guard (Green 2015a). The next summer, North Korean soldiers were said to have physically crossed the border into Changbai to maraud for food (Kim Kwang-tae and Choi Kyong-ae 2016). And again, reports in spring 2017 asserted the same (Yonhap 2017). There is no visible border wall between the two states, and the river is the effective boundary, so the ability of North Korean soldiers to vault into Chinese territory and cause distress to locals there is clear and present. However, such events are never covered in North Korea's state media, and only occasionally confirmed in China. Kim Jong-un, North Korea's otherwise ubiquitous leader, has never visited the city.

This chapter seeks to illustrate the centrality of evasion to life and work in the border region. For refugees and temporary economic migrants from North Korea, the modes of evasion are well-known. Border guards are to be avoided or bribed, as are the Changbai Public Security Bureau (PSB) and border guards (*bianfang*) on the other side. The respective states also engage in acts of evasion, by avoiding the key issues in their respective media discourses about the border, allowing bribes and smuggling through the net, and in allowing ostensibly illegal currency trading and market activities to flourish in a kind of grey zone (Roitman 2005).

Bad information and difficult research terrain

In crossing from Hyesan to Changbai, border guards themselves evade two states – the DPRK that fails to feed them, and the People's Republic of China (PRC) that seeks to hunt them down. A second evasion therefore takes place, with respect to the clear rendering of this and other incidents in what is a very difficult information environment. In other words, the truth is elusive, too.

The broad junction of PRC Changbai county with the sprawling urban acreage of Hyesan city on the DPRK side is fertile ground for rumours. Official sources of information for this section of the border are few and far between. On the PRC side, the Changbai Public Security Bureau (PSB) has a website and a microblogging account. But, as in the case of its counterpart in the PRC Korean Autonomous Prefecture in Yanbian, this information tends to skew towards the propagandistic depiction of community relations building (Shu 2016). The same is true for the limited official accounts available of Chinese People's Liberation Army activity in the border region (Yao et al. 2017). On the North Korean side, most of the information released about the DPRK side of the border has to do with new or refurbished monuments to the country's ubiquitously evoked leaders, or the building of new houses in once-flooded areas. Only in rare cases are dangers from the Chinese side of the border implied or denounced (Cathcart and Gleason 2013).

What is then left to fill the gap are single-source stories in the South Korean press about North Korean border jumpers who cause chaos in China. Typically, if these have merit, they are corroborated by the Chinese media eventually. In some cases, different media outlets pronounce the same story as having happened over one month apart and purport to 'exclusive' content, meaning that it was a rumour that spread but a key detail (the date of the incident) was wrongly altered (Duowei News 2016). These, however, are small informational errors compared to the pure speculation and single-source stories that are never corroborated or, more often, never returned to at all (*Asahi Shimbun* 2016). It is also very difficult to know, in the absence of interrogation reports or more detailed reporting on this issue in Chinese, precisely why the guards are coming across from North Korea. If it is for food, does this then hold that the entirety of the KPA is lacking in rations and low in morale, as asserted by some (Stanton 2016)? It is very difficult to confirm these stories.

Defectors have been a vital source of information in recent years in describing conditions in the border region. By far the best one for grappling with the issues of interconnected border aspects is Hyeonseo Lee, who after growing up in Hyesan spent nearly seven years in China and criss-crossed the border multiple times. Although it is rarely framed as such, Lee's memoir is particularly useful as a study of Hyesan's history and function within the border region. She relays tales told by her grandmother, who had studied in Japan, of the early months of the Korean War, when the family had to hide their family's Workers' Party of Korea party cards in fears of being executed by the American soldiers arriving on the Yalu River (Lee 2015: 7). Her family had connections thereafter in China, and her description of the city is worth quoting at length:

> When I was growing up Hyesan was an exciting place to be. Not because it was lively – nowhere in the country was noted for its theatre scene, restaurants or fashionable subcultures. The city's appeal lay in its proximity to the narrow Yalu River, Korea's ancient border with China. In a closed country like North Korea, Hyesan seemed like a city at the edge of the world. To the citizens who lived there it was a portal through which all manner of marvelous foreign-made goods – legal, illegal, and highly illegal – entered the country. This made it a thriving hub of trade and smuggling, which brought many benefits and advantages to the locals, not least of which were opportunities to form lucrative partnerships with Chinese merchants on the other side of the river, and make hard currency. At times it could seem like a semi-lawless place where the government's iron rule was not so strong. This was because almost everyone, from the municipal Party chief to the lowliest border guard, wanted a share of the riches. Occasionally, however, there were crackdowns ordered by Pyongyang, and they could be brutal. People from Hyesan were therefore more business-minded and often better off than people elsewhere in North Korea. The grown-ups would tell me we were fortunate to live there.
>
> *(Lee 2015: 11f.)*

In most defector memoirs, the border is a new zone of activity that mainly exists as an area to be passed through as quickly as possible. But for Lee it is a more centred place. Different defectors have different motivations and degrees of agency with respect to their existence in the region and their purpose of crossing. Unlike some high-profile defectors like Shin Dong-hyuk, Hyeonseo Lee's narrative has not been challenged or altered (Pilling 2013; Eichhorn 2015; Harden 2015). Acknowledging that falsehoods play directly into the production of North Korea counterpropaganda, Lee has clearly stated that defectors need to be more consistent with their life testimonies. Fortunately, the discourse on North Korea seems ready for a more *Alltagsgeschichte* approach to the border region, particularly the recognition of insights gathered from slower observation. In so doing, the role played by border guards is no doubt important, but so too is that of women. Lee's accounts of Hyesan and elements of her life story accordingly dovetail with some of the best new scholarship on female North Korean defectors being published (Kim Mikyoung 2013; Song 2013; Choi 2014; Kim Sung Kyung 2016).

Among the most intellectually combative of the new approaches comes from Eunyoung Choi, whose work attempts to reshape the discursive terrain around North Korean female border crossers, recognizing that the Sino–North Korean frontier is a highly charged geopolitical space. Choi somewhat controversially argues that international human rights organizations have overemphasized 'the irresponsible and brutal policies of North Korea and China' to the detriment of understanding 'the broader conditions that shape trafficking of North Korean women and the women's own migration experiences' (Choi 2014: 272). Data collected by human rights organizations, she implies, is primarily gathered in order to be used as a cudgel against North Korea and China; the women thus become the means to an end – critique of North Korea or the elimination of that state altogether. Drawing from a body of interviews with North Korean migrant women conducted in Yanbian between 2003 and 2007, Choi moves to recover a sense of agency with respect to North Korean migrant women. Reading Agustin (2006), Choi critiques along the way Western 'moral panic about prostitution...and the avoidance of uncomfortable truths about the willingness of many women to be trafficked' (Choi 2014: 273). Like the York University sociologist Hyun Ok Park (2014), Choi recognizes that the crossing of the Tumen River into China is not simply traumatic due to the danger of evading North Korean state penalty, but because these women

> move from a relatively closed socialist system in a totalitarian regime to a global capitalist economy where they are subject to the influence and interests of powerful state and non-state organizations, most notably, the United States, China, and South Korea, and the United Nations.
>
> *(Choi 2014: 274)*

Does such a depiction overread the Chinese border as somehow immediately representing the forces of hegemonic global capitalism? Perhaps. But even if Hyeonseo Lee's memoir implicitly critiques this notion, the book also coheres to Choi's other interviewees in the sense that there is much more at work in the border region than a binary of pure trafficking against the will of the migrant. Choi's final argument that international human rights spotlighting of the North Korean refugee issue is actually harmful to the cause of the refugees themselves by causing crackdowns, however, is both impossible to prove and indicative of the frustration felt on the limitations of the knowable in the border region.

While the legal status of North Korean border crossers is murky, the experiences of women who cross borders point to multiple and hybrid identities. Hyeonseo Lee explicitly evokes this notion by putting down roots in China, and using no fewer than seven pseudonyms. Scholar Jiyoung Song describes the progression of many such women from 'Confucian communist mothers' to 'Trafficked wives' to 'Smuggled refugees' to 'Unsettled settlers' as they cross new national frontiers (Song 2013: 160).

The new scholarship dwells on multiple and hybrid identities, both of North Korean women and North Korean migrants irrespective of gender, yet virtually none of these ideas penetrates into Chinese academic discourse or state media publications. Official academic discourse in China on female North Koreans without travel or work visas is not particularly pliant. Apart from the occasional irregular reference to a possible refugee crisis if North Korea collapses, Chinese officials tend to insist that refugees are economic migrants, pure and simple. In Chinese state media, the names given to North Koreans living illegally in China are therefore few; the defectors tend to be identified as *tuobeizhe*, 'those who have escaped from the North.' Some potential changes to these views and the policies that underpin them were hinted at in 2010 and 2012, such as the publication of US journalist Barbara Demick's prize winning book *Nothing to Envy* (2010) in Chinese, and some other semi-empathetic accounts of North Koreans roaming toward Southeast Asia in search of a visa to Seoul (Hwang 2010; Qi and Li 2012). Likewise, Hyeonseo Lee was allowed to speak critically of the North Korean regime in March 2016 in a small Beijing bookshop. Given the levels of sensitivity and control around these issues in China, such actions are surprising, but they have not and do not appear capable of bringing a new policy line into fruition.

If the Chinese official view of border illegalities is somewhat rigid, the North Korean state view presents two dominant themes. The first dwells on iconic depictions of Kimist family glory, reminding observers that the DPRK state founder Kim Il-song frequently crossed the frontier in search of national salvation and socialist revolution. The second theme presents the frontier as a great danger to average North Koreans, and a site of potential terrorism carried out against North Korean society and the statues of their leaders. After huge floods in September 2016, North Korean state media promised to remake its side of the flooded Tumen River valley into a 'socialist fairyland,' showing night after night of television coverage of similar work sites with the Korean People's Army fixing smashed infrastructure. Moving around in North Korea is still largely illegal without a special permit, meaning that these floods brought many thousands of citizens into contact with others facing similar pressures in the border region (United Nations General Assembly 2014: 7).

Fine line of legality

Is the border a lawless area, or one in which states have the upper hand? A common assumption tends to be that the state is total. Indeed, the strong focus on border security by both China and North Korea suggests that this is where a state attempts to enforce its legal authority through control over cross-border movement. There remain strong incentives for both North Koreans and Chinese to simply treat the other as if it does not exist, or to focus on controlling movement of goods and people across the rivers dividing the countries. The bilateral border between China and North Korea also has an internal component (for instance, checks at county level) within the DPRK provinces of North Hamgyong and Ryanggang in particular.

On the North Korean side, the *Gukka Anjeon Bowiebu* (State Security Department/SSD) plays an important role in border security. Within the interlocking layers of North Korean bureaucracy, it should be noted that not every action of the SSD is *ipso facto* a destruction of human rights or prosecutable by the International Criminal Court. Even undercover reporting from inside North Korea acknowledges some of the efforts of the department including cracking down on crimes such as rape, human smuggling, prostitution, and other illicit activities (Cathcart 2012; Greitens 2014: 100–103). The North Korean state was heavily involved in drug trafficking from 1999 to 2005, but state security institutions cracked down on them thereafter (Wang and Blancke 2014; Hastings 2015: 162, 175).[1]

The occasional SSD dispatch of groups of investigators into China to hunt down defectors, efforts in which the Chinese state cooperates, appear to be an attempt on the part of both states to enforce the legal prerogative of the state over border crossing. As Denkowski illustrates, the SSD also 'performs a customs function' and 'oversees border guards by civilian and military personnel, who perform customs duties with the main target of detecting spies' (Denkowski 2014: 12f). The SSD does not have steady contact with Chinese customs on the other side of the border, and 'only officers [are] authorized to cross the border to Chinese checkpoints' (Denkowski 2014: 12f). Circumstantial evidence exists that the SSD cooperated with Chinese comrades in cases involving foreign missionaries of mutual interest like Kenneth Bae and the Garratt family in Dandong (Blancke and Rosenke 2011), but there are also indications that North Korean officials distrust their Chinese counterparts deeply.

On the Chinese side of the frontier, technology is increasing in use, including more cameras along the frontier. Border guards on the North Korean side may not have ammunition (at least according to locals on the Chinese side), but on the Chinese side they are well-armed. Chinese security officials can operate with greater swiftness and confidence in part because of their technological advantages up and down the border. Infrastructure along the frontier is truly dilapidated on much of the North Korean side, making an efficient provision of border guards and rapid movement of troops very difficult indeed. Some efforts have been made in the recent past to improve this problem by Kim Jong-un (Denkowski 2015: 354). Although most of the railroad lines on the Yalu and Tumen rivers escaped bombing by the Americans in the Korean War, they are still largely moving on foundations originally put down by the Japanese in the 1920s and 1930s, and are falling apart. Efforts were underway to establish a Hyesan–Samjiyeon highway to much regime fanfare in 2015 and 2016 (Chosun Central Television broadcast, 2016), but these appear to have been cut short or the resources redirected to emergency flood relief in early September 2016.

Denkowski notes there are 'three lines of border control' on the North Korean border with China. Behind the standard border guards, fences and bunkers and occasional dog patrols, there are police foot patrols, and the third line is borderland villages of 'unarmed and politically trusted civilians' who both patrol and report upward. Interviews with former SSD agents (including border guards of company commander rank, a former counterintelligence officer, and a member of the political bureau who also supervised police) provide some of the most detailed data available in English. These interviews confirm that the SSD has more power than the local police; coordination with local agencies is therefore hierarchical and the local stations 'aid and abet the SSD's formal social control' (Denkowski 2014: 11). Although they presented deeply flawed accounts, the memoirs by two US-based reporters who were arrested for crossing the frozen Tumen River in 2009 seem to confirm as much, in that the manner of their processing confirms the layered approach (Cathcart and Gleason 2012).

However, the SSD's work and torture of illegal border crossers leads to crimes against humanity and the agency itself may be involved in large-scale drug smuggling. In his interviews with former security officials now resident in South Korea, Denkowski notes that such individuals maintain a 'fear of re-victimization and re-traumatization.' His interviews with a former SSD-Colonel indicates the bureaucracy has 'a culture of total surveillance, even within the agency directed towards each comrade by each comrade' (Denkowski 2014: 8f.).

In spite of the problems with North Korean KPA crossing the frontier illegally and dangerously as discussed earlier, there has been an increase in counter-espionage surveillance in China. At the same time, crackdowns on 'espionage' in the border region should raise questions about their implications for researchers. In November 2015, a Chinese newspaper affiliated with the People's Liberation Army reported that a 'foreign spy' who turned out to be Japanese had been arrested in the border regions of Jilin and North Korea – not for taking photos of North Korea, but for observing and photographing People's Liberation Army border outposts. The incident occurred in Changbai County, not so far from Hyesan; a local farmer reported some 'suspicious and stealthy (*guigui suisui*)' behaviour and called local border police, who took the foreigner into custody, checked his camera, and then confirmed his arrest. The report notes that 'in recent years, foreign espionage organizations activities in the border region have been absolutely rampant.' The article then called for more public understanding of the need for struggle, aid in catching spies, and vigilance of Party organizations (China Defence Daily 2015). How this activity was supposed to accord with the concurrent push for increased tourism and eco-tourism in the Mt. Paektu area was not described. Fieldwork in the region is difficult but can ameliorate some problems, although Chinese watching for spies and the notion that North Korean border guards might shoot anyone who takes their photograph also makes for a dismaying environment. Individuals like the Japanese activist Ishimaru Jiro can still go regularly to collect testimonials from contacts inside North Korea. Likewise, Christian missionaries who may be involved with refugees are surely known to the PRC immigration authorities and security officials in Yanbian, but they are generally allowed to continue to travel to Yanbian and survey the border region.

Technology cannot prevent problems with drug production and distribution purely on the Chinese side of the border; not every drug addiction or movement in Dandong or Yanbian can be laid at the feet of a North Korean partner. Accordingly, anti-drug campaigns in north-eastern border areas of China never call out the Kim regime as the source of the problem, but rather cultural decadence (Zoccatelli 2014). Nevertheless, both sides know that most North Korean drug trafficking across the frontier is done by boat (Denkowski 2014: 13). On the Chinese side of the border, the state makes efforts to shut this down, with occasional success (Greitens

2014: 23). However, announcing increase of patrols without announcing increased hauls of contraband should indicate that this activity is often futile (Liaoning Daily 2016).

Despite border security technologies in place, the 'fine line of legality' is frequently crossed. The reasons for the contravention of laws are multiple: such 'crossings' happen because border surveillance technology is not up-to-date, as a result of involvement of security guards in drug smuggling, because individuals move through the void of effective bilateral cross-border communication, because regulations around foreign espionage and even simple tourism continue to change, and due to violation of human rights. The line between legality and illegality needs to be further parsed out with respect to how the state interacts with the population on both sides of the border, and in particular on the North Korean side of the border. If lines of legality are trespassed by the ambiguities of border crossing, manifested in technologies and failures of security, so too can they be with respect to circulation of currency and illicit drugs. We therefore need to look again at the state itself – to what extent is the North Korean state a criminal actor along the frontier, complicitly or actively supporting drug-smuggling operations?

Part of the answer to this question depends on how one frames the North Korean state more generally. One means of doing so is to place at its centre the 'illicit economy' (Habib 2011). As the University of Sydney political scientist Justin Hastings notes, North Korea has an economy 'where the lines between formal and informal trade, and between licit and illicit, are blurred' (Hastings 2015: 166). The border region is indeed full of 'hybrid traders,' defined by Hastings as 'actual [DPRK] state officials who use their position to go into business for themselves.' Again, the line between state and private, and legal and illegal, is very hard to tease out here. This is why Kim Jong-un's general caution about spreading 'corruption' in North Korean officials needs to be defined contextually (Human Rights Watch 2015; Kim Jong-un 2016). Kim cannot really openly admit that officials are heavily involved in trade activity in part because they had been told after the Arduous March of the late 1990s to fend for themselves (Hastings 2015: 171).

Equally ambiguous is the state of currency on the frontier, where North Korean struggles against foreign currency seem to come and go in cycles. In a series of 2014 interviews, North Korean defectors told Christopher Green how their own foreign currency usage in North Korea had been a rational response to government currency revaluations in 2002 and 2009 (Green 2016). The Chinese Renminbi (RMB) has indeed become 'the people's money' in the border region (Greitens 2014: 97f). Chinese currency is used to price goods in private markets up and down the Tumen River valley. The norm of what some call 'yuanization' in northern Korea is not entirely a new phenomenon, though. In Hyesan, RMB were openly circulating in Ryanggang province as far back as the 1980s (Green 2016: 418, 423). Likewise, Hyesan's relatively advanced market activity in the 1980s is also noted by memoirs from two young female defectors born in that city, although they do not confirm RMB use at that time (Lee 2015: 14; Haggard 2016).

Kim Jong-un may have inherited a situation wherein Chinese currency circulates throughout his country, but the state has still taken efforts to stem it. Foreign exchange was reportedly added to the list of crimes punishable by death in North Korea in 2012 (United Nations General Assembly 2014: 2). While capital punishment may sound severe, the DPRK itself does not shy away from admitting to holding public executions, adding that such events are warranted for cases 'where a criminal committed brutal crimes and the victim or his/her family requested to confirm the execution' (United Nations General Assembly 2014: 4f). It is unclear, though, if anyone has in fact been put to death for trading in foreign currencies. Confusingly, these are the only currencies in which foreign tourists visiting North Korea are allowed to use (apart from the model Kwangbok Department Store), all in state-sanctioned locations where traders have clear licence to do so.

Human movement and hybrid identities

The Renminbi might be officially disdained in North Korea, but their capture is also a sovereign goal of the state, and officially sanctioned North Korean delegations continue to be sent abroad to obtain foreign currency. Probably tens of thousands of North Korean women have been sent to China for this purpose, living in contexts which are severely confined from the Chinese point of view, but quite liberal from the North Korean point of view (Green 2015b). In the case of North Korean restaurant workers in China, there are ample opportunities for structured and usually electronically monitored meetings with foreigners, since the clientele tend to be South Korean, Chinese, and a mix of other curious foreigners paying usually in RMB (Greitens 2014: 55).

Reportage about these enterprises is a relatively abundant genre – they exist in Hunchun, there are several in Yanbian, and they are also in Harbin, Mudanjiang, Ji'an, Dandong, Shenyang, and Changchun. However, they are relatively dynamic, close, and move easily, and quantitative data about them are almost impossible to get. The South Korean government tendency to group these activities under the rubric of North Korea's international export of 'slave labour' has tended to avoid discussing the visible function that such enterprises serve specific to the Sino–Korean border region or Northeast China (Yoon and Lee 2015). Nor are the restaurant workers linked in even sketchy ways to the drug business, which appears to be occurring along wholly separate tracks. Only in the realm of espionage are the restaurants linked to the more nefarious proclivities of the North Korean state, although again, investigations are few (Jakarta Post 2017). Likewise, if foreign-bound North Koreans are acting as 'drug mules' in other contexts (Greitens 2014: 18), it seems odd that the restaurant workers are never interpreted in quite the same way.

If we place the border at the centre of the relationship between Pyongyang and Beijing, the business activities by North Koreans in Northeast China might be better understood. Hastings urges us to better understand the relationship between the centre and the periphery (particularly the north-eastern periphery) in North Korea (Hastings 2015: 170). The individuals sent across the border have been through deep ideological training and are generally considered reliable. The funds they remit are useful for keeping living standards high in Pyongyang. And they are a tangible reminder to Chinese comrades that North Koreans are not simply problematic illegals, but stakeholders in China's economic order, if only in a small way. It is notable that in the dozen or more years that the guest worker programme has run in the restaurant sector, defections, and problems have been rare – and even a huge problem for the North Koreans with the group defection of a dozen young women from a restaurant in Ningbo, near Shanghai, in April 2016 did not devolve into public recriminations between China and North Korea. Instead, the North Korean state media has continued to call upon the United Nations and the Red Cross (at times using CNN reporter Will Ripley to amplify their messages) to return the women and insist that they were abducted by the South Korean intelligence services.

On the Chinese side, care is taken not to allow public comment or opprobrium about these facilities. North Korean women in the border region tend to be depicted in PRC state media as happy singers or stylish border guards, never sex workers or human trafficking victims. While bribes were almost certainly involved in their selection from Pyongyang, the state-sanctioned presence of North Korean female workers in China is thus not a victory for perceptions of North Korean marketization (Yoon and Lee 2015: 72–75). They tend to have two to three year contracts, the state takes somewhere between 70 and 90 per cent of their earnings, and they are generally given one afternoon per week to go to a local market with their entire unit. Their legality, however, is an indicator of limited human movement across the frontier – but their ability to acculturate, settle in China, and ultimately act as a *transfronterizo* is proscribed by the state (Martinez 2009: 91). The Sino–North Korean borderland, then, contains elements of interpenetration and cultural hybridity, both legally sanctioned and illegal.

Probably the thorniest and least clear analytical question around the frontier zone has to do with identity, even as such analysis promises a corrective to the omissions of state-driven discourse. Do North Koreans who border cross into China without the permission of either state take on a hybrid identity thereby? What about North Koreans who arrive in China without planning to transit to South Korea? Making things yet more layered are ethnic Koreans in China, some small number of whom have entered into 'defector cram schools' where they can pose as North Korean defectors so as to get more generous asylum provision in countries like the UK. There has been a great deal of writing around the issue of national identity in the border region, without much consensus even on what aspects of identity construction or nationality need to serve as the centre of the debate. Part of the basic problem comes back to issues stemming from the divided politics of the Korean peninsula: South Korea claims all North Koreans as citizens of the Republic of Korea (ROK) – but cannot assert these claims over North Koreans in China, for fear of rupturing bilateral relations altogether or prompting yet more accusations from North Korea of 'abductions' of people who are in fact trying desperately to flee to Seoul. North Korean refugees must therefore flee to a third country – typically in Southeast Asia – in order to contact ROK officials who can conduct them on to Seoul and the Hanawon (defector halfway houses). From the official standpoint of the ROK state, then, there is no purpose to be served in theorizing a transnational identity – much less a sinified Korean identity – for North Korean refugees seeking to escape permanently, vaulting out of Pyongyang's legal orbit; they are seen instead as potential citizens of the true Korean republic and its capitol in Seoul. The numbers of refugees who made it successfully to South Korea has been brought steadily down (Human Rights Watch 2015).

Conclusion

Approaching the border region with a 'state vs. anti-state' or 'resisters vs. the state' paradigm is both helpful and limiting. New research indicates how the North Korean state has itself absorbed certain aspects of marketization, to the extent of participating in illegal drug trafficking, and in exporting its largely female labour force into Chinese border areas and cities to gain hard currency. In such an environment where money is a primary incentive, the process of illegal border crossing out of North Korea inevitably results in evading state controls by bribing of border guards, no matter how strong their political training may be. The process of border crossing brings with it changes in identity for North Korean refugees, some of whom become semi-permanent exiles in the legal netherworld of China, others of whom are able to defect to South Korea in the end. But even these acts of apparent resistance are often loaded with unexpected elements: nostalgia for North Korea, a desire to engage in multiple re-crossings of the border, and even 'willingness to be trafficked,' as Eunseung Choi (2014) has argued. Full re-defection is also a possibility, and although such instances are still extremely rare, the North Korean state creates relatively persuasive narratives around those who do.

At the geopolitical level, both sides in the Sino–North Korean bilateral relationship seek to avoid airing of difficult cross-border issues, and research on security cooperation in the border region is therefore nascent. Missionaries, intelligence operatives, foreign journalists, and scholars working on either or both sides of the border therefore tend to be operate under a kind of ambiguous shadow. Whereas the Chinese side of the border has tended to be regarded as by far the easiest in which to undertake research, developments indicate that such openness is far from guaranteed. The new counter-espionage campaigns, and the tendency to clamp down on border travel at times of ostensible crisis such as occurred in April 2017, do not presage some kind of golden age for scholars engaged in borderland studies along the Tumen and Yalu River valleys.

If fieldwork is rendered difficult, theory can sometimes fill the gap. Yet if we return to cross-border activities in Hyesan, it is difficult to find behaviours that fall fully inside the theoretical ambit. For instance, a family member of Hyeonseo Lee's in the border city of Hyesan was approached by a man who knew they had ties in China. He wanted to smuggle out a particularly sensitive commodity into China: the bones of an American GI from the Korean War, for which he had heard that dealers with contacts in the USA would pay handsomely. Lee uses the anecdote to emphasize the randomness of opportunity and the entrepreneurial nature of people in Hyesan. But the anecdote indicates more than that. For North Korean citizens, there could be few things more patriotic than marshalling evidence of their nation's triumph over American imperialism; ostensibly, political credit could be obtained by providing the bones to a local revolutionary museum within the hegemony of the state's Korean War narrative. At the same time, the state has to be circumvented for material gain to accrue; no Workers' Party of Korea official is going to sanction the export of these bones. Ultimately the request was turned down, in favour of a more reliable commodity of opium, in whose practices and marketing Lee's uncle is fluent (Lee 2015: 59). The state appears and disappears in Lee's life.

Evasion is not always about hiding to avoid detection, but instead about blurred boundaries and state complicity so that there is nothing determinate to detect. The North Korean state's ambivalent approach to foreign currency as well as drug trafficking indicates as much. The contradictions and difficulties in using oral testimonies and memoir literature must be forded through, as on both sides of the Sino–North Korean frontier, the states themselves use the deliberate withholding of information as part of state control. In this environment, legal and illegal border crossers can provide a corrective to state narratives, even as individuals mirror state tactics and withhold, adapt, and reshape stories for their own survival.

Ultimately, the limited transnational cooperation engaged in by the states on both sides of the border is not put to particularly positive ends, and hybrid identity in cities as physically close as Hyesan and Changbai is more or less an idea rather than a reality. North Korea is jealous of the labour and the loyalty of its citizens, whereas China frames the region as often in patriarchal and ethnopolitical terms as in economic and security terms. Legal trade is very difficult to set up under these circumstances, and grey areas seem prone to predominate in spite of national assertions on both sides that the border is fully under control and can be rationally engaged economically. In spite of the state investment in border technology and security services, the border will continue to be the site of illegal traffic. But it will also remain an imaginative terrain for those for whom the ineluctable spread of North Korean state criminality is the key concern.

Note

1 Hastings (2015: 163) entertains a paradox: 'A country that is one of the most isolated in the world survives in part…by engaging in international commerce, and hence being tied into the global [narcotics] economy.'

References

Agustin, Laura (2006). 'The Disappearing of a Migration Category: Migrants Who Sell Sex,' *Journal of Ethnic and Migration Studies* Vol. 32, No. 1, pp. 29–47.
Asahi Shimbun (2016). 'North Korea Said to Be Dispatching Hit Teams to Kill Defectors,' 23 August.
Blancke, Stephan and Hans Rosenke (2011). 'Blut ist dicker als Wasser: Die chinesisch-nordkoreanische Militaer- und Geheimdienstkooperation,' *Zeitschrift fuer Aussen- und Sicherheitspolitik*, Vol. 4, pp. 263–294.

Cathcart, Adam (2012). 'Prostitution, Abortion, and "Flower Girls": Women in Hyesan,' *SinoNK*, 2 August.

Cathcart, Adam and Brian Gleason (2012). 'Oprah vs. Juche: Reviewing the North Korean Border Capture, Captivity and Trial of Laura Ling and Euna Lee,' *Korean Quarterly*, Vol. 15, No. 2.

Cathcart, Adam and Brian Gleason (2013). 'The Discursive Battleground for North Korean Refugees: "Double Defector" Propaganda and Emerging Sino-North Korean Frictions,' in *Peaceful Unification of the Korean Peninsula and Human Rights in North Korea*, ed. Korea-UK Forum on the Peaceful Unification of Korea (London: ROK Ministry of Unification), pp. 109–137.

China Defence Daily (2015). 'Jilin lihuo yi waiji jiandie: latan Jiefangjun bianjing bingli fenbu [Jilin province apprehends a foreign spy for unreasonably scouting the distribution of PLA strength along the border],' *Zhongguo Guofangbao*, 18 November.

Choi, Eunyoung (2014). 'North Korean Women's Narratives of Migration: Challenging Hegemonic Discourses of Trafficking and Geopolitics,' *Annals of the Association of American Geographers*, Vol. 104, No. 2, pp. 271–279.

Chosun Central Television (2016). Broadcast of 8 August.

Demick, Barbara (2010). *Nothing to Envy: Real Lives in North Korea* (London: Granta).

Denkowski, Charles A. von (2014). 'The North Korean State Security Department's Border Policing: Insecurity and Disharmony in Northeast Asia,' Lecture at the 6th Annual Conference of the Asian Criminological Society, Osaka University of Commerce, 29 June.

Denkowski, Charles A. von (2015). 'From State-Organized Crime to Legal Business: Transforming North Korea – A Criminological Approach,' in *East Asian Intelligence and Organised Crime*, ed. Stephan Blancke (Berlin: Verlag Dr. Koester), pp. 343–396.

Duowei News (2016). 'Chaoxian junren yuejing qiangjie, yu Zhongguo juncha qiangzhan [North Korean soldiers cross the border and commit robbery; engage in a gunfight with Chinese military police],' *Duowei Xinwen*, 28 July.

Eichhorn, Moritz (2015). 'Die Luegen des Kronzeugen: Shin Dong-hyuk hat ein nordkoreanisches Lager ueberlebt; Jetzt revidiert er Teile seiner Story [The lies of the key witness: Shin Dong-hyuk, who experienced a North Korean prison camp, revises part of his story],' *Die Welt*, 20 January, p. 7.

Green, Christopher (2015a). 'From the Borderland to Beijing: Chinese Civilian Shot in Changbai,' *SinoNK*, 20 September.

Green, Christopher (2015b). 'Rhetoric vs Reality: 5.24 and North Korean Workers in Dandong,' *SinoNK*, 3 December.

Green, Christopher (2016). 'The Sino-North Korean Border Economy: Money and Power Relations in North Korea,' *Asian Perspective*, Vol. 4, No. 3 (July–September), 415–434.

Greitens, Sheena Chestnut (2014). *Illicit: North Korea's Evolving Operations to Earn Hard Currency* (Washington, DC: Committee for Human Rights in North Korea).

Habib, Benjamin (2011). 'North Korea's Parallel Economies: Systemic Disaggregation Following the Soviet Collapse,' *Communist and Post-Communist Studies*, Vol. 44, No. 2, pp. 149–159.

Haggard, Stephan (2016). 'Yeonmi Park In Order to Live: A North Korean Girl's Journey to Freedom,' *North Korea: Witness to Transformation*, 13 January. https://piie.com/blogs/north-korea-witness-transformation/yeonmi-park-order-live-north-korean-girls-journey-freedom.

Harden, Blaine (2015). 'New Forward to Escape from Camp 14,' blaineharden.com.

Hastings, Justin (2015). 'The Economic Geography of North Korean Drug Trafficking Networks,' *Review of International Political Economy*, Vol. 22, No. 1, pp. 162–193.

Human Rights Watch (2015). 'North Korea: Harsher Punishments for Contact with South,' 9 February.

Hwang, Zhangpu (2010). '"Tuobeizhe" ["Defector"],' *Fenghuang Zhoukan* [Phoenix Weekly], 1 October cover story. www.51fenghuang.com/news/fengmiangushi/tuobeizhe.html.

Jakarta Post News Desk (2017). 'Police to Investigate North Korean Restaurant on Spy Activity,' *Jakarta Post*, 20 February.

Kim Jong-il (1968). 'Let Us Develop Ryanggang Province into a Firm Base for Education in Revolutionary Traditions: A Talk to Senior Officials of Ryanggang Province and Anti-Japanese Revolutionary Fighters,' 21 July, *Kim Jong Il Selected Works, Volume 1, 1964–1969* (Pyongyang: Foreign Languages Press, 1992), pp. 364–379.

Kim Jong-un (2016). 'Kim Jong Un's Letter to Teaching Staff and Students at Kim Il Sung University on 70th Anniversary of Its Founding,' *Rodong Sinmun*, 3 October.

Kim Kwang-tae and Choi Kyong-ae (2016). 'Two N. Korean Armed Deserters Arrested after Shootout with Chinese Security Sources: Source,' Yonhap News Agency, 29 July.

Kim Mikyoung (2013). 'North Korean Refugees' Nostalgia: The Border People's Narratives,' *Asian Politics & Policy*, Vol. 5, No. 4, pp. 523–542.

Kim Sung Kyung (2016). 'Mobile North Korean Women and Their Places in the Sino-North Korea Borderland,' *Asian Anthropology*, Vol. 15, No. 2, pp. 116–131.

Korean Central News Agency (2017). 'Rodong Sinmun Calls for Intensifying Anti-Imperialist and Class Education,' 6 March.

Lee, Hyeonseo, with David John (2015). *The Girl with Seven Names: A North Korean Defector's Story* (New York: Harper Collins).

Liaoning Daily (2016). 'Dandong kaizhan qiuji shuishang lianhe xunting [Dandong commences combined autumn water patrols],' *Liaoning Ribao*, 23 September.

Martinez, Ernesto (2009). 'Violence, Business and Identity in the Borderlands: Chinese-Mexicans in Mexicali, Mexico,' *Cultural Dynamics*, Vol. 21, No. 1, pp. 79–101.

Park, Hyun Ok (2014). *The Capitalist Unconscious: From Korean Unification to Transnational Korea* (New York: Columbia University Press).

Pilling, David (2013). 'Lunch with the FT: Shin Dong-hyuk,' *Financial Times*, 31 August/1 September, Life and Arts, p. 3.

Qi, Fei and Li Hao (2012). 'Caifang "Women zui xinfu" de zuozhe, Barbara Demick [Interview with Barbara Demick, author of "Nothing to Envy"],' *Fenghuang Zhoukan* [Phoenix Weekly], 1 April. http://bbs.tianya.cn/post-worldlook-455017-1.shtml.

Roitman, Janet (2005). *Fiscal Disobedience: An Anthropology of Economic Regulation in Central Africa* (Princeton: Princeton University Press).

Shu, Wenqiang (2016). 'Changbai xian gong'anju kaizhan "fupinri" fupin shijian huodong [Changbai county Public Security Bureau begins "assistance to the poor" activities],' Changbai County Government, 21 October. http://gaj.changbai.gov.cn/tpxw/149658.jhtml.

Song, Jiyoung (2013). '"Smuggled Refugees": The Social Construction of North Korean Migration,' *International Migration*, Vol. 51, No. 4, pp. 158–173.

Stanton, Joshua (2016). 'To Prevent War, Talk To North Korea's Soldiers about Rice, Peace and Freedom,' *One Free Korea*, 26 August. http://freekorea.us/2016/08/26/to-prevent-war-talk-to-north-koreas-soldiers-about-rice-peace-freedom/#sthash.HizMVnID.dpbs.

United Nations General Assembly (2014). 'Summary Prepared by the Office of the United Nations High Commissioner for Human Rights in accordance with paragraph 15(b) of the annex to Human Rights Council resolution 5/1 and paragraph 5 of the annex to Council resolution 16/21: Democratic People's Republic of Korea,' Human Rights Council Working Group on the Universal Periodic Review, Nineteenth session (28 April–9 May), Document A/HRC/WG.6/19/PRK/3 (23 January).

Wang, Peng and Stephan Blancke (2014). 'Mafia State: The Evolving Threat of North Korean Narcotics Trafficking,' *The RUSI Journal*, Vol. 159, No. 5 (October/November), pp. 52–59.

Yao, Zhang, Guo Dawei, and Liang Yonggang (2017). 'Wujing Jilin zongdui Jilin pianqu yiludu "Moguizhou" jixian xunlian jishi [An on-the-spot report of "Devil Week" Extreme Training of a Provincial Armed Police Squadron On a Stretch of Land in Jilin Province],' *Jilin Xinwenwang* (Jilin News Net) 23 March. www.jl.chinanews.com/kjww/2017-03-27/16941.html.

Yonhap (2017). 'Six Armed North Korean Soldiers Enter China,' *JoongAng Daily*, 3 March.

Yoon, Yeo-sang and Lee Seung-ju (2015). *Human Rights and North Korea's Overseas Laborers: Dilemmas and Policy Challenges* (Seoul: Database Center for North Korean Human Rights).

Zoccatelli, Giulia (2014). '"It Was Fun, It Was Dangerous": Heroin, Young Urbanites and Opening Reforms in China's Borderlands,' *International Journal of Drug Policy*, Vol. 25, pp. 762–768.

34

Border and road regimes in Central Asia

Ordering disorder at an Uzbek–Kazakh checkpoint

Rano Turaeva

The collapse of the Soviet Union in the early 1990s was visibly marked by borders and checkpoints between the newly independent republics, as well as inside most of the former Soviet Republics (Tabyshalieva 2001; Megoran 2002, 2006, 2007, 2012a, 2012b; Megoran et al. 2005; Grafe et al. 2008; Kipping 2008; Lewington 2010; Kraudzun 2012). However, it did not stop people from crossing these borders. Millions of labour migrants have since moved in the direction of Russia, Kazakhstan, and the West (the USA and Europe). Mobility and migration increased after the collapse of the Soviet Union; it is arguably the most important and visible change in the post-Soviet era. Newly installed border crossings and checkpoints along roads far away from borders rendered the state visible in new ways and put state–society relations at the centre of popular discussions (Martin 2015). For many travellers, moving outside the familiarity of the home town or district came to be seen as a dangerous endeavour. The suffering associated with such movement is nicely depicted in a popular Uzbek proverb: "*yol azobi gor azobi*" – "suffering the road is suffering the grave".

This chapter not only presents, in part, an autoethnographic account of cross-border travel from Uzbekistan to Kazakhstan, but also includes reflections based on travelling within the country in minivans, buses, and trains. Moreover, some border crossing experiences also relate to the experiences at the Tadjik–Uzbek and Uzbek–Turkmen borders. The approach I take in this chapter is comparable to Khosravi's (2010) autoethnography of illegal border crossing.

Ethnographies of border crossing and checkpoints are a cornerstone of the literature on border studies (Alvarez 1995; Van Houtum and Van Naerssen 2002; Migdal 2004). The aim of my contribution in this volume, however, is not directly to engage with this literature on borders and borderlands (Feyissa and Hoehne 2010; Khosravi 2010; Van Houtum 2010; Donnan and Wilson 2010a, b; Wastl-Walter 2012; Korf and Raeymaekers 2013; Hoehne 2015). My aim is to take border crossing experiences as an example to explore situations of uncertainty and show how uncertainty can be used as a resource. Furthermore, in this way one can uncover the complexities of ordering disorder and the establishment of power regimes in the case of border regimes. In other words, my argument in this chapter is that there is a kind of continuously established order among the obvious chaos at border crossings and checkpoints, where people have even died in the crowds. This order is not only made from the rule of law; it is regulated through unwritten rules and norms established and maintained via practices of negotiation in complex encounters.

In the precarious environment where uncertainty is not an avoidable state of mind, combined with the highly visible power of the state apparatus established along roads and on borders, travellers become a resource for both officials in uniform and for those without uniforms, as well as for entrepreneurs and a number of other residents of the border region. Uncertainty is used by all actors involved, mainly by those who are capable of benefiting from it. Distance from one's home – the safe location characterized by a safe network – is the main requirement for uncertainty. The moment a person moves away from home with its familiar social networks, he or she becomes vulnerable, feeling a lack of knowledge of the social and other structures that define the unfamiliar place. Travellers away from home have to deal with new situations and unexpected encounters, and often they are not well informed about the rules and norms in place. This particularly concerns first-time travellers on certain roads and border crossing points. In the environment of uncertainty and disorder, travellers have to negotiate and handle aggressive and power-hungry officers and negotiate their way through the checkpoints.

It is interesting to trace the process of those negotiations during which a certain kind of order within disorder is formed. State technologies of power or *dispositif* (a term which I will return to shortly) are appropriated by local security officers, as well as by citizen-passengers and drivers. The latter stand in the middle as brokers between the state and citizens negotiating the legality and legitimacy of their passing. Citizens also become active parts of the process of appropriation through their own ways of negotiating rules with officers, drivers, and brokers. State officials use existing regulation on identification documents, mobility, and registration, which was originally meant to protect the security of citizens against them, thus restricting their freedom of movement. Therefore, many have no choice but to pay for their freedom. Besides state officials, drivers also profit from these regulations; they get their share from passengers and state officials for the services they offer. The fact that state officials frequently abuse regulations provides opportunities for brokers to take a cut from the bribes they negotiate with customs officials.

This chapter is structured in the following way: I start with the presentation of the ethnographic material illuminating the complexities of border and road regimes in Central Asia. I will then highlight the importance of uncertainty as a resource in the analysis of border regimes in Central Asia and trace the formation of order amidst disorder. Furthermore, I will discuss the notion of power in more detail, using Foucault to understand border regimes and power regimes as *dispositifs*. The concluding remarks will summarize the argument.

Travelling from Tashkent to Chimkent via Chernyaevka

It is summer 2006; the temperature is as high as 35–40 degrees Celsius. I am travelling together with a female friend of mine – Lola (32). She has dyed blonde hair, is about 160 cm tall, physically well built, and slim. We both wear jeans and T-shirts and carry handbags; I also have my backpack with my laptop and some books with me. My friend looks Caucasian Armenian, her skin is fair, and she can easily pass as Russian. In comparison, I look more "local", Uzbek or Kyrgyz; she is clearly more attractive than me. We both travel on Uzbek passports and we speak Russian with each other.

Travelling both within and out of Uzbekistan is time consuming and challenging, not because of the rough roads, but rather because of the numerous checkpoints within the country as well as on the border. The checkpoints are feared for their harsh and inhumane treatment and infamous for the extortion of money by the guards. In-country border-crossing checkpoints are equipped with soldiers, customs officers and police who scrutinize passengers and vehicles. While it is not unusual to cross in private vehicles, most people travel on public buses or in shared taxis. The checkpoints were established after the independence of Uzbekistan in the early 1990s. Travelling within Uzbekistan in general is a risky business, considering the number of traffic police on the roads of towns and cities; six or seven checkpoints lie in front of us on the 719 kilometres to Almaty in Kazakhstan.

We are both heading to Almaty to get our UK visas since the embassy in Tashkent is closed temporarily. We are planning to cross into Kazakhstan at the Chernyaevka border, named after the border village. Chernyaevka is the old Soviet name for the village, which is now called Gisht-Kuprik on the Uzbek side and Zhibek Zholy on the Kazakh side. The border checkpoint, however, is still known by the old name Chernyaevka. It is located 12 kilometres from the Yunusabad area of Tashkent, from where minivans (*marshrutka*s) regularly shuttle back and forth. The *marshrutka*s leaving from Yunusabad bazaar cost 1500 sum (US$2) during the daytime and 2000 sum (US$2.50) in the evening. One can also take a taxi if one is in a hurry and has more money to spend. We opt for the *marshrutka*.

Right after our vehicle stops not far from the checkpoint (cars are not allowed to cross the border, so all passengers have to walk through it), three or four women approach us and the other passengers to offer their services. These services include: providing blank papers (A4), blank customs declaration forms, and assistance with filling out these forms. These services cost between 1000 and 1500 sum, depending on what one needs. The forms also include short-term registration papers for Kazakhstan, which allow a person to stay up to five days without further registration.

From where our *marshrutka* stops, it is still about a one kilometre walk to the border. There are some women with lots of luggage and some elderly passengers for whom this is a considerable challenge. At this point, other drivers step in and offer a lift to the other side of the border without further hassle for a price ranging from US$15 to US$35. Their prices change constantly according to the exchange rates of local currencies. However, we know that these services are illegal and therefore dangerous (Galemba 2013). If one is caught there is an additional payment for the soldier who otherwise may arrest the passengers and driver. The bribe to be paid when caught varies according to how skilfully one is able to communicate with the soldier and how "hungry" and daring the soldier is. We do not accept this kind of offer and continue to the border gates where a big crowd is queuing up.

It is already 11 am – too late for crossing given the number of travellers waiting when we arrive at the gates of the first checkpoint on the Uzbek side of the border. We stand and watch how the crowd at the gate moves and behaves. We both hope that at some point there will be a way to get through this chaotic crowd, or that the soldiers observing us would take pity on us and open another door to avoid the crowd. Lola keeps smiling and flirting with the soldiers. I am trying to find a spot where we could both squeeze through the male dominated crowd and enter the office. After two long hours we manage to squeeze into the bulk of the crowd. It is very hot and some fellow travellers complain about their weary feet, some have difficulty pushing through with their bags, and children are crying. Those with small crying children are finally allowed to enter through another door and avoid the crowd. The crowds can be dangerous for those with heart problems; local newspapers occasionally report that older women die in the crowds while crossing the Uzbek–Kazakh border.[1] In order to be able to bear the long periods of time (up to several hours) being squeezed until one finally enters the building, one either needs to be very fit or a young man. When crossing the border here, people with different passports are treated differently. People holding Kazakh or Russian passports have almost no problem crossing from both sides, whereas holders of Uzbek passports face considerable challenges.

The majority of travellers are migrants who are coming from Uzbekistan to work in Kazakhstan on construction sites or in other jobs as *mardikor* (short-term labourers). Some travellers continue their journey from Kazakhstan to Russia. They are picked up by prearranged brokers called *starshiy* at the other side of the border. The *starshiys*' job is to bring Uzbek traveller-migrants to their final destination in Russia and organize jobs and accommodation. Some of our fellow travellers are petty traders who buy products in the Kazakh bazaars to resell in Uzbekistan. This was a profitable business in the 1990s and early 2000s; more recently, however, given the corruption related to border crossing and shrinking price differences, it has lost much of its attraction.

Finally, we make it through the crowd. Lola is calm, whereas I am rather nervous to cross the border, despite the fact that neither of us has had any problems with our passports. After we enter the customs office, we hurry to complete the customs declaration and deal with the soldiers, customs and immigration officers. These officials are known to harass travellers, depending on their personality and mood. All belongings are X-rayed as well as manually checked, and if the officer in charge is in a bad mood or needs money, he will easily find fault with the individual belongings of a traveller. After the X-ray, I have the following conversation with an officer who looks at me as if I were a criminal:

CO: Open your bags, what are you transporting? What is in your laptop! Open your laptop? What is this?
RT: I have nothing in it. This is a USB stick. This is a voice recorder. This is a book about the history of an Uzbek hero.
CO: Are you a spy? Why do you have these things? For whom do you work?
RT: I am a researcher and not a spy.
CO: I will have to inform our head officer and we will investigate your stuff.
RT: Please officer, I am in a hurry, let's settle this, I am writing about the history of the region and am not a spy. I can show you all my files if you want.
CO: Follow me and bring your belongings.

Officers sometimes seem very happy if they manage to scare a person, particularly if he or she seems to have money to settle things "privately" (as in my case). Compare this conversation with the one between a shuttle trader and a customs officer, which I overheard:

CO: Open your bags! What are these things?
ST: I am a poor mother of three children. I have to feed my children. I do not have many things. Please officer let me go. I have already paid the soldiers at the gate I don't have extra money left.
CO: (looking at how she was dressed to guess if she has money) I will have to fine you for breaking the rules on import and export.
ST: Officer, please don't fine, don't confiscate. We can settle this without fines please.

In the room I am asked to follow the officer and two other officers – a man and a woman – and sit at a table. The woman searches my body and the man asks me to open my laptop. I login to the account where I have no files and the officer is obviously not sure how to handle my computer. He places the mouse into the search field within a folder and types the word "type" (for whatever reason). Zero results. My computer is set to English and he looks really lost and embarrassed. The officer who brought me to the room says: "You are a computer specialist and you do not know how to deal with it?" The specialist computer officer gives no answer; to ease the situation I offer my help. This friendly gesture makes the already nervous officers even more embarrassed and the officer who brought me to the room finally asks if I have any good quality pens for them. I hand over all the pens I have and the officers let me go.

This time I am lucky to have a computer officer who does not know how to deal with my computer and was not able to find fault and "*oformit protocol*" – "to write a protocol" – another threatening phrase in this setting, which is usually used against uninformed citizens who would interpret it as the start of big trouble that needs an urgent solution here and now.

Finally, we make it through the first building on the Uzbek side. The next building is about 150 metres away from the first. We are both tired, hungry, and thirsty. We tried to drink less in order to avoid having to use the toilets, which are outside and thus require extra time. Once on the other side of the border, the crowd in front of the Kazakh customs office has not become smaller; from time to time a soldier shouts: "Is there anybody with Kazakh or Russian passports?" Those with the right passport can pass without hassle. All others are left in the crowd for an unknown number of hours until they finally make it into the building. On the Kazakh side, similar procedures begin: custom declaration, luggage check, passport control, face control, behaviour control, etc. One can see officers in both uniform and in plain clothes (they can be recognized as non-travellers as they do not have any bags and are just standing around). While I am standing in the queue for passport control, a Kazakh officer in civilian clothes signals with his finger for me to approach him. I am not sure what to do, but move in his direction. My friend Lola has already passed passport control. The man says: "[Give] Your passport. Why are you going to Kazakhstan?" I do not know if he really is an officer in civilian clothes or just a pretender. For me, it is simply his demand ("your passport") that authorizes him and makes him an officer in my eyes. I show my passport and smile, thinking it might help. He begins to interrogate me, and my efforts to establish his identity only make him act even more pushy and arrogant. I have to show him the contents of my rucksack and my pockets, and after half an hour we settle on a "small fee" (US$20) and he lets me go. There are other "officers" in civilian clothing subjecting other passengers to similar procedures, particularly those decently dressed from whom money could be expected. I realize that I am a random catch by an officer in his out-of-office hours, out for "random hunting". At all the stations on the Kazakh side, the soldiers and officers are rude and arrogant towards non-Russians and non-citizens, often resorting to random checks, stripping, and arrogant laughter. They directly name the sum one has to pay as a bribe, sending the message of unchecked power to all surrounding people. Soldiers, with or without uniforms, shout commands to anybody passing through this space of insecurity and uncertainty.

After several long hours of this, I feel relieved when we leave the buildings of check and trial. But gender-based harassment can go further than this. Both of us are relatively attractive and nicely dressed young women, which can become at times quite dangerous when travelling without an accompanying man. This is taken as an invitation by many Central Asian men, who try to start conversations with us, often in intruding and rude ways. From my own experience in Central Asia, I often feel threatened if a man starts a conversation without me looking in his direction. Often men take refusal to continue an imposed conversation as an insult and then become very nasty, insulting, and violent. As we walk towards the taxis, two tall Kazakh men in uniform approach and stop us. "Passports!" is their clear and firm order. I naïvely hand over my passport which is still in my hand. The man grins coldly and says: "You are Uzbek, I am Kazakh. This is Kazakhstan, so I can do whatever I want here and you can do nothing." He starts moving away with my passport in his hand. I am helpless but I know that I have to get my money out quickly and buy my passport back. My friend Lola steps in and stresses that she would solve this. She runs after the two men and stops them by touching the hand of the one holding the passport. I see her skilfully winding the document from his hands, very fast, with another hand placed on his chest. She smiles and says:

> I am sure you understand women, and we have just spent several hours at the border behind us. We are tired and we are hurrying to find the next bathroom, if you kindly permit us. I am sure you will still be here when we come back and we can of course leave you our numbers.

Lola's speech is well delivered, almost as if she has trained for it beforehand. One of the soldiers writes down her number and, after having dialled it and hearing her telephone ring, they let us go. Needless to say, we would never see them again. The incident reminds us of the highly gendered nature of checkpoints.

Unwritten rules and uncertainty as recourse

The borders between Uzbekistan and Kazakhstan constitute a regime of uncertainty, and within this regime an average traveller has to be prepared to deal with the unchecked power of various official and unofficial actors. Travellers have to follow written and unwritten rules and behavioural patterns. Of course, individual positioning and skills make a difference, as shown above.

The setting of road or border regimes is made up from the environment of precarity, uncertainty, fear, liminality, and the respective attitudes of state officials, passengers, drivers, and others. By comparison, the "style" of these regimes is much more informal than in other regimes of control, which have permanent staff and their local offices, such as local police offices, for example. Road and border checkpoints, with their rotating personnel and often relatively isolated location, grant more space to exert and abuse informal power and extort money from those passing through. The rules in place maybe derived from laws and regulations; in practice, however, they are based on the routine of the interactions, exchange, and communication. There are certain unwritten rules about how to talk to an official at a checkpoint along the road, how to deal with the luggage, what to expect from the driver, where to stop to eat, and what other precautions regarding general security issues are to be taken. The fears associated with cross-border travel change depending on who is crossing the border. Earlier, before 2005, petty traders benefited from the price differences between Kazakhstan and Uzbekistan. Their products were constantly confiscated unless they paid bribes. The bribes increased and gradually made the risky travel of the traders unprofitable. Now, labour migrants make up the majority of those crossing the borders; they have their *starshiy* – the broker organizing the trip and employment at the destination – waiting on the other side of the border. The officers ask these travellers "who is your *starshiy*?" The migrants give the name of their *starshiy* and if he has good relations with the officer in charge, the traveller is spared all the trouble of those without good connections.

Uncertainty is maintained and even fostered in order to be used as a resource for economic gain by those in power – be it the middlemen offering services to avoid the state or state officials acting in the name of the state. Inter-ethnic relations and nationalistic discourse very strongly shape encounters, particularly when crossing borders. Intensified by the additional uncertainty of the travellers, this creates favourable conditions for violence and abuse.

This environment is precarious in the sense that Judith Butler (2009, 2016) describes. Butler (2009: ii) defines precarity as a "politically induced condition of maximized vulnerability and exposure for populations exposed to arbitrary state violence and to other forms of aggression that are not enacted by states and against which states do not offer adequate protection". Here it is important to distinguish between systemic qualities of risk – as in Beck's risk society model (Beck 2009) – and precarity as a structural condition where knowledge of these qualities (precarity and risk) are given.

However, in the situation of uncertainty, lack of knowledge about security is an a priori requirement for feeling insecure and in doubt (state of uncertainty). On the individual level in the situation of uncertainty (and lack of knowledge about risks), a person becomes completely dependent on others and therefore vulnerable to violence and abuse. Pelkmans (2013) highlights the intellectual aspect of doubt whereas McBrien (2013: 253) draws attention to the emotional aspect of doubt. The anthropology of uncertainty (Felson and Gmelch 1979; Boholm 2003; Samimian-Darash et al. 2012) is a field yet to be developed, and scholarly works on uncertainty and risks are still dominated by quantitative analysis (Hoffman and Hammonds 1994; Johnson and Slovic 1995), mainly in the fields of medicine, health, business, and trade.

New locations, new rules, new environments, and the absence of familial networks and family support lead to situations of uncertainty and risk, unless people are friendly to each other, state officials do not abuse their authority, and people are protected by their families and networks. In the environment of precarity, those who have no power are dependent on the mercy of those in power and who are feared as being able to abuse their power at any moment. The condition of uncertainty is maintained through constant questioning of travellers' belongings, documents, and purpose of travel. Uncertainty is a big resource, which makes it easy to gain profits in the form of money, presents, private numbers, and the attention of good-looking women.

Border regimes

Border regimes are a certain form of governance that is based on regular encounters structured through numerous and continuous interactions, rules, exchange, values, and attitudes. Regime is "the complex of institutional geography, rules, practice and animating ideas that are associated with the regulation" (Hood et al. 2001: 9). A regime-based approach to any regulatory systems of government allows us to "bring out the relationships among different parts of the regulatory system" (Hood et al. 2001: 14). Going back to the etymology of the word "regime" from the Latin "regimen", meaning "rule" or "government", the Latin *regimen* itself comes from the verb "regere", meaning "to lead straight" or "to rule". The verb *regere* has several kin words or lexemes such as "correct", "erect", "region", "rule", and "surge" (Merriam-Webster n.d.). Mobility, authoritarian rule, and uncertainty are preconditions for the establishment of border regimes in a Foucauldian (Foucault 1975 [1977], 1980) understanding of the regime as a dispersed but powerful set of institutions, practices, and objects. For instance, road or border regimes are established under the conditions of uncertainty for travellers who are outside their safe networks and who are subject to the unchecked power of those who make use of this uncertainty, namely the authorities who legitimize their authority through their uniforms, or just rhetorically through spitting out different commands such as "your passport" or "come here and show me your bags' contents".

Power is central for the functioning of any regime and Foucault's recommendation is to "escape from the limited field of juridical sovereignty and state institutions, and instead base our analysis of power on the study of the techniques and tactics of domination" (Foucault 1980: 102). In other words, power is constituted through strategies, *dispositifs*, techniques, and economy (Foucault 1978: 12).

Borders and roads are instituted and authorized by the state and made visible by the presence of state officials in uniform, guns, technology (X-ray, other equipment, papers), the power to interfere with the mobility of travellers and decide their fate, and so on (Kearney 1991; Langer 1999; Cunningham and Heyman 2004; Fassin 2011). Power, authority, and economic relations of this order are established in favour of those in power.

To understand a regime one needs to look at its context and content. The regime context is "the backdrop or setting in which regulation takes place" (Hood et al. 2001: 21). The "regime content means the policy settings, the configuration of state and other organizations directly engaged in regulating the risk, and the attitudes, beliefs, and operating conventions of the regulators" (Hood et al. 2001: 21). The elements of a regime, according to Foucault, are a *dispositif* – that is, mechanisms, techniques, and economies driven by power and power relations (Foucault 1978: 12).

Dispositif: state technologies of control

So, what kind of mechanisms, techniques, and technologies of control are used by the state in the case at hand? Citizens are required to carry their passports, since it is the only valid identification document besides a driver's licence. Male citizens at the age of military service should additionally carry their military service status certificate. These documents should not be expired nor damaged (passports can become worn out easily because of frequent use), and have a proper registration stamp (*propiska*) indicating the place where a person is registered (Turaeva 2012). These rules can be found only within small brochures of internal regulations, issued only for internal use by the security services, including the police. The rules for extra luggage when travelling within one's own country are taken from the rules which are written for those items imported to or exported from Uzbekistan and are used by state security officers at the checkpoints.

All these rules are applied differently in different contexts by police officers along roads or security officers at checkpoints. They make up what Foucault called *dispositif* – originally from Latin *dispōnāre* "'to set in order', 'to arrange', 'to dispose' or 'to form'" which "indicates a dispositional arrangement of agency, which can also be translated as a certain organisation, formation, assemblage, distribution or order" (Raffnsøe et al. 2014: 9).

According to Foucault, *dispositif* consists of tools and devices to control and manage populations. An apparatus has a target to correct and produce the desired effect (Rabinow 1984: p. xvi). Foucault states that an apparatus

> is, firstly, a thoroughly heterogeneous ensemble consisting of discourses, institutions, architectural forms, regulatory decisions, laws, administrative measures, scientific statements, philosophical, moral and philanthropic propositions – in short, the said as much as the unsaid. Such are the elements of the apparatus. The apparatus itself is the system of relations that can be established between these elements. Secondly, what I am trying to identify in this apparatus is precisely the nature of the connection that can exist between these heterogeneous elements. [...] between these elements, whether discursive or non-discursive, there is a sort of interplay of shifts of position and modifications of function which can also vary very widely. Thirdly, I understand by the term "apparatus" a sort of – shall we say – formation which has as its major function at a given historical moment that of responding to an urgent need. The apparatus thus has a dominant strategic function.
>
> *(Foucault 1980, 194–195)*

Foucault states that

> the universal juridicism of modern society seems to fix limits on the exercise of power, its universally widespread panopticism enables operation, on the underside of the law, a machinery that is both immense and minute, which supports, reinforces, multiplies the asymmetry of power and undermines the limits that are traced around the law. (Foucault 1977: 223)

A *dispositif*, as an apparatus of control and power (i.e., mechanism to exercise power), is a mechanism enabling road or border regimes function. Since these regimes are based on technologies of power and control that function like machines, they provide those actors vested with authority an opportunity to use them for their own benefit. The state of uncertainty in which travellers find themselves through this simultaneous use and abuse of power, further contribute to these mechanisms. As a *dispositif* of state control over populations, the border regimes function both to secure territory *and* bring profits. Various rules, informal practices, discourses, attitudes, and beliefs structure them. Thinking in terms of machines, apparatuses, and technologies highlights the importance of both the ruthless and non-human workings of power *and* the human emotions and attitudes contributing to the heterogeneity of the regime and its components, which at times function as machines with human faces.

Concluding remarks

Based on the ethnography of border crossing from Uzbekistan to Kazakhstan in Chernyaevka border checkpoint, I explained the mechanisms of power and institutionalization of power in the form of border regimes and road regimes where uncertainty is used as the main resource. By going into the details of the experiences of crossing borders in Central Asia, I tried to shed some light on the principles and mechanisms of power at work in the form of rhetoric, discourses, dialogues, communication, and violence in order to stop and remind them of the power of those working for the state. Travelling the roads and crossing the borders is a chaotic experience for travellers, and for those who benefit from this process it is an opportunity to play power games. The process of travelling and crossing borders is a challenge for all the actors involved, be it bribing an official, accepting bribes, negotiating, gaining, maintaining one's authority or status, gambling or performing.

Within this diversity of situations, institutional setup, and practices, there is some kind of "agreement" and the rules to play the game are both written and mostly unwritten, win or lose. What fascinated me about roads, borders, and journeys within and outside Uzbekistan, Turkmenistan, Tajikistan, and Kazakhstan is how order within disorder is being formed and maintained, as well as how uncertainty plays a crucial role as a resource within this process. This order forming border regimes is comparable to Foucault's *dispositif* of power and control, as it is constituted through techniques, strategies, institutions, and practices of power. In these settings, road regimes and border regimes are constantly negotiated, shaped, and maintained.

Note

1 A woman dies in the queue of the Uzbek-Kazakh border, published by Uzhalqharakat on 10 November 2013, http://uzxalqharakati.com/ru/archives/5877.

References

Alvarez Jr, R.R. (1995). The Mexican-US border: The making of an anthropology of borderlands. *Annual Review of Anthropology, 24*, pp. 447–470.
Beck, U. (2009). *World at risk*. Cambridge: Polity Press.
Boholm, Å. (2003). The cultural nature of risk: Can there be an anthropology of uncertainty? *Ethnos, 68*(2), pp. 159–178.
Butler, J. (2009). Performativity, precarity and sexual politics. *AIBR-Revista de Antropologia Iberoamericana, 4*(3), pp. i–xiii.
———. (2016). *Frames of war: When is life grievable?* Brooklyn, NY: Verso Books.

Cunningham, H. and Heyman, J. (2004). Introduction: Mobilities and enclosures at borders. *Identities*, *11*(3), pp. 289–302.
Donnan, H. and Wilson, T.M. (2010a). *Borderlands: Ethnographic approaches to security, power, and identity*. Lanham, MD, Boulder, CO, Toronto, New York, Plymouth: University Press of America.
Donnan, H. and Wilson, T.M. (2010b). Ethnography, security and the "frontier effect", in borderlands. In *Borderlands: Ethnographic approaches to security, power, and identity*. Hastings Donnan and Thomas M. Wilson, eds. Lanham, MD: University Press of America, pp. 1–21.
Fassin, D. (2011). Policing borders, producing boundaries. The governmentality of immigration in dark times. *Annual Review of Anthropology*, *40*, pp. 213–226.
Felson, R.B. and Gmelch, G. (1979). Uncertainty and the use of magic. *Current Anthropology*, *20*(3), pp. 587–589.
Feyissa, D. and Hoehne, M.V. (2010). *Borders and borderlands as resources in the Horn of Africa*. Woodbridge: James Currey.
Foucault, M. [1975] (1977). *Discipline and punish: The birth of the prison*. New York: Vintage.
———. (1978). *Dispositive der Macht Michel Foucault über Sexualität*. Berlin: Wissen und Wahrheit, Mrve Verlag.
———. (1980). *Power/knowledge: Selected interviews and other writings, 1972–1977*. New York: Pantheon.
Galemba, R.B. (2013). Illegality and invisibility at margins and borders. *PoLAR: Political and Legal Anthropology Review*, *36*(2), pp. 274–285.
Grafe, C., Raiser, M. and Sakatsume, T. (2008). Beyond borders—Reconsidering regional trade in Central Asia. *Journal of Comparative Economics*, *36*(3), pp. 453–466.
Hoehne, M. (2015). *Between Somaliland and Puntland: Marginalization, militarization and conflicting political visions*. Nairobi, Kenya: Rift Valley Institute.
Hoffman, F.O. and Hammonds, J.S. (1994). Propagation of uncertainty in risk assessments: The need to distinguish between uncertainty due to lack of knowledge and uncertainty due to variability. *Risk Analysis*, *14*(5), pp. 707–712.
Hood, C., Rothstein, H. and Baldwin, R. (2001). *The government of risk: Understanding risk regulation regimes*. Oxford: Oxford University Press.
Johnson, B.B. and Slovic, P. (1995). Presenting uncertainty in health risk assessment: Initial studies of its effects on risk perception and trust. *Risk Analysis*, *15*(4), pp. 485–494.
Kearney, M. (1991). Borders and boundaries of state and self at the end of empire. *Journal of Historical Sociology*, *4*(1), pp. 52–74.
Khosravi, S. (2010). *"Illegal" traveller: An auto-ethnography of borders*. New York: Springer.
Kipping, M. (2008). Can "integrated water resources management" silence Malthusian concerns? The case of Central Asia. *Water International*, *33*(3), pp. 305–319.
Korf, B. and Raeymaekers, T., eds. (2013). *Violence on the margins: States, conflict, and borderlands*. New York: Springer.
Kraudzun, T. (2012). From the Pamir frontier to international borders: Exchange relations of the borderland population. In *Subverting borders*. B. Brungs and J. Miggelbrink, eds. Wiesbaden: VS Verlag für Sozialwissenschaften, pp. 171–191.
Langer, J. (1999). "Towards a conceptualization of border: The Central European experience". In *Curtains of iron and gold. Reconstructing borders and scales of interaction*. J. Eskelinen, I. Liikanen and J. Oksa, eds. Aldershot: Ashgate, pp. S.25–42.
Lewington, R. (2010). The challenge of managing central Asia's new borders. *Asian Affairs*, *41*(2), pp. 221–236.
Martin, D. (2015). Close(r) to the edge: Anthropology of post-Soviet borderlands. *Journal of the Royal Anthropological Institute*, *21*(1), pp. 199–201.
McBrien, J. (2013). Afterword, the aftermath of doubt. In *Ethnographies of doubt: Faith and uncertainty in contemporary societies*. M. Pelkmans, ed. London: IB Tauris, pp. 251–268.
Megoran, N. (2002). *The borders of eternal friendship: The politics and pain of nationalism and identity along the Uzbekistan-Kyrgyzstan Ferghana Valley boundary, 1999-2000*. Unpublished Doctoral Dissertation, Sidney Sussex College, Cambridge, September.
———. (2006). For ethnography in political geography: Experiencing and re-imagining Ferghana Valley boundary closures. *Political Geography*, *25*(6), pp. 622–640.
———. (2007). On researching "ethnic conflict": Epistemology, politics, and a Central Asian boundary dispute. *Europe-Asia Studies*, *59*(2), pp. 253–277.

———. (2012a). Rethinking the study of international boundaries: A biography of the Kyrgyzstan–Uzbekistan boundary. *Annals of the Association of American Geographers, 102*(2), pp. 464–481.

———. (2012b). "'B/ordering' and biopolitics in Central Asia". In *A companion to border studies* (Vol. 26). T.M. Wilson and H. Donnan, eds. Hoboken, NJ: John Wiley & Sons, pp. 473–491.

Megoran, N., Raballand, G. and Bouyjou, J. (2005). Performance, representation and the economics of border control in Uzbekistan. *Geopolitics, 10*(4), pp. 712–740.

Merriam-Webster.com. (n.d.) "Regimen". Available at www.merriam-webster.com/dictionary/regimen.

Migdal, J. (2004). *Boundaries and Belonging: States and Societies in the Struggle to Shape Identities and Local Practices.* Cambridge: Cambridge University Press.

Pelkmans, Mathijs (ed.) (2013). *Ethnographies of doubt. Faith and uncertainty in contemporary societies.* London: IB Tauris.

Rabinow, P. (1984). *The Foucault reader.* New York: Pantheon Books

Raffnsøe, S., Gudmand-Høyer, M. T. and Thaning, M.S. (2014). What is a Dispositive? Copenhagen Business School, working paper.

Samimian-Darash, L., Arnoldi, J., Goldstein, D.M., Keck, F., Mathews, A.S., Redfield, P., Tellmann, U. and Samimian-Darash, L. (2012). Governing future potential biothreats: Toward an anthropology of uncertainty. *Current Anthropology, 54*(1), pp. 1–22.

Tabyshalieva, A. (2001). Central Asia: Imaginary and real borders. *Central Asia and Caucasus Analyst,* 19/19. Available at: www.cacianalyst.org/publications/analytical-articles/item/7055-analytical-articles-caci-analyst-2001-12-19-art-7055.html.

Turaeva, R. (2012). "Propiska regime in post-Soviet space; regulating mobility and residence", Central Asian Studies Institute at American University of Central Asia, Working Papers, available at: www.auca.kg/en/casiwp/.

Van Houtum, H. (2010). Waiting before the law: Kafka on the border. *Social & Legal Studies, 19*(3), pp. 285–297.

Van Houtum, H. and van Naerssen, T. (2002) Bordering, ordering and othering. *Tijdschrift voor Economische en Sociale Geografie (TESG), 93*(2), pp. 125–136.

Wastl-Walter, D. (ed.) (2012). *The Ashgate research companion to border studies.* Farnham: Ashgate Publishing.

35
Bordered spaces
Spatial strategies in a "disputed border"

Swargajyoti Gohain

It is now common to see borderlands as spaces that transcend the territorial logic of nation states. Yet, in particular instances of conflict, in territories disputed between two states, national borders tend to become reified or larger than life. In this chapter, I show how the "disputed border" introduces nuances in the general understanding of borderlands as spaces of flows. I do this in relation to my ethnographic experiences in a border region that has been at the center of territorial contention between two nation states – India and China. This is the western part of Arunachal Pradesh, consisting of Tawang and West Kameng districts, which is claimed by China as the southern extension of Tibet.

Pioneering scholars of border studies in the social sciences Michael Baud and Willem van Schendel (1997: 229) advocate treating the border not as the limits of an inflexible boundary line, but as having a more zonal quality. They adopt "a cross-border perspective, in which the region on both sides of a state border is taken as the unit of analysis." The production of linear borders, they argue, are state effects – the attempts of the state to maintain exclusive control over spaces that historically and culturally are not contained within national boundaries. While the disciplines of geography and international relations have conventionally tended to study the border in terms of the state effect (boundary lines, cartography, foreign policy, and border war), Baud and van Schendel argue for a more inclusive approach, which takes into account the triangular interactions of state, regional elite, and local people on both sides of a border, so that the border becomes the intersecting zone between a "double triangle" (Baud and van Schendel 1997).

This conceptualization of the border is consistent with the focus on fluidity, porosity, and hybridity that has come to characterize the study of borders in general in the present. Globalization, economic liberalization, and other visions for increasing connections between nation states have led to a renewed perspective toward borders as sites of liberation and possibilities, rather than as peripheries. Various studies have been carried out to analyze and predict the trends of an increasingly open, borderless world. The question, however, is moot whether indeed borderlands can live up to the promise invested in them.

I argue that the study of borders cannot be complete without a discussion of the disputed border, and of the strategies adopted by the people living in them for adapting to or transforming their living conditions. By disputed border, I mean not only a linear boundary line whose exact position is contested, but an entire border region that is claimed by both the nation states between which it lies, and which remains highly militarized. The particular dynamics between the triad of state, regional elite, and local people are very different in areas marked as disputed, which in turn generate new politics and strategies of accommodation.

It might be countered here that that the disputed border is simply a border where the state effect is much stronger compared to other borderlands, and where the role of local people and regional elite – the other two points of the triad – diminishes considerably. However, I argue that in disputed borderlands, there is both a territorial divide between the two sides of the border as well as a psychological and social divide; for reasons of security, the state has to enforce greater curbs on cross-border exchanges and commonalities. In spatial terms, it might be said that the triad of state, region, and locality is reshaped into a circular power structure, where locality and region become subsets within a statist circle of power.

Bringing disputed borders into the general framework on borders requires new formulations. If border studies includes the strategies of adaptation that border people devise in the wake of imposition of borders, then attention should be given not only to strategies of border crossing, such as cross-border trade – legal or otherwise – immigration, or cross-border ties of kinship and religion, but also to strategies where reorientation, rather than subversion of physical boundaries, is chosen.

In disputed border regions, constant military surveillance makes it more difficult to cross borders and retain cross-border ties. Under conditions of territorial dispute, the state takes a proactive stance in dissuading relations with the "other" nation, so that the other side is not only unknown but also unknowable. That is, physical patrolling of the boundary goes hand in hand with cultural policing, so that the border people are forced to shed any traces of hybridity or heterogeneity that they might have, in order to lend credence to the nationalist project. Dislocated from their cross-border networks, the border people in disputed areas are denied the avenues for border crossing. The choices for people living in disputed borderlands are adaptation and integration. Adaptation does not mean surrender to the totalizing project of the nation state. Rather, they are practices oriented toward the center rather than movement across the border.

Contextualizing border studies

The proliferation of works on the border since the 1990s has created a distinct discursive field. In this field, the border exists through its opposite; the crossing. For instance, national borders are shown up to be what they are – imaginary and imagined constructs – through acts, processes, and conditions of border crossing. The character of the border notwithstanding, that is, whether it is a border that allows friendly passage and works through official permits or whether it is a border, crossing which requires subterfuge, both function through similar metaphors. Borders are gateways or doors opening up from one unit to another.

Social anthropologist Ulf Hannerz (1997) suggests that empirical border studies have contributed to undermining the notion of nations and cultures as bounded, mutually exclusive units. According to Hannerz, this shift has caused ethnographers and other scholars to celebrate *crossing* as a sign of creativity rather than view it as an anomaly. This does not mean that in contemporary border studies the state has disappeared. But the inviolability of state borders is increasingly being recognized as a myth. As people gradually understand the border to be artificial, arbitrary, and hence problematic, they begin treating it as something to be maneuvered, perhaps subverted, or used resourcefully to their own advantage (Hannerz 1997: 537). The state thus surfaces as an entity that protects the artificial construct of the border, and thus as something that people have to work past in order to achieve crossing.

In many of the border-related works, the attempt is to expose the form of border associated with the modern nation state as contingent, through a historical retracing of origins. Unveiling the particular processes, ideas, and practices that went into the construction of a border serves to denaturalize it. This is particularly in relation to postcolonial borders, which were fashioned through imperial conquest or to serve colonial administrative designs. Thus, van Schendel (2005), in an account of the India–Bangladesh border, shows how this particular boundary was formed through the arbitrary decisions of British administrators. The boundary, called the Radcliffe Line, after Sir Cecil Radcliffe, who was in charge of deciding the boundary divisions and representing it cartographically, was later found to be empirically problematic, running as it did through shifting rivers, and nonexistent landmarks, and cutting through communal village holdings or farmlands.

Van Schendel shows how in the face of such arbitrary divisions, borderland strategies rest on "defiance and accommodation," where border people both accept the conditions of bordered, restricted existence, and creatively seek to defy/cross the border for economic and commercial gain, often through the covert support of border guards and other state agents. Clandestine border-crossing activities (smuggling and illegal immigration) constitute a "border effect" that counters the state effect (of surveillance, patrol, and territorial control). Partly as a result of the disenchantment with political borders (Hannerz 1997), crossing is seen to be the strategy of resistance for border peoples. In other words, if states and state borders are arbitrary constructs, for borderlanders forced to deal with their artificiality, subversion through crossing (legal or otherwise) is shown to be the common strategy.

Yet, how does one categorize strategies that do not include border crossing? In fact, how does one address border situations that do not allow crossing? In situations of territorial conflict between strong, hyper-national states, where constant military surveillance of border checkpoints precludes crossing, the border, rather than being outward looking, becomes inverted onto itself, forcing a similar reorientation upon the border denizens. Subject to the nationalist project of a state intent on exerting absolute control over its borders, the border people of disputed border areas experience a borderland condition without the anticipated potential for subversion through crossing. The strategies or expressions of resistance they devise have to engage with and not confront the state. Engagement involves compromise and dissimulation rather than dissent or disagreement.

I turn to a discussion of the disputed territory of Arunachal Pradesh, and specifically its western section in order to illustrate my point.

The western borderlands of Arunachal Pradesh

India and China have 2,500 miles of common frontier from northwest Kashmir to the trijunction of China, Myanmar, and India, and the two countries are in dispute regarding three main border tracts along this frontier: the "Western Sector" (Aksai Chin area) in the Ladakh province of Jammu and Kashmir, the "Central Sector," concerning certain border passes and specific places along the Indo-Tibetan border in the Indian states of Sikkim, Himachal Pradesh, and Uttaranchal, and last, but most importantly, the "Eastern Sector" in Arunachal Pradesh (Sharma 1965). Here, the Indian government claims the border to be the McMahon Line, delineated by British colonial rulers in 1914 in the Simla Convention. While the Indian and Tibetan representative signed the boundary treaty demarcating the McMahon Line as the international boundary, the Chinese representative refused to sign it, citing problems with some of its clauses. In the postcolonial period, India accepts this boundary while China disputes its legitimacy, considering it an unfair imperialist deal by the British. China claims almost 33,000 square miles south of the McMahon Line.

The Indian and Chinese governments have not engaged in direct talks about the alignment of the India–China boundary. On October 20th, 1962, the Chinese troops attacked several posts on the Indo-Tibetan border, and soon overran the districts of Tawang and West Kameng in the western part of Arunachal Pradesh. The troops remained there for two months before they were called back.

Since the 1962 war, India's boundaries with Tibet along Arunachal Pradesh have been, to all practical purposes, sealed off. The Monpas, who traditionally inhabited Tawang and West Kameng, had developed close political, commercial, and cultural links with Tibet over a period of almost three centuries since 1680, when the Fifth Dalai Lama decreed that all areas in and adjacent to the current Tawang district would be part of Tibet. Until the Indo-Tibetan boundary delineation of 1914, the Monpas were directly subject to the Tibetan government and paid taxes in the form of an agricultural levy (*khral*). Since the British took no steps to enforce the McMahon Line on the ground even after the boundary delimitation, there was a continuous flow of commodities, religious artifacts, and people after India's independence, too. Up until 1950, Tibetan officials were engaged in collecting taxes from the people of this area.

However, the change in China's government, the Dalai Lama's exile in 1959, and the subsequent boundary war between India and China led to a complete redrawing of geographical and social cartography. The Monpas were re-oriented away from their previous Tibetan networks and integrated into the new Indian nation state, as part of the North East Frontier Agency, later renamed as Arunachal Pradesh. To date, this region, along with other regions along India's northern and northeast frontiers, remains a disputed territory. The Monpas are categorized as a backward scheduled tribe of northeast India, who inhabit the geographical and social margins of the Indian nation. They no longer have access to the routes of commercial and cultural exchanges to which they were previously accustomed. Confined by the border and geographically distant from the center, they dwell in a territorial limbo.

Since 2003, under the charge of Tsona Gontse Rinpoche, political and spiritual leader, and head of the Gaden Rabye Ling Monastery in West Kameng, a section of the population began a demand for a Mon Autonomous Region, asking for separate administration for the region consisting of Tawang and West Kameng within Arunachal Pradesh. This does not require the Mon region to secede from Arunachal Pradesh, but instead, self-rule within the state. The Mon Autonomous Region Demand Committee (MARDC), formed as the pressure group to articulate this demand, points to two major problems faced by this border region in its current administrative set-up as part of Arunachal Pradesh: in cultural terms, the threat of erosion of the Tibetan Buddhist heritage of this region due to the influence of migrant Christian and other non-Buddhist populations, and in development terms, the continued backwardness of the region relative to the more developed areas of Arunachal Pradesh. The MARDC leaders allege that they cannot push for reforms in the spheres of culture and development under the present state administration of Arunachal Pradesh, which according to them, is inattentive to the special needs of this region; they argue that only autonomy would lead to change.

The demand for Mon Autonomous Region calls for the extension of the Sixth Schedule to West Kameng and Tawang districts (Constitution of Mon Autonomous Council). The Sixth Schedule is a clause within the Indian Constitution that provides for the administration of certain marginalized tribal areas as autonomous entities, by constituting a local level District Council or a Regional Council. The Sixth Schedule has its origin in a colonial policy, the Government of India Act of 1935, which segregated certain hill areas as "excluded" and "partially excluded," where administration was loose and tribal laws and customs protected. In the postcolonial period, the hill tracts of northeast India, formerly "excluded" areas, were put under the Sixth Schedule, while tribal tracts, formerly "partially excluded" areas, were put under the Fifth Schedule of the Indian Constitution (Baruah 2003). In the latter, democratic decentralization in the form of grassroots-level Panchayati Raj Institutions is in force, a system which organically links village-level bodies (Gram Sabhas) to the lower house of the Indian parliament (Lok Sabha), and was inaugurated by the first Indian prime minister, Jawaharlal Nehru in 1959 (Mathew 1995). In the Sixth Schedule, Panchayati Raj Institutions are replaced by the local government or council, which therefore makes it a stronger protective legislation than the Fifth Schedule. It protects against tribal land alienation, provides reservations in schools and government employment, and gives authority to traditional institutions to oversee land use and resolve customary disputes (McDuie-Ra 2012).

The original Sixth Schedule areas created right after independence in 1952 included many parts of what are now the four separate northeast Indian states of Meghalaya, Assam, Tripura, and Mizoram. These areas underwent significant territorial reorganization in 1971, and now the Sixth Schedule clause applies also to Ladakh in Kashmir. Three other states of northeast India, Manipur, Nagaland, and Arunachal Pradesh, do not come under the purview of this clause but have other provisions for "protective discrimination" (Baruah 2003) through which the autonomy of traditional institutions and customs are upheld.

Although Arunachal Pradesh as a whole has safeguards in place for protecting tribal customary institutions, this has proved inadequate for certain communities in the state who have a perception of being marginalized. In February 2004, the Arunachal Pradesh state legislative assembly, during a moment of internal crisis, allowed a resolution to be passed, recommending the creation of two autonomous councils under provisions of the Sixth Schedule – one being Mon region and the other comprising Tirap and Changlang districts in eastern Arunachal Pradesh known as Patkai region (*The Hindu* 2008). As of 2017, however, this resolution still lies pending in the central parliament.

From one angle, the Mon demand for autonomy appears as a manifestation of the identity politics common to northeast India. In India's northeast, ethnic identity politics, often student-led, has been a defining feature of the region, dating back to the period before national independence. Here, contestations against dominant representations of the Indian nation (Aryan/Hindu/North India-centric) and the peripheral status of the region vis-à-vis the center are expressed through insurgency movements (Nagaland since the 1940s, Mizoram in the 1960s, and Assam in the 1980s etc.). One might be inclined to cite in the case of the politics of northeast India, the thesis of Benedict Anderson (1991) regarding a modular nationalism that is transplanted from Europe to distant shores. Anderson's theoretical proposition suggests how practices travel, and in this vein, it is easy to cast the demand for Mon region as an ethnic homeland movement inspired by similar movements in northeast India. On the surface, it appears that the autonomy proposal seeks redress for problems very specific to and contained within the Mon region, such as development of infrastructure, education, healthcare, communication, and so on, increase in political participation and greater decision-making powers of the people of the region through local governance, and the preservation of indigenous local customs and traditions.

However, to conclude that the autonomy demand pertains to Monpa self-hood notions or to local development needs is to miss the larger idea of an inter-Himalayan alliance between different Tibetan Buddhist populations that various programs within the movement allude to. While the Mon autonomy demand rests on a Monpa ethnicity and speaks of local development needs, it simultaneously invokes past and present ties with Tibet and other Tibetan Buddhists in India. As Tibetan Buddhist minorities in a primarily non-Buddhist regional and national milieu, Monpas feel culturally marginalized both within Arunachal Pradesh and in the national identity. Underlying the Monpas' territorial demand is the quest for recognition, manifesting itself through linguistic revivalism, renewed interest in traditional customs and clothes, and more significantly, the evocation of their past connection with Tibet and other Tibetan Buddhists across the Himalayan region.

The Monpas' case gives the lie to a concept of border that hinges on fluidity. Geographically, Monpas are border people, but as inhabitants of a disputed border zone, they cannot engage in border-crossing activities that are considered to be a feature of borderland living. Yet, this does not mean that Monpas are passive recipients of state territorial practices. I wish to submit that the demand for autonomy through the Sixth Schedule is a border strategy of adaptation in a disputed border. The proposal for Mon autonomy does not challenge the territorial integrity of the Indian nation. It does not rest on physically crossing or remapping boundaries. It is a demand that is fully within constitutional limits, circumscribed by parameters that are already in place, and have been tested in other contexts, that is, the Sixth Schedule and the model of autonomous councils. In just over a decade since its inception, the movement has succeeded in mobilizing a big cross section of the population behind its cause. It is noteworthy that Tsona Rinpoche, who founded this movement for autonomy, met with a sudden death in 2014. The movement, however, has refused to die and surfaces from time to time in the news headlines.

I have dealt elsewhere extensively with this movement and the events surrounding it (Gohain 2013). In this chapter, I argue that the autonomous council is a spatial adaptation – a territorial compromise. The larger idea behind the demand is transnational, and transborder in spirit, for it is about an inter-Himalayan alliance of Tibetan Buddhist peoples, which cuts across regional and national boundaries. Yet, the demand itself adapts a state-given solution for marginalized communities, that of an autonomous council, which does not aspire beyond the territorial boundaries ascribed by nations. Thus, the demand accommodates the logic of the national boundary. The actual space that emerges in the various programs surrounding the autonomy demand is transnational in scope; this is not made explicit, but emerges only through ethnographic study.

Belonging beyond borders

The Monpas lived under Tibetan political authority before becoming part of India, and shared cultural, religious, commercial, and kinship ties with both Tibetans and Bhutanese. After the 1962 war, the Indian state militarily closed off border passages to China, effectively putting an end to previous trade links between the Monpas and Tibetans. In the aftermath of the war, the Indian state tried to integrate the border areas through schemes of education, development, and settlement of populations from the country's heartland. With the migration of Hindi-speaking populations from north India, as well as dissemination of a Bollywood-centered popular culture through television, Hindi gradually became the de facto lingua franca of the region. Local religious and cultural traditions were also comparatively upstaged as new festivals and performances from other parts of India became popular.

In 1987, Tsona Rinpoche returned to his home in Mon region after acquiring the highest monastic degree of Geshe Lharampa from Drepung Loseling Monastery in South India. Disturbed by the lack of development and what he thought as the corrosion of Tibetan Buddhist traditions in Mon, he devised an agenda for reforms, and became active in various social welfare efforts and reconstruction of monasteries and other Buddhist monuments. But soon, according to his own admissions and confidences by some of his associates, he realized that he could not bring about significant changes without political power, prompting him to join electoral politics. In 2003, he formally launched the Mon Autonomous Region demand.

One of the original agendas of the autonomy movement was to make Bhoti or Tibetan the language of instruction in all schools of this region, and this has been successfully implemented since Tsona Rinpoche first raised the language issue in the late 1990s. While the people of this region speak various Tibetan-related languages, which are oral in form, they have chosen to adopt as the medium of instruction the modern Tibetan language – the standardized literary Tibetan used in the curricula of universities worldwide. Despite the variation in speech forms of the different Tibetan Buddhist communities across the Himalayan region, they have a common sacred script in classical Tibetan, which is the language of the scriptures. Nowadays, additionally, some of these different communities, including the Monpas, are using the modern Tibetan language to assert a common identification with each other. In this instance, language is the medium through which a cultural politics of transnational belonging is asserted.

The Monpas also have a long history of trade with Tibet and Bhutan, which exists today only in popular memory, after physical trade declined in the wake of regulation of cross-border mobility. Elderly people in their 80s, who witnessed the last phases of Tibetan rule, recall the trade fairs that used to be held three times a year in Tsona, Tibet, to which Monpas would carry their wares. Besides trade narratives, Monpas also have oral narratives that trace cross-border kinship and marriage connections with both Tibet and Bhutan. A couple of contemporary texts have now reproduced in written form these narratives of origin and marriage, clearly positioning the Monpas as a people with transnational affiliations. Some sections of the population, and especially the monks, are increasingly stressing the Tibetan roots and Tibetan Buddhist cultural heritage of the Monpas.

Several organizations with the aim of preserving Tibetan Buddhist culture in the region have become increasingly visible and there is renewed focus on renovating and reclaiming Tibetan Buddhist sacred places within Mon in an attempt to reclaim it as part of a wider sacred geography. Huge financial investments are being made into building monasteries, monuments, and schools and higher centers for Buddhist learning, part of which are drawn from the Ministry of Culture of the Indian government but a large part from foreign sources. A systematic attempt to highlight the Monpas' wider, Tibetan Buddhist connections is evident in various spheres of the society.

A cartographic presentation of these connections would result in a spatial map that goes beyond the present national boundaries. The present movement for autonomy does not express these transnational imaginings as the demand for a homeland; indeed, it cannot, since this territorial representation challenges national and regional boundaries. Rather, the spatial map that is submitted for consideration is a conservative one that conforms to state-given provisions, that is, the Sixth Schedule. I would like to argue that this is typical of a disputed border region, where identities and belonging are not given but have to be negotiated.

Strategies in disputed borders

Disputed borders have seldom been labeled as such in the literature on borders. Mostly, discussions of militarization and occupation have served to express territorial conflict between nations or internal security. The state makes its presence felt at disputed borders through its military forces, and so, social relations are understood in relation to militarism. For example, Smadar Lavie's work among the Mzeina of South Sinai, conducted in the mid-1980s and published in 1990, is a classic case of a border region under occupation that had to shed previous elements of social life in order to adapt to life under two hostile nations. In the Arab–Israeli conflict in the 20th century, the South Sinai was a "political football tossed at least five times between Egypt and Israel" (Lavie 1990: 6).

The central question motivating Lavie's study was: how did the Mzeina Bedouins of South Sinai adapt to such a situation, where cross-border ties of any kind had to be suppressed? Disenfranchised on their own land by continual military occupations, the Mzeina could not perform their nomadic Bedouin identity, romanticized in travelers' accounts, except allegorically; "tribal identity appeared as moralistic, multi-layered narratives transcending the spatial and temporal boundaries of military occupation through symbolic defiance only, because for Mzeinas to openly confront any armed or unarmed occupier could mean beatings, jail, even death" (Lavie 1990: 7).

In another work, Michael Gilsenan (1996) writes about the transformations wrought on the Akkar region on the Lebanon–Syria borderlands. Gilsenan's book is about narratives of violence and the attempts by members of the different strata, *beys* (landlords), *aghas* (overseers, agents), and *fellahin* (sharecroppers), to narratively negotiate the disjunction between expectations and codified values of honor and martial heroism on the one hand, and everyday practices that devalue honor, on the other. It is a book about a crumbling feudal economic structure and the absorption of former lords and middlemen into the city-centric economy of Lebanon. The fact that the region is a border region is alluded to briefly, despite the fact that Gilsenan's work was carried out in a period when war ravaged the borders of Lebanon and Syria, leading to border blockades.

Gilsenan's work draws attention to the fact that in a conflicted border region, there are other processes besides crossing that become paramount – processes that require negotiation with, rather than subversion of, the state. Gilsenan chooses to focus on narratives that express the conflict felt by a people on the crossroads of modernity, and is silent about the strategies of crossing that might be present among the inhabitants of Akkar. While this does not prove that Akkar border peoples do not engage in subterranean transborder activities, it indicates that their orientation and energies are directed toward surviving within national economic networks.

A third example is Ravina Aggarwal's (2004) book on Ladakh, a disputed border region on the India–China border. Aggarwal shows how cultural performances of national holidays, festivals, films, or traditional sports such as archery competitions become sites for nation-making. Yet, even as these performances articulate state structures of power, they also expose the ambiguities of state power by generating alternative meanings.

In all the above works, border actors engage with the state (or state agents), not so that they might cross to the *other* side, but so that they could express themselves even while remaining firmly on *this* side. Secondly, these works use analytical terms such as allegory, narrative, and performances in order to show how border people in disputed borders deal with the situation, indicating that border activities and subjectivities in a disputed border zone are manifested only through a screen. Given that conditions of state rule are at their extreme in disputed border areas, the border-ness of such regions and populations is manifested not in overt subversion or crossing, but in more underlying terms. I argue that the autonomy demand discussed here is also a similar strategy by a population inhabiting a disputed territory. What is demanded is a Mon Autonomous Region, but what actually emerges in various discourses and programs is a more transnational space that extends beyond current political boundaries.

References

Aggarwal, Ravina. 2004. Beyond Lines of Control: Performance and Politics on the Disputed Borders of Ladakh, India. Durham, NC: Duke University Press.
Anderson, Benedict. 1991. Imagined Communities. (Revised version). London: Verso.
Baruah, Sanjib. 2003. "Citizens and Denizens: Ethnicity, Homelands and the Crisis of Displacement in North East India." Journal of Refugee Studies 16 (1): 44–66.

Baud, Michael and Willem van Schendel. 1997. "Toward a Comparative History of Borderlands." Journal of World History 8 (2): 211–241.

Gilsenan, Michael. 1996. Lords of the Lebanese Marches. Berkeley: University of California Press.

Gohain, Swargajyoti. 2013. "Imagined Places: Politics and Narratives in a Disputed Indo-Tibetan Borderland." Unpublished PhD Dissertation, Emory University, USA. [This is being revised for publication as Himalaya Bound: Culture, Politics, and Imagined Geographies in India's Northeast Frontier, University of Washington Press].

Hannerz, Ulf. 1997. "Borders." International Social Science of Journal 154: 537–548.

Lavie, Smadar. 1990. The Poetics of Military Occupation: Mzeina Allegories of Bedouin Identity under Israeli and Egyptian Rule. Berkeley: University of California Press.

Mathew, George. 1995. Status of Panchayati Raj in the States of India 1994. Delhi: Institute of Social Sciences.

McDuie-Ra, Duncan. 2012. Northeast Migrants in Delhi: Race, Refuge and Retail. Leiden: Amsterdam University Press.

Sharma, Surya. 1965. "The India-China Border Dispute: An Indian Perspective." The American Journal of International Law 59 (1): 16–47.

The Hindu. 2008. "Arunachal Districts Bordering China Press for Autonomy." 20 October. www.thehindu.com/todays-paper/tp-national/Arunachal-districts-bordering-China-press-for-autonomy/article15325574.ece.

van Schendel, Willem. 2005. The Bengal Borderland: Beyond State and Nation in South Asia. London: Anthem.

Index

9/11 attacks 56, 59, 408

Abraham, I. 63, 363
Afghanistan: Pamirian Borderlands 385–93; women refugees in Pakistan 33
Aga Khan III 386–7
Aga Khan IV 387, 388, 390–1
Aga Khan Development Network 387–93
Agamben, G. 352
Aggarwal, R. 452
Agnew, J. 59
Agrawal, A. 323
agriculture: agricultural expansion in Indonesia 180–7; Chinese in Russian Far East 190–9; Dungans involvement in 142–3
airports, as checkpoint 403–4, 408–9
Ak-Sai 44, 46–53
Akaev, Askar 298, 299
Akkar 452
Alibaba Group 340–1
All Burma Student Democratic Front 250–1
Almaty 140–9
Alter, J. 380
AMD programs 186
American Baptist missionaries 354, 355
Amurskaya Oblast 337–43
Anderson, B. 61, 411, 449
Andong Meas 102–3
Anglo–Dutch Treaty (1824) 168–9
Anglo–Gorkha war 232
anti-migrant politicians/policies 17–26
anticipation/recollection of violence 403, 405
Appadurai, A. 320, 326, 361, 363
Arakan: Buddhist Kingdom of 152; central and peripheral power 157–8; creation of the State of 153–4; Muslims in 154–5, 271–4; social, religious, and ethnic inter-relationships in 155–6; spirit cults in 156–7
Arnold, D. 248, 249
Arunachal Pradesh 445–52
Asad, T. 389, 392
Asian Borderlands Research Network (ABRN) 6, 62

Asian Studies, dominant subdivisions of 81
Asom Gana Parishad (AGP) 258
assemblages 243–52
Association for Borderlands Studies (ABS) 57
Association of Southeast Asian Nations (ASEAN) 57, 60
asylum 17, 19, 24, 26, 30, 246–8
Attabad landslide 121, 122
Atush 294–302
Aung San, General 221
Aung San Suu Kyi 33–4, 353
Australia: Christmas Island 24; detention facility deaths 24; externalization of border enforcement 23; forefront of maritime border enforcement 19; Rohingya migrants 24
Austronesian Sea people 267, 277–87
Awami League 258

Back Pack Health Worker Team (BPHWT) 355, 365, 368
Bae, Kenneth 426
Bakiev, Kurmanbek 299, 300
Balibar, E. 242
Baltit Fort 115, 117, 119
Bamar fishermen 267–75
Ban Rak Thai 127–38; boundaries 128–9; cold war frontier 130–1; geopolitical jigsaw 127–8; mobility 138; multicultural 131–8; traffic line 131–8
banal nationalism 44–5
Bangladesh: India border violence 25; militarization of Chittagong Hill Tracts 35; Rohingya refugees 23–4, 30, 33–4; war heroines in 32–3
Bangladesh–India border enclaves 255–65; after the exchange 259–61; creation and exchange of 256–9; India's resettlement package 260; making state space 261–2; theorizing the exchange 263
banking: banks and quasi-banks 338–9; Chinese credit cards 341 *see also* currency
Bartelson, J. 335
barter-oriented trade relations in Nepal 320–1

454

Index

Baud, M. 61, 392, 445
Bay of Bengal 23, 25
Beck, U. 439
Beech, N. 147
Bell, G. 107
Bengal borderlands 255
Bernot, Lucien and Denise 151–2
Berubari Union 257, 258
Bestor, T. 108, 110
Bharatia Janata Party (BJP) 258
Billig, M. 44–5
biodiesel/fuel 204–10
biosocial nature of body 376–83
Bishkek 141, 143, 144, 295–302
Bishop, Julie 24
Blagoveshchensk 334–43
bodies, as mobile border 403–10
Border Consortium (Thailand–Burma) 352, 358, 363
border regimes 440–1
border studies: bust to boom 59–62; contextualizing 446–7; focus on global North 58; *longue durée* take 63–4
Borneo 168–78, 180–7; border checkpoints 176 (map); osmotic pressure between states 175–6
Bourdieu, P. 296
Brambilla, C. 65
Braudel, F. 106, 107
Brenner, C.T. 58
bribes: demanded from Uyghur traders 299; Sino–North Korean border 423, 429; Sino–Russian cross-border trade 338–9; Uzbek–Kazakh border 435, 436, 439; Vietnam 309
Brooke, Charles 171, 172
Brooke, James 169, 171
Brussels and Istanbul airport attacks 404
Buddhism: Arakan 152–9; cultural roots of Monpas 448–51; moral economy and Buddhist Karen 369–71; Tibetan marriage 376–83
Bunnell, T. 57
Burma *see* Myanmar
Burman migrants 36
buses 46–8
Bush, Laura 353
Butler, J. 439

Calcutta, Hindu Bengali refugees 33
Cambodia 94–104; borderlands and development 98–101; disjointed borders 97–8; livelihoods 95–7; social movements 101–4
Cape Dato 169, 173
capitalist economy, expansion in China 202–10
case studies, ethnographic 66–7
cash: circulation in Nepal 320–3; lack of in Sino–Russian border trade 338–9 *see also* banking; currency
"ceasefire capitalism" 222, 224

celebrity humanitarianism 353
Chakma, Kalpana 35
Chalfin, B. 335
Chang, Wen-chin 109
Changbai 422–31
Changbai Public Security Bureau (PSB) 423
checkpoints 403–10; arrestability 405–6; beyond 408–9; mobile 407–8; one manifestation of border 403; as target 406–7; Uzbek–Kazakh 434–42
Chernyaevka 435–42
China: 1962 war with India 448; agricultural internationalization and modernization 197–8; agriculture in Russian far east 190–9; bordering at the international Sino–Myanmar border 222–3; cross-border livelihoods between Kazakhstan and 140–9; diplomatic relations with Kyrgyzstan restored 295; disputed border region with India 445–52; establishment of PRC 118; Go West campaign 85, 202, 205, 208; 'Going Out' policy 193, 197–8; history of Sino–Kyrgyz cross-border trade 295, 298–301; Karakoram Highway 114–24; labor export to Russia 195–7; 'One Belt, One Road 114–15; relations with ASEAN 60; routing Myanmar communication through 223; sovereign decisions on Sino–Russian border 334–43; Special Economic Zones 114; Tibetan–Hui marriage relations 376–83; township and village enterprises (TVEs) 196; Western Development scheme 299–300; Yunnan Province development 202–10
China–Pakistan Economic Corridor 114, 121–3
China–Vietnam border, women traders 36
Chittagong (Bangladesh) 35, 152
Choi, E. 424–5, 430
Choonhavan, Chatichai 57
Christmas Island 24
citizenship: Bangladesh–India enclaves 255–63; Moken in Thailand 281; Rohingya denied in Myanmar 18, 23; Thai–Burma borderland 247, 270, 273
Civilisation and Capitalism 106
Civilizing the Margins: Southeast Asian Government Policies for the Development of Minorities 81
Clastres, P. 82
Cold War 1–2, 57, 59, 67, 127–37, 181, 250, 390–1
colonialism: Anglo–Dutch Treaty (1824) 168–9; Arakan racial legacy 153–4; boundaries as legacy 22, 63; British administrators in India 447–9; Burma 221; Ismaili bureaucratic roots in 389; Ismaili political theology of development 386; militarised history of Ogasawara 412–14; Sixth Schedule (Indian Constitution) 448–9
commodity chains 106–12, 168–78, 177, 325–33
commodity exchange, Mustang 320–1
compressor-diving fishing 268, 281

455

Index

Constable, N. 37
containment 316–17, 322–3
Cooch Behar enclaves 257
Corbridge, S. 59
corruption: Sino–Russian cross-border trade 334–43; Sino–Vietnamese border 308–12
credit, Uyghur traders and 297–8
crossing, strategy of resistance for border peoples 446–7
'cultural biography' of an item 107
cultural commodities 325–33
culture of politics 230, 234, 236–8
currency: Sino–North Korean border 428–9, 431; Xinjiang banknotes 116–17 see also banking; cash
customary lands, enclosure of in Borneo 184–6
customs officers: Chernyaevka border 435–9; Sino–Russian border 337–40, 341–2

Dalai Lama 448
Darjeeling 230–3
Das, V. 32
data driven migration policing 20
Daurov, Husey 143, 144, 146
Dawei people 270–1, 272 (map)
Dayaks 171, 182, 185
De Genova, N. 248
de Maaker, E. 62
deaths: at borders 24–5; India–Bangladesh border 34
debt, Chinese traders in Vietnam 306–7
Décobert, A. 368
defectors: defector cram schools 430; source of information 423–4
Demick, B. 425
Democratic Karen Buddhist Army 355
Democratic People's Republic of Korea 422–31; border wall 22, 23; demilitarized zone 21
Deng Xiaoping 198, 291, 295
Denkowski, C.A. 426, 427
Devananda, Douglas 406
development: institutions 385–93; Jatropha expansion 202–10; roads in Nepal 315–23; West Kalimantan, Borneo 180–7
Devji, F. 389
Diamond Jubilee Investment Trust 387
disorder, Uzbek–Kazakh checkpoint 434–42
dispositif 435, 440–2
disputed border, spatial strategies in 445–52
distance-demolishing technologies 83, 204, 279
"DIY import" method, Vietnam 309–10
Domel "refugees" 281–4
domestic workers, women 36–8
Dordoi market 295, 300
Douglas, M. 379
drones 20, 21, 26

drug trafficking, Sino–North Korean border 426, 427–8
Duncan, C. 81
Dungans: agriculturalists 142–3; communities in Shaanxi province 143; diaspora people within Kazakhstan 145; effect of Sino–Soviet relations 143; fire disasters 144–5; pious Muslims 142; trade entrepreneurs 140, 145

e-commerce *see* internet and online shopping
East India Company 75, 169, 232
Economic Land Concessions (ELCs), Cambodia 99–100
"economy of grace" 390, 391, 392
Ekvall, R. 381
Elden, S. 20, 23
elephants 26
emotions 362–3, 365–7
enclaves, K10 in Myanmar 218–19, 221–2, 224–7 *see also* Bangladesh–India border enclaves
Endres, K. 308
energy, projects in China 202–10
espionage, Sino–North Korean border 427
ethnic belonging, conveyed by dress 328
ethno-religious boundaries 376–83
Eubank, Allan and Joan 354
Eubank, David 349, 354–8
Europe and the People Without History 106
European Union: asylum applications 26; new boundaries 56; Schengen Agreement 19
exceptional borders 43–4
externalization and internalization of border work 18, 19–20, 23–4

Fassin, D. 361, 362–3, 364, 367, 389, 392
federalism 230–9
fences and walls *see* walls
Ferghana Valley 42–53, 147, 294–302
firewood collection 207
Firoz Khan Noon, Prime Minister of Pakistan, 257
Fischer, A. 381
Fold, N. 181
food security, China 198, 204
foreign exchange, North Korea 428–9
forest products: Borneo 171–2; Sino–Vietnamese borderlands 202, 207
forestry, Cambodia 100
Forsyth, I. 57
Forsythe, D. 364
Foucault, M. 349, 352, 399, 435, 440, 441, 442
Free Burma Rangers 349–59, 365, 367, 368, 369; in action 357–8; founding 354; "Good Life Club" 355, 356, 357, 359
'friction of terrain' 83, 84, 202, 204
Frontex 19
'frontier constellations' 180–7

Index

Gandhi, Indira 257–8
Gandhi, Rajiv 405
Gansu Province 141, 377, 381
Gaotong Cun 203–10
Gatcha 282–4
Geiger, D. 181
gender-based harassment, Chernyaevka border 438–9
gendered nationalism 31–4
gendered violence 30, 34
Geographies at the Margins: Borders in South Asia 62
Giersch, C.P. 82
Gilgit-Baltistan 115–24, 385, 387
Gilsenan, M. 452
globalization 1, 2, 21, 22, 38, 106–12, 315–24, 445
Gohain, S. 17
Golden Triangle 127–9, 130
Google Maps 43
Gorkha kingdom 232
Gorno-Badakhshan 385–92
governmentality (Foucault) 352
Great Depression 173
Great Wall of China 20
Grundy-Warr, C. 61, 93, 220
Gukka Anjeon Bowiebu (North Korea) 426, 427
Gupta, A. 220, 338, 342

Habibur Rahman, Mohammad 25
Han Chinese: beneficiaries of Xinjiang investment 299–300; Dungan business partners 140, 142, 144, 145
Handai ethnic minority 202–10
handicrafts 326, 331
Hannerz, U. 446
Hansen, T.B. 335
Harris, T. 317
Hart, K. 321
Hastings, J. 428, 429
head tax, Dayaks 171
healthcare, emergency 351–2, 354–5
Hefner, R. 82
Heihe 334–43
hemp 326, 327, 328; cultivation ban by Chinese state 329; second-hand skirts 331
Heyman, J. 50, 51
highlands of Asia *see* Zomia
'Hindu Kush-Himalayan region' 76
Hindus/Hinduism: abducted women 32; enclave dwellers 261; world's 'last Hindu kingdom 233
Hirsch, P. 181
Historical Dictionary of the Peoples of the Southeast Asian Massif 78
Hmong people: China–Vietnam cross-border trade 312; cross-border trade networks in textiles 330–2; cultural commodities 325–6; diaspora in the United States 329; long-distance trading 331–2; manufactured textiles in Sino–Vietnamese borderlands 328–9; residents of Yên Bái 325–6; significance of clothing in Hmong society 326; textile production and cultural meanings 327–8
hobbit's beard 110–11
Hong Kong, women domestic workers in 36–7
Honghe Prefecture 202–10
Horstmann, A. 61, 362, 369
Horvath, A. 147
Hui people, Tibetan–Hui marriage relations 376–83
huizu and Han–Chinese traders 140–8
humanitarian assistance, Free Burma Rangers 349–59
humanitarian economy 362–73
Humphrey, C. 335
Hunza valley 115–25, 386–8
Hyesan 422–31

identity: biopolitical 404; checkpoints and 403–10; Moken in Nyawi 284–5; multiple and hybrid 425, 429–31
identity politics, North East India 447–50
Imagined Communities 61
India: 1962 war with China 448; anti-Indian rioting in Yangon 153; Arunachal Pradesh dispute 445–52; Border Security Force (BSF) 17, 25, 34; enclaves 255–65; Line of Control between Pakistan and 21; Look East policy 60; patriarchal communalism 32; women 32–5; women's labour migration 37
Indian Congress Party 258
Indo Nepal Treaty of Peace and Friendship 233
Indonesia: agrarian expansion Malaysian border 174–8, 180–7; women domestic workers 36–7
Ingold, T. 380
International Centre for Integrated Mountain Development 76
internet and online shopping 340–2
intifada 31
intimate militarism 42–53; becoming bordered 46–8; domesticating border guard 48–50; exceptional borders 43–4; state escalation of force 50–1
invisibility, marker of sovereignty 336, 340–2
Inwood, J. 18
Isfara River 44, 46, 47, 52
Ishimaru Jiro 427
Islam: Dungans' self-identification 142; Islamic content of Uyghur traders' practices 297–8; Tibetan Muslims 381–2
Ismaili Muslim institutions 385–93
Israel 31–2; women and Palestine border 35

jade trade 109
Jaffna 405

Index

Japan 411–20
Jatropha, plantation expansion 202–10
Jilin province 422–31
Jimenez Tovar, S. 145
Jolie, Angelina 353
Jordan, Syrian women refugees 34
Journal of Borderlands Studies 57, 58, 62

kabang 277, 281, 282, 283, 286–7
Kachin Independence Army (KIA) 221, 225, 226–7
Kachin Independence Organization (KIO) 215, 218–19, 221–7, 371
Kachin State 218–28
Kagbeni 315
kala 153–8
Kapiao 116–17
Kapuas Hulu district (Borneo) 180, 184–6
Karakoram Highway 114–24
Karasuu bazaar/market 295–301
Karen people 349–59; displaced in Thailand 247; Education Department (KED) 368; history of Christianization 354; Human Rights Group (KHRG) 358, 365, 367; Kaw Moo Raw Karen Youth Organization 250; National Liberation Army (KNLA) 250, 349, 354, 357, 358, 363, 367, 368; National Union (KNU) 249–50, 358, 363, 364, 365, 366, 367–8, 369, 371, 372; nationalist politics 249–51; nurses 356, 358; Teacher Working Group 365
Kashgar 114–24, 294, 296, 298–301
Kashmir 34–5, 400; Line of Control in 21, 22, 35
Kazakhstan: cross-border livelihoods between China and 140–9; Uzbek–Kazakh checkpoint 434–42
Keesing, F.M. 82
Keyes, C. 128
Khan, Ayub 118–19
Khatun, Felani 25, 34
Khin Nyunt, General 268
Khmer Rouge 98
Khojas 389
Khosravi, S. 434
Khruba Wong 369
Kim Jong-un 423, 426, 428
Kinh traders 331, 332
Kirat Yakthung Chumlung (KYC), 237–8
KMT army 127–38
Kong Mung Mong 127–38
Korea *see* Democratic People's Republic of Korea
Korean People's Army 422, 426
Kraska, P. 21–2
Kumaraswamy, Krishanti 405
Kyrgyzstan: Dungan people 141–9; history of Sino–Kyrgyz cross-border trade 294–302; intimate militarism 42–53

labor: Burmese migrants in Thailand 242–52; Chinese to Russian Far East 190–9
Ladakh 447, 449, 452
Laiza 222, 223, 224
land: enclosure of customary in Borneo 184–5; grabs in Cambodia 94–104; registration system Bangladesh–India border enclaves 262
language: bilingual aid to cross-border trading 325; Dai dialects 206; Hindi de facto lingua franca 450; Russian in Kazakhstan 140; Tibetan 451
Lào Cai province. 325–33
latencies, Moken people 279, 282
Lattimore, O. 82
Lau Kha border market 325
Lavie, S. 451–2
law regulations, Russian post-socialist law violation 334–43
Leach, E. 82, 152
Lebanon, women refugees 33, 34
Lee, H. 423–4, 425, 431
"leech plot" 304–13
legality/illegality, Sino–North Korean border 428
Leider, J. 153, 273
Letters from Iwo Jima (film) 418
Levi-Strauss, Claude 151
Lhasa 106–12
Liberation Tigers of Tamil Eelam 400, 404
Lim, Joo Jock 78
Limbu people 215–16, 230–9
liminality 147, 148
littorals, cultural borderland 266–75
livelihoods, definition 96
logging: Cambodia 99–100; Indonesia 182–3
Ludden, D. 129, 245
Lundu District 169–74

Madina bazaar 299, 300
Mae Aw *see* Ban Rak Thai
Mae Hong Son Province 127–38
Maguan 325–7, 330
maize 75
Malay Peninsula 266–75
Malaysia 168–78, 180–7
mandala model 81, 97, 277
Mandarin 134–5, 141, 325
Manmohan Singh, 258
Maoist insurgency (Nepal) 233–4
Maoist party, Nepal 236, 237
markets: Chinese farming in Russia far east 191–3; consumer markets Sino–Vietnamese border 325–33; failed market experiment in Vietnam 202–10
Marma people 151–2
McBrien, J. 440
McKinnon, J. 74
McMahon Line 447–8
Médecins sans Frontières (MSF) 351, 353, 371

media/press, difficult information environment 423
Megoran, N. 66
mental maps 134, 231; Arakanese social space 157
Mergui Archipelago 277–9; distribution of Moken groups in 278 (map)
meritocracy 391
Mezzadra, S. 243, 245
Michaud, J. 66, 96
Migdal, J. 134
migrants: agricultural labour from China 190–9; Burmese in Thailand 242–52; deaths of 24–6
militarism, defined 21–2
militarization 17–26, 34–6; and agricultural expansion in Indonesia 180–7; checkpoints and 403–10
military territorialization 186, 224
minivans (*marshrutka*s) 436
missionaries 349–59
Mizo people 60–1
mobile telephone, use in internet trading 341
mobility, Nepal 315–24
modernity, Nepal 315–24
Modi, Narendra 259
Mohammed Ali (Pakistani Prime Minister) 257
Moken 266–75, 277–87; belief system 280; ideology 279; Moken–Bamar mixed communities 268–9; pivot practice 280–1, 284–5; renewal of ceremonies 281–4; stateless at sea 273–4; true Zomians 287
Moken people 277–87
Mon migrants 270–1
Móng Cái 304–13
Monpa people 448–52; demand for Mon Autonomous Region 448
moral economy: conceptualizing 362–4; humanitarianism and 364–5; other components of 370; self-help, suffering and 365–7
moral legitimacy: political legitimacy and 367–8; through religious imaginary 368–70
Morris-Suzuki, T. 411
Mrauk U 155, 157–8
Mughals 256–7
mushroom trade 110
music and dance 415–20
Mustang District (Nepal) 315–24
Myanmar: border with Thailand 267–8; bordering between KIO Myanmar government 224–5; (B)ordering northern Myanmar 220–2; development of marine fisheries 267–8; externalization of border work 23–4; geopolitical frontier 127–38; *hluttaw* 226; international Sino–Myanmar border 222–3; Kachin State administrative boundaries 225–6; migrants in Thailand 242–52; Myanmar–Thailand border migrants 269; Myawaddy–Mae Sot border 361–73; Panglong Agreement 226; ritual/ethnic integration Rakhine/Arakan 151–8; Sino–Myanmar boundary 218–29
Myeik Archipelago 267–8
Mzeina Bedouins (South Sinai) 451–2

Nanyo odori 415–17, 419
National League of Democracy 372
natural resources: Cambodia 94–104; Indonesia 180–7; Malaysian Borneo 168–78
Nehru, Jawaharlal 257, 449
Neilson, B. 243, 245
Nepal 230–9, 315–24
Newman, D. 56
non-timber forest products 207, 208
Nordstrom, C. 335–6
Northeast India, economies of violence 34–6
Nothing to Envy 425
Nyawi 278 (map), 282–5
nyetsang network 316, 318–20; decline of 322

Ogasawara Islands 411–20; colonial and militarised history of 412–14; musical crossings 415–18
oil palm 174–5, 180, 183–7
'One Belt, One Road' 114–15, 124
Ong, A. 335
opium 75–6, 130
othering: in Arakanese (Rakhine) spirits cult 156–7; Chinese/Vietnamese traders 307–8; religion and 353; religious actors/faith-based NGOs framed as undesirable "others" 388
Otunbaeva, Roza 50–1

Pacific War 413–14, 416, 417, 418–19
Pakistan: development institutions and religious networks 385–93; India–Pakistan border deaths 25; proximity and China border 114–25
Pakistan (East) *see* Bangladesh
Palestine 31–2
Pamirian borderlands 385–93
Panglong Agreement (1947) 218, 221, 226
Park, Hyun Ok 425
passports 20, 65, 118–19, 404, 407, 436–7, 438–9, 441
Pelkmans, M. 440
Peluso, N. 181
Penrose, J. 134
People's Liberation Army 110, 118, 423, 427
pepper 176
Perkebunan Pusantara 184
Pha Long 325, 326, 330
Philippines, women domestic workers 36–7
Pickles, J. 248
Piliavsky, A. 66, 225
Pinkaew, L. 247
Pir Sabzali 386–7

Index

pivot system 279, 280–1, 286–7; among people of Nyawi 284–5; binomial organization in the making 285–6
Pochta Rossii 341
Political Geography 61, 62
political legitimacy, through moral legitimacy 367–8
political livelihoods 94–104
politics of culture 230, 234–9
Popescu, G. 220
positionality, concept of 267, 270–1, 273–4
power, related to uncertainty 434–42
predation, marker of sovereignty 336–40
Premadasa, Ranasinghe 405
processual histories 107–8
profit, Uyghur traders and 296–7, 298–9
proximity 114–24

Qing Empire 117, 141

Radcliffe, Sir Cecil 447
Radcliffe Line 447
Rahmon, President 45
Rambo, A.T. 80
Ratanakiri province 94–104
Redfield, P. 352, 356
Reeves, M. 147, 296
religion: conservative Christians in the USA 352; identity in Bangladesh–India border enclaves 260–1; Ismaili Muslim institutions and development 385–93; moral legitimacy through religious imaginary 368–70; Tibetan–Hui marriage relations 376–83
remittances 37
Remtilla, A. 390
Renukaruban, Velauthapillai 409
rice, processual history 108
Rigg, J. 204
Rippa, A. 92, 147
Risse, T. 57, 63
roads/transport: infrastructure development in Nepal 315–24; Karakoram Highway 114–24; Tajikistan and Kyrgyzstan border 46–8
Rohingya people 18, 23–4, 30, 33–4, 154–5, 271–4, 371
Rousseau, Jérôme 82
rubber, smuggling 173–4
Russia: Chinese agriculture in far east 190–9; sovereign decisions on the Sino–Russian border 334–43
Rutherford, D. 336
Ryanggang province 422–31

Sadan, M. 152, 225
Sama, sea nomads 285–6
Santa Claus costumes 110
Sapa 326

Sarawak 168–78, 180, 181–2, 184–5
Sather, C. 285, 286
Saudi Arabia, women's labor migration 37
Savory, Nathaniel 412, 416
Saxer, M. 120, 122
Schafer, E. 110
Schein, L. 329
Schengen Agreement 19
Schiller, N.G. 64
Schoenberger, L. 109
schooling/education, Kachin in Myanmar 224
Scott, J.C. 62, 73, 77–8, 82, 83, 85, 204, 261–2, 263, 266, 269, 279, 312, 336, 340, 342, 362, 363
sea nomads *see* Moken
Seeing Like a State 336
self-help 365
Sellato, B. 82
Sen, A. 96
shamans 281, 282
Shan State 127–38
Sharma, A. 220
Sheikh Hasina 258
Sheikh Mujib, assassination of 258
Sheller, M. 319
Shin Dong-hyuk 424
shuttle trade 334–43
Sidaway, J.D. 61, 67
Sidre 377, 378–9
Silk Road 74, 92, 111, 114, 124, 141, 145, 146, 148, 298
Simla Convention 447
Simmel, G. 403–4
Simpson, A. 335
Sinar Mas Group 184–5
Singapore, women domestic workers in 36–7
Singh, Manmohan 258
Singh, Rajnath 25
Sittwe 152, 155, 156
Sivaramakrishnan, K. 323
Sixth Schedule (Indian Constitution) 448–50
Sloping Land Conversion Programme 205
smuggling: organized smuggling companies 339–40; rubber in Borneo 173–4
social capital, accumulation of 295–7
social networks, Uyghur traders 294–302
Soguk, N. 65
Song, J. 425
Southeast Asian massif 73–4, 77 (map), 78, 79 (map), 80, 84, 94, 206, 267
sovereignty: body as an embodied cultural 380–2; Indonesian–Malaysian border 185; internal/external 221; new forms of 335–6; and security West Kalimantan: 181–3
Soviet Union: collapse of 142, 294, 298, 334–5, 337, 434; legacy in Tajikistan 389–92

Spencer, J. 52
spirit cults 156
Sri Lanka 403–9; beyond the checkpoint 408–9; civil war 404–5
starshiy (brokers) 437, 439
state, the: complicity and negotiation with 308–11; and corporate actors in China 202–10; escalation of force 50–1; institutionalization of in Nepal 320–2; non-state space within 261–2; state officials 435–42
statelessness: *vs.* positionality 273–4 *see also* Rohingya people
state–society symbiosis 172–3
Steenberg, R. 109, 292, 293
Steinberg, J. 389
Steputat, F. 335
structural violence 18
Sturgeon, J.C. 61, 209
subsidies, for biofuel technology 203, 205, 208, 209
suffering 365–7
Sugauli treaty 232
Suharto, President 166, 182, 183, 185, 186–7
suicide bombers 405–7
Sunshine Technology 205–9
surveillance technology 21, 26; Sino–North Korean border 426, 428
sushi supply chain 108, 110
Syrian refugees 30, 34

Tagliacozzo, E. 107
Tajikistan 42–53, 385–93
Tamils 404–9
Taobao 340, 341, 342
Tapp, N. 83
Tashkurgan 120, 121, 122
Tawang 448
taxes: cross-border goods Vietnam 308–11; imports into Nepal 322
Taylor, P.J. 59, 221, 322
Tenasserim region 267–8
tenth month ceremony 270
Territorial Power Domains, Southeast Asia, and China: The Geo-strategy of an Overarching Massif 78
territorialisation 230–9
Testart, A. 83
textiles, Hmong 325–33
Thailand 127–39, 242–54, 361–73; Burmese refugees in 34, 36; identities, exclusiveness, and inclusiveness 269–70; Special Economic Zones 248–9
The Art of Not Being Governed: An Anarchist History of Upland Southeast Asia 62, 77, 83, 85, 336
Thein Sein, President 222
Thompson, E.P. 361, 362–3
Thongchai, W. 61, 246

Tibet 106–13; language 451; relation to Zomia 80; Tibetan Buddhist ties with North East India 448–51; Tibetan–Hui marriage relations 376–83
TMMD program 185–6
tourism: industry in Nepal 321–2; Sapa as ethnic tourism destination 326; Sino–Russian cross-border trade 337–40; tourist handicrafts 331
trade: cultural commodities 325–33; global and Zomia 74–6; Hmong manufactured textiles 330–2; international Sino–Myanmar border 222–3; Kazakhstan and China 140–8; leech plot 304–13; shuttle 334–43; trans-Karakoram 114–25; Uyghur traders Sino–Kyrgyz border 294–302
trafficking, women Sino–North Korean border 424–5
Trans-Regional and -National Studies of Southeast Asia (TRaNS) 62
Treaty of Nanking 75
trekking companies 321
Trinamool Congress Party 258
Trump, Donald 17, 20
trust: mistrust between Chinese/Vietnamese traders 306–7; Uyghur traders and 297–8
Tsing, A. 110
Tsona Gontse Rinpoche 448, 450
Turbulent Times and Enduring Peoples: Mountain Minorities in the South-East Asian Massif 78
Turner, S. 109, 312
Turner, V. 147
Tyner, J. 18

U Thuzana 355, 369
U Vinaya 369
UN Drug Convention 1988 76
uncertainty, used as a resource 434–42
Union of Burma 153, 218, 221
United Nations High Commissioner for Refugees (UNHCR) 24, 225, 250, 371
United States: border zone defined 19; mobile checkpoints 408; US–Mexico border 1, 17, 20, 31, 50, 57
Urak Lawoi 277, 280, 285
Urry, J. 319
Uyghur traders 117–19, 294–302
Uzbekistan 42–53, 434–42

van Schendel, W. 60, 61, 62, 63, 73, 74, 76, 77, 78, 80, 266, 363, 392, 445, 447
Vandergeest, P. 181
Vietnam: Cambodia border 97–102; Hmong textile trade 325–33; 'leech plot' 304–13; New Economic Zones scheme 85
Vinokurov, E. 263
violence: border externalization 19–20, 23–4; border militarization 21–2; border walls 20–1, 22–3; death at border 24–6; types of 18
virtual bazaar 341

Index

Wadley, R.L. 61
Walker, A. 60, 109
Wallerstein, I. 107
walls 20–1, 22–3; cities 20–1; modern phenomenon 21; territorialize claim of authority and control 20; US–Mexico 17, 20 *see also* checkpoints
wastelands: Indonesian–Malaysian border 180–7; Jatropha plantation expansion 202–10
water buffalo 207, 208
water supply, Kyrgyzstan 52
West Kalimantan (Dutch West Borneo) 170 (map), 175, 180–7
West Kameng 448
Whyte, B.R. 256
Wimmer, A. 64
Winichakul, T. 129, 132, 266
Wolf, E. 106, 108
women: abducted in India 32; domestic workers 36–7; maternal contradictions 31–2; new roles in Kashmir 35; restaurant workers in China 429; traders in Vietnam 325–33; war heroines in Bangladesh 32
Woods, K. 186, 222

World Customs/Trade Organizations 335
World Wildlife Fund (WWF), 'Heart of Borneo' initiative. 184

Xinjiang 114–25, 294–302

Yadav, Ram Baran (President of Nepal) 231
yak tail trade 110–11
Yalu River 422, 424
Yamaker 182–3
Yangon 153, 227n1, 251
Yeh, E.T. 203
Yên Bái province 325–6
Yunnan Province 127, 130, 134, 202, 325, 327, 328
Yuval Davis, N. 33

Zhambyl *oblast* 141, 146
Zhang, J. 122, 312
Zhejiang 330–1
Zomia 3, 4, 62, 73–86, 266, 267, 269, 271, 273, 340, 342; definition 73, 76–80; global interconnectedness 76; Inner Zomians 280, 281; international trade 74–6; maritime 277–87; states, borders, and agency in 81–3; visual representation 74 (map), 77 (map)

PGMO 04/13/2018